THE YALE EDITION OF THE

WORKS OF SAMUEL JOHNSON

VOLUME XVIII

Johnson on the English Language

PREVIOUSLY PUBLISHED

VOLUME I, *Diaries, Prayers, and Annals*
Edited by E. L. McAdam, Jr., with Donald and Mary Hyde

VOLUME II, *The Idler and the Adventurer*
Edited by W. J. Bate, John M. Bullitt, and L. F. Powell

VOLUMES III, IV, and V, *The Rambler*
Edited by W. J. Bate and Albrecht B. Strauss

VOLUME VI, *Poems*
Edited by E. L. McAdam, Jr., with George Milne

VOLUMES VII and VIII, *Johnson on Shakespeare*
Edited by Arthur Sherbo, Introduction by Bertrand H. Bronson

VOLUME IX, *A Journey to the Western Islands of Scotland*
Edited by Mary Lascelles

VOLUME X, *Political Writings*
Edited by Donald J. Greene

VOLUME XIV, *Sermons*
Edited by Jean H. Hagstrum and James Gray

VOLUME XV, *A Voyage to Abyssinia*
Edited by Joel J. Gold

VOLUME XVI, *Rasselas and Other Tales*
Edited by Gwin J. Kolb

VOLUME XVII, *A Commentary on Mr. Pope's Principles of Morality, Or Essay on Man*
Edited by O M Brack, Jr.

SAMUEL JOHNSON

Johnson on the English Language

EDITED BY GWIN J. KOLB

AND ROBERT DEMARIA, JR.

NEW HAVEN AND LONDON: YALE UNIVERSITY PRESS

2005

Published with assistance from Charles A. Kelly, Jr.
and the Ford Foundation.

"A Short Scheme for compiling a new Dictionary of the English Language" (MS Hyde 50 (38–39)) and the fair copy of a draft of *The Plan of a Dictionary of the English Language* (MS Hyde 50 (40)) are reproduced with kind permission of The Donald and Mary Hyde Collection of Dr. Samuel Johnson, Houghton Library, Harvard University.

Set in Baskerville Roman type by
Tseng Information Systems, Inc.
Printed in the United States of America by
Vail-Ballou Press.

Library of Congress Cataloging-in-Publication Data

Johnson, Samuel, 1709–1784.
Johnson on the English language / Samuel Johnson ;
edited by Gwin J. Kolb and Robert DeMaria, Jr.
p. cm. — (The Yale edition of the works of
Samuel Johnson ; v. 18)
Includes bibliographical references.
ISBN 0-300-10672-6 (alk. paper)

1. English language—Lexicology—Early works to 1800.
2. English language—Early works to 1800.
I. Kolb, Gwin J. II. DeMaria, Robert. III. Title.
PE1611.J64 2005
423′.028—dc22 2004060114

A catalogue record for this book is available
from the British Library.

The paper in this book meets the guidelines for permanence and durability of the Committee on Production Guidelines for Book Longevity of the Council on Library Resources

10 9 8 7 6 5 4 3 2

TO THE MEMORY OF

Mary Hyde Eccles

PREFACE

This volume presents Johnson's writings on the English language that are part of his work on *A Dictionary of the English Language* (1755). In Johnson's life of writing no work is more important than his *Dictionary*. When he signed the contract to compose the *Dictionary* in 1746, he had a reputation as a journalist, small biographer, translator, and occasional poet, but his great book lifted him permanently into prominence and gave him the opportunity to complete other important projects. By the time he finished the *Dictionary,* he was the revered Mr. Rambler, the author of *The Vanity of Human Wishes,* and he was famous both in England and on the Continent as "Dictionary Johnson." He had done the work for which he would be pensioned eight years later, and he had qualifications for literary immortality that he could only burnish by his later completion of the edition of Shakespeare (1765) and the *Lives of the Poets* (1779–81).

The body of the *Dictionary* falls outside the scope of the *Yale Edition* because of its vast size. The texts presented here, however, provide all the preliminaries to Johnson's extraordinary book and thus his longest continuous philological statements. They contain Johnson's thinking about the massive task of recording English, about its structure and history, its importance in the development of English culture, its difficulties, and its lamentable instability. In addition, two of the pieces included here—namely, the *Plan* and the Preface—must be counted among Johnson's most memorable prose writings. In them Johnson not only expounds his thoughts on English, he also expresses his feelings about the labor of lexicography. Like many of Johnson's best productions, the *Plan* and the Preface brilliantly discuss their avowed subject and, at the same time, seem to present elements of an emotional and intellectual autobiography.

Despite its importance in Johnson's body of work and despite the fact that it provides most of the thinking on English of one of its greatest speakers and writers, this group of writings has never appeared in a single volume before. Moreover, the textual notes and commentary that accompany them are unprecedented. The Preface to the *Dictionary* was re-published in most later unabridged editions, as were Johnson's "History of the English Language" and his "Grammar of the English Tongue." The so-called Harrison's edition of the *Dictionary* (1786–87) also reprints Johnson's *Plan of a Dictionary of the English Language* (1747),[1] but not the two very short pieces at the end of our volume or the facsimiles of the two drafts of the *Plan* in our appendices. Harrison's edition includes, of course, the body of the *Dictionary,* but it excludes scholarly apparatus and commentary of every kind on the Preface, *Plan,* History, and Grammar.

Beginning with Sir John Hawkins in 1787, many editors and publishers have presented redactions of the *Plan* and Preface in editions of Johnson's collected works. In Volume IX of his edition, Hawkins included a section suggestively called "Philological Tracts" (pp. 163–446); the *Plan* and Preface appear under that heading, but not Johnson's History or Grammar; the other "Philological Tracts" are examples of what we would call literary criticism: parts of Johnson's edition of Shakespeare (1765) and some minor works, including the "Essay on Epitaphs" (1740). In his edition (1792), Arthur Murphy retained the contents of the section in Hawkins's "Philological Tracts" but moved them to Volume II; most later editors followed suit.[2] W. Baynes and Son reprinted the "Philological Tracts" as a separate volume in their duodecimo publication of the *Works* (1824), which, however, like the versions included in various other editions, contains no scholarly editing. With some deference to the helpful but sparse notes by learned Johnsonian anthologists like Donald Greene,[3] the same may be said about all of the many other

1. For a complete bibliographical description of all editions of the *Dictionary* published from 1755 to 1984, see *Bibliography,* pp. 410–657.

2. For a complete bibliographical description of editions of the *Works,* see *Bibliography,* pp. 1623–1712. *Bibliography* does not attempt an exhaustive list of volumes containing selections of Johnson's works, though it does include some of these (pp. 1712–20).

3. In his *Samuel Johnson* (Oxford University Press, 1984), Greene includes the Preface with some notes; in doing so, he follows Bertrand Bronson in *Samuel Johnson: Rasselas, Poems, and Selected Prose* (Holt, Rinehart and Winston, 1958) and William K.

editions of the *Plan* and Preface that have appeared in selections of Johnson's works or in broader anthologies. Because the writings in this volume have never been critically edited and because some of them may never be edited again, we have provided, both in our introductions and our notes, a far more detailed treatment of the texts than was envisioned in the original plan for the Yale Edition of the Works of Samuel Johnson.[4]

In planning the Yale Edition, the editors agreed to give some of Johnson's "philological" writings to other volumes, reserving his writings relating to the *Dictionary* for the present one. *The Plays of William Shakespeare* has its own volumes; the *Rambler* and *Idler* have theirs; and many, but not all, of Johnson's shorter essays on various "philological" or literary subjects appear in yet another volume.

Even with our scope happily thus narrowed, as editors of the present volume, we had some difficult decisions to make about what to include. A small piece called "The signification of Words how varied" was especially vexing. The essay appeared in the *Gentleman's Magazine* for February 1749 (XIX.65–66) in the form of a letter to Mr. Urban (Edward Cave), and it is signed "W.S." (suggesting the printer and publisher William Strahan).[5] The ostensible subject is the interesting fact that "the same word to which a good meaning was formerly affixed, may now have a signification directly opposite," but the letter is really a sort of advance advertisement for

---

Wimsatt, Jr., and Frank Brady in *Samuel Johnson: Selected Poetry and Prose* (University of California Press, 1977). Mona Wilson reprints both the Preface and the *Plan,* without notes, in her Reynard Library anthology of *Dr. Johnson: Prose and Poetry* (Rupert Hart-Davis, 1950).

4. In particular, we have made an effort to record nearly all textual variants in eighteenth-century editions of the texts, including some that will seem trivial to all but textual scholars; we have provided more thorough explanatory notes than appear in many of the volumes in the Yale Edition; and we have departed from the Yale Edition's stated practice of reducing capital letters and some italics to modern usage both in the texts and in quoted material in notes and introductions. We believe our practice has not caused us to fail in the stated purpose of the edition: "to produce a sound and readable text of Johnson, for use by graduate students, literary critics, literary scholars, and informed literate readers." We hope that our expanded accounts of the texts and our presentation of the texts in forms that more nearly resemble the originals will satisfy the scholar while erecting few barriers to the pleasure of the literate reader.

5. For a similar treatment of this article, see Reddick, pp. 42–43.

Johnson's *Dictionary*. Its language is mildly reminiscent of passages in Johnson's Preface lamenting the inevitability of change in language. The examples chosen by "W.S." more strongly indicate that the work emanated from Johnson's workshop, if not from his pen, because they all reappear in the illustrative quotations in the *Dictionary*. It is reasonable to assume that he had gathered these by 1748 and either passed them on to "W.S." or composed the little article himself. The article concludes, "However, it is hoped, that our language will be more fixed, and better established when the publick is favoured with a new dictionary, undertaken with that view, and adapted to answer several other valuable purposes; a work now in great forwardness." Although the article clearly reflects, if it does not belong to, a stage in the composition of the *Dictionary*, we do not include it in this edition for two reasons: although a good case could be made, the writing is not irrefutably Johnson's, and the quotations, which certainly come from Johnson's labors, belong to the body of, not the preliminaries to, the *Dictionary*.

On the other hand, we decided to include two Johnsonian introductions: to the first abridged edition—a Preface (1756)—and to the revised fourth unabridged edition—an "Advertisement" (1773). In addition, we place in the first appendix a facsimile reproduction of "A Short Scheme for compiling a new Dictionary of the English Language." This manuscript, a part of the Hyde Collection and reproduced with the kind permission of the late Mary Hyde Eccles and the Houghton Library, represents the first stage in the composition of the *Plan* and Preface. In *The R. B. Adam Library* (vol. II, 1929), the "Scheme" was reproduced, but that privately printed work has become a scarce collector's item; the technology of facsimile reproduction has improved since then; and Lady Eccles acquired a leaf that was missing at the time of the last reproduction. Our facsimile also includes a new transcription. In the second appendix, we produce in facsimile, with gratitude again to Lady Eccles, the fair copy of the *Plan* (also in *The R. B. Adam Library*), a manuscript written by an amanuensis, representing an intermediate state of composition between the "Scheme" and the published *Plan*. Unlike the former, which is in Johnson's inimitable and difficult hand, this neatly written document does not require a transcription. The two manuscripts together, along with the *Plan* and Preface, show with unique completeness a process of composition and revision in an important part of Johnson's works.

First and last among those whom we would like to acknowledge for their help in preparing this edition is Ruth Kolb. She has been very nearly a third co-editor, working on the project before Robert DeMaria, Jr., joined the team and continuing faithfully through to the conclusion of the work. She provided essential help in the laborious collations necessary to establish the texts, and she worked on every other phase of the project. Her equally essential but less tangible contributions will be mentioned last.

Among the others who furthered the progress of this volume are several scholars and friends whose deaths have deprived us of some of the pleasure we have in presenting this publication: W. J. Bate, James L. Clifford, David Eccles, Mary Hyde Eccles, J. David Fleeman, Arthur Friedman, Donald J. Greene, Allen T. Hazen, Donald F. Hyde, Paul J. Korshin, Herman W. Liebert, Maynard Mack, and Robert F. Metzdorf.

We rejoice to name many more scholars, librarians, book collectors, research assistants, secretaries, and other correspondents who may hear us offer our thanks for their important contributions: O M Brack, Jr., Lindsey Briggs, Judith Calvert, Patricia Cannon, Donald D. Eddy, James Engell, David Fairer, Vincent Giroud, Gerald M. Goldberg, Per Henningsgaard, Henry Hitchings, Park Honan, Giovanni Iamartino, Charles A. Kelly, Jr., Patricia Kenworthy, Jack Kolb, Sara Landreth, Anne McDermott, Nancy MacKechnie, John H. Middendorf, Thomas Muzyka, Edward Navakas, Graham Nicholls, Robert Parks, Steven Parks, Ronald D. Patkus, Charles E. Pierce, Claude Rawson, Allen Reddick, Bruce Redford, Edward Rosenheim, Paul T. Ruxin, Alice Schreyer, Albrecht B. Strauss, Michael Suarez, Linda Troost, Gordon Turnbull, David Vander Meulen, Blake Weathersby, Howard D. Weinbrot, and Samantha Zacher.

It is an additional pleasure to thank the many fine institutions that helped us with our work. Between us, during the course of producing this edition, we received research grants from Vassar College, the Center for Advanced Study in the Behavioral Sciences (through a grant from the Mellon Foundation), the Beinecke Rare

Books and Manuscripts Library, the Guggenheim Foundation, and the University of Chicago. In addition, we wish to thank the librarians and staff of the Bodleian Library, the British Library, the Cambridge University Libraries, the University of Chicago Libraries, the Cordell Library, the Pierpont Morgan Library, the New York Public Library, the Pembroke College Library (Oxford), the Princeton University Libraries, the Stanford University Libraries, the Vassar College Libraries, the Christopher Wren Library (Trinity College, Cambridge), and the Yale University Libraries.

In conclusion, Robert DeMaria, Jr., wishes to thank Joanne DeMaria for her sensible responses to various questions that arose about the composition of this volume, for her moral support, and for her remarkable persistence and accuracy in seeing the book through its final stages of production. Gwin Kolb wishes to repeat and extend the incalculable debt of gratitude he owes to his wife Ruth, who, as acknowledged earlier,[6] has sustained and shared his labor for more than sixty years, and to their children, Jack and Alma Dean, who have provided steady comfort for much of the same period.

6. In the Preface to his edition of *Rasselas* (*Yale* XVI.xii).

CONTENTS

INTRODUCTION

The Historical Background of the *Plan* and Preface

Three distinct traditions of lexicography influenced Johnson when he began work on the *Dictionary* in 1746: the English, the Continental (especially French), and the Latin.[1] There were many prefaces and some plans or proposals for dictionaries of various kinds in each of these traditions; together, these preliminary essays compose the generic antecedents of Johnson's *Plan* and Preface.

Specific generic antecedents for the *Plan* are conspicuous for their paucity in contrast to those available for the Preface. We have located no relevant foreign language proposals and only a few in English. Comparatively few proposals on any subject survive because they were often single sheets or half sheets of printed paper discarded by their perusers, while remaining publisher's stock met the same fate. In any case, the proposals themselves tended to be quasi-legal contractual statements declaring the size, quality, and content (in general terms) of what the author would provide in exchange for the cost of subscription to the book or edition. Often a specimen of the proposed text was included.[2] Bare proposals, therefore, are not very similar to the kind of essay Johnson provides in the *Plan*. Closer in kind are the prefaces that sometimes accompanied the proposals proper. A rare survivor in this mode is *Proposals for Printing by Subscription, the Dictionary and Concordance of F. Marius de Calasio. . . . by W. Romaine, A. M.* The one-page proposal is preceded by a ten-page preface ("To the Learned") by Romaine and an equally long "Address to the Publick" by "a Stranger to the Editor, and a Friend

1. For a complementary explanation of the historical background of the Preface and *Plan*, see Sledd-Kolb, pp. 25–32, to which we are indebted.

2. For examples of proposals, see John Feather, *English Book Prospectuses: An Illustrated History* (1984).

to Learning." The whole twenty-two page pamphlet is entitled *Some Remarks on the Progress of Learning since the Reformation* . . . (1746). The Johnsonian sound of many sentences in the "Address to the Publick," as well as the topic itself, suggest that this essay may, in fact, be Johnson's work.[3] Whether or not it is, some such proposal provided the formal model for Johnson's *Plan,* and he had had plenty of practice writing in the genre before he wrote the *Plan.* Not including "Some Remarks," Johnson had written all or part of some ten proposals before he published the *Plan* in September 1747, including proposals for his aborted translation of Paolo Sarpi's *History of the Council of Trent* (1738), Robert James's *Medicinal Dictionary* (1741), the *Harleian Catalogue* (1742), and his own edition of the *Plays of William Shakespeare* (1745).[4] None of these is as extensive as the *Plan,* and none, of course, relates to a dictionary of a language; but they clearly show Johnson's mastery of the form.

Proposals, such as the *Plan,* that relate to dictionaries are very scarce. In the John Johnson and Gough collections of pre-1801 proposals at the Bodleian Library, for example, there are only a few items that are relevant to Johnson's *Plan.*[5] Perhaps the most pertinent extant work exists in a single surviving copy at Aberystwyth

3. For an argument in favor of including "Address to the Publick" in the Johnsonian canon, see O M Brack, Jr., and Robert DeMaria, Jr., "'Some Remarks on the Progress of Learning': A New Preface by Samuel Johnson" (*New Rambler,* No. E VI [2002–2003], pp. 61–74).

4. For descriptions of proposals by SJ through 1747, see *Bibliography* 34.7PP; 37.10HAP; 38.10SP; 38GM 8/Supplement 700; 41.6JP; 42.11HP/1a; 43.12HMP; 44.9PP/1a; 45.4SP; 47.8LP; 47.8PD/1a, 1b, 2.

5. In addition to No. 77, Chambers's "Considerations," the following items in the John Johnson Collection are worthy of note: No. 1, proposals for printing Minsheu's polyglot dictionary (1627); Nos. 54–55, proposals for two versions of Davies's Welsh dictionary (1725); No. 73, proposals for the English translation of Pierre Bayle's *Dictionary Historical and Critical* (1732); No. 76a, proposals for a new edition of Estienne's *Thesaurus Linguae Latinae* (1734–35); No. 83, proposals for Lye's edition of Junius's *Etymologicum Anglicanum* (1743); No. 106, proposals for the second edition of the *Universal History* (30 May 1746); No. 108, proposals for William Guthrie's *History of England* (7 November 1746); No. 114, proposals for Guilelmus's Hebrew lexicon; and No. 120, proposals for M. Savary's *Universal Dictionary of Arts and Sciences.* Of these only 76a, 83, 106, and 108 have anything approaching the discursiveness of SJ's *Plan,* and only 108 approaches the size of his work. The complementary Gough Collection of Book Prospectuses before 1801 does not add significantly to this list. Nor does the collection from the Chetham Library in Manchester, copies of which are also housed in Bodley.

College, Wales—Ambrose Philips's *Proposals for Printing an English Dictionary, in Two Volumes in Folio; explaining the whole Language, after the following Manner* (1724?).[6] As James Sledd and Gwin Kolb observe, "Philips never completed the dictionary which he had planned, but it should be noted that his *Proposals* have much in common with Johnson's statement of his own achievement in the Preface to his octavo edition of 1756" (p. 7). Some time before Philips published his proposals, his friend Joseph Addison had conceived a design of an English dictionary, and Philips's work may be a reflection of Addison's.[7] Although he apparently never mentioned Philips's *Proposals,* Johnson knew of Addison's plan, and he received "a collection of examples selected from [John] Tillotson's works . . . by Addison" for use in the *Dictionary.* However, Johnson remarks further in his "Life" of Addison that the package of quotations "came too late to be of use, so I inspected it but slightly, and remember it indistinctly."[8] In the *Plan,* Johnson also suggests that he received a list of authors to be used as authorities in the dictionary planned by Alexander Pope (see pp. 55–56 and n. 8 below). There are strong similarities between Pope's list and Johnson's, but Pope evidently produced no proposal or plan for a dictionary.

Another proposal deserving of consideration as a possible model for Johnson's *Plan* outlines a plan for an encyclopedia rather than a dictionary of English. Johnson once told Boswell that he formed his style partly on "[Ephraim] Chambers's Proposal for his Dictionary"—meaning, perhaps, a proposal, now lost, for the first edition of Chambers's *Cyclopaedia* (1728), or, more probably, *Some Considerations Offered to the Publick, preparatory to a second Edition of Cyclopaedia: or, an Universal Dictionary of Arts and Sciences.*[9] As Sledd and Kolb showed in 1955, there are significant similarities between the topics

6. For a reprint of the *Proposals* and a discussion of their relationship to Joseph Addison's proposed dictionary, see Mary Segar, "Dictionary Making in the Early Eighteenth Century," *Review of English Studies,* VII (1931), 210–13.

7. Segar (p. 210) identifies a brief advertisement in the *Postboy* for 1–4 June 1717 as a description of Addison's project. Most notable for attention to the proposal as a precursor to SJ's *Plan* is the stated intention that "Authorities shall be quoted throughout" (p. 211).

8. *Lives,* II.113; par. 91.

9. *Life,* I.218–19; for a brief treatment of stylistic similarities between SJ's and Chambers's prefatory writings, see W. K. Wimsatt, Jr., *Philosophic Words* (1948), pp. 53–54.

and opinions in Johnson's *Plan* and Chambers's "Considerations."[1] Johnson resembles Chambers when he describes the lowly reputation of lexicographers ("Considerations," par. 22; cf. pp. 25–26 below); when he discusses his inadequacy to the task at hand and his fear of unrealistic expectations ("Considerations," par. 9; cf. p. 28 below); when he dismisses the idea of perfection in a dictionary ("Considerations," pars. 1, 4, 13; cf. p. 49 below); and when he discusses the efforts of French and Italian academies, which had the responsibility of composing the dictionaries of their respective languages ("Considerations," pars. 14, 20; cf. pp. 30, 49, 58 below). None of these similarities, however, is unique to a comparison between Johnson and Chambers. The topics had all been discussed before Chambers wrote his proposal; and, though Johnson certainly read it, when he wrote his *Plan* he probably drew on the wider tradition in which Chambers participated rather than specifically and directly on Chambers's work itself.

Although there are very few extant proposals for dictionaries, a great many prefaces contributed to the tradition of lexicographers' statements in the background of Johnson's *Plan* and Preface. In the tradition of Latin lexicography, the most important prefaces to be considered are Johann Mathias Gesner's preface to an expanded edition of Basilius Faber's *Thesaurus Eruditionis Scholasticae* (1735; first published in 1571) and the lengthy preface to the London edition of Robert Estienne's *Thesaurus Linguae Latinae* (1734–35; first published in 1531). The importance of these two dictionaries to Johnson is supported by references to them in a reader's notes on Johnson's "Scheme of an English Dictionary" (see pp. 394 and 408 below).[2] Other Latin dictionaries with prefaces expressing themes of the kind taken up in Johnson's preliminary essays include Du Cange's glossary of Medieval Latin (1678); the Latin-English-Latin dictionaries of Adam Littleton (1673), Fr. Gouldman (1664), Thomas Holyoake (1677), and Robert Ainsworth (1736); and the etymological dictionaries of Franciscus Junius and Stephen Skinner, both mentioned in Johnson's Preface (see pp. 81–82 and notes 9 and 1 below). Johnson also knew the polyglot dictionary of

1. Sledd-Kolb, pp. 19–25.

2. For a discussion of the Renaissance Latin dictionaries that SJ probably knew and their importance to him, see Paul Korshin, "Johnson and the Renaissance Dictionary," *Journal of the History of Ideas,* XXXV (1974), 300–312.

John Minsheu, *The Guide into Tongues* (1617); he probably read its preface and may have perused the very sketchy proposals for a new edition (1627; see p. xviii, n. 5 above), although they were certainly scarce by 1747.

In the Continental tradition, Johnson could well have seen the prefaces to the first (1694), second (1718), and third (1740) editions of the French Académie's *Dictionnaire*. In addition, he certainly knew the preface of Basnage de Bauval to the second (1701) and the third (1708) editions of Antoine Furetière's *Dictionnaire universel, contenant généralement tous les mots français, tant vieux que modernes et les terms de toutes les sciences et des arts* (first published 1690); all the earlier prefaces were republished in the fourth edition (1727). Johnson cites, without reference, a remark made by Basnage de Bauval in his preface (see below, p. 47, n. 9).

No Continental tradition had as much influence on Johnson as the French. He refers to the Italian Accademia della Crusca and to the reception of its dictionary, however, and he may have read the prefaces to any of the four main editions of the *Vocabolario* published before 1747 (1612, 1623, 1691, 1729–38). It is less likely that he knew of the Spanish national dictionaries because he refers only to the French and Italian productions, and there is no evidence that he read Spanish. On the other hand, the Real Academia Español published its *Diccionario de la Lengua Castellana* in 1726 with extensive prefatory material, including sections on orthography and etymology. This work, largely modeled on the French *Dictionnaire*, shows that the central issues of lexicography were being discussed widely on the Continent before Johnson began his *Dictionary of the English Language*.

If one excludes Chambers's *Cyclopaedia*, it appears that earlier dictionaries of English were less important in forming Johnson's *Plan* and Preface than either Continental or Latin works of the same kind. But prefaces were available to him in the few works concerning early English or "Teutonick" language. Chief among these must be counted George Hickes's *Linguarum Veterum Septentrionalium Thesaurus* (3 vols., 1703–05), which Johnson mined for specimens in his "History of the English Language."[3] He also consulted Henry Spelman's *Glossarium Archaeologicum* (1664) and Richard Rowland's

3. See pp. 143–48, 158–59, and 160–61 below.

(a.k.a. Verstegan) *A Restitution of Decayed Intelligence* (1605), for they are cited occasionally in his etymological notes.[4] The most important of modern English dictionaries for Johnson were Edward Phillips's *New World of English Words* (1658) and Nathan Bailey's *Dictionarium Britannicum* (1730). The second edition of Bailey's work (1736) is frequently cited in Johnson's *Dictionary,* but its bare prefatory material provides no background for his *Plan* and Preface. Phillips's preface, however, with its proclamations of the national importance of lexicography and its proto-Lockean view of language as the "*vehiculum* or Conveyancer of all good Arts" (sig. b3^{r}), is rich in the tradition in which Johnson worked. In 1749 Benjamin Martin published his dictionary *Lingua Britannica Reformata* with a preface that exceeds all earlier prefaces to English dictionaries, "a model of planning and detail."[5] This could not, obviously, have influenced Johnson's *Plan,* however, and, in fact, the influence seems to have run in the opposite direction.[6] This fact makes it unlikely that Martin's preface exerted any influence on Johnson's preface of 1755, but in the roll call of earlier prefaces to English dictionaries, Martin's deserves a prominent place.

The extent to which Johnson relied on the complex tradition of lexicographical preliminaries can be demonstrated by examining the genealogy of some of the sentiments in Johnson's *Plan* and Preface. As Chambers's *Considerations* and his Preface to his *Cyclopaedia* (5th ed., 1741) have many sentiments in common with Johnson's *Plan* and Preface, the following examination doubles as a comparison of the similarities between Johnson's and Chambers's preliminary pieces. However, it mainly shows their mutual reliance on a deep tradition of writing about lexicographical issues. For the sake of order, we have grouped the sentiments common to Johnson and Chambers into three topics: (1) characterizations of the lexicographer and his task; (2) attitudes toward the Continental academies; and (3) linguistic issues.

(1) Johnson begins both the Preface and *Plan* with statements about the pitiful status of lexicographers in the world of learning

4. See *Dictionary,* s.v. *lazy* and *vixen,* for examples; for a full account of SJ's use of earlier works on Germanic languages, see *JDTR*, pp. 20–36.

5. Starnes and Noyes, p. 150.

6. Starnes and Noyes, p. 152.

and the drudgery of their work. He follows this up at various points in both works with remarks about the "hapless" lexicographer, the unattainable goals of his task, and the painfulness of his endeavors. Likewise, in *Considerations* Chambers says,

> A Man must either be vain or silly to an uncommon Degree, that expects to raise a *Character* for Learning, by a Dictionary; a Work of Labour rather than Genius; and wherein Reputation may be lost, but none gain'd. It is known what Figure Lexicographers make in the Republick of Letters; with what Contempt they are treated by those who hold the first Rank therein; and how often, even the best of them, receive the Lash at the Hands of the Critics, for the Faults they unavoidably fall into. If the View of being useful did not operate stronger on some Minds than the Love of Fame, few would engage themselves in Works of this Kind, where all the Credit that will be allowed them, is that of being laborious Compilers.[7]

In his Preface, Chambers suggests that dictionary-making is "pioneer's work" (p. xviii), a description which may be the source of Johnson's remark in the Preface that the lexicographer is considered "the pioneer of literature, doomed only to remove rubbish and clear obstructions from the paths through which Learning and Genius press forward to conquest and glory" (p. 73 below). Both Johnson and Chambers also mention mines and shops as remote places the lexicographer must search for words ("Considerations," par. 18; Preface, p. 102 below).

The particular verbal echoes notwithstanding, Johnson drew his remarks on the drudgery of lexicography from a pervasive tradition of such comments that included Chambers's but was not limited to his. Lexicographers were ridiculed in antiquity, and Erasmus complained about the compilation of his dictionary-like *Adagia* (1500) in a tone close to Johnson's: "in other books there is often room for the mind to operate, there is the pleasure of discovery or creation, there is the possibility at any time, in any place, of completing a part of the work by sheer mental activity, and of hastening on your project by the quickness of your brain; here you are fettered to the treadmill, you cannot budge an inch, as they say, from your

7. "Considerations," par. 22.

texts. You waste your eyesight on decaying volumes covered with mould."[8] Something akin to this passage is in the background of Johnson's *Plan,* where, in one draft, he refers to lexicography as the "proper Drudgery of Asinine Industry" (p. 428 below). Likewise, Johann Mathias Gesner begins the preface to his edition of Faber's *Thesaurus* by mentioning the flight of most scholars from the uncommonly difficult and inglorious labor of lexicography: "Fugiunt laborem plerique, in difficultate haud mediocri contentum vulgo, et inglorium."[9]

Closely related to the theme of its drudgery are statements of how lexicography has wasted the private lives of lexicographers. For example, in *Catalogus Bibliothecae Harleianae* (1743–45), Johnson reprints the Latin epigraph that Henri Estienne attached to his *Thesaurus Graecae Linguae* (1572): in translation, "No one knows how much work this lexicon cost; nor would it occur to anyone to find fault with it, save that you will complain, learned reader, that Stephanus runs himself down when he complains in such lugubrious verse as this: This thesaurus has given me rags for riches and replaced the bloom of youth with the wrinkles of old-age" (II, No. 15094).

So common is this topic among dictionary writers that Paul Korshin has given it a name: "lacrimae lexicographi" (the tears of the lexicographer).[1] Perhaps the most famous contribution to the theme is Joseph Scaliger's poem written after he completed his Latin-Arabic dictionary, "In Lexicorum compilatores, inscriptum Lexico Arabico a se collecto, in Batavis."[2] Scaliger lugubriously described lexicography as a labor containing all punishments in one ("omnes/ Poenarum facies hic labor unus habet"). The lines were reprinted in the *Gentleman's Magazine* for January 1748 (p. 8). Arthur Murphy said that Johnson "communicated" the verse, which he later alluded to in *Γνῶθι Σεαυτόν*, the Latin poem he composed on the completion of his revision of his own *Dictionary* in 1773.[3]

8. *Adages,* trans. M. M. Phillips (1964), p. 198.

9. "Most flee the work, which commonly consists of no mean difficulty and wins no glory" (*Thesaurus Eruditionis Scholasticae* (1735), sig. b2^r).

1. Korshin, p. 306.

2. *Poemata omnia* (1615), p. 35; "Upon the compiling of lexicons, written in the Arabic Lexicon, collected by himself, in Holland."

3. Murphy, *An Essay on his Life and Genius* (*Works of Samuel Johnson* [1792], I.78).

Chambers refers to Scaliger's epigram in his *Considerations* (par. 23), and Johnson does so in his Preface (p. 111). But Johnson undoubtedly knew the poem from reading Scaliger, one of his heroes, and other lexicographers had also quoted it, including recent editors of Furetière's *Dictionnaire universel* (1743, p. xiv).

The magnificent and moving envoy in Johnson's Preface also belongs to the tradition of lugubrious lexicographers. In the penultimate paragraph, Johnson says, "whether I shall add any thing by my own writings to the reputation of *English* literature, must be left to time . . . but I shall not think my employment useless or ignoble, if by my assistance foreign nations, and distant ages, gain access to the propagators of knowledge, and understand the teachers of truth; if my labours afford light to the repositories of science, and add celebrity to *Bacon,* to *Hooker,* to *Milton,* and to *Boyle.*" Edward Phillips is one of the earlier lexicographers who had expressed this thought, though in much less eloquent terms: "In this work, which, for the generality of it, must stand the brunt of many a curious inquisition; both for the present, and future ages, I regard not my own fame equal to the renown and glory of the Nation."[4] When, even more famously and lugubriously, Johnson writes, "I have protracted my work till most of those whom I wished to please, have sunk into the grave, and success and miscarriage are empty sounds: I therefore dismiss it with frigid tranquillity, having little to fear or hope from censure or from praise," he draws again on a long tradition of lexicographers' complaints; specifically, he sounds much like the recent editors of Furetière's *Dictionnaire universel* (1743): "Il peut s'assurer que nous porterons sur cela [toute l'aigreur] l'indifférence jusqu' à l'insensibilité. Sans répondre à rien, nous abandonnerons au Public tous nos interêts, & le soin de juger qui a raison" (I.xiii).

(2) In their preliminary pieces, both Johnson and Chambers compare their efforts to those of the Continental academies and express some scorn in the comparison. Chambers sees his proposed

---

SJ describes Scaliger after finishing his dictionary as "tenuis pertaesus opellae, / Vile indignatus studium, nugasque molestas" (tired of the lowly task and resentful of the contemptible work, the worthless effort) (*Yale* VI.271). Scaliger's epigram is reprinted in *The Poems of Samuel Johnson,* ed. David Nichol Smith and Edward L. McAdam, Jr. (1941), p. 160.

4. *The New World of English Words* (1658), sig. C4^r.

second edition as "supplying in some Measure the Want of an *English Academy*" ("Considerations," par. 11), and hopes it will "abundantly indemnify us in the Want of what other Countries are so fond of, Royal, Imperial, Caesarian, and Ducal Academies, Palatine Societies, and the like: Splendid Names, pompous Titles, but rarely productive of Fruits answerable thereto!" (par. 20).[5] In his Preface, Johnson says, with equal disdain, "If an academy should be established for the cultivation of our stile, which I, who can never wish to see dependance multiplied, hope the spirit of *English* liberty will hinder or destroy, let them, instead of compiling grammars and dictionaries, endeavour, with all their influence, to stop the licence of translatours, whose idleness and ignorance, if it be suffered to proceed, will reduce us to babble a dialect of *France*" (Preface, pp. 108–09 below). Both writers also cite the failures of the academies to achieve perfection as an indication that perfection in dictionary-making is not to be expected from them as humble individuals. Johnson says, for example, "though therefore my performance should fall below the excellence of other dictionaries, I may obtain, at least, the praise of having endeavoured well, nor shall I think it any reproach to my diligence, that I have retired without a triumph from a contest with united academies and long successions of learned compilers" (*Plan,* p. 58 below).[6] In "Considerations," Chambers also cites the lengthy, unsuccessful efforts of the academies:

> How many Years were the *French* Academists, to the Number of Forty the choicest Wits in *France,* in composing their Dictionary? How often did they alter the Plan of it; and yet when finish'd how many Faults did Furetier find in a single Sheet publish'd as a Specimen? How many Meetings and what Ado was made in the same Academy for the Examination of a single Tragedy, the *Cid* of M. *Corneille*? Besides, of the three Works which that Academy was design'd to compose, two still remain, after near an hundred Years, untouch'd. The Case is much the same with that other celebrated Body *Della Crusca,* whose Vo-

5. For a third reference to the academies in the "Considerations," see par. 14.

6. Cf. Johnson's references to the academicians in the *Plan* (pp. 30–31 and 49 below).

> cabulary after forty Years spent in the Composition, came out with so many, and some such grievous Faults, as gave Occasion to many severe Critiques on it. (par. 14)

Chambers repeats the critique and uses it to apologize for his own deficiencies in the first paragraph of the Preface to his *Cyclopaedia* (I.ii). In his Preface, Johnson echoes the sentiment: "[I]f the aggregated knowledge, and co-operating diligence of the *Italian* academicians, did not secure them from the censure of *Beni;* if the embodied criticks of *France,* when fifty years had been spent upon their work, were obliged to change its oeconomy, and give their second edition another form, I may surely be contented without the praise of perfection" (pp. 112–13 below).

The similarities here are important and they are underlined by the way both writers use the word "perfection." Chambers uses it at least three times in his *Considerations* (pars. 1, 4, 13) with much the same tone and meaning as Johnson does in his Preface (p. 113 below) and *Plan* (p. 49 below). Both writers were responding, however, to statements in the prefaces to the French Académie's *Dictionnaire* that asserted the possibility of perfection in language and in dictionaries.[7] But this assertion runs contrary to a deeper current in lexicographical prefaces declaring the imperfection of such works. To give just one example, in his address to the reader in Thomas Holyoake's *A Large Dictionary* (1676) Thomas Lincoln lists numerous Latin lexicographers and declares that it was the fate of individuals to begin the task but of none to perfect it. The story of these lexicographers proves the aphorism "Ars longa, vita brevis." Moreover, a similar attitude toward the academies and their inevitable failures had been struck before. Publishing between the time of Chambers's *Considerations* and Johnson's *Plan,* Johann Mathias Gesner pointed out in 1735 that he was trying to succeed where whole academies with regal support had failed. The tone in which he describes the "Trivultine Societas" on the one hand and the "singuli homines" on the other is similar to Johnson's (sig. b2^{r}). The editors of Furetière's *Dictionnaire universel* (1743) also reacted to the Acadé-

7. For the Académie's pronouncement on the perfection of language, see p. 49, n. 1, below. On perfection in dictionaries, see, e.g., the Preface to the third edition of the *Dictionnaire* (1740), pars. 1–2.

mie's claims when they said, "Il n'est presque pas possible de finir absolument ces sortes d'Ouvrages" (I.v). Johnson's most scornful remark about academies is yoked to a plea made by Boileau, a major cultural figure in France who long spurned the Académie. In asking that if an academy is established, it should first "stop the licence of translatours," Johnson adapts Boileau's request that the Académie curb French translators: "les trois quarts, tout au moins, de ceux qui les [anciens] ont traduits, étaient des ignorans ou des sots."[8]

(3) Chambers and Johnson agree at many points in their preliminary essays on the important lexicographical issue of definition and related issues of language theory. Both describe the process of definition similarly, and both agree that it is impossible to define "simple words" or "simple ideas" (Chambers, Preface, pp. xiv–xv; Johnson, Preface, p. 88 below). They also agree, in Johnson's words, that "names . . . have often many ideas" (p. 91 below) and in Chambers's that "few names . . . denote only one idea" (p. xiv); and further, in the matter of definition, both think definitions should be arranged from the "literal," which is close to the etymological meaning, to the more remote and metaphorical meanings (p. xix; p. 91 below). Both also believe that "language is the instrument of science [i.e., knowledge]" (Preface, p. 79 below) in Johnson's words, or in Chambers's that it is the "immediate matter of knowledge . . . considered as communicable" (Preface, p. viii). Since words and knowledge are so tightly connected, they both believe that a dictionary can provide what Johnson calls "intellectual history" (p. 98 below), that this is a very important subject (Chambers, pp. xvii, xxii), and that, as a historian of thought, the lexicographer must "register" rather than "form" what he finds (Johnson, Preface, p. 102 below; Chambers, Preface, p. xvii).

Although the parallels between Chambers and Johnson are important, both writers were probably drawing on a superior source of linguistic theory, Book III of John Locke's *Essay concerning Human Understanding* (1690). On the matter of definition, for example, Locke could have been a source for both lexicographers when he

8. *Lives,* III.237 (par. 347), n. 4. Hill quotes *Oeuvres de M. Boileau Despréaux* [1747], V.118.

wrote, "The *Names of simple* Ideas *are not capable of any definitions*" (III.iv.4). On the numerical relationship between words and things, Locke also provides the lexicographers' model; as Johnson quotes him in illustration of *name* (noun, sense 2), Locke says, "If every particular idea that we take in, should have a distinct name, names must be endless."[9] When Johnson says, "language is the instrument of science," he is not following Chambers so much as Locke, who wrote, "words . . . [are] immediately the Signs of Mens [sic] *Ideas;* and by that means the Instruments whereby Men communicate their Conceptions" (III.ii.6). Even before Locke, however, Edward Phillips had expressed in the preface to *A New World of English Words* (1658) a similar view of the relation between words and things:

> The very Summe and Comprehension of all Learning in General, is chiefly reducible into these two grand Heads, *Words* and *Things;* and though the latter of these two be, by all men, not without just cause, acknowledged the more solid and substantial part of Learning; yet since, on the other side, it cannot be denyed but that without *Language* (which is as it were the *vehiculum* or conveyancer of all good Arts) *things* cannot well be expressed or published to the World, it must be necessarily granted, that the one is little lesse necessary, and an inseparable concomitant of the other. (sig. b3[r])

Earlier yet, John Minsheu had made similar connections in the dedication to his *Guide into Tongues* (1617). As authorities for the connection between words and things he cited Isidore of Seville and, finally, Plato. The arrangement of parts of a definition from the literal (meaning in Johnson and earlier writers, the etymological) to the figurative and metaphorical followed from this conception of language and was a convention in Latin lexicography long before Phillips, Chambers, and Johnson worked in the field.

Neither Phillips nor Locke extends his thinking on language to reach the Johnsonian conclusion that a history of words provides "intellectual history" (Preface, p. 98 below). However, that idea was expressed in the early editions of Basilius Faber's *Thesaurus Erudi-*

9. Untraced, but cf. Locke's *Essay,* III.i.3.

tis Scholasticae (1587) and even in his avowed precursor's book, the *Forum Romanum* of Secundus Curione (1561).[1]

Johnson's belief that the lexicographer's task is to "register" rather than to "form" language (Preface, p. 102 below) is uncommon in dictionaries written before his. Many dictionaries, especially those associated with academies, describe their raison d'être as the purification of language. (The motto of the Real Academia Española, for example, was "Limpia, fija y da esplendor"—it cleans, establishes, and polishes.) The fact that both Johnson and Chambers respect the common usage of words puts them on the same minority side of the lexicographical aisle. However, the position had often been taken before on broader linguistic issues. Even the French *Dictionnaire,* the earlier dictionary most concerned with controlling and correcting speech, finally acknowledged in the preface to its third edition (1740), "L'usage qui en matière de Langue, est plus fort que la raison, auroit bientôt transgressé ces lois" (p. xxix). In works broadly philological, a preference for usage as a standard of correctness in language goes back to a statement in Horace's *Ars Poetica,* which Johnson quoted (slightly incorrectly) in the *Dictionary* under "latter": "Volet usus/ Quem penes arbitrium est, & vis, & norma loquendi."[2]

In addition to those mentioned above, there are other similarities between Johnson's and Chambers's preliminary essays, but these are so widespread in earlier works that they prove little about the causal connection between the encyclopedist and the lexicographer. For example, both writers acknowledge their indebtedness to earlier lexicographers (Chambers, Preface, p. ii; Johnson, Preface, p. 87 below). Many Latin lexicographers had not only expressed their gratitude to their forerunners but had also given long lists of them.[3] Restrictions on the word list proposed by both Johnson

1. Faber's approach is outlined in the extensive preface to the London Stephanus, *Thesaurus Linguae Latinae* (1734–35). For more on this tradition of lexicography and its relation to SJ's *Dictionary,* see *JDLL,* pp. 11–16.

2. *Ars Poetica,* ll. 71–72: ". . . use will require it, in whose hands is the judgment, power, and standard of speech." The correct reading is *ius* ("law") for *vis* ("power"); we translate Johnson's incorrect quotation, not Horace.

3. For example, Thomas Holyoake, *A Large Dictionary* (1677), and Robert Ainsworth, *Thesaurus* (1736).

and Chambers, specifically the exclusion or branding of foreign words and "hard words" (barely Anglicized Latin words), had also been called for earlier. Phillips says he will distinguish between what words "are natural, and legitimate, and what spurious, and forc'st" (sig. c2^{r}). In a much more extensive way, such purity had been a concern of Latin and of all the Continental dictionaries. The French, the Italian, and the Spanish academies, for example, had all established lists of writers whose diction was "pure" before they embarked on their lexicons.

For all that the themes of Johnson and Chambers have in common, there are few stylistic similarities. This is an issue that needs clarifying because of Johnson's remark to Boswell about the stylistic importance to him of Chambers's proposal.[4] For example, in their statements of what causes the disparity between idea and performance, the voices of the two writers are obviously distinct, although their themes are much alike. Chambers says, "A thousand things interfere: lexicography, being of the nature of an art, deviates, of course, from the standard of pure reason. . . . The instruments, the materials, and forty things come into the account: the former prove out of order; the latter obstinate and untractable, or perhaps not easy to be had. In effect, the author's situation, his want of leisure or perseverance, his frailties and foibles, nay his very perfections and all conspire against it" (Preface, p. xviii). On the same subject, Johnson elaborates:

> I expect that sometimes the desire of accuracy, will urge me to superfluities, and sometimes the fear of prolixity betray me to omissions; that in the extent of such variety I shall be often bewildred, and in the mazes of such intricacy, be frequently entangled; that in one part refinement will be subtilised beyond exactness, and evidence dilated in another beyond perspicuity. Yet I do not despair of approbation from those who knowing the uncertainty of conjecture, the scantiness of knowledge, the fallibility of memory, and the unsteadiness of attention, can compare the causes of error with the means of avoiding it, and the extent of art with the capacity of man. (*Plan,* p. 59 below)

4. See p. xix above and n. 9.

In this instance and in general, Johnson's style contains more imagery than Chambers's; Johnson even approaches intellectual allegory, as the author is "betray[ed]," "entangled," and "bewildred." Characteristically, too, Johnson uses many more abstract nominal phrases to express ideas that Chambers describes with simple abstractions: Johnson has "the uncertainty of conjecture, the scantiness of knowledge, the fallibility of memory, and the unsteadiness of attention," for example, whereas Chambers speaks only of "want of leisure" before adding "or perseverance, his frailties and foibles."

It is appropriate now to draw a conclusion on the matter of Johnson's debt to Chambers and the rest of lexicographical tradition in his Preface and *Plan*. Although numerically impressive, the correspondences cited do not convince us that Chambers's preliminaries are a direct source of Johnson's writings because for nearly every correspondence there are other possible sources for Johnson's themes. Therefore it seems evident that both Johnson and Chambers were drawing on a common tradition of writings about language and lexicography. Further specific instances are documented in our notes to Johnson's *Plan* and Preface, but to summarize: the lowly reputation of lexicographers, the pains of their work (including a reference to Scaliger's poem on the subject), their inevitable failures, the heroism of their struggles in view of the fact that whole academies had been assigned the task before—all these were commonplace in lexicographical prefaces and proposals known to Johnson. Chambers's rejection of the idea of an English academy is an immediate precursor to Johnson's even more disdainful rejection of it, but such scorn had been expressed before on both sides of the Channel and it had been brewing for a long time.[5] Both Chambers's and Johnson's ideas about definition and about the relationship between language and knowledge are substantially expressed in Locke's *Essay concerning Human Understanding*, Book III.[6] The shunning of foreign words is something

5. For a history of the idea, see Hermann M. Flasdieck, *Der Gedanke einer englischen Spachakademie in Vergangenheit und Gegenwart* (1928), cited in Sledd-Kolb, pp. 20–21.

6. For studies of SJ's indebtedness to Locke, see John H. Middendorf, "Ideas vs. Words: Johnson, Locke, and the Edition of Shakespeare," in *English Writers of the Eighteenth Century*, ed. John H. Middendorf (1971), pp. 249–72; Elizabeth Hedrick, "Locke's Theory of Language and Johnson's *Dictionary*," *Eighteenth-Century Studies*,

Boileau had urged the French Académie to attend to years before Chambers and Johnson recommended it.[7] The high regard in which both writers hold "intellectual history" was at least as old as Francis Bacon;[8] expressing that regard in a dictionary was part of the Faber tradition in lexicography, although Johnson's and Chambers's view of the link between dictionaries and intellectual history is particularly close. The conviction that "shops" and "mines" are sources of legitimate vocabulary was essential to the lexicographical work of Furètiere. Considering the extent to which the correspondences between Chambers and Johnson rely on tradition, perhaps the most suggestive of the correspondences are verbal: the "shops" and "mines" mentioned above; and the fact that both describe lexicographers as "pioneers."[9]

However, these examples do not provide adequate evidence to call Chambers Johnson's source. The most that can reasonably be claimed is that Chambers is an important member of the tradition of lexicographical writings on which Johnson drew. Johnson certainly knew Chambers's work and cited it in the body of the *Dictionary* about 150 times (almost all in the first three letters of the alphabet); he drew on lexicographical tradition as Chambers had; and he agreed with him quite closely on the notion that a dictionary could express the history of ideas.

The Historical Background of the "History of the English Language"

There is little in earlier English works with which to compare Johnson's "History of the English Language."[1] Several earlier lexicographers provide a summary history of English, but they use few or no examples that illustrate their narratives. In *The New World of*

XX (1987), 422–44; and Robert DeMaria, Jr., "The Theory of Language in Johnson's *Dictionary*," in *Johnson After Two Hundred Years*, ed. Paul J. Korshin (1986), pp. 159–74.

7. See p. 109, n. 7, below.

8. *Advancement of Learning*, in *Works* (1730; 2nd ed., 1740), II.455.

9. For a note on this correspondence and a possible common source of the idea, see Preface, p. 73, n. 2, below.

1. For a lengthy treatment of Johnson's History, see Nagashima, pp. 33–88.

English Words (1658), for instance, Edward Phillips discusses the expulsion of Celtic languages from Britain, their replacement by Germanic languages, and the breadth of borrowings from other languages in English. However, he includes no texts of the language at any of the stages that he describes; he provides only examples of loan words. Cocker's *English Dictionary* (1704) cites Joseph Scaliger on the origins of European languages but contains little history of English proper. Nathan Bailey's *Universal Etymological Dictionary* (1721) discusses the "Mutation of our Language" (2nd ed. [1724], sig. a^{v}), but it provides only a few important terms and King Alfred's version of the Lord's Prayer to illustrate Old English. Bailey's *Dictionarium Britannicum* (1730) has no history at all; his second edition (1736), the dictionary on which Johnson relied most heavily in compiling his own, cites William Camden on the character of Old English and reprints some of Camden's examples of Anglo-Saxon terminology, including their equivalents for the Roman names of the months. The longest passages of early English in Bailey consist of four versions of the Lord's Prayer, only one of which is complete. Of all English dictionaries printed before 1755, Benjamin Martin's *Lingua Britannica Reformata* (1749) comes closest to providing a history of English that resembles Johnson's. Martin cites ten versions of the Lord's Prayer as it appeared in works ranging from Eadfride's Gospel (c. 700) to Barker's Bible (1610). The chronological range of Martin's examples is roughly comparable to Johnson's, but they are fewer and much shorter.

Dictionaries were not, of course, the only kinds of works to which Johnson could look for models on which to base his History of English. He knew of histories of English in historical and linguistic works of other sorts. He owned and annotated a 1636 edition of William Camden's *Remains concerning Britain* (1605), and he cited it many times in the body of the *Dictionary*. In this important work, Camden devotes a chapter to the languages of the British and cites several of the versions of the Lord's Prayer later adduced by Benjamin Martin. In *Logonomia Anglica* (1619), a philosophical grammar, Alexander Gil begins with a history of English that traces the Saxon people to Ashkenaz, the son of Gomer (Genesis 10:3). More sensibly, Gil cites a passage of the famous letter of Ælfric to Sigeferth

(c. 960) on the dangers of translating the Bible into the vernacular. Although he took it from Michael Drayton's *Polyolbion,* Gil expands his representation of early English by including a passage of Robert of Gloucester's *Metrical Chronicle* (c. 1300). Johnson himself borrows a passage of the *Metrical Chronicle* (edited by Thomas Hearne, 1724) in his History (pp. 162–73 below), and he cites two stanzas of Spenser's *Faerie Queene* written in Gil's "reformed orthography" (a phonetic spelling scheme employing many made-up letters) in his "Grammar of the English Tongue" (pp. 296–98 below). Much more useful to him than Gil's *Logonomia,* however, was George Hickes's vast three-volume *Thesaurus.* These magnificent folios served Johnson as the direct source for three of his examples in the History (see p. xxi, n. 3, above). Hickes's volumes, which are actually a collection of several works, each with its own title page, comprise a grammar of Old English (and several other medieval northern languages); their sections on the poetry of "Saxon" and "Semi-Saxon" provided Johnson with matter. These sections are more chronological than most parts of Hickes's tomes, which were not designed as histories of English, though they supplied many of the materials necessary for compiling such a work.

Although Hickes's *Thesaurus* was the single most useful book for Johnson when he was compiling the materials for his History, a portion of James Greenwood's *Essay towards a Practical English Grammar Describing the Genius and Nature of the English Tongue* (1711) provided the closest antecedent to a model for his procedure. Translating it from Latin to English, Greenwood drew on John Wallis's preface to his own English grammar; but he added many pages of specimens of English at various stages of its development. (Greenwood identifies his additions to Wallis by placing them between quotation marks.) Four subsequent editions of Greenwood's *Grammar,* each with augmented collections of historical specimens of English, were available to Johnson when he composed his History; the last and fullest was published in 1753. Greenwood, in his own preface, preliminary to his augmented version of Wallis's, acknowledges his assorted debts: "*I must here confess, that I have been very much obliged in the following Papers to Bishop* WILKINS'*s* Real Character, *Dr.* WALLIS, *Dr.* HICKES'*s* Saxon Grammar; *and I must also take notice, that in two or three Places I have made use of Mr.* LOCK'*s Expressions, because I liked them better than my own.*"[2]

Johnson's use of Wilkins is minimal (see p. 300 below), but he is generally indebted to the same predecessors as Greenwood. Most importantly, like Greenwood, Johnson both translates sections of Wallis's grammar and uses other parts of his work extensively.[3] Differences between Johnson's quotations of Wallis and Greenwood's show clearly that Johnson was making his own independent translation, but the co-dependence of Greenwood and Johnson on Wallis's grammar is striking nevertheless. Similarly, Johnson followed Greenwood's lead in quoting (within the *Dictionary*) writers like Verstegan, Camden, and Brerewood on early English. Johnson's citations of these authors are more ample than Greenwood's, so it is unlikely that he drew any of them secondhand, but the correspondences are striking. Even in its fifth edition, Greenwood's history of English by example is much thinner than Johnson's, but it comes closer to Johnson's performance than any of Johnson's other precursors.[4]

To describe Johnson's debts in his History of English, we could say then that he used Greenwood's method but adopted the larger scale of citations found in Hickes's *Thesaurus*. Ephraim Chambers seems

2. Greenwood, sig. A4^{v}; interestingly, Greenwood also thanks "*the Reverend and Learned Dr.* SAMUEL CLARK, *Rector of St.* James'*s, who did me the Honour to make Corrections to the whole Work.*" For another reference to Clarke, see Grammar, p. 290 and n. 1 below. All editions of Greenwood's *Essay* were printed with a recommendation by Isaac Watts, a writer whom Johnson admired as a practical theologian and an educator.

3. In addition to his translation of Wallis's preface, Greenwood included a translation of Wallis's "Praxis," with many additions, and his first chapter, "De Sonorum Formatione." SJ drew on several parts of Wallis's *Grammatica,* but his only direct translation (abridged and accompanied with commentary) comes from Chapter 14, "De Etymologia" (see p. 328, n. 4, below). Greenwood borrowed from this section of *Grammatica* less than SJ, and he reduced his borrowing in his revised, fourth edition of 1740 (reprinted in 1753), evidently deciding, like SJ, that Wallis's connections between sound and sense were fanciful.

4. It appears that Benjamin Martin could have taken most of his examples secondhand from Greenwood, and in *Cyclopaedia* Ephraim Chambers admits that he took almost all of his from Greenwood for his article on "English, or the English *Tongue*." Although many are versions of the Lord's Prayer, and all of them are short, Greenwood has twenty-two different selections in his history (in the fourth and fifth editions), covering the period from the ninth century to the end of the sixteenth.

to have taken all his passages from Greenwood, although some of them, like John of Trevisa's translation of Higden's *Polychronicon* (1387), come originally from Hickes's *Thesaurus*.[5] Like Johnson and Greenwood, Chambers also made heavy use of Wallis. However, his whole article is slight: the history of English proper takes up only about one folio page in the size and format of Johnson's *Dictionary*.

One other work to which Johnson is indebted remains to be mentioned. Although Thomas Warton did not cite illustrative passages, his *Observations on the Faerie Queene of Spenser* (1754) briefly summarized the history of English poetry before Edmund Spenser. Warton sent Johnson a copy of this work, and Johnson praised it in a letter dated 16 July 1754. This was just the time when he was thinking about writing his "History of the English Language," and indeed he clearly made some use of Warton's book. Like Warton, Johnson comments on Robert of Gloucester, John Gower, Chaucer, John Lydgate, Sir Thomas More, and John Skelton. Most, if not all, of these writers had been cited by earlier historians of English language and literature, but similarities between Warton's and Johnson's comments strongly suggest that Warton's work was on Johnson's desk, or in his thoughts, when he put his own History together.[6] Still, because of the conspicuousness and predominance of illustrative quotations in Johnson's History, as a whole Johnson's work is very different from Warton's. Moreover, although there are precedents for the form, the method, and the substance of Johnson's History, no earlier work in English or Latin approximates its special combination of elements and does it on anything like Johnson's scale.

Given the sheer size of Johnson's *Dictionary* and the importance of history in his treatment of English throughout the book, the singularity of his History of English is not surprising. But quite surprising is the apparent fact that no clear analogues to Johnson's His-

5. *Cyclopaedia*, s.v. "English"; *Thesaurus*, I.xvii; SJ did not include this passage in his History.

6. For a detailed study of the similarities, see Gwin J. Kolb and Robert DeMaria, Jr., "Thomas Warton's *Observations on the Faerie Queene of Spenser*, Samuel Johnson's 'History of the English Language,' and Warton's *History of English Poetry:* Reciprocal Indebtedness?" *Philological Quarterly*, LXXIV (1995), 327–35. For another treatment of the same similarities, see Nagashima, pp. 71–75.

tory exist in other languages, either among Latin or among Continental vernacular dictionaries. Many Latin dictionaries listed their authorities in the preliminary matter and often, as in the case of Faber's *Thesaurus* in 1735, organized them according to four literary or linguistic ages: gold, silver, bronze, and iron. Other lexicographers, such as Robert Ainsworth, listed the Latin authors chronologically but located the center of purity in Cicero, while finding impurities in Lucretius on one end and Cassiodorus on the other end of the time line. In all of these dictionaries, however, quotations illustrating the history of Latin appear only in the treatment of the words contained within the dictionary proper. Often enough the entries in the great Latin-Latin lexicons themselves constitute small histories of the language; but we have found nothing in these works that much resembles Johnson's History of English.[7]

There also seem to be no precedents for Johnson's History in the Continental lexicons of his time. Lodovico Antonio Muratori had assembled materials for the early history of Italian in *Antiquitates Italicae Medii Aevi* (6 vols., 1738–42), a work that Johnson noticed in the *Gentleman's Magazine* for July 1742 (p. 391), but Muratori's historical materials are not included in the *Vocabolario* of the Accademia della Crusca. The Spanish *Diccionario* (1726) contains examples of usage in both Latin and Castilian, although they are brief, and it includes a brief history of the language, but without examples. The French Académie had chosen carefully among possible sources for its word list and definitions, but it did not provide citations of those passages deemed exemplary of the best French usage in its *Dictionnaire.* The competing French dictionary of Antoine Furetière included citations of passages and some of the encyclopedic characteristics adopted by Chambers and Johnson, but no history of the language. Johnson's History is a very slender work when the examples are subtracted, and the examples themselves are somewhat carelessly copied, but the compilation and presentation of so much material in a general dictionary of a language were new, and Johnson deserves credit for richly illustrating for the first time the his-

7. There were separate treatises devoted to the history of Latin, including eighteenth-century landmark works by Johann Georg Walch of Meiningen and Johann Nicolaus Funck, but these are not combined with any lexicographical elements.

tory of a vernacular language in a book written in that language, for the benefit of a non-specialist audience.

Historical Introduction to "A Grammar of the English Tongue"

In addition to "The History of the English Language," Johnson included in his preliminary matter "A Grammar of the English Tongue." Only two earlier English dictionaries had included such a work: *A New General English Dictionary* (1735) by William Thomas Dyche and William Pardon, and Benjamin Martin's *Lingua Britannica Reformata* (1749). Furthermore, this feature is absent in the dictionaries produced by the Continental academies and in the Latin dictionaries that were most important to Johnson.[1] There are grammars of various Germanic languages, including Old English, in Hickes's *Thesaurus,* but the *Thesaurus* is a pastiche of linguistic genres rather than a conventional dictionary. Clearly, none of these works provided a model for Johnson's Grammar. The fact that Dyche-Pardon and Martin included grammars in their dictionaries is important because their existence shows that Johnson is not entirely innovative, but he owes nothing substantive to either grammarian/lexicographer. Both works are idiosyncratic and removed from the mainstream of English grammars that Johnson exemplified.

The generic antecedents of Johnson's Grammar are mostly independent publications. In *A Bibliography of the English Language from the Invention of Printing to the Year 1800,* Volume I (1965), R. C. Alston lists fifty-two separate English grammars published through 1754 (I.2–32).[2] The earliest was *William Bullokarz Pamphlet for Grammar* (1586); the most frequently reprinted was Ann Fisher's *A New Grammar* (1750). Johnson mentions neither of these works, but he alludes to four of the first eight grammars in Alston's list: Alexander Gil's *Logonomia Anglica* (1619), Charles Butler's *The English Gram-*

1. For a listing of some of these dictionaries, see above, p. xx and n. 2.

2. This number covers those written in English and those written in Latin by native speakers of English, and it includes several that appeared in more than one format, such as Benjamin Martin's *Physico-Grammatical Essay,* which also appeared in his dictionary.

mar (1633), Ben Jonson's *English Grammar* (1640), and John Wallis's *Grammatica Linguae Anglicanae* (1653). Wallis and Jonson are the grammarians on whom Johnson most often relies.[3] Of all these grammars, it is worth noting that only Gil's *Logonomia Anglica* has approximately the same organization of parts as Johnson's Grammar. Johnson divides his work into sections called "Orthography," "Etymology" (more like what is now called "word formation"), "Syntax," and "Prosody." Instead of "Orthography," Gil has a slightly broader section called "Grammaticam de literarum usu." Most of the other works have sections called "grammar" rather than "etymology"; many have a section on pronunciation, which Johnson considers part of prosody; and only Gil includes metrics, the second part of prosody according to Johnson.

Wallis and Jonson are similar in overall organization for both have sections on pronunciation, grammar, and syntax. The only difference is Wallis's addition of phonetics. However, their similarities are superficial, because the two represent important opposing tendencies in the historical background of Johnson's Grammar. Wallis is usually credited with being the first English grammarian to rebel against the widespread practice of reducing English to Latin grammar, and Jonson, though not the most rigid, was one of those against whom he rebelled. In choosing to rely on these two opposing views, Johnson suggests that his own conception is somewhere in between.

Wallis's grammar was very well established and had run to five editions before 1755. It was widely quoted and had been translated *en bloc* in James Greenwood's influential *Essay towards a Practical English Grammar* (1711).[4] Johnson was doing nothing new in borrowing from Wallis, although he was less reliant than Greenwood in his action. In the overall construction of his Grammar, Johnson displays a preference for some of Ben Jonson's older, Latinizing traits;

3. For further details on SJ's use of these grammars and others, see below, pp. 265–68. SJ used the fourth edition of Wallis's *Grammatica* (1674). For an assessment of Wallis's work and an account of the editions, see E. J. Dobson, *English Pronunciation, 1500–1700* (2d ed., 2 vols., 1968), I.218–46. We draw on Dobson's work in what follows.

4. For Johnson's use of Greenwood in his "History of the English Language," see pp. xxxv–xxxvii above.

on the other hand, he displays a progressive willingness to go even further than Wallis in the direction of empirical rather than abstract grammar. For example, in the midst of translating into his Grammar much of Wallis's section on *Etymologia*, Johnson criticizes Wallis's fancifulness in imagining correlations between sound and sense in the formation of words, and at the end of the section, he makes four highly critical, numbered observations on his historical etymologies, including the damning remark, "That Wallis's derivations are often so made, that by the same license any language may be deduced from any other" (p. 346, below). Within the *Dictionary* proper, Johnson enacts this conviction by being less speculative than earlier etymologists. Specifically, he is more reluctant to make connections based only on homophony or superficial, formal similarities; and, more steadily than earlier grammarians and lexicographers, he sees language and the transmission of words as social activities subject to all of the social changes that affect other aspects of culture.

Latinizing English grammar may be another way of imposing ideal, non-empirical categories upon it; although Johnson was not unsympathetic to Wallis's strictures on this practice, he continued it himself. He respected Wallis's critique of standard grammatical categories, but he probably shared more fully Wallis's attitude toward pronunciation, which is unusual in its respect for orthography. Throughout his philological work, Johnson displays a belief in the superiority of the written to the spoken word, and Wallis contributes to Johnson's denigration of the "merely oral."[5] For example, although the sentiment was not restricted to Wallis, Johnson agrees when he writes, "For pronunciation the best general rule is, to consider those as the most elegant speakers who deviate least from the written words" (p. 295 below). The spelling reformers whom Johnson mentions somewhat derisively in his Grammar tended to put the emphasis the other way around in their attempts to make pronunciation dictate spelling. In asserting the superiority of written language throughout his *Dictionary*, Johnson could certify the truth of his position by the fact that Wallis's work, though over a hundred years old, was still popular, while the works of the spelling reform-

5. SJ uses this phrase in his Preface (p. 75 below).

ers were becoming rare and curious volumes. Indeed, Wallis's work was so well rooted in good sense that some of his observations based on his preference for written language continued to bear fruit later in the eighteenth century: his belief in the sounding of final *e* in the fourteenth century, for example, was expanded into rules for the proper pronunciation of Chaucer's poetry by Thomas Tyrwhitt in his edition of *The Canterbury Tales* (5 vols., 1775–78).

Although Wallis is his most frequently cited English source, Johnson often silently relies on Ben Jonson's *English Grammar*.[6] Like the work of Sylburgius on Greek, which Johnson criticizes on the first page of his Grammar, Ben Jonson's work attempts to apply the principles of Petrus Ramus's Latin grammar to other languages. Ramus tried to base grammar, and indeed all arts, on experience (in opposition to scholastic a priori categories), and Jonson says on his title page that he bases his work on "his observation of the English Language now spoken."[7] Moreover, as G. A. Padley points out, "while accommodating vernacular structure to a method of analysis devised for a different type of language [i.e., Latin], [Jonson is] none the less able to cater for idiosyncrasies of English usage."[8] He omits a discussion of grammatical mood, for example, and, following the Ramist spirit (but not the letter), finds that verbs are words with number, tense, and person, all categories that can be clearly marked in English.

There were many Continental grammars of modern European languages on which Johnson could have drawn, and he shows his awareness of some of them in the opening of his section on Prosody. He specifically mentions Benedetto Buommattei's *Della lingua Toscana* (1623) and François Séraphin Regnier-Desmarais's *Traité de la grammaire française* (1705).[9]

But of greater importance to Johnson than Continental grammars were grammars of the Latin language. Of the multitude of these works the standard, which appeared in numerous editions

6. For an account of Jonson's grammar, see G. A. Padley, *Grammatical Theory in Western Europe, 1500–1700: Trends in Vernacular Grammar* (2 vols., 1985–88), I.57–66.

7. *English Grammar,* p. 463.

8. Padley, pp. 59–60.

9. See below, p. 347; for more information on Continental grammatical traditions, see Padley, passim.

and forms, was "Lily's Grammar." Johnson refers to Lily both in his Grammar and in the *Dictionary* proper.[1] However, in his treatment of grammatical terminology within the latter he generally relies on another Latin grammar, John Clarke's *New Grammar of the Latin Tongue* (1733). In fact, in the *Dictionary* itself, grammar tends automatically to mean Latin grammar. In his Grammar Johnson adjusts his presentation to account for English usage, but he does so incompletely. Thus, Johnson differs from Ephraim Chambers, whom he so often resembles, because Chambers favored a radical subordination of general grammar to particular usages: that is, he favored English usage as a standard rather than Latin's categorical rules.[2]

Unlike Chambers, Johnson was only moderately opposed to the non-empirical application of inappropriate Latin categories to English syntax and grammar, and he was unwilling to depart altogether from this activity himself. His mildly revisionist reliance on Latin grammar is exemplified in his treatment of verbal tense. Just as he refuses to find case and gender in English nouns, so Johnson refuses to break English verbs into conjugations, and he criticizes Ben Jonson for doing it: "The English verbs were divided by Ben Johnson [sic] into four conjugations, without any reason arising from the nature of the language, which has properly but one conjugation" (pp. 324–25 below). On the other hand, Johnson cannot escape the language of "conjugation," and his analysis of moods and tenses of English is not progressive. He identifies indicative, imperative, infinitive, conjunctive, and potential moods. He needs the last two, equivalents of the subjunctive and optative, in order to fit English into the patterns of Latin and Greek. For the first paradigm (*to have*), the formal differences between the conjunctive and the indicative are limited to the second- and third-person singular (*thou hast* is indicative; *thou have* and *he have* are conjunctive). The distinction of the potential depends on the use of *might, could,* and *should* as modal auxiliaries.

Unlike more progressive grammarians, Johnson does not conclude that the great differences in form and structure between Latin and English indicate that the two languages make meanings in fun-

1. For bibliographical information and for further treatment of SJ's indebtedness to Lily, see below, pp. 265–66 and n. 1.

2. For Chambers's treatment of English grammar, see *Cyclopaedia,* s.v. *English.*

damentally different ways and require, therefore, fundamentally different grammars. Wallis is more progressive than Johnson: in his treatment of verbs, for example, he avoids both the distinction of conjugations and the strict analysis of verbs according to the Latin categories. Like modern English grammarians, Wallis sees the modal auxiliaries as the particular way in which English expresses mood rather than as a version of Latin inflection. Even Ben Jonson is more progressive than Johnson on this topic, although his treatment of modal change as a function of the syntax of "verbs with verbs" is awkward. Unable to accommodate the language of Latin grammar to the highly analytical syntax of English, Johnson finds that syntax in English is nearly nonexistent. This means only that English has little inflection, but it leads Johnson to treat syntax very briefly in his Grammar.

Summing up, one can say that in describing English after the model of Latin, Johnson is conservative, but that on the whole his Grammar is neither innovative nor reactionary. In terms of grammatical tradition, Johnson's "Grammar of the English Tongue" should be seen as a step along the way to the Latin-based, compromise approaches to English grammar that were becoming dominant in mid-century England. This dominance was solidified by Robert Lowth's *Short Introduction to English Grammar* (1762), to which Johnson refers in the fourth edition of his *Dictionary* (1773) and which he later recommended, instead of his own, to a young clergyman.[3]

3. See pp. 305, 306, and nn. 1 and 6 respectively below.

SHORT TITLES AND ABBREVIATIONS

Bibliography—J. D. Fleeman (and prepared for publication by James McLaverty). *A Bibliography of the Works of Samuel Johnson: Treating His Works Published from the Beginnings to 1984*. 2 vols. Oxford, 2000.

Cyclopaedia—Ephraim Chambers. *Cyclopaedia: or an Universal Dictionary of Arts and Sciences* (1728). 5th ed. London, 1741.

Dictionary—Samuel Johnson. *A Dictionary of the English Language: in which the Words are deduced from their Originals, and Illustrated in their Different Significations by Examples from the best Writers* (1755). References to the text of the *Dictionary* proper, apart from the preliminary matter, are to the 4th ed. (London, 1773).

English Grammar—Ben Jonson. *The English Grammar*. In *Ben Jonson*. Ed. C. H. Herford, Percy and Evelyn Simpson. Vol. VIII, pp. 453–553. Oxford, 1947.

Grammatica—John Wallis. *Grammatica Linguae Anglicanae* (1653). 4th ed. Oxford, 1674.

Greenwood—James Greenwood. *An Essay towards a Practical English Grammar* (1711). 5th ed. London, 1753.

JDLL—Robert DeMaria, Jr. *Johnson's* Dictionary *and the Language of Learning*. Chapel Hill and Oxford, 1986.

JDTR—Robert DeMaria, Jr. "Johnson's *Dictionary* and the 'Teutonick' Roots of the English Language." In *Language and Civilization: A Concerted Profusion of Essays and Studies in Honour of Otto Hietsch*. Ed. Claudia Bank. Frankfurt-on-Main, 1992.

Letters—*The Letters of Samuel Johnson*. Ed. Bruce Redford. 5 vols. Princeton, 1992–94.

Life—Boswell's *Life of Johnson*. Ed. George Birkbeck Hill. Revised and enlarged by L. F. Powell. 6 vols. Oxford, 1934–50; Vols. v–vi (2d ed.), 1964.

Lives—*Lives of the English Poets by Samuel Johnson LL.D.* Ed. George Birkbeck Hill. 3 vols. Oxford, 1905.

Locke's Essay—John Locke. *An Essay concerning Human Understanding*. Ed. Peter H. Nidditch. Oxford, 1975.

Nagashima—Daisuke Nagashima. *Johnson the Philologist.* Hirakata, Osaka, Japan, 1988.

OED— *Oxford English Dictionary.* Online version: http://dictionary.oed.com/, unless otherwise noted.

"*Preliminaries*"—Gwin J. Kolb and Robert DeMaria, Jr. "The Preliminaries to Dr. Johnson's *Dictionary:* Authorial Revisions and the Establishment of the Texts." *Studies in Bibliography,* XLVIII (1995), pp. 121–33.

Reddick—Allen Reddick. *The Making of Johnson's Dictionary, 1746–73.* Cambridge, 1990.

Sale Catalogue— *The Sale Catalogue of Samuel Johnson's Library* [1785]: *A Facsimile Edition.* Ed. J. D. Fleeman. English Literary Studies, No. 2, University of Victoria, 1975.

Sledd-Kolb—James H. Sledd and Gwin J. Kolb. *Dr. Johnson's Dictionary: Essays in the Biography of a Book.* Chicago, 1955.

Starnes and Noyes—DeWitt T. Starnes and Gertrude E. Noyes. *The English Dictionary from Cawdrey to Johnson, 1604–1755.* Chapel Hill, 1946.

Thesaurus—George Hickes, *Linguarum Vett.* [*Veterum*] *Septentrionalium Thesaurum Grammatico-Criticum & Archaeologicum, Ejusdem de antiquae Literaturae Septentrionalis Utilitate Dissertationem Epistolarem.* 2 vols. Oxford, 1705.

Watkins—W. B. C. Watkins. *Johnson and English Poetry before 1660.* Princeton, 1936.

Yale—The Yale Edition of the Works of Samuel Johnson. New Haven, 1958–.

I, *Diaries, Prayers, and Annals.* Ed. E. L. McAdam, Jr., with Donald and Mary Hyde. 1958.

II, *The Idler* and *The Adventurer.* Ed. W. J. Bate, John M. Bullitt, and L. F. Powell. 1963.

III–V, *The Rambler.* Ed. W. J. Bate and Albrecht B. Strauss. 1969.

VI, *Poems.* Ed. E. L. McAdam, Jr., with George Milne. 1964.

VII–VIII, *Johnson on Shakespeare.* Ed. Arthur Sherbo. 1968.

X, *Political Writings.* Ed. Donald J. Greene. 1977.

XIV, *Sermons.* Ed. Jean Hagstrum and James Gray. 1978.

XVI, *Rasselas and Other Tales.* Ed. Gwin J. Kolb. 1990.

XVII, *A Commentary on Mr. Pope's Principles of Morality, Or Essay on Man.* Ed. O M Brack, Jr. 2004.

SIGLA USED IN THE TEXTUAL NOTES

Plan

FC—The Fair Copy of the *Plan.*
C state— The Plan of a Dictionary of the English Language. London: J. and P. Knapton, T. Longman, et al. "Chesterfield state." 1747.
non-C state— The Plan of a Dictionary of the English Language. London: J. and P. Knapton, T. Longman, et al. "Non-Chesterfield state." 1747.
47— The Plan of a Dictionary of the English Language. London: J. and P. Knapton, T. Longman, et al. Second edition. 1747.

Preface, History, Grammar, and Advertisement

55a—A Dictionary of the English Language. 2 vols. London: J. and P. Knapton, T. and T. Longman, et al. 1755.
55b—*A Dictionary of the English Language.* Second edition. 2 vols. London: J. and P. Knapton, et al. 1755–56.
65—A Dictionary of the English Language. Third edition. 2 vols. London: A. Millar, T. Longman, et al. 1765.
73—A Dictionary of the English Language. Fourth edition. 2 vols. London: W. Strahan, J. & F. Rivington, et al. 1773.
84—A Dictionary of the English Language. Fifth edition. 2 vols. London: W. & A. Strahan, J. F. & C. Rivington, et al. 1784.
85a—A Dictionary of the English Language. Sixth edition. 2 vols. London: J. F. and C. Rivington, L. Davis, et al. 1785.
85b—A Dictionary of the English Language. Seventh edition. London: J. F. and C. Rivington, L. Davis, et al. 1785.

Preface to the Abridged Edition

56—A Dictionary of the English Language. . . . Abstracted from the Folio Edition. 2 vols. London: J. Knapton, et al. 1756.

60—A Dictionary of the English Language. . . . Abstracted from the Folio Edition. Second edition. 2 vols. London: J. Knapton, et al. 1760.

66—A Dictionary of the English Language. . . . Abstracted from the Folio Edition. Third edition. 2 vols. London: J. Knapton, et al. 1766.

70—A Dictionary of the English Language. . . . Abstracted from the Folio Edition. Fourth edition. 2 vols. London: W. Strahan, et al. 1770.

73 abr.—A Dictionary of the English Language. . . . Abstracted from the Folio Edition. Fifth edition. 2 vols. London: W. Strahan, et al. 1773.

78—A Dictionary of the English Language. . . . Abstracted from the Folio Edition. Sixth edition. 2 vols. London: W. Strahan, et al. 1778.

83—A Dictionary of the English Language. . . . Abstracted from the Folio Edition. Seventh edition. 2 vols. London: W. Strahan, et al. 1783.

THE PLAN OF
A DICTIONARY OF THE ENGLISH LANGUAGE
(1747)

EDITOR'S INTRODUCTION

Composition, Publication, and Reception of the *Plan*

The composition of *The Plan of a Dictionary of the English Language* ranks among the most complicated processes of writing and revising that Johnson ever undertook. The successive stages in the composition can be described at length because two annotated manuscript drafts of the pamphlet are extant, a quantity seemingly unequalled by the preliminary stages of any other of Johnson's works. Our account is a shorter, simpler, altered version of a much more extensive treatment, readily accessible to the curious.[1]

The story begins soon after Johnson had presumably decided to accept the tentative proposal of seven important London booksellers (John and Paul Knapton, Thomas Longman and Thomas Shewell, Charles Hitch, Andrew Millar, and Robert Dodsley, who apparently initiated the proposal) that he prepare a new dictionary of the English language, or at least that he draw up a prospectus of such a work which, meeting with their approval, would lead to a formal contract (which, in the event, he and the booksellers signed on 18 June 1746).[2] Accordingly, Johnson wrote "A Short Scheme for compiling a new Dictionary of the English Language," a holograph manuscript now part of the Hyde Collection at the Houghton Library, which is reproduced (and accompanied by a printed text) in the Appendix below (pp. 378–427). Both his known habit of rapid composition and the manuscript itself suggest that the "Scheme" was drawn up only a short time before 30 April 1746, the date noted by Johnson on the last leaf, supposedly just after completing the piece.

1. See Sledd-Kolb, chap. 2 ("The Composition and Publication of *The Plan of a Dictionary*"), pp. 46–84, 211–20. Unless otherwise noted, the present discussion is drawn from this chapter.

2. *Life,* I.182–83; Sir John Hawkins, *Life of Samuel Johnson, LL.D.* (1787), p. 344n.

For a man who had "long thought" of making a dictionary and who testified repeatedly to his speed in writing, the composition of the nineteen-leaf "Scheme" was, at most, probably a matter of a few days' labor. Indeed, like "forty-eight of the printed octavo pages of the Life of Savage" (*Life,* I.166), the whole document may have been created at a single sitting.

Whatever the exact period of composition, a study of the manuscript indicates, first, that Johnson was primarily intent on setting down, quickly and systematically, his notions about the problems and practices involved in compiling a dictionary of the English language and, second, that he was not making a conscious effort to write in his most polished style. The "Scheme" originally consisted of nineteen leaves, but part of the third and all of the eighth are now missing. The remaining seventeen and one-third leaves[3] contain approximately 3,500 words arranged in some 41 paragraphs. In these paragraphs, which correspond to the "body" (pars. 7–74) of the first printed text, Johnson treated, sequentially, such topics as the choice of words for inclusion in his dictionary, spelling, pronunciation, etymology, syntax, definition, "the Distribution of words into their proper classes," and illustrative quotations. That he recorded his thoughts speedily and painlessly and without very much attention to the niceties of writing is evidenced, in varying degrees, by the clean appearance of most of the leaves, the probable omission of several words, the heavy reliance on the comma for pointing and the absence of all punctuation marks in a good many spots where one would normally expect them, the few lapses from "correct" or typically Johnsonian syntax, and the small number of revisions relative to the number made during subsequent stages in the composition of the *Plan.*

The changes that Johnson made before submitting the manuscript to readers consist almost wholly of (1) the substitution of words or phrases for the originals, (2) the correction of mistakes resulting from haste or carelessness, and (3) the

3. Leaf 9 of the "Scheme" was added to the Hyde Collection after the publication of Sledd-Kolb.

deletion of words (largely) or phrases. These changes are distributed fairly evenly throughout the document, with fourteen of the seventeen and one-third leaves each containing, roughly, from two to five.

After he had written the "Scheme" and had made changes of the sort just described, Johnson presumably passed the manuscript to at least one reader and possibly more: two different persons wrote comments on it. We can offer no conjecture about the identity of the more taciturn of the two, who seems, from the location of his remarks, to have been the second reader. But we think that the first, and much more vocal, reader was probably the bull-breeding king of Ashbourne, Johnson's close friend Dr. John Taylor. Taylor's handwriting is markedly similar to the writing of this first reader, whose comments, especially one about "your Dictionary," sound as though he were on terms of easy familiarity with the author. Moreover, we know that Johnson had earlier entrusted Taylor with the manuscript of *Irene* and that also, according to Taylor's recollection long afterward, he sent him "in the country" a draft of the *Plan*, possibly, though not certainly, the "Scheme" itself.[4]

Whether Taylor or someone else, the first reader made a total of approximately fifty sets of marks, corrections, and/or comments on the manuscript, most of them inserted between Johnson's lines or in the margins. At least one appears on every leaf except 19, which contains only three lines of text, but there are more than twice as many—roughly thirty-four to fifteen—on leaves 1–10 as there are on leaves 11–

4. See Marshall Waingrow, ed., *The Correspondence and Other Papers of James Boswell Relating to the Making of the Life of Johnson* (1969; 2d ed., 2001), p. 83, which records Taylor's memories, in a conversation with Boswell on 6 May 1785, (1) of receiving, "in the country," a draft of the *Plan* from SJ, (2) of passing it to William Whitehead, and (3) of hearing from SJ that the draft had later passed to Thomas Villiers, Earl of Clarendon, and, finally, to Lord Chesterfield. Also see *Life,* I.184–85. In his cogent article on "Johnson and Chesterfield, 1746–47" (*Studies in Burke and His Time,* XII [1970], 1677–90), Jacob Leed argues persuasively that this draft was not the fair copy of the *Plan,* as Sledd-Kolb had concluded, but may have been the "Scheme." Although it is appealing in several respects, the hypothesis fails, as Leed points out (p. 1686), to explain the seeming fact that, unlike the "Scheme," the draft in question was not written in SJ's hand.

18. About seventeen suggest various changes in phraseology, ranging from a single word to a much longer part of a sentence. Eleven other notes consist of as many terms ("Words," "Orthography," etc.) used to describe the series of topics discussed in the "Scheme" and written at the beginnings of appropriate paragraphs. Some ten are concerned—briefly, for the most part—with examples that illustrate general statements in the manuscript. Several additional alterations supply small words omitted by Johnson in writing the document.

Finally, three notes resulted from three of Johnson's generalizing remarks about his intentions in the *Dictionary*. First, he had said: "When the Orthography and Pronunciation are adjusted the *Etymology* or Derivation is next to be considered, and the words are to be placed in their different classes whether simple . . . or compound . . . whether primitive . . . or derivative" (p. 40 below). Evidently assuming that this statement disclosed Johnson's intention to arrange the words in his *Dictionary* on the basis of their etymologies, the reader argues vigorously, in his longest single note, for a strictly alphabetical arrangement. He begins by inquiring: "Is not Fabers [sic] Method quite thro', the best?" and then continues: "If the Words are not alphabetically placed, a Man must understand the Language only to find a Derivative, & then he has no Occasion for your Dictionary. This would spoil the Sale of it to Schools & Foreigners. Besides may not the Author & I differ in a Derivation, & if it should so happen, by what Rule can I find the Derivative I want? A Dictionary has no more to do wth Connection and Dependance than a Warehouse book. They are both mere Repertoriums, & if they are not such they are of no Use at all" (p. 394 below). In his second general note, the reader again directs Johnson's attention to the model for a new English dictionary provided, in classical lexicography, by Basilius Faber's *Thesaurus Eruditionis Scholasticae* (1571). Commenting on Johnson's statement, in the section on definition, that it may be "necessary to give the interpretation of the principal words in some other Languages" (p. 406 below), he says, "Look at Faber's Thesaurus" (p. 408 below). These references to Faber, together with the second reader's mention of "Stephen[s]," offer more evidence, it should be pointed out, of the inclusiveness of the lexicographical tradition—Continental as well as English—within which Johnson worked and the nature of which we have examined on pp. xvii–xxi above. In the last of his general notes, prompted by Johnson's remarks (p. 422) about the illustrative quotations to be cited in his *Dictionary,* the reader expresses precise recommendations: "All Examples should be compleat Sense & Grammar, (not the Author's whole Sense) for without that a Learner can not judge how, why, in what Sense a word is employed. At the Conclusion of each word there ought to be Examples 1 of the Elegant Uses of each Word & Phrase in which it is employed. 2. Examples of the Abuse of each Word &c. wth Cautions how to correct & avoid it" (p. 424 below).

The comments of the second reader can be treated briefly, for there are only three of them on the manuscript. Two are reactions to specific examples of kinds of usages. The third, like the note of the first reader quoted above, takes issue with Johnson's statement about placing words "in their different classes." "Whether," the second reader asks, "Stephen's Method which seems to be meant here will not be more puzzling?" (p. 394 below). "Stephen[s]" designates, of course, a member of the famous French family (Stephanus or Estienne) of classical scholars, lexicographers, and printers; and the "Method" that the reader almost certainly had in mind is the modified etymological arrangement followed in Robert Stephanus's *Thesaurus Linguae Latinae* (1531), published in four volumes at London in 1734–35.

After at least two critics had read the "Scheme," Johnson made additional changes in the manuscript. One group of approximately eight changes appears to respond to the first, and only the first, reader's remarks; a second, smaller group appears to be independent of the remarks. Neither group gives any sign of systematic revision. On the whole, Johnson was not very hospitable to the reader's suggested improvements. He accepted, naturally, all the words that he had omitted and the reader had presumably supplied. But he usually preferred his own prose to that of the reader, and the very few alternatives he accepted are slight. He also made an occasional revision of his own that seems to have been, in part at least, the consequence of the reader's proposed alterations. Apparently he was influenced only once by the reader's comments about the examples presented in the "Scheme"; and, so far as we can tell, he was not led, by the general remarks, to change any of his statements about the various aspects of preparing a dictionary.

Exclusive of those discussed above, the revisions Johnson definitely or probably made in the "Scheme" after its return from the readers number some four or five (the actual total may be larger, since it may include some changes that cannot be classified either as "pre-" or "post-reader"), are limited to five of the first seven leaves of the manuscript, and may have occurred at different times. Two of these revisions are additional passages written on the versos of leaves 4 and 7 (pp. 386, 394 below) and designed for insertion on the rectos of the same leaves. The latter passage forms the final paragraph on pronunciation in the printed *Plan* (p. 40 below); the former appears in the section on the choice of words in the *Dictionary* (p. 34 below). Two other fragmentary changes, on leaves 1 and 2 respectively (pp. 378, 380 below), show that Johnson had begun to rewrite, or at least to consider rewriting, the "Scheme." The last of this group of revisions involved both the addition, on leaf 4 (p. 384 below), of a reference to the Fourth Earl of Chesterfield's views on spelling and the crossing-through of about half the remainder of the same paragraph. Versions of this crossed-out passage and also of the rest of the paragraph eventually become the ultimate paragraph of the section on orthography (p. 35 below).

The allusion to Chesterfield constitutes the earliest documentary evidence of the Earl's influence on the composition of the *Plan*. That initial influence was hardly trifling, for Johnson's original estimate of the "settled propriety" of English spelling gives way to Chesterfield's assertion of its "great uncertainty among the best writers." As we point out below, however, Chesterfield's subsequent effects on specific parts of the *Plan* are much less significant. Although the exact date of its insertion remains unclear, the reference to Chesterfield not only belongs to the post-30 April 1746 group of revisions but was also one of the later additions to that group. Probably Johnson did not entertain the thought of addressing the *Plan* to Chesterfield until after he had reached an oral agreement with the booksellers; for he says in the fair copy of the piece that he had been "content with the Terms . . . Stipulated" (p. 430 below) until he found that his design had excited the Earl's curiosity and attracted his favor. The causes of the latter's positive interest may have been his putative perusal of an early draft of the *Plan,* possibly the "Scheme," and his ensuing conversation or conversations with Johnson about the *Dictionary*—all of these events predating his certain scrutiny of, and comment on, the fair copy of the *Plan.*[5]

The second major step in the composition of the *Plan* was the expansion of the "Scheme" into a document closely resembling the printed form of the piece. With the "Scheme" evidently close at hand, Johnson presumably wrote another holograph manuscript, beginning with the address to Chesterfield as "one of his Majesty's [George II's] Principal Secretaries of State" and concluding with one version of the final sentence in the *Plan.* The precise period of composition remains uncertain but it must have occurred after 29 October 1746, since Chesterfield did not become a secretary of state until that time. We may guess that Johnson wrote the enlarged draft during the fall of 1746 and/or the winter of 1746–47.

The manuscript itself is lost. However, a clerk's fair copy of the *Plan*—consisting, originally, of forty-six leaves (of which all except leaf 32 are extant; see pp. 428–89 below)—was almost certainly made from this manuscript. Thus we are able, by comparing the "Scheme" and the fair copy, to reconstruct most of the contents of the missing document.

A broad generalization about the lost manuscript can be drawn immediately from our comparison; in transforming

5. See Leed's article cited above.

the "Scheme" into the *Plan,* Johnson, with only one clear exception, built on what he had done already. He kept the basic form of the structure the same, so to speak, but added an entrance and exit and some new rooms. Specifically, he added (1) the introductory and closing remarks addressed to Chesterfield (pp. 428, 486–89 below); (2) the paragraph (p. 435), in the discussion of the principles governing the selection of words for the *Dictionary,* about the moral to be deduced from the reluctant admission of "Terms of Science" into the French Académie's *Dictionnaire;* (3) the statements, in the section devoted to orthography, about the "Contest . . . between Etymology and Pronunciation" (p. 443) and also about his decision (p. 444) to "make no Innovations" in spelling "without a reason sufficient to balance the Inconveniencies of Change"; (4) examples (p. 474), in the section on definition, of the varied "characters of words" that will be explained in the *Dictionary;* (5) a reply (p. 476), at the conclusion of the discussion of definition, to those persons who may consider "many of these remarks . . . trifling"; (6) the announcement (p. 482), at the end of the section on classifying words, of his decision—prompted by Chesterfield's "opinion" —to "Interpose my own Judgment" concerning "Questions of purity, or propriety"; and (7) the statement (p. 483), in the section on quotations and "Authorities," that "Mr Pope" had "chosen . . . Many of the Authours" to be cited in the *Dictionary.*

Our inferences about the presence in the lost manuscript of three other groups of paragraphs must be presented with less than perfect assurance, because portions of both the "Scheme" and the fair copy are missing; but assorted bits of evidence suggest that almost all of these paragraphs were transferred from the "Scheme" to the lost manuscript.

Aside from completely new paragraphs, additions in the lost manuscript included the lengthening of paragraphs in the "Scheme" and, occasionally, the expansion of one paragraph into two. Changes in phraseology, also producing numerous additions, ranged from the fairly common substitution of one or more words for the original to the rare recasting of almost an entire paragraph. Further, punctuation usually increased in both frequency and weight, with the pointing of some previously unmarked passages and the replacement of a good many commas by periods or semicolons. (The copyist may have introduced at least some of the changes in punctuation; it is impossible to be sure.)

Last, so far as we can tell, Johnson omitted from the lost manuscript only one sizable passage in the "Scheme" (p. 406). In the section on the definition of words, he had declared: "It may be doubted whether it be not necessary to give the interpretation of the principal words in some other Languages, which would much facilitate the use of the Dictionary to foreigners and might perhaps contribute to its use in other Countries, and would not be without advantages to the English themselves." When he came to this paragraph during the composition of the longer draft, however, he apparently decided not to use it. The reasons for his decision can only be surmised, but perhaps he was struck by the frankly commercial—and inappropriate—tone of the passage and was impressed, too, by the difficulties involved in compiling, simultaneously, a new English and multilingual dictionary. At all events, the paragraph did not appear in the expanded version of the "Scheme."

The next major phase in the composition of the *Plan* began when Johnson, supposedly as soon as he completed the lost manuscript, gave or sent it to an amanuensis for copying. Since, as will be noted shortly, the clerk had great trouble deciphering several passages, it seems likely that the document was not a model of neatness or legibility. After the amanuensis finished the fair copy (of which, to repeat, forty-five of the original forty-six leaves are extant), Johnson presumably read it through at least once, making corrections and other changes as he went along, and adding the complimentary close and his signature at the end. The nature and number of his revisions at this time cannot be estimated with any precision. Consequently, we treat all of his changes (excepting one group) later in this account. But it should be emphasized that some of the alterations described later were almost certainly madc before, not after, the fair copy had circulated among readers.

The single group of revisions examined here consists of corrections of more than twenty faulty words or passages in the fair copy. Perhaps not all these corrections were made at the same time; but, since none of the glaring mistakes rectified by them evoked comments from later readers (apparently), most, if not all, were clearly made before Johnson submitted the fair copy to anyone else. About fifteen changes resulted from the clerk's inability to read Johnson's hand or to understand the arrangement of certain passages. Six corrections add words omitted by the clerk or by Johnson himself in the manuscript that the clerk copied, while two others apparently delete superfluous words.

After he had made at least one set of revisions in the fair copy, Johnson presumably sent the manuscript to Lord Chesterfield: the holograph complimentary close and signature suggest that the document was intended for presentation to its addressee.[6] Subsequently, it was read by at least one more unidentified person.

Chesterfield made a total of eight comments on the manuscript. One of these deals with Johnson's choice of a word, three with the spelling of a word, one with morphology, one with etymology, one with syntax, and one with pronunciation (see pp. 438, 436, 448, 457, 446, 454, 464, 450). The second reader, who sometimes echoes or reinforces Chesterfield, wrote eleven remarks on the fair copy. In addition, and excluding the signs that direct attention to the notes, he made at least nineteen other marks, or sets of marks (largely red crosses and underlinings), on the manuscript. One group of four notes concerns illustrative examples in various sections of the *Plan* (see pp. 436, 448, 448, 464). Another group

6. We owe this observation to Leed (p. 1685).

of four notes criticizes the choice of expressions (see pp. 433, 436, 457, 467 below); one note concerns spelling (457). The two remaining comments express the reader's reaction to two of the general statements in the manuscript (pp. 460, 481). Last, practically all the reader's red markings query assorted aspects of the prose in the fair copy.

Fairly soon, seemingly, after its receipt by Chesterfield, the fair copy, bearing Chesterfield's and the second reader's comments, was returned to Johnson. Presumably, Johnson read it through at least one more time. He considered, as he read, the comments of the critics and made, in addition, many changes unrelated to the readers' comments. He revised relevant portions of the manuscript in response to the first seven of Chesterfield's remarks but made no change in response to the eighth. Of the second reader's twenty-odd suggestions (both notes and significant marks) independent of Chesterfield's comments, he was influenced more or less by sixteen.

Besides his certain or probable corrections of the clerk's errors and his favorable responses to the readers' suggestions, Johnson's revisions in the fair copy number well over two hundred. They appear on forty-four of the forty-five leaves, but they are most numerous on leaves 3, 12, and 21, and they include alterations in phraseology, punctuation, spelling (probably), and capitalization (apparently), as well as the deletion and addition of several sizable passages. In making certain changes, Johnson obviously aimed at enhanced precision of diction; in others, he elaborated or qualified or emphasized the meaning of the originals. Sometimes he compressed wordy, awkward expressions into smoother, more pointed phrases. Occasionally he shifted the form of a whole sentence, and here and there he increased or reduced the number of sentences in the original passage. He deleted two substantial passages—the first, and its substitute, on leaf 11 (p. 441); the second, and its much longer replacement, on leaves 35 and 34^{v} (pp. 474, 473). Aside from the latter replacement, the only other sizable addition in the fair copy consists of a qualification of Johnson's remark that his "method" of arranging illustrative quotations will amount to a record "of the gradual changes of the Language" (p. 485).

Unlike revisions involving the writing of one or more letters, Johnson's changes in punctuation cannot always be distinguished from the marks made by the clerk. Moreover, even when a particular change seems, on the basis of the difference in appearance, to be Johnson's, one cannot always decide whether it is an actual revision or merely a correction of the clerk's mistake. Nevertheless, enough indisputable evidence exists to prove that, in revising the fair copy, Johnson paid much more attention to punctuation than he had in previous stages of the composition. Specifically, he continued the practice, which we have already noted, of substituting periods for commas; and, except in the new passages he added, he tended to increase the amount of his pointing, especially of commas. Last, unless we assume that all the (roughly) twenty changes are corrections of the clerk's errors, it seems probable that he made at least a few alterations in the spelling and capitalization that he had employed in the manuscript that the clerk transcribed. Johnson's attention to the accidentals (punctuation, spelling, and capitalization) in the *Plan* suggests that, unlike some eighteenth-century authors, who relied on compositors (or other professionals) to point their texts, Johnson undertook the work himself. However, it is also true for Johnson's texts as well as other eighteenth-century texts that compositors and copyists added pointing. This was part of their job, and it was formally described in printers' manuals of the day. Hence, with regard to accidentals, various stages of composition in Johnson's *Plan* display a particularly confusing, hybrid state. We have taken this into consideration as best we can in our selection of a basic text and in our substitution of readings from other states of the text (see below, pp. 22–24).

After his final revision of the fair copy, Johnson presumably sent the document to the printer (perhaps the shop of William Strahan), where it served as copy. But, unlike the bookseller Andrew Millar on the more famous occasion connected to the *Dictionary,* he was not able to say, "Thank God

I have done with him,"[7] for a comparison of the revised fair copy and the first edition of the printed *Plan* shows that he revised extensively while he was reading the proofs of the work. About one hundred of the (approximately) 420 differences between the two versions are changes in phrasing, for which, with hardly any exceptions, Johnson himself was surely responsible. These variations in diction appear on all pages of the first edition except 1 and 20–24 (since leaf 32 of the fair copy is missing, it is impossible to determine whether any differences occur on pp. 22–23 of the printed text). As a group, they reveal Johnson engaged in putting final touches to his prose—correcting obvious mistakes, selecting more appropriate words or phrases, improving rhythms, sharpening parallel constructions, condensing loose passages—above all, avoiding glaring repetitions. Most of them are limited to the deletion, addition, or substitution of single words; but some involve the revision of phrases; and a very few consist of such alterations as the combination or multiplication of sentences.

The largest single group of differences between the fair copy and the first edition, numbering almost three hundred and appearing on every page of the latter, comprises variations in punctuation; the smallest group, with about twenty members, consists of changes in spelling. With few exceptions, pointing in the printed version is markedly heavier than that in the fair copy; two hundred of the changes, for example, signify the addition of as many commas, and a majority of the other changes consist of the substitution of semicolons for commas. One cannot assume, of course, that Johnson was responsible for all of these revisions; but since, as we have noted, he tended to punctuate more frequently in successive stages of the composition of the *Plan,* it is almost certain that he was the cause of at least some of them. Others were undoubtedly made by a compositor following printing house rules for punctuation. As for the changes in spelling, little can be inferred about the number—if, in-

7. On receiving the "last sheet" of SJ's *Dictionary,* Millar said, "'[T]hank GOD I have done with him.' 'I am glad' (replied Johnson, with a smile,) 'that he thanks GOD for any thing'" (*Life,* I.287).

deed, there were any—of Johnson's alterations. The spelling in the printed *Plan* itself is not entirely consistent; for instance, "public" appears on page 3 (p. 28), "publickly" on page 34 (p. 59); "errour" on page 29 (p. 53), "error" on page 34 (p. 59). Perhaps the most one can say, in view of the fact that he certainly made changes in spelling in the fair copy, is that Johnson may have been responsible for some of the similar changes in the printed version.

The penultimate part of our story commences soon after Johnson returned the proofs containing his final revisions to the printer. He may have done this during June or July 1747, for the publication date was early August of the same year. The pamphlet appeared in a quarto edition that includes two different settings of signature A and two different states of E1^{v}. As R. W. Chapman noted long ago, signature A was set once and then completely reset. Copies containing the original setting of signature A are labeled "Chesterfield" because this address appears at the head of page 1: "To the Right Honourable Philip Dormer, Earl of Chesterfield; One of his Majesty's Principal Secretaries of State." Copies containing the second setting are called "Non-Chesterfield" because this address does not appear on page 1. The earlier state of E1^{v} (p. 34) contains a duplication of the word *the* ("the the mazes") in ll. 1–2; the second does not contain this error. So far as we know, no copies exist that contain the "Chesterfield" setting of signature A *and* the uncorrected state of E1^{v}.

Reconstruction of the likely sequence in the printing of the first edition is relatively simple. The sheets (with sheet A in the "Chesterfield" setting) were started through the press. During the printing, a redundant expression (the repetition of "reason") on page 19 was discovered, and the erratum directing its deletion was placed on the verso of the title page; later the duplication of "the" on E1^{v} was discovered, and that error was corrected. Then the assembling of all sheets began. After the early copies had been sewn and possibly even put on the market, it was decided, probably by Johnson, to remove the address to Chesterfield on page 1 and to correct several small errors in signature A, which was entirely reset as a cancel sheet, since type had been distributed. Johnson also probably took the opportunity to make a few more revisions (see notes b, e, and f on pp. 26, 28, 29). The cancel sheet then replaced the "Chesterfield" setting of signature A in all unsewn copies. The fact that no "Chesterfield" copies, apparently, contain the duplication of "the" on page 34 ($E1^v$) may be explained thus: assuming that sheet E was piled up in the order, or roughly in the order, in which it was printed and that the sheets were assembled from the tops of the various piles, one would expect the "Chesterfield" setting of signature A to be assembled with the corrected state of $E1^v$.

Early in August 1747—almost five months after newspaper announcements had informed the public that the *Dictionary* was "*now Preparing for the Press, and in good Forwardness*"—copies presumably of both the "Chesterfield" and the "Non-Chesterfield" settings were offered for sale. By the eighth of that month, Daniel Wray the antiquary had bought one, for an undisclosed price, from Robert Dodsley, one of the publishers of the *Dictionary,* whose periodical *Museum* for 1 August carried an enthusiastic puff, along with quotations from the "Non-Chesterfield" setting. The piece was also very favorably noticed in the July–September number of the *Bibliothèque raisonné des ouvrages des savans,* published in Amsterdam. In the section entitled "Nouvelles Literaires *De Londres,*" the anonymous reviewer observed:

> Il n'est pas surprenant que peu de Nations aient de bons Dictionnaires de leur langue. La tâche est aussi pénible que peu brillante, & convient mieux à une Société qu'à un particulier. C'est à leur Académie que les François doivent tous leurs Dictionaires [sic]. Quoiqu'un pareil établissement soit jusqu'ici simplement souhaité dans cette ville, un particulier travaille depuis quelque tems à un Dictionnaire complet, & il vient d'en publier le plan dans une Lettre à Mil. *Chesterfield.* Ce Seigneur accoutumé à favoriser les projets utiles, & connaissant mieux que personne les beautés & les difficultés de sa langue, a encouragé l'Auteur qui se nomme *Johnson,* à

> poursuivre un travail aussi ingrat. Celui-ci expose dans sa Lettre la méthode & les règles qu'il a dessein de suivre. On ne peut rien ajouter à la finesse de ses vues, & à la délicatesse des détails dans les quels il entre. Son Ecrit confirme que pour être bon Critique il faut être bon Philosophe. L'histoire des mots est liée avec de la succession des idées, & il ne faut pas moins de bon sens que de lecture pour suivre une langue dans ses progrès & dans ses bisareries, qui souvent cessent le l'être, lorsqu'on en démèle les raisons Mr. *Johnson* apporte tout ce qu'il faut pour le succès, & ceux même qui ne font pas de l'Anglois une étude particuliere ne liront pas sans fruit une Lettre écrite avec une pureté & une élégance peu communes. Si l'Ouvrage est dans le mème goût, les Anglois n'auront pas à se plaindre de l'avoir longtems attendu.[8]

And in Ireland, the *Plan* soon evoked the compliment of a rival proposal from one John Maxwell, M.A. In "A Plan of Mr. Maxwell's work to be intitled The Treasure of the English Tongue" Maxwell promised great feats of lexicography to be revealed in a year and a half, including illustrative quotations from "Discourses of the most ingenious and approved Authors on the most important and curious points." Maxwell never made good on these promises.[9]

Nearer at home, Johnson's friend Thomas Birch assessed the pamphlet as "an ingenious performance, but the style is flatulent" and went on to report that Daniel Wray "has some objections to [Johnson's] Scheme, & even wrote down his Remarks upon it."[1] On the other hand, the Earl of Orrery told

8. Howard Weinbrot speculates very plausibly that this piece was written by Matthew Maty (personal communication). In any case, Maty echoed its sentiments in 1751 in a footnote to his puff of the *Rambler* (*Journal Britannique,* IV [February 1751], 235. Maty also reviewed the *Dictionary* when it appeared in 1755 (see pp. 67–68 below). For a discussion of Maty's several severe reviews of Johnson's work, see Uta Janssens, *Matthew Maty and the Journal Britannique, 1750–1755: A French View of English Literature in the Middle of the Eighteenth Century* (Amsterdam: Holland University Press, 1975), pp. 110–12.

9. Lord Orrery sent a copy of Maxwell's plan to Thomas Birch on 30 December 1747 (British Library Add. MS 4303, fols. 135–36).

1. British Library Add. MS 35,397, fol. 67^v (30 December 1747). Birch first men-

Birch that "I am much pleased with the plan: and I think the specimen is one of the best I have ever read. Most specimens disgust, rather than prejudice us in favour of the work to follow; but the language of Mr Johnson's is good, and the arguments are properly and modestly expressed. . . . I have great expectations from the performance."[2]

So far as we know, the period from late 1747 to the end of 1754 contains no notable events that have a bearing on the publication of the *Plan*. The partners in the *Dictionary* probably continued to distribute copies of the pamphlet until the supply was exhausted; in April 1755, at least one reviewer of the *Dictionary* thought that they had been circulating free copies for several years. However, no new edition of the *Plan* appeared in the seven years while Johnson was working on the contents of the *Dictionary*.

Toward the end of 1754, however, when the *Dictionary* was almost ready for publication, the booksellers resumed their advertising campaign, which had been largely dormant for almost seven years. In that campaign, the *Plan* played an active role. It appeared (in the "Non-Chesterfield" setting) in the Appendix to the *Scots Magazine* for 1754 and possibly in other places at about the same time. Then, at the end of February 1755, 1,500 copies were published in the octavo edition (printed, without the salutation from the "Chesterfield" setting). An entry in William Strahan's ledgers proves that the date of publication was 1755, although 1747 is the date on the title page. Free copies of this publication, according to newspaper advertisements, were available for the asking.

A collation of the octavo and quarto ("Chesterfield" setting) editions reveals only minor variations (restricted almost entirely to spelling and punctuation). These changes could have been made by a compositor; none of them suggests that

---

tions the *Plan* on fol. 63v (1 August 1747), saying it is "ready for publication at the Meeting of the Parliament."

2. British Library Add. MS 4303, fol. 133r; Orrery's remark is cited by Boswell, *Life*, I.185. Before he read it, Orrery mentioned the *Plan* approvingly in letters to Birch on 22 August 1747 and 19 September 1747 (British Library Add. MS 4303, fols. 126, 130).

Johnson made any changes in the text of the work. Granted that he had advance notice of the new edition, he may have decided that he had already done all he wanted to do with the *Plan*. He had written the "Scheme" and had revised parts of it both before and after readers commented on it; he had written (and probably revised) the manuscript of the *Plan* proper; he had (almost certainly) revised the fair copy both before and after it circulated among readers; he had revised proofs at least once; and, finally, he had probably made changes in signature A of the first edition during the resetting of that signature. In 1755 Johnson perhaps felt that the *Plan* should be able to speak for itself to contemporary and later audiences.

Almost simultaneously with the *Plan*'s—and the *Dictionary*'s initial—appearance in 1755, readers could also scan a four-page epitome of the former in the *Gentleman's Magazine* for April. Considerably later, Thomas Davies carried the *Plan* (and the Preface; see p. 66 below) in Volume II of his *Miscellaneous and Fugitive Pieces* (1773, 1774, 1774). Interestingly, he did so without Johnson's knowledge in 1773.[3] James Harrison followed suit in his one-volume folio edition of the *Dictionary* (1785–87). This is the only edition of the *Dictionary* with both the *Plan* and the Preface, although Matthew Maty wished both had been included in the first edition when he reviewed the *Dictionary* in the July–August 1755 number of the *Journal Britannique*.[4] Sir John Hawkins reprinted the *Plan* in his edition of the *Works* (1787), and subsequently, beginning in 1792 and continuing intermittently far into the nineteenth century, the so-called Arthur Murphy edition of *The Works of Samuel Johnson* included the *Plan*.

Excerpts from it and the Preface (see p. 67 below) also appeared in successive editions of the *Beauties of Johnson*, one of a popular group that singled out, besides Shakespeare, such eighteenth-century authors as Henry Fielding, Oliver Goldsmith, David Hume, and Laurence Sterne. The first edition (1781) was expanded in 1782, and many editions followed. A second volume was first published in 1782. The two volumes

3. *Life*, II.270–71. In the edition of 1773, the *Plan* appeared in vol. II, pp. 30–54.
4. For SJ's hostility to Maty, see *Life*, I.284 and n. 3.

combined contained eight quotations from the *Plan*, though this number seems to have shrunk to seven in the eighth edition (2 vols. in 1, 1792). An edition published in Philadelphia in 1787 provided a rare, if not unique, appearance of Johnson's philological writings in America before 1800.

Like the Preface, too (see pp. 68–69 below), the *Plan* elicited laudatory remarks, sometimes repetitious, in early biographies of Johnson both short and long. The former include: David Erskine Baker, *The Companion to the Play-House* (2 vols., 1764), II. sigs. S6–T1; James Tytler (?), *An Account of the Life and Writings of Dr. Samuel Johnson* (1774); David Erskine Baker and Isaac Reed, "Samuel Johnson" in *Biographica Dramatica* (1782); William Cooke (?), *Memoirs of the Life and Writings of Dr. Samuel Johnson* (1782); "L," *Memoirs of the Life and Writings of Dr. Samuel Johnson* (1784); William Cooke, *The Life of Samuel Johnson, LL.D.* (1785); William Shaw, *Memoirs of the Life and Writings of the Late Dr. Samuel Johnson* (1785); Joseph Towers, *An Essay on the Life, Character, and Writings of Dr. Samuel Johnson* (1786).

Of the four longer biographies two, James Boswell's (1791) and Robert Anderson's (1795), contained high praise of the *Plan*. Boswell comments: "It is worthy of observation, that the 'Plan' has not only the substantial merit of comprehension, perspicuity, and precision, but that the language of it is unexceptionably excellent; . . . and never was there a more dignified strain of compliment, than that in which he courts the attention of one who, he had been persuaded to believe, would be a respectable patron" (*Life*, I.183–84). Anderson's remarks draw heavily (pp. 74–75) on Boswell's.

On the other hand, Sir John Hawkins's assessment in his *Life* (1787) is far more reserved: "Such was [Johnson's] opinion . . . of [Lord Chesterfield's] skill in literature, his love of eloquence, and his zeal for the interests of learning, that he approached him with the utmost respect, and that he might not err in his manner of expressing it, the stile and language of that address which his plan includes are little less than adulatory" (1787, pp. 188–89). And Arthur Murphy, in his *Essay on the Life and Genius of Johnson*, the first volume of his edition of Johnson's *Works* (1792, p. 49), merely records the publication of the *Plan* as an introduction to his account of the relations between Johnson and Chesterfield.

The Text of the *Plan*

As stated above, five early partial or complete versions of the *Plan* are extant. They include, to repeat: (1) a seventeen-and-a-third-leaf manuscript (reproduced, together with a printed text, in Appendix A below) entitled "A Short Scheme for compiling a new Dictionary of the English Language," which—dated "April 30, 1746"—is written in Johnson's own hand, and corresponds to the body of the printed version; (2) a forty-five-leaf manuscript (reproduced in Appendix B below), untitled and undated, addressed "To the Right Honourable | Philip Dormer, | Earl of Chesterfield; | One of His Majesty's Principal Secretaries | of State," a fair copy, which is written in the hand of an amanuensis (but is also sprinkled with holograph revisions by Johnson) and numbers about 6,800 words; (3) the "Chesterfield" state (so called because the original setting of signature A contains the address to the Earl on p. 1) of the first (quarto) edition, published, as well as the "Non-Chesterfield" state, in August of 1747; (4) the "Non-Chesterfield" state (so called because the salutation to the Earl does not appear in the second setting of signature A) of the same edition; and (5) the octavo edition, published in February of 1755, only about six weeks prior to the appearance of the *Dictionary* itself.[5]

Neither the first nor the final version listed above furnishes a candidate for the basic text of this edition. The "Short Scheme" is exactly that—an initial draft, written rather "quickly, easily, and a bit carelessly," of the main section of

5. See Gwin J. Kolb, "Establishing the Text of Dr. Johnson's 'Plan of a Dictionary of the English Language,'" *Eighteenth-Century Studies in Honor of Donald F. Hyde,* ed. W. H. Bond (1970), pp. 81–87, which has supplied most of the material and prose in the present discussion. Since the article appeared, the Hyde Collection has acquired an additional leaf of "A Short Scheme for compiling a new Dictionary of the English Language," thus bringing the total number to seventeen and a third leaves. This list, of course, does not include the text of the aforementioned *Plan* in Thomas Davies's *Miscellaneous and Fugitive Pieces* (p. 20 above).

the completed work, which comes to nearly twice its length. The octavo edition was set, minus the address, from the "Chesterfield" state of the 1747 edition; and it shows only minor variations from that state. These variations are largely restricted to spelling and punctuation that were probably the work of a compositor according to common eighteenth-century practice. None of the differences clearly suggests Johnson's involvement in any way in the preparation of the octavo edition.

As we were guided by a wish to approximate Johnson's final intentions regarding the *Plan,* and to exclude parts of the text neither introduced nor approved by the author, the choice of the basic text presented below was therefore limited to fair copy, the "Chesterfield" state, and the "Non-Chesterfield" state. The fair copy served as printer's copy for the first edition, and so it might seem to be the logical selection, altered, of course, by the substitution of Johnson's later changes. But a collation of the fair copy and the "Chesterfield" state of the first edition reveals that Johnson scrutinized attentively—and carefully revised—the proofs of the work from beginning to end. Because the detailed results of our collation are available elsewhere,[6] we merely summarize our findings here. The differences between the fair copy and the "Chesterfield" state of the first edition in diction and punctuation point unmistakably to the printed version as the fuller realization of Johnson's intentions (displayed most precisely, it may be inferred, in his last revised proofs, now irrecoverable); the differences in spelling also indicate a slight but definite superiority in the same version with respect to accidentals; and those in capitalization afford no solid countervailing evidence in favor of the fair copy. Excluding signature A (pp. 1–8), the "Chesterfield" and "Non-Chesterfield" states of the first edition, as noted above (p. 22), consist of the same setting of type and hence are virtually identical. Because the former preceded the latter, however, we selected the "Chesterfield" state of the first edition as the basic text

6. Kolb, cited above, pp. 83–86.

of this edition and inserted substantive, apparently authorial variants from the "Non-Chesterfield" state of the text.

The "Chesterfield" state of signature A was set first, as R. W. Chapman pointed out many years ago;[7] then, "after the early copies" of the *Plan* "had been sewn and possibly even put on the market, it was decided, probably by Johnson, to remove the address to Chesterfield on page 1" (which was an awkward repetition of much of the formal title of the work) "and to correct several errors in signature A, which was entirely reset as a cancel sheet." At the same time, Johnson almost certainly "took the occasion to make a few more revisions."[8] We therefore deleted the address to Chesterfield from the present text (p. 25) but inserted into it the three other substantive differences (pp. 26, 28, 29) that appear in the "Non-Chesterfield" state. We also followed the same state in remedying two obvious misspellings, shifting two misplaced words, changing the spelling of another word, and altering the punctuation in two passages.

Finally, complying with the erratum on the verso of the title page of the first edition, we removed the phrase "or reason" on page 19 (ll. 13–14; see p. 45 below) of both states and, observing the correction in sixteen of the "Non-Chesterfield" copies of the work we have collated, also deleted the redundant "the" on page 34 (l. 1). Besides rectifying three misspellings of words that were accurately spelled in the fair copy, we have made no additional changes in the text of the "Chesterfield" state of the first edition. We have detected no passage needing emendation and, for reasons already published, remain unconvinced by W. R. Keast's argument that the paragraphs concerning "ground" (pp. 47–48 below) are not "a proper part of the final text" of the *Plan.*[9]

7. "Johnson's Plan of a *Dictionary,*" *Review of English Studies,* II (1926), 216–18.

8. Chapman, cited above.

9. Keast's argument appears in "Johnson's *Plan of a Dictionary:* A Textual Crux," *Philological Quarterly,* XXXIII (1954), 341–47; the reasons for our skepticism are recorded in Sledd-Kolb, pp. 214–15.

THE PLAN OF A DICTIONARY OF THE ENGLISH LANGUAGE (1747)

My Lord,[a1]

When first I undertook to write an English Dictionary, I had no expectation of any higher patronage than that of the proprietors of the copy, nor prospect of any other advantage than the price of my labour;[2] I knew, that the work in which I engaged is generally considered as drudgery for the blind,[3] as

a. *no address above to Lord Chesterfield in non-C state*] To the RIGHT HONOURABLE | PHILIP DORMER, | Earl of CHESTERFIELD; | One of His MAJESTY'S Principal Secretaries | of State. *C state*

---

1. For Chesterfield's role in the composition of the *Plan,* see Introduction, pp. 8–9, 12–13 above. Early in their acquaintanceship, SJ evidently received a gift of £10 from Chesterfield—but no further support. Nevertheless, in two essays in *The World* (28 November, 5 December 1754), Chesterfield hailed the forthcoming *Dictionary* as though he were its patron. SJ responded on 7 February 1755 with the "celebrated letter" to Chesterfield, repudiating the Earl's belated, probably unintentional attempt to present himself as the *Dictionary*'s patron. For additional details and interpretation, see Sledd-Kolb, pp. 85–104; Jacob Leed, "Johnson and Chesterfield: 1746–47," *Studies in Burke and His Time,* XII (1970), 1677–90; Paul J. Korshin, "The Johnson-Chesterfield Relationship: A New Hypothesis," *PMLA,* LXXXV (1970), 247–59; Howard Weinbrot, "Johnson's *Dictionary* and *The World:* The Papers of Lord Chesterfield and Richard Owen Cambridge," *Philological Quarterly,* L (1971), 663–69; and Elizabeth Hedrick, "Fixing the Language: Johnson, Chesterfield and *The Plan of a Dictionary,*" *ELH,* LV (1988), 421–42.

2. SJ's contract with the booksellers (signed on 18 June 1746) for compiling *Dictionary* specified £1575 as his payment, which included "the expence of amanuenses and paper, and other articles." After the publication of the work in 1755, the booksellers produced receipts showing that they had paid SJ "a hundred pounds & upwards more than his due." By "remitt[ing] the difference," the booksellers earned SJ's lifelong gratitude. See Hawkins, p. 344; *Life,* I.304; Murphy, *Essay* (*Works* [1792], I.78).

3. *Blind* may mean "ignorant" (*Dictionary,* sense 2) and be part of the imagery of drudgery; in the fair copy of the *Plan,* SJ called lexicography "the proper Drudgery of Asinine Industry" (see p. 428 below). *Blind* may also mean, proleptically, the literal blindness that Erasmus mentions as the result of lexi-

the proper toil of artless industry, a task that requires neither the light of learning, nor the activity of genius,[4] but may be successfully performed without any greater[b] quality than that of bearing burthens with dull patience, and beating the track of the alphabet with sluggish resolution.[5]

Whether this opinion, so long transmitted and so widely propagated,[6] had its beginning from truth and nature,[7] or from accident and prejudice, whether it be decreed by the authority of reason, or the tyranny of ignorance, that of all the candidates for literary praise, the unhappy lexicographer holds the lowest place, neither vanity nor interest incited me to enquire. It appeared that the province allotted me was of

b. greater *non-C state*] higher *C state*

---

cography (see Introduction, pp. xxiii–xxiv above). The exact meaning of the word in the passage, in fact, is blurred between the two senses. In his "Life of Milton," SJ emphasizes the extreme difficulty facing a physically blind lexicographer: "To collect a dictionary seems a work of all others least practicable in a state of blindness, because it depends upon perpetual and minute inspection and collation" (*Lives,* I.120, par. 84).

4. *Genius:* "Mental power or faculties" (*Dictionary,* sense 3).

5. Cf. the following passage: "He [Savage] knew that the track of elegy had been so long beaten that it was impossible to travel in it without treading in the footsteps of those who had gone before him" ("Life of Savage" [*Lives,* II.407, par. 249]).

6. On the tradition of "degrading" lexicography, see Introduction, pp. xxii–xxv above. With this paragraph, cf. SJ's *Adventurer* 39, par. 9 (*Yale* II.347–48) and his poem *Γνῶθι Σεαυτόν* [Know thyself], which was written after his revision of the fourth unabridged edition of *Dictionary.* Within *Dictionary* his references to lexicography are belittling but somewhat playful: see *dull* ("To make dictionaries is *dull* work"), *lexicographer* ("A harmless drudge"), *Grubstreet* ("Originally the name of a street in Moorfields in London, much inhabited by writers of small histories, dictionaries, and temporary poems; whence any mean production is called *grubstreet*"). SJ's private opinion of lexicographical labor may have been different from what he publicly professed, however; for example, he wrote to Edmund Hector on the day *Dictionary* was published, 15 April 1755: "I did not find dictionary making so very unpleasant as it may be thought" (*Letters,* I.105). And late in life he sought the contract for a revision of Ephraim Chambers's *Cyclopaedia* and said he liked that "*muddling* work" (*Life,* II.203, n. 3). On lexicographers' complaints about their suffering because of such labor, see Introduction, pp. xxiv–xxv above.

7. *Nature:* "The constitution and appearances of things" (*Dictionary,* sense 7).

all the regions of learning generally confessed to be the least delightful, that it was believed to produce neither fruits nor flowers, and that after a long and laborious cultivation, not even the barren laurel had been found upon it.[8]

Yet on this province, my Lord, I enter'd with the pleasing hope, that as it was low, it likewise would be safe. I was drawn forward with the prospect of employment, which, tho' not splendid, would be useful, and which tho' it could not make my life envied, would keep it innocent;[c] which would awaken no passion, engage me in no contention, nor throw in my way any temptation to disturb the quiet of others by censure, or my own by flattery.

I had read indeed of times, in which princes and statesmen thought it part of their honour to promote the improvement of their native tongues, and in which dictionaries were written under the protection of greatness.[9] To the patrons of such undertakings, I willingly paid the homage of believing that they, who were thus solicitous for the perpetuity of their language, had reason to expect that their actions would be celebrated by posterity, and that the eloquence which they promoted would be employed in their praise. But I considered such acts of beneficence as prodigies, recorded rather to raise wonder than expectation; and content with the terms that I had stipulated, had not suffered[d] my imagination to

c. innocent; *non-C state*] innocent, *C state*
d. suffered *non-C state*] suffer'd *C state*

8. In a letter to Thomas Birch (30 December 1747), Lord Orrery praised SJ's *Plan* but mentioned this passage as a trifling fault because "[t]he laurel is not barren, in any sense whatever; it bears fruit and flowers" (British Library Add. MS 4303, f. 133^{r}; *Life,* I.185). The entry on *laurel* in *Dictionary* includes a description of its fruit and flowers drawn from Philip Miller's *Gardener's Dictionary* (1724).

9. The first edition (1694) of the *Dictionnaire de l'Académie* was dedicated to King Louis XIV, who served as its protector, and it had been fostered earlier by Cardinal Richelieu, along with the Académie. The four editions of the Italian *Vocabolario della Crusca* published before 1755 were dedicated to rulers in the cities of publication (Venice and Florence); from the start the project had the direct support of Cardinal Bembo.

flatter me with any other encouragement, when I found that my design had been thought by your Lordship of importance sufficient to attract your favour.[1]

How far this unexpected distinction can be rated among the happy incidents of life, I am not yet able to determine. Its first effect has been to make me anxious lest it should fix the attention of the public too much upon me, and as it once happened to an epic poet of France, by raising the reputation of the attempt, obstruct the reception of the work.[2] I imagine what the world will expect from a scheme, prosecuted under your Lordship's influence, and I know that expectation, when her wings are once expanded, easily reaches heights which performance never will attain, and when she has mounted the summit of perfection, derides her follower, who dies in the pursuit.[3]

Not therefore, to raise expectation, but to repress it, I here lay before your Lordship the plan of my undertaking, that more may not be demanded than I intend, and that before it is too far advanced to be thrown into a new method, I may be advertised of its defects or superfluities. Such informations[4] I may justly hope from the emulation with which those who desire the praise of elegance and[e] discernment must contend in the promotion of a design that you, my Lord, have not

e. and *non-C state*] or *C state*

---

1. See p. 9 above.

2. For his epic poem about Henry of Navarre, *La Henriad* (1728), Voltaire enjoyed the patronage of George I and, after his death, through Chesterfield's intervention, the patronage of Queen Caroline. Her name headed an illustrious list of 343 subscribers, which included the royal family and the most notable politicians of the day. For an account of the publication of *La Henriad* in England, see *The Complete Works of Voltaire,* Vol. II, *La Henriad* (1970), ed. O. R. Taylor, 60–79.

3. Cf. *Rambler* 207 (*Yale* V.311): "the toil with which performance struggles after idea, is so irksome and disgusting, and so frequent is the necessity of resting below that perfection which we imagined within our reach, that seldom any man obtains more from his endeavours than a painful conviction of his defects, and a continual resuscitation of desires which he feels himself unable to gratify."

4. *Informations,* although not listed in *Dictionary,* appears under sense 1 of *information* ("Intelligence given; instruction") in a quotation from "[Robert] *South's Sermons.*"

thought unworthy to share your attention with treaties and with wars.[5]

In the first attempt to methodise my ideas, I found a difficulty which extended itself to the whole work. It was not easy to determine by what rule of distinction the words of this dictionary were to be chosen. The chief intent of it is to preserve the purity and ascertain the meaning of the[f] English idiom; and this seems to require nothing more than that our language be considered so far as it is our own; that the words and phrases used in the general intercourse of life, or found in the works of those whom we commonly stile polite writers, be selected, without including the terms of particular professions, since, with the arts to which they relate, they are generally derived from other nations, and are very often the same in all the languages of this part of the world. This is perhaps the exact and pure idea of a grammatical dictionary;[6] but in lexicography, as in other arts, naked science[7] is too delicate for the purposes of life. The value of a work must be estimated by its use: It is not enough that a dictionary delights the critic, unless at the same time it instructs the learner; as it is to little purpose, that an engine amuses[8] the philosopher[9] by the subtilty of its mechanism, if it requires so much knowledge in its application, as to be[g] of no advantage to the common workman.[1]

f. the *non-C state*] our *C state*
g. as to be *non-C state*] to as be *C state*

---

5. An allusion to Chesterfield's appointment on 29 October, O.S., 1746 as "one of his Majesty's [King George II's] Principal Secretaries" (Sledd-Kolb, p. 95).

6. Ephraim Chambers distinguishes the following kinds of dictionaries: "*grammatical,* as the common Dictionaries of languages; which, for one word, substitute another of equal import, but more obvious sense: *philosophical,* which give the general force or effect of words, or what is common to them in all the occasions where they occur: and *technical*" (*Cyclopaedia* I.xvii).

7. *Science:* "Knowledge" (*Dictionary,* sense 1).

8. *Amuse:* "To entertain with tranquillity; to fill with thoughts that engage the mind, without distracting it" (*Dictionary*).

9. *Philosopher:* "A man deep in knowledge, either moral or natural" (*Dictionary*).

1. An important part of SJ's audience was to be "foreigners" and "learners," as

The title which I prefix to my work has long conveyed a very miscellaneous idea, and they that take a dictionary into their hands have been accustomed to expect from it, a solution of almost every difficulty. If foreign words therefore were rejected, it could be little regarded, except by critics, or those who aspire to criticism; and however it might enlighten those that write, would be all darkness[h] to them that only read. The unlearned much oftner consult their dictionaries, for the meaning of words, than for their structures or formations; and the words that most want explanation, are generally terms of art, which therefore experience has taught my predecessors to spread with a kind of pompous[2] luxuriance over their productions.[3]

The academicians of France, indeed, rejected terms of science[4] in their first essay, but found afterwards a necessity of relaxing the rigour of their determination; and, tho' they would not naturalize them at once by a single act, permitted them by degrees to settle themselves among the natives, with little opposition, and it would surely be no proof of judgment

h. darkness *non-C state*] darkess *C state*

---

a reader of his "Scheme" admonished him (see fols. 7^v and 18^v, pp. 394, 424 below). For similar opinions, also see the second par. of SJ's Preface to the abridgment of *Dictionary* and the Introduction to that Preface (pp. 367, 363–65 below). With SJ's mechanical simile for a dictionary, cf. his remark to Francesco Sastres on 21 August 1784: "Dictionaries are like watches, the worst is better than none, and the best cannot be expected to go quite true" (*Letters,* IV.379).

2. *Pompous:* "Splendid; magnificent; grand" (*Dictionary*).

3. Earlier English dictionaries such as Edward Phillips's *New World of English Words* (1658) and Nathan Bailey's *Universal Etymological English Dictionary* (1721; 16th ed., 1755) advertised the inclusion of technical terms on their title pages. The terms lend a "pompous luxuriance" to their pages because they are usually Latinate, "hard" words. Although some critics complained about the excessive Latinity of SJ's word list, he included a smaller percentage of "hard" words and technical terms than his predecessors; see E. L. McAdam, Jr., "Inkhorn Words before Dr. Johnson," *Eighteenth-Century Studies in Honor of Donald F. Hyde,* ed. W. H. Bond (1970), pp. 187–206. SJ includes more technical terms than editions of the French *Dictionnaire* published before 1755, and his avowed intention may be described as a compromise between the French ideal of purity and his English predecessors' inclination unsystematically to include all kinds of words.

4. *Science:* "Any art or species of knowledge" (*Dictionary,* sense 4).

to imitate them in an error which they have now retracted, and deprive the book of its chief use by scrupulous distinctions.[5]

Of such words however, all are not equally to be considered as parts of our language, for some of them are naturalized and incorporated, but others still continue aliens, and are rather auxiliaries than subjects. This naturalization is produced either by an admission into common speech in some metaphorical signification, which is the acquisition of a kind of property among us, as we say the *zenith* of advancement, the *meridian* of life, the *cynosure** of neighbouring eyes;[6] or it is the consequence of long intermixture and frequent use, by which the ear is accustomed to the sound of words till their original is forgotten, as in *equator, satellites;*[7] or of the change

* *Milton.* [SJ's note]

5. After much difficulty, including the death of the first editor, Claude de Vaugelas, the *Dictionnaire de l'Académie* appeared in two volumes in 1694, fifty-seven years after it was proposed by Jean Chapelain. The Preface states that terms of arts and sciences are omitted except those that "ayant passé dans le discours ordinaire, ont formé des façons de parler figurées" (pp. xv–xvi). The *Dictionnaire* was assaulted by Antoine Furetière, even before publication, for its lack of technical terms. The Académie responded immediately with two supplementary volumes, edited by Pierre Corneille, *Dictionnaire des artes et des sciences* (1694). However, the revisions of the *Dictionnaire de l'Académie* in 1718 and 1740 admitted only slightly more technical terms into the main word list.

6. Of *zenith* no metaphorical sense or example is listed in *Dictionary.* "*Meridian* of life" may be a phrase adapted from a passage in Matthew Hale's *Primitive Origination of Mankind* (1677, p. 7), which is quoted under sense 3 of *meridian* ("the particular place or state of any thing") in *Dictionary.* Under *cynosure* ("The star near the North-Pole, by which sailors steer") SJ again quotes Milton's metaphorical use, "the *cynosure* of neighbouring eyes" (*L'Allegro,* l. 80).

7. *Dictionary* contains only the modern technical definition of *equator,* taken from John Harris, *Lexicon Technicum: or, an Universal English Dictionary of Arts and Sciences* (2 vols., 1704). The Latin word from which it is derived means only "one who equalizes" or an assayer in the phrase *aequator monetae* (*Oxford Latin Dictionary*). Of *satellite* only the modern definition appears: "A small planet revolving round a larger." The Latin word was *satelles,* singular, *satellites,* plural, meaning an escort, henchman, or associate. SJ, who says the English plural has three syllables, criticizes Pope for continuing the Latin form and giving it four syllables (sa-tel-li-tes; *Essay on Man,* I.42). SJ himself uses the word in a sense that could be taken as either radical or derivative in the Preface to Shakespeare (par. 121): "These elevations and depressions of renown . . . , since they are not

of a foreign to an English termination, and a conformity to the laws of the speech into which they are adopted, as in *category, cachexy, peripneumony.*[8]

Of those which yet continue in the state of aliens, and have made no approaches towards assimilation, some seem necessary to be retained, because the purchasers of the dictionary will expect to find them. Such are many words in the common law, as *capias, habeas corpus, præmunire, nisi prius:*[9] such are some terms of controversial divinity, as *hypostasis;*[1] and of physick,[2] as the names of diseases; and in general all terms which can be found in books not written professedly upon particular arts, or can be supposed necessary[i] to those who do not regularly study them. Thus when a reader not skilled in physick happens in Milton upon this line,

i. necessary *non-C state*] nenessary *C state*

escaped by the highest and brightest of mankind, may surely be endured with patience by criticks and annotators, who can rank themselves but as the satellites of their authours" (*Yale* VII.99).

8. The Greek source of *category* is κατηγορία, as SJ indicates in *Dictionary.* Noting that the Greek word behind *cachexy* is καχεξία, he takes his definition from John Arbuthnot, *Practical Rules of Diet in the Various Constitutions and Diseases of Human Bodies* (1732): "A general word to express a great variety of symptoms; most commonly it denotes such a distemperature of the humours, as hinders nutrition, and weakens the vital and animal functions" (p. 381). For *peripneumony* ("An inflammation of the lungs") SJ gives *peripneumonia* as the main spelling and derives the word from Greek περί and πνεύμων.

9. In *Dictionary,* SJ takes his definition from John Cowell, *The Interpreter* (1607; rev. White Kennet, 1701); he italicizes *capias* to show that it is unassimilated (see p. 33 below): "A writ of two sorts, one before judgment, called *capias ad respondendum,* in an action personal, if the sheriff, upon the first writ of distress, return that he has no effects in his jurisdiction. The other is a writ of execution after judgment." *Habeas corpus* and *nisi prius* ("A judicial writ, which lieth in case where the inquest is panelled and returned before the justices of the bank; the one party or the other making Petition to have this writ for the ease of the country") receive the same treatment, except that *nisi prius* is not italicized. *Præmunire* is spelled *Premunire,* italicized, and defined "1. A writ in the common law, whereby a penalty is incurrable, as infringing some statute," without reference to Cowell. SJ usually reduces the Latin digraph *æ* to *e.* He discusses the subject in *Dictionary* under *æ,* which he calls "A diphthong of very frequent use in the Latin language, which seems not properly to have any place in the English."

1. *Dictionary* does not italicize *hypostasis:* "1. Distinct substance. 2. Personality. A term used in the doctrine of the Holy Trinity."

2. *Physick:* "The science of healing" (*Dictionary*).

. . . pining atrophy,
Marasmus, and wide-wasting pestilence.

he will with equal expectation look into his dictionary for the word *marasmus,* as for *atrophy,* or *pestilence,* and will have reason to complain if he does not find it.[3]

It seems necessary to the completion of a dictionary design'd not merely for critics but for popular use, that it should comprise, in some degree, the peculiar words of every profession; that the terms of war and navigation should be inserted so far as they can be required by readers of travels, and of history; and those of law, merchandise and mechanical trades, so far as they can be supposed useful in the occurrences of common life.[4]

But there ought, however, to be some distinction made between the different classes of words, and therefore it will be proper to print those which are incorporated into the language in the usual character, and those which are still to be considered as foreign, in the italick letter.[5]

Another question may arise, with regard to appellatives, or the names of species. It seems of no great use to set down the words, *horse, dog, cat, willow, alder, dasy, rose,* and a thousand others, of which it will be hard to give an explanation not more obscure than the word itself.[6] Yet it is to be consid-

---

3. *Marasmus, pestilence,* and *atrophy* are not italicized in *Dictionary.* However, *marasmus* is defined with close attention to the Greek root μαραινεῖν (to waste), "A consumption, in which persons waste much of their substance." These lines from *Paradise Lost* (XI.486–87) are quoted under *marasmus* and *atrophy.*

4. For definitions of "terms of war and navigation," SJ used *A Military Dictionary explaining All Difficult Terms in Martial Discipline, Fortification, and Gunnery . . . to which is likewise added, a Sea-Dictionary of all the terms of Navigation* (1708). See, e.g., *crowfoot, petard,* and *ponton.* For legal terms, he used John Cowell, *The Interpreter* (rev. White Kennet, 1701); for mechanical trades, Joseph Moxon, *Mechanick Exercises* (2 vols., 1678–80 and 1683–84). He used no special dictionary of commerce.

5. This distinction is made in *Dictionary* but not thoroughly or very consistently.

6. *Dictionary* contains a multitude of such terms: *horse,* for instance, being defined as "A neighing quadruped, used in war, and draught and carriage"; *dog* as "A domestick animal remarkably various in his species; comprising [seven breeds], with many others. The larger sort are used as a guard; the less for

ered, that[j] if the names of animals be inserted, we must admit those which are more known, as well as those with which we are, by accident, less acquainted; and if they are all rejected, how will the reader be relieved from difficulties produced by allusions to the crocodile, the chamæleon,[k] the ichneumon, and the hyæna?[7] If no plants are to be mentioned, the most pleasing part of nature will be excluded, and many beautiful epithets be unexplained. If only those which are less known are to be mentioned, who shall fix the limits of the reader's learning? The importance of such explications appears from the mistakes which the want of them has occasioned. Had Shakespear had a dictionary of this kind, he had not made the *woodbine* entwine the *honeysuckle;*[8] nor would Milton, with such assistance, have disposed so improperly of his *ellops* and his *scorpion.*[9]

j. that *non-C state*] that, *C state*
k. chamæleon, *FC*] camæleon, *47*

---

sports"; and *cat* as "A domestick animal that catches mice, commonly reckoned by naturalists the lowest order of the leonine species." The definitions show an advance over Nathan Bailey's *Dictionarium Britannicum,* where *cat,* for example, is only "a domestic creature that kills mice." The treatment of plants benefitted markedly from the use of large passages in Philip Miller's *Gardener's Dictionary* (1731), some providing the only definitions of entries, others supplementing SJ's short definitions.

7. *Dictionary* includes all four words, the first two being defined by lengthy excerpts from Augustin Calmet, *Dictionnaire historique . . . de la Bible* (2d ed., 4 vols., 1730) and, for *chameleon* (sic), also one from "Bacon's Natural History, N° 360." For more details about the borrowings from Calmet, see W. K. Wimsatt, Jr., *Philosophic Words* (1948), p. 151. *Ichneumon* is defined as "A small animal that breaks the eggs of the crocodile" and *hyena* (sic) as "An animal like a wolf, said fabulously to imitate human voices."

8. They are two names, of course, for the same plant. *Dictionary* does not quote the erroneous passage from *A Midsummer Night's Dream:*

> So doth the woodbine, the sweet
>   honeysuckle,
> Gently entwist; the female ivy so
> Enrings the barky fingers of the
>   elm. (IV.i.39–41)

But in his edition of the plays (1765) SJ comments, "Shakespeare perhaps only meant, so the leaves involve the flower, using 'woodbine' for the plant and 'honesuckle' for the flower; or perhaps Shakespeare made a blunder" (*Yale* VII.155).

9. *Dictionary* defines *elops* (sic) as "A fish; reckoned however by *Milton* among the serpents," and cites *Paradise Lost,* X.525:

Besides, as such words, like others, require that their accents should be settled, their sounds ascertained, and their etymologies deduced, they cannot be properly omitted in the dictionary. And though the explanations of some may be censured as trivial, because they are almost universally understood, and those of others as unnecessary, because they will seldom occur, yet it seems not proper to omit them, since it is rather to be wished that many readers should find more than they expect, than that one should miss what he might hope to find.

When all the words are selected and arranged, the first part of the work to be considered is the ORTHOGRAPHY, which was long vague and uncertain, which at last, when its fluctuation ceased, was in many cases settled but by accident, and in which, according to your Lordship's observation, there is still great uncertainty among the best critics;[1] nor is it easy to state a rule by which we may decide between custom and reason, or between the equiponderant authorities of writers alike eminent for judgment and accuracy.

The great orthographical contest has long subsisted between etymology and pronunciation. It has been demanded, on one hand, that men should write as they speak; but as it has been shewn that this conformity never was attained in any language, and that it is not more easy to perswade men to agree exactly in speaking than in writing, it may be asked with equal propriety, why men do not rather speak as they write. In France, where this controversy was at its greatest height, neither party, however ardent, durst adhere steadily to their own rule; the etymologist was often forced to

---

Scorpion and asp, and amphisbena dire,
Cerastes horn'd, hydrus, and *elops* drear,
And dipsas.

Sense 1 of *scorpion* is "A reptile much resembling a small lobster, but that his tail ends in a point with a very venomous sting." However, sense 4 is "A sea fish. *Ainsworth.*"

1. Although the "observation" seems to be absent in his writings published before 1747, Chesterfield's concern regarding current English cacography appears in his letters to his son and elsewhere (sec Sledd-Kolb, pp. 90, 223).

spell with the people; and the advocate for the authority of pronunciation, found it sometimes deviating so capriciously from the received use of writing, that he was constrained to comply with the rule of his adversaries, lest he should lose[1] the end by the means, and be left alone by following the croud.[2]

When a question of orthography is dubious, that practice has, in my opinion, a claim to preference, which preserves the greatest number of radical letters, or seems most to comply with the general custom of our language.[3] But the chief rule which I propose to follow, is to make no innovation, without a reason sufficient to balance the inconvenience of change; and such reasons I do not expect often to find. All change is of itself an evil, which ought not to be hazarded but for evident advantage; and as inconstancy is in every case a mark of weakness, it will add nothing to the reputation of our tongue.[4] There are, indeed, some who despise the inconve-

1. lose *FC*] loose *47*

---

2. The Préface to the *Dictionnaire* of 1694 states that analogy and etymology are the criteria of its orthography, except where usage is decisive (par. 16). Before and especially after publication, there were debates on the propriety of this decision. In *Lettre sur l'ortografe* (1694), for example, l'abbé Dangeau proposed a radical reform based on pronunciation. In *l'Art de bien parler françois* (1696), Nicolas de La Toûche summed up the arguments and arrived at a critique of them similar to SJ's remarks. Pronunciation and more popular usage gained ground in the second edition of the *Dictionnaire* (1718), and in the Préface to the third edition (1740) the editors stated bluntly: "On entreprendroit en vain de l'assujétir à une orthographe systémique. . . . L'usage qui en matière de Langue, est plus fort que la raison, auroit bientôt transgressé ces lois" (par. 15). For an account of the *Dictionnaire*'s support of the old orthography, see Ferdinand Brunot, *Histoire de la langue Française,* vol. IV (1913), pp. 142–49, to which we are indebted. Discussion of the orthographical controversy appears in Paul Pellisson-Fontanier and Pierre-Joseph Thoulier, abbé d'Olivet, *Histoire de l'Académie* (3d ed., 1748), but SJ may have used primary sources.

3. This sentence suggests SJ's preference for etymological spelling and analogical construction, where usage is not decisive. He acts on this preference in *Dictionary* and reiterates it in the Preface (pp. 75–78 below), but his willingness to accept established usage, strong initially, grew stronger between 1747 and 1755.

4. Cf. the restatement of this principle in the Preface (p. 78 below), where SJ apparently refers to the following comment in Richard Hooker's *Of the Laws of Ecclesiastical Polity,* IV.xiv.1:

niencies of confusion, who seem to take pleasure in departing from custom, and to think alteration desirable for its own sake, and the reformation of our orthography, which these writers have attempted, should not pass without its due honours, but that I suppose they hold singularity its own reward, or may dread the fascination of lavish praise.[5]

The present usage of spelling, where the present usage can be distinguished, will therefore in this work be generally followed, yet there will be often occasion to observe, that it is in itself inaccurate, and tolerated rather than chosen; particularly, when by a change of one letter, or more, the meaning of a word is obscured, as in *farrier*, for *ferrier,* as it was formerly written, from *ferrum* or *fer;*[6] in *gibberish* for *gebrish,* the jargon of Geber, and his chymical followers, understood by none but their own tribe.[7] It will be likewise sometimes proper to trace back the orthography of different ages, and shew by what gradations the word departed from its original.[8]

Closely connected with orthography is PRONUNCIATION, the stability of which is of great importance to the duration of a language, because the first change will naturally begin by corruptions in the living speech. The want of certain rules for the pronunciation of former ages, has made us wholly igno-

---

"Laws, as all other things human, are many times full of imperfection, and that which is supposed behooveful unto men, proveth oftentime most pernicious. . . . But true withal it is, that alteration, though it be from worse to better, hath in it inconveniences, and those weighty" (Donald Greene, *The Politics of Samuel Johnson* [1960], p. 314). SJ quotes parts of the passage in *Dictionary* to illustrate the meanings of *imperfection, behooveful,* and *alteration.*

5. *Fascination:* "The power or act of bewitching; enchantment; unseen inexplicable influence" (*Dictionary*). See an equally satirical brief history of English attempts at spelling reform in the Grammar (pp. 295–301 below).

6. In *Dictionary,* SJ derives the word from "*ferrier,* French; *ferrarius,* Latin" without mentioning the more basic *ferrus* (Medieval Latin, *horseshoe*) or *ferrum* (Latin, *iron*).

7. *OED* lists the spelling *geberish,* but modern lexicographers reject SJ's etymology, preferring to describe the word as onomatopoeic. On SJ's knowledge of "Geber" (Jabir ibn Hayyan, Abu Musa, an eighth-century Arab alchemist labeled "the father of modern chemistry") and other "chymical" writers, see Gwin J. Kolb and Robert DeMaria, Jr., "Dr. Johnson's Etymology of *Gibberish,*" *Notes and Queries,* XLV (March 1998), 72–74.

8. Our search—certainly not exhaustive—has disclosed no example of such "tracing" in *Dictionary.*

rant of the metrical art of our ancient poets; and since those who study their sentiments regret the loss of their numbers, it is surely time to provide that the harmony of the moderns may be more permanent.[9]

A new pronunciation will make almost a new speech, and therefore since one great end of this undertaking is to fix the English language, care will be taken to determine the accentuation of all polysyllables by proper authorities, as it is one of those capricious phænomena which cannot be easily reduced to rules. Thus there is no antecedent reason for difference of accent in the two words *dolorous* and *sonorous,* yet of the one Milton gives the sound in this line,

> He pass'd o'er many a region *dolorous,*

and that of the other in this,

> *Sonorous* metal blowing martial sounds.[1]

It may be likewise proper to remark metrical licences, such as contractions, *generous, gen'rous, reverend, rev'rend;* and coalitions, as *region, question.*[2]

But it is still more necessary to fix the pronunciation of monosyllables, by placing with them words of correspondent sound, that one may guard the other against the danger of that variation, which to some of the most common, has already happened, so that the words *wound,* and *wind,* as they

9. "Wholly ignorant" is an exaggeration. Although Thomas Tyrwhitt's edition of *The Canterbury Tales* (5 vols., 1775–78) was the first to recover Chaucer's metrics, pieces of the puzzle had been previously assembled by others; for example, John Wallis understood the pronunciation of Middle English final *e* (see Introduction, p. xlii above), and some of Chaucer's admirers used this knowledge to defend his numbers. The pronunciation and prosody of English poets from the seventh through the thirteenth centuries were less well understood.

1. *Paradise Lost,* II.619 and I.540; quoted under *dolorous* and *sonorous,* respectively, in *Dictionary.* SJ usually indicates the pronunciation of a word by inserting an accent mark (´) after the vowel of the stressed syllable: e.g., "do´lorous" and "sono´rous."

2. In *Dictionary* SJ, while not explicitly remarking "metrical licences," quotes examples of *gen'rous* in works by a total of six poets, of *rev'rend* in a line by Pope, and of coalesced last two vowels (*region* and *question*) in works by a total of five poets.

are now frequently pronounced, will not rhyme to *sound,* and *mind.* It is to be remarked that many words written alike are differently pronounced, as *flow,* and *brow,* which may be thus registred, *flow, woe, brow, now,* or of which the exemplification may be generally given by a distich.[3] Thus the words *tear* or lacerate, and *tear* the water of the eye, have the same letters, but may be distinguished thus, *tear, dare; tear, peer.*[4]

Some words have two sounds, which may be equally admitted, as being equally defensible by authority. Thus *great* is differently used.

> For Swift and him despis'd the farce of state,
> The sober follies of the wise and *great.* Pope.

> As if misfortune made the throne her seat,
> And none could be unhappy but the *great.* Rowe.[5]

The care of such minute particulars may be censured as trifling, but these particulars have not been thought unworthy of attention in more polished languages.

---

3. In *Dictionary* SJ, although not regularly fixing "the pronunciation of monosyllables," provides (1) two distiches from Dryden and one from Swift in which *wind* ("any tract of air") rhymes with *mind* but (2) no rhymes in his illustrative quotations for *wound.* He also cites one couplet for *brow,* three couplets for *to flow*—all four from Dryden—to indicate their pronunciation.

4. Under sense 2 of *to tear* ("To laniate; to wound with any sharp point drawn along"), SJ includes a rhyme with *hair* from Shakespeare. At the beginning of his entry for the noun *tear* ("The water which violent passion forces from the eyes"), he comments, "*ea* in this word is pronounced *ee,*" but he provides no exemplary distich.

5. On 28 March 1772, answering remarks by Boswell, SJ replied in part: "'what entitles [Thomas] Sheridan [in his pronouncing *General Dictionary of the English Language,* which was not published until 1780, although its *Scheme* appeared in 1762] to fix the pronunciation of English? He has, in the first place, the disadvantage of being an Irishman: and if he says he will fix it after the example of the best company, why they differ among themselves. I remember an instance: when I published the Plan for my Dictionary, Lord Chesterfield told me that the word *great* should be pronounced so as to rhyme to *state;* and Sir William Yonge sent me word that it should be pronounced so as to rhyme to *seat,* and that none but an Irishman would pronounce it *grait.* Now here were two men of the highest rank, the one, the best speaker in the House of Lords, the other, the best speaker in the House of Commons, differing entirely'" (*Life,* II.161). SJ enters the couplets from Pope (*Epistle to Robert Earl of Oxford,* ll. 9–10) and Nicholas Rowe (Prologue to *The Fair Penitent,* ll. 3–4) in illustration of sense 9 of *great.*

The accuracy of the French, in stating the sounds of their letters, is well known; and, among the Italians, Crescembeni has not thought it unnecessary to inform his countrymen of the words, which, in compliance with different rhymes, are allowed to be differently spelt, and of which the number is now so fix'd, that no modern poet is suffered to encrease it.[6]

When the orthography and pronunciation are adjusted, the ETYMOLOGY OR DERIVATION is next to be considered, and the words are to be distinguished according to their different classes, whether simple, as *day, light,* or compound as *day-light;* whether primitive, as, to *act,* or derivative, as *action, actionable, active, activity.* This will much facilitate the attainment of our language,[7] which now stands in our dictionaries a confused heap of words without dependence, and without relation.[8]

When this part of the work is performed, it will be necessary to inquire how our primitives are to be deduced from foreign languages, which may be often very successfully performed by the assistance of our own etymologists. This search will give occasion to many curious disquisitions, and sometimes perhaps to conjectures, which, to readers unacquainted with this kind of study, cannot but appear improbable and capricious. But it may be reasonably imagined, that what is so much in the power of men as language, will very often be

---

6. In *L'istoria della volgar poesia* (6 vols., 1714, I.402–11), Giovanni Mario Crescimbeni includes a section on "ortographia nelle Poesie Volgari," and elsewhere he censures alternate spellings introduced for the sake of rhyme in the sixteenth century (I.379–80). We have not located the specific regulations to which SJ refers, however, despite the generous assistance of Giovanni Iamartino of the University of Milan. In 1755 SJ was involved in Giuseppe Baretti's borrowing at least one of Crescimbeni's books from Thomas Warton (*Letters,* I.92).

7. *Attainment:* "The act or power of attaining" (*Dictionary,* sense 2).

8. In the etymological section of many entries in *Dictionary,* SJ refers compound or derivative words to their simpler forms, but he does not classify words as "simple," "compound," "primitive," or "derivative." This section of the *Plan* seems to contain the last vestiges of SJ's earlier intention to organize his entries according to their radical forms. See "Scheme," fol. 7, and the reader's remark on the verso (pp. 392, 394 below).

capriciously conducted. Nor are these disquisitions and conjectures to be considered altogether as wanton sports of wit,[9] or vain shews of learning; our language is well known not to be primitive or self-originated, but to have adopted words of every generation, and either for the supply of its necessities, or the encrease of its copiousness, to have received additions from very distant regions; so that in search of the progenitors of our speech, we may wander from the tropic to the frozen zone, and find some in the vallies of Palestine and some upon the rocks of Norway.[1]

Beside the derivation of particular words, there is likewise an etymology of phrases. Expressions are often taken from other languages, some apparently, as to *run a risque, courir un risque;*[2] and some even when we do not seem to borrow their words; thus, to *bring about* or accomplish, appears an English phrase, but in reality our native word *about* has no such import, and it is only a French expression, of which we have an example in the common phrase, *venir à bout d'une affaire.*[3]

In exhibiting the descent of our language, our etymologists seem to have been too lavish of their learning, having traced almost every word through various tongues, only to shew what was shewn sufficiently by the first derivation. This practice is of great use in synoptical lexicons, where mutilated and doubtful languages are explained by their affinity to others more certain and extensive, but is generally superfluous in English etymologies.[4] When the word is easily de-

9. *Wit:* "Imagination: quickness of fancy" (*Dictionary,* sense 2).

1. In fact, very few of SJ's etymologies invoke semitic languages (see *sack* and *cabal* for rare examples). Many more invoke Norse or Old Icelandic.

2. This phrase is not separately treated under either *run* or *risk,* although it appears in three illustrative quotations under *risk.*

3. Cf. *about,* adv. (*Dictionary,* after sense 9): "Some of these phrases seem to derive their original from the French *à bout; venir à bout d'une chose.*"

4. In preparing etymologies in *Dictionary,* SJ consulted at least these synoptical works: Meric Casaubon, *De Quatuor Linguis Commentationis, Pars Prior: Quae, De Lingua Hebraica: et, De Lingua Saxonica* (1650); James Howell, *Lexicon Tetraglotton* (1660); and John Minsheu, *The Guide into Tongues: Ductor in Linguas* (1617). But his main sources of etymologies were the less synoptic works of Franciscus Junius (*Etymologicum Anglicanum,* 1743) and Stephen Skinner (*Etymologicon Linguae Anglicanae,* 1671); see Preface, pp. 81–82. He also avoids synoptic

duced from a Saxon original, I shall not often enquire further, since we know not the parent of the Saxon dialect, but when it is borrowed from the French, I shall shew whence the French is apparently derived. Where a Saxon root cannot be found, the defect may be supplied from kindred languages, which will be generally furnished with much liberality by the writers of our glossaries;[5] writers who deserve often the highest praise, both of judgment and industry, and may expect at least to be mentioned with honour by me, whom they have freed from the greatest part of a very laborious work, and on whom they have imposed, at worst, only the easy task of rejecting superfluities.

By tracing in this manner every word to its original, and not admitting, but with great caution, any of which no original can be found, we shall secure our language from being overrun with *cant,* from being crouded with low terms, the spawn of folly or affectation, which arise from no just principles of speech, and of which therefore no legitimate derivation can be shewn.[6]

When the etymology is thus adjusted, the ANALOGY of our language is next to be considered; when we have discovered whence our words are derived, we are to examine by what rules they are governed, and how they are inflected through their various terminations. The terminations of the English

---

etymologies, i.e., chains of related words in other languages imagined to be closer to the first, God-given language. SJ does not reject the theory of one original language, but he believes that if it existed, it is lost in obscurity; see *Dictionary* (s.v. *sack*).

5. SJ used at least the following works, which are, partly or wholly, glossaries of early or early modern English: William Baxter, *Glossarium Antiquitatum Britannicarum* (1719); William Camden, *Remains concerning Britain* (1636); Thomas Hearne, ed., *Robert of Gloucester's Chronicle* (1724); Henry Spelman, *Glossarium Archaiologicum* (1664); John Hughes, ed., *The Works of Mr. Edmund Spenser* (1715); John Urry, ed., *The Works of Geoffrey Chaucer* (1721); Thomas Hanmer, ed., *The Works of William Shakespear* (1743–44).

6. Among the censorious terms employed in *Dictionary* are *cant* (sense 2: "A particular form of speaking peculiar to some certain class or body of men"), *low,* and *mean,* the latter sometimes denoting the absence of an ascertainable etymology. For more details, see Harold Byron Allen, "Samuel Johnson and the Authoritarian Principle in Linguistic Criticism" (Ph.D. diss., University of Michigan, 1940).

are few, but those few have hitherto remained unregarded by the writers of our dictionaries. Our substantives are declined only by the plural termination, our adjectives admit no variation but in the degrees of comparison, and our verbs are conjugated by auxiliary words, and are only changed in the preter tense.[7]

To our language may be with great justness applied the observation of *Quintilian,* that speech was not formed by an analogy sent from heaven. It did not descend to us in a state of uniformity and perfection, but was produced by necessity and enlarged by accident, and is therefore composed of dissimilar parts, thrown together by negligence, by affectation, by learning, or by ignorance.[8]

Our inflections therefore are by no means constant, but admit of numberless irregularities, which in this dictionary will be diligently noted. Thus *fox* makes in the plural *foxes,* but *ox* makes *oxen. Sheep* is the same in both numbers. Adjectives are sometimes compared by changing the last syllable, as *proud, prouder, proudest;* and sometimes by particles prefixed, as *ambitious, more* ambitious, *most* ambitious. The forms of our verbs are subject to great variety; some end their preter tense in *ed,* as I *love,* I *loved,* I have *loved,* which may be called the regular form, and is followed by most of our verbs of southern original.[9] But many depart from this rule, without agreeing in any other, as I *shake,* I *shook,* I have *shaken,* or *shook* as it is sometimes written in poetry; I *make,* I *made,* I have

---

7. Cf. similar comments in Grammar, pp. 306, 307, 315 below.

8. *Institutio Oratoria,* 1.6.16–17: remarking irregularity in the form of Latin words, Quintilian writes, "Non enim, cum primum fingerentur homines, Analogia demissa caelo formam loquendi dedit, sed inventa est, postquam loquebantur, et notatum in sermone quid quoque modo caderet. Itaque non ratione nititur sed exemplo, nec lex est loquendi sed observatio, ut ipsam analogian nulla res alia fecerit quam consuetudo." (It is not the case that heaven-sent analogy provided the form of speech when men were first created; rather, this form was discovered by men when they were speaking and marking the way the words terminate. Thus it is based not on reason but on example, and there is no law of speech but observation; in sum, nothing but custom makes what we call analogy.) Cf. Preface, p. 79 and n. 4 below.

9. *Southern* means Latin or one of the Romance languages.

made; I *bring,* I *brought;* I *wring,* I *wrung,* and many others, which, as they cannot be reduced to rules, must be learned from the dictionary rather than the grammar.[1]

The verbs are likewise to be distinguished according to their qualities, as actives from neuters;[2] the neglect of which has already introduced some barbarities in our conversation, which, if not obviated by just animadversions, may in time creep into our writings.

Thus, my Lord, will our language be laid down, distinct in its minutest subdivisions, and resolved into its elemental principles. And who upon this survey can forbear to wish, that these fundamental atoms of our speech might obtain the firmness and immutability of the primogenial and constituent particles of matter, that they might retain their substance while they alter their appearance, and be varied and compounded, yet not destroyed.[3]

But this is a privilege which words are scarcely to expect; for, like their author, when they are not gaining strength, they are generally losing it. Though art may sometimes prolong their duration, it will rarely give them perpetuity, and their changes will be almost always informing us, that language is the work of man, of a being from whom permanence and stability cannot be derived.

Words having been hitherto considered as separate and unconnected, are now to be likewise examined as they are ranged in their various relations to others by the rules of SYNTAX or construction, to which I do not know that any regard has been yet shewn in English dictionaries, and in which the grammarians can give little assistance.[4] The syntax of this

---

1. *Dictionary* contains forms for many irregular plurals, preterites, past participles, comparatives, and superlatives.

2. *Dictionary* regularly provides separate entries for the "active" (transitive) and "neuter" (intransitive) senses of verbs.

3. This sentence glances at the kind of "philosophical" (scientific) or rational language proposed by such linguistic projectors as Leibnitz and John Wilkins; but the next paragraph stresses the changeability of languages, "the work" of unstable man. Elsewhere—e.g., Preface to Shakespeare (*Yale* VII.107, par. 145)—SJ refers to words or other elements of language as "atoms."

4. *Syntax:* "That part of Grammar which teaches the construction of words" (*Dictionary,* sense 2); SJ discusses

language is too inconstant to be reduced to rules, and can be only learned by the distinct consideration of particular words as they are used by the best authors. Thus, we say, according to the present modes of speech, the soldier died *of* his wounds, and the sailor perished *with* hunger; and every man acquainted with our language would be offended by a change of these particles, which yet seem originally assigned by chance, there being no reason to be drawn from grammar[m] why a man may not, with equal propriety, be said to dye *with* a wound or perish *of* hunger.

Our syntax therefore is not to be taught by general rules, but by special precedents; and in examining whether Addison has been with justice accused of a solecism in this passage,

> The poor inhabitant ———
> Starves in the midst of nature's bounty curst,
> And in the loaden vineyard *dies for thirst.*

it is not in our power to have recourse to any established laws of speech, but we must remark how the writers of former ages have used the same word, and consider whether he can be acquitted of impropriety, upon the testimony of Davies, given in his favour by a similar passage.

> She loaths the watry glass wherein she gaz'd,
> And shuns it still, although *for thirst she dye.*[5]

m. *The erratum on the verso of the title-page of 47 directs that* or reason *be deleted from the phrase* grammar or reason

---

syntax very briefly in his Grammar (see p. 347 below), limiting his treatment to matters of inflection, which alone he considered proper to grammar. Consistent with these remarks, SJ lists many combinations of verbs and prepositions as separate senses of the verbs in *Dictionary*.

5. Both the passage of Addison ("A Letter from Italy, to the right Honourable Charles Lord Halifax in the year 1701," ll. 113 and 117–18) and that by Sir John Davies (*Nosce Teipsum*, ll. 119–20) are quoted in *Dictionary* under *to die*, sense 5 ("*For* commonly before a privative, and *of* before a positive cause; these prepositions are not always truely [sic] distinguished"). We do not know who accused Addison of a solecism, but a reader of SJ's "Scheme" commented on the passage (see p. 402, below).

When the construction of a word is explained, it is necessary to pursue it through its train of PHRASEOLOGY, through those forms where it is used in a manner peculiar to our language, or in senses not to be comprised in the general explanations; as from the verb *make,* arise these phrases, to *make love,* to *make an end,* to *make way,* as he *made way* for his followers, the ship *made way* before the wind; to *make a bed,* to *make merry,* to *make a mock,* to *make presents,* to *make a doubt,* to *make out an assertion,* to *make good* a breach, to *make good* a cause, to *make nothing* of an attempt, to *make lamentation,* to *make a merit,* and many others which will occur in reading with that view, and which only their frequency hinders from being generally remarked.[6]

The great labour is yet to come, the labour of interpreting these words and phrases with brevity, fulness and perspicuity; a task of which the extent and intricacy is sufficiently shewn by the miscarriage of those who have generally attempted it. This difficulty is encreased by the necessity of explaining the words in the same language, for there is often only one word for one idea; and though it be easy to translate the words *bright, sweet, salt, bitter,* into another language, it is not easy to explain them.[7]

With regard to the INTERPRETATION many other questions have required consideration. It was some time doubted whether it be necessary to explain the things implied by particular words. As under the term *baronet,* whether instead of this explanation, *a title of honour next in degree to that of baron,* it would be better to mention more particularly the creation, privileges and rank of baronets; and whether under the word *barometer,* instead of being satisfied with observing that it is *an instrument to discover the weight of the air,* it would be fit to spend a few lines upon its invention, construction and principles.[8]

---

6. *Dictionary* lists such combinations as separate senses of the main word.

7. Although abandoning his original intention of using foreign languages in his definitions (see "Scheme," fol. 12, p. 406 below), SJ sometimes draws on Latin and Greek words and phrases for further explanations of words in *Dictionary;* for examples, see *JDLL,* pp. 114–15.

8. In *Dictionary* the definition of *baronet* comes from John Cowell, *The In-*

It is not to be expected that with the explanation of the one the herald should be satisfied, or the philosopher with that of the other; but since it will be required by common readers, that the explications should be sufficient for common use, and since without some attention to such demands the dictionary cannot become generally valuable, I have determined to consult the best writers for explanations real as well as verbal, and perhaps I may at last have reason to say, after one of the augmenters of Furetier, that my book is more learned than its author.[9]

In explaining the general and popular language, it seems necessary to sort the several senses of each word, and to exhibit first its natural and primitive signification, as

To *arrive,* to reach the shore in a voyage. He *arrived* at a safe harbour.

Then to give its consequential meaning, *to arrive,* to reach any place whether by land or sea; as, he *arrived* at his country seat.

Then its metaphorical sense, to obtain any thing desired; as, he *arrived* at a peerage.

Then to mention any observation that arises from the comparison of one meaning with another; as, it may be remarked of the word *arrive,* that in consequence of its original and etymological sense, it cannot be properly applied but to words signifying something desirable; thus, we say a man *arrived* at happiness, but cannot say without a mixture of irony, he *arrived* at misery.[1]

Ground, the earth, generally as opposed to the air or water. He swam till he reached *ground.* The bird fell to the *ground.*

Then follows the accidental or consequential signification,

---

terpreter (rev. White Kennet, 1701), the much longer one for *barometer* from John Harris, *Lexicon Technicum* (1704).

9. "Enfin mon livre (si j'ai quelque droit de l'appeller ainsi) est beaucoup plus sçavant que moi." "Préface de M. Basnage de Bauval, pour la second [1701] & la troisieme Edition [1708] de ce Dictionnaire" [first published 1690] in *Dictionnaire universel, contenant généralement tous les mots français tant vieux que modernes et les termes de toutes les sciences et des arts,* 4 vols. (1727), I. sig. ***2^r.

1. The entry for *arrive* in *Dictionary* resembles this treatment.

in which *ground* implies any thing that lies under another; as, he laid colours upon a rough *ground.* The silk had blue flowers on a red *ground.*

Then the remoter or metaphorical signification; as, the *ground* of his opinion was a false computation. The *ground* of his work was his father's manuscript.[2]

After having gone through the natural and figurative senses, it will be proper to subjoin the poetical sense of each word, where it differs from that which is in common use; as, *wanton* applied to any thing of which the motion is irregular without terror, as

In *wanton* ringlets curl'd her hair.[3]

To the poetical sense may succeed the familiar; as of *toast,* used to imply the person whose health is drunk.

The wise man's passion, and the vain man's *toast.* Pope.[4]

The familiar may be followed by the burlesque; as of *mellow,* applied to good fellowship.

In all thy humours whether grave, or *mellow.* Addison.[5]

Or of *bite* used for *cheat.*

——— More a dupe than wit,
Sappho can tell you, how this man was *bit.* Pope.[6]

And lastly, may be produced the peculiar sense, in which a word is found in any great author. As *faculties* in Shakespeare signifies the powers of authority.

2. *Dictionary* distinguishes twenty senses of *ground.*

3. *Wanton:* "Quick, and irregular of motion," *Dictionary,* sense 5, illustrated by *Paradise Lost,* IV.304–07, which contain a correct version ("Dishevell'd, but in wanton ringlets wav'd") of this line.

4. *Toast:* "A celebrated woman whose health is often drunk" (*Dictionary,* sense 3), illustrated partly by this line (*The Rape of the Lock,* V.10).

5. *Mellow:* "Drunk; melted down with drink" (*Dictionary,* sense 4), illustrated partly by this line (*Spectator* 68, par. 3), the first of a four-line translation of Martial, *Epigrams,* 12.47.

6. *To Bite:* "To cheat; to trick; to defraud: a low phrase" (*Dictionary,* sense 6), not illustrated by these lines (*Epistle to Dr. Arbuthnot,* ll. 368–69).

——— This Duncan
Has born his *faculties* so meek, has been
So clear in his great office, that &*c*.[7]

The signification of adjectives, may be often ascertained by uniting them to substantives, as *simple swain, simple sheep;* sometimes the sense of a substantive may be elucidated by the epithets annexed to it in good authors, as the *boundless ocean,* the *open lawns,* and where such advantage can be gained by a short quotation it is not to be omitted.[8]

The difference of signification in words generally accounted synonimous, ought to be carefully observed; as in *pride, haughtiness, arrogance;*[9] and the strict and critical meaning ought to be distinguished from that which is loose and popular; as in the word *perfection,* which though in its philosophical and exact sense, it can be of little use among human beings, is often so much degraded from its original signification, that the academicians have inserted in their work *the perfection of a language,* and with a little more licentiousness might have prevailed on themselves to have added *the perfection of a dictionary.*[1]

There are many other characters of words which it will be of use to mention. Some have both an active and passive signification, as *fearful,* that which gives or which feels terror,

7. *Faculties:* "Power; authority" (*Dictionary,* s.v. *faculty,* sense 8), illustrated by these lines (*Macbeth* I.vii.16–18).

8. *Dictionary* usually abandons these intentions. Rare exceptions refer to epithets in foreign languages (see, e.g., *gold,* sense 3).

9. After examining *Dictionary* entries for *pride* (8 senses), *proud* (9 senses), *haughtiness* (1 sense), *haughty* (3 senses), *arrogance* (1 sense), and *arrogant* (1 sense), we conclude that SJ only intermittently clarified "the difference of signification in words generally accounted synonimous."

1. Obviously thinking of the French "academicians," SJ may be referring to the following passage: "On dira peutestre qu'on ne peut jamais s'asseurer qu'une Langue vivante soit parvenuë à sa derniere perfection; Mais ce n'a pas esté le sentiment de Ciceron, qui aprés avoir fait de longues reflexions sur cette matiere, n'a pas fait difficulté d'avancer que de son temps la Langue Latine estoit arrivée à un degré d'excellence où l'on ne pouvoit rien adjouster. Nous voyons qu'il ne s'est pas trompé et peutestre n'aura-t-on pas moins de raison de penser la mesme chose en faveur de la Langue Françoise" (*Dictionnaire de l'Académie Française* [2 vols., 1694], Préface, par. 5). *Dictionary* does not make this distinction concerning "perfection."

a *fearful prodigy*, a *fearful hare*.[2] Some have a personal, some a real meaning, as in opposition to *old* we use the adjective *young* of animated beings, and *new* of other things.[3] Some are restrained to the sense of praise, and others to that of disapprobation, so commonly, though not always, we *exhort* to good actions, we *instigate* to ill;[4] we *animate, incite* and *encourage* indifferently to good or bad. So we usually *ascribe* good, but *impute* evil; yet neither the use of these words, nor perhaps of any other in our licentious language, is so established as not to be often reversed by the correctest writers.[5] I shall therefore, since the rules of stile, like those of law, arise from precedents often repeated, collect the testimonies on both sides, and endeavour to discover and promulgate the decrees of custom, who has so long possessed, whether by right or by usurpation, the sovereignty of words.[6]

It is necessary likewise to explain many words by their opposition to others; for contraries are best seen when they stand together. Thus the verb *stand* has one sense as opposed to *fall*, and another as opposed to *fly*;[7] for want of attending to which distinction, obvious as it is, the learned Dr. Bentley has squandered his criticism to no purpose, on these lines of Paradise Lost.

——— In heaps
Chariot and charioteer lay over-turn'd,
And fiery foaming steeds. What *stood, recoil'd,*

2. *Fearful:* "Afraid. It has *of* before the object of fear" (*Dictionary,* sense 2); "Terrible; dreadful; frightful; impressing fear" (sense 4); neither distinguishes "active" and "passive" senses.

3. *Dictionary* makes this distinction only under *new* (sense 1).

4. *Exhort:* "To incite by words to any good action" (*Dictionary*); *instigate:* "To urge to ill; to provoke or incite to a crime" (ibid.).

5. *Dictionary* makes this distinction only for *impute;* a quotation under each word (from John Rogers and the King James Bible, respectively) shows the exception to the general usage.

6. An echo of the well-known lines from Horace, quoted in *Dictionary* (s.v. *latter*) as "*Volet usus / Quem penes arbitrium est, & vis, & norma loquendi*" (*Ars Poetica,* ll. 72–73); in the translation of Philip Francis (1743), "If custom will, whose arbitrary sway, / Words, and the forms of language must obey."

7. *Dictionary* exhibits these contraries in the definitions of *to stand,* senses 4 and 11, respectively.

O'erwearied, through the faint Satanic host,
Defensive scarce, or with pale fear surpris'd
Fled ignominious ———

"Here," says the critic, "as the sentence is now read, we find that what *stood, fled,*" and therefore he proposes an alteration, which he might have spared if he had consulted a dictionary, and found that nothing more was affirmed than that those *fled* who did *not fall.*[8]

In explaining such meanings as seem accidental and adventitious, I shall endeavour to give an account of the means by which they were introduced. Thus to *eke out* any thing, signifies to lengthen it beyond its just dimensions by some low artifice, because the word *eke* was the usual refuge of our old writers when they wanted a syllable.[9] And *buxom,* which means only *obedient,* is now made, in familiar phrases, to stand for *wanton,* because in an antient form of marriage, before the reformation, the bride promised complaisance and obedience in these terms, "I will be bonair and *buxom* in bed and at board."[1]

I know well, my Lord, how trifling many of these remarks will appear separately considered, and how easily they may give occasion to the contemptuous merriment of sportive idleness, and the gloomy censures of arrogant stupidity; but

---

8. SJ refers to the following note in Richard Bentley's edition of Milton's *Paradise Lost* (1732), p. 196:

> What stood, recoil'd . . . or *Fled ignominious.*] This Sentence is inexplicable. What Contradiction is that, *what stood, fled*? And yet that is the plain Syntax, as it now stands. And what's THROUGH *the Host*? Some wrong must have been done to our Author here. To come at his Meaning and Intention, the whole Paragraph must be reform'd. This way may be one:
>
> *And fiery foamy steeds.* Yet somewhile stood
> *The faint* Satanic *Host;* o'erwearied stood
> *Defensive scarce: then with pale fear surpris'd,*
> *Then first with fear surpris'd,* &c.

Johnson quotes, incorrectly, *Paradise Lost* VI.389–95.

9. This explanation is repeated under *to eke* (*Dictionary,* sense 4).

1. In the *Sarum Manual* (1554), e.g., the wife promises "to be bonere and buxum in bedde and at the borde till death us depart" (*Manuale ad Usum per Celebris Ecclesie Sarisburiensis,* fol. 48^{r}). SJ's remark is repeated in *Dictionary,* s.v. *buxom.*

dulness it is easy to despise, and laughter it is easy to repay. I shall not be solicitous what is thought of my work by such as know not the difficulty or importance of philological studies, nor shall think those that have done nothing qualified to condemn me for doing little. It may not, however, be improper to remind them, that no terrestrial greatness is more than an aggregate of little things, and to inculcate after the Arabian proverb, that drops added to drops constitute the ocean.[2]

There remains yet to be considered the DISTRIBUTION of words into their proper classes, or that part of lexicography which is strictly critical.

The popular part of the language, which includes all words not appropriated to particular sciences, admits of many distinctions[n] and subdivisions; as, into words of general use;[o] words employed chiefly in poetry; words obsolete; words which are admitted only by particular writers, yet not in themselves improper; words used only in burlesque writing; and words impure and barbarous.

Words of general use will be known by having no sign of particularity, and their various senses will be supported by authorities of all ages.

The words appropriated to poetry will be distinguished by some mark prefixed, or will be known by having no authorities but those of poets.[3]

n. distinctions *FC*] dictinstions *47*
o. use; *emend.*] use ; *47*

---

2. The second section (entitled "Fabulae Locmani Sapientis") of Thomas Erpenius's *Arabicae Linguae Tyrocinium* (1656) includes proverbs and adagia, all translated into Latin. Adagium I reads, "Principium arboris est officulum" (a tiny thing is the beginning of a tree); the second, added by the editor, reads, "Gutta addita gutta evadit stagnum" (drop added to drop results in a large pool), p. 66. For similar comments, see *Rambler* 43 (par. 10), *Yale* III.235; *Rasselas, Yale* XVI.58: "Great works are performed, not by strength, but perseverance: yonder palace was raised by single stones, yet you see its height and spaciousness. He that shall walk with vigour three hours a day will pass in seven years a space equal to the circumference of the globe."

3. In *Dictionary* no "words appropriated to poetry" are distinguished by marks, but the meanings of numerous words (some also labeled "not in use") are illustrated solely by lines from poems; e.g., *to able, to abode, abreast, to*

Of antiquated or obsolete words, none will be inserted but such as are to be found in authors who wrote since the accession of Elizabeth, from which we date the golden age of our language;[4] and of these many might be omitted, but that the reader may require, with an appearance of reason, that no difficulty should be left unresolved in books which he finds himself invited to read, as confessed and established models of stile. These will be likewise pointed out by some note of exclusion, but not of disgrace.[5]

The words which are found only in particular books, will be known by the single name of him that has used them; but such will be omitted, unless either their propriety, elegance, or force, or the reputation of their authors affords some extraordinary reason for their reception.[6]

Words used in burlesque and familiar compositions, will be likewise mentioned with their proper authorities, such as *dudgeon* from Butler, and *leasing* from Prior, and will be diligently characterised by marks of distinction.[7]

Barbarous or impure words and expressions, may be branded with some note of infamy, as they are carefully to be eradicated wherever they are found; and they occur too frequently even in the best writers. As in Pope,

——— *in* endless errour *hurl'd.*
'Tis these that early taint the female soul.[8]

---

abrook ("not in use"), *to accoil* ("out of use"), and *aconite* ("commonly used in poetical language for poison in general").

4. *Dictionary* usually cites "authors who wrote since the accession [1558] of Elizabeth," Sir Philip Sidney (1554–1586) being the earliest quoted very often. However, Roger Ascham (1515–1568) is quoted about a hundred times, and other earlier writers occasionally. See *JDTR,* pp. 20–36.

5. *Dictionary* dubs a substantial number of words "obsolete" or "not in use."

6. *Dictionary* includes many such words (perhaps the greatest number from Dryden), sometimes even though condemning them (e.g., *falsify,* sense 4).

7. In *Dictionary* neither *dudgeon* nor *leasing* is "characterised by marks of distinction," although the entry for *dudgeon* includes two passages from Samuel Butler's *Hudibras* and that for *leasing* one from Matthew Prior's *Alma; or the Progress of the Mind.* On the other hand, the entry for *grannam* ("Grandmother") states, "only used in burlesque works."

8. *Essay on Man,* II.17; *The Rape of the Lock,* I.87. Neither line is cited in *Dictionary.*

In Addison,

> Attend to what a *lesser* muse indites.[9]

And in Dryden,

> A dreadful quiet felt, and *worser* far
> Than arms ———[1]

If this part of the work can be well performed, it will be equivalent to the proposal made by Boileau to the academicians, that they should review all their polite writers, and correct such impurities as might be found in them, that their authority might not contribute, at any distant time, to the depravation of the language.[2]

With regard to questions of purity, or propriety, I was once in doubt whether I should not attribute too much to myself in attempting to decide them, and whether my province was to extend beyond the proposition of the question, and the display of the suffrages on each side; but I have been since determined[3] by your Lordship's opinion, to interpose my own judgment, and shall therefore endeavour to support what appears to me most consonant to grammar and reason. Au-

---

9. "To the Right Honourable Sir John Somers" (l. 19); not cited in *Dictionary* where *lesser* is defined as "A barbarous corruption of *less,* formed by the vulgar from the habit of terminating comparatives in *er;* afterward adopted by poets, and then by writers of prose, till it has all the authority which a mode originally erroneous can derive from custom." Passages are quoted from Spenser, Shakespeare, Thomas Burnet, Locke, John Woodward, and Pope.

1. *Astraea Redux,* ll. 3–4; included, along with lines from Shakespeare, in *Dictionary* where *worser* is defined as "A barbarous word, formed by corrupting *worse* with the usual comparative termination."

2. Cf. the following remarks which Thoulier d'Olivet recorded and published in his *Histoire de l'Académie* (2d ed., 2 vols., 1730 [II.121–22]) and which appeared in Boileau's works beginning in 1740 (*Oeuvres* [5 vols., 1747], V.117): "Quoi, dit-il, l'Académie ne voudra-t-elle jamais connoître ses forces? Toujours bornée a son Dictionnaire, quand donc prendra-t-elle l'essor? Je voudrois que la France pût avoir ses Auteurs Classiques, aussi-bien que l'Italie. Pour cela, il nous faudroit un certain nombre de Livres qui fussent déclaré exemts de fautes, quant au Stile. Quel est le Tribunal, qui aura le droit de prononcer là-dessus, si ce n'est l'Académie?"

3. *To determine:* "To influence the choice" (*Dictionary,* sense 5).

sonius thought that modesty forbad him to plead inability for a task to which Cæsar had judged him equal.

> Cur me posse negem posse quod ille putat?[4]

And I may hope, my Lord, that since you, whose authority in our language is so generally acknowledged, have commissioned me to declare my own opinion, I shall be considered as exercising a kind of vicarious jurisdiction, and that the power which might have been denied to my own claim, will be readily allowed me as the delegate of your Lordship.[5]

In citing authorities, on which the credit of every part of this work must depend, it will be proper to observe some obvious rules, such as of preferring writers of the first reputation to those of an inferior rank, of noting the quotations with accuracy, and of selecting, when it can be conveniently done, such sentences, as, besides their immediate use, may give pleasure or instruction by conveying some elegance of language, or some precept of prudence, or piety.[6]

It has been asked, on some occasions, who shall judge the judges?[7] And since with regard to this design, a question may arise by what authority the authorities are selected, it is necessary to obviate it, by declaring that many of the writers whose testimonies will be alleged, were selected by Mr. Pope, of whom I may be justified in affirming, that were he still

---

4. *Ausonius* 1.4 (ll. 9–12) directed to Emperor Augustus Theodosius I:

> scribere me Augustus iubet et mea carmina poscit
> paene rogans: blando vis latet imperio.
> non habeo ingenium, Caesar sed iussit: habebo.
> cur me posse negem, posse quod ille putat?

(Augustus orders me to write and requests my poems, beseeching me often: but the power lies in the flattering command. I have no genius, but should Caesar give the order, I will have it. Why should I deny that I am capable of what he thinks I can do?)

5. For Chesterfield's response to Johnson's flattering concession, see p. 58, n. 6 below.

6. Cf. SJ's later comments (Preface, pp. 93–94 below) on the "pleasure or instruction" afforded by *Dictionary*'s illustrative passages.

7. The question of "who shall judge the judges" is at least as old as Juvenal, *Satires* 6.O31–32 ("quis custodiet ipsos custodes"), and it has been traced to Plato's similar question about the guardians in his ideal state (*Republic*, 403e).

alive, solicitous as he was for the success of this work, he would not be displeased that I have undertaken it.[8]

It will be proper that the quotations be ranged according to the ages of their authors, and it will afford an agreeable amusement, if to the words and phrases which are not of our own growth, the name of the writer who first introduced them can be affixed, and if, to words which are now antiquated, the authority be subjoined of him who last admitted them. Thus for *scathe* and *buxom,* now obsolete, Milton may be cited.

——— The mountain oak
Stands *scath'd* to heaven ———[9]

——— He with broad sails
Winnow'd the *buxom* air ———[1]

8. According to Joseph Spence, in his *Observations, Anecdotes, and Characters of Books and Men* (1820; ed. James M. Osborn [2 vols., 1966], I.170–71, 374–75), Pope selected in 1744—the year of his death—a list of prose writers and began a list of poets to be used as authorities in an English dictionary. Later, SJ, whose poem *London* (1738) Pope admired (*Life,* I.128–29) and whose candidacy for a master's degree he had supported (ibid., 133, 143), received Pope's lists—"probably" from Robert Dodsley, Boswell stated (ibid., 182–83). SJ's indebtedness to these lists remains unknown. But the following figures suggest a likely influence. Of Pope's twenty prose writers, counting the four "authorities for familiar dialogues," fifteen are cited frequently in *Dictionary;* the remaining five are Lord Bolingbroke, Nathaniel Hooke, Conyers Middleton, John Vanbrugh, and Hobbes. Hobbes is excluded because SJ "did not like his principles" (*Early Biographies,* p. 82), and Bolingbroke, whose principles Johnson also disliked (see *Dictionary,* s.v. *irony*), only creeps in as a correspondent of Pope. There are two quotations from Hooke and one from Vanbrugh in *Dictionary* (s.v. *cat o'nine tails; to give* [v.n.], sense 1; and *round,* sense 6, respectively) and none from Middleton. Although Pope specifically rejected him "as too affected," Sir Walter Ralegh is cited in *Dictionary.* Of Pope's nine poets, all are cited frequently except John Fletcher, who comes in three times, with his collaborator Francis Beaumont. Altogether, the evidence, we conclude, justifies SJ's "affirmation" of Pope's attitude regarding SJ's work on *Dictionary.*

9. *Paradise Lost,* I.612–13: "As when Heaven's fire / Hath *scath'd* the forest oaks, or mountain pines"; under *to scathe* in *Dictionary* SJ notes, "Both the verb and the noun are now obsolete."

1. *Paradise Lost,* V.269–70: "with quick fan / Winnows the buxom air"; in *Dictionary* SJ defines *buxom* as "Obedient; obsequious."

By this method every word will have its history, and the reader will be informed of the gradual changes of the language, and have before his eyes the rise of some words, and the fall of others. But observations so minute and accurate are to be desired rather than expected, and if use be carefully supplied, curiosity must sometimes bear its disappointments.[2]

This, my Lord, is my idea of an English dictionary, a dictionary by which the pronunciation of our language may be fixed, and its attainment facilitated; by which its purity may be preserved, its use ascertained, and its duration lengthened.[3] And though, perhaps, to correct the language of nations by books of grammar, and amend their manners by discourses of morality, may be tasks equally difficult; yet as it is unavoidable to wish, it is natural likewise to hope, that your Lordship's patronage may not be wholly lost; that it may contribute to the preservation of antient, and the improvement of modern writers; that it may promote the reformation of those translators, who for want of understanding the characteristical difference of tongues, have formed a chaotic dialect of heterogeneous phrases;[4] and awaken to the care of purer

2. *Dictionary* does not present the "history" of nearly all the words it lists. For some of the reasons for its failure to do so, see Preface, pp. 91–92 below. Nevertheless, its entries display the histories of words much more fully than those in earlier English dictionaries, and *OED* both adopted and extended its concept of lexicography.

3. To Albert C. Baugh and Thomas Cable (*A History of the English Language* [4th ed., p. 268], as well as other historians of the English language, this sentence is prime evidence of Johnson's prescriptivism and the similarity of his attempts to those of the continental academies. Cf. SJ's altered "expectation" in Preface, pp. 104–05 below.

4. Cf. the still more severe comments on translators and their work in Preface, pp. 108–09 below). Yet *Dictionary* quotes passages from many translations, including George Chapman's and Pope's Homer, Dryden's Vergil, Juvenal, and (in prose) Charles Alphonse Dufresnoy's poem *De Arte Graphice;* and, above all others, the King James Bible, which is cited about 5,000 times. Subsequently, SJ wrote an impassioned letter to William Drummond on 13 August 1766, supporting a translation of the Bible into Scots Gaelic (*Letters,* I.268–71). And later, of course, in *Lives* he extolled the translations of Dryden (pars. 223, 226, 306, 312–13) and Pope (pars. 93 ["the English *Iliad* . . . is certainly the noblest version of poetry which the world has ever seen"], 345, 348).

diction, some men of genius, whose attention to argument makes them negligent of stile, or whose rapid imagination, like the Peruvian torrents, when it brings down gold, mingles it with sand.[5]

When I survey the plan which I have laid before you, I cannot, my Lord, but confess, that I am frighted at its extent, and, like the soldiers of Cæsar, look on Britain as a new world, which it is almost madness to invade.[6] But I hope, that though I should not complete the conquest, I shall at least discover the coast, civilize part of the inhabitants, and make it easy for some other adventurer to proceed farther, to reduce them wholly to subjection, and settle them under laws.

We are taught by the great Roman orator, that every man should propose to himself the highest degree of excellence, but that he may stop with honour at the second or the third:[7] though therefore my performance should fall below the excellence of other dictionaries, I may obtain, at least, the praise of having endeavoured well, nor shall I think it any reproach to my diligence, that I have retired without a triumph from a contest with united academies and long successions of learned compilers. I cannot hope in the warmest moments, to preserve so much caution through so long a work, as not

5. The entry for Peru in Emanuel Bowen's *A Complete System of Geography* (2 vols., 1747) includes the following passage: as certain rivers "come from Mountains where there are Gold Mines, they carry some Grains of that Metal [gold] along with the Sand" (II.578). In Aphra Behn's *Oroonoko* (London, 1688, pp. 181–82), the phenomenon is reported to occur in Surinam.

6. SJ refers to the Emperor Claudius, whose forces, under the command of Aulus Plautius, invaded Britain in 43 A.D. In his history of Rome (60.19.2–4), Dio Cassius describes the succession of events, beginning with the troops' refusal (caused by fear of an uncivilized world) to go ashore and ending with their enthusiastic agreement to do so, after a stirring speech by a slave named Narcissus. In the first (No. 100; 28 November 1754) of his two *World* essays on the *Dictionary,* Lord Chesterfield responded to SJ's comments here and in his earlier reference to Ausonius (see pp. 54–55, above): "I will not only obey him like an old Roman, as my dictator, but, like a modern Roman, I will implicitly believe in him [SJ] as my pope, and hold him to be infallible while in the chair." Also see Introduction, pp. 8–9 above.

7. Cicero, *Orator* 1.3–4; SJ expresses the same opinion about perfection elsewhere—e.g. pp. 28, 49 above; *Rambler* 169 (par. 5), *Yale* V.131; *Adventurer* 85 (par. 18), *Yale* II.416–17.

often to sink into negligence, or to obtain so much knowledge of all its parts, as not frequently to fail by ignorance. I expect that sometimes the desire of accuracy, will urge me to superfluities, and sometimes the fear of prolixity betray me to omissions; that in the extent of such variety I shall be often bewildred, and in the[p] mazes of such intricacy, be frequently entangled; that in one part refinement will be subtilised beyond exactness, and evidence dilated in another beyond perspicuity. Yet I do not despair of approbation from those who knowing the uncertainty of conjecture, the scantiness of knowledge, the fallibility of memory, and the unsteadiness of attention, can compare the causes of error with the means of avoiding it, and the extent of art with the capacity of man; and whatever be the event of my endeavours, I shall not easily regret an attempt which has procured me the honour of appearing thus publickly,

My Lord,
Your Lordship's
Most Obedient,
and
Most Humble Servant,
SAM. JOHNSON.

p. *see Editor's Introduction, p. 16, ll. 22–26, above*

A DICTIONARY OF THE ENGLISH LANGUAGE (1755)

THE PREFACE

A HISTORY OF THE ENGLISH LANGUAGE

A GRAMMAR OF THE ENGLISH TONGUE

Composition

The date of Johnson's decision to include in his *Dictionary* a preface, history of the language, and grammar is unclear. None of the three versions of his *Plan of a Dictionary* (1747)—the "Short Scheme" (pp. 378–427 below), the fair copy (pp. 428–89 below), and the published *Plan* (pp. 25–59 above)—alludes to the front matter of the projected work. However, by 1747 a number of dictionaries, counting both bilingual and English, contained one or more of the same preliminary pieces; so it is possible that from the beginning of his enterprise Johnson intended to provide a preface, a history, and a grammar for his readers.[1] If he had not reached his decision earlier, he may well have been prompted to make it on his scrutiny of Benjamin Martin's *Lingua Britannica Reformata* (1749), which includes all three features (as well as numerous divided and numbered definitions) and which he examined soon after its appearance, perhaps even before.[2]

Speculation aside, the initial known reference to the Preface, History, and Grammar—and obvious proof of his intention—occurs in the note preceding Johnson's prayer for 3 April 1753: "I began the 2d vol of my Dictionary, room being left in the first for Preface, Grammar & History none of them yet begun."[3] In the absence of subsequent authorial and non-authorial comments about the production of the three works, one must reconstruct the probable stages from several pieces of indirect evidence.

On 16 July 1754, Johnson wrote his friend Thomas Warton, Fellow of Trinity College, Oxford: "my book [the *Dictionary*] . . . now draws towards its end, but . . . I cannot finish [it] to my

1. See Sledd-Kolb, pp. 11–12, 208.
2. Ibid., p. 43.
3. *Yale* I.50.

mind without visiting the libraries of Oxford which I therefore hope to see in about a fortnight. I know not how long I shall stay or where I shall lodge, but shall be sure to look for you at my arrival, and we shall easily settle the rest."[4]

Because his preparation of the word list was mostly completed by the summer of 1754, investigators have inferred that Johnson went to Oxford chiefly for the purpose of consulting libraries and scholars about the substance of his preliminaries and that he composed the pieces toward the end of the summer and/or during the fall of 1754.[5]

Presumably soon after his arrival, writing a letter (lacking both an identifying place and date) to William Strahan, the frequent printer and publisher of his works, he recorded what is apparently his only surviving description of his researches there: "My journey will come to very little beyond the satisfaction of knowing that there is nothing to be done, and that I leave few advantages here to those that shall come after me."[6] Much later, providing James Boswell with materials for his *Life of Johnson* (1791), Thomas Warton obligingly communicated, in addition to a number of his (annotated) letters from Johnson, a fuller account of Johnson's activities while at Oxford. "He came . . . within a fortnight [after 16 July 1754], and stayed about five weeks. He lodged at a house called Kettel-hall, near Trinity College. But during this visit at Oxford, he collected nothing in the libraries for his Dictionary." Nevertheless, Warton goes on to say, among other things, that the residence of Francis Wise, the Radclivian Librarian, contained "an excellent library; particularly, a valuable collection of books in Northern literature with which Johnson was often very busy."[7]

Warton's remarks naturally arouse inquiries regarding the possible links between Johnson's reading in Wise's library (and elsewhere), his supposed conversations with Wise and other Oxford scholars, and his relationships with Warton (in-

4. *Letters,* I.81–82.
5. See Sledd-Kolb, pp. 109–10; Reddick, pp. 74–75.
6. *Letters,* I.82.
7. *Life,* I.270, n. 5; 271–74, esp. 273.

cluding the latter's works), on one hand, and the contents of his Preface, History, and Grammar, on the other.

Besides general references to the "northern languages," "northern literature," and "Teutonick" tongues and etymologies, the Preface contains such specific statements as "from arbitrary representation of sounds by letters proceeds that diversity of spelling observable in the *Saxon* remains," "anomalous plurals of nouns and preterites of verbs, which in the *Teutonick* dialects are very frequent," "our words of one syllable are very often *Teutonick,*" and "of words undoubtedly *Teutonick* the original is not always to be found in any ancient language." It is possible, we suppose, but are far from certain, that these and other statements were founded on Johnson's inspection of materials in Wise's library. Otherwise, since numerous other parts of the Preface exhibit similarities to the pronouncements of earlier English and Continental lexicographers, it appears that Johnson gained little, if anything, for the Preface from the libraries and scholars at Oxford.[8]

On the other hand, we are led to conjecture that Johnson, having (we guess) put together his History and Grammar, sat down, replete with pertinent facts, generalizations, and memories—some pleasant, some more painful—and wrote the profoundly moving Preface at one or two sittings, drawing for his long footnote (pp. 82–83 below) on Stephen Skinner's *Etymologicon Linguae Anglicanae* (1671) and Franciscus Junius's *Etymologicum Anglicanum* (ed. Edward Lye, 1743) during the process. In support of our conjecture, we stress his extraordinary memory, talent for "ranging particulars under generals,"[9] and quickness in writing. Furthermore, we are confident that his unsurpassed skill and speed in composing prefaces resulted, partly, from his long cultivation of the genre: between 1735 (to his translation of Father Jerome Lobo's *Voyage to Abyssinia*) and 1754 (to vol. XXIV of the *Gentlemen's Magazine*), the number came to about twelve, at least.[1]

8. See *JDTR,* pp. 20–36.

9. "Preface to Rolt's Dictionary," *The Works of Samuel Johnson* (1825), V.251; Allen T. Hazen, *Samuel Johnson's Prefaces and Dedications* (1937), pp. 198–200.

1. See Fleeman, *Bibliography,* 35.2LV/1a; 38.4PM/1a; 39.10CP/1a; 40GM10/p. iii;

And in 1756, although he "never saw the man, and never read the book," he, knowing "very well what such a Dictionary should be . . . wrote a Preface" to Richard Rolt's *Dictionary of Trade and Commerce.*[2]

Publication and Reception

The Preface made its appearance in the first edition of the *Dictionary* (1755) as well as in the proprietors' later seven unabridged editions published in the eighteenth century (1755–56, 1765, 1773, 1784, 1785, 1785, 1799) and those published in the nineteenth. It also appeared in the three Dublin unabridged editions and issues (1775, 1777, 1798–97), Harrison's edition (1785–87), and Jarvis and Fielding's edition (1785–86).

A more significant indicator of its appeal was its inclusion in the following abridgments: four Dublin editions and issues (1758, 1764, 1766, 1768); J. Mifflin's London edition (1778), which also contained the History; the proprietors' edition and issue of 1792; and the Edinburgh edition and issue of 1797 and 1798.

The Preface began its independent existence in vol. II of Thomas Davies's *Miscellaneous and Fugitive Pieces* (1773, 1774, 1774) and apparently in a French translation by Diderot. In a letter to his friend William Johnson Temple, dated 6 December 1775, Boswell wrote: "I have seen the Preface to his [Johnson's] Dictionary translated by Diderot." But neither C. B. Tinker nor Thomas Crawford was able "to trace this translation."[3] Then the Preface became a part of Sir John

---

41GM11/p. iii; 42GM12/pp. iii–iv; 43.1CBH; 43GM13/p. iii; 44.4HM/1; 44 GM14/p. iii; 48.4DP/1; 49.12LEM/1a; 53.2GMI/1; 53GM23/p. iii; Hazen, pp. 43, 171, 77; NCBEL, II (1971), cols. 1136–39, 1143–44.

2. *Life,* I.359.

3. See *The Correspondence of James Boswell and William Johnson Temple,* vol. I (1756–1777), ed. Thomas Crawford (1997), p. 403 n. 5. Thanks to Howard Weinbrot, we are aware of reviews in the *Journal Britannique* (see n. 5 below) and in the *Journal étranger* (December 1756; pp. 111–74), in which the whole Preface is rendered in French. We have no evidence that the piece was written by Diderot, but perhaps this is the work that Boswell saw.

Hawkins's edition of Johnson's collected *Works* (1787) and of Arthur Murphy's counterpart in 1792 (1793, 1796).

A passage from it is quoted in the Preface to the first edition of *The Beauties of Johnson* (1781). This first edition was slightly expanded in 1782, and many editions followed. A second volume was published in 1782, along with the third (called the "fifth") edition of the first volume. The two volumes together contained seventeen quotations from the Preface. This number held steady through the eighth edition (2 vols. in 1, 1792).

Additional proof of the widely favorable reaction accorded the Preface occurs both in initial reviews of the *Dictionary* and in the early biographies of its compiler. Specifically, the largest single parts of the notices in the *Gentleman's Magazine,* the *London Magazine,* the *Monthly Review,* and *Scots Magazine* consist of excerpts from it. The article in the *Gentleman's Magazine* (XXV [April 1755], p. 150), probably by John Hawkesworth,[4] also praises the work for "shewing" Johnson's "great" relevant "knowledge," for being "written with the utmost purity and elegance," and for "delight[ing] the passenger without detaining him by the way." The *London Magazine* (XXIV [April 1755], p. 193) states that the "extracts from" the "preface will best shew the nature of his work," "the difficulties of its execution," and "the truest idea of its merits, and its imperfections." The piece in the *Monthly Review* (XII [April 1755], p. 293), perhaps by Sir Tanfield Leman, in its second paragraph introduces passages "from our learned compiler's preface" by saying that they provide "an account of what he has intended." And the *Scots Magazine* reprints (XVII [April 1755], p. 177) the passage in the *Gentleman's Magazine* that contains the warm praise of the Preface. The *Journal étranger* in July 1755 reviewed the *Dictionary* favorably and translated passages from the Preface, "qui," it declared, "annonce beaucoup de sçavoir" (p. 132). But the review by Matthew Maty in the *Journal Britannique,* for July and August

4. For a discussion of the review, see John Lawrence Abbott, *John Hawkesworth, Eighteenth-Century Man of Letters* (1982), pp. 103, 186.

1755, is critical both of Johnson's prose style and of many of the sentiments expressed in the Preface. He also suggests that Johnson did not reprint the *Plan* in the *Dictionary* because he wished to hide his debt to Chesterfield.[5]

The early biographies about Johnson can be divided into minor—earlier—and major—later. Four of the first group quote from and/or praise the Preface: Isaac Reed and/or George Steevens, *An Account of the Writings of Dr. Samuel Johnson* . . . (1784–85, quotations); William Shaw, *Memoirs of the Life and Writings of the Late Dr. Samuel Johnson* (1785, quotations and praise); Joseph Towers, *Essay on the Life, Character, and Writings of Dr. Samuel Johnson* (1786, quotations and praise); and James Harrison (?), *The Life of Dr. Samuel Johnson* (1786, a quotation and praise).

The second group of biographies, more inclusive than the first, repeat, and in two cases extend, the laudatory comments noted above. In his *Life* (1787, p. 343), Sir John Hawkins remarks: "let the piteous description of [Johnson's] circumstances and feelings, which the preface contains, induce us to bury our resentment of a few petulant expressions, in the reflection, that this stupendous compilation was undertaken and completed by the care and industry of a single person."

James Boswell's assessment (*Life,* I.291) ranks foremost among all these biographies in its detailed treatment of the Preface. "I believe," he declares, "there are few prose compositions in the English language that are read with more delight, or are more impressed upon the memory, than that preliminary discourse. One of its excellences has always struck me with peculiar admiration; . . . the perspicuity with which he has expressed abstract scientifick notions." Next, citing an example of this "perspicuity," Boswell in the following eight paragraphs refers to the Preface seven times.

In his *Essay on the Life and Genius of Dr. Johnson* (1792,

5. *Journal Britannique,* XVII (July/August 1755), pp. 217–44. Maty also mentions the *Plan* in his review (see above, p. 20 and note 4).

p. 166), Arthur Murphy points out that, although the *Dictionary* "does not properly fall within the province of this essay . . . the preface will be found in this edition. He who reads the close of it, without acknowledging the force of the pathetic and sublime, must have more insensitivity in his composition than usually falls to the share of man."

Lastly, in his *Life of Samuel Johnson* (1795; 3rd ed., 1814, p. 226), Robert Anderson, after quoting its conclusion, describes the Preface as "a splendid specimen of eloquent composition, equally correct in the diction and in the principle," which "contains an elaborate and comprehensive view of his subject, a correct estimate of the duties of a perfect lexicographer, and a fair apology for the imperfections of his work." Then, echoing Murphy's opinion given above, he declares that "the conclusion is so irresistably pathetic that it is impossible to read the passage without shedding a tear."

Most, not all, of the remaining critical reactions we have collected express or imply warm admiration for the Preface. Listed chronologically, these laudatory remarks begin with Joseph Warton's succinct assessment in his letter of 16 May 1755 to his brother Thomas: "His [Johnson's] preface is fine."[6] Second is the tribute of Giuseppe Baretti, Johnson's good friend, who in his *Italian Library* (1757, p. 304) declared: "the preface, prefixed to [the *Dictionary*], is even superior for elegance and power of thinking to ours [the preface to *Vocabolario degli Accademici della Crusca*]."[7] Third, while he was in Leipzig, Boswell's journal entry for 4 October 1764 noted that Professor Johann Christoph Gottsched, "one of the most distinguished *literati* in this country . . . said the Preface to Johnson's *Dictionary* was one of the best pieces he had ever read. Said he, 'He knows his subject to the bottom.'"[8]

Another group of references consists of quotations from

6. *The Correspondence of Thomas Warton,* ed. David Fairer (1995), p. 50.

7. Johnson contributed to at least the first paragraph of the preface to Baretti's *Italian Library* (see *Bibliography,* pp. 707–08).

8. *Boswell on the Grand Tour: Germany and Switzerland,* 1764, ed. F. A. Pottle (1953), pp. 125–26.

the Preface that are usually accompanied by favorable comments. The earliest of these occurs in Thomas Warton's letter of 19 April 1755 to his brother Joseph, which, besides citing a passage, dubbed the Preface "noble"—but added that "I fear [it] will disgust, by the expressions of [Johnson's] consciousness of superiority, and of his contempt of patronage."[9]

Later works containing both one or more quotations and/or favorable remarks include: Thomas Sheridan, *British Education: or, The Source of the Disorders of Great Britain* (1756); Joseph Priestley, *A Course of Lectures on the Theory of Language and Universal Grammar* (1762); George Campbell, *The Philosophy of Rhetoric* (1776); John Fell, *An Essay towards an English Grammar* (1784); Thomas Sheridan, *A General Dictionary of the English Language* (1780; sigs. A2^r and B2^r); John Horne Tooke, *The Diversions of Purley, Part I* (1786; pp. 267–68: after calling Johnson's *Dictionary* "the most imperfect and faulty, and the least valuable of any of his productions . . . ," Horne Tooke continues, "I rejoice however, that though the least valuable, he found it the most profitable: for I could never read his preface without shedding a tear"); James Boswell, *The Correspondence and Other Papers of James Boswell Relating to the Making of the "Life of Johnson"* (2d ed., 2001; Philip Metcalfe's undated contribution expresses a sympathy with the conclusion of Johnson's Preface similar to that expressed by Tooke, p. 455); James Thomson Callender, *Deformities of Dr. Samuel Johnson* (1782, p. 54): "that whole preface is a piece of the most profound nonsense, which ever insulted the common sense of the world."

Disregarding this harsh and insensitive appraisal, we conclude, keenly aware of its many reprintings—complete and partial—and the many approving comments about it, that the Preface met overall with an exceedingly favorable early reception, which presaged its later outstanding place in the Johnsonian canon.

9. *Correspondence of Thomas Warton,* ed. Fairer, p. 43.

The Text

No manuscript of the Preface is known to exist. At the end of his pioneering essay on the printed text, W. R. Keast, having collated the first four proprietors' (London) editions[1] and having stated his concurrence, which we share, with the Greg-Bowers theory of "copy-text," summarizes: "Future editors must . . . adopt the text of the first edition as their copy-text and introduce into it the two sets of Johnsonian revisions from the second and fourth editions, together with such changes in the accidentals from these texts as seem necessary for correctness or consistency."[2] Unlike other editors of volumes in the Yale Edition of the Works of Samuel Johnson, we too are in general agreement with the Greg-Bowers theory, but we are not strict adherents. We departed from the Greg copy-text in choosing the Chesterfield state of the *Plan* as our basic text, instead of the fair copy. However, for Johnson's Preface, as well as for the History and Grammar, we have selected the earliest known version, which in all these cases is the first edition of the *Dictionary*.[3]

Examining anew editions one through four as well as the proprietors' fifth (1784),[4] sixth (1785), and seventh (1785),[5] the latter for possible rectification of errors, we have arrived at the same general conclusion, although our estimate of vari-

1. (1) Published on 15 April 1755; (2) 1755, set from the first edition and revised by SJ; (3) 1765, set from the second edition and unrevised; and (4) 1773, set from the first edition and revised by SJ.

2. W. R. Keast, "The Preface to *A Dictionary of the English Language:* Johnson's Revision and the Establishment of the Text," *Studies in Bibliography,* V (1952–53), 129–46, p. 146.

3. W. W. Greg's seminal essay is "The Rationale of Copy-Text," *Studies in Bibliography* III (1950–51), 19–36. For a brief summary of Greg's theory and its adaptation by Fredson T. Bowers, see William Proctor Williams and Craig S. Abbott, *An Introduction to Bibliographical and Textual Studies* (1999), pp. 82–83.

4. Fleeman states that, although the date of "1784" appears on the title pages of the two volumes, the work "was printed in October, 1783" (*Bibliography,* p. 435).

5. Fleeman differentiates the 1785 setting of type: it was published in three distinct forms: in sixpence weekly numbers, in two volumes quarto, and in one volume folio, called the "Seventh" edition, also dated 1785 (*Bibliography,* p. 440). We collated Gwin Kolb's copies of the seven editions.

ants has differed from Keast's in two instances. We have accepted sixty-three of his suggested readings, including his emendation of *fall* for *full* on p. 89 below; but have rejected his choice of *betwixt* rather than *between* on p. 77 below (we have found *betwixt* neither elsewhere in the Preface nor in the *Plan of a Dictionary*, the History, the Grammar, and Johnson's letters) and his emendation of *semi* for *fair* on p. 86 below (we have adopted *far*, proposed by the reviewer of the *Dictionary* in the *Monthly Review*). Moreover, we have (1) made decisions on three variants about which Keast was undecided (pp. 130, 131); (2) selected the replacement on p. 83 below of a semicolon for a comma that appears in the second, third, and fourth editions and which Keast overlooked; and (3) recorded twelve accidental variants that appear only in the third edition, unrevised, to repeat, by Johnson.[6]

Because the Preface has not hitherto undergone critical editing and may not do so again for a long time, we, concluding that the data may be useful to other students, have recorded all the variants, both substantive and accidental, in the first four editions. (Our sigla for these editions are *55a*, *55b*, *65*, and *73*). In this and other ways we follow our somewhat modified version of the normal style of the Yale Edition (see our Preface, p. xi and n. 4).

6. These two paragraphs are a shortened version of a section of our article "Preliminaries," pp. 121–22.

PREFACE

It is the fate of those who toil at the lower employments of life, to be rather driven by the fear of evil, than attracted by the prospect of good; to be exposed to censure, without hope of praise; to be disgraced by miscarriage, or punished for neglect, where success would have been without applause, and diligence without reward.

Among these unhappy mortals is the writer of dictionaries; whom mankind have considered, not as the pupil, but the slave of science,[1] the pioneer[a][2] of literature,[3] doomed only to remove rubbish and clear obstructions from the paths through which Learning and Genius[b] press forward to conquest and glory, without bestowing a smile on the humble drudge[4] that facilitates their progress.[5] Every other authour may aspire to praise; the lexicographer can only hope to escape reproach, and even this negative recompence[c] has been yet granted to very few.

a. pioneer *55b, 65*] pionier *55a, 73*
b. paths through which Learning and Genius press *73*] paths of Learning and Genius, who press *55a, 55b, 65*
c. recompence *55b, 65*] recompense *55a, 73*

---

1. *Science:* See *Plan,* p. 29, n. 7, above.

2. *Pioneer:* "One whose business is to level the road, throw up works, or sink mines in military operations" (*Dictionary*). In the preface to *Cyclopaedia,* Ephraim Chambers describes dictionary-making in the same terms: "sinking, and working under-ground . . . mere drudgery, and pioneer's work; difficult to carry on, dubious of success, and overlooked when done" (I.xviii). Cf. the following remark in Thomas Wilson's *Many Advantages of a Good Language to any Nation* (1724): "though the low Parts of [the work] are but like cleaning the Streets, or mending the High-ways, yet . . . the Tongue as well as the Feet wants an easy and smooth Path to walk in" (p. 5).

3. *Literature:* "Learning; skill in letters" (*Dictionary*).

4. Cf. SJ's definition of *lexicographer* in *Dictionary:* "A writer of dictionaries; a harmless drudge, that busies himself in tracing the original, and detailing the signification of words."

5. On the supposed degradation of lexicography, see *Plan,* pp. 25–26 above.

I have, notwithstanding this discouragement, attempted a dictionary of the *English* language, which, while it was employed in the cultivation of every species of literature, has itself been hitherto neglected;[d] suffered to spread, under the direction of chance, into wild exuberance;[e] resigned to the tyranny of time and fashion;[f] and exposed to the corruptions of ignorance, and caprices of innovation.

When I took the first survey of my undertaking, I found our speech copious without order, and energetick without rules: wherever I turned my view, there was perplexity to be disentangled, and confusion to be regulated; choice was to be made out of boundless variety, without any established principle of selection; adulterations were to be detected, without a settled test of purity;[g] and modes of expression to be rejected or received, without the suffrages of any writers of classical reputation or acknowledged authority.

Having therefore no assistance but from general grammar,[6] I applied myself to the perusal of our writers; and noting whatever might be of use to ascertain or illustrate any word or phrase, accumulated in time the materials of a dictionary, which, by degrees, I reduced to method, establishing to myself,[h] in the progress of the work, such rules as experience and analogy[7] suggested to me; experience, which practice and observation were continually increasing; and analogy, which, though in some words obscure, was evident in others.

In adjusting the ORTHOGRAPHY, which has been to this

d. neglected; *73*] neglected, *55a, 55b, 65*
e. exuberance; *73*] exuberance, *55a, 55b, 65*
f. fashion; *73*] fashion, *55a, 55b, 65*
g. purity; *55a, 73*] purity, *55b, 65*
h. myself, *55a, 55b, 73*] myself *65*

6. Unlike "universal . . . grammar" (see Grammar, p. 278 below), "general grammar" is not a technical term but means merely "common" or "usual" grammar (*Dictionary*, s.v. *general*, sense 9).

7. *Analogy:* "By grammarians, it is used to signify the agreement of several words in one common mode; as, from *love* is formed *loved,* from *hate, hated,* from *grieve, grieved*" (*Dictionary,* sense 3). Also see *Plan,* pp. 42–43 above.

time unsettled and fortuitous, I found it necessary to distinguish those irregularities that are inherent in our tongue, and perhaps coeval with it, from others which the ignorance or negligence of later writers has produced. Every language has its anomalies, which, though inconvenient, and in themselves once unnecessary, must be tolerated among the imperfections of human things, and which require only to be registered,[i] that they may not be increased, and ascertained, that they may not be confounded: but every language has likewise its improprieties and absurdities, which it is the duty of the lexicographer to correct or proscribe.

As language was at its beginning merely oral,[8] all words of necessary or common use were spoken before they were written; and while they were unfixed by any visible signs, must have been spoken with great diversity, as we now observe those who cannot read to catch sounds imperfectly, and utter them negligently. When this wild and barbarous jargon was first reduced to an alphabet, every penman endeavoured to express, as he could, the sounds which he was accustomed to pronounce or to receive, and vitiated in writing such words as were already vitiated in speech. The powers of the letters,[9] when they were applied to a new language, must have been vague and unsettled, and therefore different hands would exhibit the same sound by different combinations.

From this uncertain pronunciation arise in a great part the various dialects of the same country, which will always be observed to grow fewer, and less different, as books are multiplied; and from this arbitrary representation of sounds

i. registered, *73*] registred, *55a, 55b, 65*

---

8. "Merely oral" and "a word used only in speech" are phrases of disapprobation that SJ scatters throughout *Dictionary.* The prejudice against oral speech was common to the age. SJ is close to the beliefs of the French, as described by Ferdinand Brunot: "Car on en viendra à proclamer que le peuple, maître tout puissant des langues, n'a point de droits sur l'écriture, et bientôt, d'erreur en erreur, on prétendra que c'est l'écriture qui règle la langue parlée" (*Histoire de la langue Française,* IV [1913], 145).

9. The "powers" of a letter are its potential sounds. See Grammar, p. 277 below.

by letters, proceeds that diversity of spelling observable in the *Saxon* remains,[1] and I suppose in the first books of every nation, which perplexes or destroys analogy, and produces anomalous formations, that,[j] being once incorporated, can never be afterward dismissed or reformed.

Of this kind are the derivatives *length* from *long, strength* from *strong, darling* from *dear, breadth*[k] from *broad,* from *dry, drought,* and from *high, height,* which *Milton,* in zeal for analogy, writes *highth;*[2] *Quid te exempta juvat spinis de pluribus una;* to change all would be too much, and to change one is nothing.[3]

This uncertainty is most frequent in the vowels, which are so capriciously pronounced, and so differently modified, by accident or affectation, not only in every province, but in every mouth, that to them, as is well known to etymologists, little regard is to be shewn in the deduction of one language from another.

Such defects are not errours in orthography, but spots of barbarity impressed so deep in the *English* language, that criticism can never wash them away;[l] these, therefore, must be permitted to remain untouched:[m] but many words have[n] been altered by accident, or depraved by ignorance, as the pronunciation of the vulgar has been weakly followed; and some still continue to be variously written, as authours differ in their care or skill: of these it was proper to enquire the true orthography, which I have always considered as depend-

j. that, *73*] which, *55a, 55b, 65*
k. *breadth 55a, 55b, 73*] *breadth, 65*
l. away; *55a, 55b, 65*] away: *73*
m. untouched: *55a, 55b, 65*] untouched; *73*
n. likewise *omitted 55b, 65*] likewise *55a, 73*

1. SJ very occasionally provides evidence of this diversity of spelling in *Dictionary* (see, e.g., *many*).

2. In *Dictionary* under *height* (sense 1), SJ cites *Paradise Lost,* I.92, but he "corrects" Milton's spelling.

3. Horace, *Epistles,* II.2.212: "What good does it do you to pluck out a single one of many thorns" (Loeb Library translation).

ing on their derivation,[4] and have therefore referred them to their original languages: thus I write *enchant, enchantment, enchanter,* after the *French,* and *incantation* after the *Latin;* thus *entire* is chosen rather than *intire,* because it passed to us not from the *Latin integer,* but from the *French entier.*

Of many words it is difficult to say whether they were immediately received from the *Latin* or the *French,* since at the time when we had dominions in *France,* we had *Latin* service in our churches. It is, however, my opinion, that the *French* generally supplied us; for we have few *Latin* words, among the terms of domestick use, which are not *French;* but many *French,* which are very remote from *Latin.*

Even in words of which the derivation is apparent, I have been often obliged to sacrifice uniformity to custom; thus I write, in compliance with a numberless majority, *convey* and *inveigh, deceit* and *receipt, fancy* and *phantom;* sometimes the derivative varies from the primitive, as *explain* and *explanation, repeat* and *repetition.*

Some combinations of letters having the same power are used indifferently without any discoverable reason of choice, as in *choak, choke; soap, sope; fewel, fuel,* and many others; which I have sometimes inserted twice, that those who search for them under either form, may not search in vain.[5]

In examining the orthography of any doubtful word, the mode of spelling by which it is inserted in the series of the dictionary, is to be considered as that to which I give, perhaps not often rashly, the preference.[6] I have left, in the examples, to every authour his own practice unmolested, that the reader may balance suffrages, and judge between[o] us: but

o. between *55a, 73*] betwixt *55b, 65*

4. SJ decides the "true orthography" only where the precedent is ambiguous. He is contemptuous of spelling reform (see Grammar, pp. 295–301 below).

5. *Dictionary* includes both spellings of SJ's three examples.

6. In the three examples given above, SJ prefers *choke* and *soap* but provides full entries for *fewel* and *fuel.*

this question is not always to be determined by reputed or by real learning; some men, intent upon greater things, have thought little on sounds and derivations; some, knowing in the ancient tongues, have neglected those in which our words are commonly to be sought. Thus *Hammond* writes *fecibleness*[7] for *feasibleness,* because I suppose he imagined it derived immediately from the *Latin;* and some words, such as *dependant, dependent; dependance, dependence,* vary their final syllable, as one or another[p] language is present to the writer.[8]

In this part of the work, where caprice has long wantoned without controul, and vanity sought praise by petty reformation, I have endeavoured to proceed with a scholar's reverence for antiquity, and a grammarian's regard to the genius[9] of our tongue. I have attempted few alterations, and among those few, perhaps the greater part is from the modern to the ancient practice; and I hope I may be allowed to recommend to those, whose thoughts have been, perhaps,[q] employed too anxiously on verbal singularities, not to disturb, upon narrow views, or for minute propriety, the orthography of their fathers. It has been asserted, that for the law to be *known,* is of more importance than to be *right.*[1] Change, says *Hooker,* is not made without inconvenience, even from worse to better.[2] There is in constancy and stability a general and lasting advantage, which will always overbalance the slow improvements of gradual correction. Much less ought our written language to comply with the corruptions of oral utterance,[3] or copy that which every variation of time or place makes different from itself, and imitate those changes, which

p. another *73*] other *55a, 55b, 65*
q. been, perhaps, *55a, 55b, 65*] been perhaps *73*

---

7. *Dictionary,* although frequently quoting passages from Henry Hammond's *Of Fundamentals* and *A Practical Catechism* (*Works;* 4 vols., 1684), lists neither *fecibleness* nor *feasibleness.*

8. *Dictionary* lists all four examples, and the entries for *dependent* and *dependence* contain the same comment as that in the latter half of this sentence.

9. *Genius:* "Nature; disposition" (*Dictionary,* sense 5).

1. Untraced.

2. See *Plan,* p. 36 and n. 4 above.

3. Cf. *Plan,* p. 37 above.

will again be changed, while imitation is employed in observing them.

This recommendation of steadiness and uniformity does not proceed from an opinion, that particular combinations of letters have much influence on human happiness; or that truth may not be successfully taught by modes of spelling fanciful and erroneous: I am not yet so lost in lexicography, as to forget that *words are the daughters of earth, and that things are the sons of heaven.*[4] Language is only the instrument of science, and words are but the signs of ideas:[5] I wish, however, that the instrument might be less apt to decay, and that signs might be permanent, like the things which they denote.

In settling the orthography, I have not wholly neglected the pronunciation, which I have directed, by printing an accent upon the acute or elevated syllable. It will sometimes be found, that the accent is placed by the authour quoted, on a different syllable from that marked in the alphabetical series; it is then to be understood, that custom has varied, or that the authour has, in my opinion, pronounced wrong. Short directions are sometimes given where the sound of letters is irregular; and if they are sometimes omitted, defect in such minute observations will be more easily excused, than superfluity.[6]

In the investigation both of the orthography and signification of words, their ETYMOLOGY was necessarily to be con-

---

4. If this is a quotation, it remains untraced. Italics in SJ's works do not necessarily indicate quotation (e.g., see *Taxation No Tyranny* in *Yale* X.411 and n. 2.) The ancient idea occurs in Quintilian (see *Plan,* p. 43, n. 8, above), but apparently the closest verbal parallel is in Samuel Madden's poem *Boulter's Monument* (1745), which SJ corrected: "Words are men's Daughters but God's sons are things" (l. 377)—a parallel which L. R. M. Strachan pointed out in *Notes and Queries,* CLXXXIII (1942), 27.

5. Cf. the treatment of the relationship between ideas and words in Locke's *Essay* (III.ii ["*Of the Signification of Words*"]), especially this passage: "Words . . . [are] immediately the Signs of Mens [sic] *Ideas;* and by that means, the Instruments whereby Men communicate their Conceptions" (sect. 6).

6. In making *Dictionary,* SJ did less work on pronunciation than he originally intended; see *Plan,* pp. 38–39, nn. 2, 3, above.

sidered, and they were therefore to be divided into primitives and derivatives. A primitive word, is that which can be traced no further to any *English* root; thus *circumspect, circumvent, circumstance, delude, concave,* and *complicate,* though compounds in the *Latin,* are to us primitives. Derivatives, are all those that can be referred to any word in *English* of greater simplicity.

The derivatives I have referred to their primitives, with an accuracy sometimes needless; for who does not see that *remoteness* comes from *remote, lovely* from *love, concavity* from *concave,* and *demonstrative* from *demonstrate*? but[r] this grammatical exuberance the scheme of my work did not allow me to repress. It is of great importance,[s] in examining the general fabrick of a language, to trace one word from another, by noting the usual modes of derivation and inflection; and uniformity must be preserved in systematical works, though sometimes at the expence of particular propriety.

Among other derivatives I have been careful to insert and elucidate the anomalous plurals of nouns and preterites of verbs, which in the *Teutonick* dialects are very frequent, and,[t] though familiar to those who have always used them, interrupt and embarrass the learners of our language.

The two languages from which our primitives have been derived are the *Roman* and *Teutonick:* under the *Roman* I comprehend the *French* and provincial tongues;[7] and under the *Teutonick* range the *Saxon, German,*[8] and all their kindred dialects. Most of our polysyllables are *Roman,* and our words of one syllable are very often *Teutonick.*

In assigning the *Roman* original, it has perhaps sometimes happened that I have mentioned only the *Latin,* when the word was borrowed from the *French;* and considering myself

r. but *55a, 73*] But *55b, 65*
s. importance, *55b, 65*] importance *55a, 73*
t. and, *55a, 55b, 65*] and *73*

7. "Provincial tongues": the languages of Italy, Spain, and the other provinces of the Roman Empire.

8. *German:* see Grammar, p. 279, n. 4, below.

as employed only in the illustration of my own language, I have not been very careful to observe whether the *Latin* word be pure or barbarous, or the *French* elegant or obsolete.

For the *Teutonick* etymologies I am commonly indebted to *Junius* and *Skinner,* the only names which I have forborn to quote when I copied their books;[9] not that I might appropriate their labours or usurp their honours, but that I might spare a perpetual repetition by one general acknowledgment. Of these, whom I ought not to mention but with the reverence due to instructors and benefactors, *Junius* appears to have excelled in extent of learning, and *Skinner* in rectitude of understanding. *Junius* was accurately skilled in all the northern languages, *Skinner* probably examined the ancient and remoter dialects only by occasional inspection into dictionaries; but the learning of *Junius* is often of no other use than to show him a track by which he may deviate from his purpose, to which *Skinner* always presses forward by the shortest way. *Skinner* is often ignorant, but never ridiculous: *Junius* is always full of knowledge; but his variety distracts his judgment, and his learning is very frequently disgraced by his absurdities.[1]

The votaries of the northern muses will not perhaps easily restrain their indignation, when they find the name of *Junius* thus degraded by a disadvantageous comparison; but whatever reverence is due to his diligence, or his attainments, it

9. SJ refers to Stephen Skinner, *Etymologicon Linguae Anglicanae* (1671), and Franciscus Junius, *Etymologicum Anglicanum,* ed. Edward Lye (1743), which supply the vast majority of Germanic, or "Teutonick," etymologies in *Dictionary.* For other sources of SJ's Germanic etymologies, see *JDTR,* pp. 20–36. The names of Junius and Skinner are sometimes given and sometimes "forborn" in Johnson's Germanic etymologies, but Junius's and Skinner's own named sources are frequently reduced to "some" and "others" (e.g., see *Dictionary,* s.v. *almanack*).

1. This kind of comparative evaluation, stemming from the comparison of Demosthenes and Cicero in Longinus (*On the Sublime* 12.4–5, trans. W. H. Fyfe and Donald Russell [1995], 209) and Plutarch ("Comparison of Demosthenes and Cicero," *Lives,* trans. Bernadotte Perrin [1919; rpt. 1994], VII.210–21), appears elsewhere in SJ's literary criticism (see, e.g., the comparison between Pope and Dryden in the "Life of Pope," *Lives,* III.220–23, pars. 303–11 and the comparison of Vergil and Homer in the "Life of Dryden," I.447–48, par. 304).

can be no criminal degree of censoriousness to charge that etymologist with want of judgment, who can seriously derive *dream* from *drama,* because *life is a drama, and a drama is a dream;* and who declares with a tone of defiance, that no man can fail to derive *moan* from *μόνος, monos, single* or *solitary,* who[u] considers that grief naturally loves to be *alone**.

u. *monos, single* or *solitary,* who *73*] *monos,* who *55a, 55b, 65*

*[SJ's note:] That I may not appear to have spoken too irreverently of *Junius,* I have here subjoined a few Specimens of his etymological extravagance.

BANISH, *religare, ex banno vel territorio exigere,* in *exilium agere.* G. *bannir.* It. *bandire,* bandeggiare. H. *bandir.* B. bannen. Ævi medii scriptores bannire dicebant. V. Spelm. in Bannum & in Banleuga. Quoniam verò regionum urbiumque; limites arduis plerumque montibus, altis fluminibus, longis denique flexuosisque angustissimarum viarum amfractibus includebantur, fieri potest id genus limites *ban* dici ab eo quod *Βαννάται* & *Βάνναтροι* Tarentinis olim, sicuti tradit Hesychius, vocabantur *αί λοξοὶ καὶ μὴ ἰθυτενεῖς ὁδοι,* "obliquæ ac minimè in rectum tendentes viæ." Ac fortasse quoque huc facit quod *Βανοὺς,* eodem Hesychio teste, dicebant *ὄρη στραγγύλη,* montes arduos.

[Banish, to bind fast, from *banno,* to send out of the region by means of a public notice, to put into exile. Gallic, *bannir.* Italian, *bandire, bandeggiare.* Spanish, *bandir.* Belgian, *bannen.* Medieval writers said *bannire.* See [Henry] Spelman [*Glossarium Archaiologicum,* 1664] on *bannum* and *banleuga.* Because in truth the boundaries of regions and of cities were for the most part inclosed by steep mountains and deep rivers with long turnings and windings and with the ruggedness of very narrow paths, it is possible that this kind of boundary was made to be called a *ban* from what were once called *Βαννάται* and *Βάνναтροι* among the Tarentines. As Hesychius tells us, they were called the *crisscross* and *not straight* roads: "crisscross roads, and very rarely keeping straight." But perhaps the word came about because, according to the same Hesychian testimony, they called the confining peaks or difficult mountains, *Βανούς.*]

EMPTY, emtie, *vacuus, inanis.* A. S. Æmtig. Nescio an sint ab *ἐμέω* vel *εμετάω.* Vomo, evomo, vomitu evacuo. Videtur interim etymologiam hanc non obscurè firmare codex Rush. Mat. xii. 22. ubi antiquè scriptum invenimus gemoeted hit emetig. "Invenit eam vacantem."

[Empty, emtie, void, devoid of. Anglo-Saxon, *æmtig.* I know not but they might be from *ἐμέω* or *ἐμετάω,* to vomit or throw up, or to evacuate by vomiting. Also, this appears to be the etymology which the codex Rushworthianus appears to confirm at Matthew xii. 22 where we find written in the old way, "gemoeted hit æmtig," that is, "it was found empty."]

HILL, *mons, collis.* A. S. hyll. Quod videri potest abscissum ex *κολώνη* vel *κολωνὸς.* Collis, tumulus, locus in plano editior. Hom. Il. b. v. 811, *ἔστι δέ τις προπάροιθε πόλεος*

Our knowledge of the northern literature is so scanty, that of words undoubtedly *Teutonick* the original is not always to be found in any ancient language;[v] and I have therefore inserted *Dutch* or *German* substitutes, which I consider not as radical but parallel, not as the parents, but sisters of the *English*.[2]

The words which are represented as thus related by descent or cognation, do not always agree in sense; for it is incident to words, as to their authours,[w] to degenerate from their ancestors, and to change their manners when they change their country. It is sufficient, in etymological enquiries, if the senses of kindred words be found such as may easily pass into

v. language; *55b, 65, 73*] language, *55a*
w. authours, *55a, 55b, 73*] authors *65*

αἰπεῖα, κολώνη. Ubi authori brevium scholiorum *κολώνη* exp. *τόπος εἰς ὕψος ἀνηκων, γεώλοφος ἐξοχή*.

[Hill, mountain, hill. Anglo-Saxon *hyll*, which may seem cut out of *κολώνη* or *κολωνὸς*, or *collis*, a hill, a place on a plain which is more prominent. Homer, *Iliad*, book 5, line 811, "There is a certain steep place or hill in front of the city." Here the scholiast explains *κολώνη* as a place rising to a height, a prominence crested with earth.]

NAP, *to take a nap. Dormire, condormiscere.* Cym. heppian. A. S. hnæppan. Quod postremum videri potest desumptum ex *κνέφας*, obscuritas, tenebræ: nihil enim æque solet concilare somnum, quàm caliginosa profundæ no[c]tis obscuritas.

[Nap, to take a nap. To sleep, to take a nap. Welsh, *heppian*. Anglo-Saxon *hnæppan*, which may ultimately derive from *κνέφας* (darkness, night) because nothing is so likely to bring on sleep as the pitchy darkness of deep night.]

STAMMERER, Balbus, blæsus. Goth. STAMMS. A. S. stamer, stamur. D. stam. B. stameler. Su. stamma. Isl. stamr. Sunt a *στωμυλεῖν* vel *στωμύλλειν*, nimiâ loquacitate alios offendere; quod impeditè loquentes libentissimè garrire soleant; vel quòd aliis nimii semper videantur, etiam parcissimè loquentes.

[Stammerer, one who is tongue-tied or has a speech impediment. Gothic, *stamms*. Anglo-Saxon, *stamer, stamur*. Danish, *stam*. Belgian, *stameler*. Swedish, *stamma*. Islandic, *stamr*. These are all from *στωμυλεῖν* or *στωμύλλειν* (to offend others with too much talking) because those speaking with an impediment are accustomed to jabber most freely. Or it may be because they always seem to others to be jabbering excessively, even when they are saying very little.]

---

2. See History, p. 126 below.

each other, or such as may both be referred to one general idea.

The etymology, so far as it is yet known, was easily found in the volumes where it is particularly and professedly delivered; and, by proper attention to the rules of derivation, the orthography was soon adjusted. But to COLLECT the WORDS of our language was a task of greater difficulty: the deficiency of dictionaries was immediately apparent; and when they were exhausted, what was yet wanting must be sought by fortuitous and unguided excursions into books, and gleaned as industry should find, or chance should offer it, in the boundless chaos of a living speech. My search, however, has been either skilful or lucky; for I have much augmented the vocabulary.[3]

As my design was a dictionary,[x] common or appellative, I have omitted all words which have relation to proper names; such as *Arian, Socinian, Calvinist, Benedictine, Mahometan;* but have retained those of a more general nature, as *Heathen, Pagan.*[4]

Of the terms of art I have received such as could be found either in books of science or technical dictionaries; and have often inserted, from philosophical writers,[5] words which are supported perhaps only by a single authority, and which being not admitted into general use, stand yet as candidates or probationers, and must depend for their adoption on the suffrage of futurity.

x. dictionary, *55a, 73*] dictionary *55b, 65*

---

3. According to Starnes and Noyes (p. 185), SJ's word list is actually smaller than that of Nathan Bailey's *Dictionarium Britannicum* (1730 and 1736), but Bailey (and especially Scott-Bailey [1755]) included many "obsolete terms, proper names, and . . . highly specialized scientific, religious, and other terms" that SJ rejected.

4. There are rare exceptions to this rule: e.g., *Grubstreet* and *Lichfield.*

5. In *Dictionary, philosopher* is defined as "A man deep in knowledge, either moral or natural"; sense 1 of *natural* is "Produced or effected by nature; not artificial." See also W. K. Wimsatt, Jr., *Philosophic Words* (1948), which usually—but not always (p. 5)—equates "philosophic" with "scientific."

The words which our authours have introduced by their knowledge of foreign languages, or ignorance of their own, by vanity or wantonness, by compliance with fashion,[y] or lust of innovation, I have registred as they occurred, though commonly only to censure them, and warn others against the folly of naturalizing useless foreigners to the injury of the natives.

I have not rejected any by design, merely because they were unnecessary or exuberant; but have received those which by different writers have been differently formed, as *viscid,* and *viscidity, viscous,* and *viscosity.*

Compounded or double words I have seldom noted, except when they obtain a signification different from that which the components have in their simple state. Thus *highwayman, woodman,* and *horsecourser,*[6] require an explication; but of *thieflike* or *coachdriver* no notice was needed, because the primitives contain the meaning of the compounds.

Words arbitrarily formed by a constant and settled analogy, like diminutive adjectives in *ish,* as *greenish, bluish,* adverbs in *ly,* as *dully, openly,* substantives in *ness,* as *vileness, faultiness,* were less diligently sought, and sometimes[z] have been omitted, when I had no authority that invited me to insert them; not that they are not genuine and regular offsprings of *English* roots, but because their relation to the primitive being always the same, their signification cannot be mistaken.

The verbal nouns in *ing,* such as the *keeping* of the *castle,* the *leading* of the *army,* are always neglected, or placed only to illustrate the sense of the verb, except when they signify things as well as actions, and have therefore a plural number, as *dwelling, living;* or have an absolute and abstract signification, as *colouring, painting, learning.*

The participles are likewise omitted, unless, by signifying

y. fashion, *55a, 55b, 65*] fashion *73*
z. and sometimes *73*] and many sometimes *55a, 55b, 65*

---

6. *Horsecourser:* "1. One that runs horses, or keeps horses for the race. 2. A dealer in horses" (*Dictionary*).

rather habit or quality[a] than action, they take the nature of adjectives; as a *thinking* man, a man of prudence; a *pacing* horse, a horse that can pace: these I have ventured to call *participial adjectives.*[7] But neither are these always inserted, because they are commonly to be understood, without any danger of mistake, by consulting the verb.

Obsolete words are admitted, when they are found in authours not obsolete, or when they have any force or beauty that may deserve revival.[8]

As composition is one of the chief characteristicks[b] of a language, I have endeavoured to make some reparation for the universal negligence of my predecessors, by inserting great numbers of compounded words, as may be found under *after, fore, new, night, far,*[c] and many more. These, numerous as they are, might be multiplied, but that use and curiosity are here satisfied, and the frame of our language and modes of our combination are amply[d] discovered.

Of some forms of composition, such as that by which *re* is prefixed to note *repetition,* and *un* to signify *contrariety* or *privation,* all the examples cannot be accumulated, because the

a. habit or quality *73*] qualities *55a, 55b, 65*

b. characteristicks *55a, 55b, 73*] characteristics *65*

c. *far emendation proposed by the reviewer of SJ's Dictionary in the Monthly Review,* XII (1755), 300, n. 14] *fair omitted 55b, 65; fair, 55a, 73*

d. combination are amply *55b, 65*] combination amply *55a, 73*

---

7. *Dictionary* does not list *thinking* and *pacing* as adjectives, and SJ's Grammar does not mention "participial adjectives," but the phrase is used in *Dictionary* (e.g., *exceeding, feeling, fighting*).

8. This recalls part of the epigraph of the *Dictionary* from Horace, *Epistles,* II.ii.115–16:

> Obscurata diu populo bonus eruet, atque
> Proferet in lucem speciosa vocabula rerum

("Terms long lost in darkness the good poet will unearth for the people's use and bring into the light," trans. H. R. Fairclough [1929], pp. 433–35). In his illustrative quotations under the words *obsolete, laudably,* and *practice,* SJ printed Dryden's version of the thought: "*Obsolete* words may be *laudably* revived, when they are more sounding, or more significant than those in *practice*" (*Satires of Juvenal* [1697], Dedication, *The Works of John Dryden,* vol. IV, *Poems 1693–96,* ed. A. B. Chambers, William Frost, and Vinton A. Dearing [1974], p. 15).

use of these particles, if not wholly arbitrary, is so little limited, that they are hourly united[e] to new words as occasion requires, or is imagined to require them.

There is another kind of composition more frequent in our language than perhaps in any other, from which arises to foreigners the greatest difficulty. We modify the signification of many verbs[f] by a particle subjoined; as to *come off,* to escape by a fetch; to *fall on,* to attack; to *fall off,* to apostatize; to *break*[g] *off,* to stop abruptly; to *bear out,* to justify; to *fall in,* to comply; to *give over,* to cease; to *set off,* to embellish; to *set in,* to begin a continual tenour; to *set out,* to begin a course or journey; to *take off,* to copy; with innumerable expressions of the same kind, of which some appear wildly irregular, being so far distant from the sense of the simple words, that no sagacity will be able to trace the steps by which they arrived at the present use. These I have noted with great care; and though I cannot flatter myself that the collection is complete, I have perhaps[h] so far assisted the students of our language, that this kind of phraseology will be no longer insuperable; and the combinations of verbs and particles, by chance omitted, will be easily explained by comparison with those that may be found.

Many words yet stand supported only by the name of *Bailey, Ainsworth, Philips,* or the contracted *Dict.* for *Dictionaries* subjoined:[i] of these I am not always certain that they are seen[j] in any book but the works of lexicographers.[9] Of such I have

e. united *55b, 65*] affixed *55a, 73*
f. verbs *55a, 55b, 65*] words *73*
g. to *break 55b, 65, 73*] *to break 55a*
h. I have perhaps *55b, 65*] I believe I have *55a, 73*
i. subjoined: *55a, 55b, 65*] subjoined; *73*
j. seen *55b, 65*] read *55a, 73*

9. Nathan Bailey, *Dictionarium Britannicum* (2d ed., 1736); Edward Phillips, *The New World of English Words* (1658); Robert Ainsworth, *Thesaurus Linguae Latinae Compendius* (1736). SJ used the second edition of Bailey (see Sledd-Kolb, pp. 4, 207 n. 4); it is uncertain which edition of the others he used. On his exclusion of "dictionary words," see *Plan,* p. 30, n. 3, above. Such complaints about the earlier dictionaries were common. For example, in the Preface to *Cyclopaedia,* Ephraim Chambers remarks, "The truth is, a fourth part of the words in some of our popular Dictionaries, stand on no better authority than the

omitted many, because I had never read them; and many I have inserted, because they may perhaps exist, though they have escaped my notice: they are, however, to be yet considered as resting only upon the credit of former dictionaries. Others, which I considered as useful, or know to be proper, though I could not at present support them by authorities, I have suffered to stand upon my own attestation, claiming the same privilege with my predecessors of being sometimes credited without proof.

The words, thus selected and disposed, are grammatically considered:[k] they are referred to the different parts of speech; traced, when they are irregularly inflected, through their various terminations; and illustrated by observations, not indeed of great or striking importance, separately considered, but necessary to the elucidation of our language, and hitherto neglected or forgotten by *English* grammarians.[1]

That part of my work on which I expect malignity most frequently to fasten, is the *Explanation;* in which I cannot hope to satisfy those, who are perhaps not inclined to be pleased, since I have not always been able to satisfy myself. To interpret a language by itself is very difficult; many words cannot be explained by synonimes, because the idea signified by them has not more than one appellation; nor by paraphrase, because simple ideas cannot be described.[2] When the nature of things is unknown, or the notion unsettled and indefinite, and various in various minds, the words by which such notions are conveyed, or such things denoted, will be ambiguous and perplexed.[3] And such is the fate of hapless lexicography, that not only darkness, but light, impedes and distresses it; things may be not only too little, but too much known, to be happily illustrated. To explain, requires the use

k. considered: *55a, 55b, 65*] considered; *73*

---

single practice of some one fanciful author; who has met with Dictionary-writers fond enough to take his frippery off his hands, and expose them to the public for legitimate goods" (I.xx).

1. See *Plan,* p. 42 above.

2. Cf. the statement in Locke's *Essay* (III.iv.4): "The *Names of simple* Ideas *are not capable of any definitions.*"

3. For an extended discussion of these problems, see Locke, *Essay,* III ("Of Words").

of terms less abstruse than that which is to be explained, and such terms cannot always be found; for as nothing can be proved but by supposing something intuitively known, and evident without proof,[4] so nothing can be defined but by the use of[l] words too plain to admit a definition.

Other words there are, of which the sense is too subtle and evanescent to be fixed in a paraphrase; such are all those which are by the grammarians termed *expletives,* and, in dead languages, are suffered to pass for empty sounds, of no other use than to fill a verse, or to modulate a period, but which are easily perceived in living tongues to have power and emphasis, though it be sometimes such as no other form of expression can convey.[5]

My labour has likewise been much increased by a class of verbs too frequent in the *English* language, of which the signification is so loose and general, the use so vague and indeterminate, and the senses detorted so widely from the first idea, that it is hard to trace them through the maze of variation, to catch them on the brink of utter inanity, to circumscribe them by any limitations, or interpret them by any words of distinct and settled meaning:[m] such are *bear, break, come, cast, fall,*[n] *get, give, do, put, set, go, run, make, take, turn, throw.* If of these the whole power is not accurately delivered, it must be remembered, that while our language is yet living, and variable by the caprice of every tongue[o] that speaks it, these words are hourly shifting their relations, and can no more be

l. but by the use of *55a, 73*] but by supposing some *55b, 65*
m. meaning: *55a, 55b, 65*] meaning; *73*
n. *fall emended by W. R. Keast, Review of English Studies, n.s.,* IV (1953), 52–53] *full 55a, 55b, 65, 73, 84, 85a, 85b, 87*
o. tongue *55b, 65*] one *55a, 73*

4. Cf. the following comment attributed to Locke in *Dictionary* under sense 1 of *intuition* ("Sight of any thing; used commonly of mental view. Immediate knowledge"): "The truth of these propositions we know by a bare simple intuition of the ideas, and such propositions are called self-evident" (untraced).

5. The definition of *expletive* in *Dictionary* does not include reference to their value, although the illustrative quotation from Swift ("These are not only useful expletives to matter, but great ornaments of style" [untraced]) clearly indicates it.

ascertained in a dictionary,[p] than a grove, in the agitation of a storm, can be accurately delineated from its picture in the water.[6]

The particles are among all nations applied with so great latitude, that they are not easily reducible under any regular scheme of explication: this difficulty is not less, nor perhaps greater, in *English,* than in other languages.[7] I have laboured them with diligence, I hope with success; such at least as can be expected in a task, which no man, however learned or sagacious, has yet been able to perform.

Some words there are which I cannot explain, because I do not understand them; these might have been omitted very often with little inconvenience, but I would not so far indulge my vanity as to decline this confession: for when *Tully* owns himself ignorant whether *lessus,* in the twelve tables, means a *funeral song,* or *mourning garment;*[8] and *Aristotle* doubts whether *οὔρευς*, in the Iliad, signifies a *mule,* or *muleteer,*[9] I may surely,[q] without shame, leave some obscurities to happier industry, or future information.

The rigour of interpretative lexicography requires that *the*

p. dictionary, *55a, 55b, 73*] dictionary *65*
q. surely, *73*] freely, *55a, 55b, 65*

6. Cf. *Adventurer* 95 (par. 13), *Yale* II.428–29: "the passions, from whence arise all the pleasures and pains that we see and hear of, if we analize the mind of man, are very few; but those few agitated and combined, as external causes shall happen to operate, and modified by prevailing opinions and accidental caprices, make such frequent alterations on the surface of life, that the show while we are busied in delineating it, vanishes from the view."

7. Cf. Locke's *Essay* (III.vii.4): "[particles] are all *marks of some Action, or Intimation of the Mind;* and therefore to understand them rightly, the several views, postures, stands, turns, limitations, and exceptions, and several other Thoughts of the Mind, for which we have either none, or very deficient Names, are diligently to be studied. Of these, there are a great variety, much exceeding the number of Particles, that most Languages have, to express them by: and therefore it is not to be wondred that most of these Particles have divers, and sometimes almost opposite significations."

8. Cicero (*Tully*) cites conflicting authorities but expresses a preference for "dolorous wailing," "lugubrem eiulationem" (*Laws,* II.23.59).

9. Aristotle, *Poetics* 1461a, 9–11; *Iliad,* I.50 is at issue, but the choices for translating *οὔρευς* are "mules" and "sentinels."

explanation, and the word explained, should be always reciprocal; this I have always endeavoured, but could not always attain. Words are seldom exactly synonimous;[r] a new term was not introduced, but because the former was thought inadequate: names, therefore, have often many ideas, but few ideas have many names.[1] It was then necessary to use the proximate word, for the deficiency of single terms can very seldom be supplied by circumlocution; nor is the inconvenience great of such mutilated interpretations, because the sense may easily be collected entire from the examples.[2]

In every word of extensive use, it was requisite to mark the progress of its meaning, and show by what gradations of intermediate sense it has passed from its primitive to its remote and accidental signification; so that every foregoing explanation should tend to that which follows, and the series be regularly concatenated from the first notion to the last.

This is specious, but not always practicable; kindred senses may be so interwoven, that the perplexity cannot be disentangled, nor any reason be assigned why one should be ranged before the other. When the radical idea branches out into parallel ramifications, how can a consecutive series be formed of senses in their nature collateral? The shades of meaning sometimes pass imperceptibly into each other; so that though on one side they apparently differ, yet it is impossible to mark the point of contact. Ideas of the same race, though not exactly alike, are sometimes so little different, that no words can express the dissimilitude, though the mind easily perceives it, when they are exhibited together; and sometimes there is such a confusion of acceptations, that dis-

r. synonimous; *55a, 73*] synonymous; *55b, 65*

1. Cf. Locke as SJ quotes him in illustration of *name* (noun, sense 2): "If every particular idea that we take in, should have a distinct name, names must be endless" (untraced, but compare Locke's *Essay,* III.i.3).

2. Such a view led Charles Richardson to complain that SJ's method tends "to interpret the import of the context, and not to explain the individual meaning of the word" (*A New Dictionary of the English Language* [2d ed., 2 vols., 1839], I.38).

cernment is wearied, and distinction puzzled, and perseverance herself hurries to an end, by crouding together what she cannot separate.

These complaints of difficulty will, by those that have never considered words beyond their popular use, be thought only the jargon of a man willing to magnify his labours, and procure veneration to his studies by involution and obscurity. But every art is obscure to those that have not learned it: this uncertainty of terms, and commixture of ideas, is well known to those who have joined philosophy with grammar; and if I have not expressed them very clearly, it must be remembered that I am speaking of that which words are insufficient to explain.

The original sense of words is often driven out of use by their metaphorical acceptations, yet must be inserted for the sake of a regular origination. Thus I know not whether *ardour* is used for *material heat,* or whether *flagrant,* in *English,* ever signifies the same with *burning;* yet such are the primitive ideas of these words, which are therefore set first, though without examples, that the figurative senses may be commodiously deduced.

Such is the exuberance of signification which many words have obtained, that it was scarcely possible to collect all their senses; sometimes the meaning of derivatives must be sought in the mother term, and sometimes deficient explanations of the primitive may be supplied in the train of derivation. In any case of doubt or difficulty, it will be always proper to examine all the words of the same race; for some words are slightly passed over to avoid repetition, some admitted easier and clearer explanation than others, and all will be better understood, as they are considered in greater variety of structures and relations.

All the interpretations of words are not written with the same skill, or the same happiness: things equally easy in themselves, are not all equally easy to any single mind. Every writer of a long work commits errours, where there appears neither ambiguity to mislead, nor obscurity to confound him; and in a search like this, many felicities of expression will be casually overlooked, many convenient parallels will be forgotten, and many particulars will admit improvement from a mind utterly unequal to the whole performance.

But many seeming faults are to be imputed rather to the nature of the undertaking, than the negligence of the performer. Thus some explanations are unavoidably reciprocal or circular, as *hind, the female of the stag; stag, the male of the hind:* sometimes easier words are changed into harder, as *burial* into *sepulture* or *interment, drier* into *desiccative, dryness* into *siccity* or *aridity, fit* into *paroxysm;* for the easiest word, whatever it be, can never be translated into one more easy. But easiness and difficulty are merely relative, and if the present prevalence of our language should invite foreigners to this dictionary,[3] many will be assisted by those words which now seem only to increase or produce obscurity. For this reason I have endeavoured frequently to join a *Teutonick* and *Roman* interpretation, as to CHEER,[s] to *gladden,* or *exhilarate,* that every learner of *English* may be assisted by his own tongue.

The solution of all difficulties, and the supply of all defects, must be sought in the examples,[t] subjoined to the various senses of each word, and ranged according to the time of their authours.

When first I collected these authorities, I was desirous that every quotation should be useful to some other end than the illustration of a word; I therefore extracted from philosophers principles of science; from historians remarkable facts; from chymists complete processes;[4] from divines striking exhortations; and from poets beautiful descriptions. Such is

s. CHEER, *55b, 65, 73*] CHEER *55a*
t. examples, *55a, 73*] examples *55b, 65*

---

3. In the "Short Scheme," SJ—and one reader—mention the possible "sale" of *Dictionary* to "foreigners" (see pp. 406, 394 below), but SJ omitted his comment in later versions of the *Plan;* for additional details see Sledd-Kolb, p. 66.

4. *Process:* "Methodical management of any thing" (*Dictionary,* sense 4); the first illustrative quotation reads: "Experiments, familiar to chymists, are unknown to the learned, who never read chymical *processes.* [Robert] *Boyle.*"

design, while it is yet at a distance from execution. When the time called upon me to range this accumulation of elegance and wisdom into an alphabetical series, I soon discovered that the bulk of my volumes would fright away the student, and was forced to depart from my scheme of including all that was pleasing or useful in *English* literature, and reduce my transcripts very often to clusters of words, in which scarcely any meaning is retained; thus to the weariness of copying, I was condemned to add the vexation of expunging.[5] Some passages I have yet spared, which may relieve the labour of verbal searches, and intersperse with verdure and flowers the dusty desarts of barren philology.[6]

The examples, thus mutilated, are no longer to be considered as conveying the sentiments or doctrine of their authours; the word for the sake of which they are inserted, with all its appendant clauses, has been carefully perserved; but it may sometimes happen, by hasty detruncation, that the general tendency of the sentence may be changed: the divine may desert his tenets, or the philosopher his system.[7]

Some of the examples have been taken from writers who were never mentioned as masters of elegance or models of stile; but words must be sought where they are used; and in what pages, eminent for purity, can terms of manufacture or agriculture be found?[8] Many quotations serve no other pur-

---

5. For a detailed reconstruction of SJ's recasting his initial conception of *Dictionary,* see Reddick, chaps. 3 and 4.

6. "Intersperse . . . philology": cf. William Walker, *English Examples of the Latine Syntaxis* (1683), sig. A8^r: "Temper all discourses of philology with interspersions of morality," which is the illustrative passage for *philology* in *Dictionary.*

7. Although SJ frequently edits his sources, he very rarely changes the meaning. See Gwin and Ruth Kolb, "The Selection and Use of the Illustrative Quotations in Dr. Johnson's *Dictionary,*" in *New Aspects of Lexicography,* ed. Howard D. Weinbrot (1972), pp. 61–72; *JDLL,* pp. 62, 271; Anne McDermott, "Textual Transformations: *The Memoirs of Martinus Scriblerus* in Johnson's *Dictionary,*" *Studies in Bibliography,* XLVIII (1995), 133–48, pp. 144–47.

8. SJ may be thinking of the encyclopedias he used for material on these subjects, such as Ephraim Chambers's *Cyclopaedia* (4th ed., 1741, or 7th ed., 1751–52), John Harris's *Lexicon Technicum* (5th ed., 1736), and Philip Miller's *Gardeners Dictionary* (1731). He also drew extracts from Joseph Moxon's *Mechanick Exercises* (1678), for example, and Thomas Tusser's *Art of Husbandry* (1557).

pose, than that of proving the bare existence of words,[u] and are therefore selected with less scrupulousness than those which are to teach their structures and relations.

My purpose was to admit no testimony of living authours, that I might not be misled by partiality, and that none of my cotemporaries might have reason to complain; nor have I departed from this resolution, but when some performance of uncommon excellence excited my veneration, when my memory supplied me, from late books, with an example that was wanting, or when my heart, in the tenderness of friendship, solicited admission for a favourite name.[9]

So far have I been from any care to grace my pages with modern decorations, that I have studiously endeavoured to collect examples and authorities from the writers before the restoration, whose works I regard as *the wells of English undefiled,*[1] as the pure sources of genuine diction. Our language, for almost a century, has, by the concurrence of many causes, been gradually departing from its original *Teutonick* character, and deviating towards a *Gallick* structure and phraseology, from which it ought to be our endeavour to recal it, by making our ancient volumes the ground-work of stile, admitting among the additions of later times, only such as may supply real deficiencies, such as are readily adopted by the genius of our tongue, and incorporate easily with our native idioms.[2]

u. existence of words, *55a, 55b, 73*] existence words, *65*

9. Among the "favourite names" that gained admission in 1755 were David Garrick (s.v. *fabulist, nowadays, prudish*), Charlotte Lennox (s.v. *to suppose,* sense 4, and *singular,* sense 3, e.g., for citations of *The Female Quixote*), Samuel Richardson (s.v. *to glisten* and *to romance,* for examples), William Law (s.v. *gewgaw* and *devotion,* sense 5, for examples), and Samuel Johnson (s.v. *to medicate* and *instillation,* sense 3, e.g., for citations of the *Rambler*).

1. Edmund Spenser, *Faerie Queene,* IV. 2.32.8: "Dan *Chaucer,* well of English undefyled."

2. In deploring the supposed gallicizing of the English language, SJ repeats a long-standing complaint. Richard Verstegan (in *A Restitution of Decayed Intelligence* [1605]), John Hare (in *St. Edwards Ghost* [1643]), John Wallis (in *Grammatica),* and Stephen Skinner (in *Etymologicon Linguae Anglicanae* [1671]), were among the commentators who expressed similar opinions; for details, see R. F. Jones, *The Triumph of the English*

But as every language has a time of rudeness antecedent to perfection, as well as of false refinement and declension,[3] I have been cautious lest my zeal for antiquity might drive me into times too remote, and croud my book with words now no longer understood. I have fixed *Sidney*'s work for the boundary, beyond which I make few excursions.[4] From the authours which rose in the time of *Elizabeth,* a speech might be formed adequate to all the purposes of use and elegance. If the language of theology were extracted from *Hooker* and the translation of the Bible; the terms of natural knowledge[5] from *Bacon;* the phrases of policy,[6] war, and navigation from *Raleigh;* the dialect of poetry and fiction from *Spenser* and *Sidney;* and the diction of common life from *Shakespeare,*[7] few

---

Language (1953), pp. 241–42, 248–50, 260–61. Early in the eighteenth century (1713), Henry Felton declared, "In *English* . . . I would have all *Gallicisms* . . . avoided, that our Tongue may be sincere, that we may keep to our own Language, and not follow the *French* Mode in our Speech, as we do in our Cloaths" (*A Dissertation on Reading the Classicks and Forming a Just Style,* pp. 98–99); in *Dictionary,* under *Gallicism,* SJ includes a shortened version of this passage. In 1752, SJ's friend William Guthrie stated in the preface to his translation, *Cicero's Epistles to Atticus,* "*English,* of all modern languages, is the best fitted to support the Dignity of great Writing, when it can work itself clear of those Gallicisms, which has polluted its Current for these hundred Years past" (I.xiii–xiv). Again in *Dictionary,* SJ censured at least twenty-four gallicisms, from *adroitness* to *transpire* (verb neuter, 2); for the complete list, see Harold B. Allen, "Samuel Johnson and the Authoritarian Principle in Linguistic Criticism," (Ph.D. diss., Univ. of Michigan, 1940), section 5.114.

3. SJ shares these notions concerning the "perfection" and "declension" of living languages with the Accademia della Crusca and the French Académie as well as with other earlier writers on language; for a longer discussion, see Sledd-Kolb, pp. 25–28.

4. See *Plan,* p. 53, n. 4, above.

5. *Natural knowledge:* science, especially natural history; see *Dictionary,* s.v. *disquisition:* "The royal society had a good effect, as it turned many of the greatest geniuses of that age to the *disquisitions* of natural knowledge. *Addison's Spectator.*"

6. *Policy:* "1. The art of government, chiefly with respect to foreign powers. 2. Art; prudence; management of affairs; strategem" (*Dictionary*).

7. Cf. SJ's Preface to Shakespeare: "the dialogue of this authour . . . seems scarcely to claim the merit of fiction, but to have been gleaned by diligent selection out of common conversation, and common occurrences"; "If there be . . . in every nation, a stile which never becomes obsolete . . . ; this stile is probably to be sought in the common intercourse of life. . . . there is a conversation above grossness and below refinement, where propriety resides, and where this

ideas would be lost to mankind, for want of *English* words, in which they might be expressed.

It is not sufficient that a word is found, unless it be so combined as that its meaning is apparently determined by the tract[8] and tenour of the sentence; such passages I have therefore chosen, and when it happened that any authour[v] gave a definition of a term, or such an explanation as is equivalent to a definition, I have placed his authority as a supplement to my own, without regard to the chronological order, that is otherwise observed.

Some words, indeed, stand unsupported by any authority, but they are commonly derivative nouns or adverbs, formed from their primitives by regular and constant analogy, or names of things seldom occurring in books, or words of which I have reason to doubt the existence.

There is more danger of censure from the multiplicity than paucity of examples; authorities will sometimes seem to have been accumulated without necessity or use, and perhaps some will be found, which might, without loss, have been omitted.[9] But a work of this kind is not hastily to be charged with superfluities: those quotations,[w] which to careless or unskilful perusers appear only to repeat the same sense, will often exhibit, to a more accurate examiner, diversities of signification, or, at least, afford different shades of the same meaning: one will shew the word applied to persons, another to things; one will express an ill, another a good, and a third

v. authour *55a, 55b, 73*] author *65*
w. quotations, *73*] quotations *55a, 55b, 65*

poet seems to have gathered his comick dialogue" (*Yale* VII.63, 70).

8. *Tract:* "Continuity; any thing protracted, or drawn out to length" (*Dictionary,* sense 3). An illustrative quotation from William Holder reads, in part, "in *tract* of speech a dubious word is easily known by the coherence with the rest."

9. In a letter to Daniel Wray of 23 May 1755, Thomas Edwards agreed that SJ's "needless number of authorities is intolerable, were these properly reduced, and the long articles from Miller and Chambers together with the monsters from the Dictionaries left out, the work for ought I know might be brought into half the compass it now takes"; see *JDLL,* pp. 7, 267.

a neutral sense; one will prove the expression genuine from an ancient authour;[x] another will shew it elegant from a modern: a doubtful authority is corroborated by another of more credit; an ambiguous sentence is ascertained by a passage clear and determinate; the word, how often soever repeated, appears with new associates and in different combinations, and every quotation contributes something to the stability or enlargement of the language.

When words are used equivocally, I receive them in either sense; when they are metaphorical, I adopt them in their primitive acceptation.

I have sometimes, though[y] rarely, yielded to the temptation of exhibiting a genealogy of sentiments, by shewing how one authour[z] copied the thoughts and diction of another: such quotations are indeed little more than repetitions, which might justly be censured, did they not gratify the mind, by affording a kind of intellectual history.[1]

The various syntactical structures occurring in the examples have been carefully noted; the licence or negligence with which many words have been hitherto used, has made our stile capricious and indeterminate; when the different combinations of the same word are exhibited together, the pref-

x. authour; *55a, 55b, 73*] author; *65*
y. though *55a, 73*] tho' *55b, 65*
z. authour *55a, 55b, 73*] author *65*

1. Both in "An Account of the Harleian Library" ([1742], par. 12) and in *Rasselas* (*Yale* XVI.113), Johnson expresses a high regard for intellectual history. Catalogues of books, he says in the former, are of great importance to "those whom curiosity has engaged in the study of literary history, and who think the intellectual revolutions of the world more worthy of their attention, than the ravages of tyrants." For an example of the kind of "intellectual history" SJ refers to here, see *Dictionary* (*friendless*, sense 1):

To some new clime, or to thy native sky,
Oh *friendless* and forsaken virtue fly.
Dryden's Aurengzebe [I.i.]
To what new clime, what distant sky,
Forsaken, *friendless*, will ye fly?
Pope ["Two Chorus's to the Tragedy of *Brutus*," ll. 13–14]

Cf. *break* (verb neuter, sense 19)—James Howell and Robert South; *slight* (adjective, sense 1)—Dryden and Pope; *rover* (sense 4)—Joseph Glanvill and Robert South.

erence is readily given to propriety, and I have often endeavoured to direct the choice.

Thus have I laboured by settling[a] the orthography, displaying[b] the analogy, regulating[c] the structures, and ascertaining[d] the signification of *English* words, to perform all the parts of a faithful lexicographer: but I have not always executed my own scheme, or satisfied my own expectations. The work, whatever proofs of diligence and attention it may exhibit, is yet capable of many improvements: the orthography which I recommend is still controvertible, the etymology which I adopt is uncertain, and perhaps frequently erroneous; the explanations are sometimes too much contracted, and sometimes too much diffused, the significations are distinguished rather with subtilty than skill, and the attention is harrassed with unnecessary minuteness.

The examples are too often injudiciously truncated, and perhaps sometimes, I hope very rarely, alleged in a mistaken sense; for in making this collection I trusted more to memory, than, in a state of disquiet and embarrassment, memory can contain, and purposed[e] to supply at the review what was left incomplete in the first transcription.[2]

Many terms appropriated to particular occupations, though necessary and significant, are undoubtedly omitted;[3] and of the words most studiously considered and exemplified, many senses have escaped observation.

Yet these failures, however frequent, may admit extenua-

a. by settling *73*] to settle *55a, 55b, 65*
b. displaying *73*] display *55a, 55b, 65*
c. regulating *73*] regulate *55a, 55b, 65*
d. ascertaining *73*] ascertain *55a, 55b, 65*
e. purposed *55a, 55b, 73*] proposed *65*

2. Many slightly inaccurate quotations suggest SJ's use of his memory in supplying illustrative quotations, but since he is often as accurate as a copyist, it is impossible to say how much he relied on his memory. He also included a great many passages transcribed by his amanuenses; for an extended account, see Reddick, pp. 29–44, 56–58, 61–65, 70.

3. SJ largely neglected musical terminology, for example; see *JDLL,* pp. 217–18.

tion and apology. To have attempted much is always laudable, even when the enterprize is above the strength that undertakes it: To rest below his own aim is incident to every one whose fancy is active, and whose views are comprehensive;[4] nor is any man satisfied with himself because he has done much, but because he can conceive little. When first I engaged in this work, I resolved to leave neither words nor things unexamined, and pleased myself with a prospect of the hours which I should revel away in feasts of literature, the[f] obscure recesses of northern learning, which I should enter and ransack,[g] the treasures with which I expected every search into those neglected mines to reward my labour, and the triumph with which I should display my acquisitions to mankind. When I had thus enquired into the original of words, I resolved to show likewise my attention to things; to pierce deep into every science, to enquire the nature of every substance of which I inserted the name, to limit every idea by a definition strictly logical, and exhibit every production of art or nature in an accurate description, that my book might be in place of all other dictionaries whether appellative or technical. But these were the dreams of a poet doomed at last to wake a lexicographer.[5] I soon found that it is too late to look for instruments, when the work calls for execution, and that whatever abilities I had brought to my task, with those I must finally perform it. To deliberate whenever I doubted, to enquire whenever I was ignorant, would have protracted the undertaking without end, and, perhaps, without much improvement; for I did not find by my first experiments, that what I had not of my own was easily to be obtained: I saw that one enquiry only gave occasion to another, that book referred to book, that to search was not always to find, and to find was not always to be informed; and that thus

f. literature, the *55a, 55b, 65*] literature, with the *73*
g. ransack, *55a, 55b, 65*] ransack; *73*

---

4. See *Plan,* p. 58, n. 7, above.
5. On the tradition of degrading lexicography, see Introduction, pp. xxii–xxv, and *Plan,* pp. 25–27, above.

to persue perfection, was, like the first inhabitants of Arcadia, to chace the sun, which, when they had reached the hill where he seemed to rest, was still beheld at the same distance from them.[6]

I then contracted my design, determining to confide in myself, and no longer to solicit auxiliaries, which produced more incumbrance than assistance: by this I obtained at least one advantage, that I set limits to my work, which would in time be ended,[h] though not completed.[7]

Despondency has never so far prevailed as to depress me to negligence; some faults will at last appear to be[i] the effects of anxious diligence and persevering activity. The nice and subtile[j] ramifications of meaning were not easily avoided by a mind intent upon accuracy, and convinced of the necessity of disentangling combinations, and separating similitudes. Many of the distinctions which to common readers appear useless and idle, will be found real and important by men versed in the[k] school philosophy, without which no dictio-

h. ended, *73*] finished, *55a, 55b, 65*
i. appear to be *55a, 55b, 73*] appear to *65*
j. subtile *55b, 65*] subtle *55a, 73*
k. versed in the *55a, 55b, 73*] versed in *65*

6. The grief produced in "fabulous" men by the initial darkness on earth is mentioned or glanced at, as E. E. Duncan-Jones has noted (*TLS,* 3 April 1959, p. 193), in Manilius's *Astronomica,* i.66–70 ("The sun, when night came on, withdrawn, they griev'd, / As dead, and joy'd next morn when he reviv'd" [*The First Booke of M. Manilius,* trans. Thomas Creech (1697), p. 5]); Statius's *Thebaid* iv.282–84); Lucretius's *De rerum natura,* v. 973–76; and Marvell's *The First Anniversary of the Government under O. C.,* ll. 337–40. Cf. *Rasselas* (*Yale* XVI.127 and n. 3). SJ's image seems conflated with Pope's analogy in the *Essay on Criticism,* which SJ called "perhaps the best that English poetry can shew" (*Lives,* III.229, par. 329):

In fearless youth we tempt the heights of Arts,
While from the bounded level of our mind
Short views we take, nor see the lengths behind;
But more advanc'd, behold with strange surprise
New distant scenes of endless science rise!
. . . .
Th' increasing prospect tires our wand'ring eyes,
Hills peep o'er hills, and Alps on Alps arise. (ll. 219–32)

7. See Reddick for an account of SJ's changing "design" of *Dictionary.*

nary shall ever[l] be accurately compiled, or skilfully examined.[8]

Some senses however there are, which, though not the same, are yet so nearly allied, that they are often confounded. Most men think indistinctly, and therefore cannot speak with exactness; and consequently some examples might be indifferently put to either signification: this uncertainty is not to be imputed to me, who do not form, but register the language; who do not teach men how they should think, but relate how they have hitherto expressed their thoughts.[9]

The imperfect sense of some examples I lamented, but could not remedy, and hope they will be compensated by innumerable passages selected with propriety, and preserved with exactness; some shining with sparks of imagination, and some replete with treasures of wisdom.

The orthography and etymology, though imperfect, are not imperfect for want of care, but because care will not always be successful, and recollection or information come too late for use.

That many terms of art and manufacture are omitted, must be frankly acknowledged; but for this defect I may boldly allege that it was unavoidable: I could not visit caverns to learn the miner's language, nor take a voyage to perfect my skill in the dialect of navigation, nor visit the warehouses of merchants, and shops of artificers, to gain the names of commodities, utensils,[m] tools and operations, of which no mention is found in books; what favourable accident, or easy enquiry brought within my reach, has not been neglected;

l. shall ever *73*] ever shall *55a, 55b, 65*
m. commodities, utensils, *55b, 65*] wares, *55a, 73*

---

8. SJ seems to be thinking of such scholastic distinctions as those of genus, species, and differentia. Locke discusses the usefulness of these categories in defining words; see Locke's *Essay,* III.iii. 10–19.

9. Contrast SJ's comments at the end of the *Plan* (p. 57 above), especially the paragraph beginning, "This, my Lord, is my idea of an English dictionary, a dictionary by which the pronunciation of our language may be fixed, and its attainment facilitated; by which its purity may be preserved, its use ascertained, and its duration lengthened."

but it had been a hopeless labour to glean up words, by courting living information, and contesting with the sullenness of one, and the roughness of another.

To furnish the academicians *della Crusca* with words of this kind, a series of comedies called *la Fiera,* or *the Fair,* was professedly written by *Buonaroti;*[1] but I had no such assistant, and therefore was content to want what they must have wanted likewise, had they not luckily been so supplied.

Nor are all words which are not found in the vocabulary, to be lamented as omissions. Of the laborious and mercantile part of the people, the diction is in a great measure casual and mutable; many of their terms are formed for some temporary or local convenience, and though current at certain times and places, are in others utterly unknown. This fugitive cant, which is always in a state of increase or decay, cannot be regarded as any part of the durable materials of a language, and therefore must be suffered to perish with other things unworthy of preservation.

Care will sometimes betray to the appearance of negligence. He that is catching opportunities which seldom occur, will suffer those to pass by unregarded,[n] which he expects hourly to return; he that is searching for rare and remote things, will neglect those that are obvious and familiar: thus many of the most common and cursory words have been inserted with little illustration, because in gathering the authorities, I forbore to copy those which I thought likely to occur whenever they were wanted. It is remarkable that, in reviewing my collection, I found the word SEA unexemplified.[2]

Thus it happens, that in things difficult there is danger from ignorance, and in things easy from confidence; the

n. unregarded, *55b, 65, 73*] unreguarded, *55a*

1. Michelangolo Buonarroti's *La Fiera Commedia* is a five-day play, or "series" of plays, first performed at the Uffizi Palace during carnival in 1618. Many of the characters are commercial traders and artisans.

2. Before publication, however, SJ managed to find sixteen illustrative quotations for the five senses of the word, a fact that strongly suggests that at least some of the examples had been collected by his amanuenses.

mind, afraid of greatness, and disdainful of littleness, hastily withdraws herself from painful searches, and passes with scornful rapidity over tasks not adequate to her powers, sometimes too secure for caution, and again too anxious for vigorous effort; sometimes idle in a plain path, and sometimes distracted in labyrinths, and dissipated by different intentions.

A large work is difficult because it is large, even though all its parts might singly be performed with facility; where there are many things to be done, each must be allowed its share of time and labour, in the proportion only which it bears to the whole; nor can it be expected, that the stones which form the dome of a temple, should be squared and polished like the diamond of a ring.[3]

Of the event of this work, for which, having laboured it with so much application, I cannot but have some degree of parental fondness, it is natural to form conjectures. Those who have been persuaded to think well of my design, will require[o] that it should fix our language, and put a stop to those alterations which time and chance have hitherto been suffered to make in it without opposition. With this consequence I will confess that I flattered myself for a while;[4] but now begin to fear that I have indulged expectation which neither reason nor experience can justify. When we see men grow old and die at a certain time one after another, from century to

o. design, will require *73*] design, require *55a, 55b, 65*

3. SJ makes similar comments in *Rambler* 43 (par. 10; *Yale* III.235): "All the performances of human art, at which we look with praise or wonder, are instances of the resistless force of perseverance: it is by this that the quarry becomes a pyramid, and that distant countries are united with canals"; and *Rasselas* (*Yale* XVI.58): "Great works are performed, not by strength, but perseverance: yonder palace was raised by single stones, yet you see its height and spaciousness." The latter remark, George L. Barnett has pointed out (*Notes & Queries*, CCL [1956], 485–86), echoes a passage in Cicero's *De senectute* vi.17.

4. See *Plan*, p. 38, above. This passage is important to historians of English who recognize that by the end of his labors SJ understood the overwhelming power of usage, although he may have set out to reform and regularize it (see, e.g., Thomas Pyles, *The Origin and Development of the English Language* [1964], pp. 212–13).

century, we laugh at the elixir that promises to prolong life to a thousand years; and with equal justice may the lexicographer be derided, who being able to produce no example of a nation that has preserved their words and phrases from mutability, shall imagine that his dictionary can embalm his language, and secure it from corruption and decay, that it is in his power to change sublunary nature, and[p] clear the world at once from folly, vanity, and affectation.

With this hope, however, academies have been instituted, to guard the avenues of their languages, to retain fugitives, and repulse intruders; but their vigilance and activity have hitherto been vain; sounds are too volatile and subtile for legal restraints; to enchain syllables, and to lash the wind, are equally the undertakings of pride, unwilling to measure its desires by its strength.[5] The *French* language has visibly changed under the inspection of the academy; the stile of *Amelot*'s translation of father *Paul* is observed by *Le Courayer* to be *un peu passé;*[q][6] and no *Italian* will maintain, that the diction of any modern writer is not perceptibly different from that of *Boccace, Machiavel,* or *Caro.*[7]

Total and sudden transformations of a language seldom happen; conquests and migrations are now very rare: but there are other causes of change, which, though slow in their operation, and invisible in their progress, are perhaps as much superiour to human resistance, as the revolutions of

p. and *73*] or *55a, 55b, 65*
q. *passé; 55b, 65*] *passè; 55a, 73*

5. An allusion to Xerxes' attempt to lash and enchain the Hellespont (Herodotus, *History,* VII.35, 54). The phrases "to enchain syllables, and to lash the wind" and the reference to "pride" echo ll. 232 and 230 of SJ's *Vanity of Human Wishes,* which are based on Juvenal's Tenth Satire (ll. 180–81). Also in *Adventurer* 137 (par. 6; *Yale* II.488), SJ translates Juvenal's lines, and in a conversation on 21 April 1773, he quotes the Latin original (*Life,* II.227).

6. Pierre François le Courayer, who translated Paolo Sarpi's *Istoria del Concilio Tridentino* (1619) in 1736, makes this remark in his preface (p. xiii) about Sieur Abraham-Nicholas Amelot de la Houssaie's translation. SJ used le Courayer's work in beginning his aborted translation of Sarpi's *Istoria* in 1738 (see *Life,* I.135 and n. 1).

7. Annibal Caro (1507–66), translator of the *Aeneid.*

the sky, or intumescence of the tide. Commerce, however necessary, however lucrative, as it depraves the manners, corrupts the language; they that have frequent intercourse with strangers, to whom they endeavour to accommodate themselves, must in time learn a mingled dialect, like the jargon which serves the traffickers on the *Mediterranean* and *Indian* coasts. This will not always be confined to the exchange, the warehouse, or the port, but will be communicated by degrees to other ranks of the people, and be at last incorporated with the current speech.[8]

There are likewise internal causes equally forcible. The language most likely to continue long without alteration, would be that of a nation raised a little, and but a little, above[r] barbarity, secluded from strangers, and totally employed in procuring the conveniencies of life; either without books, or, like some of the *Mahometan* countries, with very few: men thus busied and unlearned, having only such words as common use requires, would perhaps long continue to express the same notions by the same signs. But no such constancy can be expected in a people polished by arts, and classed by subordination,[9] where one part of the community is sustained and accommodated by the labour of the other. Those who have much leisure to think, will always be enlarging the stock of ideas, and every increase of knowledge, whether real or fancied, will produce new words, or combinations of words. When the mind is unchained from necessity, it will range after convenience; when it is left at large in the fields of speculation, it will shift opinions; as any custom is disused, the words that expressed it must perish with it; as any opinion grows popular, it will innovate speech in the same proportion as it alters practice.

r. little, above *55a, 55b, 65*] little above *73*

---

8. In his preface to Richard Rolt's *New Dictionary of Trade and Commerce* (1756), SJ further asserted that "There is no man who is not in some degree a merchant" (par. 24).

9. SJ usually expressed the notion of subordination as being conducive to human happiness; see *Life,* VI, Index, s.v. *subordination.*

As by the cultivation of various sciences, a language is amplified, it will be more furnished with words deflected from their original sense; the geometrician will talk of a courtier's zenith, or the excentrick virtue of a wild hero, and the physician of sanguine expectations and phlegmatick delays.[1] Copiousness of speech will give opportunities to capricious choice, by which some words will be preferred, and others degraded; vicissitudes of fashion will enforce the use of new, or extend the signification of known terms. The tropes of poetry will make hourly encroachments, and the metaphorical will become the current sense: pronunciation will be varied by levity or ignorance, and the pen must at length comply with the tongue; illiterate[2] writers will at one time or other, by publick infatuation, rise into renown, who, not knowing the original import of words, will use them with colloquial licentiousness, confound distinction, and forget propriety. As politeness increases, some expressions will be considered as too gross and vulgar for the delicate, others as too formal and ceremonious for the gay and airy;[3] new phrases are therefore adopted, which must, for the same reasons, be in time dismissed. *Swift,* in his petty treatise on the *English* language, allows that new words must sometimes be introduced, but proposes that none should be suffered to become obsolete.[4] But what makes a word obsolete, more than general agree-

1. As noted above (p. 31, n. 6), *Dictionary* lists no metaphorical sense or usage of *zenith,* but it lists both for *eccentrick* [sic], *sanguine,* and *phlegmatick.*

2. *Illiterate:* "Unlettered; untaught; unlearned, unenlightened by science" (*Dictionary*).

3. *Airy:* "Gay; sprightly; full of mirth; vivacious; lively; spirited; light of heart" (*Dictionary,* sense 8). SJ once called Mrs. Cholmondeley "a very airy lady" (*Life,* V.248).

4. *A Proposal for Correcting, Improving and Ascertaining the English Tongue, in a Letter to the Earl of Oxford* (1712): "But, where I say that I would have our Language, after it is duly correct, always to last; I do not mean that it should never be enlarged: Provided, that no Word, which a [regulating] Society shall give a Sanction to, be afterwards antiquated and exploded, they may have Liberty to receive whatever new ones they shall find Occasion for" (*Prose Works of Jonathan Swift,* ed. Herbert Davis, IV [1957], 15). In his "Life of Swift," SJ describes the *Proposal* as "written without much knowledge of the general nature of language, and without any accurate enquiry into the history of other tongues" (*Lives,* III.16, par. 40).

ment to forbear it? and how shall it be continued, when it conveys an offensive idea, or recalled again into the mouths of mankind, when it has once become unfamiliar by disuse, and unpleasing by unfamiliarity.[s]

There is another cause of alteration more prevalent than any other, which yet in the present state of the world cannot be obviated. A mixture of two languages will produce a third distinct from both,[t] and they will always be mixed, where the chief part of education, and the most conspicuous accomplishment, is skill in ancient or in foreign tongues. He that has long cultivated another language, will find its words and combinations croud upon his memory; and haste or[u] negligence, refinement or[v] affectation, will obtrude borrowed terms and exotick expressions.

The great pest of speech is frequency of translation.[5] No book was ever turned from one language into another, without imparting something of its native idiom; this is the most mischievous and comprehensive innovation; single words may enter by thousands, and the fabrick of the tongue continue the same, but new phraseology changes much at once; it alters not the single stones of the building, but the order of the columns. If an academy should be established for the cultivation of our stile, which I, who can never wish to see dependance multiplied, hope the spirit of *English* liberty will hinder or destroy,[6] let them, instead of compiling grammars and dictionaries, endeavour, with all their influence, to stop

s. once . . . unfamiliarity. *73*] once by disuse become unfamiliar, and by unfamiliarity unpleasing. *55a, 55b, 65*
t. both, *55a, 73*] both; *55b, 65*
u. or *55b, 65*] and *55a, 73*
v. or *55b, 65*] and *55a, 73*

5. Yet *Dictionary* contains many illustrative quotations drawn from translations, including Pope's Homer, which SJ later said had "tuned the English tongue" (*Lives,* "Pope," III.238, par. 348). For additional details, see *Plan,* p. 57, n. 4, above. In *Idlers* 68, 69 (*Yale* II.211–17), SJ wrote a short narrative of the "art of translation" from the ancients to Dryden.

6. Cf. SJ's comment in his "Life of Roscommon" (*Lives,* I.233, par. 17): "We live in an age in which it is a kind of publick sport to refuse all respect that cannot be enforced. The edicts of an English academy would probably be read

the licence of translatours, whose idleness and ignorance,[7] if it be suffered to proceed, will reduce us to babble a dialect of *France*.[8]

If the changes that we fear be thus irresistible, what remains but to acquiesce with silence, as in the other insurmountable distresses of humanity? it[w] remains that we retard what we cannot repel, that we palliate what we cannot cure.[9] Life may be lengthened by care, though death cannot be ultimately defeated: tongues, like governments, have a natural tendency to degeneration;[1] we have long preserved our constitution, let us make some struggles for our language.

In hope of giving longevity to that which its own nature forbids to be immortal, I have devoted this book, the labour of years, to the honour of my country, that we may no longer yield the palm of philology, without a contest,[x] to the nations of the continent. The chief glory of every people arises from its authours:[2] whether I shall add any thing by my own writings to the reputation of *English* literature, must be left to time: much of my life has been lost under the pressures of

w. it *55a, 55b, 65*] It *73*
x. philology, . . . contest, *73*] philology to *55a;* philology without a contest *55b, 65*

---

by many, only that they might be sure to disobey them." For Arthur Murphy's contrary opinion, see *Johnsonian Miscellanies,* I.436–37. In his "Considerations Preparatory to a Second Edition," Ephraim Chambers, whose attitude toward academies resembles Johnson's, hopes that the new, collaborative edition of his *Cyclopaedia* will "abundantly indemnify us in the Want of what other Countries are so fond of, Royal, Imperial, Caesarian, and Ducal Academies, Palatine Societies, and the like: Splendid Names, pompous Titles, but rarely productive of Fruits answerable thereto!" (p. 4; par. 20).

7. SJ's appeal to a hypothetical "Academy" resembles Boileau's plea that the Académie improve French translators: "les trois quarts, tout au moins, de ceux qui les [anciens] ont traduits, étaient des ignorans ou des sots" (*Lives,* III.237, n. 4, Hill quoting *Oeuvres de Boileau* [1747], V.118).

8. For SJ's opposition to gallicisms, see p. 95 and n. 2 above.

9. Cf. *Rambler* 32 (par. 6; *Yale* III.175): "The cure for the greatest part of human miseries is not radical, but palliative."

1. Cf. *Idler* 63 (par. 6; *Yale* II.197): "Language proceeds, like every thing else, thro' improvement to degeneracy."

2. Cf. SJ's assessment as reported by Dr. William Maxwell: "Intellectual pre-eminence . . . was the highest superiority [in a nation]; and . . . every nation derived their highest reputation from the splendour and dignity of their writers" (*Life,* II.125).

disease;[3] much has been trifled away;[4] and much has always been spent in provision for the day that was passing over me;[5] but I shall not think my employment useless or ignoble, if by my assistance foreign nations, and distant ages, gain access to the propagators of knowledge, and understand the teachers of truth; if my labours afford light to the repositories of science, and add celebrity to *Bacon,* to *Hooker,* to *Milton,* and to *Boyle.*[6]

When I am animated by this wish, I look with pleasure on my book, however defective, and deliver it to the world with the spirit of a man that has endeavoured well. That it will immediately become popular I have not promised to myself: a few wild blunders, and risible absurdities,[7] from which no work of such multiplicity was ever free, may for a time furnish folly with laughter, and harden ignorance in contempt; but useful diligence will at last prevail, and there never can be wanting some who distinguish desert; who will consider that no dictionary of a living tongue ever can be perfect, since while it is hastening to publication, some words are budding, and some falling away; that a whole life cannot be spent upon syntax and etymology, and that even a whole life would not be sufficient; that he, whose design includes whatever language can express, must often speak of what he does not understand; that a writer will sometimes be hurried by eager-

---

3. Late in his life, SJ wrote to his friend Edmund Hector: "My Health has been from my twentieth year such as has seldom afforded me a single day of ease" (*Letters,* V.7); for additional evidence of his often poor emotional and physical health, see *Letters,* V. Index, Samuel Johnson, s.v. *health.*

4. For evidence of SJ's tendency to waste time, see *Life,* VI. Index, Samuel Johnson, s.v. *idleness* and *indolence.*

5. While he compiled *Dictionary,* SJ's writings included the *Rambler* and *Adventurer* essays and pieces in the *Gentleman's Magazine* and *Preceptor.* Moreover, his *Vanity of Human Wishes* and his play *Irene* (also produced on stage) were published during the same period. For a full description of these and other compositions, see *Bibliography,* pp. 140–410.

6. All four writers provide many illustrative passages in *Dictionary.* With Johnson's assertion that he puts national glory above personal interest, compare Edward Phillips, *The New World of English Words* (1658): "In this work, which, for the generality of it, must stand the brunt of many a curious inquisition; both for the present, and future ages, I regard not my own fame equal to the renown and glory of the Nation" (sig. c4).

7. For some of these mistakes, see *Life,* I.293–96, 300.

ness to the end, and sometimes faint with weariness under a task, which *Scaliger* compares to the labours of the anvil and the mine;[8] that what is obvious is not always known, and what is known is not always present; that sudden fits of inadvertency will surprize vigilance, slight avocations will seduce attention, and casual eclipses of the mind[y] will darken learning; and that the writer shall often in vain trace his memory at the moment of need, for that which yesterday he knew with intuitive readiness, and which will come uncalled into his thoughts to-morrow.[9]

In this work, when it shall be found that much is omitted, let it not be forgotten that much likewise is performed; and though no book was ever spared out of tenderness to the authour, and the world is little solicitous to know whence proceeded the faults of that which it condemns; yet it may gratify curiosity to inform it, that the *English Dictionary* was written with little assistance of the learned,[1] and without any patronage of the great;[2] not in the soft obscurities of retirement,[3]

y. of the mind *55a, 73*] *omitted 55b, 65*

8. Joseph Scaliger, "In Lexicorum compilatores, inscriptum Lexico Arabico a se collecto, in Batavis" (To the compilers of Dictionaries, inscribed in the Arabic Lexicon he himself compiled, in Holland) (*Poemata Omnia* [1615], p. 35); for more on SJ's references to Scaliger's epigram, see our Introduction, p. xxiv above.

9. *To-morrow:* "To. *preposition* . . . 26. *To day, to night, to morrow,* are used, not very properly, as substantives in the nominative and other cases" (*Dictionary*).

1. Glossing this phrase in *Life* (I.292), Boswell remarks that, according to SJ, "the only aid which he received was a paper containing twenty etymologies, sent to him by a person then unknown, who he was afterwards informed was Dr. [Zachary] Pearce, Bishop of Rochester."

2. SJ refers to his relations with Philip Dormer Stanhope, Fourth Earl of Chesterfield; for which, see *Plan,* p. 25, n. 1, above. One sentence in the "celebrated" letter to the Earl (7 February 1755) reads: "I hope it is no very cinical asperity not to confess obligation where no benefit has been received, or to be unwilling that the Public should consider me as owing that to a Patron, which Providence has enabled me to do for myself" (*Letters* I.96). Later, in his revision of *The Vanity of Human Wishes* for Robert Dodsley's *Collection of Poems* (March 1755), SJ substituted *patron* for *garret* in the following couplet (ll. 159–60): "There mark what ills the scholar's life assail, / Toil, envy, want, the patron, and the jail" (*Yale* VI.99).

3. *Retirement:* "Private way of life" (*Dictionary,* sense 2).

or under the shelter of academick bowers,[4] but amidst inconvenience and distraction, in sickness and in sorrow.[5] It[z] may repress the triumph of malignant criticism to observe, that if our language is not here fully displayed, I have only failed in an attempt which no human powers have hitherto completed. If the lexicons of ancient tongues, now immutably fixed, and comprised in a few volumes, are[a] yet, after the toil of successive ages, inadequate and delusive; if the aggregated knowledge, and co-operating diligence of the *Italian* academicians, did not secure them from the censure of *Beni;*[6] if the embodied criticks of *France,* when fifty years had been spent upon their work, were obliged to change its oeconomy, and give their second edition another form,[7] I may surely be

z. sorrow. It *73*] sorrow: and it *55a, 55b, 65*
a. are *55b, 65*] be *55a, 73*

4. SJ is probably thinking of such friends at Oxford University as William Adams, later Master of Pembroke College; Thomas Warton, fellow of Trinity College; and Francis Wise, Radclivian Librarian. Despite this remark, in his letter of thanks to George Huddesford, Vice Chancellor of Oxford, for his honorary M.A. (26 February 1755; *Letters,* I.98–99), SJ describes himself as "umbratic[us]" (one who is shaded, an academic).

5. See p. 110, n. 3, above.

6. Paolo Beni attacked the first edition of the *Vocabolario della Crusca* the year it was published (1612), in *L'anticrusca overo Il Paragone dell'Italiana Lingua: nel qualsi mostra chiaramente che l'Antica sia inculta e rozza: e la Moderna regolata e gentile.* As the title suggests, Beni objected to the preference shown by the Accademia for the "rustic" language of Dante, Petrarch, and Boccaccio, for he favored the "refined" language of modern writers, particularly Ariosto. In his "Considerations" Ephraim Chambers likewise stresses the defects of the works of the Académie and the Accademia: "How many Years were the *French* Academists, to the Number of Forty the choicest Wits in *France,* in composing their Dictionary? How often did they alter the Plan of it; and yet when finish'd how many Faults did *Furetière* find in a single Sheet publish'd as a Specimen? . . . The Case is much the same with that other celebrated Body Della Crusca, whose Vocabulary after forty Years spent in the Composition, came out with so many, and such grievous Faults, as gave Occasion to many severe Critiques on it" (p. 3; par. 14).

7. "On en a changé tout la forme" (*Dictionnaire* [2d ed., 1718], Préface, par. 8). In particular, the editors strengthened the alphabetization of the book by listing many words separately that had earlier appeared under their root forms. For example, as they explain in par. 12, the word *absoudre* now appears early in volume I, whereas in the first edition it was only listed in volume II under *soudre.* At one point SJ was uncertain whether to follow the method of listing words adopted by the first or the second edition of the *Dictionnaire.* See *Plan,* p. 40,

contented without the praise of perfection, which, if I could obtain, in this gloom of solitude,[8] what would it avail me? I have protracted my work till most of those whom I wished to please,[b] have sunk into the grave,[9] and success and miscarriage are empty sounds: I therefore dismiss it with frigid tranquillity, having little to fear or hope from censure or from praise.[1]

b. please, *55a, 55b, 65*] please *73*

n. 8, above and "Scheme," pp. 392 and 394 below.

8. "Gloom of solitude": a phrase SJ, who disliked solitude intensely (see *Life,* Index, "Samuel Johnson I," s.v. *solitude*), used several times in his writings; see *Ramblers* 124 (par. 2; *Yale* IV.296) and 159 (par. 1; *Yale* V.81); Sermon 1 (par. 1; *Yale* XIV.3).

9. SJ refers particularly to the death of his wife Elizabeth (Tetty) on 17 March 1752, but he may also have in mind his dear friend Gilbert Walmesley of Lichfield who died on 3 August 1751 (*Life,* I.234, 81 n. 2).

1. This somber conclusion sounds like the penultimate paragraph of the preface to the six-volume edition of Furetière's *Dictionnaire universel* (1743); see Introduction, p. xxv above.

EDITOR'S INTRODUCTION TO "THE HISTORY OF THE ENGLISH LANGUAGE"

Composition

"The History of the English Language" consists largely of illustrative passages ranging from "the age of *Alfred* to that of *Elizabeth.*" Of the total of forty texts cited, twenty-seven also provided illustrative quotations for the *Dictionary*'s word list (first edition) and/or were owned by Johnson (the commencement of ownership being uncertain, however). Consequently, the presence of the whole group—but not necessarily all the authors (see p. 119 below)—in the History has been presumed to be unrelated, and possibly antecedent, to Johnson's activities in Oxford in the summer of 1754 when he visited Thomas Warton with the avowed intention of researching the History.

The thirteen remaining passages were probably drawn from the following works: six from the 1717 edition of *Tottel's Miscellany* (*Poems of Henry Howard, Earl of Surrey . . . with the Poems of Sir Thomas Wiat, and others his Famous Contemporaries*), one from Christopher Rawlinson's edition of King Alfred's translation of Boethius's *Consolation of Philosophy* (*An. Manl. Sever. Boethi Consolationis Philosophiae* [1698]), one from Thomas Mareschall's edition of the West-Saxon Gospels, sometimes called Alfred's Gospels (*Quatuor D. N. Jesu Christi Euangeliorum versiones perantiquae duae* . . . [1665, 1664]),[1] one from John Lewis's edition of John Wyclif's translation of the

1. Since the volume also contains the Gothic Bible of Bishop Ulfilas, or Wulfila (ca. 350), SJ apparently based his remarks about the Bible (the Codex Argenteus at the University of Uppsala), which he calls "the silver book" (p. 126 below), on Mareschall's edition. Edward Lye's edition of *Sacrorum Evangeliorum versio Gothica ex codice Argenteo* appeared in 1750, and *Sale Catalogue* lists a copy (no. 534). But SJ was seemingly unacquainted with Lye's edition until well after 1754, for he mentions it first in a revised sentence in the fourth edition (1773) of the History (p. 126 below).

New Testament (1731), one from Edmund Gibson's edition of *The Anglo-Saxon Chronicle* (1692), one from George Colvile's translation of Boethius's *Consolation of Philosophy* (1556), one from Sir John Fortescue-Aland's edition of Sir John Fortescue's *Difference between an Absolute and Limited Monarchy* (1714), and one from the 1736 edition of John Skelton's *Workes.*[2] Pending the improbable discovery of relevant information, it seems impossible to determine when Johnson selected these works for use in the History and whether the presence of these excerpts owed anything to his 1754 stay in Oxford.

It seems certain, too, that we will never know exactly when Johnson (the choices were his, we assume) selected any of the passages cited in the History. But, as the textual notes below (pp. 128–31) show, the transcriber(s) and the proofreader(s) —not Johnson, we think—displayed scant competence in discharging their tasks. Moreover, someone (a copyist?), perhaps offended by the mixture of the sacred and the profane, consistently eliminated the names of God and Christ from the text of Sir Thomas More's "A merry iest" (see pp. 212, 217, 219 below).

His choice of illustrative passages apart, Johnson's composition of the History chiefly involved his selection and description of the authors providing the passages; his borrowing, with due acknowledgment, the chart of "Gothick" languages from George Hickes's *Institutiones Grammaticae Anglo-Saxonicae et Moeso-Gothicae* (1689); his remarks on Bishop Ulfilas's translation (ca. 350) of the Gospels, included in the famous Codex Argenteus at the University of Uppsala; and his brief observations on the origin and development of the English language up to the reign (1558–1603) of Elizabeth I. Unlike some, at least, of his predecessors, Johnson cited both prose writers and poets (the latter outnumbering the former) to exemplify particular stages in the history of his native tongue.[3]

2. Bibliographical identifications of the texts used by Johnson, except Colvile and Fortescue, were made by W. B. C. Watkins, *Johnson and English Poetry before 1660* (1936), pp. 109–110, 85, 86, 110, 85, 108–09, respectively.

3. See, for example, Nathan Bailey, *Universal Etymological English Dictionary* (13th ed., 1749) I, Introduction; Ephraim Chambers, *Cyclopaedia,* s.v. "English."

We have found no approximations of the list of prose writers in earlier chronological surveys. But the list of poets partly resembles that in the "backward glance at English poetry from Spenser's age" which forms a section (pp. 227–38) of Thomas Warton's *Observations on the Faerie Queene of Spenser* (March 1754), a book Johnson commented on admiringly in his letter (16 July 1754) to Warton partially quoted above. For example, both Warton and Johnson, initially referring to earlier English poets as "bards," single out—in the same order—Robert of Gloucester, John Gower, Chaucer, John Lydgate, Sir Thomas More, and John Skelton.

Furthermore, portions of Warton's and Johnson's remarks about these authors are comparable, though far from identical. For instance, according to Warton, the rhyming "chronicle of Robert of Glocester [sic], who wrote . . . about the year 1280," is a specimen of "the last dregs of that kind of composition which was practic'd by the British bards" (p. 227). Similarly, Johnson says that "*Robert of Gloucester,*" who employed rhyme and "is placed by the criticks in the thirteenth century, seems to have used a kind of intermediate diction, neither *Saxon* nor *English;* in his work therefore we see the transition exhibited" (p. 162 below).

Again, Warton points out that "Gower and Chaucer were reputed the first English poets, because they first introduc'd INVENTION into our poetry." He adds, "Chaucer . . . deserves to be rank'd as one of the first English poets, on another account; his admirable artifice in painting the manners" (p. 228). For Johnson, Gower, "the first of our authours, who can be properly said to have written *English*" and who "calls *Chaucer* his disciple, . . . may . . . be considered as the father of our poetry." Of Chaucer, Johnson comments in part, "The history of our language is now brought to the point at which the history of our poetry is generally supposed to commence, the time of the illustrious *Geoffry Chaucer,* who may perhaps, with great justice, be stiled the first of our versifiers who wrote poetically" (p. 182).

Still again, in his relatively extended discussion of Lydgate, Warton remarks that the poet "succeeded" Gower, Chaucer, and the writer of *Piers Plowman;* that "his principal performances" were "the FALL OF PRINCES, and STORY of Thebes"; that he was a "Monk of Bury"; and that he "is the first English poet who can be red [sic] without hesitation and difficulty" (pp. 228–29, 230, 232). Johnson states that "*Lydgate* was a monk of *Bury*, who wrote about the same time with *Chaucer*. Out of his prologue to his third book of the *Fall of Princes* a few stanzas are selected, which, being compared with the style of his two contemporaries [Gower and Chaucer], will show that our language was then not written by caprice, but was in a settled state" (p. 206).

Fourth, Warton merely lists "Sir Thomas More" as one of the "great names" ("Colet, dean of St. Paul's, Cheke," and Ascham are also mentioned) affording luster to the age of Henry VIII, "perhaps the first which England ever saw, that may with propriety be styled classical" (p. 234). Johnson introduces excerpts from More's works by remarking, "Of the works of Sir *Thomas More* it was necessary to give a larger specimen [than that of works by Sir John Fortescue], both because our language was then in a great degree formed and settled, and because it appears from *Ben Johnson,* that his works were considered as models of pure and elegant style. The tale, which is placed first ["A merry iest how a sergeant would learne to playe the frere"] . . . will show what an attentive reader will, in perusing our old writers, often remark, that the familiar and colloquial part of our language, being diffused[4] among those classes who had no ambition of refinement, or affectation of novelty, has suffered very little change" (p. 210).

Lastly, of John Skelton, Warton writes, "In this age [of Henry VIII] flourish'd John Skelton, who . . . contributed not the least share of improvement to what his ancestors had left him; nor do I perceive that his versification is in any degree more polish'd than that of his immediate predecessor, [Stephen] Hawes. His best pieces . . . are his CROWNE of LAURELL, and BOWGE OF COURT. But the genius of this

4. We have emended the first (folio) edition reading of "disused" to the second (folio) edition reading of "diffused"; see our article "Preliminaries."

author seems little better qualify'd for picturesque, than for satyrical poetry; in the former, he wants invention, grace, and dignity; in the latter, wit, and good manners" (p. 234). Johnson devotes a single sentence to Skelton: "At the same time with Sir *Thomas More* lived *Skelton,* the poet laureate of *Henry* VIII. from whose works it seems proper to insert a few stanzas, though he cannot be said to have attained great elegance of language." The "few stanzas" are taken from Skelton's "prologue to the Bouge of Courte" (p. 248).

Summarizing and making our inference explicit, we believe that the composition of Johnson's History owed something to Warton's *Observations;* specifically, Johnson's choice of authors to be quoted, and his comments about these authors were influenced to some, perhaps only slight, degree by Warton's "backward glance" at English poetry. More than this, we think, cannot be validly concluded.[5]

We are also confident that during his 1754 visit to Oxford, Johnson's talks with Warton embraced the *Dictionary* (including the History)—the cause, after all, of Johnson's visit—and to speculate that the exchanges touched on relevant parts of Warton's *Observations* and the contents of his short outline, "Plan of the History of English Poetry."[6] The latter shares with Johnson's History the same sequential mention of the British "bards" named above. Nevertheless, despite these surmises, the fact remains that Warton's precise aid to Johnson's composition of the History will never be known. The date and circumstances of his writing the other portions of the History are also uncertain. However, all of his seventeen comments (including those discussed above) are brief, with six being single, medium-length sentences. Consequently, remembering his remarkable ability—demonstrated repeatedly—to

5. Our discussion of the probable indebtedness of SJ's History to Warton's *Observations* is drawn from our article "Thomas Warton's *Observations on the Faerie Queene of Spenser,* Samuel Johnson's 'History of the English Language,' and Warton's *History of English Poetry:* Reciprocal Indebtedness?" *Philological Quarterly,* LXXIV (1995), 327–35, to which the reader is referred for additional details.

6. The "Plan" was written in the early 1750s; see David Fairer, "The Origins of Warton's *History of English Poetry,*" *Review of English Studies,* new ser., XXXII (1981), 42–45.

compose rapidly, we guess that, having chosen (and had copied) the illustrative passages, Johnson produced the entire History at one sitting in the late summer or fall of 1754.

Publication and Reception

After its appearance in the first edition of the folio *Dictionary* (1755), the History was included in the proprietors' seven unabridged editions published during the remainder of the eighteenth century (1755–56, 1765, 1773, 1784, 1785, 1785, 1799) as well as in most of the unabridged versions of the nineteenth century. It was also contained in the following non-proprietorial complete editions and reissues: three Dublin (1775, 1777, 1797); Harrison's (1785–87); and Jarvis and Fielding's (1785–86). It was carried, too, in four editions and reissues of the Dublin abridgment (1758, 1764, 1768, 1768). Finally, the History (also the Preface and Grammar; see p. 66 above) appeared in the abridgment "Printed for J. Mifflin" (1778).[7]

Besides this record of its appearances, other kinds of evidence throw light on the early reception of the History. Chronologically, the first were positive remarks in reviews of the *Dictionary*. According to the *Gentleman's Magazine*, the History "regularly trace[s]" the course of "our language . . . from the old *Gothic* and *Teutonic* to modern *English*."[8] The *Monthly Review*, more laudatory and detailed, summarizes the History and concludes that Johnson has traced "briefly, but clearly, the alterations and improvements in our language, down to the reign of *Elizabeth;* and has all along illustrated his observations by apposite samples of the different modes of orthography and style."[9] The *Journal étranger* (July 1755) printed the same remarks in French (pp. 148–49).

7. For complete bibliographical descriptions of these editions, see *Bibliography*, pp. 410–52 and 497.

8. *Gentleman's Magazine*, XXV (April 1755), p. 150.

9. *Monthly Review*, XII (April 1755), p. 323; Benjamin Christie Nangle (*The Monthly Review, First Series, 1749–1789* [1934], p. 134) identifies the author as Sir Tanfield Leman.

Instead of publishing a fresh appraisal of the *Dictionary,* the *Scots Magazine* reprinted extracts from the Preface and the word list; from the *Gentleman's Magazine* (including the remarks about the History); and from the *Monthly Review* (including the comments about the History).[1]

Probably the first work to borrow from the History was its counterpart in the Joseph Nichol Scott–Nathan Bailey *New Universal Etymological Dictionary* (1755); as Philip B. Gove pointed out many years ago (1939), their History "copies, paraphrases, and reworks" Johnson's original, "with the indebtedness of a servile but dully alert mind."[2]

Our (limited) search has located only two other instances of the appearance of Johnson's History in other books: the French *Encyclopédie* Supplément (1776, s.v. *Anglois*) and G. M. C. Denina's "Comment la langue angloise s'est formée de la celtique & anglo-saxonne" (1796).[3]

Surveying this sparse body of evidence, we infer that the History's early reception, although positive, was decidedly restricted. But it is occasionally mentioned (see pp. 268–69 below) in references to the Grammar of the English Tongue, which attracted considerably more attention.

The Text

No manuscript of the History is known to exist. In preparing our text, we collated the first seven proprietors' unabridged editions.[4] The result confirmed our presumptive inclination toward the first edition as our copy-text, and it further disclosed that Johnson (slightly) revised only the

1. *Scots Magazine,* XVII (April 1755), pp. 177–85.

2. Philip B. Gove, "Notes on Serialization and Competitive Publishing: Johnson's and Bailey's Dictionaries, 1755," *Oxford Bibliographical Society, Proceedings & Papers,* V (1936–39), p. 314.

3. L. F. Powell, "Johnson and the *Encyclopédie,*" *Review of English Studies,* II (1926), pp. 335–37; Denina's article appears in *Mémoirs de l'Académie Royale* (Berlin), *Classe des belles–lettres* (1796), p. 64 (Sledd-Kolb, pp. 180, 244).

4. For the list, see p. xlvii above. We collated Gwin Kolb's copies of all the editions. For a study of differences in copies of the first edition, see William B. Todd, "Variants in Johnson's *Dictionary,* 1755," *Book Collector,* XIV (Summer 1965), pp. 212–13.

fourth edition. Four substantive changes (pp. 125, 126, 127, 182 below) in this edition are certainly authorial; of these Arthur Sherbo records the second, and Daisuke Nagashima the first, second, and fourth.[5] We have also adopted one substantive correction (p. 210 below) in the second, third, and fourth editions; and one (p. 183 below) appearing only in the third edition.

Although retaining most of the accidental readings in the first edition, we have accepted, for sundry reasons, a few in the second, third, and fourth editions. Finally, we have found nothing in Johnson's prose that requires emendation, and we believe that the hazardous task of emending the numerous quoted passages exceeds our editorial responsibilities. But wherever mistakes obstruct a reader's comprehension of the text we have supplied correct readings in our textual notes. And, since the History has not hitherto undergone critical editing and probably will not do so again for a long time, we, concluding that the data may be useful to other students, have recorded all the variants, substantive and accidental, in the first four editions.[6]

Italics and capitals in works quoted in the Introduction and annotation follow the style of the Yale Edition of the Works of Samuel Johnson. Printing the text of Johnson's "History of the English Language" presented some problems unprecedented in the Yale Edition because Johnson employed unusual typography for his representation of early English. We have not set out to reproduce Johnson's typography, but we have imitated him, as well as modern resources allowed, wherever we judged typography to be verging in any way on spelling. Hence, we do not use the so-called gothic letters of the font that Johnson used to represent his specimens of early English, except where the forms themselves are the subject of Johnson's presentation, as in his inventories of let-

5. Sherbo, "1773: The Year of Revision," *Eighteenth-Century Studies*, VII (1973–74), pp. 28–29; Nagashima, p. 36.

6. This paragraph and the preceding one form a condensed, altered version of a section of "Preliminaries," pp. 130–32, to which the reader seeking more detailed information is referred.

ters. In the belief that they represent significant differences in spelling, we retain the Old English and Middle English letters, ash (æ, Æ), thorn (þ, Þ), eth (ð, Đ), wynn (ƿ, Ƿ), yogh (ȝ, Ȝ), and vocalic y (ý). We have also retained abbreviations common in printed and scribal versions of Old English texts, although it has not proved possible in all cases to represent these exactly as Johnson did. Like Johnson, we use] for *and*, a long mark over a vowel to indicate a succeeding nasal (*m* or *n*), and ꝥ to indicate *þæt*. The actual abbreviation represents a stylized *t* drawn diagonally over a *þ*. In a few other abbreviations, however, Johnson employed combinations of diagonal lines and consonants which we could not duplicate. In these cases, we represent the consonant and place it next to the one on which it was drawn in the original typography.

In all cases in the History, we preferred Johnson's transcription to the text of his sources, although he is sometimes inaccurate both because of his printer's limited typographical resources and because he and/or his amanuenses made many errors. (We note small but significant errors, those that change meaning, in the textual notes. More complex divergences between Johnson's texts and their sources are given in the commentary.) However, when presented with alternatives among various editions of the specimen texts in the History, we have chosen those that best represent Johnson's source. In addition, on rare occasions, for the sake of sense, we have inserted in the text a missing letter or word in brackets. To the parts of the following works that are originally Johnson's, we have applied our somewhat modified version of the normal procedure observed by the Yale Edition (see our Preface, p. xi and n. 4).

THE HISTORY OF THE ENGLISH LANGUAGE

Though the *Britains* or *Welsh* were the first possessors of this island, whose names are recorded, and are therefore in civil[1] history always considered as the predecessors of the present inhabitants; yet the deduction of the *English* language, from the earliest times of which we have any knowledge to its present state, requires no mention of them: for we have so few words, which can, with any probability, be referred[a] to *British* roots, that we justly regard the *Saxons* and *Welsh,* as nations totally distinct.[2] It has been conjectured, that when the *Saxons* seized this country, they suffered the *Britains* to live among them in a state of vassalage, employed in the culture of the ground, and other laborious and ignoble services. But it is scarcely possible, that a nation, however depressed, should have been mixed with another in considerable numbers without[b] some communication of their tongue, and therefore it may, with great reason, be imagined, that those, who were not sheltered in the mountains, perished by the sword.

The whole fabrick and scheme of the *English* language is *Gothick* or *Teutonick:* it is a dialect of that tongue, which prevails over all the northern countries of *Europe,* except those

a. referred *55b, 65, 73*] refered *55a*
b. mixed with another . . . without *73*] mixed in considerable numbers with the *Saxons* without *55a, 55b, 65*

1. *Civil:* "Relating to the community; political; relating to the city or government" (*Dictionary,* sense 1).

2. SJ was unusual in recognizing this distinction. A few earlier scholars had made it, including Richard Verstegan, whose *Restitution of Decayed Intelligence* (1605) is cited occasionally in *Dictionary,* and John Free in *An Essay towards an History of the English Tongue* (1749), but some confusion about it appeared in Paul Henri Mallet's *Introduction à l'Histoire de Dannemarc* (1755), and was not cleared up until 1770, when Bishop Thomas Percy translated Mallet's work and added introductory material and notes supporting the distinction SJ asserts.

where the *Sclavonian*[3] is spoken. Of these languages Dr. *Hickes* has thus exhibited the genealogy.[4]

GOTHICK,

ANGLO-SAXON,[c]	FRANCICK,	CIMBRICK,[5]
Dutch,	German.	Islandick,
Frisick,		Norwegian,
English.		Swedish,[d]
		Danish.

Of the *Gothick,* the only monument remaining is a copy of the gospels somewhat mutilated, which, from the silver with which the characters are adorned, is called the *silver book.* It is now preserved at *Upsal,* and having been twice published before, has been lately reprinted at *Oxford,* under the inspection of Mr. *Lye,* the editor of *Junius.*[e][6] Whether the diction of this

c. ANGLO-SAXON, *55a, 55b, 65*] ANGLO SAXON, *73*
d. Swedish, *55b, 65, 73*] Swedish. *55a*
e. and . . . *Junius. 73*] and has been twice published. *55a, 55b, 65*

---

3. In *Cyclopaedia,* part of the entry for "SCLAVONIC" reads:

> [T]he language of the Sclavi, an antient people of Scythia Europaea; who, about the year 518, quitting their native country, ravaged Greece and established the kingdoms of Poland and Moravia, and at last settled in Illyria; which thence took the name of *Sclavonia.* . . .
>
> The *Sclavonic* is held, after the Arabic, the most extensive language in the world: it is spoke from the Adriatic to the north sea, and from the Caspian to Saxony, by a great variety of people . . . ; *viz.* the Polish, Russian, Hungarian, etc.

4. Hickes, *Institutiones* (1689), sig. B3^{v}. SJ translated the names from Hickes's Latin but excluded *Scotica,* which followed *Anglica* (English). The chart was earlier reprinted in Greenwood, p. 38.

5. Hickes also calls it *Cimbro-Gothic. Cimbri* was the Roman name for the Germanic tribes living in the area of Jutland. Hickes's chart suggests that by *Cimbrick* he may mean Old Scandinavian.

6. The Codex Argenteus at the University of Uppsala contains the Gothic Bible of Bishop Ulfilas, or Wulfila. As the textual note below indicates, the reference to the edition, *Sacrorum Evangeliorum versio Gothica* (1750), edited by Edward Lye, who also edited Franciscus Junius's *Etymologicum Anglicanum* (see Preface, p. 81, n. 9, above), was added in the fourth edition of *Dictionary.* At least two editions of Ulfilas's Bible were published earlier: *Quotuor D. N. Jesu Christi Euangeliorum versiones perantiquae duae* (1665, 1664), whence SJ drew his selection from Alfred's Gospels (see pp.

venerable manuscript be purely *Gothick,* has been doubted; it seems however to exhibit the most ancient dialect now to be found of the *Teutonick* race, and the *Saxon,* which is the original of the present *English,* was either derived from it, or both have descended[f] from some common parent.[7]

What was the form of the *Saxon* language, when, about the year 450, they first entered[g] *Britain,* cannot now be known. They seem to have been a people without learning, and very probably without an alphabet; their speech therefore, having been always cursory and extemporaneous, must have been artless and unconnected, without any modes of transition or involution of clauses; which abruptness and inconnection[8] may be observed even in their later writings. This barbarity may be supposed to have continued during their wars with the *Britains,* which for a time left them no leisure for softer studies;[9] nor is there any reason for supposing it abated, till the year 570, when *Augustine* came from *Rome* to convert them to Christianity.[1] The Christian religion always implies or

f. both have descended *73*] both descended *55a, 55b, 65*
g. entered *65, 73*] entred *55a, 55b*

133–43 below); and *D. N. Jesu Christi S.S. Evangelia ab Ulfila Gothorum,* ed. George Stiernhielm (Stockholm, 1671).

7. SJ's remarks reflect his reading of the arguments concerning Gothic in Lye's edition. Both Erik Benzelius, whose emended text of the Bible with his Latin commentary Lye edited, and Lye rejected the notion that the true language of the work was Theotish, though they recognized, like modern scholars, that Wulfila's Gothic is loaded with Greekisms; see Elfriede Stutz, *Gotische Literaturdenkmäler* (1966), cited in Herwig Wolfram, *History of the Goths* (1979; trans. Thomas J. Dunlap, 1988, p. 80). However, throughout SJ's life, there was doubt about the place of Gothic in the history of languages. For example, Junius believed that Greek and Gothic were closely related dialects descended from the original language spoken by mankind before the disaster at Babel. Hickes retained Junius's thesis about the antiquity of Gothic, but omitted his mythology (*Thesaurus,* I.i.sig. P2[v]; *Institutiones,* sig. B3[r]). SJ's notion that Gothic and Anglo-Saxon might be the offspring of a common parent may come from J. G. Graevius's life of Junius, which Lye prefixed to his edition of Junius's *Etymologicum Anglicanum,* sig. D2[v]; see preceding note.

8. *Inconnection* does not appear in *Dictionary; inconnexedly* is defined as "Without any connexion or dependance. Little used."

9. The relevant meaning of *soft* is "civil" (*Dictionary,* sense 7).

1. The date of Augustine's arrival in

produces a certain degree of civility and learning; they then became by degrees acquainted with the *Roman* language, and so gained, from time to time, some knowledge and elegance, till in three centuries they had formed a language capable of expressing all the sentiments of a civilised[2] people, as appears by king *Alfred*'s paraphrase or imitation of *Boethius*, and his short preface, which I have selected as the first specimen of ancient *English*.[3]

CAP. I.

On ðære tide þe Gotan of Siððiu mæʒþe piþ Romana rice ʒepin upahofon. ⁊ miþ heora cýninʒum. Rædʒota and Eallerica pæron hatne. Romane buriʒ abræcon. and eall Italia rice ꝥ is betpux þam muntum ⁊ Sicilia ðam ealonde in anpald ʒerehton. ⁊ þa æʒter[h] þam foresprecenan cýninʒum Ðeodric fenʒ to þam ilcan rice.[i] se Ðeodric pæf[j] Amulinʒa. he pæs Cristen. þeah he on þam Arrianiscan ʒedpolan ðurhpunode. He ʒehet Romanum his freondscipe. spa ꝥ hi mostan heora ealdrihta pýrðe beon. Ac he þa ʒehat spiðe ýfele ʒelæste. ⁊ spiðe praþe ʒeendode mid maneʒum mane. ꝥ pæs to eacan oþrum unarimedum ýflum. ꝥ he Iohannes þone papan het ofslean. Ða pæs sum consul. ꝥ pe heretoha hataþ. Boetius pæs haten. se pæs in boccræftum ⁊ on

h. *A mistake for* æfter
i. rice. *55a, 55b*] rice *65, 73*
j. *A mistake for* pæs

England is regularly given as 597 and easily derived from Bede's *Historia Ecclesiastica Gentis Anglorum* (chaps. 24–25).

2. *Civilised* is not a headword in *Dictionary,* but it appears in a quotation illustrative of *to civilize,* which SJ defines, "To reclaim from savageness and brutality; to instruct in the arts of regular life." SJ "would not admit *civilization,* but only *civility*" in *Dictionary* (*Life,* II.155).

3. King Alfred's Boethius, chaps. 1, 2, and part of 3: *An. Manl. Sever. Boethi Consolationis Philosophiae, libri V, Anglo-Saxonice redditi ab Alfredo, inclyto Anglo-Saxonum Rege. Ad apographum Junianum expressos edidit Christophorus Rawlinson* (1698), pp. 1–3 (see Watkins, p. 85). For our handling of typographical problems in this text, see our Introduction, pp. 122–23. SJ translated parts of Boethius in *Rambler* essays 6, 7, 96, 143, 178; and in 1765, in collaboration with Hester Thrale, he undertook a complete translation of the *Consolation,* but gave it up in deference to another translator (*Yale* VI.257–63).

poruld þeapum se rihtpisesta. Se ða onʒeat þa maniʒfealdan ýfel þe se cýninʒ Ðeodric piþ þam Cristenandome ⁊ piþ þam Romaniscum pitum dýde. he þa ʒemunde ðara eþnessa ⁊ þara ealdrihta ðe hi under ðam Caserum hæfdon heora ealdhlaford-dum. Ða onʒan he smeaʒan ⁊ leorniʒan on him selfum hu he ꝥ rice ðam unrihtpisan cýninʒe aferran mihte. ⁊ on rýht ʒeleaffulra and on rihtpisra anpald ʒebrinʒan. Sende þa diʒellice ærendʒepritu to þam Casere to Constantinopolim. þær is Creca heah burʒ ⁊ heora cýnestol. for þam se Casere pæs heora ealdhlaford cýnnes. bædon hine þæt he him to heora Cristendome ⁊ to heora ealdrihtum ʒefultumede. Ða ꝥ onʒeat se pælhreopa cýninʒ Ðeodric. ða het he hine ʒebrinʒan on carcerne ⁊ þær inne belucan. Ða hit ða ʒelomp ꝥ se arpýrða pæs on spa micelre nearanesse becom. þa pæs he spa micle spiðor on his Mode ʒedrefed. spa his Mod ær spiðor to þam poruld sælþum unʒepod[k] pæs. ⁊ he ða nanre frofre be innan þam carcerne ne ʒemunde. ac he ʒefeoll nipol of dune on þa flor. ⁊ hine astrehte spiþe unrot. and ormod hine selfne onʒan pepan ⁊ þus sinʒende cpæþ.[4]

k. *A misconstruction of* ʒepunod

4. Chapter 1. In the days when the Goths from Sythia raised an armed conflict against the Romans, they were led by kings named Rædgota and Alaric. They sacked Rome itself and held in thrall the whole kingdom of Italy from the mountains to the island of Sicily. Then, after those aforementioned kings, Theodoric took control of the same region. This Theodoric was a descendant of Amul; he was a Christian, although he persisted in the Arian heresy. He promised such friendship to the Romans as would enable them to retain their ancient rights, but he kept that promise in a truly evil way, and he ended very wickedly with many crimes. In particular, besides other, innumerable wicked deeds, he ordered the murder of Pope John. There was a certain consul, or what we call a leader, who was named Boethius. Both in scholarship and in civic duty he was most just. When he came to understand the many wicked deeds that King Theodoric had perpetrated against the Christian community and against the counsellors of the Romans, he remembered the privileges and ancient rights that they had enjoyed under their old lords, the Caesars. Then he began to ponder and to consider privately how he could take the power away from that unrighteous king and bring in the proper rule of the faithful and righteous. Then he secretly sent letters to Caesar in Constantinople, the chief city of the Greeks and their capital. As this Caesar was the ancestral lord of their people, Boethius's letters asked him to further their Christianity and their ancient privileges. When the cruel King Theodoric found out about Boethius's plea, he ordered

CAP. II.

Ða hoð[l] þe ic precca ȝeo lustbærlice sonȝ. ic sceal nu heofiende sinȝan. ⁊ mid spi[5] unȝeradum pordum ȝesettan. þeah ic ȝeo hpilum ȝecoplice funde. ac ic nu pepende ⁊ ȝisciende of ȝeradra porda misfo. me ablendan þas unȝetreopan poruld sælþa. ⁊ me þa forletan spa blindne on þis dimme hol. Ða bereafodon ælcere lustbærnesse þa ða ic him æfre betst trupode, ða pendon hi me heora bæc to and me mid ealle fromȝepitan. To phon sceoldan la mine friend seȝȝan þæt ic ȝesæliȝ mon pære. hu mæȝ se beon ȝesæliȝ se ðe on ðam ȝesælþum ðurhpuman[m] ne mot:[6]

CAP. III.

Ða ic þa ðis leoþ. cpæð Boetius. ȝeomriende asunȝen hæfde. ða com ðær ȝan in to me heofencund Pisdom. ⁊ ꝥ min murnende Mod mid his pordum ȝeȝrette. ⁊ þus cpæþ. Hu ne eart þu se mon þe on minre scole pære afed ⁊ ȝelæred. Ac hponon purde þu mid þissum poruld sorȝum þus spiþe ȝespenced. buton ic pat ꝥ þu hæfst ðara pæpna to hraþe forȝiten[n] ðe ic þe ær sealde. Ða

l. *A mistake for* lioð
m. *A mistranscription of* ðurhwunian
n. forȝiten *55a, 65, 73*] ȝorȝiten *55b*

---

him to be taken to prison and locked up. So it came to pass that this reverend man was brought to such a distressed state. He was so much the more sorely troubled because his spirit had formerly enjoyed considerable worldly comfort. He recalled nothing comforting in the prison. He fell down flat on the floor and lay prostrate in deep sorrow. He bemoaned his desperate state and thus singing said.

5. spi is a mistake in Johnson's source for spiþe.

6. Chapter 2. "The lays that I used as a pilgrim to recite so eagerly I must now sing sadly and set with lyrics all out of tune. Although I used to compose smoothly, now, weeping and sobbing, I fail to hit upon suitable words. False worldly pleasure has blinded me and abandoned me eyeless in this dark hole. The very things in which I always most trusted have taken all joy away; they have turned their back on me and departed from me altogether. Oh, to what purpose did my friends say that I was a fortunate man? How can one who cannot remain amidst worldly pleasures ever be fortunate?"

clipode se Ƿisdom ⁊ cƿæþ. Geƿitaþ nu aƿirʒede ƿoruld sorʒa of mines þeʒenes Mode. forþam ʒe sind þa mæstan sceaþan. Lætaþ hine eft hƿeorfan to minum larum. Ða eode se Ƿisdom near. cƿæþ Boetius. minum hreoƿsiendan ʒeþohte. ⁊ hit sƿa moƿolil[o] hƿæt hƿeʒa uparærde. adriʒde þa minenes Modes eaʒan. and hit fran bliþum ƿordum. hƿæþer hit oncneoƿe his fostermodor. mid ðam þe ða ꝥ Mod ƿiþ beƿende. ða ʒecneoƿ hit sƿiþe sƿeotele his aʒne modor. ꝥ ƿæs se Ƿisdom þe hit lanʒe ær týde ⁊ lærde. ac hit onʒeat his lare sƿiþe totorenne ⁊ sƿiþe tobrocenne mid dýsiʒra hondum. ⁊ hine þa fran hu ꝥ ʒeƿurde. Ða andsƿýrde se Ƿisdom him ⁊ sæde. ꝥ his ʒinʒran hæfdon hine sƿa totorenne. þær þær hi teohhodon ꝥ hi hine eallne habban sceoldon. ac hi ʒeʒaderiað monifeald dýsiʒ on þære fortruƿunʒa. ⁊ on þam ʒilƿe butan heora hƿelc eft to hýre bote ʒecirre:·[7]

This may perhaps be considered as a specimen of the *Saxon* in its highest state of purity, for here are scarcely any words borrowed from the *Roman* dialects.[8]

Of the following version of the gospels the age is not cer-

o. *A mistake for* niowul

7. Chapter 3. "When," said Boethius, "I had sung this song, lamenting, then there came walking in to me heavenly Wisdom and greeted my anxious soul with her words. She said, 'How now? Are you not the man who in my school was nourished and taught? Then, how is it that you are so beaten down with worldly sorrows, unless, as I perceive, you have rashly forsaken the weapons I gave you earlier in life?' Then Wisdom spoke out and said, 'Depart now, accursed worldly sorrows, from the mind of my servant, for you are the worst enemy. Let him turn again to my teachings.'"

"When Wisdom came in upon my sorrowful train of thought," said Boethius, "and had raised my mind somewhat from its prostrate state, she wiped my mind's eyes, and with sweet words she asked my mind whether it recognized its foster mother. Thereupon my mind turned to her. Then it indeed clearly recognized its own mother as that same Wisdom who had long before trained it and taught it. But my mind noticed that Wisdom's learning was all torn up, all ruined at the hands of fools, and it asked Wisdom how this happened. Wisdom answered, saying that her young followers had torn and ruined her in this fashion when they were determined that they would have all of her. 'But in their presumption and vainglory they will collect a heap of folly, unless each of them submits again to Wisdom's remedies.'"

8. *Roman dialects:* Romance languages, especially French.

tainly known, but it was probably written between the time of *Alfred* and that of the *Norman* conquest, and therefore may properly be inserted here.

Translations seldom afford just specimens of a language, and least of all those in which a scrupulous and verbal interpretation is endeavoured, because they retain the phraseology and structure of the original tongue;[9] yet they have often this convenience, that the same book, being translated in different ages, affords opportunity of marking the gradations of change, and bringing one age into comparison with another. For this purpose I have placed the *Saxon* version and that of *Wickliffe,* written about the year 1380, in opposite columns; because the convenience of easy collation seems greater than that of regular chronology.

9. With this assessment of translations, cf. Preface, pp. 108–09 above.

LUCÆ,[p] CAP. I.[1]

Forðam þe pitodlice maneʒa
þohton þara þinʒa race ʒe-
endebýrdan þe on us
ʒefýllede sýnt.
2 Spa us betæhtun þa ðe
hit of frýmðe ʒesapon. and
þære spræce þenas pæron.
3 Me ʒeþuhte [of-fýliʒde
from fruma] ʒeornlice
eallum. [mið] endebýrdnesse
pritan ðe. þu ðe selusta
Theophilus.
4 Ðæt þu oncnape þara
porda soðfæstnesse. of þam
ðe þu ʒelæred eart:·
5 On Herodes daʒum
Iudea cýnincʒes. pæs sum
sacerd on naman Zacharias.

LUK, CHAP. I.[2]

In the dayes of Eroude kyng
of Judee ther was a prest
Zacarye by name: of the sort

p. LUCÆ, *55b*] LUCÆ *55a, 65, 73*

1. Alfred's Gospels, Luke 1; see p. 126, n. 6, above. SJ excludes from his version the interpolated instructions concerning the days of the Christian year on which the passages were to be read.

2. John Wyclif, Luke 1; *The New Testament,* trans. John Wyclif, ed. John Lewis (1731), pp. 35–36 (Watkins, p. 110). SJ added the verse numbers but omitted the first four verses, which we supply for the sake of completeness from *The Gospels, Gothic, Anglo-Saxon, Wycliffe, and Tyndale Versions,* ed. Joseph Bosworth, 4th ed. (1907), p. 267:

Forsothe for manye men enforceden to ordeyne the tellyng of thingis, whiche ben fillid in us,

2 As thei that seyn atte the bigynnyng, and weren ministris of the word bitaken,

3 It is seen also to me, havynge alle thingis diligentli bi order, to write thee, thou best Theofile,

4 That thou knowe the treuthe of tho wordis, of whiche thou art lerned.

of Abian tune. ⁊ his ƿif ƿæs of Aarones dohtrum. and hýre nama ƿæs Elizabeth:·

6 Soðlice hiȝ ƿæron butu rihtƿise beforan Gode. ȝanȝende on eallum his bebodum ⁊ rihtƿisnessum butan ƿrohte:·

7 And hiȝ næfdon nan bearn. forþam ðe Elizabeth ƿæs unberende. ⁊ hý on hýra daȝum butu forð-eodun:·[q]

8 Soðlice ƿæs ȝeƿorden þa Zacharias hýs sacerdhades breac on his ȝeƿrixles endebýrdnesse beforan Gode.

9 Æfter ȝeƿunan þæs sacerdhades hlotes. he eode ꝥ he his offrunȝe sette. ða he on Godes tempel eode.

10 Eall ƿerod þæs folces ƿæs ute ȝebiddende on þære offrunȝe timan:·

11 Ða ætýƿde him Drihtnes enȝel standende on þæs ƿeofodes spiðran healfe.

12 Ða ƿeard Zacharias ȝedrefed ꝥ ȝeseonde. ⁊ him eȝe onhreas:·

13 Ða cƿæð se enȝel him to. Ne ondræd þu ðe Zacharias. forþam þin ben is ȝehýred. ⁊ þin ƿif Elizabeth þe sunu cenð. and þu nemst hýs naman Iohannes.

of Abia, and his wyf was of the doughtris of Aaron: and hir name was Elizabeth.

2 An bothe weren juste bifore God: goynge in alle the maundementis and justifyingis of the Lord withouten playnt.

3 And thei hadden no child, for Elizabeth was bareyn and bothe weren of greet age in her dayes.

4 And it bifel that whanne Zacarye schould do the office of presthod in the ordir of his course to fore God.

5 Aftir the custom of the presthod, he wente forth by lot and entride into the temple to encensen.

6 And at the multitude of the puple was without forth and preyede in the our of encensying.

7 And an aungel of the Lord apperide to him: and stood on the right half of the auter of encense.

8 And Zacarye seynge was afrayed: and drede fel upon him.

9 And the aungel sayde to him, Zacarye drede thou not: for thy preier is herd, and Elizabeth thi wif schal bere to thee a sone: and his name schal be clepid Jon.

q. forð-eodun *55a, 65, 73*] ȝorð-eodun *55b*

14 ⁊ he býð þe to ȝefean ⁊ to blisse. ⁊ maneȝa on hýs acennednesse ȝefaȝniað:·

15 Soðlice he býð mære beforan Drihtne. and he ne drincð ƿin ne beor. ⁊ he bið ȝefýlled on haliȝum Gaste. þonne ȝýt of his modor innoðe.

16 And maneȝa Israhela bearna he ȝecýrð to Drihtne hýra Gode.

17 And he ȝæð toforan him on ȝaste ⁊ Elias mihte. ꝥ he fædera heortan to hýra bearnum ȝecýrre. ⁊ unȝeleaffulle to rihtƿisra ȝleapscýpe. Drihtne fulfremed folc ȝeȝearƿian:·

18 Ða cƿæð Zacharias to þam enȝele. Hƿanun ƿat ic þis. ic eom nu eald. and min ƿif on hýre daȝum forðeode:·

19 Ða andsƿarode him se enȝel. Ic eom Gabriel. ic þe stande beforan Gode. and ic eom asend ƿið þe sprecan. ⁊ þe þis bodian.

20 And nu þu bist suƿiȝende. ⁊ þu sprecan ne

10 And joye and gladyng schal be to thee: and manye schulen have joye in his natyvyte.

11 For he schal be great bifore the Lord: and he schal not drinke wyn ne sydyr, and he schal bc fulfild with the holy gost yit of his modir wombe.

12 And he schal converte manye of the children of Israel to her Lord God.

13 And he schal go bifore[s] in the spiryte and vertu of Helye: and he schal turne the hertis of the fadris to the sonis, and men out of beleeve: to the prudence of just men, to make redy a perfyt puple to the Lord.

14 And Zacarye seyde to the aungel: wherof schal Y wyte this? for Y am old: and my wyf hath gon fer in hir dayes.

15 And the aungel answerde and seyde to him, for Y am Gabriel that stonde nygh bifore God, and Y am sent to thee to speke and to evangelise to thee these thingis, and lo thou schalt be doumbe.

16 And thou schalt not mowe speke, til[t] into the day

s. *The necessary word* him *appears after* bifore *in the original.*

t. til *55a, 65, 73*] till *55b*

miht oð þone[r] dæʒ þe þas
þinʒ ʒepurðað. forþam þu
minum pordum ne ʒelýfdest.
þa beoð on hýra timan
ʒefýllede:·

21 And ꝥ folc pæs
Zachariam ʒe-anbidiʒende.
and pundrodon ꝥ he on þam
temple læt pæs:·

22 Ða he ut-eode ne mihte
he him to-sprecan. ⁊ hiʒ
oncneopon ꝥ he on þam
temple sume ʒesihtðe ʒeseah.
⁊ he pæs bicniende hým. ⁊
dumb þurhpunede:·

23 Ða pæs ʒeporden þa his
þenunʒa daʒas ʒefýllede
pæron. he ferde to his huse:·

24 Soðlice æfter daʒum
Elizabeth his pif ʒe-eacnode.
and heo bediʒlude hiʒ fif
monþas. ⁊ cpæð.

25 Soðlice me Drihten
ʒedýde þus. on þam daʒum
þe he ʒeseah minne hosp
betpux mannum afýrran:·

26 Soðlice on þam sýxtan
monðe pæs asend Gabriel se
enʒel fram Drihtne on Galilea
ceastre. þære nama pæs
Nazareth.

27 To bepeddudre fæmnan

in which these thingis
schulen be don,[u] for thou
hast not beleved to my
wordis, whiche schulen be
fulfild in her tyme.

17 And the puple was
abidynge Zacarye: and thei
wondriden that he taryede in
the temple.

18 And he gede out and
myghte not speke to hem:
and thei knewen that he
hadde seyn a visioun in the
temple, and he bekenide to
hem: and he dwellide stille
doumbe.

19 And it was don whanne
the dayes of his office weren
fulfillid: he wente into his
hous.

20 And aftir these dayes
Elizabeth his wif conseyvede
and hidde hir fyve monethis
and seyde.

21 For so the Lord dide to
me in the dayes in whiche he
biheld to take awey my
reprof[w] among men.

22 But in the sixte
monethe the aungel Gabriel
was sent from God: into a
cytee of Galilee whos name
was Nazareth.

23 To a maydun weddid to

r. þone *55a, 55b, 73*] pone *65*
u. don, *55b*] don. *55a, 65, 73*
w. reprof *55a, 65, 73*] reproof *55b*

anum pere. þæs nama þæs[v] Iosep. of Dauides huse. ⁊ þære fæmnan nama pæs Maria:·

28 Ða cpæð se enʒel inʒanʒende. Hal pes þu mid ʒýfe ʒefýlled. Drihten mid þe. ðu eart ʒebletsud on pifum:·

29 Þa[x] pearð heo on his spræce ʒedrefed. and þohte hpæt seo ʒretinʒ pære:·

30 Ða cpæð se enʒel. Ne ondræd þu ðe Maria. soðlice þu ʒýfe mid Gode ʒemettest.

31 Soðlice nu. þu on innode[y] ʒe-eacnast. and sunu censt. and his naman Hælend ʒenemnest.

32 Se bið mære. ⁊ þæs hehstan sunu ʒenemned. and him sýlð Drihten God his fæder Dauides setl.

33 And he ricsað on ecnesse on Iacobes huse. ⁊ his rices ende ne bið:·

34 Ða cpæð Maria to þam enʒle. hu ʒepýrð þis. forþam ic pere ne oncnape:·

a man: whos name was Joseph of the hous of Dauith, and the name of the maydun was Marye.

24 And the aungel entride to hir, and sayde, heil ful of grace the Lord be with thee: blessid be thou among wymmen.

25 And whanne sche hadde herd: sche was troublid in his word, and thoughte what manner salutacioun this was.

26 And the aungel seid to hir, ne drede not thou Marye: for thou hast founden grace anentis God.

27 Lo thou schalt conseyve in wombe, and schalt bere a sone: and thou schalt clepe his name Jhesus.

28 This shall be gret: and he schal be clepid the sone of higheste, and the Lord God schal geve to him the seete of Dauith his fadir.

29 And he schal regne in the hous of Jacob withouten ende, and of his rewme schal be noon ende.

30 And Marye seyde to the aungel, on what maner schal this thing be don? for Y knowe not man.

v. *A mistake for* paes

x. Þa *55a, 55b, 65*] Ha *73*

y. *A mistake for* innoðe

35 Ða andsparode hýre se enʒel. Se halʒa Gast on þe becýmð. ⁊ þæs heahstan miht þe ofer-sceadað. and forþam ꝥ haliʒe þe of þe acenned bið. bið Godes sunu ʒenemned.

36 And nu. Elizabeth þin maʒe sunu on hýre ýlde ʒeacnode. and þes monað is hýre sýxta. seo is unberende ʒenemned.

37 Forþam nis ælc pord mid Gode unmihtelic:·

38 Ða cpæð Maria. Her is Drihtnes þinen. ʒepurðe me æfter þinum porde:· And se enʒel hýre fram-ʒepat:·

39 Soðlice on þam daʒum aras Maria ⁊ ferde on muntland mid ofste. on Iudeiscre ceastre.

40 ⁊ eode into Zacharias huse. ⁊ ʒrette Elizabeth:·

41 Ða pæs ʒeporden þa Elizabeth ʒehýrde Marian ʒretinʒe. ða ʒefaʒnude ꝥ cild on hýre innoðe. and þa pearð Elizabeth haliʒum Gaste ʒefýlled.

42 ⁊ heo clýpode mýcelre

31 And the aungel answerde and seyde to hir, the holy Gost schal come fro above into thee: and the vertu of the higheste schal ouer schadowe thee: and therfore[z] that holy thing that schal be borun of thee: schal be clepide the sone of God.

32 And to[a] Elizabeth thi cosyn, and sche also hath conseyved a sone in hir eelde, and this monethe is the sixte to hir that is clepid bareyn.

33 For every word schal not be impossyble anentis God.

34 And Marye seide to the hond maydun of the Lord: be it doon to me aftir thi word; and the aungel departide fro hir.

35 And Marye roos up in tho dayes and wente with haste into the mountaynes into a citee of Judee.

36 And sche entride into the hous of Zacarye and grette Elizabeth.

37 And it was don as Elizabeth herde the salutacioun of Marye the young childe in hir wombe gladide, and Elizabeth was fulfild with the holy Gost.

38 And cryede with a gret

z. therfore *55a, 55b, 73*] therefore *65*
a. to *is a mistake for* lo.

stefne. and cƿæð. Ðu eart betƿux ƿifum ʒebletsud. and ʒebletsud is þines innoðes ƿæstm.

43 ⁊ hƿanun is me þis. ꝥ mines Drihtnes modor to me cume:·

44 Sona sƿa þinre ʒretinʒe stefn on minum earum[b] ʒeƿorden ƿæs. þa fahnude [in ʒlædnise] min cild on minum innoþe.

45 And eadiʒ þu eart þu þe ʒelýfdest. ꝥ fulfremede sýnt þa þinʒ þe þe fram Drihtne ʒesæde sýnd:·[c]

46 Ða cƿæð Maria. Min saƿel mærsað Drihten.

47 ⁊ min ʒast ʒeblissude on Gode minum Hælende.

48 Forþam þe he ʒeseah his þinene ead-modnesse. soðlice[d] heonun-forð me eadiʒe secʒað ealle cneoressa.

49 Forþam þe me mýcele þinʒ dýde se ðe mihtiʒ is. ⁊ his nama is haliʒ.

50 ⁊ his mild-heortnes of cneoresse on cneoresse hine ondrædendum:·

51 He ƿorhte mæʒne on his earme. he to-dælde þa

voice and seyde, blessid be thou among wymmen and blessid be[e] the fruyt of thy wombe.

39 And whereof is this thing to me, that the modir of my Lord come to me?

40 For lo as the vois of thi salutacioun was maad in myn eeris: the yong child gladide in joye in my wombe.

41 And blessid be thou that hast beleeved: for thilke thingis that ben seid of the Lord to thee schulen be parfytly don.

42 And Marye seyde, my soul magnifieth the Lord.

43 And my spiryt hath gladid in God myn helthe.

44 For he hath behulden the mekenesse of his hand-mayden: for lo for this alle generatiouns schulen seye that I am blessid.

45 For he that is mighti hath don to me grete thingis, and his name is holy.

46 And his mersy is fro kyndrede into kyndredis to men that dreden him.

47 He made myght in his arm, he scateride proude

b. earum *55a, 65, 73*] eorum 55
c. sýnd *55a, 65, 73*] synd *55b*
d. soðlice *55a, 55b, 65*] oð lice *73*
e. be *55a, 55b, 73*] by *65*

ofer-modan on mode hýra heortan.

52 He apearp þa rican of setlc. and þa eað-modan upahof.

53 Hinȝriȝende he mid ȝodum ȝefýlde. ⁊ ofer-mode idele forlet.

54 He afenȝ Israhel his cniht. ⁊ ȝemunde his mild-heortnesse.[f]

55 Spa he spræc to urum fæderum. Abrahame and his sæde on á peoruld:·

56 Soðlice Maria punude mid hýre spýlce þrý monðas. ⁊ ȝepende þa to hýre huse:-

57 Ða pæs ȝefýlled Elizabethe cenninȝ-tid. and heo sunu cende.[g]

58 ⁊ hýre nehcheburas ⁊ hýre cuðan ꝥ ȝehýrdon. ꝥ Drihten his mild-heortnesse mid hýre mærsude ⁊ hiȝ mid hýre blissodon:-

59 Ða on þam ehteoðan dæȝe hiȝ comon ꝥ cild ýmbsniðan. and nemdon hine his fæder naman Zachariam:-

60 Ða andsparode his modor. Ne se soðes. ac he bið Iohannes ȝenemned:-

61 Ða cpædon hi to hýre.

men with the thoughte of his herte.

48 He sette doun myghty men fro seete and enhaunside meke men.

49 He hath fulfillid hungry men with goodis, and he has left riche men voide.

50 He havynge mynde of his mercy took up Israel his child,

51 As he hath spokun to oure fadris, to Abraham, and to his seed into worldis.

52 And Marye dwellide with hir as it were thre monethis and turned agen into his hous.

53 But the tyme of beringe child was fulfillid to Elizabeth, and sche bar a son.

54 And the neyghbouris and cosyns of hir herden that the Lord hadde magnyfied his mercy with hir, and thei thankiden him.

55 And it was doon in the eightithe day thei camen to circumside the child, and thei clepiden him Zacarye by the name of his fadir.

56 And his modir answeride and seide, nay; but he schal be clepid Jon.

57 And thei seiden to hir,

f. mild-heortnesse *55a, 55b, 65*] mild heortnesse *73*

g. cende. *55a, 65, 73*] cende, *55b*

Nis nan on þinre mæʒðe
þýssum naman ʒenemned:·
62 Ða bicnodon hi to his
fæder. hpæt he polde hýne
ʒenemnedne beon:·
63 Þa prat he ʒebedenum
pex-brede. Iohannes is his
nama. ða pundrodon hiʒ
ealle:·
64 Ða pearð sona his muð
⁊ his tunʒe ʒe-openod. ⁊ he
spræc. Drihten bletsiʒende:·

65 Ða pearð eʒe ʒeporden
ofer ealle hýra nehcheburas.[h]
and ofer ealle Iudea muntland pæron þas pord
ʒepidmærsode.
66 ⁊ ealle þa ðe hit
ʒehýrdon. on hýra heortan
settun ⁊ cpædon. Þenst ðu
hpæt býð þes cnapa. pitodlice
Drihtnes hand pæs mid him:·

67 And Zacharias his fæder
pæs mid haleʒum Gaste
ʒefýlled. ⁊ he piteʒode and
cpæð.
68 Gebletsud sý Drihten
Israhela God. forþam þe he
ʒeneosude. ⁊ his folces
alýsednesse dýde.
69 And he us hæle horn
arærde on Dauides huse his
cnihtes.
70 Spa he spræc þurh his

for no man is in thi kynrede
that is clepid this name.
58 And thei bikenyden to
his fadir, what he wolde that
he were clepid.
59 And he axinge a poyntel
wroot seiynge, Jon is his
name, and alle men
wondriden.
60 And annoon his mouth
was openyd and his tunge,
and he spak and blesside
God.
61 And drede was maad on
all hir neighbouris, and all
the wordis weren puplischid
on alle the mounteynes of
Judee.
62 And alle men that
herden puttiden in her herte,
and seiden what manner
child scal this be, for the
hond of the Lord was with
him.
63 And Zacarye his fadir
was fulfillid with the holy
Gost, and profeciede and
seide.
64 Blessid be the Lord God
of Israel, for he has visitid
and maad redempcioun of his
puple.
65 And he has rered to us
an horn of helthe in the hous
of Dauith his child.
66 As he spak by the

h. nehcheburas. *55a, 65, 73*] nehcheburas, *55b*

haleȝra ƿiteȝena muð. þa ðe of ƿorldes frým ðe spræcon.

71 ⁊ he alýsde us of urum feondum. and of ealra þara handa þe us hatedon.

72 Mild-heortnesse to ƿýrcenne mid urum fæderum. ⁊ ȝemunan his haleȝan cýðnesse.

73 Hýne uý[i] to sýllenne þone að þe he urum fæder Abrahame spor.

74 Ðæt ƿe butan eȝe. of ure feonda handa alýsede. him þeoƿian

75 On haliȝnesse beforan him eallum urum daȝum:·

76 And þu cnapa bist þæs hehstan ƿiteȝa ȝenemned. þu ȝæst beforan Drihtnes ansýne[j] his ƿeȝas ȝearƿian.

77 To sýllene his folce hæle ȝeƿit on hýra sýnna forȝýfnesse.

78 Ðurh innoðas ures Godes mild-heortnesse.[k] on þam he us ȝeneosude of eastdæle up-sprinȝende.[l]

79 Onlýhtan þam þe on þýstrum ⁊ on deaðes sceade[m]

mouth of hise holy prophetis that weren fro the world.

67 Helth fro oure enemyes, and fro the hond of alle men that hatiden us.

68 To do mersy with oure fadris, and to have mynde of his holy testament.

69 The grete ooth that he swoor to Abraham our fadir,

70 To geve himself to us, that we without drede delyvered fro the hond of oure enemyes serve to him,

71 In holynesse and rightwisnesse before him, in alle our dayes.

72 And thou child schalt be clepid the profete of the higheste, for thou schalt go before the face of the Lord to make redy hise weyes.

73 To geve science of heelth to his puple into remissioun of her synnes.

74 By the inwardeness of the mersy of oure God, in the which he springyng up fro on high hath visited us.

75 To geve light to them that sitten in derknessis, and

i. *A mistake for* us

j. ansýne *55a, 65, 73*] ansyne *55b*

k. mild-heortnesse. *55a, 65, 73*] mild-heortnesse, *55b*

l. up-sprinȝende *55a, 65, 73*] up-sýrinȝende *55b*

m. A mistake for sceades

sittað. ure fet to ʒereccenne on sibbe peʒ:·

80 Soðlice se cnapa peox. ⁊ pæs on ʒaste ʒestranʒod. ⁊ pæs on pestenum oð þone dæʒ hýs ætýpednessum on Israhel:·

in schadowe of deeth, to dresse oure feet into the weye of pees;

76 And the child wexide, and was confortid in spiryt, and was in desert placis till to the day of his schewing to Ysrael.

Of the *Saxon* poetry some specimen is necessary, though our ignorance of the laws of their metre and the quantities of their syllables, which it would be very difficult, perhaps impossible, to recover, excludes us from that pleasure which the old bards undoubtedly gave to their contemporaries.

The first poetry of the *Saxons* was without rhyme, and consequently must have depended upon the quantity of their syllables;[n] but they began in time to imitate their neighbours,[3] and close their verses with correspondent sounds.

The two passages,[o] which I have selected, contain apparently the rudiments of our present lyrick measures, and the writers may be justly considered as the genuine ancestors of the *English* poets.

He mai him sore adreden,
Ðæt he ðanne ore bidde ne muʒen,
Uor ꝥ bilimfeð ilome.
He is pis ꝥ bit and bote
And bet biuoren dome.

n. syllables; *55a, 55b, 65*] syllables: *73*
o. passages, *55a, 55b, 65*] passages *73*

3. *neighbours:* SJ may mean the Scandinavians, which would be historically plausible (see *The New Princeton Encyclopedia of Poetry and Poetics* [1993], s.v. *rhyme*). George Hickes, the source of SJ's specimen texts in this section, attributes the origins of rhyme in English to the decay of the ancient Saxon language and its mixture with "old Danish"; he says this led to a breakdown of the quantitative basis of the meter, which was compensated by the addition of rhyme (*Thesaurus* I.i.197–98, 222). Modern scholars attribute the appearance of rhyme in Old English to Latin or Irish influences.

Deað com on ðis midelard
Ðurð ðæs defles onde,
And senne and sosȝe[p] and ispinc,
On se and on londe.[4]

Ic am elder ðanne ic pes,
A pintre ⁊ ec a lore.
Ic ealdi more ðanne ic dede,
Mi pit oȝhte to bi more.[5]

Se þ hine selue uorȝet,
Uor piue oþer uor childe.
He sal comen on euele stede,
Bute ȝod him bi milde.[6]

Ne hopie pif to hire pere,
Ne pere to his piue.
Bi for him selue eurich man,
Ðaer pile he bieð alíue.[7]

p. *A mistake for* sorȝe

4. He may be so powerfully afraid that he shall not in that hour be able to pray. Often it happens so. Thus, he is wise who prays and repents and amends himself before judgment day. Death came into the world through the Devil's malice, as did sin and sorrow and toil, in the sea and on the land. (This is an anonymous lyric, printed as an example of alliteration in "semi-Saxonic" verse from MS Bodleian, Digby 4, in *Thesaurus,* I.i.196 [*Sale Catalogue,* no. 89; Watkins, p. 86]. Pieces of the lines appear in the *Poema Morale* [following]; SJ reprinted lines 4–5 of the quotation in *Dictionary* under *to boot.* He also cites line 4 [and translates it] in his *Miscellaneous Observations on Macbeth* [1745], *Yale* VII.10.)

5. I am older than I was in years and also in learning. I have aged more than I have done; my knowledge ought to be greater (stanza I). (This and the following stanzas are drawn from Hickes's selection of 191 quatrains he found in MS Bodleian, Digby A.4, and Trinity College, Lambeth Codex MS homil. Semi-Sax., *Thesaurus* I.i.222–24. A better text of the whole group of lines, with nine additional stanzas, appears in British Library, MS Egerton, 613, and has been critically edited from that source as "A Moral Ode" by Hans Marcus in "Das frümittelenglische 'Poema morale,'" *Palaestra* 194 [Leipzig, 1934], 55–230, to whose German translation we are indebted.)

6. The man who forgets himself for the sake of a wife or a child shall come to no good unless God pities him (XIII).

7. A wife should not trust in her husband, nor a man in his wife. Everyone should be for themselves as long as they are alive (XV).

Eurich man mid þ he haueð,
Mai beȝȝen heueriche.
Se ðe lesse ⁊ se ðe more,
Here aider iliche.[8]

Heuene and erðe he ouersieð,
His eȝhen bið fulbriht.
Sunne ⁊ mone ⁊ alle sterren,
Bieð ðiestre on his lihte.[9]

He pot hƿet ðencheð and hƿet doþ,
Alle quike ƿihte.
Nis no louerd ſpich is x̄ist,
Ne no kinȝ ſpich is drihte.[1]

Heuene ⁊ erðe ⁊ all ðat is,
Biloken is on his honde.
He deð al þ his ƿille is,
On sea and ec on londe.[2]

He is ord albuten orde,
And ende albuten ende.
He one is eure on eche stede,
Wende ƿer ðu ƿende.[3]

He is buuen us and bineðen,
Biuoren and ec bihind.
Se man þ ȝodes ƿille deð,
Hie mai hine aihƿar uinde.[4]

---

8. Every man with what he has may purchase heaven. Those who are less and those who are more considerable are there both alike (XXXI).

9. He superintends heaven and earth; his eyes are so beaming bright that the Sun and Moon and all the stars go dark under his gaze (XXXVI).

1. He knows what all living beings think and do. There is no master such as Christ nor any king like the Lord (XXXVIII).

2. Heaven and earth and all that exists is enclosed in his hand. He does everything that is his will on sea and on land (XXXIX).

3. He is the first without a beginning and the last without an end. He is always in every place no matter where one might go (XLI).

4. He is above us and beneath us, before us and behind. Whoever does the will of God can always find Him (XLII).

Eche rune he iherð,
And pot eche dede.
He ðurh siȝð eches iðanc,
Wai hpat sel us to rede.[5]

Se man neure nele don ȝod,
Ne neure ȝod lif leden.
Er deð ⁊ dom come to his dure,
He mai him sore adreden.[6]

Hunȝer ⁊ ðurst hete ⁊ chele,
Ecðe and all unhelðe.
Ðurh deð com on ðis midelard,
And oðer uniselðe.[7]

Ne mai non herte hit iþenche,
Ne no tunȝe telle.
Hu muchele pinum and hu uele,
Bieð inne helle.[8]

Louie God mid ure hierte,[q]
And mid all ure mihte.
And ure emcristene spo us self,
Spo us lereð drihte.[9]

Sume ðer habbeð lesse merȝðe,
And sume ðer habbeð more.

q. hierte, *65*] hierte. *55a, 55b, 73*

---

5. He hears every secret and he knows of every deed. He penetrates every heart. Oh! what shall our counsel be? (XLIII).

6. Whoever never wishes to do good nor ever lead a good life, before death and judgment come to his door, he may fear for himself most sorely (LVIII). (The last line of this section repeats the first line of the previous selection [p. 143 and n. 3 above]; SJ skips section XLIX, which contains more of the earlier lines.)

7. Hunger and thirst, heat and cold, pain and all disease came into this world along with death and other sorrows (XCVI).

8. Heart may not feel nor tongue tell how much and how many are the punishments in Hell (CXXXVIII).

9. Let us love God with all our heart and with all our might, and let us love our fellow Christian as ourself, as God teaches us (CXLVIII).

Ech efter ðan ƫ he dede,
Efter ƫ he spanc sore.[1]

Ne sel ðer bi bred ne pin,
Ne oþer kennes este.
God one sel bi eches lif,
And blisce and eche reste.[2]

Ne sal ðar bi scete ne scrud,
Ne porldes pele none.
Ac si merȝþe ƫ men us bihat,
All sall ben ȝod one.[3]

Ne mai no merȝþe bi spo muchel,
Spo is ȝodes isihðe.
Hi is soþ sune and briht,
And dai bute nihte.[4]

Ðer is pele bute pane,
And reste buten ispinche.
Se ƫ mai and nele ðeder come,
Sore hit sel uorðenche.[5]

Ðer is blisce buten tpeȝe,
And lif buten deaðe.
Ðet eure sullen punie ðer,
Bliðe hi bieþ and eaðe.[6]

Ðer is ȝeuȝeþe buten elde,
And elde buten unhelþe.

1. Some in heaven have less glory and others more, each according to his deeds, according to the performance of his hard labors (CLXXII).

2. There shall be neither bread nor wine in Heaven, nor any other kinds of provisions. God alone shall be the life of each, the joy, and also the peace (CLXXIII).

3. There shall be neither cloth nor clothing, nor any worldly wealth, but all the glory that men have promised us shall be in God alone (CLXXIV).

4. No glory can be as great as the sight of God. He is truly both the Sun and light and day without night (CLXXV).

5. There is wealth without poverty and rest without labor. Whoever is able but wishes not to come thither shall sorely regret it (CLXXVI).

6. There is joy without uncertainty and life without death. Whoever shall come to live there shall be happy and easy (CLXXVII).

Nis ðer forȝe[r] ne sor non,
Ne non uniselðe.[7]

Ðer me sel drihten isen,
Spo ase he is mid ipisse.
He one mai and sel al bien,
Enȝles and mannes blisce.[8]

To ðare blisce us brinȝ ȝod,
Ðet rixeð buten ende.
Ðanne he ure saula unbint,
Of lichamlice bend.[9]

Crist ȝeue us lede spich lif,
And habbe spichne ende.
Ðet pe moten ðider cumen,
Ðanne pe hennes pende.[1]

About the year 1150, the *Saxon* began to take a form in which the beginning of the present *English* may be plainly discovered; this change seems not to have been the effect of the *Norman* conquest, for very few *French* words are found to have been introduced in the first hundred years after it; the language must therefore have been altered by causes like those which, notwithstanding the care of writers and societies instituted to obviate them, are even now daily making innovations in every living language. I have exhibited a specimen of the language of this age from the year 1135 to 1140 of the

r. *A mistake for* sorge

7. There is youth without age and age without sickness. There is neither sorrow nor suffering nor any misery at all (CLXXVIII).

8. There shall I see the Lord as He is truly in his glory. He alone can and shall be all, the joy of angels and men (CLXXIX).

9. Bring us to that joy, God, who rules without end. Then shall our souls be loosed from their fleshly bonds (CXC).

1. Christ grant us to lead such a life and to have such an end that we can arrive in heaven when we go from here (CXCI).

Saxon chronicle, of which the latter part was apparently written near the time to which it relates.[2]

Ðis ʒære for þe kinʒ Stephne ofer sæ to Normandi. ⁊ þer pes under-fanʒen. forði ꝥ hi penden ꝥ sculde ben alsuic alse þe eom pes. ⁊ for he hadde ʒet his tresor. ac he to-deld[s] it ⁊ scatered sotlice. Micel hadde Henri kinʒ ʒadered ʒold ⁊ sýluer. and na ʒod ne dide me for his saule þar of. Ða þe kinʒ Stephne to Enʒla-land com þa macod he his ʒaderinʒ æt Oxene-ford. ⁊ þar he nam þe biscop Roʒer of Seres-beri. ⁊ Alexander biscop of Lincoln. ⁊ te Canceler Roʒer hise neues. ⁊ dide ælle in prisun. til hi jafen up here castles. Ða þe suikes underʒæton ꝥ he milde man þas[t] ⁊ softe ⁊ ʒod. ⁊ na justisc ne dide. þa diden hi alle punder. Hi hadden him manred maked and aðes suoren. ac hi nan treuðe ne heolden. alle he pæron for-sporen. ⁊ here treoðes for-loren. for æuric rice man his castles makede and aʒænes him heolden. and fýlden þe land full of castles. Hi suencten suiðe þe precce men of þe land mid castel-peorces. þa þe castles paren maked. þa fýlden hi mid deoules and ýuele men. Ða namen hi þa men þe hi penden ꝥ ani ʒod hefden. baðe be nihtes and be dæies. carl-men ⁊ pimmen. and diden heom in prisun efter ʒold and sýluer. ⁊ pined heom un-tellendlice pininʒ. for ne pæren næure nan martýrs spa pined alse hi pæron. Me henʒed up bi þe fet and smoked heom mid ful smoke. me henʒed bi þe þumbes. oðer bi þe hefed. ⁊ henʒen brýniʒes on her fet. Me dide cnotted strenʒes abuton here hæued. ⁊ uurýðen[u] to ꝥ it ʒæde to þe hærnes. Hi diden heom in quarterne þar nadres ⁊ snakes ⁊ pades pæron

s. to-deld *55a*] to deld *55b, 65, 73*
t. *A mistake for* pas
u. uurýðen *55a, 73*] uurdðen *55b, 65*

---

2. Anglo-Saxon Chronicle; *Chronicon Saxonicum,* ed. Edmund Gibson (1692), *The Peterborough Chronicle* for the years 1137–40 (SJ's date, 1135, is a mistake), pp. 238–44 (Watkins, p. 85). Our translation makes use of the notes in Cecily Clark's edition, *The Peterborough Chronicle, 1070–1154* (2d ed., 1970), and draws heavily on the translations of Harry A. Rositzke's *The Peterborough Chronicle* (1951) and Dorothy Whitelock's *The Anglo-Saxon Chronicle* (1961).

inne. ⁊ drapen heom spa. Sume hi diden in crucet hus.[v] ꝥ is in an ceste ꝥ pas scort ⁊ nareu. ⁊ un-dep.[w] ⁊ dide scærpe stanes þer inne. ⁊ þrenȝde þe man þær inne. ꝥ hi bræcon alle þe limes. In mani of þe castles pæron lof ⁊ ȝrī. ꝥ pæron sachenteȝes[x] ꝥ tpa oðer þre men hadden onoh to bæron onne. ꝥ pas spa maced ꝥ is fæstned to an beom. ⁊ diden an scærp iren abuton þa mannes þrote ⁊ his hals. ꝥ he ne mihte nopiderpardes ne sitten. ne lien. ne slepen. oc bæron al ꝥ iren. Mani þusen hi drapen mid hunȝær. J ne canne. ⁊ ne mai tellen alle þe pundes. ne alle þe pines ꝥ hi diden precce men on his land.[y] ⁊ ꝥ lastede þa XIX. pintre pile Stephne pas kinȝ. ⁊ æure it pas uuerse and uuerse. Hi læidenȝæildes on þe tunes æureū pile. ⁊ clepeden it tenserie. þa þe precce men ne hadden nan more to ȝiuen. þa ræueden hi and brendon alle þe tunes. ꝥ pel þu mihtes faren all adæis fare sculdest þu neure finden man in tune sittende. ne land tiled. Ða pas corn dære. ⁊ flec.[3] ⁊ cæse. ⁊ butere.[z] for nan ne pæs o þe land. Wrecce men sturuen of hunȝær. sume jeden on ælmes þe paren sum pile rice men. sum fluȝen ut of lande. Wes næure ȝæt mare preccehed on land. ne næure heðen men perse ne diden þan hi diden. for ouer siðon ne for-baren[a] hi nouðer circe. ne cýrceiærd. oc nam al þe ȝod ꝥ þar inne pas. ⁊ brenden sýðen þe cýrce ⁊ alteȝædere. Ne hi ne for-baren biscopes land. ne abbotes. ne preostes. ac ræueden muneces. ⁊ clerekes. ⁊ æuric man oðer þe ouer mýhte. Gif tpa men oðer þre coman ridend to an tun. al þe tunscipe fluȝæn for heom. penden ꝥ hi pæron ræueres. Ðe biscopes ⁊ lered men heom cursede æure. oc pas heom naht þar of. for hi pæron all for-cursæd ⁊ for-suoren ⁊ forloren. War sæ me tilede. þe erðe ne bar nan corn. for þe land pas all for-don mid suilce dædes. ⁊ hi sæden openlice ꝥ Crist slep. ⁊ his halechen.

v. crucet hus *73*] crucet-hus 55a, *55b, 65*
w. un-dep *55a, 73*] un dep *55b, 65*
x. *A mistake for* racheteȝes
y. *SJ's source reads* þis land.
z. butere. *55a, 73*] butere *55b, 65*
a. for-baren *55a, 55b, 73*] for baren *65*

---

3. Clark makes "flec" the more sensible "flesc."

Suilc ⁊ mare þanne ƿe cunnen sæin. ƿe þolenden XIX. ƿintre for ure sinnes. On al þis ýuele time heold Martin abbot his abbotrice XX. ƿinter.[b] ⁊ half ʒær. ⁊ VIII. dæis. mid micel suinc. ⁊ fand þe munekes. ⁊ te ʒestes al ꝥ heom behoued. ⁊ heold mýcel carited in the hus. and þoð ƿeðere ƿrohte on þe circe ⁊ sette þar to landes ⁊ ƿentes.[c] ⁊ ʒoded it suýðe and læt it refen. and brohte heom into þe neƿæ mýnstre on s. Petres mæsse-dæi mid micel ƿurtscipe. ꝥ ƿas anno ab incarnatione Dom. MCXL. a combustione loci XXIII. And he for to Rome ⁊ þær ƿæs ƿæl underfanʒen fram þe Pape Euʒenie. ⁊ beʒæt thare priuileʒies. an of alle þe landes of þabbot-rice. ⁊ an oðer of þe landes þe lien to þe circe-ƿican. ⁊ ʒif he lenʒ moste liuen. alse he mint to don of þe horder-ƿýcan. And he beʒæt in landes ꝥ rice men hefden mid strenʒþe. of Willelm Malduit þe heold Roʒinʒham þæ castel he ƿan Cotinʒham ⁊ Estun. ⁊ of Huʒo of Waltuile he ƿan Hýrtlinʒb. ⁊ Staneƿiʒ. ⁊ LX. sold. of Aldeƿinʒle ælc ʒær. And he makede manie munekes. ⁊ plantede ƿiniærd. ⁊ makede manie ƿeorkes. ⁊ ƿende þe tun betere þan it ær ƿæs. and ƿæs ʒod munec ⁊ ʒod man. ⁊ forði hi luueden God and ʒode men. Nu ƿe ƿillen sæʒen sum del ƿat belamp on Stephne kinʒes time. On his time þe Judeus of Nor-ƿic bohton an Cristen cild beforen Estren. and pineden him alle þe ilce pininʒ ꝥ ure Drihten ƿas pined. and on lanʒ-fridæi him on rode henʒen for ure Drihtnes luue. ⁊ sýðen býrieden him. Wenden ꝥ it sculde ben for-holen. oc ure Drihtin atýƿede ꝥ he ƿas hali martýr. ⁊ to[4] munekes him namen. ⁊ bebýried him heʒlice. in ðe mýnstre. ⁊ he maket þur ure Drihtin ƿunderlice and mani-fældlice miracles. ⁊ hatte he s. Willelm:·[5]

b. ƿinter. *55a, 73*] ƿinter *55b, 65*
c. *A mistake for* rentes

4. Clark sees that "to" is probably a mistake for "te."

5. [1137] This year King Stephen went across the sea to Normandy and was received there because they thought he would be just like his uncle and because he had acquired his treasure. But Stephen distributed and scattered his treasure about foolishly. [Then again,] King Henry had amassed much gold and silver and no good was done thereby for his soul.

When King Stephen returned to England, he made his assembly in Oxford. There he took Roger, the Bishop of Sarum, Alexander, Bishop of Lincoln,

On þis ȝær com Dauid kinȝ of Scotland mid ormete færd to þis land polde pinnan þis land. ⁊ him com toȝænes Willelm eorl

---

and Chancellor Roger, his nephew, and put them all in prison until they gave up their castles. While the traitors had believed that he was a mild, gentle, and good man who inflicted no punishment, they had committed all sorts of atrocities. They had done [Stephen] homage and sworn oaths to him, but they did not keep their pledge. They were all forsworn and their pledges forsaken, for each powerful man had built castles and fortified them against [Stephen], and they had filled the land full of castles. They had worked the poor men of the realm hard with castle-building. When the castles had been made, they had filled them with devils and evil men. Then, by day and by night, they had taken the men whom they thought owned any goods, men and women, and put them in prison for the sake of gold and silver. They punished them with unspeakable tortures. Never were any martyrs as tortured as these were. They were hung by the feet and choked with foul smoke; they were hung by the thumbs; and some were hung by the head while coats of mail were hung on their feet. Knotted strings were twisted about their heads until it went to the brain. They put them in confines infested with serpents, snakes, and toads, killing them in that way. Some they put in the torture house, that is, a box that was short, narrow, and shallow. They inserted sharp stones and pressed the man inside so that they broke all of his limbs. In many of the castles there were chains and halters so heavy that two or three men had all they could handle to carry one [set]. This instrument was so arranged—fastened to a beam, with the sharp iron placed around the man's throat and neck—that one could not move at all—neither sit, nor lie, nor sleep—but he had to bear the weight of all that iron. They also starved to death many thousands of people. I may not and cannot tell of all the atrocities and tortures they committed against the poor men of this land.

Their wickedness occupied nineteen years of Stephen's reign and it grew worse and worse all the time. Time and again they levied taxes on the towns and called it protection money. When the poor men had no more to give, then they despoiled the town and burned it all up. The result was that you could travel all day long and never find anyone occupying a town, nor was the land under cultivation. Then grain became very expensive, along with meat, cheese, and butter, because there was none to be had off the land. Poor people died of hunger. Some who once were rich went begging; some fled the land. Things had never been more wretched in the land, nor ever had the heathens done anything worse than these men were doing. Time and again they spared neither church nor churchyard, but took all the goods that were inside and burned down the church along with everything else. They spared neither a bishop's property, nor that of an abbot or a priest. They ravaged the goods of monks and clerks and of everyone else that they could. If two or three men came riding into a town, the whole village fled for home believing that they were plunderers. The bishops along with the rest of the clergy excommunicated these bad men constantly, but it was nothing to them because they were already wholly excommunicated and forsworn and damned rebels and outlaws.

Wherever it was tilled, the earth bore no fruit because the land was entirely ruined with such deeds. They said

of Albamar þe þe[d] kinȝ adde beteht Euor-ƿic. ⁊ to oðer æuez men mid fæu men ⁊ fuhten ƿid heom. ⁊ flemden þe kinȝ æt te standard. ⁊ sloȝen suiðe micel of his ȝenȝe:·[6]

On þis ȝær ƿolde þe kinȝ Stephne tæcen Rodbert eorl of Gloucestre. þe kinȝes sune Henries. ac he ne mihte for he ƿart it ƿar. Ða efter hi þe lenȝten þesterede[e] þe sunne ⁊ te dæi abuton nontid dæjes. þa men eten ꝥ me lihtede candles to æten bi. ⁊ ꝥ ƿas XIII.[f] kln. April. ƿæron men suiðe ofƿundred. Ðer efter ford-feorde Willelm Ærce-biscop of Cantƿar-býriȝ. ⁊ te kinȝ makede Teobald Ærce-biscop. þe ƿas abbot in þe Bec. Ðer efter

d. þe þe *55a, 73*] þe *55b, 65*
e. *A mistake for* ƿestrede
f. XIII. *55a, 73*] XIII *55b, 65*

---

openly that Christ and all his saints were asleep. We suffered more of such things than we can possibly express for nineteen years for our sins.

Throughout this evil time Abbot Martin held his abbacy, for twenty years, six months, and eight days, with great effort. He provided his monks and his guests all that they needed and maintained a great deal of almsgiving and feasts for the poor in the house. Nevertheless, he worked on the church, added lands and rents, improved it richly and had it roofed. He most worshipfully led his monks into the new abbey on St. Peter's Day. That was in the year 1140 after the incarnation of the Lord and twenty-three years after the place had been consumed in flames.

Abbot Martin then went to Rome and was there well received by Pope Eugene and acquired the rights to all the lands of the abbacy and of other lands that belonged to the office of the sacristan. If he had lived long, he would have done the same for the office of treasurer. He also acquired lands that powerful men had held by force. From William Malduit of Rockingham Castle he got Cottingham and Easton and from Hugo of Waltervile he got Irthlingborough and Stanwick and from Aldwinkle sixty shillings per year. In addition, he made monks of many men, planted vineyards, and performed many works. He made the town better than it ever was. He was a good monk and a good man, and therefore God and good men loved him.

Now we will report some of the things that happened in King Stephen's time. In his time the Jews of Norwich bought a Christian child before Easter and tortured him in all the same ways that our Lord was tortured. And on Good Friday they hung him on a cross, for the love of our Lord, and then they buried him. They believed that their deed would be concealed, but our Lord demonstrated that he was a holy martyr and the monks took him and had him buried with religious rites in the monastery. Through our Lord he performed many wonderful miracles, and he was called St. William.

6. [1138] In this year King David of Scotland came to this land with an enormous army; he meant to conquer this realm. Against him went Earl William of Albamar, to whom the king had given York, and the other loyal men with a few troops. They fought with them and put the king to flight at the standard and killed a great many of his followers.

pæx suiðe micel uuerre betuýx þe kinȝ ⁊ Randolf eorl of Cæstre noht forði ꝥ he ne jaf him al ꝥ he cuðe axen him. alse he dide alle oðre. oc æfre þe mare iaf heom þe pærse hi pæron him. Ðe eorl heold Lincol aȝænes þe kinȝ. ⁊ benam him al ꝥ he ahte to hauen. ⁊ te kinȝ for þider ⁊ besætte him ⁊ his broðer Willelm de R . . . are[7] in þe castel. ⁊ te eorl stæl ut ⁊ ferde efter Rodbert eorl of Gloucestre. ⁊ broht him þider mid micel ferd. and fuhten spiðe on Candel-masse-dæi aȝenes heore lauerd. ⁊ namen him. for his men him suýken ⁊ fluȝæn. and læd him to Bristope and diden þar in prisun. ⁊ . . . teres.[8] Ða pas all Enȝle-land stýred mar þan ær pæs. and all ýuel pæs in lande. Ðer efter com þe kinȝes dohter Henries þe hefde ben Emperic on Alamanie.[g] ⁊ nu pæs cuntesse in Anȝou. ⁊ com to Lundene. ⁊ te Lundenissce folc hire polde tæcen ⁊ scæ fleh. ⁊ forles þas micel:· Ðer efter þe biscop of Win-cestre Henri. þe kinȝes broðer Stephnes. spac pid Rodbert eorl ⁊ pid þemperice and spor heom aðas ꝥ he neure ma mid te kinȝ his broðer polde halden. ⁊ cursede alle þe men þe mid him heolden. and sæde heom ꝥ he polde iiuen heom up Win-cestre. ⁊ dide heom cumen þider. Ða hi þær inne pæren þa com þe kinȝes cuen . . .[9] hire strenȝðe ⁊ besæt heom. ꝥ þer pæs inne micel hunȝær. Ða hi ne lenȝ ne muhten þolen. þa stali hi ut ⁊ fluȝen. ⁊ hi purðen par piðuten ⁊ folecheden heom. and namen Rodbert eorl of Glou-cestre and ledden him to Rouecestre. and diden him þare in prisun. and te emperice fleh into an mýnstre. Ða feorden ða pise men betpýx. þe kinȝes freond ⁊ te eorles freond. and sahtlede sua ꝥ me sculde leten ut þe kinȝ of prisun for þe eorl. ⁊ te eorl for þe kinȝ. ⁊ sua diden. Siðen ðer efter sathleden þe kinȝ ⁊ Randolf eorl at Stan-ford ⁊ aðes sporen and treuðes fæston ꝥ her nouðer sculde besuiken oðer. ⁊ it ne for-stod naht. for þe kinȝ him siðen nam in Hamtun. þurhe picci ræd. ⁊ dide him in prisun. ⁊ ef sones he let him ut þurhe pærse red to ꝥ foreparde ꝥ he suor on halidom. ⁊ ȝýsles fand. ꝥ

g. Alamanie *55a, 55b, 65*] Alamame *73*

---

7. Gibson correctly conjectures "Romare."

8. Gibson conjectures "cweateres," but Clark supplies the better "in feteres."

9. Gibson conjectures "mid" and Clark adds "al."

he alle his castles sculde iiuen up. Sume he iaf up and sume ne iaf he noht. and dide þanne pærse ðanne he hær sculde. Ða pas Enȝle-land suiðe to-deled. sume helden mid te kinȝ. ⁊ sume mid þemperice. for þa þe kinȝ pas in prisun. þa penden þe eorles ⁊ te rice men ꝥ he neure mare sculde cumme ut. ⁊ sæhtleden pýd þemperice. ⁊ brohten hire into Oxen-ford. and iauen hire þe burch:· Ða ðe kinȝ pas ute. þa herde ꝥ sæȝen. and toc his feord ⁊ besæt hire in þe tup.[h] ⁊ me læt hire dun on niht of þe tup[i] mid rapes. ⁊ stal ut ⁊ scæ fleh ⁊ iæde on fote to Walinȝ-ford. Ðær efter scæ ferde ofer sæ. ⁊ hi of Normandi penden alle fra þe kinȝ to þe eorl of Anȝæu. sume here þankes ⁊ sume here un-þankes[j] for he besæt heom til hi aiauen up here castles. ⁊ hi nan helpe ne hæfden of þe kinȝ. Ða ferde Eustace þe kinȝes sune to France. ⁊ nam þe kinȝes suster of France to pife. pende to biȝæton Normandi þær þurh. oc he spedde litel. ⁊ be ȝode rihte. for he pas an ýuel man. for pare se he. . . .[1] dide mare ýuel þanne ȝod. he reuede þe landes ⁊ læide mic . . . . . . .s[2] on. he brohte his. pif to Enȝle-land. ⁊ dide hire in þe caste[k] . . . . . . teb.[3] ȝod pimman scæ pæs. oc scæ hedde litel blisse mid him. ⁊ xpist ne polde ꝥ he sculde lanȝe rixan. ⁊ pærd ded and his moder beien. ⁊ te eorl of Anȝæu pærd ded. ⁊ his sune Henri toc to þe rice. And te cuen of France to-dælde fra þe kinȝ. ⁊ scæ com to þe iunȝe eorl Henri. ⁊ he toc hire to piue. ⁊ al Peitou mid hire. Ða ferde he mid micel færd into Enȝle-land. ⁊ pan castles. ⁊ te kinȝ ferde aȝenes him micel mare ferð. ⁊ þoð-pæþere futen hi noht. oc ferden þe Ærce-biscop ⁊ te pise men betpux heom. ⁊ makede ꝥ sahte ꝥ te kinȝ sculde ben lauerd ⁊ kinȝ pile he liuede. ⁊ æfter his dæi pare Henri kinȝ. ⁊ he helde him for fader ⁊ he him for sune. and sib ⁊ sæhte sculde ben betpýx heom ⁊ on al Enȝle-land. Ðis and te oðre foruuardes þet hi makeden suoren to halden þe

h. *A mistake for* tur
i. *Another mistake for* tur
j. un-þankes *55a, 55b, 65*] un þankes *73*
k. caste *55a, 65, 73*] caŝ te *55b*

1. Gibson correctly conjectures "com he."

2. Gibson correctly conjectures "micel geldes."

3. Clark reads "castel on Cantebyrig"; Gibson does not comment on this lacuna.

kinȝ ⁊ te eorl. and te biscop. ⁊ te eorles. ⁊ ricemen alle. Đa ƿas þe eorl underfanȝen æt Win-cestre and æt Lundene mid micel ƿurtscipe. and alle diden him man-red. and suoren þe pais to halden. and hit ƿard sone suiðe ȝod pais sua ꝥ neure ƿas here. Đa ƿas ðe kinȝ strenȝere þanne he æuert her ƿas. ⁊ te eorl ferde ouer sæ. ⁊ al folc him luuede. for he dide ȝod justise ⁊ makede pais:·[4]

---

4. [1140] In this year King Stephen wanted to capture Robert, Earl of Gloucester, King Henry's son, but he could not do it because the earl became aware of [the plan]. The following Lent the sun and the daylight grew dark. When men were eating, candles were lit to sup by, and that was March 20th. People were truly astonished. After that William, Archbishop of Canterbury, died and the king made Theobald, who was the abbot of Bec [in Normandy], the Archbishop.

After that there came a very big war between the king and Randolph, Earl of Chester, not because he did not give him all that he could ask of him, as he did for all others: but, the more he gave them, the worse they treated him. The earl fortified Lincoln against the king and deprived him of all that [the king] should have had. The king went there and laid siege to [Randolph] and his brother William of Roumare [Earl of Lincoln] in the castle. Yet, the earl stole away and went after Robert, Earl of Gloucester, and brought him back with a large armed force. They fought hard against their liege lord on Candelmas Day [2 February 1141] and captured him because his men failed him and fled. They took him to Bristol and put him in prison and in irons. Then all England was more agitated than ever, and all kinds of evil were in the land.

Then King Henry's daughter, who had been Empress of Germany and was now the Countess of Anjou, came to London. The people of London wanted to take her captive, but she fled, leaving much [wealth] there.

Then Henry, Bishop of Winchester, King Stephen's brother, spoke with Earl Robert and with the empress. He swore oaths to them that he no longer would support his brother the king, and he excommunicated all those who were loyal to him. He also told them that he would give up Winchester to them, and he arranged for them to come there. When they were therein [in Winchester Castle], the king's queen arrived with all her strength and besieged them, and caused a great deal of hunger within [the walls]. When they could no longer endure, they stole out and fled, but those on the outside [the queen's troops] found out and followed them. They captured Robert of Gloucester and took him to Rochester and had him thrown in prison, but the empress fled to a monastery. Then counselors went between them, friends of the king and friends of the earl, and arranged that the king should be released from prison in exchange for the earl and the earl in exchange for the king. And they made it so.

Then, after that, the king and Earl Randolph conferred at Stanford and swore oaths and gave their words that neither would deceive the other. But it did not last at all because the king then captured [Randolph] at Hampton, through a wicked plan, and threw him in prison. But soon, following a worse

Nearly about this time, the following pieces of poetry seem to have been written, of which I have inserted only short fragments; the first is a rude attempt at the present measure of eight syllables, and the second is a natural introduction to *Robert of Gloucester,* being composed in the same measure, which, however rude and barbarous it may seem, taught the way to the *Alexandrines* of the *French* poetry.

---

plan, he let him out on condition that he swear on the sacrament and offer hostages as security that he would surrender all of his castles. Some he surrendered and some he did not, and then he did worse things than he had previously done.

Then England was truly divided: some sided with the king and some with the empress. The reason for this is that when the king was in prison, the earls and other powerful men thought he would never come out, and they made covenants with the empress. They invited her to Oxford and gave her the town. When the king got out [of prison], he heard this reported and gathered his forces and besieged her in the tower. But at night she was let down out of the tower by means of ropes, and she escaped. She fled and went on foot to Wallingford. Afterwards she went abroad, and all the people of Normandy turned from the king to the Earl of Anjou, some of them gladly and some of them grudgingly, when he besieged them until they surrendered their castles, having received no help from the king.

Then the king's son, Eustace, went to France and married the sister of the King of France, thinking by that means to gain Normandy. However, he enjoyed little success, and by good right, because he was an evil man. Wherever he went he did more harm than good. He appropriated lands and levied heavy taxes. He brought his wife to England and put her in Canterbury castle. She was a good woman, but she had little joy of [her husband], and Christ did not ordain that he should rule for long: both he and his mother died.

Then the Earl of Anjou died, and his son Henry took the throne. The Queen of France then separated from the king and went to the young earl Henry; he took her in marriage and all Poitou with her. Then he took a large force into England and won castles. The king brought up a greater army against him, but nevertheless they did not fight. The archbishop and the counselors interceded and made a pact providing that the king should be the liege lord and king while he lived, and after his day Henry would be king. [Henry] would consider [the king] his father, and the king think of him as his son and brother, and there would be peace and reconciliation between them and all throughout England. The king, the earl, the bishops, and the earls, and all the rich landholders swore to respect this [pact] and all the other conditions that they had made. Then the earl was received in Winchester and in London with great honor; all paid him homage and swore to keep the peace. And it soon became such a good peace as never was kept here [before]. Then the king was stronger than he ever had been here. The earl went abroad and everyone loved him because he was just and made peace.

FUR in see bi west spaýnge.[5]
Is a lond ihote cokaýgne.[l]
Đer nis lond under heuenriche.
Of wel of godnis hit iliche.
Đoý paradis be miri and briýt.
Cokaýgn is of fairir siýt.
What is þer in paradis.
Bot grasse and flure and greneris.
Đoý þer be ioi and gret dute.
Đer nis met bote frute.
Đer nis halle bure no bench.
Bot watir man is þursto quench.
Beþ þer no men but two.
Helý and enok also.
Clinȝlich[m] maý hi go.
Whar þer woniþ men no mo.

l. cokaýgne *55a, 73*] cockaygne *55b, 65*
m. Clinȝlich *55a, 73*] Clinglich *55b, 65*

5. The opening of "The Land of Cockayne," an anonymous lyric of 192 lines that appears in *Thesaurus,* I.i.231–33 (Watkins, p. 86). The poem comes from the manuscript Harley 913, now in the British Library, and has often been reedited. See R. H. Robbins, *Historical Poems of the XIVth and XVth Centuries* (1959), pp. 121–27, and J. S. Bennett and G. V. Smithers, *Early Middle English Verse and Prose* (1966), pp. 136–44 and 336–41. SJ quotes the first two lines of the poem (with slightly different spelling) in *Dictionary* under *cockney,* citing Hickes's footnote on *cockaygne* (l. 2):

"Nunc *coquin, coquine.* Quæ olim apud Gallas otio, gulæ & ventri deditos, *ignavum, ignavam, desidiosum, desidiosam, segnem* significabant. Hinc *urbanos* utpote à rusticis laboribus ad vitam sedentariam, & desidiosam avocatos pagani nostri olim *cokaignes,* quod nunc scribitur *cockneys,* vocabant. Et poëta hic noster in monachos & moniales, ut segne genus hominum, qui desidiæ dediti, ventri indulgebant, & coquinæ amatores erant, malevolentissime invehitur, monasteria & monasticam vitam in descriptione terræ *cockaineæ,* parabolice perstringens."

(Now *coquin* or *coquine,* which in French used to mean those given to laziness, gluttony, and lust, that is, idleness, pleasure-seeking, ease. Hence it became the name of a city-dweller who had turned from hard rural labors to a city life of ease; so our country-folk called those gone off to pleasure *cokaignes,* which is now written "cockneys." And our poet [of the "Land of Cockayne"] here viciously inveighs against monks and nuns as the kind of people who are lazy, who are given over to pleasure, indulge in sex, and are lovers of fine cookery; in his description of the land of Cockayne he satirizes, by analogy, monasteries and monastic life.)

In cokaýgne is met and drink.
Wiþute care how and swink.
Đe met is[n] trie þe drink so clere.[o]
To none russin and sopper.
I sigge for soþ boute were.
Đer nis lond on erþe is pere.
Under heuen nis lond i wisse.
Of so mochil ioi and blisse.
Đer is mani swete siýte.
Al is dai nis þer no niýte.
Đer nis baret noþer strif.
Nis þer no deþ ac euer lif.
Đer nis lac of met no cloþ.
Đer nis no man no woman wroþ.
Đer nis serpent wolf no fox.
Hors no capil. kowe no ox.
Đer nis schepe no swine no gote.
No non horwýla god it wote.
Noþer harate noþer stode.
Đe land is ful of oþer gode.
Nis þer flei fle no lowse.
In cloþ in toune bed no house.
Đer nis dunnir slete no hawle.
No non vile worme no snawile.
No non storm rein no winde.
Đer nis man no woman blinde.
Ok al is game ioi ant gle.
Wel is him þat þer mai be.
Đer beþ rivers gret and fine.
Of oile melk honi and wine.
Watir seruiþ þer to noþing.
Bot to siýt and to waussing.[6]

n. is *55a, 73*] if *55b, 65,*
o. clere. *55a, 55b*] clere: *65, 73*

---

6. Far in the sea, west of Spain
There is a land called Cockayne.
No land under heaven
In wealth or virtue is its like.
Though paradise is happy and
bright,

SANCTA MARGARETTA.[7]

Olde ant ýonge i preit ou oure folies for to lete.
Ðenchet on god þat ýef ou wit oure sunnes to bete.

Cockayne is a fairer sight.
What is there in paradise
Except grass and flowers and greenery.
Though there is joy and great pleasure,
There is no food but fruit.
There is neither hall nor bench—
Only water to quench one's thirst.
There are only two men there—
Elijah and also Enoch.
Virtuously can they live
Where no other men dwell.
In Cockayne there is meat and drink
Without any trouble or labor.
The meat is choice, the drink very clear.
Tea and supper are two meals, not one.
I tell you truly there were both.
There is no land on earth to compare.
Under heaven there is no land I know
With so much joy and happiness.
There is many a pleasant sight.
It is always daytime there and never night.
There is neither war nor strife.
There is no death, just eternal life.
There is no lack of food or clothing.
There is not an angry man or woman.
There is not a single snake, wolf, or fox,
Neither horse nor mare, cow nor ox.
There is not a sheep, nor pig, nor goat,
Nor any grooms, God knows.
There is neither stable nor stud farm.
The land is full of other good things.
There is not a fly, flea, or louse.
In the town mews there is not a bed or house.
There is no loud sounding sleet or hail,
Not a single vile worm or snail,
Neither storm, rain, nor wind.
There is not a blind man or woman,
But all is pleasure, joy, and glee.
Happy is the lot of whoever may there be.
There are large and small rivers there
Of oil, milk, honey, and wine.
Water has there no use
Except for viewing and washing.

7. The opening of "Vita Santae Margaretae," an anonymous lyric of 312 lines that appears in *Thesaurus* I.i.224–31. The story was told in a number of Middle English poems; this version survives in several manuscripts, of which Hickes chose Trinity College, Cambridge 323. It was edited along with several other Middle English versions of the Life of St. Margaret by Oswald Cockayne in *Seinte Marherete: The Meiden ant Martyr in Old English* (1862; rpt. Early English Text Society, 1866). For further bibliographical information, see Charlotte D'Evelyn and Frances A. Foster, "Saints' Legends," in *A Manual of the Writings in Middle English, 1050–1500*, ed. J. Burke Severs, Vol. 2 (1970), 606–08.

Here[p] mai tellen ou. wid wordes feire ant[q] swete.
Ðe vie of one meidan. was hoten Maregrete.
Hire fader was a patriac. as ic ou tellen maý.
In auntioge wif eches i ðe false laý.
Deve godes ant doumbe. he served nitt ant daý.
So deden moný oþere. þat singet weilaweý.
Theodosius was is nome. on crist ne levede he noutt.
He levede on þe false godes. ðat ƿeren wid honden wroutt.
Ðo þat child sculde christine ben. ic[r] com him well in þoutt.
E bed wen it were ibore. to deþe it were ibroutt.
Ðe moder was an heþene wif þat hire to wýman bere.
Ðo þat child ibore was. nolde ho hit furfare.
Ho sende it into asýe. wid messagers ful ýare.
To a norice þat hire wiste. ant sette hire to lore.
Ðe norice þat hire wiste. children aheuede seuene.
Ðe eitteþe was maregrete. cristes maý of heuene.
Tales ho ani tolde. ful feire ant ful euene.
Wou ho þoleden martirdom. sein Laurence ant seinte Steuene.[8]

p. *SJ's transcription omits* i, *the subject of the sentence, which appears after* Here *in the original.*
q. ant *55a*] and *55b, 65, 73*
r. *A mistake for* it

8. Old and young alike, I beg you to abandon your follies.
Think on God who gave you intelligence in order to heal your sins.
Here I shall relate to you, in plain and pleasant words,
The life of one maiden, whose name was Margaret.
Her father was a patriarch, as I can tell you.
In Antioch he chose a wife according to a corrupt law.
Night and day he worshipped deaf and dumb gods,
As did many others who sing wellaway.

Theodosius was his name. He did not believe in Christ at all.

In these fragments, the adulteration of the *Saxon* tongue, by a mixture of the *Norman*, becomes apparent; yet it is not so much changed by the admixture of new words, which might be imputed to commerce with the continent, as by changes of its own forms[s] and terminations; for which no reason can be given.[9]

Hitherto the language used in this island, however different in successive time, may be called *Saxon;* nor can it be expected, from the nature of things gradually changing, that any time can be assigned, when the *Saxon* may be said to cease, and the *English* to commence. *Robert of Gloucester* however, who is placed by the criticks in the thirteenth century, seems to have used a kind of intermediate diction, neither *Saxon* nor *English;* in his work therefore we see the transition exhibited, and, as he is the first of our writers in rhyme, of whom any large work remains, a more extensive quotation is extracted. He writes apparently in the same measure with the foregoing authour of St. *Margarite,* which,[t] polished into greater exactness, appeared to our ancestors so suitable to

s. forms *55a, 73*] form *55b, 65*
t. which, *55b, 65*] which *55a, 73*

He believed in the false gods that were made by human hands.
When the thought came to him that the child would be Christian,
From the bed whence it was born, he ordered it put to death.

The mother was a heathen wife. Two women took [the baby] to her.
Since the child was born alive, she did not want it to die.
She contrived to send it to a sanctuary with well-provisioned attendants.
[She sent the child] to a wet-nurse whom she knew and accounted her lost.

The nurse that she knew had seven children.
Margaret was the eighth. A Christian maiden from heaven,
She listened calmly and sweetly to tales that anyone told
About how St. Lawrence and St. Stephen suffered martyrdom.

9. In his *Seinte Marherete* (pp. 74–96), Oswald Cockayne provides a description of these changes (mostly leveling and truncating of Old English inflectional endings and changes in the pronouns), which refutes the notion, prevalent from Camden through Hickes, SJ, and Thomas Warton, that the English language was properly called Saxon before it became English.

the genius of the *English* language, that it was continued in use almost to the middle of the seventeenth century.[1]

Of þe batayles of Denemarch, þat hii dude in þys londe
Þat[u] worst were of alle oþere, we mote abbe an honde.
Worst hii were. vor oþere adde somwanne ýdo,
As Romeýns & Saxons, &[v] wel wuste þat lond þerto.
Ac hii ne kepte[w] ýt holde noȝt, bote robbý, and ssende,
And destrue, & berne, & sle, & ne couþe abbe non ende.
And bote lute ýt nas worþ, þeý hii were ouercome ýlome.
Vor mýd ssýpes and gret poer as prest efsone hii come.
Kýng Adelwolf of þýs lond kýng was tuentý ȝer.
Þe Deneýs come bý hým rýuor þan hii dude er.
Vor in þe al our vorst ȝer of ýs kýnedom
Mýd þre & þrýttý ssýpuol men her prince hýder come,
And at Souþhamtone[x] arýued[y] an hauene bý Souþe.
Anoþer gret ost þulke týme arýuede[z] at Portesmouþe.
Þe kýnȝ nuste weþer kepe, at delde ýs ost atuo.
Þe Denes adde þe maýstre. þo al was ýdo,
And bý Estangle &[a] Lýndeseýe hii wende vorþ atte laste,
And so hamward al bý Kent, & slowe & barnde vaste.

u. *Cap.* Þ *emend. here and at the beginning of all subsequent lines in this passage where small* þ *appears*
v. & *55a, 73*] and *55b, 65*
w. kepte *55a, 73*] kept *55b, 65*
x. Souþhamtone *55a, 73*] Souþamtone *55b, 65*
y. arýued *55a, 73*] aryuede *55b, 65*
z. arýuede *55b, 65, 73*] aryuede *55a*
a. & *55a*] and *55b, 65, 73*

1. *Robert of Gloucester's Chronicle,* ed. Thomas Hearne (2 vols., 1724), I.260–67 (Watkins, p. 108). Hearne's, which was the first complete edition, uses several manuscript sources for establishing the text: Harleian MS 201, Coll of Arms, Arundel 58, Cotton Calig A.xi, and a Bodleian MS with notes on it by his friend James West (see Edward Donald Kennedy, *A Manual of the Writings in Middle English* (8 vols., 1989), *Chronicles,* VIII.2798). In *Dictionary,* SJ cites Robert under *lither* (sense 2) and *shrew,* and Hearne's glossary to this edition under *stoniness* (sense 1). In our section on his composition of the History (pp. 115–20) above, we discuss SJ's possible indebtedness to Thomas Warton's *Observations on Spenser's Faerie Queene,* beginning with Robert of Gloucester and ending with John Skelton; for Warton's comments on Robert of Gloucester, see p. 117 above.

Aȝen wýnter hii wende hem. anoþer[b] ȝer eft hii come.
And destrude Kent al out, and Londone nome.
Þus al an ten ȝer þat lond hii broȝte þer doune,
So þat in þe teþe ȝer of þe kýnge's croune,
Al býsouþe hii come alond, and þet folc of Somersete
Þoru þe býssop Alcston and þet folc of Dorsete
Hii come & smýte an bataýle, & þere, þoru Gode's grace,
Þe Deneýs were al býneþe, & þe lond folc adde þe place,
And more prowesse dude þo, þan þe kýng mýȝte býuore,
Þeruore gode lond men ne beþ noȝt al verlore.
Þe kýng was þe boldore þo, & aȝen hem þe more drou,
And ýs foure godes sones woxe vaste ý nou,
Edelbold and Adelbryȝt, Edelred and Alfred.
Þýs was a stalwarde tem, & of gret wýsdom & red,
And kýnges were al foure, & defendede wel þýs lond,
An Deneýs[c] dude ssame ýnou, þat me volwel vond.
In syxteþe ȝere of þe kýnge's kýnedom
Is eldeste sone Adelbold gret ost to hým nome,
And ýs fader also god, and oþere heye men al so,
And wende aȝen þýs Deneýs, þat muche wo adde ý do.
Vor myd tuo hondred ssýpes & an alf at Temse mouþ hii come,
And Londone, and Kanterburý, and oþer tounes nome,
And so vorþ in to Soþereýe, & slowe & barnde vaste,
Þere þe kýng and ýs sone hem mette atte laste.
Þere was bataýle strong ýnou ýsmýte in an þrowe.
Þe godes kýnȝtes leýe adoun as gras, wan medeþ mowe.
Heueden, (þat were of ýsmýte,) & oþer lýmes also,
Flete in blode al fram þe grounde, ar þe bataýle were ýdo.
Wanne þat blod stod al abrod, vas þer gret wo ý nou.
Nýs ýt reuþe vorto hure, þat me so volc slou,
Ac our suete Louerd atte laste ssewede ýs suete grace,
And sende þe Cristýne Englýsse men þe maýstrýe in þe place,
And þe heþene men of Denemarch býneþe were echon.

b. anoþer *55a, 73*] another *55b, 65*
c. Deneýs *55b, 65, 73*] Deneys *55a*

Nou nas þer ȝut in Denemarch Cristendom non;
Þe kýng her after to holý chýrche ýs herte þe more drou,
And teþeȝede wel & al ýs lond, as hii aȝte, wel ý nou.
Seýn Swýthýn at Wýnchestre býssop þo was,
And Alcston at Sýrebourne, þat amendede muche þýs cas.
Þe kýng was wel þe betere man þoru her beýre red,
Tuentý wýnter he was kýng, ar he were ded.
At Wýnchestre he was ýbured, as he ȝut lýþ þere.
Hýs tueýe sones he ȝef ýs lond, as he býȝet ham ere.
Adelbold, the eldore, þe kýnedom of Estsex,
And suþþe Adelbrýȝt, Kent and Westsex.
Eýȝte hondred ȝer ýt was and seuene and fýftý al so,
After þat God anerþe com, þat þýs dede was ýdo.
Boþe hii wuste bý her týme wel her kýnedom,
At þe vyfte ȝer Adelbold out of þýs lyue nome.
At Ssýrebourne he was ýbured, & ýs broþer Adelbrýȝt
His kýnedom adde after hým, as lawe was and rýȝt.
Bý ýs daye þe verde com of þe heþene men wel prout,
And Hamtessyre and destrude Wýnchestre al out.
And þat lond folc of Hamtessyre her red þo nome
And of Barcssyre, and foȝte and þe ssrewen ouercome.
Adelbrýȝt was kýng[d] of Kent ȝeres folle tene,
And of Westsex bote výue, þo he deýde ých wene.

Adelred was after hým kýng ý mad in þe place,
Eyȝte[e] hondred & seuene & sýxtý as in þe ȝer of grace.
Þe vorste ȝer of ýs kýnedom þe Deneýs þýcke com,
And robbede and destrude, and cýtes vaste nome.
Maýstres hii adde of her ost, as ýt were dukes, tueýe,
Hýnguar and Hubba, þat ssrewen were beýe.
In Est Angle hii býleuede, to rest hem as ýt were,
Mýd her ost al þe wynter, of þe vorst ȝere.
Þe oþer ȝer hii dude hem vorþ, & ouer Homber come,
And slowe to grounde & barnde, & Euerwýk nome.
Þer was bataýle strong ý nou, vor ýslawe was þere
Osryc kýng of Homberlond, & monýe þat with hým were.

d. kýng *55b, 65, 73*] kyng *55a*
e. Eyȝte *55a, 55b, 65*] Eýȝte *73*

Þo Homberlond was þus ýssend, hii wende & tounes nome.
So þat atte laste to Estangle aȝen hým come.
Þer hii barnde & robbede, & þat folc to grounde slowe,
And, as wolues among ssep, reulých hem to drowe.
Seýnt Edmond was þo her kýng, & þo he seý þat deluol cas
Þat me morþrede so þat folc, & non amendement nas,
He ches leuere to deýe hýmsulf, þat such sorwe to ýseý.
He dude hým vorþ among ýs son, nolde he noþýg fle.
Hii nome hým & scourged hým, & suþþe naked hým bounde
To a tre, & to hým ssote, & made hým moný a wounde,
Þat þe arewe were on hým þo þýcce, þat no stede nas býleuede.
Atte laste hii martred hým, & smýte of ýs heued.
Þe sýxte ȝer of þe crounement of Aldered þe kýng
A nýwe ost com into þýs lond, gret þoru alle þýng,
And anon to Redýnge robbede and slowe.
Þe king and Alfred ýs broþer nome men ýnowe,
Mette hem, and a bataýle smýte vp Assesdoune.
Þer was moný moder chýld, þat sone laý þer doune.
Þe bataýle ýlaste vorte nýȝt, and þer were aslawe
Výf dukes of Denemarch, ar hii wolde wyþ drawe,
And mony þousend of oþer men, & þo gonne hii to fle;
Ac hii adde alle ýbe assend, ȝýf þe nýȝt nadde ý be.
Tueye bataýles her after in þe sulf ȝere
Hii smyte, and at boþe þe heþene maýstres were.
Þe kýng Aldered sone þo þen weý of deþ nome,
As ýt vel, þe výftý ȝer of ýs kýnedom.
At Wýmbourne he was ýbured, as God ȝef þat cas,
Þe gode Alfred, ýs broþer, after hým kýng was.

Alfred, þýs noble man, as in þe ȝer of grace he nom
Eýgte hondred & sýxtý & tuelue þe kýnedom.
Arst he adde at Rome ýbe, &, vor ýs grete wýsdom,
Þe pope Leon hým blessede, þo he þuder com,
And þe kýnge's[f] croune of hýs[g] lond, þat in þýs lond ȝut ýs:

f. kýnge's *55a, 55b, 73*] kýnges *65*
g. *A mistake for* þys

And he led hým to be kýng, ar he kýng were ýwýs.
An he was kýng of Engelond, of alle þat þer come,
Þat vorst þus ýlad was of þe pope of Rome,
An suþþe oþer after hým of þe erchebýssopes echon.
So þat hýuor[h] hým pore kýng nas þer non.
In þe Souþ sýde of Temese nýne bataýles he nome
Aȝen þe Deneýs þe vorst ȝer of ýs kýnedom.
Nýe ȝer he was þus in þýs lond[i] in bataýle & in wo,
An ofte sýþe aboue was, and býneþe oftor mo;
So longe, þat hým nere bý leuede bote þre ssýren in ýs hond,
Hamtessyre, and Wýltessyre, and Somersete,[j] of al ýs lond.
A daý as he werý was, and asuoddrýnge hým nome
And ýs men were ýwend auýsseþ, Seyn Cutbert to hym com.
"Ich am," he seyde, "Cutbert, to þe ýcham ýwend
To brýnge þe gode týtýnges. Fram God ýcham ýsend.
Vor þat folc of þýs lond to sýnne her wýlle al ȝeue,
And ȝut nolle herto her sýnnes býleue
Þoru me & oþer halewen, þat in þýs lond were ýbore;
Þan vor ȝou býddeþ God, wanne we beþ hým býuore,
Hour Louerd mýd ýs eýen[k] of milce on þe lokeþ þeruore,
And þý poer þe wole ȝýue aȝen, þat þou ast neý verlore.
And þat þou þer of soþ ýse, þou ssalt abbe tokýnýnge.
Vor þým men, þat beþ ago to daý auýssynge,
In lepes & in coufles so muche vyss hii ssolde hým brynge,
Þat ech man wondrý ssall of so gret cacchýnge.
And þe mor vor þe harde vorste, þat þe water ýfrore hýs,
Þat þe more aȝen þe kunde of vyssýnge ýt ýs.
Of serue ýt wel aȝen God, and ýlef me ys messager,
And þou ssall þý wýlle abýde, as ýcham ýtold her."
As þýs kýng herof awoc, and of þýs sýȝte þoȝte,
Hys výssares come to hým, & so gret won of fyss hým broȝte,
Þat wonder ýt was, & namelýche vor þe weder was so colde.
Þo lýuede þe god man wel, þat Seyn Cutbert adde ýtold.

h. *A mistake for* bývor
i. þýs lond *55a, 55b, 73*] þýs-lond *65*
j. Somersete, *55a, 55b, 73*] Somersete *65*
k. eýen *55a*] eyen *55b, 65, 73*

In Deuenýssyre þer after arýuede of Deneýs
Þre and tuentý ssýpuol men, all aȝen þe peýs,
Þe kýnge's broþer of Denemarch duc of ost was.
Oure kýnge's men of Engelond mette hem bý cas,
And smýte þer an bataýle, and her gret duc slowe,
And eyȝte hondred & fourtý men, & her caronýes to drowe.
Þo kynȝ Alfred hurde þýs, ýs herte gladede þo,
Þat lond folc to hým come so þýcke so ýt mýȝte go,
Of Somersete, of Wýltessýre, of Hamtessýre þerto,
Euere as he wende, and of ýs owe folc al so.
So þat he adde poer ýnou, and atte laste hii come,
And a bataýle at Edendone aȝen þe Deneýs nome,
And slowe to grounde, & wonne þe maýstre of the velde.
Þe kýng & ýs grete duke býgonne hem to ȝelde
To þe kýnȝ Alfred to[l] ýs[m] wýlle, and ostages toke,
Vorto wende out of ýs lond, ȝýf he ýt wolde loke;
And ȝut þerto, vor ýs[n] loue, to auonge Cristendom.
Kýng Gurmund, þe hexte kýng, vorst þer to come.
Kýng Alfred ýs godfader was. & ýbaptýsed ek þer were
Þrettý of her hexte dukes. and muche of þat folc þere
Kýng Alfred hem huld wýþ hým tuelf dawes as he hende,
And suþþe he ȝef hem large ȝýftes, and let hým wende.
Hii, þat nolde Cristyn be, of lande flowe þo,
And byȝonde see in France dude wel muche wo.
Ȝut þe ssrewen come aȝen, and muche wo here wroȝte.
Ac þe kýnȝ Alfred atte laste to ssame hem euere broȝte.
Kýng Alfred was þe wýsost kýnȝ, þat long was býuore.
Vor þeý me segge þe lawes beþ in worre týme vorlore,
Nas ýt noȝt so hiis daýe. vor þeý he in worre were,
Lawes he made rýȝtuollore, and strengore þan er were.
Clerc he was god ynou, and ȝut, as me telleþ me,
He was more þan ten ȝer old, ar he couþe ýs abece.
Ac ýs gode moder ofte smale ȝýftes hým tok,
Vor to byleue oþer ple, and loký on ýs boke.
So þat bý por clergýe ýs rýȝt lawes he wonde,

l. to *55a, 55b, 73*] in *65*
m. ýs *55a, 55b*] ys *65, 73*
n. ýs *55a, 55b*] ys *65, 73*

Þat neuere er nere ý mad, to gouerný ýs lond.
And vor þe worre was so muche of þe luþer Deneýs,
Þe men of þýs sulue lond were of þe worse peýs.
And robbede and slowe oþere, þeruor he býuonde,
þat þer were hondredes in eche contreýe of ýs lond,
And in ech toune of þe hondred a teþýnge were also,
And þat ech man wyþoute gret lond in teþýnge were ýdo,
And þat ech man knewe oþer þat in teþýnge were,
And wuste somdel of her stat, ȝýf me þu vp[2] hem bere.
So streýt he was, þat þeý me ledde amýdde weýes heýe
Seluer, þat non man ne dorste ýt nýme, þey he ýt seye.
Abbeýs he rerde moný on, and moný studes ýwýs.
Ac Wynchestrye he rerde on, þat nýwe munstre ýcluped ýs.
Hýs lýf eýȝte and tuentý ȝer in ýs kýnedom ýlaste.
After ýs deþ he was[o] ýbured at Wýnchestre atte laste.[3]

o. was *55a*] wos *55b, 65, 73*

---

2. Hearne notes and prefers the Cottonian ms reading "þufþe" (theft) to "þu vp."

3. Because of the Danish assaults made on this land,
the worst of all others, we had to abide foreign rule.
They were the worst; although others had done somewhat,
as the Romans and Saxons, they thoroughly controlled the land.
But they did not keep it secure at all; they just plundered, and ravaged,
and destroyed, and burned, and killed, and could stand no limits.
And it mattered little to them if they should quickly be overcome,
for soon they came again with ships and a great army all prepared.
King Æthelwulf was king of this land for twenty years.
Under him, the Danes came more often than they had before.
In what was easily our worst year during his reign
their prince came here with thirty-three ships full of men,
docking at Southampton, a southern port.
Another great army docked at Portsmouth at the same time.
The king did not know whether to maintain his force whole or divide it in two.
The Danes had the upper hand, no matter what was done,
and they went forth finally by way of East Anglia and Lindsey,
and then homeward through Kent where they slew and burned with speed.
In winter they went home again, but they came the next year too,
and devastated Kent entirely and took London.
Thus in ten years they brought the land there down.
So in the tenth year of the king's reign,
when they landed in the south, the people of Somerset,

led by Bishop Alcston, and the people of Dorset
came and fought a battle, and there, by the grace of God,
the Danes were defeated, and the peasants took control.
Thus they gained more honor than the king could earlier.
On that account, good peasants should not be forlorn.
The king was all the bolder, however, and went against them all the more.
Then his four sons had grown up enough,
Æthelbald and Æthelberht, Æthelred and Alfred.
They made a stalwart team, of great wisdom and good counsel.
All four were kings and defended this land well.
Nevertheless the Danes did plenty of wickedness, as I have full well found.
In the sixteenth year of the king's reign
his eldest son Æthelbald gathered a great army,
including his good father and other high-ranking men,
and went against the Danes who had done so much evil.
They had come into the mouth of the Thames with two hundred and fifty ships
and taken London and Canterbury and other towns.
They had then gone into the south and slain and burned widely.
There the king and his son finally encountered them.
There a very fierce battle was fought in a short time.
The good knights lay down like grass when a meadow is mown.
Heads, which had been cut off, and other body parts too,
drenched the ground in blood before the battle was done.
When the slaughter was known far and wide, there was very great sorrow.
Is it not a pity to hear that such men were killed?
But our sweet Lord finally showed us his sweet grace
and gave the Christian Englishmen the upperhand in the battle,
and the heathen men of Denmark were all thrown down.
There was not yet at that time any Christianity in Denmark.
Thereafter the king's affections were more drawn to the holy church,
and he properly instructed all his land, as he ought, and very firmly.
Saint Swithun was then the Bishop of Winchester
and Ealhstan was at Sherborne; these provided much help.
On account of their counsel alone the king was very much improved.
For twenty years he was king before he died.
He was buried at Winchester where he lies still.
He gave his land to the two of his sons who had been born first.
He gave Æthelbald, the elder, the kingdom of Essex
and Æthelberht, afterward, Kent and Wessex.
Eight hundred and fifty-seven years
after God was born on earth this deed was done.
In their time both wasted their kingdom badly,
but in the fifth year of his reign Æthelbald was taken out of this life.
He was buried at Sherborne, and his brother Æthelberht
gained his kingdom after him, as was lawful and right.

In his day the militia acquitted
themselves well in battle against
the heathens;
they cleaned out Hampshire and
Winchester.
Although the people of Hampshire
had accepted [Danish] rule,
like the people of Berkshire, they
fought and overthrew the tyrants.
Æthelberht was king of Kent for the
following ten years
but of Wessex only five, when he
died, I believe.

Æthelred was made king in his
place,
in the year of our Lord eight
hundred and sixty-seven.
The Danes undertook a heavy
invasion in the first year of his
reign.
They plundered and destroyed, and
they took many cities.
They had two leaders of their army,
dukes, as it were,
Hynguar and Hubba who were both
tyrants.
They stopped in East Anglia to rest
up, as it appeared,
with their troops, for the whole
winter of the first year.
The next year they went forth and
crossed the Humber
and slew and burned things to the
ground and captured York.
The fighting there was very fierce,
because slain there were
Osric king of Northumbria and
many who were with him.
When Northumbria was destroyed,
they went on and took towns.
In the end they came again to East
Anglia.
There they burned and robbed and
killed the people down to
nothing.
Like wolves among sheep, pitiful to
see, they drew them off.
Saint Edmund was then their king.
He perceived that doleful
situation
in which the people were being
murdered without recourse;
he preferred to die himself rather
than to witness such sorrow.
He went forth with his son; he did
not wish to flee at all.
They captured him and beat him
and then bound him naked
to a tree; they shot at him and gave
him many wounds.
The arrows were so thick on him
that no place was left for them.
Finally they martyred him and cut
off his head.
In the sixth year after King
Æthelred's coronation
a new army, great in all respects,
attacked this land,
and plundered and slaughtered in
Reading.
The king and his brother Alfred got
together a large force,
encountered them, and joined
battle with them near Ashdown.
There many a mother's child soon
lay down in death.
The battle lasted until night, and
slain there were
five Danish dukes before they
retreated,
and many thousands of other men,
even though they began to flee.
But they had all been killed, if night
had not fallen.
Two battles thereafter in the same
year of his reign
they fought, and in both the
heathens had the victory.
Then King Æthelred soon took the
path of death,
as it happened, in the fifth year of
his reign.
He was buried at Wimborne, as God
provided.

Alfred the Good, his brother, was king after him.
Alfred, this noble man, then in the year of grace
eight hundred and seventy-two, inherited the kingdom.
Earlier he had visited Rome and for his great wisdom
Pope Leo blessed him, when he came thither,
and he blessed the king's crown of his land, which is still in this land.
He anointed him king before he was king, I believe.
Then he was king of England, of all who came there,
he who was the first king to be consecrated by the Pope at Rome
and then, after him, by all the archbishops.
For this reason there was before him no pure king.
South of the Thames he engaged in nine battles
with the Danes in the first year of his reign.
For nine years he was continually in battle and in grief;
he often had the upper hand, but more often he was beaten down.
This went on so long that he was left with but three shires in his control:
Hampshire, Wiltshire, and Somerset were all of this land he had.
One day when he was weary and a faintness was overtaking him
while his men were out fishing, Saint Cuthbert came to him.
"I am," he said, "Cuthbert. I am sent to you
to bring you good news. I am sent from God.
Because the people of this land are entirely given over to sin,
and have not yet desired to set sin aside
through the help of me and other saints who were born in this land;
because you prayed to God when we came before him,
our Lord looks on you with merciful eyes,
and he wishes to give you again your power, which has nearly forsaken you.
And so that you may truly see this, you shall have a sign.
Those men who went fishing today
shall bring in so many fish in baskets and tubs
that each one shall wonder at the size of the catch.
They shall wonder the more since the water is frozen because of the hard frost:
thus the kind of fishing available is against the size of the catch.
Worship God well for it and believe me his messenger,
and you shall continue according to your wishes, as I have here said."
As the king was waking and thinking on this vision,
his fishermen came to him and so great a catch of fish brought him
that it was a miracle, especially because the weather was so cold.
Then the good man lived well, as Saint Cuthbert foretold.
In Devonshire then came the Danes,
twenty three ships full of men, a direct breach of the peace.
The king of Denmark's brother was the duke of the army.
Our king of England's men happened to encounter them,
and fought in battle there, and killed their great duke
as well as eight hundred and forty men; they drew away their carcasses.
When King Alfred heard this, his heart was happy.

Countrymen came to him in as great numbers as they could,
from Somerset, Wiltshire, and Hampshire,
wherever he went, and also from among people in his own county.
As a result he had great power, and finally his forces gathered
and fought a battle against the Danes at Ethandun.
They killed them down to nothing and carried the day.
The [Danish] king and his great duke yielded
to the will of King Alfred: he took hostages
against their departure from the land, if they would see to it,
and on condition that they would, for his love, accept the rule of Christ.
King Gurmund, the high king, was the first to come [for conversion].
King Alfred acted as his godfather, and also baptized there were
thirty of their highest dukes. Many of their people there
King Alfred kept with him for twelve days while he entertained,
and then he gave them great gifts and let them go.
Those who did not wish to be Christians fled the land
and beyond the sea in France did much mischief.
Yet again the wicked heathens came and caused sorrow here,
but finally King Alfred cast them all down in disgrace.
King Alfred was the wisest king in a very long time.
Although it is said that in wartime laws are forgotten,
it was not so in his day. Although he was engaged in war,
he made the the laws more just and stronger than they were before.
He was a very good scholar and yet, as I have heard,
He was more than ten years old before he learned his abc's.
His good mother often gave him little presents
so that he would stop playing and concentrate on his books.
As a result [of his studies] he made his just laws through pure clerical knowledge,
the likes of which had never been made for the government of this land.
Although there had been so much war with the wicked Danes,
the men of this very land were [before Alfred] worse off in peace.
Some robbed and murdered others. Therefore he contrived
the establishment of hundreds in each county of his land.
In each town of the hundred he set up a tithing and
arranged that each man without great land was committed to the tithing,
and that all knew the others that were in the tithing,
and might know pretty well their condition, if people bore their thefts.
So strict was [Alfred] that even if men left silver in the highway
no one dared to pick it up, even when he saw it.
He built many abbeys and many houses indeed.
He also built up Winchester to such an extent that it was called a new church.
He lived to reign for twenty-eight years.
After his death he was finally interred at Winchester.

Sir *John Mandeville* wrote, as he himself informs us, in the fourteenth century, and his work, which comprising a relation of many different particulars, consequently required the use of many words and phrases, may be properly specified in this place. Of the following quotations, I have chosen the first, because it shows, in some measure, the state of *European* science[4] as well as of the *English* tongue; and the second, because it is valuable for the force of thought and beauty of expression.[5]

In that lond, ne in many othere bezonde that, no man may see the sterre transmontane, that is clept the sterre of the see, that is unmevable, and that is toward the Northe, that we clepen the lode sterre. But men seen another sterre, the contrarie to him, that is toward the Southe, that is clept Antartyk. And right as the schip men taken here[6] avys here, and governe hem be the lode sterre, right so don schip men bezonde the parties, be the sterre of the Southe, the which sterre apperethe not to us. And this sterre, that is toward the Northe, that wee clepen the lode sterre, ne apperethe not to hem. For whiche cause, men may wel perceyve, that the lond and the see ben of rownde schapp and forme. For the partie of the firmament schewethe in o contree, that schewethe not in another contree. And men may well preven be experience and sotyle compassement of wytt, that zif a man fond passages be schippes, that wolde go to serchen the world, men myghte go be schippe alle aboute the world, and aboven and benethen. The whiche thing I prove thus, aftre that I have seyn. For I have been toward the parties of Braban, and beholden the Astrolabre, that the sterre that is clept the

4. *Science:* "Knowledge" (*Dictionary,* sense 1).

5. *The Voiage and Travaile of Sir John Maundevile. Kt.* . . . (1725), pp. 217–26 and 382–84 (Watkins, p. 108). The edition of 1725 is based on MS Cotton, Titus C.xvi, which has continued to be the principal source in later editions. See *Mandeville's Travels,* ed. M. C. Seymour (1967), with a glossary to which we are indebted. SJ cites Mandeville in *Dictionary* under *cattle.* SJ also cites Mandeville in his notes on Shakespeare (*Yale* VIII.792 and 1020).

6. *Here:* their.

transmontayne, is 53 degrees highe. And more forthere in Almayne and Bewme, it hathe 58 degrees. And more forthe toward the parties septemtrioneles, it is 62 degrees of heghte, and certyn mynutes. For I my self have mesured it by the Astrolabre. Now schulle ze knowe, that azen the Transmontayne, is the tother sterre, that is clept Antartyke; as I have seyd before. And tho 2 sterres ne meeven nevere. And be hem turnethe alle the firmament, righte as dothe a wheel, that turnethe be his axille tree: so that tho sterres beren the firmament in 2 egalle parties; so that it hathe als mochel aboven, as it hathe benethen. Aftre this, I have gon toward the parties meridionales, that is toward the Southe: and I have founden, that in Lybye, men seen first the sterre Antartyk. And so fer I have gon more[p] in tho contrees, that I have founde that sterre more highe; so that toward the highe Lybye, it is 18 degrees of heghte, and certeyn minutes (of the whiche, 60 minutes maken a degree) aftre goynge be see and be londe, toward this contree, of that I have spoke, and to other yles and londes bezonde that contree, I have founden the sterre Antartyk of 33 degrees of heghte, and mo mynutes. And zif I hadde had companye and schippynge, for to go more bezonde, I trowe wel in certyn, that wee scholde have seen alle the roundnesse of the firmament alle aboute. For as I have seyd zou be forn, the half of the firmament is betwene tho 2 sterres: the whiche halfondelle I have seyn. And of the tother halfondelle, I have seyn toward the Northe, undre the Transmontane 62 degrees and 10 mynutes; and toward the partie meridionalle, I have seen undre the Antartyk 33 degrees and 16 mynutes: and thanne the halfondelle of the firmament in alle, ne holdethe not but 180 degrees. And of tho 180, I have seen 62 on that o part, and 33 on that other part, that ben 95 degrees, and nyghe the halfondelle of a degree; and so there ne faylethe but that I have seen alle the firmament, saf 84 degrees and the halfondelle of a degree; and that is not the fourthe part of the firmament. For the 4 partie of the roundnesse of the firmament

p. *SJ's transcription omits the word* forthe, *which appears after* more *in the original.*

holt 90 degrees: so there faylethe but 5 degrees and an half, of the fourthe partie. And also I have seen the 3 parties of alle the roundnesse of the firmament, and more zit 5 degrees and an half. Be the whiche I seye zou certeynly, that men may envirowne[7] alle the erthe of alle the world, as wel undre as aboven, and turnen azen to his contree, that hadde companye and schippynge and conduyt: and alle weyes he scholde fynde men, londes, and yles, als wel as in this contree. For zee wyten welle, that thei that ben toward the Antartyk, thei ben streghte, feet azen feet of hem, that dwellen undre the transmontane;[q] als wel as wee and thei that dwellyn under us, ben feet azenst feet. For alle the parties of see and of lond han here appositees, habitables or trepassables, and thei of this half and bezond half. And wytethe wel, that aftre that, that I may parceyve and comprehende, the londes of Prestre[r] John, emperour of Ynde ben undre us. For in goynge from Scotlond or from Englond toward Jerusalem, men gon upward alweys. For oure lond is in the lowe partie of the erthe, toward the West: and the lond of Prestre John is the lowe partie of the erthe, toward the Est: and thei han there the day, whan wee have the nyghte, and also highe to the contrarie, thei han the nyghte, whan wee han the day. For the erthe and the see ben of round forme and schapp, as I have seyd beforn. And that that[s] men gon upward to o cost, men gon dounward to another cost. Also zee have herd me seye, that Jerusalem is in the myddes of the world; and that may men preven and schewen there, be a spere, that is pighte in to the erthe, upon the hour of mydday, whan it is equenoxium, that schewethe no schadwe on no syde. And that it scholde ben in the myddes of the world, David wytnessethe it in the Psautre, where he seythe, Deus operatus est salut· in medio terre.[8] Thanne thei that parten fro the parties of

q. transmontane *55a, 73*] Transmontane *55b, 65*
r. Prestre *55a, 73*] Preste *55b, 65*
s. that that *55a, 55b, 65*] than that *73*

---

7. *Envirowne:* encircle.
8. God has worked our salvation in the middle of the earth (Vulgate Bible, *Liber Psalmorum,* 73.12).

the West, for to go toward Jerusalem, als many iorneyes as thei gon upward for to go thidre, in als many iorneyes may thei gon fro Jerusalem, unto other confynyes of the superficialtie of the erthe bezonde. And whan men gon bezonde tho iourneyes, towarde Ynde and to the foreyn yles, alle is envyronynge the roundnesse of the erthe and of the see, undre oure contrees on this half. And therfore hathe it befallen many tymes of o thing, that I have herd cownted, whan I was zong; how a worthi man departed sometyme from oure contrees, for to go serche the world. And so he passed Ynde, and the yles bezonde Ynde, where ben mo than 5000 yles: and so longe he wente be see and lond, and so enviround the world be many seysons, that he fond an yle, where he herde speke his owne langage, callynge on oxen in the plowghe, suche wordes as men speken to bestes in his owne contree: whereof he hadde gret mervayle: for he knewe not how it myghte be. But I seye, that he had gon so longe, be londe and be see, that he had envyround alle the erthe, that he was comen azen envirounynge, that is to seye, goynge aboute, unto his owne marches, zif he wolde have passed forthe, til he had founden[t] his contree and his owne knouleche.[9] But he turned azen from thens, from whens he was come fro; and so he loste moche peynefulle labour, as him self seyde, a gret while aftre, that he was comen hom. For it befelle aftre, that he wente in to Norweye; and there tempest of the see toke him; and he arryved in an yle; and whan he was in that yle, he knew wel, that it was the yle, where he had herd speke his owne langage before, and the callynge of the oxen at the plowghe: and that was possible thinge. But how it semethe to symple men unlerned, that men ne mowe not go undre the erthe, and also that men scholde falle toward[u] the hevene, from undre! But that may not be, upon lesse, than wee mowe falle toward hevene, fro the erthe, where wee ben. For fro

t. founden *55a, 73*] foundee *55b, 65*
u. toward *55a, 73*] towarde *55b, 65*

9. *Knouleche:* knowledge, culture.

what partie of the erthe, that men duelle, outher aboven or benethen, it semethe alweyes to hem that duellen, that thei gon more righte than ony other folk. And righte as it semethe to us, that thei ben undre us, righte so it semethe hem, that wee ben undre hem. For zif a man myghte falle fro the erthe unto the firmament; be grettere resoun, the erthe and the see, that ben so grete and so hevy, scholde fallen to the firmament: but that may not be: and therfore seithe oure Lord God, Non timeas me, qui suspendi terrā ex nichilo?[1] And alle be it, that it be possible thing, that men may so envyronne alle the world, natheles of a 1000 persones, on ne myghte not happen to returnen in to his contree. For, for the gretnesse of the erthe and of the see, men may go be a 1000 and a 1000 other weyes, that no man cowde redye[2] him perfitely toward the parties that he cam fro, but zif it were be aventure and happ, or be the grace of God. For the erthe is fulle large and fulle gret, and holt in roundnesse and aboute envyroun, be aboven and be benethen 20425 myles, aftre the opynyoun of the olde wise astronomeres. And here seyenges I repreve noughte. But aftre my lytylle wyt, it semethe me, savynge here reverence, that it is more.[v] And for to have bettere understondynge, I seye thus, be ther ymagyned a figure, that hathe a gret compas; and aboute the poynt of the gret compas, that is clept the centre, be made another litille compas: than aftre, be the gret compas devised be lines in manye parties; and that alle the lynes meeten at the centre; so that in as many parties, as the grete compas schal be departed, in als manye, schalle be departed the litille, that is aboute the centre, alle be it, that the spaces ben lesse. Now thanne, be the gret compas represented for the firmament, and the litille compas represented for the erthe. Now thanne the firmament is devysed, be astronomeres, in 12 signes; and every signe is de-

v. more. *55b, 65, 73*] more, *55a*

1. "Do you not fear me, who has suspended the earth [in the heavens] from nothing" (recalls Vulgate Bible, *Liber Job,* 26.7).

2. *Redye:* direct.

vysed in 30 degrees, that is 360 degrees, that the firmament hathe aboven. Also, be the erthe devysed in als many parties, as the firmament; and lat every partye answere to a degree of the firmament: and wytethe it wel, that aftre the auctoures of astronomye, 700 furlonges of erthe answeren to a degree of the firmament; and tho ben 87 miles and 4 furlonges. Now be that here multiplyed be 360 sithes; and than thei ben 31500[w] myles, every of 8 furlonges, aftre myles of oure contree. So moche hathe the erthe in roundnesse, and of heghte enviroun, aftre myn opynyoun and myn undirstondynge. And zee schulle undirstonde, that aftre the opynyoun of olde wise philosophres and astronomeres, oure countree ne Irelond ne Wales ne Scotlond ne Norweye ne the other yles costynge to hem, ne ben not in the superficyalte cownted aboven the erthe; as it schewethe be alle the bokes of astronomye. For the superficialtee of the erthe is departed in 7 parties, for the 7 planetes: and tho parties ben clept clymates. And oure parties be not of the 7 clymates: for thei ben descendynge toward the West. And also these yles of Ynde, which beth evene azenst us, beth noght reckned in the climates: for thei ben azenst us, that ben in the lowe contree. And the 7 clymates strecchen hem envyrounynge the world.

II.[3] And I John Maundevylle knyghte aboveseyd, (alle thoughe I bē unworthi) that departed from oure contrees and passed the see, the zeer of grace 1322. that have passed manye londes and manye yles and contrees, and cerched manye fulle straunge places, and have ben in many a fulle gode honourable companye, and at many a faire dede of armes, (alle be it that I dide none myself, for myn unable insuffisance) now I am comen hom (mawgree my self) to reste: for gowtes, artetykes, that me distreynen, tho diffynen the ende of my labour,[4] azenst my wille (God knowethe.) And

w. 31500 *55a, 73*] 315000 *55b, 65*

---

3. This is the beginning of Chapter CIX.

4. For gout and arthritis have confined me and brought my labors to an end. . . .

thus takynge solace in my wrecched reste, recordynge the tyme passed, I have fulfilled theise thinges and putte hem wryten in this boke, as it wolde come in to my mynde, the zeer of grace 1356 in the 34 zeer that I departede from oure contrees. Wherfore I preye to alle the rederes and hereres of this boke, zif it plese hem, that thei wolde preyen to God for me: and I schalle preye for hem. And alle tho that seyn for me a Pater noster, with an Ave Maria, that God forzeve me my synnes, I make hem partneres and graunte hem part of alle the gode pilgrymages and of alle the gode dedes, that I have don, zif ony be to his plesance: and noghte only of tho, but of alle that evere I schalle do unto my lyfes ende. And I beseche Almyghty God, fro whom alle godenesse and grace comethe fro, that he vouchesaf, of his excellent mercy and habundant grace, to fulle fylle hire soules with inspiracioun of the Holy Gost, in makynge defence of alle hire gostly enemyes here in erthe, to hire salvacioun, bothe of body and soule; to worschipe and thankynge of him, that is three and on, with outen[x] begynnynge and withouten[y] endynge; that is, with outen[z] qualitee, good, and with outen[a] quantytee, gret; that in alle places is present, and alle thinges contenynynge; the whiche that no goodnesse may amende, ne non evelle empeyre; that in perfeyte trynytee lyvethe and regnethe God, be alle worldes and be alle tymes. Amen, Amen, Amen.

The first of our authours, who can be properly said to have written *English*,[5] was Sir *John Gower*, who, in his *Confession of a Lover*, calls *Chaucer* his disciple, and may therefore be considered as the father of our poetry.[6]

x. with outen *55a, 55b*] withouten *65, 73*
y. withouten *55a, 55b, 65*] without *73*
z. with outen *55a, 55b, 65*] withouten *73*
a. with outen *55a, 55b, 65*] withouten *73*

5. The notion that English is a purer language, succeeding cruder Saxon and Normano-Saxon languages, was received in Elizabethan times (most memorably in Spenser's phrase "the wells of English undefyl'd") and passed on through Hickes and SJ to Warton and beyond.

6. *Io. Gower de Confessione Amantis* (1554), Prologue, fol. 3[v]; *Sale Catalogue,*

Nowe for to speke of the commune,
It is to drede of that fortune,
Which hath befalle in sondrye londes:
But ofte for defaute of bondes
All sodeinly, er it be wist,
A tunne, whan his lie arist[7]
Tobreketh, and renneth all aboute,
Whiche els shulde nought gone out.
And eke full ofte a littell skare
Vpon a banke, er men be ware,
Let in the streme, whiche with gret peine,
If any man it shall restreine.
Where lawe failleth, errour groweth.
He is not wise, who that ne troweth.
For it hath proued oft er this.
And thus the common clamour is
In euery londe, where people dwelleth:
And eche in his complainte telleth,
How that the worlde is miswent,
And therevpon his argument
Yeueth euery man in sondrie wise:
But what man wolde him selfe auise
His conscience, and nought misuse,
He maie well at the first excuse
His god, whiche euer stant in one,
In him there is defaute none
So must it stande vpon vs selue,
Nought only vpon ten ne twelue,

---

no. 583. But Watkins points out (pp. 36, 106) that in the *Confessione* the supposed speaker of these lines ("'Grete well Chaucer, when ye mete, / As my disciple and my poete'") is Venus, not Gower the author, and that later in *Idler* 63, par. 10 (*Yale* II.198), SJ, after making a similar remark ("Gower, whom Chaucer calls his master"), goes on to declare: "Gower . . . seems justly to claim the honour which has been hitherto denied him, of shewing his countrymen that something more was to be desired [than merely versified prose], and that English verse might be exalted into poetry." In *Dictionary,* under *to feague,* SJ cites Gower's use of "*To feige,* for to censure."

7. *A tunne, whan his lie arist:* A barrel when its lees rise [in fermentation].

But plenarly vpon vs all.[b]
For man is cause of that shall fall.

The history of our language is now brought to the point at which the history of our poetry is generally supposed to commence, the time of the illustrious *Geoffry Chaucer,* who may perhaps, with great justice, be stiled the first of our versifyers who wrote poetically.[8] He does not however appear to have deserved all the praise which he has received, or all the censure that he has suffered. *Dryden,* who, mistaking[c] genius[9] for learning, in confidence of his abilities, ventured to write of what he had not examined, ascribes to *Chaucer* the first refinement of our numbers, the first production of easy and natural rhymes, and the improvement of our language, by words borrowed from the more polished languages of the continent.[1]

b. all. *55a, 55b, 73*] all, *65*
c. who, mistaking . . . , in *73*] who mistakes . . . , and, in *55a, 55b, 65*

---

8. Cf. Dryden's remark in his Preface to the *Fables* (1700): "As [Chaucer] is the Father of *English* Poetry, so I hold him in the same Degree of Veneration as the *Grecians* held *Homer,* or the *Romans Virgil*" (*Works of John Dryden,* ed. Vinton Dearing, VII [2000], 33). For a comparison of SJ's and Warton's comments on Chaucer, Gower, and Lydgate, see our article "Thomas Warton's *Observations on the Faerie Queene of Spenser,* Samuel Johnson's 'History of the English Language,' and Warton's *History of English Poetry:* Reciprocal Indebtedness?" *Philological Quarterly* LXXIV (1995), pp. 328–29. SJ once contemplated producing an edition of Chaucer with an etymological glossary (*Life* IV.381, n. 1).

9. *Genius:* "Mental power or faculties" (*Dictionary,* sense 3).

1. See n. 8, above, which raises the possibility that SJ knew Dryden's similar remark. SJ's comments clearly refer to Dryden's Preface to the *Fables,* where Dryden asserts, among many other things, that "[Boccaccio] and Chaucer . . . refin'd their Mother-Tongues"; that "*Chaucer* . . . first adorn'd and amplified our barren Tongue from the *Provençall* [Old French], which was then the most polish'd of all the Modern Languages"; that "From *Chaucer* the Purity of the *English* Tongue began"; and that "the Verse of *Chaucer* . . . is not Harmonious to us; but . . . They who liv'd with him, and some time after him, thought it Musical; and it continues so even in our Judgment, if compar'd with the Numbers of *Lidgate* and *Gower,* his Contemporaries." Dryden goes on to say, erroneously, that Thomas Speght, in his edition (1598) of Chaucer, was wrong in asserting the essential correctness of Chaucer's versification and that "some thousands of his Verses . . . are lame for want of half a foot, and sometimes a whole one" (ed. Dearing, VII.26, 30, 34). In his remarks, SJ may not summarize Dryden quite accurately, but see p. 183, note 3, below.

Skinner contrarily blames him in harsh terms for having vitiated his native speech by *whole cartloads of foreign words.*[2] But he that reads the works of *Gower* will find smooth numbers and easy rhymes, of which *Chaucer* is supposed to have been the inventor, and the *French* words, whether good or bad, of which *Chaucer* is charged as the importer. Some innovations he might probably make, like others, in the infancy of our poetry, which the paucity of books does not allow[d] us to discover with particular exactness;[3] but the works of *Gower* and *Lydgate* sufficiently evince, that his diction was in general like that of his contemporaries: and some improvements he undoubtedly made by the various dispositions of his rhymes, and by the mixture of different numbers, in which he seems to have been happy and judicious. I have selected several specimens both of his prose and verse; and among them, part of his translation of *Boetius,* to which another version, made in the time of queen *Mary,* is opposed. It would be improper to quote very sparingly an author[e] of so much reputation, or to make very large extracts from a book so generally known.

d. does not allow *65*] does allow *55a, 55b, 73*
e. author *73*] authour *55a, 55b, 65*

---

2. Stephen Skinner, *Etymologicon Linguae Anglicanae* (1671), sig. B3[r]: "*Chaucerus* poeta, pessimo exemplo, integris vocum plaustris ex eadem Gallia in nostram Linguam invectis, eam, nimis antea à Normannorum victoria adulteratam, omni fere nativa gratia et nitore spoliavit." (By his very bad example Chaucer the poet almost ruined the native grace and elegance of our language—it had much earlier been adulterated by the Norman conquest—when he brought in a whole waggonload of words from that same French.)

3. Cf. Dryden's statement that Chaucer "liv'd in the Infancy of our Poetry and that nothing is brought to Perfection at the first" (ed. Dearing, VIII.34).

CHAUCER.[4]

Alas! I wepyng am constrained to begin verse of sorowfull matter, that whilom in florishyng studie made delitable ditees. For lo! rendyng muses of Poetes enditen to me thinges to be writen, and drerie teres. At laste no drede ne might overcame tho muses, that thei ne werren fellowes, and foloweden my waie, that is to saie, when I was exiled, thei that weren of my youth whilom welfull and grene, comforten now sorowfull wierdes[6] of me olde man: for elde is comen unwarely upon me, hasted by the harmes that I have, and sorowe hath commaunded his age to be in me. Heres hore aren shad overtime-

COLVILE.[5]

I that in tyme of prosperite, and floryshing studye, made pleasaunte and delectable dities, or verses: alas now beyng heauy and sad ouerthrowen in aduersitie, am[f] compelled to fele and tast heuines and greif. Beholde the muses Poeticall, that is to saye: the pleasure that is in poetes verses, do appoynt me, and compel me to writ these verses in meter, and the sorowfull verses do wet my wretched face with very waterye teares, yssuinge out of my eyes for sorowe. Whiche muses no feare without doute could ouercome, but that they wold folow me in my iourney of exile or banishment. Sometyme the ioye

f. am *55a, 55b, 73*] and *65*

---

4. SJ drew his quotations from John Urry's edition of *The Works of Geoffrey Chaucer . . . Together with a Glossary* (1721); see Watkins, pp. 92–93. In *Dictionary,* Chaucer is cited from Urry's edition or from Junius's *Etymologicum Anglicanum,* under *to con, dam* (mother), *defend* (sense 4), *donjon, drotchel, erke, grin* ("A snare; a trap"), *gourd* (sense 2), *to mucker, quaint* (sense 2), *rote* (sense 1), *shall* (origin of), *to sneap, spick and span* (origin of), *tackle* (sense 1), and *welkin* (sense 1); some of these are noted by Allen Walker Reade in "The History of Lexicography," in *Lexicography: An Emerging International Profession* (1986), pp. 28–50.

5. *Boetius de Consolationae Philosophiae,* trans. George Colvile, alias Coldewel (1556), Book I.

6. *Wierdes:* fate.

liche upon my hed: and the slacke skinne trembleth of mine empted bodie. Thilke deth of men is welefull, that he ne cometh not in yeres that be swete, but cometh to wretches often icleped: Alas, alas! with how defe an ere deth cruell turneth awaie fro wretches, and naieth for to close wepyng eyen. While fortune unfaithfull favoured me with light godes, that sorowfull houre, that is to saie, the deth, had almoste drente myne hedde: but now for fortune cloudie hath chaunged her decevable chere to mewarde, myne unpitous life draweth along ungreable dwellynges. O ye my frendes, what, or whereto avaunted ye me to ben welfull? For he that hath fallin, stode in no stedfast degre.

of happy and lusty delectable youth dyd comfort me, and nowe the course of sorowfull olde age causeth me to reioyse. For hasty old age vnloked for is come vpon me with al her incommodities and euyls, and sorow hath commaunded and broughte me into the same old age, that is to say: that sorowe causeth me to be olde, before my time come of olde age. The hoer heares do growe vntimely vpon my heade, and my reuiled skynne trembleth my flesh, cleane consumed and wasted[g] with sorowe. Mannes death is happy, that cometh not in youth, when a man is lustye, and in pleasure or welth: but in time of aduersitie, when it is often desyred. Alas Alas howe dull and deffe be the eares of cruel death vnto men in misery that would fayne dye: and yet[h] refusythe to come and shutte vp theyr carefull wepyng eyes. Whiles that false fortune fauoryd me with her transitorye goodes, then the howre of death had almost ouercom[i] me. That is to say

g. wasted *55a, 73*] waste *55b, 65*
h. and yet *55a, 73*] add yet *55b, 65*
i. ouercom *55a, 73*] ouercome *55b, 65*

deathe was redy to oppresse me when I was in prosperitie. Nowe for by cause that fortune beynge turned, from prosperitie into aduersitie (as the clere day is darkyd with cloudes) and hath chaungyd her deceyuable countenaunce: my wretched life is yet prolonged and doth continue in dolour. O my frendes why haue you so often bosted me, sayinge that I was happy when I had honor possessions riches, and authoritie whych be transitory thynges. He that hath fallen was in no stedefast degre.

In the mene while, that I still record these thynges with my self, and marked my wepelie complainte with office of poinctell: I saugh stondyng aboven the hight of myn hed a woman of full grete reverence, by semblaunt. Her eyen brennyng, and clere, seyng over the common might of menne, with a lively colour, and with soche vigour and strength that it ne might not be nempned, all were it so, that she were full of so grete age, that menne woulden not trowen in no manere, that she were of our elde.

The stature of her was of

Whyles that I considerydde pryuylye with my selfe the thynges before sayd, and descrybed my wofull complaynte after the maner and offyce of a wrytter, me thought I sawe a woman stand ouer my head of a reuerend countenaunce, hauyng quycke and glysteryng clere eye, aboue the common sorte of men in lyuely and delectable coloure, and ful of strength, although she semed so olde that by no meanes she is thought to be one of this oure tyme, her stature is of douteful knowledge, for nowe she shewethe
herselfe at the commen

doutous Judgemente,[j] for sometyme she constrained and shronke her selven, like to the common mesure of menne: And sometyme it semed,
that she touched the heven with the hight of her hedde. And when she hove her hedde higher, she perced the self heven, so that the sight of menne lokyng was in ydell: her[k] clothes wer maked of right delie thredes, and subtel craft of perdurable matter. The whiche clothes she had woven with her owne handes, as I knewe well after by her self declaryng, and shewyng to me the beautie: The whiche clothes a darknesse of a forleten and dispised elde had dusked and darked, as it is wonte to darke by smoked Images.

In the netherest hemme and border of these clothes menne redde iwoven therein a Grekishe A. that signifieth the life active, and above that letter, in the hiest bordure, a Grekishe C. that signifieth the life contemplatife. And betwene these two letters there were seen degrees

length or statur of men, and other whiles she semeth so high, as though she touched heuen with the crown of her hed. And when she wold stretch
fourth her hed hygher, it also perced thorough heauen, so that mens syghte coulde not attaine to behold her. Her vestures or cloths were perfyt of the finyste thredes, and subtyll workemanshyp, and of substaunce permament, whych vesturs she had wouen with her own hands as I perceyued after by her owne saiynge. The kynde or beawtye of the whyche vestures, a certayne darkenes or rather ignoraunce of oldenes forgotten hadde obscuryd and darkened, as the smoke is wont to darken Images that stand nyghe the smoke. In the lower parte of the said vestures was read the greke letter P. wouen whych signifyeth practise or actyffe, and in the hygher part of the vestures the greke letter.[l]
T. whych estandeth for theorica, that signifieth speculacion or contemplation. And betwene both the sayd letters

j. Judgemente, *55a, 55b, 73*] judgemente *65*
k. her *55a, 55b, 65*] ner *73*
l. letter. *55a*] letter *55b, 65, 73*

nobly wrought, in maner of ladders, by whiche degrees menne might climben from the netherest letter to the upperest: nathelesse handes of some men hadden kerve that clothe, by violence or by strength, and

everiche manne of 'hem had borne awaie soche peces, as he might getten. And forsothe this foresaied[n] woman bare smale bokes in her right hande, and in her left hand she bare a scepter. And when she sawe these Poeticall muses approchyng about my bed, and endityng wordes to my wepynges, she was a litle amoved, and

glowed with cruell eyen. Who (qð she) hath suffered approchen to this sike manne these commen strompettes, of which is the place that menne callen Theatre, the whiche onely ne asswagen not his sorowes with remedies, but thei would feden and norishe hym with swete venime? Forsothe, that ben tho that with thornes, and prickynges of talentes of affeccions, whiche that ben nothyng fructuous nor profit-

were sene certayne degrees, wrought after the maner of ladders, wherein was as it were a passage or waye in steppes or degrees from the lower part wher the letter.[m] P. was which is

vnderstand from practys or actyf, unto the hygher parte wher the letter T. was whych is vnderstand speculacion or contemplacion. Neuertheles the handes of some vyolente persones had cut the sayde vestures and had taken awaye certayne pecis thereof, such as euery one coulde catch. And she her selfe dyd bare in her ryght hand litel bokes, and in

her lefte hande a scepter, which foresayd phylosophy (when she saw the muses poetycal present at my bed, spekyng sorrowful wordes to my wepynges) beyng angry sayd (with terrible or frownynge countenaunce) who suffred these crafty harlottes to com to thys sycke man? whych can help hym by no means of hys griefe by any kind of medicines, but rather increase the same with swete poyson. These be they that

m. letter. *55a*] letter *55b, 65, 73*
n. foresaied *55a, 73*] forsaied *55b, 65*

able, distroien the Corne,[o] plentuous of fruictes of reson. For thei holden hertes of men in usage, but thei ne deliver no folke fro maladie. But if ye muses had withdrawen fro me with your flatteries any unconnyng and unprofitable manne, as ben wont to finde commenly emong the peple, I would well suffre the lasse grevously. For why, in soche an unprofitable man myne ententes were nothyng endamaged. But ye withdrowen fro me this man, that hath ben nourished in my studies or scoles of Eleaticis, and of Academicis in Grece. But goeth now rather awaie ye Mermaidens, whiche that ben swete, till it be at the last, and suffreth this man to be cured and heled by my muses, that is to say, by my notefull sciences. And thus this companie of muses iblamed casten wrothly the chere dounward to the yerth, and shewing by rednesse ther shame, thei passeden sorowfully the thresholde. And I of whom the sight plounged in teres was darked, so that I ne might not know what that woman was, of so Im-

doo dystroye the fertile and plentious commodytyes of reason and the fruytes thereof wyth their pryckynge thornes, or barren affectes, and accustome or subdue mens myndes with sickenes, and heuynes, and do not delyuer or heale them of the same. But yf your flatterye had conueyed or wythdrawen from me, any vnlernyd man as the comen sorte of people are wonte to be, I coulde haue ben better contentyd, for in that my worke should not be hurt or hynderyd. But you haue taken and conueyed from me thys man that hath ben broughte vp in the studyes of Aristotel and of Plato.[p] But yet get you hence maremaids (that seme swete untyll you haue brought a man to deathe) and suffer me to heale thys my man wyth my muses or scyences that be holsome and good. And after that philosophy had spoken these wordes the sayd companye of the musys poeticall beynge rebukyd and sad, caste down their countenaunce to the grounde, and by blussyng confessed their shamfastnes, and went out

o. Corne, *55a, 55b, 73*] corne *65*
p. Plato. *55b, 65, 73*] Plato *55a*

perial aucthoritie, I woxe all abashed and stonied, and cast my sight doune to the yerth, and began still for to abide what she would doen afterward. Then came she nere, and set her doune upon the utterest corner of my bed, and she beholdyng my chere, that was cast to the yerth, hevie and grevous of wepyng, complained with these wordes (that I shall saine) the perturbacion of my thought.

of the dores. But I (that had my syght dull and blynd wyth wepyng, so that I knew not what woman this was hauyng soo great aucthoritie) was amasyd or[q] astonyed, and lokyng downeward, towarde the grounde, I began pryvylye to look what thyng she would saye ferther, then she had said. Then she approching and drawynge nere vnto me, sat downe vpon the vttermost part of my bed, and lokyng vpon my face sad with weping, and declynyd toward the earth for sorow, bewayled the trouble of my minde wyth these sayinges folowynge.

q. or *55a, 73*] and *55b, 65*

The conclusions of the ASTROLABIE.[7]

This book (written to his son in the year of our Lord 1391, and in the 14 of King Richard II.) standeth so good at this day, especially for the horizon of Oxford, as in the opinion of the learned it cannot be amended, says an Edit. of Chaucer.[8]

Lytel Lowys my sonne, I perceve well by certaine evidences thyne abylyte to lerne scyences, touching nombres and proporcions, and also well consydre I thy besye prayer in especyal to lerne the tretyse of the astrolabye. Than for as moche as a philosopher saithe, he wrapeth hym in his frende, that condiscendeth to the ryghtfull prayers of his frende: therfore I have given the a sufficient astrolabye for oure orizont, compowned after the latitude of Oxenforde: upon the whiche by mediacion of this lytell tretise, I purpose to teche the a certaine nombre of conclusions, pertainynge to this same instrument. I say a certaine nombre of conclusions for thre causes, the first cause is this. Truste wel that al the conclusions that have be founden, or ells possiblye might be founde in so noble an instrument as in the astrolabye, ben unknowen perfitely to anye mortal man in this region, as I suppose. Another cause is this, that sothely in any cartes of the astrolabye that I have ysene, ther ben some conclusions, that wol not in al thinges perfourme ther behestes: and some of 'hem ben to harde to thy tender age of ten yere to conceve. This tretise divided in five partes, wil I shewe the wondir light rules and naked wordes in Englishe, for Latine ne canst thou nat yet but smale, my litel sonne. But neverthelesse suffiseth to the these trewe conclusyons in Englishe, as well[r] as suffiseth to these

r. well *55a, 73*] wel *55b, 65*

7. *Works,* ed. Urry, pp. 439–40 (Watkins, p. 93).

8. Urry's introduction (Watkins 92–93); SJ's "an Edit." changes Urry's "the last Edit.," which refers to J. H.'s reissue (1687) of Speght's edition of 1602.

noble clerkes grekes these same conclusions in greke, and to the Arabines in Arabike, and to Jewes in Hebrewe, and to the Latin folke in Latýn:[s] whiche Latyn folke had 'hem firste out of other divers langages, and write 'hem in ther owne tonge, that is to saine in Latine.

And God wote that in all these languages and in manye mo, have these conclusyons ben sufficientlye lerned and taught, and yet by divers rules, right as divers pathes leden divers folke the right waye to Rome.

Now wol I pray mekely every person discrete, that redeth or hereth this lityl tretise to have my rude ententing excused, and my superfluite of wordes, for two causes. The first cause is, for that curious endityng and harde sentences is ful hevy at ones, for soch a childe to lerne. And the seconde cause is this, that sothely me semeth better to writen unto a childe twise a gode sentence, than he foriete it ones. And, Lowis, if it be so that I shewe the in my lith Englishe, as trew conclusions touching this mater, and not only as trewe but as many and subtil conclusions as ben yshewed in latin, in any comon tretise of the astrolabye, conne me the more thanke, and praye God save the kinge, that is lorde of this langage, and all that him faith bereth, and obeieth everiche in his degree, the more and the lasse. But consydreth well, that I ne usurpe not to have founden this werke of my labour or of myne engin. I n'ame but a leude compilatour of the laboure of olde astrologiens, and have it translated in myn englishe onely for thy doctrine: and with this swerde shal I slene envy.

The first party.[t]

The first partye of this tretise shall reherce the figures, and the membres of thyne astrolaby, bycause that thou shalte have the greter knowinge of thine owne instrument.

The seconde party.[u]

The seconde partye shal teche the to werken the very practike of the foresaid conclusions, as ferforthe and also narowe

s. Latýn *55a*] Latyn *55b, 65, 73*
t. party *55a, 55b, 73*] partye *65*
u. party *55a, 55b, 73*] partye *65*

as may be shewed in so smale an instrument portatife aboute. For wel wote every astrologien, that smallest fractions ne wol not be shewed in so smal an instrument, as in subtil tables calculed for a cause.

The PROLOGUE of the TESTAMENT of LOVE.[9]

Many men there ben, that with eres openly sprad so moche swalowen the deliciousnesse of jestes and of ryme, by queint knittinge coloures, that of the godenesse or of the badnesse of the sentence take they litel hede or els none.

Sothelye dulle witte and a thoughtfulle soule so sore have mined and graffed in my spirites, that soche craft of enditinge woll nat ben of mine acquaintaunce. And for rude wordes and boistous percen the herte of the herer to the inrest point, and planten there the sentence of thinges, so that with litel helpe it is able to spring, this boke, that nothynge hath of the grete flode of wytte, ne of semelyche colours, is dolven with rude wordes and boistous, and so drawe togiðer to maken the catchers therof ben the more redy to hent[1] sentence.

Some men there ben, that painten with colours riche and some with wers, as with red inke, and some with coles and chalke: and yet is there gode matter to the leude peple of thylke chalkye purtreyture, as 'hem thinketh for the time, and afterward the syght of the better colours yeven to 'hem more joye for the first leudenesse.[v] So sothly this leude clowdy occupacyon is not to prayse, but by the leude, for comenly leude leudenesse commendeth. Eke it shal yeve sight that other precyous thynges shall be the more in reverence. In Latin and French hath many soveraine wittes had grete delyte to endite, and have many noble thinges fulfilde, but certes there ben some that speken ther poisye mater in Frenche, of whiche speche the Frenche men have as gode a fantasye as we have in heryng of Frenche mens Englishe. And many termes there ben in Englyshe, whiche unneth we Englishe

v. leudenesse *55a, 65, 73*] leudnesse *55b*

---

9. *Works,* ed. Urry, pp. 478–79.

1. *Hent:* take hold of.

men connen declare the knowleginge: howe should than a Frenche man borne? soche termes connejumpere in his matter, but as the jay chatereth Englishe. Right so truely the understandyn of Englishmen woll not stretche to the privie termes in Frenche, what so ever we bosten of straunge langage. Let than clerkes enditen in Latin, for they have the propertie of science, and the knowinge in that facultie: and lette Frenche men in ther Frenche also enditen ther queint termes, for it is kyndely to ther mouthes; and let us shewe our fantasies in such wordes as we lerneden of our dame's tonge. And although this boke be lytel thank worthy for the leudnesse in travaile, yet soch writing exiten men to thilke thinges that ben necessarie: for every man therby may as by a perpetual myrrour sene the vices or vertues of other, in whyche thynge lightly may be conceved to eschue perils, and necessaries to catch, after as aventures have fallen to other peple or persons.

Certes the soverainst thinge of desire and most creture resonable, have or els shuld have full appetite to ther perfeccyon: unresonable bestes mowen not, sithe reson hath in 'hem no workinge: than resonable that wol not, is comparisoned to unresonable, and made lyke 'hem. Forsothe the most soveraine and finall[w] perfeccion of man is in knowynge of a sothe, withouten any entent decevable, and in love of one very God, that is inchaungeable, that is to knowe, and love his creator.

Nowe principally the mene to brynge in knowleging and lovynge his creatour, is the consideracyon of thynges[x] made by the creatour, wher through by thylke thinges that ben made, understandynge here to our wyttes, arne the unsene pryvities of God made to us syghtfull and knowinge, in our contemplacion and understondinge. These thinges than forsothe moche bringen us to the ful knowleginge sothe, and to the parfyte love of the maker of hevenly thynges. Lo! David saith: thou haste delited me in makinge, as who saith, to have

w. finall *55a, 55b, 65*] final *73*
x. thynges *55a, 55b, 73*] thinges *65*

delite in the tune how God hat lent me in consideracion of thy makinge. Wherof Aristotle in the boke de Animalibus, saith to naturell philosophers: it is a grete likynge in love of knowinge ther cretoure: and also in knowinge of causes in kindelye thynges, considrid forsothe the formes of kindelye thinges and the shap, a gret kyndely love we shulde have to the werkman that 'hem made. The crafte of a werkman is shewed in the werk. Herefore trulie the philosophers with a lyvely studie manie noble thinges, righte precious, and worthy to memorye, writen, and by a gret swet and travaille to us leften of causes the properties in natures of thinges, to whiche therfore philosophers it was more joy, more lykinge, more herty lust in kindely vertues and matters of reson the perfeccion by busy study to knowe, than to have had all the tresour, al the richesse, al the vaine glory, that the passed emperours, princes, or kinges hadden. Therfore the names of 'hem in the boke of perpetuall memorie in vertue and pece arne writen; and in the contrarie, that is to saine, in Styxe the foule pitte of helle arne thilke pressed that soch godenes hated. And bicause this boke shall be of love, and the prime causes of stering in that doinge with passions and diseses for wantinge of desire, I wil that this boke be cleped the testament of love.

But nowe thou reder, who is thilke that will not in scorne laughe, to here a dwarfe or els halfe a man, say he wil[y] rende out the swerde of Hercules handes, and also he shulde set Hercules Gades a mile yet ferther, and over that he had power of strength to pull up the spere, that Alisander the noble might never wagge, and that passinge al thinge to ben mayster of Fraunce by might, there as the noble gracious Edwarde the thirde for al his grete prowesse in victories ne might al yet conquere?

Certes I wote well, ther shall be made more scorne and jape of me, that I so unworthely clothed altogither in the cloudie cloude of unconning, wil putten me in prees to speak of love, or els of the causes in that matter, sithen al the grettest clerkes

y. wil *55a, 73*] will *55b, 65*

han had ynough to don, and as who saith gathered up clene toforne 'hem, and with ther sharp sithes of conning al mowen and made therof grete rekes and noble, ful of al plenties to fede me and many an other. Envye forsothe commendeth noughte his reson, that he hath in hain, be it never so trusty. And although these noble repers, as gode workmen and worthy ther hier, han al draw and bounde up in the sheves, and made many shockes, yet have I ensample to gaðer the smale crommes, and fullin ma walet of tho that fallen[z] from the bourde among the smalle houndes, notwithstanding the travaile of the almoigner, that hath draw up in the cloth al the remissailes, as trenchours, and the relefe to bere to the almesse. Yet also have I leve of the noble husbande Boece, although I be a straunger of conninge to come after his doctrine, and these grete workmen, and glene my handfuls of the shedynge after ther handes, and yf me faile ought of my ful, to encrese my porcion with that I shal drawe by privyties out of shockes; a slye servaunte in his owne helpe is often[a] moche commended; knowynge of trouthe in causes of thynges, was more hardier in the firste sechers, and so sayth Aristotle, and lighter in us that han folowed after. For ther passing study han freshed our wittes, and oure[b] understandynge han excited in consideracion of trouth by sharpenes of ther resons. Utterly these thinges be no dremes ne japes, to throwe to hogges, it is lyfelych mete for children of trouth, and as they me betiden whan I pilgramed out of my kith in wintere, whan the wether out of mesure was boistous, and the wyld wynd Boreas, as his kind asketh, with dryinge coldes maked the wawes of the ocean se so to arise unkindely over the commune bankes that it was in point to spill all the erthe.

z. fallen *55a, 73*] falled *55b, 65*
a. often *55a, 65, 73*] ofteh *55b*
b. oure *55a, 73*] oue *55b, 65*

The PROLOGUES of the CANTERBURY Tales of CHAUCER, from the MSS.[2]

When that Aprilis with his shouris sote,
The drought of March had percid to the rote,
And bathid every veyn in such licour,
Of which vertue engendrid is the flour.
When Zephyrus eke, with his swetè breth
Enspirid hath, in every holt and heth
The tender croppis; and that the yong Sunn
Hath in the Ramm his halvè cours yrunn:
And smalè foulis makin melodye,
That slepin allè night with opin eye,
(So prickith them nature in ther corage)
Then longin folk to go on pilgrimage:
And palmers for to sekin strangè strondes,
To servin hallowes couth in sondry londes:
And specially fro every shir'is end
Of England, to Canterbury they wend,
The holy blisfull martyr for to seke,
That them hath holpin, whan that they were seke.
Befell that in that seson on a day
In Southwerk at the Tabberd as I lay,
Redy to wendin on my pilgrimage
To Canterbury, with devote corage,
At night wer come into that hostery
Wele nine and twenty in a cumpany
Of sundrie folk, by aventure yfall
In felaship; and pilgrimes wer they all;
That toward Canterbury wouldin ride.
The chambers and the stablis werin wide,
And well[c] we werin esid at the best:
And shortly whan the sunnè was to rest,

c. well *55a, 73*] wel *55b, 65*

---

2. *Works,* ed. Urry, pp. 1–2, including the title (Watkins, p. 93).

So had I spokin with them everych one,
That I was of ther felaship anone;
And madè forward erli for to rise,
To take our weye, ther as I did devise.
But nathless while that I have time and space,
Er' that I farther in this talè pace,
Methinkith it accordaunt to reson,
To tell you allè the condition
Of ech of them, so as it semid me,
And which they werin, and of what degree,
And eke in what array that they wer in:
And at a knight then woll I first begin.

The Knight.

A knight ther was, and that a worthy man,
That fro the timè that he first began
To ridin out, he lovid[d] Chevalrie,
Trouth and honour, fredome and curtesy.
Full worthy was he in his lord'is[e] werre,
And thereto had he riddin nane more ferre
As well in Christendom, as in Hethness;
And evyr honoured for his worthiness.
At Alessandre'[f] he was whan it was won;
Full oft timis he had the bord begon
Abovin allè naciouns in Pruce;
In Lettow had he riddin, and in Luce,
No Christen-man so oft of his degree
In Granada; in the sege had he be
Of Algezir, and ridd in Belmary;
At Leyis was he, and at Sataly,
Whan that they wer won; and in the grete see
At many'a noble army had he be:
At mortal battails had he ben fiftene,
And foughtin for our feith at Tramesene,
In listis thrys, and alwey slein his fo.

d. lovid *55a, 55b, 73*] loved *65*
e. lord'is *55a, 55b, 65*] lordis *73*
f. Alessandre' *55a, 55b, 65*] Alessandre *73*

This ilke worthy knight had[g] ben also
Sometimis with the lord of Palathy,
Ayens anothir hethin in Turky;
And evirmore he had a sov'rane prize;
And though that he was worthy, he was wise;
And of his port as meke as is a maid,
He nevir yet no villany ne said
In all his life unto no manner wight:
He was a very parfit gentil knight.
But for to tellin you of his array,
His hors wer good; but he was nothing gay,[h]
Of fustian he werid a gipon,
Allè besmottrid with his haburgeon.
For he was late ycome from his viage,
And wentè for to do his pilgrimage.

The HOUSE of FAME.
The First Boke.[3]

Now herkin, as I have you saied,
What that I mette or I abraied,
Of December the tenith daie,
When it was night, to slepe I laie,
Right as I was wonte for to doen,
And fill aslepè wondir sone,
As he that was werie forgo
On pilgrimagè milis two
To the corps of sainct Leonarde,
To makin lithe that erst was harde.
But as me slept me mette I was
Within a temple' imade of glas,
In whiche there werin mo images
Of golde, standyng in sondrie stages,

g. had *55a, 73*] hath *55b, 65*
h. gay, *55a, 73*] gay; *55b, 65*

3. *Works,* ed. Urry, pp. 459–60 (Watkins, p. 93).

Sette in mo riche tabirnacles,
And with perrè[4] mo pinnacles,
And mo curious portraituris,
And queint manir of figuris
Of golde worke, then I sawe evir.
        But certainly I n'ist nevir
Where that it was, but well wist I
It was of Venus redily
This temple, for in purtreiture
I sawe anone right her figure
Nakid yfletyng in a se,
And also on her hedde parde
Her rosy garland white and redde,
And her combe for to kembe her hedde,
Her dovis, and Dan Cupido
Her blindè sonne, and Vulcano,
That in his face ywas full broune.
        But as I romid up and doune,
I founde that on the wall there was
Thus writtin on a table' of bras.
        I woll now syng, if that I can,
The armis, and also the man,
That first came through his destine
Fugitife fro Troye the countre
Into Itaile, with full moche pine,
Unto the strondis of Lavine,
And tho began the storie' anone,
As I shall tellin you echone.
        First sawe I the distruccion
Of Troie, thorough the Greke Sinon,
With his false untrue forswerynges,
And with his chere and his lesynges,
That made a horse, brought into Troye,
By whiche[i] Trojans loste all ther[j] joye.

i. whiche *55a, 55b, 73*] which *65*
j. ther *55a, 55b, 65*] their *73*

4. *Perrè:* precious stones.

And aftir this was graved, alas!
How Ilions castill assailed was,
And won, and kyng Priamus slain,
And Polites his sonne certain,
Dispitously of Dan Pyrrhus.
And next that sawe I howe Venus,
When that she sawe the castill brende,
Doune from hevin she gan discende,
And bade her sonne Æneas fle,
And how he fled, and how that he
Escapid was from all the pres,
And toke his fathre', old Anchises,
And bare hym on his backc awaie,
Crying alas and welawaie!
The whiche Anchises in his hande,
Bare tho the goddis[5] of the lande
I mene thilke that unbrennid were.
Then sawe I next that all in fere
How Creusa, Dan Æneas wife,
Whom that he lovid all his life,
And her yong sonne clepid Julo,
And eke Ascanius also,
Fleddin eke, with full drerie chere,
That it was pite for to here,
And in a forest as thei went
How at a tournyng of a went
Creüsa was iloste, alas!
That rede not I, how that it was
How he her sought, and how her ghoste
Bad hym to flie the Grekis hoste,
And saied he must into Itaile,
As was his destinie, sauns faile,
That it was pitie for to here,
When that her spirite gan appere,

5. Urry has "Goddis." SJ's text often capitalizes *God* when the Judeo-Christian deity is meant, and prints "pagan" *gods* with a lower case *g*, regardless of the irregular practice of SJ's sources.

The wordis that she to hym saied,
And for to kepe her sonne hym praied.
    There sawe I gravin eke how he
His fathir eke, and his meinè,
With his shippis began to saile
Toward the countrey of Itaile,
As streight as ere thei mightin go.
    There sawe I eke the, cruill Juno,
That art Dan Jupiter his wife,
That hast ihatid all thy life
Merciless all the Trojan blode,
Rennin and crie as thou were wode
On Æolus, the god of windes,
To blowin out of allè kindes
So loudè, that he should ydrenche
Lorde, and ladie, and grome, and wenche
Of all the Trojanis nacion,
Without any' of ther savacion.
    There sawe I soche tempest arise,
That evèry herte might agrise[k]
To se it paintid on the wall.
    There sawe I eke gravin withall,
Venus, how ye, my ladie dere,
Ywepyng with full wofull chere
Ypravid[l] Jupiter on hie,
To save and kepin that navie
Of that dere Trojan Æneas,
Sithins that he your sonne ywas.

Gode counsaile of CHAUCER.[6]

Flie fro the prese and dwell with sothfastnesse,
    Suffise unto thy gode though it be small,

k. agrise *55a, 73*] agrise, *55b, 65*
l. Yprayid *55a, 55b, 65*] Ypraid *73*

6. *Works,* ed. Urry, p. 548 (Watkins, p. 93).

For horde hath hate, and climbyng tikilnesse,
Prece hath envie, and wele it brent oer all,
Savour no more then[m] the behovin shall,
Rede well thy self, that othir folke canst rede,
And trouthe the shall delivir it 'is no drede.

Painè the not eche crokid to redresse,
In trust of her that tournith as a balle,
Grete rest standith in litil businesse,
Beware also to spurne again a nalle,
Strive not as doith a crocke with a walle,
Demith thy self[n] that demist othir's dede,
And trouthe the shall deliver it 'is no drede.

That the is sent receve in buxomenesse;
The wrastlyng of this worlde askith a fall;
Here is no home, here is but wildirnesse,
Forthe pilgrim, forthe o best out of thy stall,
Loke up on high, and thanke thy God of all,
Weivith thy luste and let thy ghost the lede,
And trouthe the shall delivir, it 'is no drede.

Balade of the village without paintyng.[7]

This wretchid world'is transmutacion
As wele and wo, nowe pore, and now honour,
Without ordir or due discrecion
Govirnid is by fortun'is errour,
But nathèlesse the lacke of her favour
Ne maie not doe me syng though that I die,
J'ay tout perdu, mon temps & mon labeur
For finally fortune I doe defie.

Yet is me left the sight of my resoun
To knowin frende fro foe in thy mirrour,
So moche hath yet thy tournyng up and doun,

m. then *55a, 55b, 65*] than *73*
n. thy self *55a, 73*] thyself *55b, 65*

7. *Works,* ed. Urry, pp. 548–49.

I taughtin me to knowin in an hour,
But truily no force of thy reddour[8]
To hym that ovir hymself hath maistrie,
My suffisaunce yshal be my succour,
For finally fortune I do defie.

O Socrates, thou stedfast champion,
She ne might nevir be thy turmentour,
Thou nevir dreddist her oppression,
Ne in her chere foundin thou no favour,
Thou knewe wele the disceipt of her colour,
And that her moste worship is for to lie,
I knowe her eke a false dissimulour,
For[o] finally fortune I do defie.

The answere of Fortune.

No man is wretchid but hymself it wene,
He that yhath hymself hath suffisaunce,
Why saiest thou then I am to the so kene,
That hast thy self out of my govirnaunce?
Saie thus grant mercie of thin habundaunce,
That thou hast lent or this, thou shalt not strive,
What wost thou yet how I the woll avaunce?
And eke thou hast thy bestè frende alive.

I have the taught division betwene
Frende of effecte, and frende of countinaunce,
The nedith not the gallè of an hine,
That curith eyin derke for ther penaunce,
Now seest thou clere that wer in ignoraunce,
Yet holt thine anker, and thou maiest arive
There bountie bereth the key of my substaunce,
And eke thou haste thy bestè frende alive.
How many have I refused to sustene,
Sith I have the fostrid in thy plesaunce?

o. For *55b, 65, 73*] Tor *55a*

8. *Reddour:* violence.

Wolt thou then make a statute on thy quene,
That I shall be aie at thine ordinaunce?
Thou born art in my reign of variaunce,
About the whele with othir must thou drive
My lore is bet, then wicke is thy grevaunce,
And eke thou hast thy bestè frende alive.

The answere to Fortune.

Thy[p] lore I dampne, it is adversitie,
My frend maist thou not revin[9] blind goddesse,
That I thy frendis knowe I thanke it the,
Take 'hem again, let 'hem go lie a presse,
The nigardis in kepyng ther richesse
Pronostike is thou wolt ther toure assaile,
Wicke appetite cometh aie before sickenesse,
In generall this rule ne maie not faile.

Fortune.

Thou pinchist at my mutabilitie,
For I the lent a droppe of my richesse,
And now me likith to withdrawin me,
Why shouldist thou my roialtie oppresse?
The se maie ebbe and flowin more and lesse,
The welkin hath might to shine, rain, and haile,
Right so must I kithin[1] my brotilnesse,
In generall this rule ne maie not faile.

The Plaintiffe.

Lo, the' execucion of the majestie,
That all purveighith of his rightwisenesse,
That samè thyng fortune yclepin ye,
Ye blindè bestis full of leudèness!
The heven hath propirtie of sikirness,
This worldè hath evir restlesse travaile,
The last daie is the ende of myne entresse,
In generall this rule ne maie not faile.

p. Thy *55a, 55b, 73*] The *65*

---

9. *Revin:* bereave.

1. *Kithin:* show.

Th' envoye of Fortune.

Princes I praie you of your gentilnesse,
Let not this man and me thus crie and plain,
And I shall quitin you this businesse,
And if ye liste releve hym of his pain,
Praie ye his best frende of his noblenesse
That to some bettir state he maie attain.[2]

Lydgate was a monk of *Bury*, who wrote about the same time with *Chaucer*. Out of his prologue to his third book of the *Fall of Princes* a few stanzas are selected, which, being compared with the style of his two contemporaries, will show that our language was then not written by caprice, but was in a settled state.[3]

Like a pilgrime which that goeth on foote,
And hath none horse to releue his trauayle,
Whote, drye and wery, and may find no bote
Of wel cold whan thrust doth hym assayle,
Wine nor licour, that may to hym auayle,
Tight[q] so fare I which in my businesse,
No succour fynde my rudenes to redresse.

I meane as thus, I haue no fresh licour
Out of the conduites of Calliope,
Nor through Clio in rhethorike no floure,
In my labour for to refresh me:
Nor of the susters in noumber thrise three,
Which with Cithera on Parnaso dwell,
They neuer me gaue drinke once of their wel.

Nor of theyr springes clere and christaline,
That sprange by touchyng of the Pegase,
Their fauour lacketh my making ten lumine

q. *A mistake for* Right

2. SJ omits the remaining fifty-nine lines of the "Balade."

3. *A Treatise excellent and compendious, shewing and declaring, in maner of Tragedy, the Falles of Sondry most notable Princes . . .* (1554), Prologue, Book 3, fols. 66^{v}–7^{r} (Watkins, pp. 107–08). For Warton's comments on Lydgate, see pp. 117–18, above. SJ's copy of *The Fall of Princes* is no. 627 in *Sale Catalogue.*

I fynde theyr bawme of so great scarcitie,
To tame their tunnes with some drop of plentie
For Poliphemus throw his great blindnes,
Hath in me derked of Argus the brightnes.
Our life here short of wit the great dulnes
The heuy soule troubled with trauayle,
And of memorye the glasyng brotelnes,
Drede and vncunning haue made a strong batail
With werines my spirite to assayle,
And with their subtil creping in most queint
Hath made my spirit in makyng for to feint.
And ouermore, the ferefull frowardnes
Of my stepmother called obliuion,
Hath a bastyll of foryetfulnes,
To stoppe the passage, and shadow my reason
That I might haue no clere direccion,
In translating of new to quicke me,
Stories to write of olde antiquite.
Thus was I set and stode in double werre
At the metyng of feareful wayes tweyne,
The one was this, who euer list to lere,
Whereas good wyll gan me constrayne,
Bochas taccomplish for to doe my payne,
Came ignorauncc, with a menace of drede,
My penne to rest I durst not procede.

Fortescue was chief justice of the Common-Pleas, in the reign of king *Henry* VI. He retired in 1471.[r] after the battle of Tewkesbury, and probably wrote most of his works in his privacy. The following passage is selected from his book of the *Difference between an absolute and limited Monarchy*.[4]

r. 1471. *55a, 55b, 65*] 1471, *73*

4. John Fortescue, *The Difference between an Absolute and Limited Monarchy; as it more particularly regards the English Constitution,* ed. Sir John Fortescue-Aland (1714), chap. 2, "*Why one King reynith* Regaliter tantum, *and another reynith,* Politice and Regaliter," pp. 7–14. In the eighteenth century, this book carried republican political implications. Its description of the Saxon people as freedom-loving and anti-tyrannical made it one of Thomas Jefferson's favorite

Hyt may peraventure be marvelid by some men, why one Realme is a Lordshyp only *Royall,* and the Prynce thereof rulyth yt by his Law, callid *Jus Regale;* and another Kyngdome is a Lordschip, *Royal*[s] *and Politike,* and the Prince thereof rulyth by a Lawe, callyd *Jus Politicum & Regale;* sythen thes two Princes beth of egall Astate.

To this dowte it may be answeryd in this manner; The first Institution of thes twoo Realmys, upon the Incorporation of them, is the Cause of this diversyte.

When Nembroth by Might, for his own Glorye, made and incorporate the first Realme, and subduyd it to hymself by Tyrannye, he would not have it governyd by any other Rule or Lawe, but by his own Will; by which and for th' accomplishment thereof he made it. And therfor, though he had thus made a Realme, holy Scripture denyyd to cal hym a Kyng, *Quia Rex dicitur a Regendo;*[5] Whych thyng he dyd not, but oppressyd the People by Myght, and therfor he was a Tyrant, and callid *Primus Tyrannorum.* But holy Writ callith hym *Robustus Venator coram Deo.*[6] For as the Hunter takyth the wyld beste for to scle and eate hym; so Nembroth subduyd to him[t] the People with Might, to have their service and their goods, using upon them the Lordschip that is callid *Dominium Regale tantum.*[7] After hym Belus that was callid first a Kyng, and after hym his Sone Nynus, and after hym other Panyms; They, by Example of Nembroth, made them Realmys, would not have them rulyd by other Lawys than by their own Wills. Which Lawys ben right good under good Princes; and their Kyngdoms a[u] then most resemblyd to the Kyngdome of God, which reynith upon Man, rulyng him by hys own Will. Wherfor many Crystyn Princes usen the same Lawe; and therfor

s. *Royal 55a, 73*] *Royall 55b, 65*
t. him *55a, 55b, 73*] hym *65*
u. *A mistake for* ar

books; see Stanley Hauer, "Thomas Jefferson and the Anglo-Saxon Language," *PMLA,* XCVIII (1983), 879–98.

5. A king is so called by virtue of ruling.

6. A powerful hunter in the presence of God.

7. Absolute authority.

it is, that the Lawys sayen, *Quod Principi placuit Legis habet vigorem.*[8] And thus I suppose first beganne in Realmys, *Dominium tantum Regale.* But afterward, whan Mankynd was more mansuete, and better disposyd to Vertue, Grete Communalties, as was the Feliship, that came into this Lond with Brute, wyllyng to be unyed and made a Body Politike callid a Realme, havyng an Heed to governe it; as after the Saying of the Philosopher, every Communaltie unyed of many parts must needs have an Heed; than they chose the same Brute to be their Heed and Kyng. And they and he upon this Incorporation and Institution, and onyng of themself into a Realme, ordeynyd the same Realme so to be rulyd and justyfyd by such Lawys,[v] as they al would assent unto; which Law therfor is callid *Politicum;* and bycause it is mynystrid by a Kyng, it is callid *Regale. Dominium Politicum dicitur quasi Regimen, plurium Scientia, sive Consilio ministratum.*[9] The Kyng of Scotts reynith upon his People by this Lawe, *videlicet, Regimine Politico & Regali.*[1] And as Diodorus Syculus saith, in his Boke *de priscis*[w] *Historiis,*[2] The Realme of Egypte is rulid by the same Lawe, and therfor the Kyng therof chaungith not his Lawes, without the Assent of his People. And in like forme as he saith is ruled the Kyngdome of Saba, in Felici Arabia, and the Lond of *Libie;* And also the more parte of al the Realmys in *Afrike.* Which manner of Rule and Lordship, the sayd Diodorus in that Boke, praysith gretely. For it is not only good for the Prince, that may thereby[x] the more sewerly[3] do Justice, than by his owne Arbitriment; but it is also good for his People that receyve therby, such Justice as they desyer themself. Now as

v. Lawys *55a, 55b, 65*] Laws *73*
w. *priscis 55a, 55b, 73*] *Priscis 65*
x. thereby *55a, 55b, 73*] therby *65*

8. What is pleasing to the prince has the strength of a law.

9. Political authority is said to be a kind of government with the acknowledgment of the many or administered by a governing body.

1. That is, by an authority both political and regal.

2. *De priscis Historiis,* "On Ancient History," a Latin version of the title of Diodorus Siculus's Greek universal history, Βιβλιοθηκη Ιστορικης, "A Library of History"; on the relationship of Egyptian kings to the law, see Book I, chaps. 70–74.

3. *Sewerly:* surely, with confidence.

me seymth, it ys shewyd opinly ynough, why one Kyng rulyth and reynith on his People[y] *Dominio tantum Regali,* and that other reynith *Dominio Politico & Regali:* For that one Kyngdome beganne, of and by, the Might of the Prince, and that other beganne, by the Desier and Institution of the People of the same Prince.

Of the works of Sir *Thomas More* it[z] was necessary to give a larger specimen, both because our language was then in a great degree formed and settled, and because it appears from *Ben Johnson,* that his works were considered as models of pure and elegant style.[4] The tale, which is placed first, because earliest written, will show what an attentive reader will, in perusing our old writers, often remark, that the familiar and colloquial part of our language, being diffused[a] among those classes who had no ambition of refinement, or affectation of novelty, has suffered very little change. There is another reason why the extracts from this author[b] are more copious: his works are carefully and correctly printed, and may therefore be better trusted than any other edition of the *English* books of that, or the preceding ages.[5]

y. People *55a, 73*] people *55b, 65*
z. it *55a, 55b, 73*] is *65*
a. diffused *55b, 65, 73*] disused *55a*
b. author *73*] authour *55a, 55b, 65*

4. In Book 2 of *English Grammar* (pp. 528–53), Ben Jonson frequently cites Sir Thomas More to illustrate correct English syntax, but Chaucer, Gower, Lydgate, and Ascham are about equally prominent.

5. SJ used *The Workes of Sir Thomas More . . . wrytten by him in the Englysh tonge,* ed. William Rastell (1557): he owned this edition (*Sale Catalogue,* no. 474), and it was the only one that included all the pieces here reprinted. However, puzzling variants in the first selection can be accounted for neither in later printed versions nor in the one known manuscript. Apparently SJ or his amanuensis, or his printer, bowdlerized the text by removing the names *God* and *Christ,* evidently thinking the context inappropriate for inclusion of these holy names. We note these deviations in our textual notes below, and we make use of the facsimile, text, and glossarial notes in *The English Workes of Sir Thomas More,* vol. 1, ed. W. E. Campbell (1931). SJ cited More in the first edition of *Dictionary* under *further* and in the fourth and later editions under *eisel* and *delectation,* which come from More's translation of Pico Mirandola. See Watkins, p. 50, but Wat-

A merry iest how a sergeant would learne to playe the frere.
Written by maister Thomas More in hys youth.[6]

Wyse men alway,
Affyrme and say,
That best is for a man:
Diligently,
For to apply,
The busines that he can,
And in no wyse,
To enterpryse,
An other faculte,
For he that wyll,
And can no skyll,
Is neuer lyke to the.
He that hath lafte,
The hosiers crafte,
And falleth to making shone,
The smythe that shall,
To payntyng fall,
His thrift is well nigh done.
A blacke draper,
With whyte paper,
To goe to writyng scole,
An olde butler,
Becum a cutler,
I wene shall proue a fole.
And an olde trot,
That can I wot,[c]
Nothyng but kysse the cup,

c. *SJ substitutes* I wot *for* god wot *in* Workes.

kins errs in asserting that More's prose is cited in *Dictionary* "27 times . . . under the letters E and F alone." Most or all of these are from the Christian Platonist Henry More's *An Antidote against Atheisme* and *Divine Dialogues*. Directly after he finished *Dictionary*, SJ may have considered writing a critical biography of Thomas More. In an effort to collect manuscript material in the Bodleian Library, he wrote to Thomas Warton on 7 August 1755 (*Letters* I.112–13).

6. "A Merry iest," *Workes*, sigs. ¶i^{r}–ii^{v}.

With her phisick,
Wil kepe one sicke,
    Tyll she haue[d] soused hym vp.
A man of lawe,
That neuer sawe,
    The wayes to bye and sell,
Wenyng to ryse,
By marchaundise,
    I wish[e] to spede hym well.
A marchaunt eke,
That wyll goo seke,
    By all the meanes he may,
To fall in sute,
Tyll he dispute,
    His money cleane away,
Pletyng the lawe,
For euery strawe,
    Shall proue a thrifty man,
With bate and strife,
But by my life,
    I cannot tell you whan.
Whan an hatter
Wyll go smatter,
    In philosophy,
Or a pedlar,
Ware[f] a medlar,
    In theology,
All that ensue,
Suche craftes new,
    They driue so farre a cast,
That euermore,
They do therfore,
    Beshrewe themselfe at last.
This thing was tryed

d. haue *55a, 55b, 65*] have *73*
e. *SJ substitutes* I wish *for* I pray god *in* Workes.
f. *A mistake for* waxe

And verefyed,
        Here by a sergeaunt late,
That thriftly was,
Or he coulde pas,
        Rapped about the pate,
Whyle that he would
See how he could,[g]
        A little play the frere:
Now yf you wyll,
Knowe how it fyll,
        Take hede and ye shall here.
It happed so,
Not long ago,
        A thrifty man there dyed,
An hundred pounde,
Of nobles rounde,
        That had he layd a side:
His sonne he wolde,
Should haue this golde,
        For to beginne with all:
But to suffise
His chylde, well thrise,
        That money was to smal.
Yet or this day
I have hard say,
        That many a man certesse,
Hath with good cast,
Be ryche at last,
        That hath begonne with lesse.
But this yonge manne,
So well beganne,
        His money to imploy,
That certainly,
His policy,
        To see it was a joy,
For lest sum blast,

g. could, *55a, 55b, 73*] could *65*

Myght ouer cast,
        His ship, or by mischaunce,
Men with sum wile,
Myght hym begyle,
        And minish his substaunce,
For to put out,
All maner dout,
        He made a good puruay,
For euery whyt,
By his owne wyt,
        And toke an other way:
First fayre and wele,
Therof much dele,
        He dygged it in a pot,
But then him thought,
That way was nought,
        And there he left it not.
So was he faine,
From thence agayne,
        To put it in a cup,
And by and by,
Couetously,
        He supped it fayre vp,
In his owne brest,
He thought it best,
        His money to enclose,
Then wist he well,
What euer fell,
        He coulde it neuer lose.
He borrowed then,
Of other men,
        Money and marchaundise:
Neuer payd it,
Up he laid it,
        In like maner wyse.
Yet on the gere,
That he would were,

He reight[7] not what he spent,
So it were nyce,
As for the price,
Could him not miscontent.
With lusty sporte,
And with resort,
Of ioly company,
In mirth and play,
Full many a day,
He liued merely.
And men had sworne,
Some man is borne,
To haue a lucky howre,
And so was he,
For such degre,
He gat and suche honour,
That without dout,
Whan he went out,
A sergeaunt well and fayre,
Was redy strayte,
On him to wayte,
As sone as on the mayre.
But he doubtlesse,
Of his mekenesse,
Hated such pompe and pride,
And would not go,
Companied so,
But drewe himself a side,
To saint Katharine,
Streight as a line,
He gate him at a tyde,
For deuocion,
Or promocion,

7. *Reight:* from *reck,* to heed; Rastell's text contains the more common "rought."

There would he nedes abyde.
There spent he fast,
Till all were past,
And to him came there meny,
To aske theyr det,
But none could get,
The valour of a peny.
With visage stout,
He bare it out,
Euen vnto the harde hedge,
A month or twaine,
Tyll he was faine,
To laye his gowne to pledge.
Than was he there,
In greater feare,
Than ere that he came thither,
And would as fayne,
Depart againe,
But that he wist not whither.
Than after this,
To a frende of his,
He went and there abode,
Where as he lay,
So sick alway,
He myght not come abrode.
It happed than,
A marchant man,
That he ought money to,
Of an officere,
Than gan enquere,
What him was best to do.
And he answerde,
Be not aferde,
Take an accion therfore,
I you beheste,
I shall hym reste,
And than care for no more.
I feare quod he,

It wyll not be,
        For he wyll not come out.
The sergeaunt said,
Be not afrayd.[h]
        It shall be brought about.
In many a game,
Lyke to the same,
        Haue I bene well in vre,
And for your sake,
Let me be bake,
        But yf I do this cure.
Thus part they both,
And foorth then goth,
        A pace this officere,
And for a day,
All his array,
        He chaunged with a frere.
So was he dight,
That no man might,
        Hym for a frere deny,
He dopped and dooked,
He spake and looked,
        So religiously.
Yet in a glasse,
Or he would passe,
        He toted and he peered,
His harte for pryde,
Lepte in his syde,
        To see how well he freered.
Than forth a pace,
Unto the place,
        He goeth withouten shame[i]
To do this dede,
But now take hede,
        For here begynneth the game.

h. afrayd. *55a*] afrayd, *55b, 65, 73*
i. *SJ substitutes* withouten shame *for* in goddes name *in* Workes.

He drew hym ny,
And softely,
    Streyght at the dore he knocked:
And a damsell,
That hard hym well,
    There came and it vnlocked.
The frere sayd,
Good spede fayre mayd,
    Here lodgeth such a man,
It is told me:
Well syr quod she,
    And yf he do what than.
Quod he maystresse,
No harme doutlesse:
    It longeth for our order,
To hurt no man,
But as we can,
    Euery wight to forder.
With hym truly,
Fayne speake would I.
    Sir quod she by my fay,
He is so sike,
Ye be not lyke,
    To speake with hym to day.
Quod he fayre may,
Yet I you pray,
    This much at my desire,
Vouchesafe to do,
As go hym to,
    And say an austen frere[j]
Would with hym speke,
And matters breake,
    For his auayle certayn.
Quod she I wyll,
Stonde ye here styll,
    Tyll I come downe agayn.
Vp is she go,

j. frere *55a, 55b, 73*] frere, *65*

And told hym so,
As she was bode to say,
He mistrustying,
No maner thyng,
Sayd mayden go thy way,
And fetch[k] him[l] hyder,
That we togyder,
May talk. A downe she gothe,
Vp she hym brought,
No harme she thought,
But it made some folke wrothe.
This officere,
This fayned frere,
Whan he was come aloft,
He dopped than,
And grete this man,
Religiously and oft.
And he agayn,
Ryght glad and fayn,
Toke hym[m] there by the hande,
The frere than sayd,
Ye be dismayd,
With trouble I understande.
In dede quod he,
It hath with me,
Bene better than it is.[n]
Syr quod the frere,
Be of good chere,
Yet shall it after this.[8]
But I would now,

k. fetch *55a, 73*] feth *55b, 65*
l. him *55a, 55b, 73*] hym *65*
m. hym *55a, 55b, 73*] him *65*
n. is. *55a, 73*] is, *55b, 65*

---

8. SJ's text omits the following six lines:

For Christes sake,
Loke that you take,
No thought within your brest:
God may tourne all,
And so he shall
I trust unto the best.

Comen with you,
In counsayle yf you please,
Or ellys nat
Of matters that,
Shall set your heart at ease.
Downe went the mayd,
The marchaunt[o] sayd,
Now say on gentle frere,
Of thys tydyng,
That ye me bryng,
I long full sore to here.
Whan there was none,
But they alone,
The frere with euyll grace,
Sayd, I rest the,
Come on with me,
And out he toke his mace:
Thou shalt obay,
Come on thy way,
I have the in my clouche,
Thou goest not hence,
For all the pense,
The mayre hath in his pouche.
This marchaunt there,
For wrath and fere,
He waxyng welnygh wood,
Sayd horson thefe,
With a mischefe,
Who hath taught[p] the thy good.
And with his fist,
Vpon the lyst,[9]
He gaue hym such a blow,
That backward downe,
Almost in sowne,

o. marchaunt *55a, 73*] marchaut *55b;* marchant *65*
p. hath taught *55b, 65, 73*] hathtaught *55a*

---

9. *Lyst:* ear.

The frere is ouerthrow.
Yet was this man,
Well fearder than,
Lest he the frere had slayne,
Tyll with good rappes,
And heuy clappes,
He dawde hym vp agayne.
The frere toke harte,
And vp he starte,
And well he layde about,
And so there goth,
Betwene them both,
Many a lusty clout.
They rent and tere,
Eche others here,
And claue togyder fast,
Tyll with luggyng,
And with tuggyng,
They fell downe bothe at last.
Than on the grounde,
Togyder rounde,
With many a sadde stroke,
They roll and rumble,
They turne and tumble,
As pygges do in a poke.
So long aboue,
They heue and shoue,
Togider that at last,
The mayd and wyfe,
To breake the strife,
Hyed them vpward fast.
And whan they spye,
The captaynes lye,
Both waltring[1] on the place,
The freres hood,
They pulled a good,

1. *Waltring:* rolling.

Adowne about his face.
Whyle he was blynde,
The wenche behynde,
Lent him leyd on the flore,
Many a ioule,
About the noule,
With a great batyldore.
The wyfe came yet,
And with her fete,
She holpe to kepe him downe,
And with her rocke,
Many a knocke,
She gaue hym on the crowne.
They layd his mace,
About his face,
That he was wood[2] for payne:
The fryre frappe,
Gate many a swappe,
Tyll he was full nygh slayne.
Vp they hym lift,
And with yll thrift,
Hedlyng a long the stayre,
Downe they hym threwe,
And sayde adewe,
Commende[q] us to the mayre.
The frere arose,
But I suppose,
Amased was his hed,
He shoke his eares,
And from grete feares,
He thought hym well yfled.
Quod he now lost,
Is all this cost,
We be neuer the nere.

q. *The original reads* commaund.

2. *wood:* mad.

Ill mote he be,[r]
That caused me,
To make my self a frere.
Now masters all,
Here now I shall,
Ende there as I began,
In any wyse,
I would auyse,
And counsayle euery man,
His owne craft vse,
All newe refuse,
And lyghtly let them gone:
Play not the frere,
Now make good chere,
And welcome euerych one.

A ruful lamentacion (writen by master Thomas More in his youth) of the deth of quene Elisabeth mother to king Henry the eight, wife to king Henry the seuenth, and eldest doughter to king Edward the fourth, which quene Elisabeth dyed in childbed in February in the yere of our Lord 1503, and in the 18 yere of the raigne of king Henry the seuenth.[3]

O ye that put your trust and confidence,
In worldly ioy and frayle prosperite,
That so lyue here as ye should neuer hence,
Remember death and loke here vppon me.
Ensaumple I thynke there may no better be.
Your selfe wotte well that in this realme was I,
Your quene but late, and lo now here I lye.
Was I not borne of olde worthy linage?
Was not my mother queene[s] my father kyng?

r. *The original reads* the, *which means* to thrive.
s. queene *55a, 55b, 65*] queene, *73*

3. "A Ruful Lamentacion," *Workes,* sigs. ¶iiii^r–[v]^r.

Was I not a kinges fere[4] in marriage?
Had I not plenty of euery pleasaunt thyng?
Mercifull god this is a straunge reckenyng:
Rychesse, honour, welth, and auncestry?[t]
Hath me forsaken and lo now here I ly.
        If worship myght haue kept me, I had not gone.
If wyt myght haue me saued, I neded not fere.
If money myght haue holpe, I lacked none.
But O good God what vayleth all this gere.
When deth is come thy mighty messangere,
Obey we must there is no remedy,
Me hath he sommoned, and lo now here I ly.
        Yet was I late promised otherwyse,
This yere to liue in welth and delice.
Lo where to commeth thy blandishyng promyse,
O false astrolagy and deuynatrice,
Of goddes secretes makyng thy selfe so wyse.
How true is for this yere thy prophecy.
The yere yet lasteth, and lo nowe[u] here I ly.
        O bryttill welth, as[v] full of bitternesse,
Thy single pleasure doubled is with payne.
Account my sorow first and my distresse,
In sondry wyse, and recken there agayne,
The ioy that I haue had, and I dare sayne,
For all my honour, endured yet haue I,
More wo then welth, and lo now here I ly.
        Where are our castels, now where are our towers,
Goodly Rychmonde sone art thou gone from me,
At Westminster that costly worke of yours,
Myne owne dere lorde now shall I neuer see.
Almighty god vouchesafe to graunt that ye,
For you and your children well may edefy.

t. auncestry? *55a*] auncestry, *55b, 65, 73*
u. nowe *55a, 73*] now *55b, 65*
v. *The original reads* ay.

---

4. *Fere:* wife.

My palyce bylded is, and lo now here I ly.
Adew myne owne dere spouse my worthy lorde,
The faithfull loue, that dyd vs both combyne,
In mariage and peasable concorde,
Into your handes here I cleane resyne,
To be bestowed vppon your children and myne.
Erst wer you father, and now must ye supply,
The mothers part also, for lo now here I ly.
Farewell my doughter lady Margerete.
God wotte full oft it greued hath my mynde,[w]
That ye should go where we should seldome[x] mete.
Now am I gone, and haue left you behynde.
O mortall folke that we be very blynde.
That we least feare, full oft it is most nye,
From you depart I fyrst, and lo now here I lye.
Farewell Madame my lordes worthy mother,
Comfort your sonne, and be ye of good chere.
Take all a worth, for it will be no nother.
Farewell my doughter Katherine late the fere,
To prince Arthur myne owne chyld so dere,
It booteth not for me to wepe or cry,
Pray for my soule, for lo now here I ly.
Adew lord Henry my louyng sonne adew.
Our lorde[y] encrease your honour and estate,
Adew my doughter Mary bright of hew,
God make you vertuous wyse and fortunate.
Adew swete hart my litle doughter Kate,
Thou shalt swete babe suche[z] is thy desteny,
Thy mother neuer know, for lo now here I ly.
Lady Cicyly Anne and Katheryne,
Farewell my welbeloved sisters three,
O lady Briget other sister myne,
Lo here the ende of worldly vanitee.

w. mynde, *55a, 55b, 73*] mynde. *65*
x. seldome *55a, 55b, 73*] seldom *65*
y. lorde *55a, 73*] lord *55b, 65*
z. suche *55a, 55b, 73*] such *65*

Now well are ye that earthly foly flee,
And heuenly thynges loue and magnify,
Farewell and pray for me, for lo now here I ly.
A dew[a] my lordes, a dew[b] my ladies all,
A dew[c] my faithful seruauntes euerych one,
A dew[d] my commons whom I neuer shall,[e]
See in this world[f] wherfore to the alone,
Immortall god verely three and one,
I me commende. Thy infinite mercy,
Shew to thy seruant, for lo now here I ly.

Certain meters in English written by master Thomas More in hys youth for the boke of fortune, and caused them to be printed in the begynnyng of that boke.[5]

The wordes of Fortune to the people.

Mine high estate power and auctoritie,
If ye ne know, enserche and ye shall spye,
That richesse, worship, welth, and dignitie,
Joy, rest, and peace, and all thyng fynally,
That any pleasure or profit may come by,
To mannes comfort, ayde, and sustinaunce,
Is all at my deuyse and ordinaunce.
Without my fauour there is nothyng wonne.
Many a matter haue I brought at last,
To good conclusion, that fondly was begonne.
And many a purpose, bounden sure and fast
With wise prouision, I haue ouercast.
Without good happe there may no wit suffise.
Better is to be fortunate than wyse.

a. A dew *55a, 55b, 65*] Adew *73*
b. a dew *55a, 55b, 65*] adew *73*
c. A dew *55a, 55b, 65*] Adew *73*
d. A dew *55a, 55b, 65*] Adew *73*
e. shall, *55a, 55b*] shall *65, 73*
f. world *55a, 55b*] world, *65, 73*

---

5. "Certain meters": "The Wordes of Fortune to the People," *Workes,* sigs. ¶[v]^{v}–[vi]^{r}.

And therefore hath there some men bene or this,
My deadly foes and written many a boke,
To my disprayse. And other cause there nys,
But for me list not frendly on them loke.
Thus lyke the fox they fare that once forsoke,
The pleasaunt grapes, and gan for to defy them,
Because he lept and yet could not come by them.
But let them write theyr labour is in vayne.
For well ye wote, myrth, honour, and richesse,
Much better is than penury and payne.
The nedy wretch that lingereth in distresse,
Without myne helpe is euer comfortlesse,
A wery burden odious and loth,
To all the world, and eke to him selfe both.
But he that by my fauour may ascende,
To mighty power and excellent degree,
A common wele to gouerne and defende,
O in how blist condicion standeth he:
Him self in honour and felicite,
And ouer that, may forther and increase,
A region hole in ioyfull rest and peace.
Now in this poynt there is no more to say,
Eche man hath of him self the gouernaunce.
Let euery wight than folowe his owne way,
And he that out of pouertee and mischaunce,
List for to liue, and wyll him selfe enhaunce,
In wealth and richesse, come forth and wayte on me.
And he that wyll be a beggar, let hym be.

THOMAS MORE to them that trust in Fortune.[6]

Thou that are prowde of honour[g] shape or kynne,[h]
That hepest vp this wretched worldes treasure,

g. honour *55a, 55b, 65*] honour, *73*
h. kynne, *55a, 55b, 73*] kynne *65*

6. "Thomas More to Them that Trust in Fortune," *Workes,* sigs. ¶[vi]^r–[viii]^r.

Thy fingers shrined with gold, thy tawny skynne,
With fresh apparyle garnished out of measure,
And wenest to haue fortune at thy pleasure,
Cast vp thyne eye, and loke how slipper chaunce,
Illudeth her men with chaunge and varyaunce.
Sometyme she loketh as louely[i] fayre and bright,
As goodly Uenus mother of Cupyde.
She becketh and she smileth on euery wight.
But this chere fayned, may not long abide.
There cometh a cloude, and farewell all our pryde.
Like any serpent she beginneth to swell,
And looketh as fierce as any fury of hell.
Yet for all that we brotle men are fayne,
(So wretched is our nature and so blynde)
As soone as Fortune list to laugh agayne,
With fayre countenaunce and disceitfull mynde,
To crouche and knele and gape after the wynde,
Not one or twayne but thousandes in a rout,
Lyke swarmyng bees come flickeryng her aboute.
Then as a bayte she bryngeth forth her ware,
Siluer, gold, riche perle, and precious stone:
On whiche the mased people gase and stare,
And gape therefore, as dogges doe for the bone.
Fortune at them laugheth, and in her trone
Amyd her treasure and waueryng rychesse,
Prowdly she houeth[7] as lady and empresse.
Fast by her syde doth wery labour stand,
Pale fere also, and sorow all bewept,
Disdayn and hatred on that other hand,
Eke restles watche fro slepe with trauayle kept,
His eyes drowsy and lokyng as he slept.
Before her standeth daunger and enuy,
Flattery, dysceyt, mischiefe and tiranny.
About her commeth all the world to begge.

i. louely *55a, 55b, 65*] louely, *73*

---

7. *Houeth:* presides.

He asketh lande, and he to pas would bryng,
This toye and that, and all not worth an egge:
He would in loue prosper aboue all thyng:
He kneleth downe and would be made a kyng:
He forceth[8] not so he may money haue,
Though all the worlde accompt hym for a knaue.
Lo thus ye see diuers heddes, diuers wittes.
Fortune alone as diuers as they all,
Vnstable here and there among them flittes:
And at auenture downe her giftes fall,
Catch who so may she throweth great and small
Not to all men, as commeth sonne or dewe,
But for the most part, all among a fewe.
And yet her brotell giftes long may not last.
He that she gaue them, loketh prowde and hye.
She whirlth about and pluckth away as fast,
And geueth them to an other by and by.
And thus from man to man continually,
She vseth to geue and take, and slily tosse,
One man to wynnyng of an others losse.
And when she robbeth one, down goth his pryde.
He wepeth and wayleth and curseth her full sore.
But he that receueth it, on that other syde,
Is glad, and blesth her often tymes therefore.
But in a whyle when she loueth hym no more,
She glydeth from hym, and her giftes to.[j]
And he her curseth, as other fooles do.[k]
Alas the folysh people can not cease,
Ne voyd her trayne, tyll they the harme do fele.
About her alway, besely they preace.
But lord how he doth thynk hym self full wele.
That may set once his hande vppon her whele.
He holdeth fast: but vpward as he flieth,

j. to. *55a, 55b, 65*] to, *73*
k. do. *55b, 65, 73*] do, *55a*

8. *Forceth:* cares.

She whippeth her whele about, and there he lyeth.
Thus fell Julius from his mighty power.
Thus fell Darius the worthy kyng of Perse.
Thus fell Alexander the great conquerour.
Thus many mo then I may well reherse.
Thus double fortune, when she lyst reuerse
Her slipper fauour fro them that in her trust,
She fleeth her wey and leyeth them in the dust.
She sodeinly enhaunceth them aloft.
And sodeynly mischeueth all the flocke.
The head that late lay easily and full soft,
In stede of pylows lyeth after on the blocke.
And yet alas the most cruell proude mocke:
The deynty mowth that ladyes kissed haue,
She bryngeth in the case to kysse a knaue.
In chaungyng of her course, the chaunge shewth this,
Vp startth a knaue, and downe there falth a knight,
The beggar ryche, and the ryche man pore is.
Hatred is turned to loue, loue to despyght.
This is her sport, thus proueth she her myght.
Great boste she maketh yf one be by her power,
Welthy and wretched both within an howre.
Pouertee that of her giftes wyl nothing take,
Wyth mery chere, looketh vppon the prece,
And seeth how fortunes houshold goeth to wrake.
Fast by her standeth the wyse Socrates.[l]
Arristippus, Pythagoras, and many a lese.[m]
Of olde philosophers. And eke agaynst the sonne
Bekyth hym poore Diogenes in his tonne.
With her is Byas, whose countrey lackt defence,
And whylom of their foes stode so in dout,
That eche man hastely gan to cary thence,
And asked hym why he nought caryed out.
I bere quod he all myne with me about:
Wisedom he ment, not fortunes brotle fees.

l. Socrates. *55a, 55b, 73*] Socrates, *65*
m. lese. *55a*] lese, *55b, 65;* lese *73*

For nought he counted his that he might leese.[9]
Heraclitus eke, lyst felowship to kepe
With glad pouertee, Democritus also:
Of which the fyrst can neuer cease but wepe,
To see how thick the blynded people go,
With labour great to purchase care and wo.
That other laugheth to see the foolysh apes,
Howe earnestly they walk about theyr capes.[n]
Of this poore sect, it is comen vsage,
Onely to take that nature may sustayne,
Banishing cleane all other surplusage,
They be content, and of nothyng complayne.
No nygarde eke is of his good so fayne.
But they more pleasure haue a thousande folde,
The secrete draughtes of nature to beholde.
Set fortunes servauntes by them and ye wull,
That one is free, that other euer thrall,
That one content, that other neuer full.[o]
That one in suretye, that other lyke to fall.
Who lyst to aduise them bothe, parceyue he shall,
As great difference between them as we see,
Betwixte wretchednes and felicite.
Nowe[p] haue I shewed you bothe: these[q] whiche ye lyst,
Stately fortune, or humble pouertee:
That is to say, nowe lyeth[r] it in your fyst,
To take here bondage, or free libertee.
But in thys poynte and ye do after me,
Draw you to fortune, and labour her to please,
If that ye thynke your selfe to well at ease.
And fyrst vppon the louely shall she smile,

n. *The original reads* japes.
o. full. *55a, 73*] full, *55b, 65*
p. Nowe *55a, 73*] Now *55b, 65*
q. *A mistake for* chese
r. lyeth *55a, 55b, 73*] lieth *65*

---

9. *Leese:* lose.

And frendly on the cast her wandering eyes,
Embrace the in her armes, and for a whyle,
Put the and kepe the in a fooles paradise:
And foorth with all what so thou lyst deuise,
She wyll the graunt it liberally parhappes:
But for all that beware of after clappes.
Recken you neuer of her fauoure sure:
Ye may in clowds as easily trace an hare,
Or in drye lande cause fishes to endure,
And make the burnyng fyre his heate to spare,
And all thys worlde in compace to forfare,[1]
As her to make by craft or engine stable,
That of her nature is euer variable.
Serue her day and nyght as reuerently,
Vppon thy knees as any seruaunt may,
And in conclusion, that thou shalt winne thereby
Shall not be worth thy servyce I dare say.
And looke yet what she geueth the to day,
With labour wonne she shall happly to morow[s]
Pluck it agayne out of thyne hande with sorow.
Wherefore yf thou in suretye lyst to stande,
Take pouerties parte and let prowde fortune go,
Receyue nothyng that commeth from her hande.
Loue maner and vertue: they be onely tho.
Whiche double fortune may not take the fro.
Then mayst thou boldly defye her turnyng chaunce:[t]
She can the neyther hynder nor auaunce.
But and thou wylt nedes medle with her treasure,
Trust not therein, and spende it liberally.
Beare the not proude, nor take not out of measure.
Bylde not thyne house on heyth vp in the skye.
None falleth farre, but he that climbeth hye,
Remember nature sent the hyther bare,
The gyftes of fortune count them borowed ware.

s. morow *55a, 55b, 73*] morow. *65*
t. chaunce: *55b, 65, 73*] chaunce*: 55a*

1. *Forfare:* perish.

THOMAS MORE to them that seke Fortune.[2]

Who so delyteth to prouen and assay,
Of waveryng fortune the vncertayne lot,
If that the aunswere please you not alway,
Blame ye not me: for I commaunde you not,
Fortune to trust, and eke full well ye wot,
I haue of her no brydle in my fist,
She renneth loose, and turneth where she lyst.
The rollyng dyse in whome your lucke doth stande,
With whose vnhappy chaunce ye be so wroth,
Ye knowe your selfe came neuer in myne hande.
Lo in this ponde be fyshe and frogges both.
Cast in your nette: but be you liefe or lothe,
Hold you content as fortune lyst assyne:
For it is your owne fishyng and not myne.
And though in one chaunce fortune you offend,
Grudge not there at, but beare a mery face.
In many an other she shall it amende.
There is no manne so farre out of her grace,
But he sometyme hath comfort and solace:
Ne none agayne so farre foorth in her fauour,
That is full satisfyed with her behauiour.
Fortune is stately, solemne, prowde, and hye:
And rychesse geueth, to haue seruyce therefore.
The nedy begger catcheth an halfpeny:
Some manne a thousande pounde, some lesse some more.
But for all that she kepeth euer in store,
From euery manne some parcell of his wyll,
That he may pray therfore[u] and serue her styll.
Some manne hath good, but chyldren hath he none.
Some man hath both, but he can get none health.
Some hath al thre, but vp to honours trone,
Can he not crepe, by no maner of stelth.

u. therfore *55a, 55b, 73*] therefore *65*

2. "Thomas More to Them that Seke Fortune," *Workes,* sig. ¶[viii]$^{r-v}$.

To some she sendeth, children, ryches, welthe,
Honour, woorshyp, and reuerence all hys lyfe:[v]
But yet she pyncheth hym with a shrewde wyfe.
Then for asmuch as it is fortunes guyse,
To graunt no manne all thyng that he wyll axe,
But as her selfe lyst order and deuyse,
Doth euery manne his parte diuide and tax,
I counsayle you eche one trusse vp your packes,
And take no thyng at all, or be content,
With suche rewarde as fortune hath you sent.
All thynges in this boke that ye shall rede,
Doe[w] as ye lyst, there shall no manne you bynde,
Them to beleue, as surely as your crede.
But notwithstandyng certes in my mynde,
I durst well swere, as true ye shall them fynde,
In euery poynt eche answere by and by,
As are the iudgementes of astronomye.

The Descripcion of RICHARD the thirde.[3]

Richarde the third sonne, of whom we nowe entreate, was in witte and courage egall with either of them, in bodye and prowesse farre vnder them bothe, little of stature, ill fetured of limmes, croke backed, his left shoulder much higher than his right, hard fauoured of visage, and such as is in states[4] called warlye, in other menne otherwise, he was malicious, wrathfull, enuious, and from afore his birth, euer frowarde. It is for trouth reported, that the duches his mother had so much a doe in her trauaile, that shee coulde not bee deliuered of hym vncutte: and that hee[x] came into the

v. lyfe *55a, 55b, 65*] life *73*
w. Doe *55a, 55b, 73*] Do *65*
x. hee *55a, 73*] he *55b, 65*

3. "The Descripcion of Richard the thirde" is the first of several consecutive passages quoted here from *The history of king Richard the thirde, Workes,* sigs. c.iii[r]–[v][v]; pp. 37–42.

4. *States:* "Person[s] of high rank" (*Dictionary,* sense 15); SJ cites this passage (mutatis) as a gloss on *principality* in *Two Gentlemen of Verona* II.iv. 148 (*Yale* VII.166).

worlde[y] with the feete forwarde, as menne bee borne outwarde, and (as the fame runneth) also not vntothed, whither menne of hatred reporte aboue the trouthe, or elles that nature chaunged her course in hys beginninge, whiche in the course of his lyfe many thinges vnnaturallye committed. None euill captaine was hee in the warre, as to whiche his disposicion was more metely then for peace. Sundrye victories hadde hee, and sommetime ouerthrowes, but neuer in defaulte as for his owne parsone, either of hardinesse or polytike order, free was hee called of dyspence, and sommewhat aboue hys[z] power liberall, with large giftes hee get him vnstedfaste frendeshippe, for whiche hee was fain to pil and spoyle in other places, and get him stedfast hatred. Hee was close and secrete, a deepe dissimuler, lowlye of counteynaunce, arrogant of heart, outwardly coumpinable where he inwardely hated, not letting to kisse whome hee thoughte to kyll: dispitious and cruell, not for euill will alway, but after for ambicion, and either for the suretie or[a] encrease of his estate. Frende and foo was muche what indifferent, where his aduauntage grew, he spared no mans deathe, whose life withstoode his purpose. He slewe with his owne handes king Henry the sixt, being prisoner in the Tower, as menne constantly saye, and that without commaundement or knoweledge of the king, whiche woulde vndoubtedly yf he had entended that thinge, haue appointed that boocherly office, to some other then his owne borne brother.

Somme wise menne also weene, that his drift couertly conuayde, lacked not in helping furth his brother of Clarence to his death: whiche hee resisted openly, howbeit somwhat (as menne deme) more faintly then he that wer hartely minded to his welth. And they that thus deme, think that he long time in king Edwardes life, forethought to be king in that case the king his brother (whose life hee looked that euil[b] dyete shoulde shorten) shoulde[c] happen to decease (as in dede he

y. worlde *55a, 73*] world *55b, 65*
z. hys *55a, 55b, 73*] his *65*
a. or *55a, 73*] and *55b, 65*
b. euil *55a, 55b, 65*] euill *73*
c. shoulde *55a, 55b, 73*] should *65*

did) while his children wer yonge. And thei deme, that for thys intente he was gladde of his brothers death the duke of Clarence, whose life must nedes haue hindered hym so entendynge, whither the same duke of Clarence hadde kepte him true to his nephew the yonge king, or enterprised to be kyng himselfe. But of al this pointe, is there no certaintie, and whoso diuineth vppon coniectures, maye as wel shote to farre as to short. How beit this haue I by credible informacion learned, that the selfe nighte in whiche kynge[d] Edwarde died, one Mystlebrooke longe ere mornynge, came in greate haste to the house of one Pottyer dwellyng in Reddecrosse strete without Crepulgate: and when he was with hastye rappyng quickly letten in, hee shewed vnto Pottyer that kynge Edwarde was departed. By my trouthe manne quod Pottier then wyll my mayster the duke of Gloucester bee kynge. What cause hee hadde soo to thynke harde it is to saye, whyther hee being toward him, anye thynge knewe that hee suche thynge purposed, or otherwyse had anye inkelynge thereof: for hee was not likelye to speake it of noughte.

But nowe[e] to returne to the course of this hystorye, were it that the duke of Gloucester hadde of old foreminded this conclusion, or was nowe at erste thereunto moued, and putte in hope by the occasion of the tender age of the younge princes, his nephues (as opportunitye and lykelyhoode of spede, putteth a manne in courage of that hee neuer entended) certayn is it that hee contriued theyr destruccion, with the vsurpacion of the regal dignitye vppon hymselfe. And for as muche as hee well wiste and holpe to mayntayn, a long continued grudge and hearte brennynge betwene the quenes kinred and the kinges blood eyther partye enuying others authoritye, he nowe thought that their deuision shoulde bee (as it was in dede) a fortherlye begynnynge to the pursuite of his intente, and a sure ground for the foundacion of al his building yf he might firste vnder the pretext of reuengynge of olde displeasure, abuse the anger and ygnor-

d. kynge *55a, 55b, 73*] kyng *65*
e. nowe *55a, 55b, 73*] now *65*

aunce of the tone partie, to the destruccion of the tother: and then wynne to his purpose as manye as he coulde: and those that coulde not be wonne, myght be loste ere they looked therefore. For of one thynge was hee certayne, that if his entente were perceiued, he shold soone haue made peace beetwene the bothe parties, with his owne bloude.

Kynge Edwarde in his life, albeit that this discencion beetwene hys frendes sommewhat yrked hym: yet in his good health he sommewhat the lesse regarded it, because hee thought whatsoeuer busines shoulde falle betwene them, hymselfe should alwaye bee hable to rule bothe the parties.

But in his last sicknesse, when hee receiued his naturall strengthe soo sore enfebled, that hee dyspayred all recouerye, then hee consyderynge the youthe of his chyldren, albeit hee nothynge lesse mistrusted then that that happened, yet well forseynge that manye harmes myghte growe by theyr debate, whyle the youth of hys children shoulde lacke discrecion of themself[f] and good counsayle,[g] of their frendes, of whiche either party shold counsayle for their owne commodity and rather by pleasaunte aduyse too wynne themselfe fauour, then by profitable aduertisemente to do the children good, he called some of them before him that were at variaunce, and in especyall the lorde marques Dorsette the quenes sonne by her fyrste housebande, and Richarde the lorde Hastynges, a noble man, than lorde chaumberlayne agayne whome the quene specially grudged, for the great fauoure the kyng bare hym, and also for that shee[h] thoughte hym secretelye familyer with the kynge in wanton coumpanye. Her kynred also bare hym sore, as well for that the kynge hadde made hym captayne of Calyce (whiche office the lorde Ryuers, brother to the quene[i] claimed of the kinges former promise)[j] as for diuerse other great giftes whiche[k] hee re-

f. themself *55a, 73*] themself, *55b, 65*
g. counsayle, *55a*] counsayle *55b, 65, 73*
h. shee *55a, 55b, 73*] she *65*
i. quene *55a*] quene, *55b, 65, 73*
j. promyse) *55b, 65*] promyse *55a, 73*
k. whiche *55a, 55b, 65*] which *73*

ceyued, that they loked for. When these lordes with diuerse other of bothe the parties were comme in presence, the kynge liftinge vppe himselfe and vndersette with pillowes, as it is reported on this wyse sayd vnto them, My lordes, my dere kinsmenne and alies, in what plighte I lye you see, and I feele. By whiche the lesse whyle I looke to lyue with you, the more depelye am I moued to care in what case I leaue you, for such as I leaue you, suche bee my children lyke to fynde you. Whiche if they shoulde (that Godde forbydde) fynde you at varyaunce, myght happe to fall themselfe at warre ere their discrecion woulde serue to sette you at peace. Ye se[l] their youthe, of whiche I recken the onely suretie to reste in youre concord.[m] For it suffiseth not that al you loue them, yf eche of you hate other.[n] If they wer menne, your faithfulnesse happelye woulde suffise. But childehood must be maintained by mens authoritye, and slipper youth vnderpropped with elder counsayle, which neither they can haue, but ye geue it, nor ye geue it, yf ye gree not. For wher eche laboureth to breake that the other maketh, and for hatred of ech of others parson, impugneth eche others counsayle, there must it nedes bee long ere anye good conclusion goe forwarde. And also while either partye laboureth to be chiefe, flattery shall haue more place then plaine and faithfull aduyse, of whyche muste needes ensue the euyll bringing vppe of the prynce, whose mynd in tender youth infect, shal redily fal to mischief and riot, and drawe down with this noble realme[o] to ruine,[p] but if grace turn him to wisdom:[q] which if God send, then thei that by euill menes before pleased him best, shal after fall farthest out of fauour, so that euer at length euil driftes dreue to nought, and good plain wayes prosper. Great variaunce hath ther long bene betwene you, not alway for great causes.

l. se *55a, 73*] see *55b, 65*
m. concord. *55b, 65, 73*] concord, *55a*
n. other. *55b, 65, 73*] other, *55a*
o. realme *55a, 73*] relme *55b, 65*
p. ruine, *55a, 73*] ruine: *55b, 65*
q. wisdom: *55a, 73*] wisdom, *55b, 65*

Sometime a thing right wel intended, our misconstruccion turneth vnto worse or a smal displeasure done vs, eyther our owne affeccion or euil tongues agreueth. But this wote I well ye neuer had so great cause of hatred, as ye[r] haue of loue. That we be al men, that we be christen men, this shall I leaue for prechers to tel you (and yet I wote nere whither any preachers wordes ought more to moue you, then his that is by and by gooying to the place that thei all preache of.) But this shal I desire you to remember, that the one parte of you is of my bloode, the other of myne alies, and eche of yow with other, eyther of kinred[s] or affinitie, whiche spirytuall kynred of affynyty, if the sacramentes of Christes churche, beare that weyghte with vs that woulde Godde thei did, shoulde no lesse moue vs to charitye, then the respecte of fleshlye consanguinitye. Oure Lorde forbydde, that you loue together the worse, for the selfe cause that you ought to loue the better. And yet that happeneth. And no where fynde wee so deadlye debate, as amonge them, whyche by nature and lawe moste oughte to agree together. Suche a pestilente serpente is ambicion and desyre of vaine glorye and soueraintye, whiche amonge states where he once entreth crepeth foorth so farre, tyll with deuision and variaunce hee turneth all to mischiefe. Firste[t] longing to be nexte the best, afterwarde egall with the beste, and at laste chiefe and aboue the beste. Of which immoderate appetite of woorship, and thereby of debate and dissencion what losse, what sorowe, what trouble hathe[u] within these fewe yeares growen in this realme, I praye Godde as well forgeate as wee well[v] remember.

Whiche thinges yf I coulde as well haue foresene, as I haue with my more payne then pleasure proued, by Goddes blessed Ladie (that was euer his othe) I woulde neuer haue won the courtesye of mennes knees, with the losse of soo many heades. But sithen thynges passed cannot be gaine

r. ye *55a, 55b, 73*] he *65*
s. kinred *55a, 73*] kindred *55b, 65*
t. Firste *55a, 73*] First *55b, 65*
u. hathe *55a, 73*] hath *55b, 65*
v. well *55a, 73*] wel *55b, 65*

called, muche oughte wee the more beware, by what occasion we haue taken soo greate hurte afore, that we eftesoones fall not in that occasion agayne. Nowe be those griefes passed, and all is (Godde be thanked) quiete, and likelie righte wel to prosper in wealthfull peace vnder youre coseyns my children, if Godde sende them life and you loue. Of whyche[w] twoo thinges, the lesse losse wer they by whome thoughe Godde dydde hys pleasure, yet shoulde the realme[x] alway finde kinges and paraduenture as good kinges. But yf you among youre[y] selfe in a childes reygne fall at debate, many a good man shall perish and happely he to, and ye to, ere thys land finde peace again. Wherfore in these last wordes that euer I looke to speak with you: I exhort you and require you al, for the loue that you haue euer borne to me, for the loue that I haue euer born to you, for the loue that our Lord beareth to vs all, from this time forwarde, all grieues forgotten, eche of you loue other. Whiche I verelye truste you will, if ye any thing earthly regard, either Godde or your king, affinitie or kinred, this realme, your owne countrey, or your owne surety. And therewithal the king no longer enduring to sitte vp, laide him down on his right side, his face towarde them: and none was there present that coulde refrain from weping. But the lordes recomforting him with as good wordes as they could, and answering for the time as thei thought to stand with his pleasure, there in his presence (as by their wordes appered)[z] ech forgaue other, and ioyned their hands together, when (as it after appeared by their dedes) their hearts wer far a sonder. As sone as the king was departed, the noble prince his sonne drew toward London, which at the time of his decease, kept his houshold at Ludlow in Wales. Which countrey being far of from the law and recourse to iustice,[a] was begon to be farre oute of good

w. whyche *55a, 73*] whiche *55b, 65*
x. realme *55a, 73*] realme, *55b, 65*
y. youre *55a, 73*] your *55b, 65*
z. appered) *73*] appered *55a, 55b, 65*
a. iustice *55a, 73*] justice *55b, 65*

wyll and waxen wild, robbers and riuers walking at libertie vncorrected. And for this encheason the prince was in the life of his father sente thither, to the end that the authoritie of his presence,[b] should refraine euill disposed parsons fro the boldnes of their formar[c] outerages, to the gouernaunce and ordering of this yong prince at his sending thyther, was there appointed Sir Antony Woduile lord Riuers and brother vnto the quene, a right honourable man, as valiaunte of hande as politike in counsayle. Adioyned wer there vnto him other of the same partie, and in effect euery one as he was nerest of kin vnto the quene, so was planted next about the prince. That drifte by the quene not vnwisely deuised, whereby her bloode mighte of youth be rooted in the princes fauor,[d] the duke of Gloucester turned vnto their destruccion, and vpon that grounde set the foundacion of all his vnhappy building. For whom soeuer he perceiued, either at variance with them, or bearing himself their fauor, hee brake vnto them, some by mouth, som by writing and[e] secret messengers, that it neyther was reason nor in any wise to be suffered, that the yong king their master and kinsmanne, shoold bee in the handes and custodye of his mothers kinred, sequestred in maner from theyr compani and attendance, of which eueri one ought him as faithful seruice as they, and manye of them far more honorable part of kin then his mothers side: whose blood (quod he) sauing the kinges pleasure, was ful vnmetely to be matched with his: whiche nowe to be as who say remoued from the kyng, and the lesse noble to be left aboute him, is (quod he) neither honorable to hys magestie, nor vnto vs, and also to his grace no surety to haue the mightiest of his frendes from him, and vnto vs no little ieopardy, to suffer our welproued euil willers, to grow in ouergret authoritie with the prince in youth, namely which is lighte of beliefe and sone perswaded. Ye remember I trow king Edward himself,

b. presence, *55a, 73*] presence *55b, 65*
c. formar *55a, 55b, 65*] former *73*
d. fauor *55a, 73*] fauour *55b, 65*
e. and *55a, 73*] or *55b, 65*

albeit he was a manne of age and of discrecion, yet was he in manye thynges ruled by the bende, more then[f] stode either with his honour, or our profite, or with the commoditie of any manne els, except onely the immoderate aduauncement of them selfe. Whiche whither they sorer thirsted after their owne weale, or our woe, it wer hard I wene to gesse. And if some folkes frendship had not holden better place with the king, then any respect of kinred, thei might peraduenture easily haue be trapped and brought to confusion somme of vs ere this. Why not as easily as they haue done some other alreadye, as neere of his royal bloode as we. But our Lord hath wrought his wil, and thanke be to his grace that peril is paste. Howe be it as great is growing, yf wee suffer this yonge kyng in oure enemyes hande, whiche without his wyttyng, might abuse the name of his commaundement, to ani of our vndoing, which thyng God and good prouision forbyd. Of which good prouision none of us hath any thing the lesse nede, for the late made attonemente, in whiche the kinges pleasure hadde more place then the parties willes. Nor none of vs I beleue is so vnwyse, ouersone to truste a newe frende made of an olde foe, or to think that an houerly kindnes, sodainely contract in one houre continued, yet scant a fortnight, shold be deper setled in their stomackes: then a long accustomed malice many yeres rooted.

With these wordes and writynges and suche other, the duke of Gloucester sone set a fyre, them that were of themself ethe to kindle, and in especiall twayne, Edwarde duke of Buckingham, and Richarde lorde Hastinges and chaumberlayn, both men of honour and of great power. The tone by longe succession from his ancestrie, the tother by his office and the kinges fauor. These two not bearing eche to other so muche loue, as hatred bothe vnto the quenes parte: in this poynte accorded together wyth the duke of Gloucester, that they wolde vtterlye amoue fro the kynges companye, all his mothers frendes, vnder the name of their enemyes. Vpon this concluded, the duke of Gloucester vnderstandyng,

f. then *55a, 55b, 73*] than *65*

that the lordes whiche at that tyme were aboute the kyng, entended to bryng him vppe to his coronacion, accoumpanied with suche power of theyr frendes, that it shoulde[g] bee harde for hym to brynge his purpose to passe, without the gathering and great assemble of people and in maner of open warre, whereof the ende he wiste was doubtuous, and in which the kyng being on their side, his part should haue the face and name of a rebellion: he secretly therefore by diuers meanes, caused the quene to be perswaded and brought in the mynd, that it neither wer nede, and also shold be ieopardous, the king to come vp strong. For where as nowe euery lorde loued other, and none other thing studyed vppon, but aboute the coronacion and honoure of the king: if the lordes of her kinred shold[h] assemble in the kinges name muche people, thei should geue the lordes atwixte whome and them hadde bene sommetyme debate, to feare and suspecte, leste they shoulde gather thys people, not for the kynges sauegarde whome no manne enpugned,[i] but for theyr destruccion, hauying more regarde to their olde variaunce, then their newe attonement. For whiche cause thei shoulde assemble on the other partie muche people agayne for their defence, whose power she wyste wel farre stretched. And thus should all the realme fall on a rore. And of al the hurte that therof should ensue, which was likely not to be litle, and the most harme there like to fal wher she lest would, all the worlde woulde put her and her kinred in the wyght, and say that thei had vnwyselye and vntrewlye also, broken the amitie and peace that the kyng her husband so prudentelye made, betwene hys kinne and hers in his death bed, and whiche the other party faithfully obserued.

The quene being in this wise perswaded, suche woorde sente vnto her sonne, and vnto her brother being aboute the kynge, and ouer that the duke of Gloucester hymselfe and other lordes the chiefe of hys bende, wrote vnto the kynge

g. shoulde *55a, 55b, 73*] should *65*
h. shold *55a, 55b, 73*] should *65*
i. enpugned *55a*] empugned *55b, 65, 73*

soo reuerentelye,[j] and to[k] the queenes frendes,[l] there soo louyngelye, that they nothynge earthelye mystrustynge, broughte the kynge vppe in greate haste, not in good spede, with a sober coumpanye. Nowe was the king in his waye to London gone, from Northampton, when these dukes of Gloucester and Buckyngham came thither. Where remained behynd, the lorde Ryuers[m] the kynges vncle, entendyng on the morowe to folow the kynge, and bee with hym at Stonye Stratford [n] miles thence, earely or hee departed. So was there made that nyghte muche frendely chere betwene these dukes and the lorde[o] Riuers a greate while. But incontinente after that they were oppenlye with greate courtesye departed, and the lorde Riuers lodged, the dukes secretelye with a fewe of their moste priuye frendes, sette them downe in counsayle, wherin[p] they spent a great parte of the nyght. And at their risinge in the dawnyng of the day, thei sent about priuily to their seruantes in their innes and lodgynges about, geuinge them commaundemente to make them selfe shortely readye, for their lordes wer to horsebackward. Vppon whiche messages, manye of their folke were attendaunt, when manye of the lorde Riuers seruantes were vnreadye. Nowe hadde these dukes taken also into their custodye the kayes of the inne, that none shoulde passe foorth without theyr licence.

And ouer this in the hyghe waye towarde[q] Stonye Stratforde where the kynge laye, they hadde beestowed certayne of theyr folke, that shoulde sende[r] backe agayne, and compell to retourne, anye manne that were gotten oute of Northampton toward[s] Stonye Stratforde, tyll they should geue other lycence. For as muche as the dukes themselfe entended

j. reuerentelye *55a, 73*] reuerentlye *55b, 65*
k. to *55a, 55b, 73*] too *65*
l. frendes, *55a, 73*] frendes *55b, 65*
m. Ryuers *55a, 73*] Riuers *55b, 65*
n. *SJ's transcription reproduces the blank space in the original.*
o. lorde *55a, 55b, 65*] lord *73*
p. wherin *55a, 55b, 73*] wherein *65*
q. towarde *55a, 73*] toward *55b, 65*
r. sende *55a, 55b, 65*] send *73*
s. toward *55a, 55b, 73*] towarde *65*

for the shewe of theire dylygence, to bee the fyrste[t] that shoulde that daye attende vppon the kynges highnesse oute of that towne: thus bare they folke in hande. But when the lorde Ryuers vnderstode the gates closed, and the wayes on euerye side besette, neyther hys seruauntes nor hymself suffered to go oute, parceiuyng well so greate a thyng without his knowledge not begun for noughte, comparyng this maner present with this last nightes chere, in so few houres so gret a chaunge marueylouslye misliked. How be it sithe hee coulde not geat awaye, and keepe himselfe close, hee woulde not, leste he shoulde seeme to hyde himselfe for some secret feare of hys owne faulte, whereof he saw no such cause in hym self: he determined vppon the suretie of his own conscience, to goe boldelye to them, and inquire what thys matter myghte meane. Whome as soone as they sawe, they beganne to quarrell with hym, and saye, that hee intended to sette distaunce beetweene the kynge and them, and to brynge them to confusion, but it shoulde not lye in hys power. And when hee beganne (as hee was a very well spoken manne) in goodly wise to excuse himself, they taryed not the ende of his aunswere, but shortely tooke him and putte him in warde, and that done, foorthwyth wente to horsebacke, and tooke the waye to Stonye Stratforde. Where they founde the kinge with his companie readye to leape on horsebacke, and departe forwarde, to leaue that lodging for them, because it was to streighte for bothe coumpanies. And as sone as they came in his presence, they lighte adowne with all their companie aboute[u] them. To whome the duke of Buckingham saide, goe afore gentlemenne and yeomen, kepe youre rowmes. And thus in goodly arraye, thei came to the kinge, and on theire knees in very humble wise, salued his grace; whiche receyued them in very ioyous and amiable maner, nothinge earthlye knowing nor mistrustinge as yet. But euen by and by in his presence, they piked a quarell to the lorde Richard Graye, the kynges other brother by his mother, sayinge that hee with

t. fyrste *55a, 55b, 73*] fyrst *65*
u. aboute *55a, 55b, 73*] about *65*

the lorde marques his brother and the lorde Riuers his vncle, hadde coumpassed to rule the kinge and the realme, and to sette variaunce among the states, and to subdewe and destroye the noble blood of the realm. Toward the accoumplishinge whereof, they sayde that the lorde Marques hadde entered into the Tower of London, and thence taken out the kinges treasor, and sent menne to the sea. All whiche thinge these dukes wiste well were done for good purposes and necessari by the whole counsaile at London, sauing that sommewhat thei must sai. Vnto whiche woordes, the king[v] aunswered, what my brother Marques hath done I cannot saie. But in good faith I dare well aunswere for myne vncle Riuers and my brother here, that thei be innocent of any such matters. Ye my liege quod the duke of Buckingham thei haue kepte theire dealing in these matters farre fro the knowledge of your good grace. And foorthwith thei arrested the lord Richarde and Sir Thomas Waughan knighte, in the kinges presence, and broughte the king and all backe vnto Northampton, where they tooke againe further counsaile. And there they sent awaie from the kinge whom it pleased them, and sette newe seruantes aboute him, suche as lyked better them than him. At whiche dealinge hee wepte and was nothing contente, but it booted not. And at dyner the duke of Gloucester sente a dishe from his owne table to the lord Riuers, prayinge him to bee of good chere, all should be well inough. And he thanked the duke, and prayed the messenger to beare it to his nephewe the lorde Richard with the same message for his comfort, who he thought had more nede of coumfort,[w] as one to whom such aduersitie was straunge. But himself had been al his dayes in vre therewith, and therfore coulde beare it the better. But for al this coumfortable courtesye of the duke of Gloucester he sent the lord Riuers and the lorde Richarde with Sir Thomas Vaughan into the Northe countrey into diuers places to prison, and afterward al to Pomfrait, where they were in conclusion beheaded.

v. king *55a, 73*] sting *55b;* kinge *65*
w. coumfort *55a, 55b, 65*] comfort *73*

A letter written with a cole by Sir THOMAS MORE to hys doughter maistres MARGARET ROPER, within a whyle after he was prisoner in the Towre.[5]

Myne own good doughter, our lorde be thanked I am in good helthe of bodye, and in good quiet of minde: and of worldly thynges I no more desyer then[x] I haue. I beseche hym make you all mery in the hope of heauen. And such thynges as I somewhat longed to talke with you all, concerning the worlde to come, our Lorde put theim into your myndes, as I truste he dothe and better to by hys holy spirite: who blesse you and preserue you all. Written wyth a cole by your tender louing father, who in hys pore prayers forgetteth none of you all[y] nor your babes, nor your nurses, nor your good husbandes, nor your good husbandes shrewde wyues, nor your fathers shrewde wyfe neither, nor our other frendes. And thus fare ye hartely well for lacke of paper.

THOMAS MORE, knight.

Two short ballettes which Sir THOMAS MORE made for hys pastime while he was prisoner in the Tower of London.[6]

LEWYS the lost louer.

Ey flatering fortune, loke thou neuer so fayre,
Or neuer so plesantly begin to smile,
As though thou wouldst my ruine all repayre,
During my life thou shalt me not begile.
Trust shall I God, to entre in a while.[z]
Hys hauen or heauen sure and vniforme.
Euer after thy calme, loke I for a storme.

x. then *55a, 55b, 73*] than *65*
y. all *55a, 55b, 65*] all, *73*
z. while. *55a, 55b, 73*] while *65*

5. "A letter," *Workes,* p. 1430.
6. "Two short ballettes," *Workes,* pp. 1432–33.

DAUY the dycer.

Long was I lady Lucke[a] your seruing man,
And now haue lost agayne all that I gat,
Wherfore whan I thinke on you nowe[b] and than,
And in my mynde remember this and that,
Ye may not blame me though I beshrew your cat,[7]
But in fayth I blesse you agayne a thousand times,
For lending me now some laysure to make rymes.

At the same time with Sir *Thomas More* lived *Skelton,* the poet laureate of *Henry* VIII. from whose works it seems proper to insert a few stanzas, though he cannot be said to have attained great elegance of language.[8]

The prologue to the Bouge of Courte.

In Autumpne whan the sonne in vyrgyne
By radyante hete enryped hath our corne
Whan[c] Luna full of mutabylyte
As Emperes the dyademe hath worne
Of our pole artyke, smylynge halfe in scorne
At our[d] foly,[e] and our vnstedfastnesse
The time whan Mars to warre hym dyd dres,
I callynge to mynde the greate auctoryte
Of poetes olde, whiche full craftely
Vnder as couerte termes as coulde be
Can touche a trouth, and cloke subtylly
With fresshe vtteraunce full sentencyously
Dyuerse in style some spared not vyce to wryte

a. Lucke *55a, 73*] Luke *55b, 65*
b. nowe *55a, 55b, 73*] now *65*
c. Whan *55a, 73*] When *55b, 65*
d. our *55a, 65, 73*] out *55b*
e. foly, *55a, 73*] foly *55b, 65*

7. *Cat:* perhaps a kind of cheating or deception sometimes practiced in games of chance (see *Dictionary,* s.v. *cat in the pan; OED,* s.v. *cat* III.12).

8. John Skelton, *Pithy Pleasaunt and Profitable Workes* (1736), "Prologue to the *Bouge of Court,*" ll. 1–35, pp. 59–60 (Watkins, pp. 108–09); SJ prints five of the eighteen stanzas. Cf. Warton's comment that Skelton "contributed not the least share of improvement to what his ancestors had left him" (see p. 118 above).

Some of mortalitie nobly dyd endyte
Whereby I rede, theyr renome and theyr fame
Maye neuer dye, but euermore endure
I was sore moued to a forse the same
But ignoraunce full soone dyde me dyscure
And shewed that in this arte I was not sure
For to illumine she sayd I was to dulle
Aduysynge me my penne awaye to pulle
And not to wryte, for he so wyll atteyne
Excedyng ferther than his connynge is
His heed maye[f] be harde, but feble is brayne
Yet haue I knowen suche er this
But of reproche surely he maye[g] not mys
That clymmeth hyer than he may fotinge haue
What and he slyde downe, who shall him saue?
Thus vp and downe my mynde was drawen and cast
That I ne wyste what to do was beste
So sore enwered that I was at the laste
Enforsed to slepe, and for to take some reste
And to lye downe as soone as I my dreste
At Harwyche porte slumbrynge as I laye
In myne hostes house called powers keye[h]

Of the wits that flourished in the reign of *Henry* VIII. none has been more frequently celebrated than the earl of *Surry;* and this history would therefore have been imperfect without some specimens of his works, which yet it is not easy to distinguish from those of Sir *Thomas Wyat* and others, with which they are confounded in the edition that has fallen into my hands.[9] The three first are, I believe, *Surry*'s; the rest, being of the same age, are selected, some as examples of different

f. maye *55a, 55b, 73*] may *65*
g. maye *55a, 55b, 73*] may *65*
h. keye *55a, 73*] keye. *55b, 65*

9. *The Poems of Henry Howard, Earl of Surrey . . . with the poems of Sir Thomas Wiat, and others;* i.e., *Tottel's Miscellany* (1557); rpt. 1717 (Watkins, pp. 109–10). SJ corrected many typographical errors and made a number of minor emendations in the faulty 1717 edition of *Tottel's Miscellany* that had "fallen into [his] hands."

measures, and one as the oldest composition which I have found in blank verse.

Description of Spring, wherein eche thing renewes, save only the lover.[1]

The soote season that bud, and bloome fourth bringes,
With grene hath cladde the hyll, and eke the vale,
The Nightingall with fethers new she singes;
The turtle to her mate hath told her tale:
Somer is come, for every spray now springes.[i]
The hart hath hunge hys olde head on the pale,
The bucke in brake his winter coate he flynges;
The fishes flete with newe repayred scale:
The adder all her slough away she flynges,
The swift swallow pursueth the flyes smalle,
The busy bee her honey how she mynges;
Winter is worne that was the floures bale.
And thus I see among these pleasant thynges
Eche care decayes, and yet my sorrow sprynges.

Descripcion of the restless estate of a lover.[2]

When youth had led me half the race,
That Cupides scourge had made me runne;
I looked back to meet the place,
From whence my weary course begunne:
    And then I saw howe my desyre
Misguiding me had led the waye,
Myne eyne to greedy of theyre hyre,
Had made me lose a better prey.
    For when in sighes I spent the day,
And could not cloake my grief with game;
The boyling smoke dyd still bewray,

i. springes. *55a, 65*] springes, *55b, 73*

1. "Description of Spring," p. 3.
2. "Descripcion of the restless estate of a lover," pp. 3–4.

The present heat of secret flame:
And when salt teares do bayne my breast,
Where love his pleasent traynes hath sown,
Her beauty hath the fruytes opprest,
Ere that the buddes were spronge and blowne.
And when myne eyen dyd still pursue,
The flying chase of theyre request;
Theyre greedy looks dyd oft renew,
The hydden wounde within my breste.
When every loke these cheekes might stayne,
From dedly pale to glowing red;
By outward signes appeared playne,
To her for helpe my hart was fled.
But all to late Love learneth me,
To paynt all kynd of Colours new;
To blynd theyre eyes that else should see
My speckled chekes with Cupids hew.
And now the covert brest I clame,
That worshipt Cupide secretely;
And nourished hys sacred flame,
From whence no blairing sparks do flye.

Descripcion of the fickle Affections, Pangs, and Sleightes of Love.[3]

Such wayward wayes hath Love, that most part in discord
Our willes do stand, whereby our hartes but seldom do accord:
Decyte is hys delighte, and to begyle and mocke
The simple hartes which he doth strike with froward divers stroke.
He causeth th' one to rage with golden burning darte,
And doth alay with Leaden cold, again the others harte.
Whose gleames of burning fyre and easy sparkes of flame,

3. "Descripcion of the fickle Affections," pp. 4–6.

In balance of unequal weyght he pondereth by ame
From easye ford where I myghte wade and pass full well,
He me withdrawes and doth me drive, into a depe dark hell:
And me witholdes where I am calde and offred place,
And willes me that my mortal foe I do beseke of Grace;
He lettes me to pursue a conquest welnere wonne
To follow where my paynes were lost, ere that my sute begunne.
So by this means I know how soon a hart may turne
From warre to peace, from truce to stryfe, and so agayne returne.
I know how to content my self in others lust,
Of little stuffe unto my self to weave a webbe of trust:
And how to hyde my harmes with sole dyssembling chere,
Whan in my face the painted thoughtes would outwardly appeare.
I know how that the bloud forsakes the face for dred,
And how by shame it staynes agayne the Chekes with flamyng red:
I know under the Grene, the Serpent how he lurkes:
The hammer of the restless forge I wote eke how it workes.
I know and con by roate the tale that I woulde tell
But ofte the woordes come fourth awrye of him that loveth well.
I know in heate and colde the Lover how he shakes,
In synging how he doth complayne, in sleeping how he wakes
To languish without ache, sickelesse for to consume,
A thousand thynges for to devyse, resolvynge of his fume;
And though he lyste to see his Ladyes Grace full sore
Such pleasures as delyght hys[j] Eye, do not his helthe restore.
I know to seke the tracte of my desyred foe,
And fere to fynde that I do seek, but chiefly this I know,

j. hys *55a, 55b, 65*] his *73*

That Lovers must transfourme into the thynge beloved,
And live (alas! who would believe?) with sprite from Lyfe removed.
I knowe in harty sighes and laughters of the spleene,
At once to chaunge my state, my will, and eke my colour clene.
I know how to deceyve my self wythe others helpe,
And how the Lyon chastised is, by beatynge of the whelpe.
In standynge nere the fyre, I know how that I frease;
Farre of I burne, in bothe I waste, and so my Lyfe I leese.
I know how Love doth rage upon a yeylding mynde,
How smalle a ncte may take and mase a harte of gentle kynde:
Or else with seldom swete to season hepes of gall,
Revived with a glympse of Grace old sorrowes to let fall.
The hydden[k] traynes I know, and secret snares of Love,
How soone a loke will prynte a thoughte that never may remove.
The slypper state I know, the sodein turnes from welthe[l]
The doubtfull hope, the certaine wooe, and sure despaired helthe.

A praise of his ladie.[4]

Geve place you ladies and be gone,
Boast not your selves at all,
For here at hande approcheth one,
Whose face will stayne you all.
The vertue of her lively lookes
Excels the precious stone,
I wishe to have none other bookes

k. hydden *55a, 65, 73*] hidden *55b*
l. welthe *55a, 55b, 73*] welthe, *65*

---

4. "A praise of his ladie," anonymous, ll. 1–28, p. 145.

To reade or look upon.
In eche of her two christall eyes,
Smyleth a naked boy;
It would you all in heart suffise
To see that lampe of joye.
I think nature hath lost the moulde,
Where she her shape did take;
Or else I doubte if nature coulde
So fayre a creature make.
She may be well comparde
Unto the Phenix kinde,
Whose like was never seene nor heard,
That any man can fynde.
In lyfe she is Diana chast
In trouth Penelopey,
In woord and eke in dede stedfast;
What will you more we say:
If all the world were sought so farre,
Who could finde suche a wight,
Her beauty twinkleth lyke a starre
Within the frosty night.

The Lover refused of his love, embraceth vertue.[5]

My youthfull yeres are past,
My joyfull dayes are gone,
My lyfe it may not last,
My grave and I am one.
My Myrth[m] and joyes are fled,
And I a Man in wo,
Desirous to be ded,
My misciefe[n] to forgo.

m. Myrth *55a, 55b, 65*] myrth *73*
n. misciefe *55a, 65, 73*] misceife *55b*

5. "The Lover refused," anonymous (1557 editions read "Death" instead of "Vertue" in the title), pp. 152–53.

I burne and am a colde,
I freese amyddes the fyer,
I see she doth witholde
That is my honest[o] desyre.
I see my helpe at hande,
I see my lyfe also,
I see where she doth stande
That is my deadly fo.
I see how she doth see,
And yet she wil be blynde,
I see in helpyng me,
She sekes and will not fynde.
I see how she doth wrye,
When I begynne to mone,
I see when I come nye,
How fayne she would be gone.
I see what wil[p] ye more,
She will me gladly kill,
And you shall see therfore
That she shall have her will.
I cannot live with stones,
It is too hard a foode,
I wil be dead at ones
To do my Lady good.

The Death of ZOROAS, an Egiptian astronomer, in the first fight that Alexander had with the Persians.[6]

Now clattring armes, now raging broyls of warre,
Gan passe the noys of dredfull trumpetts clang,
Shrowded with shafts, the heaven with cloude of dartes,
Covered the ayre. Against full fatted bulles.[q]
As forceth kyndled yre the lyons keene,

o. *The original reads* most.
p. wil *55a, 65, 73*] will *55b*
q. bulles. *55a, 65*] bulles, *55b, 73*

6. "The Death of Zoroas," ascribed to Nicholas Grimald, pp. 258–60.

Whose greedy gutts the gnawing hunger prickes;
So Macedons against the Persians fare,
Now corpses hyde the purpurde soyle with blood;
Large slaughter on eche side, but Perfes more,
Moyst fieldes bebled,[r] theyr heartes and numbers bate,
Fainted while they gave backe, and fall to flighte.
The litening Macedon by swordes, by gleaves,[7]
By bandes and troupes of footemen, with his garde,
Speedes to Dary, but hym his merest kyn,
Oxate preserves with horsemen on a plumpe
Before his carr, that none his charge should give.
Here grunts, here groans, eche where strong youth is spent:
Shaking her bloudy hands, Bellone among
The Perses soweth all kind of cruel death:
With throte yrent[s] he roares, he lyeth along
His entrailes with a launce through gryded quyte,
Hym smytes the club, hym woundes farre stryking bowe,
And him the sling, and him the shining sword;
He dyeth, he is all dead, he pantes, he restes.
Right over stoode in snowwhite armour brave,
The Memphite Zoroas, a cunnyng clarke,
To whom the heaven lay open as his booke;
And in celestiall bodies he could tell
The moving meeting light, aspect, eclips,
And influence, and constellations all;
What earthly chaunces would betyde, what yere,
Of plenty storde, what signe forewarned death,
How winter gendreth snow, what temperature
In the prime tyde doth season well the soyle,
Why summer burnes, why autumne hath ripe grapes,
Whither the circle quadrate may become,
Whether our tunes heavens harmony can yelde
Of four begyns among themselves how great

r. *The original reads* be bled.
s. yrent *73*] yent *55a, 55b, 65; the original reads* ycut.

7. *Gleaves:* spears or soldiers armed with spears (*OED,* s.v. *glaive*).

Proportion is; what sway the erryng[t] lightes
Doth send in course gayne that fyrst movyng heaven;
What[u] grees one from another distant be,
What starr doth lett the hurtfull fyre to rage,
Or him more mylde what opposition makes,
What fyre doth qualifye Mavorses[8] fyre,
What house eche one doth seeke, what plannett raignes
Within this heaven sphere, nor[v] that small thynges
I speake, whole heaven he closeth in his brest.
This sage then in the starres hath spyed the fates
Threatned him death without delay, and, sith,
He saw he could not fatall order chaunge,
Foreward he prest in battayle, that he might
Mete with the rulers of the Macedons,
Of his right hand desirous to be slain,
The bouldest borne, and worthiest in the feilde;
And as a wight, now wery of his lyfe,
And seking death, in fyrst front of his rage,
Comes desperately to Alexanders face,
At him with dartes one after other throwes,
With recklesse wordes and clamour him provokes,
And sayth, Nectanaks bastard shamefull stayne
Of mothers bed, why losest thou thy strokes,
Cowardes among, Turn thee to me, in case
Manhood there be so much left in thy heart,
Come fight with me, that on my helmet weare
Apollo's laurell both for learninges laude,
And eke for martiall praise, that in my shielde
The seven fold Sophie of Minerve contein,
A match more mete, Syr King, then any here.
The noble prince amoved takes ruth upon
The wilfull wight, and with soft words ayen,
O monstrous man (quoth he) what so thou art,

t. erryng *55a, 55b, 73*] errying *65*
u. What *55b*] What, *55a, 65, 73*
v. *The original reads* or.

8. *Mavorses:* Mars's (*OED,* s.v. *Mavors*).

I pray thee live, ne do not with thy death
This lodge of Lore, the Muses mansion marre;
That treasure house this hand shall never spoyle,
My sword shall never bruise that skilfull[w] brayne,
Long gather'd heapes of science sone[x] to spill;
O how fayre fruites may you to mortall men
From Wisdoms garden give; how many may
By you the wiser and the better prove:
What error, what mad moode, what frenzy thee
Perswades to be downe, sent to depe[y] Averne,
Where no artes flourish, nor no knowledge vailes
For all these sawes. When thus the sovereign said,
Alighted Zoroas with sword unsheathed,
The careless king there smoate above the greve,
At th' opening of his quishes[9] wounded him,
So that the blood down trailed on the ground:
The Macedon perceiving hurt, gan gnashe,
But yet his mynde he bent in any wise
Hym to forbeare, sett spurrs unto his stede,
And turnde away, lest anger of his smarte
Should cause revenger hand deale balefull blowes.[z]
But of the Macedonian chieftaines knights,
One Meleager could not bear this sight,
But ran upon the said Egyptian rude,[a]
And cutt him in both knees: he fell to ground,
Wherewith a whole rout came of souldiours sterne,
And all in pieces hewed the sely seg,[1]
But happely the soule fled to the starres,
Where, under him, he hath full sight of all,
Whereat he gazed here with reaching looke.

w. skilfull *55a, 65, 73*] skillful *55b*
x. *The original reads* some.
y. *The original reads* kepe.
z. blowes. *55a, 65, 73*] blowes, *55b*
a. *The original reads* reuk, *an obsolete form of* rook, *applied to persons as an abusive term.*

---

9. *Quishes:* "armor for protecting the front part of the thighs" (*OED*, s.v. *cuisse*).

1. *Seg:* a man, only used contemptuously by this date (*OED*, s.v. *segge*).

The Persians waild such sapience to forgoe,
The very sone the Macedonians wisht
He would have lived, king Alexander selfe
Demde him a man unmete to dye at all;
Who wonne like praise for conquest of his Yre,
As for stoute men in field that day subdued,
Who princes taught how to discerne a man,
That in his head so rare a jewel beares,
But over all those same Camenes, those same,
Divine Camenes, whose honour he procurde,
As tender parent doth his daughters weale,
Lamented, and for thankes, all that they can,
Do cherish hym deceast, and sett him free,
From dark oblivion of devouring death.

Barclay wrote about 1550; his chief work is the *Ship of Fooles*, of which the following extract will shew his style.[2]

Of Mockers and Scorners, and false Accusers.

O Heartless fooles, haste here to our doctrine,
Leaue off the wayes of your enormitie,
Enforce you to my preceptes to encline,
For here shall I shewe you good and veritie:
Encline, and ye finde shall great prosperitie,
Ensuing the doctrine of our fathers olde,
And godly lawes in valour worth great golde.
Who that will followe the graces manyfolde
Which are in vertue, shall finde auauncement:
Wherfore[b] ye fooles that in your sinne are bolde,
Ensue ye wisdome, and leaue your lewde intent,
Wisdome is the way of men most excellent:
Therfore haue done, and shortly spede your pace,

b. Wherfore *55a, 55b, 73*] Wherefore *65*

2. Alexander Barclay first published his translation of Sebastian Brant's *Stultifera Navis* as *The Shyp of folys of the worlde* (1509). SJ's text is *Stultifera Navis . . . The Ship of Fooles* (1570), which includes some of Barclay's other poetry, fols. 80^v–82^r (*Sale Catalogue*, no. 278; Watkins, pp. 90–91).

To quaynt your self and company with grace.
    Learne what is vertue, therin is great solace,
Learne what is truth, sadnes and prudence,
Let grutche[3] be gone, and grauitie purchase,
Forsake your folly and inconuenience,
Cease to be fooles, and ay to sue offence,
Followe ye vertue, chiefe roote of godlynes,
For it and wisedome is ground of clenlynes.
    Wisedome and vertue two thinges are doubtles,
Whiche man endueth with honour speciall,
But suche heartes as slepe in foolishnes
Knoweth nothing, and will nought know at all:
But in this little barge in principall
All foolish mockers I purpose to repreue,
Clawe he his backe that feeleth itche or greue.
    Mockers and scorners that are harde of beleue,
With a rough combe[c] here will I clawe and grate,
To proue if they will from their vice remeue,
And leaue their folly, which causeth great debate:
Suche caytiues spare neyther poore man nor estate,
And where their selfe are moste worthy[d] derision,
Other men to scorne is all their most condition.
    Yet are mo fooles of this abusion,
Whiche of wise men despiseth the doctrine,
With mowes, mockes, scorne, and collusion,
Rewarding rebukes for their good discipline:
Shewe to suche wisdome, yet shall they not encline
Unto the same, but set nothing therby,
But mocke thy doctrine, still or openly.
    So in the worlde it appeareth commonly,
That who that will a foole rebuke or blame,
A mocke or mowe shall he haue by and by:
Thus in derision haue fooles their speciall game.

c. combe *55a, 65, 73*] comb *55b*
d. *The original reads* worthy of derision.

3. *grutche:* "'Murmuring' of the conscience; uneasiness or disturbance of mind; scruple, doubt, misgiving" (*OED*, s.v. *grudge*, 2).

Correct a wise man that woulde eschue ill name,
And fayne would learne, and his lewde life amende,
And to thy wordes he gladly shall intende.
If by misfortune a rightwise man offende,
He gladly suffereth a iuste correction,
And him that him teacheth taketh for his frende,
Him selfe putting mekely unto subiection,
Folowing his preceptes and good direction:
But yf that one a foole rebuke or blame,
He shall his teacher hate, slaunder and diffame.
Howbeit his wordes oft turne to his own shame,
And his owne dartes retourne to him agayne,
And so is he sore wounded with the same,
And in wo endeth, great misery and payne.
It also proued full often is certayne,
That they that on mockers alway their mindes cast,
Shall of all other be mocked at the last.
He that goeth right, stedfast, sure, and fast,
May him well mocke that goeth halting and lame,
And he that is white may well his scornes cast,
Agaynst a man of Inde: but no man ought to blame
Anothers vice, while he vseth the same.
But who that of sinne is cleane in deede and thought,
May him well scorne whose liuing is starke nought.
The scornes of Naball full dere should haue been bought,
If Abigayl his wife discrete and sage,
Had not by kindnes right crafty meanes sought,
The wrath of Dauid to temper and asswage.
Hath not two beares in their fury and rage
Two and fortie children rent and torne,
For they the prophete Helyseus did scorne.
So might they curse the time that they were borne,
For their mocking of this prophete diuine:
So many other of this sort often mourne
For their lewde mockes, and fall into ruine.
Thus is it foly for wise men to encline,
To this lewde flocke of fooles, for see thou shall
Them moste scorning that are most bad of all.

The Lenuoy of Barclay to the fooles.

Ye mocking fooles that in scorne set your ioy,
Proudly despising Gods punition:[e]
Take ye example by Cham the sonne of Noy,
Which laughed his father vnto derision,
Which him after cursed for his transgression,
And made him seruaunt to all his lyne and stocke.
So shall ye caytifs at the conclusion,
Since ye are nought, and other scorne and mocke.

About the year 1553 wrote Dr. *Wilson,* a man celebrated for the politeness of his style, and the extent of his knowledge: what was the state of our language in his time, the following may be of use to show.[4]

Pronunciation is an apte orderinge bothe of the voyce, countenaunce, and all the whole bodye, accordynge to the worthines of suche woordes and mater as by speache are declared. The vse hereof is suche for anye one that liketh to haue prayse for tellynge his tale in open assemblie, that hauing a good tongue, and a comelye countenaunce, he shalbe[f] thought to passe all other that haue the like vtteraunce: thoughe they haue much better learning. The tongue geueth a certayne grace to euerye matter, and beautifieth the cause in like maner, as a swete soundynge lute muche setteth forthe a meane deuised ballade. Or as the sounde of a good instrumente styrreth the hearers, and moueth muche delite, so a cleare soundyng voice comforteth muche our deintie eares, with muche swete melodie, and causeth vs to allowe the matter rather for the reporters sake, then the reporter for the matters sake. Demosthenes therfore, that famouse oratour,

e. punition: *55a, 65, 73*] punition; *55b*
f. shalbe *55a*] shal be *55b, 65, 73*

4. Thomas Wilson, *The Arte of Rhetorique* (1553), "Of Pronunciation," fols. 116ᵛ–117ʳ; in 1765 SJ gave George Steevens a copy of Wilson's *Arte* (see J. D. Fleeman, *A Preliminary Handlist of Copies of Books Associated with Dr. Samuel Johnson* [1984], no. 284).

beyng asked what was the chiefest point in al oratorie, gaue the chiefe and onely praise to Pronunciation; being demaunded, what was the seconde, and the thirde, he stil[g] made answere,[h] Pronunciation, and would make none other aunswere, till they lefte askyng, declaryng hereby that arte without vtteraunce can dooe nothyng, vtteraunce without arte can dooe right muche. And no doubte that man is in outwarde apparaunce halfe a good clarke, that hath a cleane tongue, and a comely gesture of his body. Æschines lykwyse beyng bannished his countrie through Demosthenes, when he had redde to the Rhodians his own oration, and Demosthenes aunswere thereunto, by force whereof he was bannished, and all they marueiled muche at the excellencie of the same: then (q d Æschines)[5] you would have[i] marueiled muche more if you had heard hymselfe speak it. Thus beyng cast in miserie and bannished for euer, he could not but geue such great[j] reporte of his[k] deadly and mortal ennemy.

Thus have I deduced the *English* language from the age of *Alfred* to that of *Elizabeth;* in some parts imperfectly for want of materials; but I hope, at least, in such a manner that its progress may be easily traced, and the gradations observed, by which it advanced from its first rudeness to its present elegance.

g. stil *55a, 65, 73*] still *55b*
h. answere, *55a, 55b, 73*] answere *65*
i. have *55a, 55b, 73*] haue *65*
j. great *55a, 65, 73*] greate *55b*
k. *The original reads* his most deadly.

5. *q d:* an abbreviation for *quod,* "quoth" or "said."

EDITOR'S INTRODUCTION TO "A GRAMMAR OF THE ENGLISH TONGUE"

Composition

Like his History, Johnson's Grammar consists largely of two kinds of materials, borrowed (either explicit or implied) and authorial. The first embraces a variety of concepts, distinctions, and examples drawn from other grammars; illustrative quotations together with the names of their writers and titles of their works; and miscellaneous remarks of, and allusions to, other authors. The second consists of Johnson's own prose and examples.

In the initial one-sentence paragraph, Johnson defines *grammar* ("*the art of using words properly*") and names its "four parts" ("Orthography, Etymology, Syntax, and Prosody"). He then acknowledges, and justifies, his indebtedness to "the common grammarians," who also seem to be the source of the "terms" he employs. These "grammarians" almost certainly refer to the compilers and successive, mainly anonymous, editors and augmenters of "Lily's Grammar." An amalgam, incorporating works by William Lily and John Colet, "Lily's Grammar" is composed of a Latin part, first published as *Institutio Compendiaria Totius Grammaticae* (1540), and an English part, first published as *An Introduction of the Eight Parts of Speech* (1542). The former became known as the "Grammar" or "Common Grammar," while the latter was called the "Accidence."[1] In its various forms "Lily's Grammar" was the most popular such textbook in Britain for several centuries and it contains the same definition of *grammar* and the "division and order" of its chief parts as does Johnson's Grammar.

1. For information on the composition and publication of "Lily's Grammar," see A. W. Pollard and G. R. Redgrave, *A Short-Title Catalogue of Books Printed in England, Scotland, and Ireland and of English Books Printed Abroad, 1475–1640*, 3 vols., 2d ed., revised by K. Pantzer (1976), II.62–64.

In this work Johnson may refer to "Lily's Grammar" as many as four times. He seems to be including it in his reference when he mentions "the common grammarians" (p. 275) whom he follows in defining *grammar* and ordering its parts; "grammarians" whose "established practice . . . requires that I should here treat of the Syntax" (p. 347); "grammarians" who term *s* "*suæ potestatis litera*" (a letter that makes its own sound; p. 290); and "the grammarians" who "numbered" *f* "among the semi-vowels" (p. 286). When Johnson uses the word "powers" to describe the potential sounds of a letter (p. 277), he is adapting the language of the "common grammarians"; but here, as arguably in all the other instances cited, the reference may be indirect because so many grammars were based on "Lily's."

The presence of "Lily's Grammar" in the body of Johnson's *Dictionary* increases the probability of his awareness of it in composing his Grammar. There he cites nine quotations from the English part: once as *Introduction to Grammar* (*to let* [hinder], v.a., sense 2) and eight times as *Accidence: wretch,* sense 1; *speech,* sense 2; *signification,* sense 2; *it,* sense 1; *him,* sense 2; *impersonal; ground,* sense 13; and *gain,* adj. Three of these quotations (those under *it, him,* and *impersonal*) appear only in the fourth edition of the *Dictionary.*

Of course, because it is a grammar of the Latin language, "Lily"'s usefulness to Johnson was limited. His more important sources are grammars of English. Of these the leading contributor by far was the *Grammatica Lingua Anglicana* (1653) of John Wallis, "learned and sagacious," as Johnson says, "to whom every English grammarian owes a tribute of reverence" (p. 305). Wallis wrote in Latin but Johnson translated his remarks into English before including them in the *Dictionary.* The fourth (1674) was apparently the only edition of Wallis's *Grammatica* Johnson used in creating his own work. Therefore it is the edition cited below.

The translated passages begin with a phrase concerning the vowel *e* on p. 280 (n. 6), and they recur with increasing frequency to p. 328 (see notes on pp. 324–28), when they become almost continuous, to p. 346 (see notes on pp. 334,

338), at which point they cease. The last reference to Wallis appears on p. 348.

Compared to his borrowings from Wallis's *Grammatica,* Johnson's debts to other books, including grammars, are minor. Ben Jonson's *Grammar* provides three explicit references and a single possible reference (pp. 324–25, 347, 348, 292, n. 4). James Greenwood's *Essay towards a Practical English Grammar* supplies one definite and two possible references (pp. 278, 286, 343). Charles Butler's *Feminin' Monarchi', or the Histori of Bee's* (pp. 298–99) and John Wilkins's *Essay towards a Real Character and a Philosophical Language* contribute one reference each—as well as one illustrative quotation (pp. 298–99, 300). In the fourth edition of the *Dictionary* (1773), Robert Lowth's *Short Introduction to English Grammar* furnishes two (pp. 305, 306) references.

Each of the following works, listed according to their appearance in the text, supplies one reference: Fridericus Sylburgius's *Rudimenta Graecae Linguae* (p. 275); Thomas Erpenius's *Arabicae Linguae Tyrocinium* (p. 278); Sir Thomas Smith's *De Recta et Emendata Linguae Anglicanae Scriptione, Dialogus* (p. 296); and Alexander Gil, the Elder's *Logonomia Anglica* (pp. 296–98). Three works—Benedetto Buommattei's *Della Lingua Toscana* (p. 347), Abbé François Séraphin Régnier-Desmarais's *Traité de la grammaire française* (p. 347), and Christopher Cooper's *Grammatica Linguae Anglicanae* (p. 348)—are only mentioned.

Finally, William Holder's *Elements of Speech* (p. 283, n. 9), Samuel Clarke's edition of the first twelve books of Homer's *Iliad* (p. 290, n. 1), and George Hickes's *Thesaurus* (p. 305, n. 2) *may* be the sources of three short passages.

The largest group of contributions consists of forty-eight quotations (counting the two specified above) that illustrate statements by Johnson on innovations in spelling (five), particular grammatical usages (twenty-one), and forms of versification (twenty-two). Of the twenty-eight authors cited, Milton ranks first (with eight, pp. 300, 303, 309, 309, 309, 311, 313, 353); followed by Dryden (five, pp. 303, 304, 351, 353–54, 358); then come Pope and Michael Drayton (three each:

pp. 296, 306, 356; 351, 351–53, 355–56); and Spenser, Shakespeare, the Bible, and Vergil (two each: 297, 305; 302, 323; 303, 324; 304, 305) conclude the list. Listed according to their appearance in the text, the remainder are: Chaucer, John Ray, Roger Ascham, Sir Francis Bacon, Sir Henry Wotton, Ben Jonson, Izaak Walton, Thomas Deloney, Edmund Waller, George Chapman, Elijah Fenton, David Lewis, Samuel Wesley, Walter Pope, Edward Ward, Joseph Addison, Matthew Prior, Richard Glover, John Gay, and Lewis Theobald. At least twenty of the quotations, including Milton's eight and Shakespeare's two, also appear in the main *Dictionary*—a fact that, bolstered by much additional evidence, supports our unsurprising conclusion that Johnson, in composing the Grammar, drew on material in his word list.

Publication and Reception

After its appearance in the folio *Dictionary* (1755), the Grammar was printed along with the History in most subsequent unabridged editions and one of the abridged editions.[2] However, only the Grammar was included in the first edition of the proprietors' abridgment (1756). It continued to be unaccompanied by the History in at least these later editions and reissues: 1760, 1766, 1770, 1773, 1778, 1783, 1786, 1790, 1792, 1792 (also the Preface: see p. 66 above), 1794, 1797, 1798, 1799.[3]

Besides this record of its appearances, there are other kinds of evidence concerning the early reception of the Grammar. In several early reviews, the Grammar was mentioned along with the History.[4] The *Gentleman's Magazine* noted merely that the *Dictionary* includes a "grammar, which, however short, contains more than all that went before it." The *Monthly Review* notes that Johnson's "grammar is concise,

2. See our introduction to the History (p. 120 above).

3. For further information about the contents of the abridged *Dictionary*, see *Bibliography*, pp. 486–556.

4. For references to these reviews, see our introduction to the History (pp. 120–21 above).

yet far from being obscure; several of his remarks are uncommon, if not new, and all of them deserving particular attention. The *prosody* is treated with an accuracy we do not remember to have met with in other grammarians." The *Journal étranger* (July 1755) translated these remarks into French (p. 149). In a later article, dominated by a translation of the Preface (December 1756), the *Journal* briefly mentions both the History and Grammar.

As it had borrowed the History, the Joseph Nichol Scott–Nathan Bailey *New Universal Etymological Dictionary* (1755) also borrowed the Grammar. Philip B. Gove pointed out that Scott-Bailey's Grammar "remains too close [to Johnson's] to be called anything but downright copying, with alterations."[5]

Subsequently and unsurprisingly, since grammars of English far outnumber histories, Johnson's Grammar was a far more frequent lender than his History. Although we have located only two works that borrow from the History,[6] we have found a large number of publications, not all of them grammars, which are explicitly or evidently indebted, in widely different amounts, to Johnson's Grammar. The following works—more could be added, of course—illustrate the variety and sizes, from very small to very extensive, of the borrowings and the kinds of evaluative responses they elicited. Divided according to the latter, the list includes groups containing (1) no assessments of any kind (Lewis Brittain, *Rudiments of English Grammar,* 1788; Thomas Coar, *A Grammar of the English Tongue,* 1796); (2) wholly or largely positive comments (John Burn, *A Practical Grammar of the English Language,* 1766; Daniel Fenning, *A New Grammar of the English Language,* 1771; Anselm Bayly, *A Plain and Complete Grammar of the English Language,* 1772; John Fell, *An Essay towards an English Grammar,* 1784; (3) A mixture of positive and negative comments (James Buchanan, *The British Grammar,* 1762; Joseph Priestley, *A Course of Lectures on the Theory of Language and Universal Grammar,* 1762; Robert Nares, *Elements of Orthoepy,*

5. For the reference to Gove's remark, see above, p. 121.
6. For the borrowers of the History, see above, p. 121.

1784; Charles Coote, *Elements of the Grammar of the English Language,* 1788); and (4) wholly or largely negative comments (A. F. Slack [Anne Fisher], *A Practical English Grammar,* 18th ed., 1779; J. C. Adelung, *Neues Grammatisch–Kritisches Wörterbuch der Englischen Sprache für die Deutschen,* 1783–1796; Alexander Bicknell, *The Grammatical Wreath,* 1790; John Walker, *A Critical Pronouncing Dictionary,* 1791; Peter Walkden Fogg, *Elementa Anglicana,* 2 vols., 1792).

Still another group of reactions, without any borrowings, express, at best, neutral and, at worst, wholly unfavorable generalizations about the Grammar. In the Preface to his *Short Introduction to English Grammar* (1762), Robert Lowth remarks on the poverty of Johnson's treatment of the syntax of English, while suggesting that it may be appropriate to the subject: "*The Construction of this Language is so easy and obvious, that our Grammarians have thought it hardly worth while to give us any thing like a regular and systematical Syntax. The last* English *Grammar that hath been presented to the public, and by the Person best qualified to have given us a perfect one, comprises the whole Syntax in ten lines. The reason, which he assigns for being so very concise in this part, is, 'because our Language has so little inflection, that its Construction neither requires nor admits many rules.' In truth, the easier any subject is in its own nature, the harder it is to make it more easy by explanation.*"[7] Writing about Johnson's Grammar in a letter to his brother Joseph on 19 April 1755, Thomas Warton observed the slightness of the work more critically than Lowth: "There is a grammar prefix'd and the history of the language is pretty full; but you may plainly perceive strokes of laxity and indolence."[8] Six years later, in the Preface to his *Rudiments of English Grammar* Joseph Priestley wrote: "I must not conclude this preface, without making my acknowledgements to Mr. *Johnson,* whose admirable dictionary has been of the greatest use to me in the study of our language. It is pity he had not formed as just, and as ex-

7. *Short Introduction,* pp. iv–v; see Sledd-Kolb, p. 179.
8. *Correspondence of Thomas Warton,* ed. Fairer, p. 43.

tensive an idea of English grammar."[9] In the severest judgment of all, John Horne Tooke declares: "yet it must be confessed, that [Johnson's] *Grammar* and *History* and Dictionary of what *he calls* the English language, are in all respects (except the bulk of the latter) most truly contemptible performances; and a reproach to the learning and industry of a nation, which could receive them with the slightest approbation."[1]

The Text

No manuscript of the Grammar is known to exist. In preparing our text, we collated the first seven proprietors' unabridged editions[2] and the first seven proprietors' abridged (octavo) editions.[3] Our examination of the latter revealed no signs of authorial revisions. But our collation of the former showed that Johnson revised both the third edition (more extensively than anyone, apparently, has previously realized) and the fourth, which two earlier researchers also scrutinized.[4] At the same time, the collation validated our presumptive inclination toward the first edition as our copy-text. Into it we have introduced all the substantive and accidental variants from the third and fourth editions that seem authorial; the differences range from certainly Johnsonian to possibly so, and the last group, we are keenly aware, rest on very

9. *Rudiments* (1761), p. xxiii; see Sledd-Kolb, p. 178.

1. *Diversions of Purley* (1786), Part I, p. 268n.

2. For the list, see p. xlvii above.

3. The first (1756) of these was set from the first unabridged edition, the second octavo (1760) from the first, the third (1766) from the third unabridged, the fourth (1770) from the third octavo, the fifth (1773) from the fourth octavo, the sixth (1778) from the fourth unabridged, and the seventh (1783) from the sixth octavo. We collated Gwin Kolb's copies of all the unabridged and abridged editions.

4. In his article cited above (p. 122, n. 5), Arthur Sherbo, seemingly the only previous person to mention Johnson's changes in the third edition, notes (p. 19) the modification of his original comment about the letter *H* (p. 287 below). Sherbo cites (pp. 19, 20, 29–33) thirty-four substantive changes in the fourth edition; Nagashima (pp. 20, 35–36, 146–48) somewhat fewer but with certain exclusions. Our count is seventy-seven.

slender evidence. In addition, for assorted reasons we have adopted various other accidental variants in the third and fourth editions. For assorted reasons, too, we have introduced into our text a number of readings, both substantive and accidental, from the unrevised second, fifth, and sixth unabridged editions.

We have emended the text by altering five words: three (pp. 340, 342, 344 below) to the correct ones in John Wallis's *Grammatica Linguae Anglicanae* (4th ed., 1674), from which Johnson borrowed these and numerous other parts of his Grammar;[5] two (p. 287 below) from common nouns to proper names, in accordance with the context. Believing that the hazardous task exceeded our editorial responsibilities, we have not emended the passages which Johnson quoted from other writers. However, since the Grammar has not hitherto undergone critical editing and probably will not do so again for a long time, we, concluding that the data may be useful to other students, have recorded all the variants, substantive and accidental, in the first four editions.[6]

Printing the text of Johnson's Grammar presented unusual problems because of the presence of unconventional and sometimes obscure typography. As in our edition of the History, we have not tried to reproduce Johnson's typography but to represent it in available forms wherever typography seemed to verge on orthography. The special difficulties we faced in printing Johnson's representation of passages from spelling reformers are recorded in the notes on those passages.[7] Also, as in the History, we have preferred Johnson's transcription to the text of his sources, although this has meant reproducing many errors. However, when presented with alternatives among various editions of the specimen texts in the Grammar, we have chosen those that best represent Johnson's source. In addition, on rare occasions, for the

5. See Introduction, pp. xl–xlii above.

6. These two paragraphs form a condensed, altered version of sections of "Preliminaries" (pp. 122–30), to which the reader seeking more information is referred.

7. See pp. 296, nn. 7, 9; 298, n. 6; 300, n. 6, below.

sake of sense, we have inserted in the text a missing letter or word in brackets. To the parts of the following works that are originally Johnson's, we have applied our somewhat modified version of the normal procedure observed by the Yale Edition (see our Preface, p. xi, n. 4).

A GRAMMAR OF THE ENGLISH TONGUE

GRAMMAR, which is *the art of using words properly,*[1] comprises four parts; Orthography, Etymology, Syntax, and Prosody.

In this division and order of the parts of grammar I follow the common grammarians, without enquiring whether a fitter distribution might not be found.[2] Experience has long shown this method to be so distinct as to obviate confusion, and so comprehensive as to prevent any inconvenient omissions. I likewise use the terms already received, and already understood, though perhaps others more proper might sometimes be invented. Sylburgius, and other innovators, whose new terms have sunk their learning into neglect, have left sufficient warning against the trifling ambition of teaching arts in a new language.[3]

---

1. Cf. *Grammar* (sense 1, *Dictionary*): "The science of speaking correctly; the art which teaches the relations of words to each other."

2. In this and the preceding sentences, SJ seems to be drawing, directly or indirectly, on "Lily's Grammar," a composite work incorporating grammatical works by John Lily and John Colet. See Introduction, pp. 265–66 above. Although we do not represent it, all the early editions of *Dictionary* employed smaller type in this paragraph and in numerous others throughout the *Grammar,* presumably for matters SJ considered less important than the rest (and also possibly to save space).

3. Fridericus Sylburgius describes his *Rudimenta Graecae Linguae, ad Postremam Rameae Grammatices Editionem Conformata* (1582) as both a "compendium" and a "supplement" (fol. iii^{v}) to the innovative grammar of Petrus Ramus. A copy of the *Rudimenta* is listed in the *Harleian Catalogue* (II, no. 15432), which SJ helped to compile (see *Life,* I.154), with a laudatory remark by the eminent scholar Gerhard Johann Vossius. In the *Sale Catalogue* (no. 115) of SJ's library may be a copy of Sylburgius's Greek and Latin version of the works of Justin Martyr.

PART I.
Of ORTHOGRAPHY.[a]

§ I.[b] Orthography is *the art of combining letters into syllables, and syllables into words.* It therefore teaches previously the form and sound of letters.

The letters of the English language are,

Saxon.[c][4]	Roman.	Italick.	Old English.	Name.
A a	A a	*A a*	𝔄 𝔞	*a*
B b	B b	*B b*	𝔅 𝔟	*be*
C c	C c	*C c*	ℭ 𝔠	*see*
D ꝺ	D d	*D d*	𝔇 𝔡	*dee*
Є e	E e	*E e*	𝔈 𝔢	*e*
F ꝼ	F f	*F f*	𝔉 𝔣	*eff*
Ᵹ ᵹ	G g	*G g*	𝔊 𝔤	*jee*
Ƕ h	H h	*H h*	ℌ 𝔥	*aitch*
I i	I i	*I i*	𝔦	*i*
	J j	*J j*	ℑ 𝔧	*j* consonant, or *ja*
K k	K k	*K k*	𝔎 𝔨	*ka*
L l	L l	*L l*	𝔏 𝔩	*el*
M m	M m	*M m*	𝔐 𝔪	*em*
N n	N n	*N n*	𝔑 𝔫	*en*
O o	O o	*O o*	𝔒 𝔬	*o*
P p	P p	*P p*	𝔓 𝔭	*pee*
Q cp	Q q	*Q q*	𝔔 𝔮	*cue*
R ꞃ	R r	*R r*	ℜ 𝔯 2[d]	*ar*

a. PART I.| Of ORTHOGRAPHY. *65*] *absent 55a, 55b, 73*

b. §I. *65*] *absent 55a, 55b, 73*

c. Saxon *and letters of the alphabet 73;* Saxon *and letters of the alphabet included at the end of the Grammar in editions 1–8 (1756–86) of abridged Dictionary*] Saxon *and letters of the alphabet absent 55a, 55b, 65*

d. 2 *73*] 2 *absent 55a, 55b, 65*

4. SJ used this font for several passages in the History (see pp. 128–29). We reproduce it as closely as possible, retaining, contrary to our usual practice, all the antiquated letter forms. See Introduction, p. 272.

S ꞅ	S ſ s	*S ſ s*	𝔖 ſ 𝔰	*ess*
T ꞇ	T t	*T t*	𝔗 𝔱	*tee*
U u	U u	*U u*	𝔲	*u*
V v	V v	*V v*	𝔙 𝔳	*v* consonant, or *va*
Ƿ ƿ	W w	*W w*	𝔚 𝔴	double *u*
X x	X x	*X x*	𝔛 𝔵	*ex*
Y ẏ	Y y	*Y y*	𝔜 𝔶	*wy*
Z z	Z z	*Z z*	ℨ 𝔷	*zed,* more commonly *izzard* or *uzzard,* that is,[e] *s hard*

To these may be added certain combinations of letters universally used in printing; as ct, ſt, fl, ſl, ſb, ſk, ff, ſſ, ſi, ſſi, fi, ffi, ffl, and &, or *and per ſe, and. ct, ſt, fl, ſl, ſb, ſk, ff, ſſ, ſi, ſſi, fi, ffi, ffl, &.* 𝔠𝔱, ſ𝔱, 𝔣𝔩, ſ𝔩, 𝔣𝔣, ſſ, ſ𝔦, ſſ𝔦, 𝔣𝔦, 𝔣𝔣𝔦, &.

Our letters are commonly reckoned twenty-four, because anciently *i* and *j,* as well as *u* and *v,* were expressed by the same character; but as those letters, which had always different powers,[5] have now different forms, our alphabet may be properly said to consist of twenty-six letters.[6]

None of the consonants[f] have a double form, except the small[g] ſ, *s;* of which ſ is used in the beginning and middle, and *s* at the end.

Vowels are five, a, e, i, o, u.

e. is, *55a, 55b, 65*] is *73*
f. the consonants *65*] the small consonants *55a, 55b, 73*
g. except the small *65*] except ſ, s; *55a, 55b, 73*

5. *Powers:* potential sounds, a usage based on the Latin *potestas* in the "common grammarians" (see n. 2 above) but not in *Dictionary.*

6. In *Dictionary,* SJ, although stating that the pairs *I–J* and *U–V* are each "two letters," nevertheless follows "the old custom" (entry for *V*) of ordering them under *I* and *V,* respectively. This "custom" apparently continued until Robert Gordon Latham published his revision of the Todd-Johnson *Dictionary* (1866–70), which changed the two-letter list to four.

Such is the number generally received; but for *i* it is the practice to write *y* in the end of words, as *thy, holy;* before *i*, as from *die, dying;* from *beautify, beautifying;* in the words *says, days, eyes;* and in words derived from the Greek, and written originally with *υ*, as *system, σύστημα, sympathy, συμπάθεια.*

For *u* we often write *w* after a vowel, to make a diphthong; as *raw, grew, view, vow, flowing, lowness.*

The sounds of all the letters are various.

In treating on the letters, I shall not, like some other grammarians, enquire into the original of their form as an antiquarian;[h][7] nor into their formation and prolation[8] by the organs of speech, as a mechanick,[9] anatomist, or physiologist; nor into the properties and gradations[i] of sounds, or the elegance or harshness of particular combinations, as a writer of universal and transcendental grammar.[1] I consider the English alphabet only as it is English; and even in this narrow disquisition[j] I follow the example of former grammarians,[2] perhaps with more reverence than judgment, because by writing in English I suppose my reader already acquainted with the English language; and consequently able to pronounce the letters, of which I teach the pronunciation;[k] and because of sounds in general it may be observed, that words

h. antiquarian; *55a, 55b, 65*] antiquarian: *73*
i. gradations *65*] gradation *55a, 55b, 73*
j. disquisition 73] view *55a, 55b, 65*
k. and consequently . . . pronunciation; *73*] language; and because *55a, 55b, 65*

7. *Antiquary,* but not *antiquarian,* is listed in *Dictionary.*

8. *Prolation:* "Pronunciation; utterance" (sense 1, *Dictionary*).

9. *Mechanick:* "An adherent of the doctrine of mechanism [mechanistic or Cartesian philosophy]" (*OED,* sense B, 5, citing SJ's schoolfellow and associate Robert James, *Dissertation on Fevers* [1748]); this meaning is not in *Dictionary.*

1. Among the grammars that treat "universal" matters and which SJ knew are John Wallis's *Grammatica,* John Wilkins's *Essay towards a Real Character and a Philosophical Language* (1668), William Holder's *Elements of Speech* (1669), Benjamin Martin's *Physico-Grammatical Essay on the Propriety and Rationale of the English Tongue* (1748; reprinted in his dictionary, *Lingua Britannica Reformata* [1749]), and James Harris's *Hermes* (1751).

2. The principal source is *Grammatica,* pp. 33–53. Greenwood, which is very reliant on Wallis's *Grammatica,* is a secondary source.

are unable to describe them. An account therefore of the primitive and simple letters is useless almost alike to those who know their sound, and those who know it not.

§II.[l] Of VOWELS.

A.

A has three sounds, the slender, open, and broad.

A slender is found in most words, as *face, mane;* and in words ending in *ation,* as *creation, salvation, generation.*

The *a* slender is the proper English *a,* called very justly by Erpenius,[m] in his Arabick Grammar, *a Anglicum cum e mistum,* as having a middle sound between the open *a* and the *e*.[3] The French have a similar sound in the word *pais,* and in their *e* masculine.

A open is the *a* of the Italian, or nearly resembles it; as *father, rather, congratulate, fancy, glass.*

A broad resembles the *a* of the German;[4] as *all, wall, call.*

Many words pronounced with *a* broad were anciently written with *au,* as *sault,*[n] *mault;* and we still say *fault, vault.* This was probably the Saxon sound, for it is yet retained in the northern dialects, and in the rustick pronunciation; as *maun* for *man, haund* for *hand.*

The short *a* approaches to the *a* open, as *grass.*

The long *a,* if prolonged by *e* at the end of the word, is always slender, as *graze, fame.*

A forms a diphthong only with *i* or *y,* and *u* or *w.* *Ai* or *ay,*

l. §II. 65] §II. absent *55a, 55b,* 73
m. Erpenius, *55a, 73*] Erpenius *55b, 65*
n. *sault 65*] *fault, 55a, 55b, 73*

3. Thomas Erpenius, *Arabicae Linguae Tyrocinium* (1656), pt. 1, p. 19.

4. In some of SJ's sources, *German* may be equivalent to High Dutch, and *Dutch* may mean low Dutch or Belgian, but both words had assumed something like their modern usages by 1755 (see *OED*). Moreover, in his etymological notes within *Dictionary* and in the Preface (p. 83 above), SJ seems to make the modern distinction. Perhaps the best record of the evolving distinction is in R. C. Alston, *Bibliography of the English Language* (corrected rpt., 1974); see II. 74–125, which covers work on English written for German and Dutch speakers.

as in *plain, wain, gay, clay,* has only the sound of the long and slender *a,* and differs not in the pronunciation from *plane, wane.*

Au or *aw* has the sound of the German *a,* as *raw, naughty.*

Ae is sometimes found in Latin words not compleatly[o] naturalised or assimilated, but is no English diphthong; and is more properly expressed by single *e,* as *Cesar, Eneas.*[5]

E.

E is the letter which occurs most frequently in the English language.

E is long, as in *scēne;* or short, as in *cĕllar, sĕparate, cĕlebrate, mĕn, thĕn.*

It is always short before a double consonant, or two consonants, as in *vĕx, pĕrplexity,*[p] *relĕnt, mĕdlar, rĕptile, sĕrpĕnt, cĕllar, cĕssation, blĕssing, fĕll, fĕlling, dĕbt.*

E is always mute at the end of a word, except in monosyllables that have no other vowel, as *the;* or proper names, as *Penelope, Phebe, Derbe;*[6] being used to modify the foregoing consonant, as *since, once, hedge, oblige;* or to lengthen the preceding vowel, as *băn, bāne; căn, cāne; pĭn, pīne; tŭn, tūne; rŏb, rōbe; pŏp, pōpe; fĭr, fīre; cŭr, cūre; tŭb, tūbe.*

Almost all words which now terminate in consonants ended anciently in *e,* as *year, yeare;*[q] *wildness, wildnesse;* which *e* probably had the force of the French *e* feminine, and constituted

o. compleatly *55a, 73*] completely *55b, 65*
p. as . . . *pĕrplexity, 73*] consonants, *relĕnt, 55a, 55b, 65*
q. *yeare; 55a, 65, 73*] *yeare, 55b*

---

5. Under Æ in *Dictionary,* SJ is, unusually, more expansive than he is in the Grammar: Æ is defined as "A diphthong of very frequent use in the Latin language, which seems not properly to have any place in the English; since the *æ* of the Saxons has been long out of use, being changed to *e* simple, to which, in words frequently occurring, the *æ* of the Romans is, in the same manner, altered, as in *equator, equinoctial,* and even in *Eneas.*"

6. As noted above (p. 266) and as Nagashima points out (p. 97), this remark about the letter *E* appears to be a condensation of a passage in *Grammatica* (p. 40).

a syllable with its associate consonant; for, in old editions, words are sometimes divided thus, *clea-re, fel-le, knowled-ge*. This *e* was perhaps for a time vocal or silent in poetry as convenience required; but it has been long wholly mute. Camden in his *Remains*[r] calls it the silent *e*.[7]

It does not always lengthen the foregoing vowel, as *glŏve, lĭve, gĭve.*

It has sometimes in the end of words a sound obscure, and scarcely perceptible, as *open, shapen, shotten, thistle, participle, lucre.*[s]

This faintness of sound is found when *e* separates a mute from a liquid, as in *rotten;* or follows a mute and liquid, as in *cattle.*[t]

E forms a diphthong with *a,* as *near;* with *i,* as *deign, receive;* and with *u* or *w,* as *new, flew.*

Ea sounds like *e* long, as *mean;* or like *ee,* as *dear, clear, near.*

Ei is sounded like *e* long, as *seize, perceiving.*

Eu sounds as *u* long and soft.

E, a, u[u] are combined in *beauty* and its derivatives, but have only the sound of *u.*

E may be said to form a diphthong by reduplication, as *agree, sleeping.*

Eo is found in *yeomen,* where it is sounded as *e* short; and in *people,* where it is pronounced like *ee.*

r. in his *Remains 73*] Camden calls *55a, 55b, 65*
s. *participle, lucre. 73*] *participle, metre, lucre. 55a, 55b, 65*
t. This . . . *cattle. 73*] *lucre. 55a, 55b, 65*
u. *E, a, u 55a, 73*] E, *a, u 55b*] *E a u 65*

7. William Camden, *Remaines concerning Britaine* (1636); see R. D. Dunn's ed. (1984), "Languages," in which Camden defends English orthography (p. 32). SJ's copy of the 1636 edition, which the Folger Library possesses, contains his notes and marginalia (David Fleeman, *A Preliminary Handlist of Copies of Books associated with Dr. Samuel Johnson* [1984], no. 37). "*E* mutum" or "mute e" is Wallis's term in *Grammatica* (p. 44).

I.

I has a sound, long, as *fīne;* and short, as *fĭn.*

That is eminently observable in *i,* which may be likewise remarked in other letters, that the short sound is not the long sound contracted, but a sound wholly different.

The long sound in monosyllables is always marked by the *e* final, as *thĭn, thīne.*

I is often sounded before *r* as a short *u;* as *flirt, first, shirt.*

It forms a diphthong only with *e,* as *field, shield,* which is sounded as the double *ee;* except *friend,* which is sounded as *frĕnd.*

I is joined with *eu* in *lieu,* and *ew* in *view;* which triphthongs are sounded as the open *u.*

O.

O is long, as *bōne, ōbedient, corrōding;* or short, as *blŏck, knŏck, ŏblique, lŏll.*

Women is pronounced *wimen.*

The short *o* has sometimes the sound of a close *u,* as *son, come.*

O coalesces into a diphthong with *a,* as *moan, groan, approach; oa* has the sound of *o* long.

O is united to *e* in some words derived from Greek, as *œconomy;* but *oe* being not an English diphthong, they are better written as they are sounded, with only *e, economy.*[8]

---

8. Under *Oe* in *Dictionary,* SJ states: "This combination of vowels does not properly belong to our language, nor is ever found but in words derived from the Greek, and not yet wholly conformed to our manner of writing: *œ* has in such words the sound of *E.*" Nevertheless, he lists six words beginning with *œ.* On the other hand, he records "economy" in *Dictionary* and comments: "This word is often written, from its derivation, *œconomy;* but *œ* being no diphthong in English, it is placed here with the authorities for different orthography." These "authorities" include Jeremy Taylor, Dryden, Swift, Henry Hammond, Jonson, and Richard Blackmore. In the Preface (p. 112 above), SJ or his compositor spells the word "oeconomy."

With *i,* as *oil, soil,*[v] *moil, noisome.*

This coalition of letters seems to unite the sounds of the two letters as far as two sounds can be united without being destroyed, and therefore approaches more nearly than any combination in our tongue to the notion of a diphthong.[9]

With *o,* as *boot, hoot, cooler; oo* has the sound of the Italian *u.*

With *u* or *w,* as *our, power, flower;* but in some words has only the sound of *o* long, as in *soul, bowl, sow, grow.* These different sounds are used to distinguish different significations; as *bow,* an instrument for shooting; *bow,* a depression of the head: *sow,* the she of a boar; *sow,* to scatter seed: *bowl,* an orbicular body;[1] *bowl,* a wooden vessel.

Ou is sometimes pronounced like *o* soft, as *court;* sometimes like *o* short, as *cough;* sometimes like *u* close, as *could;* or *u* open, as *rough, tough;* which use only can teach.

Ou is frequently used in the last syllable of words which in Latin end in *or,* and are made English, as *honour, labour, favour,* from *honor, labor, favor.*

Some late innovators[2] have ejected the *u,* without considering that the last syllable gives the sound neither of *or* nor *ur,* but a sound between them, if not compounded of both; besides that they are probably derived to us from the French nouns in *eur,* as *honeur, faveur.*

v. *soil, 55a, 55b, 73*] *soil; 65*

9. Cf. the following passage (cited inaccurately under *diphthong* in *Dictionary*) from William Holder's *Elements of Speech* (1669), p. 93: "we see, how many disputes, their [*i, u, ou*] simple and ambiguous nature hath created among the *Grammarians,* and how it has begot the mistake concerning *Diphthongs;* they being all, that are accompted properly such, compounded either with *i, u,* or *ou* and are, as I conceive, *Syllables* and not *Diphthongs* (as it is intended to be signified by that word:). . . ."

1. *Bowl:* "[*boule,* Fr. It is pronounced as *cow, howl.*] A round mass, which may be rolled along the ground" (*Dictionary*).

2. John Milton, e.g.; see below, p. 299, n. 4.

U.

U is long in *ūse, confūsion;* or short, as *ŭs, concŭssion.*

It coalesces with *a, e, i, o;* but has rather in these combinations the force of the *w,* as[w] *quaff, quest, quit, quite, languish;* sometimes in *ui* the *i* loses its sound, as in *juice.* It is sometimes mute before *a, e, i, y,* as *guard, guest, guise, buy.*

U is followed by *e* in *virtue,* but the *e* has no sound.

Ue is sometimes mute at the end of a word, in imitation of the French,[x] as *prorogue, synagogue, plague, vague, harangue.*

Y.

Y is a vowel, which, as Quintilian observes of one of the Roman letters, we might want without inconvenience, but that we have it.[3] It supplies the place of *i* at the end of words, as *thy;* before an *i,* as *dying;* and is commonly retained in derivative words where it was part of a diphthong in the primitive; as *destroy, destroyer; betray, betrayed, betrayer; pray, prayer; say, sayer; day, days.*

Y being the Saxon vowel ý, which was commonly used where *i* is now put, occurs very frequently in all old books.

GENERAL RULES.

A vowel in the beginning or middle syllable, before two consonants, is commonly short, as *ŏppŏrtunity.*

In monosyllables a single vowel before a single consonant is short, as *stăg, frŏg.*[y]

Many is pronounced as if it were written *manny.*[z]

w. *w,* as *73*] *w* consonant, as *55a, 55b, 65*
x. French, *55a, 73*] French; *55b, 65*
y. *stăg, frŏg. 84*] *stag, frog. 55a, 55b, 65, 73*
z. *Many . . . manny. 73*] *frog. 55a, 55b, 65*

3. Quintilian mentions *k, q,* and *x,* "not to mention the mark of the aspirate," *h;* see *Institutio Oratoria,* I.iv.9 and I.vii.10.

§III.[a] Of CONSONANTS.

B.

B has one unvaried sound, such as it obtains in other languages.

It is mute in *debt, debtor, subtle, doubt, lamb, limb, dumb, thumb, climb, comb, womb.*

It is used before *l* and *r,* as *black, brown.*

C.

C has before *e* and *i* the sound of *s;* as *sincerely, centrick, century, circular, cistern, city, siccity:* before *a, o,* and *u,* it sounds like *k,* as *calm, concavity, copper, incorporate, curiosity, concupiscence.*

C might be omitted in the language without loss, since one of its sounds might be supplied by *s,* and the other by *k,* but that it preserves to the eye the eytmology of words, as *face* from *facies, captive* from *captivus.*[4]

Ch has a sound which is analysed into *tsh,* as *church, chin, crutch.* It is the same sound which the Italians give to the *c* simple before *i* and *e,* as *citta, cerro.*

Ch is sounded like *k* in words derived from the Greek, as *chymist, scheme, choler. Arch* is commonly sounded *ark* before a vowel, as *archangel;* and with the English sound of *ch* before a consonant, as *archbishop.*

Ch, in some French words not yet assimilated, sounds like *sh,* as *machine, chaise.*

C, having no determinate sound,[b] according to English orthography, never ends a word; therefore we write *stick, block,*

a. §III. *65*] §III. *absent 55a, 55b, 73*
b. *C,* having . . . sound, *73*] *C,* according *55a, 55b, 65*

4. See SJ's note on *King Lear,* II.ii.59: "Thou whoreson zed! thou unnecessary letter!" SJ considered emending the text to read "C" because "C is a letter unnecessary in our alphabet, one of its two sounds being represented by S, and one by K" (*Yale* VIII.674–75).

which were originally *sticke, blocke.* In such words *C* is now mute.[c][5]

It is used before *l* and *r,* as *clock, cross.*

D.[d]

Is uniform in its sound, as *death, diligent.*

It is used before *r,* as *draw, dross;* and *w,* as *dwell.*

F.

F, through[e] having a name beginning with a vowel, is[f] numbered by the grammarians among the semi-vowels,[6] yet has this quality of a mute, that it is commodiously sounded before a liquid, as *flask, fly, freckle.*[7] It has an unvariable sound, except that *of* is sometimes spoken nearly as *ov.*

G.

G has two sounds, one hard, as in *gay, go, gun;* the other soft, as in *gem, giant.*

At the end of a word it is always hard, *ring, snug, song, frog.*

Before *e* and *i* the sound is uncertain.

G before *e* is soft, as *gem, generation,* except in *gear, geld,*[g] *geese, get, gewgaw,* and derivatives from words ending in *g,* as

c. *blocke.* In . . . mute. *65*] *blocke,* . . . . *C* . . . mute. *55a, 55b, 73*

d. D. *73*] D *55a, 55b, 65*

e. through *emend.* (passage from Greenwood)] though 55a, 55b, 65, 73, 84, 85a, 85b

f. vowel, is *65*] vowel, it is *55a, 55b, 73*

g. *geld, 73*] *gold, 55a, 55b, 65*

5. In the *Life* (IV.31), SJ is reported as remarking: "Imlac in 'Rasselas,' I spelt with a *c* at the end, because it is less like English, which should always have the Saxon *k* added to the *c.*" However, under the entry for *C* in *Dictionary* he says nothing about *c* never ending an English word.

6. Greenwood divides consonants into mutes (*b, c, d, g, p, q, t, z*) and semi-vowels (*f, h, l, m, n, r, s, x*). "A *Mute,*" says Greenwood, "is a Letter which makes no Sound without a *Vowel* added" (p. 265).

7. The "liquids," as Greenwood notes (p. 265), are *l, m, n,* and *r.*

singing, stronger, and generally before *er* at the end of words, as *finger.*

G is mute before *n,* as *gnash, sign, foreign.*

G before *i* is hard, as *give,* except in *giant, gigantick, gibbet, gibe, giblets, Giles, Gill,*[h] *gilliflower, gin, ginger, gingle,* to which may be added *Egypt* and *gypsy.*[i]

Gh in the beginning of a word has the sound of the hard *g,* as *ghostly;* in the middle, and sometimes at the end, it is quite silent, as *though, right, sought,* spoken *tho', rite, soute.*

It has often at the end the sound of *f,* as *laugh;* whence *laughter* retains the same sound in the middle; *cough, trough, sough, tough, enough, slough.*[j]

It is not to be doubted, but that in the original pronunciation *gh* had the force of a consonant, deeply guttural, which is still continued among the Scotch.

G is used before *h, l,* and *r.*

H.

H is a note of aspiration, and shows that the following vowel must be pronounced with a strong emission of the breath, as[k] *hat, horse.*

It seldom begins[l] any but the first syllable, in which it is always sounded with a full breath, except in *heir, herb, hostler, honour, humble, honest, humour,* and their derivatives.

It sometimes begins middle or final syllables in words compounded, as *blockhead;* or derived from the Latin, as *comprehended.*[m]

h. *Giles, Gill emend.* (*in accordance with the context; also see* gill [*Dictionary,* sense 7])] *giles, gill, 55a, 55b, 65, 73, 84, 85a, 85b*

i. *gingle,* to . . . *gypsy. 73*] *gingle, gipsy. 55a, 55b, 65*

j. *enough, slough. 55a, 73*] *enough. 55b, 65*

k. as *55b, 65, 73*] at *55a*

l. seldom begins *73*] seldom, perhaps never, begins *55a, 55b;* seldom, . . . except in compounded words, begins *65. SJ's revisions of this sentence, as well as his addition of the next sentence below, were almost certainly prompted by John Wilkes's article in the* Public Advertiser *(of an uncertain date), which lists numerous words refuting SJ's original statement. See Introduction above, p. 271, n. 4.*

m. derivatives. It . . . *comprehended.* 73] derivatives. *55a, 55b, 65*

J.[8]

J consonant sounds uniformly like the soft *g*, and is therefore a letter useless, except in etymology, as *ejaculation, jester, jocund, juice.*

K.

K has the sound of hard *c*, and is used before *e* and *i*, where, according to English analogy, *c* would be soft, as *kept, king, skirt, skeptick,* for so it should be written, not *sceptick,* because *sc* is sounded like *s*, as in *scene.*[n]

It is used before *n*, as *knell, knot,* but totally loses its sound in modern pronunciation.[o]

K is never doubled; but *c* is used before it to shorten the vowel by a double consonant, as *cŏckle, pĭckle.*

L.

L has in English the same liquid sound as in other languages.

The custom is to double the *l* at the end of monosyllables, as *kill, will, full.* These words were originally written *kille, wille, fulle;* and when the *e* first grew silent, and was afterwards omitted, the *ll* was retained, to give force, according to the analogy of our language, to the foregoing vowel.

L is sometimes mute, as in *calf, half, halves, calves, could, would, should, psalm, talk, salmon, falcon.*

The Saxon, who delighted in guttural sounds, sometimes aspirated the *l* at the beginning of words, as hlaf, *a loaf,* or *bread;* hlaford, *a lord;* but this pronunciation is now disused.

n. sceptick, because . . . *scene.* *73*] *sceptick 55a, 55b, 65*
o. in . . . pronunciation. *73*] sound. *55a, 55b, 65*

---

8. Under the entry in *Dictionary* for *I–J*, SJ states: "*I*, is in English considered both as a vowel and consonant; though, since the vowel and consonant differ in their form as well as sound, they may be more properly accounted two letters.
I vowel has a long sound . . . ; and a short sound. . . .
J consonant has invariably the same sound with that of *g* in *giant*. . . ."

Le at the end of words is pronounced like a weak *el,* in which the *e* is almost mute, as *table, shuttle.*

M.

M has always the same sound, as *murmur, monumental.*

N.

N has always the same sound, as *noble, manners.*

N is sometimes mute after *m,* as *damn, condemn, hymn.*

P.

P has always the same sound, which the Welsh and Germans confound with *B.*

P is sometimes mute, as in *psalm,* and between *m* and *t,* as *tempt.*

Ph is used for *f* in words derived from the Greek, as *philosopher, philanthropy, Philip.*

Q.

Q, as in other languages, is always followed by *u,* and has a sound which our Saxon ancestors well expressed by cp, *cw,* as *quadrant, queen, equestrian, quilt, enquiry, quire, quotidian. Qu* is never followed by *u.*[p]

Qu is sometimes sounded, in words derived from the French, like *k,* as *conquer, liquor, risque, chequer.*[q]

R.

R has the same rough snarling sound as in other tongues.

The Saxons used often to put *h* before it, as before *l* at the beginning of words.

p. *Qu . . . u. 55a, 55b, 73] quotidian. 65*

q. *chequer. ends the par. 55a, 55b, 73] Qu* is never followed by *u. 65*

Rh is used in words derived from the Greek, as *myrrh, myrrhine, catarrhous, rheum, rheumatick, rhyme.*

Re, at the end of some words derived from the Latin or French, is pronounced like a weak *er,* as *theatre, sepulchre.*

S.

S has a hissing sound, as *sibilation, sister.*

A single *s* seldom ends any word, except the third person of verbs, as *loves, grows;* and the plurals of nouns, as *trees, bushes, distresses;* the pronouns *this, his, ours, yours, us;* the adverb *thus;* and words derived from Latin, as *rebus, surplus;* the close being always either in *se,* as *house, horse,* or in *ss,* as *grass, dress, bliss, less,* anciently *grasse, dresse.*

S single, at the end of words, has a grosser sound, like that of *z,* as *trees, eyes,* except *this, thus, us, rebus, surplus.*

It sounds like *z* before *ion,* if a vowel goes before, as *intrusion;* and like *s,* if it follows a consonant, as *conversion.*

It sounds like *z* before *e* mute, as *refuse,* and before *y* final, as *rosy;* and in those words, *bosom, desire, wisdom, prison, prisoner, presént, présent,*[r] *damsel, casement.*

It is the peculiar quality of *s,* that it may be sounded before all consonants, except *x* and *z,* in which *s* is comprised, *x* being only *ks,* and *z* a hard or gross *s.* This *s* is therefore termed by grammarians *suæ*[s] *potestatis litera;*[t9] the reason of which the learned Dr. Clarke erroneously supposed to be, that in some words it might be doubled at pleasure.[1] Thus we find in several languages:

r. *presént, présent, 55b, 65*] *présent, presènt, 55a; présent, present, 73*
s. *suæ 55a, 73*] *sue 55b, 65*
t. *litera; 55a, 73*] *litera, 55b, 65*

9. See *Institutio Compendiaria* (1540), sig. Bi[v].

1. In the first half of the eighteenth century, two Clarkes were dubbed "learned": John, a schoolmaster at Hull and a grammatical writer cited many times in *Dictionary* (see *Notes and Queries,* 11th series, IX [1914], 11); and the far better known Samuel, rector of St. James's, Westminster, whom SJ admired but said he omitted from *Dictionary* (which nevertheless quotes him under *credulity* and *justification*) because of his near Arianism (*Life,* IV.416 n. 2).

Σβέννυμι, scatter, sdegno, sdrucciolo, sfavellare, σφὶγξ, sgombrare, sgranare, shake, slumber, smell, snipe,[u] *space, splendour, spring, squeeze, shrew, step, strength, stramen, stripe, sventura,*[v] *swell.*[2]

S is mute in *isle, island, demesne, viscount.*

T.

T has its customary sound, as *take, temptation.*

Ti before a vowel has the sound of *si,* as *salvation,* except an *s* goes before, as *question,* excepting likewise derivatives from words ending in *ty,*[w] as *mighty, mightier.*

Th has two sounds; the onc soft, as *thus, whether;* the other hard, as *thing, think.* The sound is soft in these words, *then, thence,* and *there,* with their derivatives and compounds; and in *that,*[x] *these, thou, thee, thy, thine, their, they, this, those,*[y] *them, though, thus,* and in all words between two vowels, as *father, whether;* and between *r* and a vowel, as *burthen.*

In other words it is hard, as *thick, thunder, faith, faithful.* Where it is softened at the end of a word, an *e* silent must be added, as *breath, breathe; cloth, clothe.*

u. *snipe, 73*] *strife, 55a, 55b, 65*
v. *stramen, . . . sventura, 73*] *stramen, sventura, 55a, 55b, 65*
w. from . . . *ty, 73*] from *y, 55a, 55b, 65*
x. compounds; and in *73*] compounds, *that 55a, 55b, 65*
y. *those, 84*] *these, 55a, 55b, 65, 73*

Neither "learned" Dr. Clarke ever commented explicitly on the principle, so far as we know, but Clarke says doubling of *s* is *multum licita* in his note on *Iliad* I.67 in his edition of Homer (1729).

2. These examples, drawn from Greek, English, and Italian, show that an *s* sound can precede the sounds of "all consonants, except *x* and *z*"; the definitions of the foreign words are as follows: *Σβέννυμι*: quench, put out; *sdegno:* disdain; *sdrucciolo:* sliding, slippery; *sfavellare:* to misspeak, from *favellare* or a mistake for *svafillare,* to shine; *σφίγξ*: sphinx; *sgombrare:* to depart; *sgranare:* to burst open; *stramen:* straw; *sventura:* misfortune.

V.

V has a sound of near affinity to that of *f, vain, vanity.*

From *f* in the Islandick alphabet, *v* is only distinguished by a diacritical point.[3]

W.

Of *w,* which in diphthongs is often an undoubted vowel, some grammarians have doubted whether it ever be a consonant; and not rather as it is called a double *u* or *ou,* as *water* may be resolved into *ouater;*[4] but letters of the same sound are always reckoned consonants in other alphabets: and it may be observed, that *w* follows a vowel without any hiatus or difficulty of utterance, as *frosty winter.* Yet I am of opinion that both *w* and *y* are always vowels, because they cannot after a vowel be used with the sound which is supposed to make them consonants.[z5]

Wh has a sound accounted peculiar to the English, which the Saxons better expressed by hƿ, *hw,* as *what, whence, whiting;* in *whore* only, and sometimes in *wholesome, wh* is sounded like a simple *h.*

X.

X begins no English word;[6] it has the sound of *ks,* as *axle, extraneous.*

z. Yet . . . consonants. *65*] *winter. 55a, 55b, 73*

3. See Runolph Jonas, "Grammaticae Islandicae Rudimenta," in *Thesaurus,* Part III, p. 3. Jones makes the ancient Islandic alphabet out of runic characters.

4. "Some grammarians" who treat *w* as *ou* include Ben Jonson, who writes "*ou*-ine" and "*ou*-ant" as examples (*English Grammar,* 478–79). In making this statement, SJ follows Wallis, who likewise says of *w,* "a quibusdam pro vocali fuit habita" (*Grammatica,* p. 15).

5. SJ follows Ben Jonson in so classifying *w* and *y,* but his reason seems to be his own (see *English Grammar,* 479–80). SJ seems to contradict himself in his treatment of *y,* below, but he also reaffirms the reason for his belief that *y* and *w* are vowels.

6. Cf. entry for *X* in *Dictionary:* "*X* Is

Y.

Y, when it follows a consonant, is a vowel; when it precedes either vowel or diphthong, is a consonant, as *ye*,[a] *young*. It is thought by some to be in all cases a vowel.[7] But it may be observed of *y* as of *w*, that it follows a vowel without any hiatus, as *rosy youth*.

The chief argument by which *w* and *y* appear to be always vowels is, that the sounds which they are supposed to have as consonants, cannot be uttered after a vowel, like that of all other consonants; thus we say, *tu, ut; do, odd;* but in *wed, dew*, the two sounds of *w* have no resemblance of each other.[b]

a. consonant, as *ye, 65*] consonant, *ye, 55a, 55b, 73*
b. The . . . other. *73*] *youth. 55a, 55b*] It may . . . *youth*, but yet that it cannot be sounded after a vowel. *65*

---

a letter, which, though found in Saxon words, begins no word in the English language." Isaac Watts and probably other commentators made the same statement before SJ. In his *Art of Reading and Writing English* (7th ed., 1751), Watts (whose biography SJ wrote for the *Lives of the Poets*), having arrived at the letter X in a list of "Moral Instructions" for school children, "beginning with every Letter of the Alphabet," says: "*X* Excuse but with truth, The follies of youth." His "Note" below reads: "*The Letter* X *begins no English Word, so that we must begin that Line with* Ex; *unless the Reader will chuse this instead of it,* (viz.).

> X is such a cross letter, Balks my
> morals and metre. (p. 20)

Much later, in his note on SJ's statement, J. H. Todd remarks: "None really English; but attempts have been made to anglicize a few words beginning with *x*" (*Dictionary*, Todd's ed. [1818], IV, Grammar, s.v. *X*). Similarly, Robert Gordon Latham, the last editor of *Dictionary*, declares at the conclusion of his entry on the letter *X:* "Indeed, it is mainly, perhaps only, as the equivalent of the Greek ξ that the letter, as an initial, has any use" (1882; vol. II, pt. II). And the *OED* summarizes: "Words having initial x . . . in English are nearly all of Greek origin; a few . . . have x representing early Sp[anish] *x* (now *j*)." So, SJ's generalization seems to be essentially accurate.

7. Ben Jonson says Y "Is also meere *Vowellish* in our tongue, and hath only the power of an *i.* even where it obtaines the seat of a *Consonant*" (*English Grammar,* 479).

Z.

Z begins no word originally English;[8] it has the sound,[c] as its name *izzard* or *s hard* expresses, of an *s* uttered with closer compression of the palate by the tongue, as *freeze, froze.*

In orthography I have supposed *orthoepy,*[9] or *just utterance of words,* to be included; orthography being only the art of expressing certain sounds by proper characters. I have therefore observed in what words any of the letters are mute.

Most of the writers of English grammar have given long tables of words pronounced otherwise than they are written, and seem not sufficiently to have considered, that of English, as of all living tongues, there is a double pronunciation, one cursory and colloquial, the other regular and solemn. The cursory pronunciation is always vague and uncertain, being made different in different mouths by negligence, unskilfulness, or affectation. The solemn pronunciation, though by no means immutable and permanent, is yet always less remote from the orthography, and less liable to capricious innovation. They have however generally formed their tables according to the cursory speech of those with whom they happened to converse; and concluding that the whole nation combines to vitiate language in one manner, have often established the jargon of the lowest of the people as the model of speech.[1]

c. sound, *55b, 65, 73*] sound *55a*

---

8. Cf. the entry for *z* in *Dictionary:* "Z, Is found in the Saxon alphabets, set down by Grammarians, but is read in no word originally Teutonick: its sound is uniformly that of an hard S. No word of English original begins with Z." The list of words under *Z* bears out SJ's remarks.

9. *Orthoepy* does not appear in *Dictionary;* sense 1 of *orthography* is: "The part of grammar which teaches how words should be spelled."

1. SJ probably refers to the lists of homophones that were common after Charles Butler's *The English Grammar* (1633), sigs. a1^{v}–d2^{v}. For discussion of these tables, see E. J. Dobson, *English Pronunciation, 1500–1700* (2d ed., 1968), I.395–421; Dobson's criticism of Butler resembles SJ's.

For pronunciation the best general rule is, to consider those as the most elegant speakers who deviate least from the written words.

There have been many schemes offered for the emendation and settlement of our orthography, which, like that of other nations, being formed by chance, or according to the fancy of the earliest writers in rude ages, was at first very various and uncertain, and is yet sufficiently irregular.[2] Of these reformers some have endeavoured to accommodate orthography better to the pronunciation, without considering that this is to measure by a shadow, to take that for a model or standard which is changing while they apply it.[3] Others, less absurdly indeed, but with equal unlikelihood of success, have endeavoured to proportion the number of letters to that of sounds, that every sound may have its own character, and every character a single sound.[4] Such would be the orthography of a new language to be formed by a synod of grammarians upon principles of science.[5] But who can hope to prevail on nations to change their practice, and make all their old books useless? or what advantage would a new orthography procure equivalent to the confusion and perplexity of such an alteration?

Some of these schemes I shall however exhibit, which may be used according to the diversities of genius,[6] as a guide to reformers, or terrour to innovators.

---

2. Cf. *Plan* (p. 35 above): "ORTHOGRAPHY was long vague and uncertain . . . was in many cases settled but by accident and . . . according to [Lord Chesterfield's] observation, there is still great uncertainty among the best critics."

3. Cf. Preface (pp. 78–79 above): "Much less ought our written language to comply with the corruptions of oral utterance, or copy that which every variation of time or place makes different from itself, and imitate those changes, which will again be changed, while imitation is employed in observing them."

4. To give "every character a single sound" was a chief goal of Alexander Gil's reformed spelling in *Logonomia Anglica* (1619). For a discussion of Gil's system, see Dobson, I.137–38.

5. *Science:* "Art attained by precepts, or built on principles" (*Dictionary,* sense 3).

6. *Genius:* "Disposition of nature by which any one is qualified for some peculiar employment" (*Dictionary,* sense 4).

One of the first who proposed a scheme of regular orthography, was Sir Thomas Smith, secretary of state to Queen Elizabeth, a man of real learning, and much practised in grammatical disquisitions.[7] Had he written the following lines according to his scheme, they would have appeared thus:[d]

> At length Erasmus, that great injur'd name,
> The glory of the priesthood, and the shame,
> Stemm'd the wild torrent of a barb'rous age,
> And drove those holy Vandals off the stage.[8]

> At lengð Erasmus, ðat grët ïnȝurd nâm,
> Δe glorï of ðe prësthüd, and ðe zâm,
> Stemmd ðe *w*ild torrent of a barb'rous âȝ,[e]
> And dröv ðös höli Vandals öff ðe stâȝ.

After him another mode of writing was offered by Dr. Gill, the celebrated master of St. Paul's school in London; which I cannot represent exactly for want of types, but will approach as nearly as I can by means of characters now in use, so as[f] to make it understood, exhibiting two stanzas of Spenser in the reformed orthography.[9]

d. thus: *65, 73*] thus. *55a, 55b*
e. âȝ, *55b, 65, 73*] âȝ. *55a*
f. use, so as *73*] use as *55a;* use so as *55b, 65*

7. See Smith's *De Recta et Emendata Linguae Anglicae Scriptione, Dialogus* (Paris, 1568). Smith's orthographic system comprises thirty-four letters: "Of which," he writes in Latin, "nineteen are Roman, *a, b, c, d, e, f, g, h, i, l, m, n, o, p, q, r, s, t, u.* Four are Greek, *k, x, u* [English y], *z.* Six are English, e [i:], D [ð], v [v or voiceless f], ˚ [j], s [sh], Σ [w]" (fol. 52ʳ). Smith, besides listing long and short forms for *a, e, i, o, u,* and a third, extra long *e,* also uses a total of five diacritical marks (¨, ", ˆ, ˜, ¯) to show the relative length of the long vowels. SJ's transliteration, which we preserve, contains many errors, especially in the use of the diacriticals.

8. Alexander Pope, *Essay on Criticism,* ll. 693–96; quoted in part under both *stem* and *torrent* in *Dictionary.*

9. Alexander Gil, *Logonomia Anglica,* p. 117. In trying to represent this passage, we offer an approximation based on *Dictionary*'s often faulty transcription, rather than Gil's text. For example, Gil distinguished between *j* and *i* (a long descender without a hook at the bottom), which SJ does not, and he used three different *h*'s, whereas SJ gives him only two. Gil proposed to reform English spelling by employing multiple characters for each letter and diacritical marks for the vowels. His second edition (1621) acknowledged the failure of his radical

Spenser, book iii. canto 5.[1]

Unthankful wretch, said he, is this the meed,
With which her sovereign mercy thou dost quite?
Thy life she saved by her gracious deed;
But thou dost ween with villanous despight,
To blot her honour, and her heav'nly light.
Die, rather die, than so disloyally,
Deem of her high desert, or seem so light.
Fair death it is to shun more shame; then die.
Die, rather die, than ever love disloyally.
But if to love disloyalty it be,
Shall I then hate her, that from deathes door
Me brought? ah! far be such reproach from me.
What can I less do, than her love therefore,
Sith I her due reward cannot restore?
Die, rather die, and dying do her serve,
Dying her serve, and living her adore.
Thy life she gave, thy life she doth deserve;
Die, rather die, than ever from her service swerve.

Vnɧ*a*nkful wrɛɔ, s*a*id hj, iz ðis ðe mjd,
Wiɧ wiɔ her so𝔳er*a*in mɛrsi ðou dust qujt?
Đj ljf ɼj s*ɑ*𝔳ɛd bj hɛr grasius djd;
But ðou dust wen wiɧ 𝔳ilɛnus dispjt,
Tu blot hɛr honor, *a*nd hɛr he𝔳nlj li*h*t.[g]
Dj, r*a*ðer dj, ðen so dislòi*a*lj,[h]
Djm of hɛr hi*h* dɛzɛrt, or sjm so li*h*t.
F*a*ir deɧ it iz tu ɼun m*ω*r ɼ*ã*m; ðɛn dj.
Dj, raðer dj, ðɛn *ɛ*𝔳ɛr lu𝔳 disloi*a*lj.

But if tu lu𝔳 disloi*a*ltj it bj,
Sal I ðɛn h*ã*t hɛr ðat from dɛðez d*ωr*
Mj brou*h*t? *a*h! f*a*r bj suɔ rɛproɔ from mj.

g. li*h*t. *55a, 55b, 73*] li*h*t: *65*
h. dislòi*a*lj, *55b, 65, 73*] disloi*a*lj. *55a*

innovations by using fewer new letters and diacriticals.

1. *The Faerie Queene,* III.v.45–46.

Wat k*a*n I lɛs du ðɛn hɛr luʋ ðɛrf*ωr*,
Si*h* I her du rɛw*a*rd kanot rest*ωr*?
Dj, r*a*ðer dj, and dji3 du hɛr sɛrʋ,
Dji3 hɛr sɛrʋ, and liʋi3 hɛr ad*ωr*.
Ðj ljf ꝛj g*ã*ʋ, ðj ljf ꝛj du*h* dɛzɛrʋ.[i]
Dj, r*a*ðɛr dj,[j] ðɛn ɛʋɛr from hɛr sɛrʋis swɛrʋ.

Dr. Gill was followed by Charles Butler, a man who did not want an understanding which might have qualified him for better employment. He seems to have been more sanguine than his predecessors, for he printed his book according to his own scheme; which the following specimen will make easily understood.[2]

But whensoever you have occasion to trouble their patience, or to come among them being troubled, it is better to stand upon your guard, than to trust to their gentleness. For the safeguard of your face, which they have most mind unto, provide a pursehood, made of coarse boultering,[3] to be drawn and knit about your collar, which for more safety is to be lined against the eminent parts with woollen cloth. First cut a piece about an inch and a[k] half broad, and half a yard long, to reach round by the temples and forehead, from one ear to the other; which being sowed in his place, join unto it two

i. dezerv. *55a*] dezerv; *55b, 65, 73*
j. dj, *85a*] di, *55a, 55b, 65, 73, 84*
k. a *55a, 73*] an *55b, 65*

2. *The Feminin' Monarchi', or the Histori of Bee's* (1634), pp. 12–13. Earlier Butler had published this work in conventional spelling (1609), though the text varies as well as the orthography. (SJ's regular spelling version is his own transliteration.) After explaining some of the typographical details, a note in the phonetic spelling edition from "Ðe Printer to ðe Reader" (sig. ¶4[v]) refers the reader to Butler's *English Grammar* (1633). Butler signifies "aspiration" by putting a dash through the consonants *d, t, c, k, g, p, s,* and *w*. He also adds the digraphs double *e* and double *o,* for a total of thirty-six characters in his alphabet, plus an inverted apostrophe for silent, or as he calls it, "quiescent" *e*. We reproduce *Dictionary*'s very inaccurate transcription, although its typographical choices obscure Butler's system.

3. *Boultering:* "The fabric used for bolters or sieves" (*OED*, s.v. *boltering*), not in *Dictionary*.

short pieces[l] of the same breadth under the eyes, for the balls of the cheeks, and then set an other[m] piece about the breadth of a shilling against the top of the nose. At other times, when they are not angered, a little piece half a quarter broad, to cover the eyes and parts about them, may serve though it be in the heat of the day.

Bet penfoëver you hav' occasion to trubble ðeir patienc', or to c*oo*m among ðem b*ee*ing trubled, it is better to stand upon your gard, ðan to trust to ðeir gentlenes. For ðe saf'gard of your fac', piɔ ðey hav' most mind' unto, provid' a purseh*oo*d, mad' of c*oo*rse boultering, to b*ee* drawn and knit about your collar, piɔ for mor' saf'ty is to b*ee* lined against ð' eminent parts wiƈ w*oo*llen cloƈ. First cut a p*ee*c' about an inɔ and a half broad, and half a yard long, to reaɔ round by ðe temples and for'head, from one ear to ðe oðer; piɔ b*ee*ing sowed in his plac', join unto it two ʃort p*ee*ces of the sam breadƈ under ðe eys, for the bals of ðe ch*ee*ks,[n] and then set an oðer p*ee*c' about ðe breadƈ of a ʃilling against the top of ðe nose. At oðer tim's, pen ðey ar' not angered, a little piec' half a quarter broad, to cover ðe eys and parts about them, may serve ðowʒ it be in the heat of ðe day. *Butler on the Nature and Properties of Bees,* 1634.

In the time of Charles I. there was a very prevalent inclination to change the orthography; as appears, among other books, in such editions of the works of Milton as were published by himself.[4] Of these reformers every man had his own

l. pieces *55b, 65, 73*] peces *55a*
m. an other *55a, 55b, 73*] another *65*
n. ch*ee*ks, *73*] *cheeks*, *55a, 55b, 65*

4. SJ may overestimate the control Milton had over the spellings that appear in his works. Milton did, however, use many reformed spellings, and his works reflect this, albeit somewhat inconsistently. For a discussion of Milton's spelling and a list of his probable preferences, based on holograph sources, see John T. Shawcross, "The Texts of Milton's Works" in *The Riverside Milton,* ed. Roy Flanagan (1998), pp. xi–xxxii.

scheme; but they agreed in one general design of accommodating the letters to the pronunciation, by ejecting such as they thought superfluous. Some of them would have written these lincs thus:

——— All the erth
Shall then be paradis, far happier place
Than this of Eden, and far happier dais.[5]

Bishop Wilkins afterwards, in his great work of the philosophical language, proposed, without expecting to be followed, a regular orthography; by which the Lord's prayer is to be written thus:

Y*ov*r Fádher h*ov*itsh art in héven, h*a*lloëd bi dhyi n*á*m, dhyi cingdým cým, dhy *ov*ill bi dýn in erth as it is in héven, &c.[6]

We have since had no general reformers; but some ingenious men have endeavoured to deserve well of their country, by writing *honor* and *labor* for *honour* and *labour, red* for *read* in the preter-tense, *sais* for *says, repete* for *repeat, explane* for *explain,* or *declame* for *declaim.*[7] Of these it may be said, that as

---

5. *Paradise Lost* XII, 463–65. The transposition of *then* and *all* may indicate that SJ is remembering these lines, although the first two, included under *paradise* in *Dictionary* read correctly, "'The earth / Shall all be paradise, far happier place.'" An example of a spelling reformer active "In the time of Charles I" (1625–1649) who favored the orthography in SJ's example is Richard Hodges. For an account of Hodges's orthographical writings, including *A Special Help to Orthography* (1643) see Dobson, I.167–73.

6. In *An Essay towards a Real Character and a Philosophical Language* (1668), John Wilkins presents his phonetic orthography without any exhortations for its use: "According to this establishment of Letters, if the *Lords Prayer* or *Creed* were to be written according to our present pronunciation of it, they should be each of them thus Lettered: . . ." (p. 373). This example of phonetic spelling is neither the "real character" nor the "philosophical language." The typography is approximate (with Greek *ov* representing a vertical digraph for omicron-upsilon common in eighteenth-century Greek typography). SJ's text, which we reproduce, contains several small errors.

7. With the exception of *sais,* these spellings are all recorded by *OED* as occurring in the seventeenth or eighteenth centuries and used by various authors. SJ clearly prefered *honour* over

they have done no good, they have done little harm; both because they have innovated little, and because few have followed them.

The English language has properly no dialects; the stile of writers has no professed diversity in the use of words, or of their flexions, and terminations, nor differs but by different degrees of skill or care. The oral diction is uniform in no spacious country, but has less variation in England than in most other nations of equal extent. The language of the northern counties retains many words now out of use, but which are commonly of the genuine Teutonick race, and is uttered with a pronunciation which now seems harsh and rough, but was probably used by our ancestors. The northern speech is therefore not barbarous but obsolete. The speech in the western provinces seems to differ from the general diction rather by a depraved pronunciation,[8] than by any real difference which letters would express.[o]

PART II.[p]

ETYMOLOGY.

ETYMOLOGY teaches the deduction of one word from another, and the various modifications by which the sense of the same word is diversified; as *horse, horses;* I *love,* I *loved.*

o. The English . . . express. *73*] them. *55a, 55b, 65*
p. PART II. *65*] PART II. *absent 55a, 55b, 73*

honor, and as remarks recorded in the *OED* suggest, this word was a kind of shibboleth for testing commitment to conventional spelling in the mid-eighteenth century.

8. To *deprave:* "To vitiate; to corrupt; to contaminate" (*Dictionary*). By "the western provinces," SJ probably means Ireland because he defines *province,* following the Latin usage of the word, as "A conquered country" (*Dictionary*); this would seem to exclude the other possibilities, Devon and Cornwall, or the American colonies.

§I.[q] *Of the* ARTICLE.

The English have two articles, *an* or *a,* and *the.*

AN, A.

A has an indefinite signification, and means *one,* with some reference to more; as, *This is a good book,* that is, *one among the books that are good. He was killed by a sword,* that is, *some sword. This is a better book for a man than a boy,* that is, *for one of those that are men than one of those that are boys. An army might enter without resistance,* that is, *any army.*

In the senses in which we use *a* or *an* in the singular, we speak in the plural without an article; as, *these are good books.*

I have made *an* the original article, because it is only the Saxon *an,*[r] or æn, *one,* applied to a new use, as the German *ein,* and the French *un;* the *n* being cut off before a consonant in the speed of utterance.[9]

Grammarians of the last age direct, that *an* should be used before *h;*[1] whence it appears that the English anciently aspirated less. *An* is still used before the silent *h,* as *an herb, an honest man:* but otherwise *a;* as,

A horse, *a* horse, my kingdom for *a* horse.
Shakespeare.[2]

An or *a* can only be joined with a singular, the correspondent plural is the noun without an article, as *I want* a *pen, I want pens:* or with the pronominal adjective *some,* as *I want* some *pens.*[s]

q. §I. *65*] §I. *absent 55a, 55b, 73*
r. *an 55a, 55b, 73*] an *65*
s. *An . . . pens. 73*] *Shakespeare. 55a, 55b, 65*

9. This observation may be an original contribution to English grammar; see H. G. Baker, "The Contribution of John Wallis to the Methods and Materials of English Grammarians" (Ph.D. diss., Univ. of Michigan, 1937), p. 385.

1. The *OED* reports, "*An* . . . was regular before *h* down to 17th c., as *an house, an happy, an hundred*" (s.v. *an,* a.[2]). However, we have not located a grammarian who "direct[s]" this; all those we have consulted recommend *a* before sounded *h.*

2. *Richard III,* V.iv.7; cited under *horse* in *Dictionary.*

THE has a particular and definite signification.

The fruit
Of that forbidden tree, whose mortal taste
Brought death into *the* world.

Milton.[3]

That is, *that particular fruit,* and *this world in which we live.* So *He giveth fodder for* the *cattle, and green herbs for* the *use of man;*[4] that is, for *those beings that are cattle,* and *his use that is man.*

The is used in both numbers.

I am as free as Nature first made man,
Ere *the* base laws of servitude began,
When wild in woods *the* noble savage ran. *Dryden.*[t5]

Many words are used without articles; as,

1. Proper names, as *John, Alexander, Longinus, Aristarchus, Jerusalem, Athens, Rome, London.* GOD is used as a proper name.

2. Abstract names, as *blackness, witchcraft, virtue, vice, beauty, ugliness, love, hatred, anger, goodnature, kindness.*

3. Words in which nothing but the mere being of any thing is implied: This is not *beer,* but *water;* This is not *brass,* but *steel.*

§II.[u] *Of* NOUNS SUBSTANTIVES.

The relations of English nouns to words going before or following are not expressed by *cases,* or changes of termination, but as in most of the other European languages by prepositions, unless we may be said to have a genitive case.

t. *Dryden. 65*] *Dryd. 55a, 55b, 73*
u. §II. *65*] §II. *absent 55a, 55b, 73*

3. *Paradise Lost,* I.1–3; cited under *mortal* (sense 2) in *Dictionary.*

4. Psalms 104.14.

5. *The Conquest of Granada,* Pt. 1, I.i. 207–9.

	Singular.
Nom. Magister,	*a* Master, *the* Master.
Gen. Magistri,	*of a* Master, *of the* Master, *or* Masters, *the* Masters.
Dat. Magistro,	*to a* Master, *to the* Master.
Acc. Magistrum,	*a* Master, *the* Master.
Voc. Magister,	Master, *O* Master.
Abl. Magistro,	*from a* Master, *from the* Master.

	Plural.
Nom. Magistri,	Masters, *the* Masters.
Gen. Magistrorum,	*of* Masters, *of the* Masters.
Dat. Magistris,	*to* Masters, *to the* Masters.
Acc. Magistros,	Masters, *the* Masters.
Voc. Magistri,	Masters, *O* Masters.
Abl. Magistris,	*from* Masters, *from the* Masters.

Our nouns are therefore only declined thus:

Master,	*Gen.* Masters.	*Plur.* Masters.
Scholar,	*Gen.* Scholars.	*Plur.* Scholars.

These genitives are always written with a mark of elision, *master's, scholar's,* according to an opinion long received, that the *'s* is a contraction of *his,* as *the soldier's valour,* for *the soldier* his *valour:* but this cannot be the true original, because *'s* is put to female nouns, *Woman's beauty;* the *Virgin's delicacy; Haughty Juno's unrelenting hate:*[6] and collective nouns, as *Women's passions; the rabble's insolence; the multitude's folly;* in all these cases it is apparent that *his* cannot be understood. We say likewise, *the foundation's strength, the diamond's lustre, the winter's severity;* but in these cases *his* may be understood, *he* and *his* having formerly been applied to neuters in the place now supplied by *it* and *its.*[7]

---

6. Dryden's *Aeneas* (1697), I.2.

7. Joseph Addison repeated the popular derivation of *'s* from *his* in *Spectator* 135 par. 8 ("I might here observe, that the same single Letter [*s*] on many occasions does the Office of a whole Word, and represents the *His* and *Her* of our Forefathers"), but it had been debunked as early as Alexander Hume's *Of the Orthographie and Congruitie of the British*

The learned and sagacious[v] Wallis, to whom every English grammarian owes a tribute of reverence, calls this modification of the noun an *adjective possessive;*[8] I think with no more propriety than he might have applied the same to the genitive in *equitum decus, Trojæ oris,*[9] or any other Latin genitive. Dr. Lowth, on the other part, supposes the possessive pronouns *mine* and *thine* to be genitive cases.[w1]

This termination of the noun seems to constitute a real genitive indicating possession. It is derived to us from those who declined smið, *a smith;* Gen. smiðes, *of a smith;* Plur. smiðes, or smiðas, *smiths;* and so in two other of their seven declensions.[2]

It is a further confirmation of this opinion, that in the old poets both the genitive and plural were longer by a syllable than the original word; *knitis,* for *knight's,* in Chaucer; *leavis,* for *leaves,* in Spenser.[3]

v. and sagacious *73*] learned, the sagacious *55a, 55b, 65*
w. Dr. . . . cases. *73*] genitive. *55a, 55b, 65*

Tongue (1617), lib. 2, cap. 5, par. 7 (see Dobson, *English Pronunciation,* I.317). The apostrophe stands for the *e* of the Old English genitive ending *es,* which was no longer pronounced in Middle English. *His* is the Old English neuter genitive singular, but this classification is not relevant to the etymology of possessive *'s,* which SJ does not seem to understand.

8. "Adjectivum *Possessivum* libet appellare," *Grammatica,* pp. 69, 101.

9. *equitum decus,* "The dignity of the cavalry," perhaps inaccurately recalling *decus equestris,* "the honor of equestrian (rank)," Velleius Paterculus, *History of Rome,* II.cxviii.2; *Trojae . . . ab oris,* "from the shores of Troy," *Aeneid,* I.1.

1. Robert Lowth, *A Short Introduction to English Grammar* (1762), pp. 35–36, which calls the case "possessive" rather than "genitive," and which SJ recommended, along with other works, to the young Daniel Astle as part of his studies (*Life* IV.311).

2. Hickes declines smið thus (*Linguarum Vett.* I.i.10), but he settles on six for the number of declensions in Anglo-Saxon; these plus the irregulars would make seven.

3. *Knightes* appears often in Chaucer as a trisyllabic word (*Canterbury Tales,* I (A) 3127, for example). *Leaves* is usually one syllable in Spenser (as in *Amoretti,* I.i, which SJ cites in *Dictionary* under *leaf*), but once, at least, it is a dissyllable (*Faerie Queene,* V.xii.13.6). Even seventeenth-century orthopoeists, such as Alexander Gil, recognized it as poetic and archaic when the *-es* plural was made a separate syllable. For additional details, see Dobson, *English Pronunciation,* II.882–83. SJ's *-is* spellings represent pronunciation, not earlier forms of the words.

When a word ends in *s,* the genitive may be the same with the nominative, as *Venus temple.*

The plural is formed by adding *s,* as *table, tables; fly, flies; sister, sisters; wood, woods;* or *es* where *s* could not otherwise be sounded, as after *ch, s, sh, x, z;* after *c* sounded like *s,* and *g* like *j;* the mute *e* is vocal before *s,* as *lance, lances; outrage, outrages.*

The formation of the plural and genitive singular is the same.

A few words yet make the plural in *n,* as *men, women, oxen, swine,* and more anciently *eyen* and *shoon.* This formation is that which generally prevails in the Teutonick dialects.

Words that end in *f* commonly form their plural by *ves,* as *loaf, loaves; calf, calves.*

Except a few, *muff, muffs; chief, chiefs.* So *hoof, roof, proof, relief, mischief, puff, cuff, dwarf, handkerchief, grief.*

Irregular plurals are *teeth* from *tooth, lice* from *louse, mice* from *mouse, geese* from *goose, feet* from *foot, dice* from *die, pence* from *penny, brethren* from *brother, children* from *child.*

Plurals ending in *s* have for the most part[x] no genitives; but we say, Womens *excellencies,* and *Weigh the* mens *wits against the* ladies *hairs.* Pope.[4]

Dr. Wallis thinks *the Lord's*[y] *house* may be said for *the house of Lords;* but such phrases are not now in use; and surely an English ear rebels against them.[5] They would commonly produce a troublesome ambiguity, as *the Lord's house* may be the *house of Lords,* or *the house of* a *Lord.* Besides that the mark of elision is improper, for in *the Lord's*[y] *house* nothing is cut off.

Some English substantives, like those of many other languages, change their termination as they express different sexes, as *prince, princess; actor, actress; lion, lioness; hero, heroine.*[yy] To these mentioned by Dr. Lowth[6] may be added *arbitress, poetess, chauntress, duchess, tigress, governess, tutress, peeress, authoress, traytress,* and perhaps others. Of these variable termi-

x. for . . . part *73*] have no *55a, 55b, 65*
y. *Lord's emend.* (as in Wallis)] *Lords' 55a, 55b, 65, 73, 84, 85a, 85b*
yy. *heroine* 85a] *heroines 55, 55a, 65, 73*

4. *Rape of the Lock,* V.72 (mutatis).
5. *Grammatica,* p. 70.
6. *A Short Introduction* (1762), p. 30.

nations we have only a sufficient number to make us feel our want, for when we say of a woman that she is a *philosopher,* an *astronomer,* a *builder,* a *weaver,* a *dancer,* we perceive an impropriety in the termination which we cannot avoid; but we can say that she is an *architect,* a *botanist,* a *student,* because these terminations have not annexed to them the notion of sex. In words which the necessities of life are often requiring, the sex is distinguished not by different terminations but by different names, as a *bull,* a *cow;* a *horse,* a *mare; equus, equa;* a *cock,* a *hen;* and sometimes by pronouns prefixed, as *a* he-*goat, a* she-*goat.*[z]

§III.[a] *Of* ADJECTIVES.

Adjectives in the English language are wholly indeclinable; having neither case, gender, nor number, and being added to substantives in all relations without any change; as, *a good woman, good women, of a good woman; a good man, good men, of good men.*

The Comparison of Adjectives.

The comparative degree of adjectives is formed by adding *er,* the superlative by adding *est,* to the positive; as,[b] *fair,* fair*er,* fair*est; lovely,* loveli*er,* loveli*est; sweet,* sweet*er,* sweet*est; low,* low*er,* low*est; high,* high*er,* high*est.*

Some words are irregularly compared; as *good, better, best; bad, worse, worst; little, less, least; near, nearer, next; much, more, most; many* (or *moe*), *more* (for *moer*), *most* (for *moest*); *late, latter,*[c] *latest* or *last.*

z. They would . . . she-*goat. 73*] They would . . . she-*goat. absent 55a, 55b, 65*

a. §III. *65*] §III. *absent 55a, 55b, 73*

b. as, *55a, 55b, 65*] as *73*

c. *latter, 55a, 73*] *later, 55b, 65. In* Dictionary, later *does not appear as a separate entry, although under* late *SJ comments:* "in the comparative *latter* for *later,* in the superlative *latest* or *last.*" *Under* latter, *SJ remarks:* "This is the comparative of *late,* though universally written with *tt,* contrary to analogy, and to our own practice in the superlative *latest.* When the thing of which the comparison is made is mentioned, we use *later;* as, *this fruit is* later *than the rest;* but *latter* when no comparison is expressed, but the reference is merely to time; as, *those are* latter *fruits.*"

Some comparatives form a superlative by adding *most,* as *nether, nethermost; outer, outmost;*[d] *under, undermost; up, upper, uppermost; fore, former, foremost.*

Most is sometimes added to a substantive, as *topmost, southmost.*

Many adjectives do not admit of comparison by terminations, and are only compared by *more* and *most,* as *benevolent, more benevolent, most benevolent.*

All adjectives may be compared by *more* and *most,* even when they have comparatives and superlatives regularly formed; as *fair; fairer,* or *more fair; fairest,* or *most fair.*

In adjectives that admit a regular comparison, the comparative *more* is oftener[e] used than the superlative *most,*[f] as *more fair* is oftener written for *fairer,* than *most fair* for *fairest.*

The comparison of adjectives is very uncertain; and being much regulated by commodiousness of utterance, or agreeableness of sound, is not easily reduced to rules.

Monosyllables are commonly compared.

Polysyllables, or words of more than two syllables, are seldom compared otherwise than by *more* and *most,* as *deplorable, more deplorable, most deplorable.*

Dissyllables are seldom compared if they terminate in *some,* as *fulsome, toilsome;* in *ful,* as[g] *careful, spleenful, dreadful;* in *ing,* as *trifling, charming;* in *ous,* as *porous;* in *less,* as *careless, harmless;* in *ed,* as *wretched;* in *id,* as *candid;* in *al,* as *mortal;* in *ent,* as *recent, fervent;* in *ain,* as *certain;* in *ive,* as *missive;*[7] in *dy,* as *woody;* in *fy,* as *puffy;* in *ky,* as *rocky,* except *lucky;* in *my,* as *roomy;* in *ny,* as *skinny;* in *py,* as *ropy,* except *happy;* in *ry,* as *hoary.*

d. *outmost 55a, 55b, 65, 73, 84*] *outermost 85a. In the first five unabridged editions of* Dictionary, outmost, *derived from "out* and *most," is defined as* "Remotest from the middle"; outermost, "superlative, from *outer," is defined as* "Remotest from the midst."

e. oftener *55a, 65, 73*] often *55b*

f. *most, 55a, 65, 73*] *more, 55b*

g. as *73*] *as 55a, 55b, 65*

---

7. *Missive:* "Such as is sent" or "Used at distance" (*Dictionary,* senses 1 and 2).

Some comparatives and superlatives are yet found in good writers formed without regard to the foregoing rules; but in a language subjected so little and so lately to grammar, such anomalies must frequently occur.

So *shady* is compared by *Milton*.

> She in *shadiest* covert hid,
> Tun'd her nocturnal note.
>
> *Parad. Lost.*[h8]

And *virtuous*.

> What she wills to say or do,
> Seems wisest, *virtuousest*, discreetest, best.
>
> *Parad. Lost.*[i9]

So *trifling*, by *Ray*, who is indeed of no great authority.

> It is not so decorous, in respect of God, that he should immediately do all the meanest and *triflingest* things himself, without making use of any inferior or subordinate minister.
>
> *Ray on the Creation.*[j1]

Famous, by *Milton*.

> I shall be named among the *famousest*
> Of women, sung at solemn festivals.
>
> *Milton's Agonistes.*[k2]

h. *Parad. Lost. 55a, 73*] *Milton. 55b, 65*
i. *Parad. Lost. 55a, 73*] *Milton. 55b, 65*
j. *Creation 55b, 65, 73*] *Creaiton 55a*
k. *Milton's Agonistes. 55a, 73*] *Milton. 55b, 65*

8. III.39–40 (*mutatis*); cited under *shady* in *Dictionary*.

9. VIII.549–50 (*mutatis*); cited under *virtuous* in *Dictionary*.

1. John Ray, *The Wisdom of God Manifested in the Works of the Creation* (1691; 3d ed., 1701), p. 55 (*mutatis*). This passage is not cited under *trifle* in *Dictionary* (but it is cited under *decorous*), and *triflingest* does not appear under *trifling* or as an independent entry. However, despite SJ's low estimate of his "authority," Ray's work provided illustrative quotations throughout *Dictionary*.

2. *Samson Agonistes*, 982–83; cited under *famous* in *Dictionary*.

Inventive, by *Ascham.*

Those have the *inventivest* heads for all purposes, and roundest tongues in all matters.

Ascham's Schoolmaster.[l3]

Mortal, by *Bacon.*

The *mortalest* poisons practised by the West Indians,[m] have some mixture of the blood, fat, or flesh of man.

Bacon.[4]

Natural, by *Wotton.*

I will[n] now deliver a few of the properest and *naturallest* considerations that belong to this piece.

Wotton's Architecture.[o5]

Wretched, by *Johnson.*

The *wretcheder* are the contemners of all helps; such as presuming on their own naturals, deride diligence, and mock at terms when they understand not things.

Ben[p] *Johnson.*[6]

l. *Ascham's Schoolmaster. 55a, 73*] *Ascham. 55b, 65*
m. West Indians, *55a, 73*] West-Indians, *55b, 65*
n. will *55a, 73*] shall *55b, 65*
o. *Wotton's Architecture. 55a, 73*] *Wotton. 55b, 65*
p. *Ben 55b, 65, 73*] *B. 55a*

3. Roger Ascham, *The Schoolmaster,* ed. James Upton (1743), p. 145; cited under *inventive* in *Dictionary.*

4. Francis Bacon, *Natural History,* in *Works* (4th ed., 1740), III.6; cited under *mortal* in *Dictionary.*

5. Sir Henry Wotton, *The Elements of Architecture* (1624), p. 79; cited under *natural* in *Dictionary.*

6. Ben Jonson, *Timber* (in *Ben Jonson,* ed. C. H. Herford, Percy and Evelyn Simpson, Vol. VIII [1947], pp. 555–649), p. 586 (*mutatis*); not cited under *natural* (n.) in *Dictionary,* which under *wretcheder* cites a quotation from Hooker's *Lawes of Ecclesiastical Politie.*

Powerful, by *Milton.*

We have sustain'd one day in doubtful fight,
What heav'n's great King hath *pow'rfullest*[q] to send
Against us from about his throne.

Paradise Lost.[r7]

The termination in *ish* may be accounted in some sort a degree of comparison, by which the signification is diminished below the positive, as *black, blackish,* or tending to blackness; *salt, saltish,* or having a little taste of salt: they therefore admit no comparison. This termination is seldom added but to words expressing sensible qualities, nor often to words of above one syllable, and is scarcely used in the solemn or sublime style.

§IV.[s] *Of* PRONOUNS.

Pronouns, in the English language,[t] are, *I, thou, he,* with their plurals *we, ye, they;*[u] *it, who, which, what, whether, whosoever, whatsoever, my, mine, our, ours, thy, thine, your, yours, his, her, hers, their, theirs, this, that, other, another,* the *same, some.*[v]

The pronouns personal are irregularly inflected.

	Singular.	Plural.
Nom.	I	We
Accus. and other oblique cases.	Me	Us
Nom.	Thou	Ye
Oblique.	Thee	You

q. *pow'rfullest 55a, 73*] *powerfullest 55b, 65*
r. *Paradise Lost. 55a, 73*] *Milton. 55b, 65*
s. §IV. *65*] §IV. *absent 55a, 55b, 73*
t. language, *55a, 55b, 65*] language *73*
u. *they; 73*] *they, 55a, 55b, 65*
v. *same, some. 73*] *same. 55a, 55b, 65*

7. VI.423–26 (*mutatis*); cited under *powerful* in *Dictionary.*

You is commonly used in modern writers for *ye,* particularly in the language of ceremony, where the second person plural is used for the second person singular, *You are my friend.*

	Singular.	Plural.	
Nom.	He	They	Applied to masculines.
Oblique.	Him	Them	
Nom.	She	They	Applied to feminines.
Oblique.	Her	Them	
Nom.	It	They	Applied to neuters or things.
Oblique.	Its	Them	

For *it* the practice of ancient writers was to use *he,* and for *its, his.*[8]

The possessive pronouns, like other adjectives, are without cases or change of termination.

The possessive of the first person is *my, mine, our, ours;* of the second, *thy, thine, your,*[w] *yours;* of the third, from *he, his,* from *she, her,* and *hers,* and in the plural *their, theirs,* for both sexes.

Our, yours, hers, theirs, are used when the substantive preceding is separated by a verb, as *These are* our *books. These books are* ours. Your *children excel* ours *in stature, but* ours *surpass* yours *in learning.*

Ours, yours, hers, theirs, notwithstanding their seeming plural termination, are applied equally to singular and plural substantives, as *This book is* ours. *These books are* ours.

Mine and *thine* were formerly used before a vowel, as *mine*

w. *your, 85a*] *you, 55a, 55b, 65, 73, 84*

8. As the genitive singular of the OE neuter singular *hit* (later, *it*), *his* went out of use in the sixteenth century and was replaced by *its* or *it's* in the seventeenth century. The use of *he* for things that have no natural gender continued into the nineteenth century, but *he* was never a form of the neuter singular nominative *it* or *hit*. See *OED,* s.v. *he* and *it.*

amiable lady; which though now disused in prose, might be still properly continued in poetry,[x] they are used as *ours* and *yours,* when they are referred to a substantive preceding, as, *thy* house is larger than *mine,* but *my* garden is more spacious than *thine.*[y]

Their and *theirs* are the possessives likewise of *they,* when *they* is the plural of *it,*[z] and are therefore applied to things.

Pronouns relative are, *who, which, what, whether, whosoever, whatsoever.*

Sing. and Plur.	Sing. and Plur.
Nom. Who	*Nom.* Which
Gen. Whose	*Gen.* Of which, *or* whose
Other oblique cases. Whom	*Other oblique cases.* Which

Who is now used in relation to persons, and *which* in relation to things; but they were anciently confounded. At least it was common to say, the man *which,* though I remember no example of, the thing *who.*[a]

Whose is rather the poetical than regular genitive of *which:*

The fruit
Of that forbidden tree, *whose* mortal taste
Brought death into the world.

Milton.[9]

Whether is only used in the nominative and accusative cases; and has no plural, being applied only to *one* of a number, commonly to one of two, as, Whether *of these is left I know not.* Whether *shall I choose?* It is now almost obsolete.[1]

x. poetry, *55a, 73*] poetry: *55b, 65*
y. preceding, . . . *thine. 73*] preceding. *55a, 55b, 65*
z. of *they,* . . . *it, 73*] likewise of *it,* and . . . things. *55a, 55b, 65*
a. At . . . *who. 73*] confounded. *55a, 55b, 65*

9. *Paradise Lost* I.1–3; cited under *mortal* in *Dictionary.*

1. *Dictionary* says nothing about *whether* being obsolete.

What, whether relative or interrogative, is without variation.

Whosoever, whatsoever, being compounded of *who* or *what,* and *soever,* follow the rule of their primitives.

		Singular.	Plural.
In all cases,	{	This	These
		That	Those
		Other	Others
		Whether	

The plural *others* is not used but when it is referred to a substantive preceding, as *I have sent* other *horses. I have not sent the same horses, but* others.

Another, being only *an other,* has no plural.

Here, there, and *where,* joined with certain particles, have a relative and pronominal use. *Hereof, herein, hereby, hereafter, herewith, thereof, therein, thereby, thereupon, therewith, whereof, wherein, whereby, whereupon, wherewith,* which signify, *of this, in this,* &c. *of that, in that,* &c. *of which, in which,* &c.

Therefore and *wherefore,* which are properly,[b] *there for* and *where for, for that, for which,* are now reckoned conjunctions, and continued in use. The rest seem to be passing by degrees into neglect, though proper, useful, and analogous. They are referred both to singular and plural antecedents.

There are two more words used only in conjunction with pronouns, *own* and *self.*

Own is added to possessives, both singular and plural, as *my* own *hand, our* own *house.* It is emphatical, and implies a silent contrariety or opposition; as, *I live in my own house,* that is, *not in a hired house. This I did with my own hand,* that is, *without help,* or *not by proxy.*

Self is added to possessives, as *myself, yourselves;* and some-

b. properly, *55a, 73*] properly *55b, 65*

times to personal pronouns, as *himself, itself, themselves.* It then, like *own,* expresses emphasis and opposition, as *I did this myself,* that is, *not another;* or it forms a reciprocal pronoun, as[c] *We hurt ourselves by vain rage.*

Himself, itself, themselves, is supposed by Wallis to be put by corruption, for *his self, it' self, their selves;* so that *self* is always a substantive.[2] This seems justly observed, for we say, *He came himself; Himself shall do this;* where *himself* cannot be an accusative.

§V.[d] *Of the* Verb.

English verbs are active, as *I love;* or neuter, as *I languish.*[3] The neuters are formed like the actives.

Most verbs signifying *action*[e] may likewise signify *condition* or *habit,* and become *neuters,* as *I love,* I am in love; *I strike,* I am now striking.

Verbs have only two tenses inflected in their terminations, the present, and simple preterite; the other tenses are compounded of the auxiliary verbs *have, shall, will, let, may, can,* and the infinitive of the active or neuter verb.

The passive voice is formed by joining the participle preterite to the substantive verb, as *I am loved.*

c. as *55a, 73*] as, *55b, 65*
d. §V. *65*] §V. *absent 55a, 55b, 73*
e. *action 73*] *action, 55a, 55b, 65*

2. *Grammatica,* pp. 79–80; Wallis's spelling is *his-self, its-self, their-selves,* with his hyphens indicating word separations lacking in common, corrupt speech.

3. SJ's distinction between *active* and *neuter* verbs seems to correspond to the modern distinction between transitive and intransitive verbs. However, Ben Jonson expresses it as a difference in "*times*": "*Active,* whose Participle past may be joyned with the Verbe *am:* as, *I am loved. Thou art hated. Neuter,* which cannot be so coupled: as *Pertaine. Dye. Live*" (*English Grammar,* 516). *Dictionary* entries for verbs are marked *v.a.* (verb active) or *v.n.* (verb neuter), but SJ refers to "transitive" verbs in his brief "Syntax" (see p. 347 below).

To have.[f] Indicative Mood.

Present Tense.

Sing. *I* have; *thou* hast;[g] *he* hath *or* has;
Plur. *We* have; *ye* have;[h] *they* have.

Has is a termination corrupted from *hath,* but now more frequently used both in verse and prose.

Simple Preterite.

Sing. *I* had; *thou* hadst;[i] *he* had;
Plur. *We* had; *ye* had;[j] *they* had.

Compound Preterite.

Sing. *I* have had; *thou* hast had;[k] *he* has *or* hath had;[l]
Plur. *We* have had;[m] *ye* have had;[n] *they* have had.

Preterpluperfect.

Sing. *I* had had; *thou* hadst had;[o] *he* had had;
Plur. *We* had had; *ye* had had;[p] *they* had had.

Future.

Sing. *I* shall have; *thou* shalt have;[q] *he* shall have;[r]
Plur. *We* shall have; *ye* shall have;[s] *they* shall have.

f. *have. 55b, 65, 73*] *Have. 55a*
g. *I* . . . ; . . . ; *73*] *I* . . . , . . . , *55a, 55b, 65*
h. *We* . . . ; . . . ; *73*] *We* . . . , . . . , *55a, 55b, 65*
i. *I* . . . ; . . . ; *73*] *I* . . . , . . . , *55a, 55b, 65*
j. *We* . . . ; . . . ; *73*] *We* . . . , . . . , *55a, 55b, 65*
k. *I* . . . ; . . . ; *73*] *I* . . . , . . . , 55a, 55b, 65
l. has . . . had; *73*] has had; *55a, 55b, 65*
m. have had; *73*] have had, *55b, 65;* have have had, *55a*
n. *ye* . . . ; *73*] *ye* . . . , *55a, 55b, 65*
o. *I* . . . ; . . . ; *73*] *I* . . . , . . . , *55a, 55b, 65*
p. *We* . . . ; . . . ; *73*] *We* . . . , . . . , *55a, 55b, 65*
q. *I* . . . ; . . . ; *73*] *I* . . . , . . . , *55a, 55b, 65*
r. have; *55a, 73*] have. *55b, 65*
s. *We* . . . ; . . . ; *73*] *We* . . . , . . . , *55a, 55b, 65*

Second Future.

Sing. *I* will have; *thou* wilt have;[t] *he* will have;
Plur. *We* will have; *ye* will have;[u] *they* will have.

By reading these future tenses may be observed the variations of *shall* and *will*.

Imperative Mood.

Sing. Have, *or* have *thou;*[v] let *him* have;
Plur. Let *us* have; have, *or* have *ye;*[w] let *them* have.

Conjunctive Mood.

Present.

Sing. *I* have; *thou* have;[x] *he* have;
Plur. *We* have; *ye* have;[y] *they* have.

Preterite simple as in the Indicative.

Preterite compound.

Sing. *I* have had; *thou* have had;[z] *he* have had;
Plur. *We* have had; *ye* have had;[a] *they* have had.

Future.

Sing. *I* shall have;[b] as in the Indicative.

Second Future.

Sing. *I* shall have had; *thou* shalt have had;[c] *he* shall have had;

t. *I* . . . ; . . . ; *73*] *I* . . . , . . . , *55a, 55b, 65*
u. *We* . . . ; . . . ; *73*] *We* . . . , . . . , *55a, 55b, 65*
v. Have, . . . *thou; 73*] Have . . . thou, *55b, 65;* Have . . . *thou, 55a*
w. Let . . . ; . . . , . . . ; *73*] Let . . . , . . . *ye, 55a, 55b, 65*
x. *I* . . . ; . . . ; *73*] *I* . . . , . . . , *55a, 55b, 65*
y. *We* . . . ; . . . ; *73*] *We* . . . , . . . , *55a, 55b, 65*
z. *I* . . . ; *thou* . . . ; *85a*] *I* . . . ; *they* . . . ; *73*] *I* . . . , *they* . . . , *55a, 55b, 65*
a. *We* . . . ; . . . ; *73*] *We* . . . , . . . , *55a, 55b, 65*
b. *I* . . . ; *73*] *I* . . . , *55a, 55b, 65*
c. *I* . . . ; . . . ; *73*] *I* . . . , . . . , *55a, 55b, 65*

Plur. *We* shall have had; *ye* shall have had;[d] *they* shall have had.

Potential.

The potential form of speaking is expressed by *may, can,* in the present; and *might, could,* or *should,* in the preterite, joined with the infinitive mood of the verb.

Present.

Sing. *I* may have; *thou* mayst have;[e] *he* may have;
Plur. *We* may have; *ye* may have;[f] *they* may have.

Preterite.

Sing. *I* might have; *thou* mightst have;[g] *he* might have;
Plur. *We* might have; *ye* might have;[h] *they* might have.

Present.

Sing. *I* can have; *thou* canst have;[i] *he* can have;
Plur. *We* can have; *ye* can have;[j] *they* can have.

Preterite.

Sing. *I* could have; *thou* couldst have;[k] *he* could have;
Plur. *We* could have; *ye* could have;[l] *they* could have.

In like manner *should* is united to the verb.

There is likewise a double *Preterite.*

Sing. *I* should have had; *thou* shouldst have had; *he* should have had.[m]

d. *We* . . . ; . . . ; *73*] *We* . . . , . . . , *55a, 55b, 65*
e. *I* . . . ; . . . ; *73*] *I* . . . , . . . , *55a, 55b, 65*
f. *We* . . . ; . . . ; *73*] *We* . . . , . . . , *55a, 55b, 65*
g. *I* . . . ; . . . ; *73*] *I* . . . , . . . , *55a, 55b, 65*
h. *We* . . . ; . . . ; *73*] *We* . . . , . . . , *55a, 55b, 65*
i. *I* . . . ; . . . ; *73*] *I* . . . , . . . , *55a, 55b, 65*
j. *We* . . . ; . . . ; *73*] *We* . . . , . . . , *55a, 55b, 65*
k. *I* . . . ; . . . ; *73*] *I* . . . , . . . , *55a, 55b, 65*
l. *We* . . . ; . . . ; *73*] *We* . . . , . . . , *55a, 55b, 65*
m. *I* . . . ; . . . ; . . . had. *73*] *I* . . . , . . . , . . . had; *55a, 55b, 65*

Plur. *We* should have had; *ye* should have had;[n] *they* should have had.

In like manner we use, *I might* have had; *I could* have had, *&c.*

Infinitive Mood.

Present.	To have.	*Preterite.*	To have had.
Participle present.	Having.	*Participle preter.*	Had.

Verb Active. *To Love.*

Indicative. *Present.*

Sing. *I* love; *thou* lovest; *he* loveth,[o] *or* loves;
Plur. *We* love; *ye* love;[p] *they* love.

Preterite simple.

Sing.	*I* loved; *thou* lovedst;[q] *he* loved;	
Plur.	*We* loved; *ye* loved;[r] *they* loved.	
Preterperfect compound.[s]	*I* have loved, *&c.*	
Preterpluperfect.	*I* had loved, *&c.*	
Future.	*I* shall love, *&c.*	*I* will love, *&c.*

Imperative.

Sing. Love, *or* love *thou;*[t] let *him* love;
Plur. Let *us* love; love, *or* love *ye;*[u] let *them* love.

Conjunctive. *Present.*

Sing.	*I* love; *thou* love;[v] *he* love;
Plur.	*We* love; *ye* love;[w] *they* love.

n. *We* . . . ; . . . ; *73*] *We* . . . , . . . , *55a, 55b, 65*
o. *I* . . . ; . . . ; . . . , *73*] *I* . . . , . . . , *he* loveth *55a, 55b, 65*
p. *We* . . . ; . . . ; *73*] *We* . . . , . . . , *55a, 55b, 65*
q. *I* . . . ; . . . ; *73*] *I* . . . , . . . , *55a, 55b, 65*
r. *We* . . . ; . . . ; *73*] *We* . . . , . . . , *55a, 55b, 65*
s. *compound. 84*] *compared. 55a, 55b, 65, 73*
t. Love, . . . ; *73*] Love . . . , *55a, 55b, 65*
u. Let . . . ; . . . , . . . ; *73*] Let . . . , . . . , *55a, 55b, 65*
v. *I* . . . ; . . . ; *73*] *I* . . . , . . . , *55a, 55b, 65*
w. *We* . . . ; . . . ; *73*] *We* . . . , . . . , *55a, 55b, 65*

Preterite simple, as in the Indicative.
Preterite compound. *I* have loved, *&c.*
Future. *I* shall love, *&c.*
Second Future. *I* shall have loved, *&c.*

Potential.

Present. *I* may *or* can love, *&c.*
Preterite. *I* might, could, *or* should love, *&c.*
Double Pret. *I* might, could, *or* should have loved, *&c.*

Infinitive.

Present.	To love.	*Preterite.*	To have loved.
Participle present.	Loving.	*Participle past.*	Loved.

The passive is formed by the addition of the participle preterite, to the different tenses of the verb *to be,* which must therefore be here exhibited.

Indicative. *Present.*

Sing. *I* am; *thou* art;[x] *he* is;
Plur. *We* are, *or* be; *ye* are, *or* be; *they* are,[y] *or* be.
The plural *be* is now little in use.

Preterite.

Sing. *I* was; *thou* wast *or* wert;[z] *he* was;
Plur. *We* were; *ye* were;[a] *they* were.

Wert is properly of the conjunctive mood, and ought not to be used in the indicative.

Preterite compound. *I* have been, *&c.*
Preterpluperfect. *I* had been, *&c.*
Future. *I* shall or will be, *&c.*

x. *I* . . . ; . . . ; *73*] *I* . . . , . . . , *55a, 55b, 65*
y. *We* . . . , . . . ; . . . , . . . ; . . . are, *73*] *We* . . . , . . . , . . . are *55a, 55b, 65*
z. *I* . . . ; . . . ; *73*] *I* . . . , . . . , *55a, 55b, 65*
a. *We* . . . ; . . . ; *73*] *We* . . . , . . . , *55a, 55b, 65*

Imperative.

Sing. Be *thou;* let *him* be;
Plur. Let *us* be; be *ye;* let *them* be.

Conjunctive. *Present.*

Sing. *I* be; *thou* beest;[b] *he* be;
Plur. *We* be; *ye* be;[c] *they* be.

Preterite.

Sing.	*I* were; *thou* wert;[d] *he* were;
Plur.	*We* were; *ye* were;[e] *they* were.
Preterite compound.	*I* have been, *&c.*
Future.	*I* shall have been, *&c.*

Potential.

I may *or* can; would, could, *or* should be; could, would, *or* should have been, *&c.*

Infinitive.

Present.	To be.	*Preterite.*	To have been.
Participle pres.	Being.	*Participle preter.*	Having been.

Passive Voice. Indicative Mood.

I am loved, *&c.* *I* was loved, *&c.* *I* have been loved, *&c.*

Conjunctive Mood.

If *I* be loved, *&c.* If *I* were loved, &*c.* If *I* shall have been loved, *&c.*

Potential Mood.

I may *or* can be loved, *&c.* *I* might, could, *or* should be loved, *&c.*
I might, could, *or* should have been loved, *&c.*

b. *I* . . . ; . . . ; *73*] *I* . . . , . . . , *55a, 55b, 65*
c. *We* . . . ; . . . ; *73*] *We* . . . , . . . , *55a, 55b, 65*
d. *I* . . . ; . . . ; *73*] *I* . . . , . . . , *55a, 55b, 65*
e. *We* . . . ; . . . ; *73*] *We* . . . , . . . , *55a, 55b, 65*

Infinitive.

Present. To be loved. *Preterite.* To have been loved.
Participle. Loved.

There is another form of English verbs, in which the infinitive mood is joined to the verb *do* in its various inflections, which are therefore to be learned in this place.

To Do.

Indicative. *Present.*

Sing. *I* do; *thou* dost;[f] *he* doth;
Plur. *We* do; *ye* do;[g] *they* do.

Preterite.

Sing. *I* did; *thou* didst;[h] *he* did;
Plur. *We* did; *ye* did;[i] *they* did.
Preterite, &c. *I* have done, *&c.* *I* had done, *&c.*
Future. *I* shall *or* will do, *&c.*

Imperative.

Sing. Do *thou;*[j] let *him* do;
Plur. Let *us* do; do *ye;*[k] let *them*[l] do.

Conjunctive. *Present.*

Sing. *I* do; *thou* do;[m] *he* do;
Plur. *We* do; *ye* do;[n] *they* do.

The rest are as in the indicative.
Infinitive. To do; to have done.
Participle pres. Doing. *Participle preter.* Done.

f. *I* . . . ; . . . ; *73*] *I* . . . , . . . , *55a, 55b, 65*
g. *We* . . . ; . . . ; *73*] *We* . . . , . . . , *55a, 55b, 65*
h. *I* . . . ; . . . ; *73*] *I* . . . , . . . , *55a, 55b, 65*
i. *We* . . . ; . . . ; *73*] *We* . . . , . . . , *55a, 55b, 65*
j. *thou; 73*] *thou, 55a, 55b, 65*
k. Let . . . ; . . . ; *73*] Let . . . , . . . , *55a, 55b, 65*
l. *them 55b, 65, 73*] them *55a*
m. *I* . . . ; . . . ; *73*] *I* . . . , . . . , *55a, 55b, 65*
n. *We* . . . ; . . . ; *73*] *We* . . . , . . . , *55a, 55b, 65*

Do[o] is sometimes used superfluously, as, *I* [p] do *love, I* did *love;* simply for *I love,* or *I loved;* but this is considered as a vitious mode of speech.

It is sometimes used emphatically; as,

> *I* do *love thee, and when I love thee not,*
> *Chaos is come again.* Shakespeare.[4]

It is frequently joined with a negative; as, *I like her, but I* do *not love her; I wished him success, but* did *not help him.* This, by custom at least, appears more easy, than the other form of expressing the same sense by a negative adverb after the verb, *I like her, but* love *her* not.[q]

The Imperative prohibitory is seldom applied in the second person, at least in prose, without the word *do;* as, *Stop him, but* do *not hurt him; Praise beauty, but* do *not dote on it.*

Its chief use is in interrogative forms of speech, in which it is used through all the persons; as, Do *I live?* Dost *thou strike me?* Do *they rebel?* Did *I complain?* Didst *thou love her?* Did *she die?* So likewise in negative interrogations; Do *I not yet grieve?* Did *she not die?*

Do and *did* are thus used only for the present and simple preterite.[r]

There is another manner of conjugating neuter[s] verbs, which, when it is used, may not improperly denominate them *neuter passives,* as they are inflected according to the passive form by the help of the verb substantive[t] *to be.* They answer nearly to the reciprocal[5] verbs in French; as,

o. *Do 55b, 65, 73*] *I do 55a*
p. *I 55a, 55b, 73*] I *65*
q. This . . . not. *73*] *him. 55a, 55b, 65*
r. *Do* . . . preterite. *73*] *Do* is thus used only in the simple tenses. *55a, 55b, 65*
s. neuter *55a, 65, 73*] neuters *55b*
t. substantive *55b, 65, 73*] sustantive *55a*

---

4. *Othello* III.iii.91–92. Cf. sense 10 of *to do* (v.n.) in *Dictionary:* "Sometimes emphatically," with these lines providing the illustrative passage.

5. *Reciprocal:* reflexive.

I am risen, surrexi, *Latin;* Je me suis levé, *French.*
I was walked out, exieram; Je m'etois promené.

In like manner we commonly express the present tense; as, I am going, *eo.* I am grieving, *doleo.* She is dying, *illa moritur.* The tempest is raging, *furit procella.* I am pursuing an enemy, *hostem insequor.* So the other tenses, as, *We were walking, ἐτυγχάνομεν περιπατοῦντες,*[6] *I*[u] *have been walking, I had been walking, I shall* or *will be walking.*

There is another manner of using the active participle, which gives it a passive signification; as, The grammar is now printing, *grammatica jam nunc chartis imprimitur.* The brass is forging, *æra excuduntur.* This is, in my opinion, a vitious expression, probably corrupted from a phrase more pure, but now somewhat obsolete: *The book is* a *printing, The brass is* a *forging; a* being properly *at,* and *printing* and *forging* verbal nouns signifying action, according to the analogy of this language.[7]

The indicative and conjunctive moods are by modern writers frequently confounded, or rather the conjunctive is wholly neglected, when some convenience of versification does not invite its revival. It is used among the purer writers of former times[v] after *if, though, ere, before, till* or *until,*[w] *whether, except, unless, whatsoever, whomsoever,*[x] and words of wishing; as, *Doubtless thou art our father,* though *Abraham* be *ignorant of us, and Israel* acknowledge *us not.*[8]

Of IRREGULAR VERBS.

The English verbs were divided by Ben Johnson into four conjugations, without any reason arising from the nature of

u. *I 55a, 55b, 73*] I *65*
v. of . . . times *73*] writers after *55a, 55b, 65*
w. *till* or *until, 73*] *before, whether, 55a, 55b, 65*
x. *whomsoever, 55a, 73*] *whomsoever; 55b, 65*

6. ἐτυγχάνομεν περιπατοῦντες: "we happened to be walking" or "it chanced that we were walking."

7. As he indicates under *A* in *Dictionary* (sense 3), SJ takes the notion from *Grammatica* (pp. 66–67) that *a* derives from *at* in this formation.

8. Isaiah 63:16.

the language, which has properly but one conjugation, such as has been exemplified; from which all deviations are to be considered as anomalies, which are indeed in our monosyllable Saxon verbs and the verbs derived from them very frequent; but almost all the verbs which have been adopted from other languages, follow the regular form.[9]

Our verbs are observed by Dr. Wallis to be irregular only in the formation of the preterite, and its participle.[1] Indeed, in the scantiness of our conjugations, there is scarcely any other place for irregularity.

The first irregularity, is a slight deviation from the regular form, by rapid utterance or poetical contraction: the last syllable *ed* is often joined with the former by suppression of *e;* as, *lov'd* for *loved;* after *c, ch, sh, f, k, x,* and after the consonants[y] *s, th,* when more strongly pronounced, and sometimes after *m, n, r,* if preceded by a short vowel, *t* is used in pronunciation, but very seldom in writing, rather than *d;* as *plac't, snatch't, fish't, wak't, dwel't, smel't;* for *plac'd,*[z] *snatch'd, fish'd, wak'd, dwel'd, smel'd;* or *placed, snatched, fished, waked, dwelled, smelled.*

Those words which terminate in *l* or *ll,* or *p,* make their preterite in *t,* even in solemn language; as *crept, felt, dwelt;* sometimes after *x, ed* is changed into *t;* as, *vext:* this is not constant.

A long vowel is often changed into a short one; thus, *kept, slept, wept, crept, swept;* from the verbs, to *keep,* to *sleep,* to *weep,* to *creep,* to *sweep.*

Where *d* or *t* go before, the additional letter *d* or *t,* in this

y. consonants *55a, 55b, 73*] consonants, *65*
z. *plac'd, 73*] *plac'd 55a, 55b, 65*

9. *English Grammar,* 516–24; Jonson makes the point about adopted words falling into the first or regular conjugation. He confesses the weakness of his scheme in dividing the irregular verbs into three conjugations, but it is rationally based on the sorts of vowel and consonant changes required to form the past tense.

1. "Tota quae sequitur Anomalia non nisi praeteriti Imperfecti temporis, & Participii Passivi formationem spectat" (p. 91). SJ's dependence on *Grammatica* is particularly great in this section and the next; for an assessment, see Nagashima, pp. 108–15.

contracted form, coalesce into one letter with the radical *d* or *t:* if *t* were the radical, they coalesce into *t;* but if *d* were the radical, then into *d* or *t,* as the one or the other letter may be more easily pronounced: as, *read, led, spread, shed, shred, bid, hid, chid, fed, bled, bred, sped, strid, rid;* from the verbs, to *read,* to *lead,* to *spread,* to *shed,* to *shread,* to *bid,* to *hide,* to *chide,* to *feed,* to *bleed,* to *breed,* to *speed,* to *stride,* to *slide,*[a] to *ride.* And thus, *cast, hurt, cost, burst, eat, beat, sweat, sit, quit, smit, writ, bit, hit, met, shot;* from the verbs, to *cast,* to *hurt,* to *cost,* to *burst,* to *eat,* to *beat,* to *sweat,* to *sit,* to *quit,* to *smite,* to *write,* to *bite,* to *hit,* to *meet,* to *shoot.* And in like manner, *lent, sent, rent, girt;* from the verbs, to *lend,* to *send,* to *rend,* to *gird.*

The participle preterite or passive is often formed in *en,* instead of *ed;* as *been, taken, given, slain, known,* from the verbs to *be,* to *take,* to *give,* to *slay,* to *know.*

Many words have two or more participles, as not only[b] *written, bitten, eaten, beaten, hidden, chidden, shotten, chosen, broken;* but likewise *writ, bit, eat, beat, hid, chid, shot, chose, broke,* are promiscuously used in the participle, from the verbs to *write,* to *bite,* to *eat,* to *beat,* to *hide,* to *chide,* to *shoot,* to *choose,* to *break,* and many such like.

In the same manner *sown, shewn, hewn, mown, loaden, laden,* as well as *sow'd, shew'd, hew'd, mow'd, loaded, laded,* from the verbs to *sow,* to *shew,* to *hew,* to *mow,* to *load,* or *lade.*

Concerning these double participles it is difficult to give any rule; but he shall seldom err who remembers, that when a verb has a participle distinct from its preterite, as *write, wrote, written,* that distinct participle is more proper and elegant, as *The book is* written, is better than *The book is* wrote. *Wrote* however may be used in poetry; at least if we allow any authority to poets, who, in the exultation of genius, think themselves perhaps intitled to trample on grammarians.[c2]

a. slid *does not appear in the preceding list in editions 1–7 of unabridged* Dictionary.

b. only *55a, 55b, 73*] only, *65*

c. wrote. *Wrote . . .* grammarians. *73*] wrote, though *wrote* may be used in poetry. *55a, 55b, 65*

2. Cf. Dryden's comment (cited in part under *grammatical* in *Dictionary*) in the Preface to his translation (1695) of *De Arte Graphica* (1668) by Charles

There are other anomalies in the preterite.

1. *Win, spin, begin, swim, strike, stick, sing, sting, fling, ring, wring, spring, swing, drink, sink, shrink, stink, come, run, find, bind, grind, wind,* both in the preterite imperfect and participle passive, give *won, spun, begun, swum, struck, stuck, sung, stung, flung, rung, wrung, sprung, swung, drunk, sunk, shrunk, stunk,*[d] *come, run, found, bound, ground, wound.* And most of them are also formed in the preterite by *a,* as *began, rang, sang, sprang, drank, came, ran,* and some others; but most of these are now obsolete.[3] Some in the participle passive likewise take *en,* as *stricken, strucken, drunken, bounden.*

2. *Fight, teach, reach, seek, beseech, catch, buy, bring, think, work,* make *fought, taught, raught, sought, besought, caught, bought, brought, thought, wrought.*

But a great many of these retain likewise the regular form, as *teached, reached, beseeched, catched, worked.*

3. *Take, shake,*[e] *forsake, wake, awake, stand, break, speak, bear, shear, swear, tear, weave, cleave, strive, thrive, drive, shine, rise, arise, smite, write, bide, abide, ride, choose, chuse, tread, get, beget, forget, seethe,* make in both preterite and participle *took, forsook, woke, awoke, stood, broke, spoke, bore, shore, swore, tore, wore,*[f] *wove, clove, strove, throve, drove, shone, rose,*[g] *arose, smote, wrote, bode, abode, rode, chose, trode, got, begot, forgot, sod.* But we say likewise, *thrive, rise, smit, writ, abid, rid.* In the preterite some are likewise formed by *a,* as *brake, spake, bare, share, sware, tare, ware, clave, gat, begat, forgat,* and perhaps some others, but more

d. *stunk, 65*] *hung, 55a, 55b, 73*
e. shook *does not appear in the succeeding list in editions 1–7 of unabridged* Dictionary.
f. wear *does not appear in the preceding list in editions 1–7 of unabridged* Dictionary.
g. *rose, 55a, 55b, 73*] *rose; 65*

Alphonse Dufresnoy and Roger de Piles: "Even of words, which are their province, [pedants] seldom know more than the Grammatical construction, unless they are born with a Poetical Genius, which is a rare Portion amongst them" ("*De Arte Graphica*" and *Shorter Works,* ed. A. E. Wallace Maurer and George R. Guffey [vol. XX, *California Edition of the Works of John Dryden,* 1989], pp. 72–73).

3. SJ takes his examples from *Grammatica* (pp. 95–96), but Wallis describes this form of the preterite as "rarius" (less common) rather than "obsolete." SJ's addition is justifiable; he may be thinking of such verbs as *cling, fling, sling* (1 Sam. 17:49), and *swing.* See Otto Jespersen, *A Modern English Grammar,* VI.5.1(7).

rarely. In the participle passive are many of them formed by *en,* as *taken, shaken, forsaken, broken, spoken, born, shorn, sworn, torn, worn, woven, cloven, thriven, driven, risen, smitten, ridden, chosen, trodden, gotten, begotten, forgotten, sodden.* And many do likewise retain the analogy in both, as *waked, awaked, sheared, weaved, leaved, abided, seethed.*

4. *Give, bid, sit,* make in the preterite *gave, bade, sate;* in the participle passive, *given, bidden, sitten;* but in both *bid.*

5. *Draw, know, grow, throw, blow, crow* like a cock, *fly, slay, see, ly,* make their preterite *drew, knew, grew, threw, blew, crew, flew, slew, saw, lay;* their participles passive by *n, drawn, known, grown,*[h] *thrown, blown, flown, slain, seen, lien, lain.* Yet from *flee* is made *fled;* from *go, went,* from the old *wend,* the participle is *gone.*[i]

§VI.[j] *Of* Derivation.

That the English language may be more easily understood, it is necessary to enquire how its derivative words are deduced from their primitives, and how the primitives are borrowed from other languages. In this enquiry I shall sometimes copy Dr. Wallis, and sometimes endeavour to supply his defects, and rectify his errours.[4]

Nouns are derived from verbs.

The thing implied in the verb as done or produced, is commonly either the present of the verb; as, to love, *love;* to fright, a *fright;* to fight, a *fight;* or the preterite of the verb, as, to strike, I strick *or* strook, a *stroke.*

The action is the same with the participle present, as *loving, frighting, fighting, striking.*

h. *known, grown, 55b, 65, 73*] *known, snown, grown, 55a*
i. *wend,* the . . . is *gone. 73*] *wend,* and the participle *gone. 55a, 55b, 65*
j. §VI. *65*] §VI. *absent 55a, 55b, 73*

4. Wallis calls this part of grammar *etymologia.* It was greatly expanded in succeeding editions through the fifth (1699); *Grammatica,* pp. 101–34. SJ translates and condenses *Grammatica* in this section, including his examples.

The agent, or person acting, is denoted by the syllable *er* added to the verb, as *lover, frighter, striker.*

Substantives, adjectives, and sometimes other parts of speech, are changed into verbs: in which case the vowel is often lengthened, or the consonant softened; as, a house, *to house;* brass, *to braze;* glass, *to glaze;* grass, *to graze;* price, *to prize;* breath, *to breathe;* a fish, *to fish;*[5] oyl, *to oyl;* further, *to further;* forward, *to forward;* hinder, *to hinder.*

Sometimes the termination *en* is added, especially to adjectives; as, haste, *to hasten;* length, *to lengthen;* strength, *to strengthen;* short, *to shorten;* fast, *to fasten;* white, *to whiten;* black, *to blacken;* hard, *to harden;* soft, *to soften.*

From substantives are formed adjectives of plenty, by adding the termination *y;* as, a louse, *lousy;* wealth, *wealthy;* health, *healthy;* might, *mighty;* worth, *worthy;* wit, *witty;* lust, *lusty;* water, *watery;* earth, *earthy;* wood, a wood, *woody;* air, *airy;* a heart, *hearty;* a hand, *handy.*

From substantives are formed adjectives of plenty, by adding the termination *ful,* denoting abundance; as, joy, *joyful;* fruit, *fruitful;* youth, *youthful;* care, *careful;* use, *useful;* delight, *delightful;* plenty, *plentiful;* help, *helpful.*

Sometimes, in almost the same sense, but with some kind of diminution thereof, the termination *some* is added, denoting *something,* or *in some degree;* as, delight, *delightsome;* game, *gamesome;* irk, *irksome;* burden, *burdensome;*[k] trouble, *troublesome;* light, *lightsome;* hand, *handsome;* alone, *lonesome;* toil, *toilsome.*

On the contrary, the termination *less* added to substantives, makes adjectives signifying want; as[l] *worthless, witless, heartless, joyless, careless, helpless.* Thus comfort, *comfortless;* sap, *sapless.*

Privation or contrariety is very often denoted by the par-

k. burden, *burdensome; 55a, 73*] burthen, *burthensome; 55b, 65*
l. as *55a, 73*] as, *55b, 65*

5. *To fish* and the succeeding examples of verbs in this paragraph do not contrast with the pronunciation of their sources. This is clear on examination of the corresponding, longer list in *Grammatica* (pp. 101–02), which includes some marks of accentuation.

ticle *un* prefixed to many adjectives, or *in* before words derived from the Latin; as, pleasant, *unpleasant;* wise, *unwise;* profitable, *unprofitable;* patient, *impatient.* Thus *unworthy, unhealthy, unfruitful, unuseful,* and many more.

The original English privative is *un;* but as we often borrow from the Latin, or its descendants, words already signifying privation, as *inefficacious, impious, indiscreet,* the inseparable particles *un* and *in* have fallen into confusion, from which it is not easy to disentangle them.

Un is prefixed to all words originally English, as *untrue, untruth, untaught, unhandsome.*

Un is prefixed to all participles made privative adjectives, as *unfeeling, unassisting, unaided, undelighted, unendeared.*

Un ought never to be prefixed to a participle present, to mark a forbearance of action, as *unsighing;* but a privation of habit, as *unpitying.*

Un is prefixed to most substantives which have an English termination, as *unfertileness, unperfectness,* which, if they have borrowed terminations, take *in* or *im,* as *infertility, imperfection; uncivil, incivility; unactive, inactivity.*

In borrowing adjectives, if we receive them already compounded, it is usual to retain the particle prefixed, as *indecent,*[m] *inelegant, improper;* but if we borrow the adjective, and add the privative particle, we commonly prefix *un,* as *unpolite, ungallant.*

The prepositive particles *dis* and *mis,* derived from the *des* and *mes* of the French, signify almost the same as *un;* yet *dis* rather imports contrariety than privation, since it answers to the Latin preposition *de. Mis* insinuates some error, and for the most part may be rendered by the Latin words *male* or *perperam.* To like, *to dislike;* honour, *dishonour;* to honour, to grace, *to dishonour, to disgrace;* to deign, *to disdeign;* chance, hap, *mischance, mishap;* to take, *to mistake;* deed, *misdeed;* to use, *to misuse;* to employ, *to misemploy;* to apply, *to misapply.*

Words derived from Latin written with *de* or *dis* retain the

m. *indecent, 73*] *indecency, 55a, 55b, 65*

same signification, as *distinguish,* distinguo; *detract,* detraho; *defame,* defamo; *detain,* detineo.

The termination *ly* added to substantives, and sometimes to adjectives, forms adjectives that import some kind of similitude or agreement, being formed by contraction of *lick* or *like.*

A giant, *giantly, giantlike;* earth, *earthly;* heaven, *heavenly;* world, *worldly;* God, *godly;* good, *goodly.*

The same termination *ly* added to adjectives, forms adverbs of like signification; as, beautiful, *beautifully;* sweet, *sweetly;* that is, *in a beautiful manner; with some degree of sweetness.*

The termination *ish* added to adjectives, imports diminution; and added to substantives, imports similitude or tendency to a character; as, green, *greenish;* white, *whitish;* soft, *softish;* a thief, *thievish;* a wolf, *wolvish;* a child, *childish.*

We have forms of diminutives in substantives, though not frequent; as, a hill, *a hillock;* a cock, *a cockrel;* a pike, *a*[n] *pickrel;* this is a French termination: a goose, *a gosling;* this is a German termination: a lamb, *a lambkin;* a chick, *a chicken;* a man, *a manikin;* a pipe, *a pipkin;* and thus *Halkin,* whence the patronimick *Hawkins, Wilkin, Thomkin,* and others.

Yet still there is another form of diminution among the English, by lessening the sound itself, especially of vowels; as there is a form of augmenting them by enlarging, or even lengthening it; and that sometimes not so much by the change[o] of the letters, as of their pronunciation; as, *sup, sip, soop, sop, sippet,* where, besides the extenuation of the vowel, there is added the French termination *et;*[p] *top, tip;*[q] *spit, spout; babe, baby, booby, βοῦπαις; great* pronounced long, especially if with a stronger sound, *grea-t; little* pronounced long, *leetle; ting, tang, tong,* imports a succession of smaller and then greater sounds; and so in *jingle, jangle, tingle, tangle,* and many other made words.

n. *a pickrel 85a*] *pickrel 55a, 55b, 65, 73, 84*
o. by the change *55b, 65*] by change *55a, 73*
p. *et; 55a, 73*] *et: 55b, 65*
q. *tip; 55a, 55b, 73*] *tip, 65*

Much however of this is arbitrary and fanciful, depending wholly on oral utterance, and therefore scarcely worthy the notice of Wallis.[6]

Of concrete adjectives are made abstract substantives, by adding the termination *ness,* and a few in *hood* or *head,* noting character or qualities; as, white, *whiteness;* hard, *hardness;* great, *greatness;* skilful, *skilfulness, unskilfulness; godhead, manhood, maidenhead, widowhood, knighthood, priesthood, likelihood, falsehood.*

There are other abstracts, partly derived from adjectives, and partly from verbs, which are formed by the addition of the termination *th,* a small change being sometimes made; as, long, *length;* strong, *strength;* broad, *breadth;* wide, *width;*[r] deep, *depth;* true, *truth;* warm, *warmth;* dear, *dearth;* slow, *slowth;* merry, *mirth;* heal, *health;* well, weal, *wealth;* dry, *droughth;* young, *youth;* and so moon, *month.*

Like these are some words derived from verbs; dy, *death;* till, *tilth;* grow, *growth;* mow, later *mowth,*[7] after *mow'th;*[s] commonly spoken and written later *math,* after *math;* steal, *stealth;* bear, *birth;* rue, *ruth;* and probably *earth* from to *ear* or *plow;* fly, *flight;* weigh, *weight;* fray, *fright;* to draw, *draught.*

These should rather be written *flighth, frighth,* only that custom will not suffer *h* to be twice repeated.[t]

The same form retain *faith, spight, wreathe, wrath, broth, froth, breath, sooth, worth, light, wight,* and the like, whose primitives are either entirely obsolete, or seldom occur. Perhaps they are derived from *fey* or *foy, spry, wry, wreak, brew, mow,*[8] *fry, bray, say, work.*

r. broad, . . . *width;* 73] broad, wide, *breadth, width;* 55a, 55b, 65

s. *mow'th;* 55a, 73] *mowth;* 55b, 65

t. custom . . . repeated. 73] custom prevails, lest *h* should be twice repeated. 55a, 55b, 65

6. This remark is consistent with SJ's regular position on sound and sense in poetry: see, e.g., *Ramblers* 92 (*Yale* IV. 121–30) and 94 (*Yale* IV.135–43); *Idlers* 60 (par. 12; *Yale* II.188–89), 61 (pars. 5–6; *Yale* IV.191–92), and "Life of Pope" (*Lives* III.230–32, pars. 330–34).

7. *mowth:* "the portion of a crop that has been [or may be] mowed" (*OED*), not in *Dictionary;* in *Grammatica* (p. 109) the word is *later-mow'th,* followed by *after-mow'th.*

8. SJ omits the corresponding substantive, which *Grammatica* gives (p. 110)

Some ending in *ship* imply an office, employment, or condition; as, *kingship, wardship, guardianship, partnership, stewardship, headship, lordship.*

Thus *worship,* that is, *worthship;* whence *worshipful,* and *to*[u] *worship.*

Some few ending in *dom, rick, wick,* do especially denote dominion, at least state or condition; as *kingdom, dukedom, earldom, princedom, popedom, christendom, freedom, wisdom, whoredom, bishoprick, bailywick.*

Ment and *age* are plainly French terminations, and are of the same import with us as among them, scarcely ever occurring,[w] except in words derived from the French, as[x] *commandment, usage.*

There are in English often long trains of words allied by their meaning and derivation; as, *to beat, a bat, batoon, a battle, a beetle, a battle-door, to batter, batter,*[y] a kind of glutinous composition for food, made by *beating* different bodies into one mass.[z9] All these are of similar signification, and perhaps derived from the Latin *batuo.* Thus *take, touch, tickle, tack, tackle;* all imply a local conjunction, from the Latin *tango, tetigi, tactum.*

From *two* are formed *twain, twice, twenty, twelve, twins, twine, twist, twirl, twig, twitch, twinge, between, betwixt, twilight, twibil.*[1]

The following remarks, extracted from Wallis, are ingenious, but of more subtlety than solidity, and such as perhaps might in every language be enlarged without end.[2]

u. and *to 73*] *to 55a, 55b, 65*
v. as *55a, 73*] as, *55b, 65*
w. occurring *73*] occuring *55a, 55b, 65*
x. as *55a, 73*] as, *55b, 65*
y. *batter, 73*] *butter, 55a, 55b, 65*
z. food, . . . mass. *73*] food. *55a, 55b, 65*

as *moth* and glosses as "tinea" (Latin, moth) and places between *broth* and *froth.* Perhaps SJ omitted this word because it is inexplicable as a derivative of *mow,* but he should then have removed its corresponding verb as well.

9. Cf. *Dictionary,* s.v. *Batter:* "A mixture of several ingredients beaten together with some liquor; so called from its being so much beaten."

1. *Twibil:* "A halbert" (*Dictionary*).

2. With these remarks, cf. SJ's atti-

Sn usually imply[a] the *nose,* and what relates to it. From the Latin *nasus* are derived the French *nes* and the English *nose;* and *nesse,* a promontory, as projecting like a nose. But as if from the consonants *ns* taken from *nasus,* and transposed, that they may the better correspond, *sn* denote[b] *nasus;* and thence are derived many words that relate to the nose, as *snout, sneeze, snore, snort, snear, snicker, snot, snivel,*[c] *snite,*[3] *snuff, snuffle, snaffle, snarle, snudge.*[4]

There is another *sn,* which may perhaps be derived from the Latin *sinuo,* as *snake, sneak, snail, snare;* so likewise *snap* and *snatch, snib,*[5] *snub.*

Bl imply[d] a *blast;* as, *blow, blast, to blast, to blight,* and, metaphorically, *to blast* one's reputation; *bleat,*[6] *bleak,* a *bleak* place, to look *bleak* or weather-beaten, *bleak, blay,*[7] *bleach, bluster, blurt, blister, blab, bladder, bleb, blister,*[8] *blabber-lip't,*[9] *blubber-cheek't, bloted,*[1] *blote-herrings, blast, blaze, to blow,* that is, *blossom, bloom;* and perhaps *blood* and *blush.*

In the native words of our tongue is to be found a great agreement between the letters and the thing signified; and therefore the sounds of letters smaller, sharper, louder, closer, softer, stronger, clearer, more obscure,[e] and more stridulous, do very often intimate the like effects in the things signified.[2]

a. imply *73*] implies *55a, 55b, 65*
b. denote *73*] denotes *55a, 55b, 65*
c. *snivel 55b, 65*] *snevil 55a, 73*
d. imply *73*] implies *55a, 55b, 65*
e. obscure, *55a, 55b, 73*] obsure *65*

---

tude toward representative verse (p. 332, n. 6 above).

3. *Snite:* "A snipe. This is perhaps the true name; but *snipe* prevails" (*Dictionary*).

4. *To Snudge:* "To lie idle, close or snug" (*Dictionary*).

5. *To Snib:* "To check; to nip; to reprimand" (*Dictionary*).

6. *Bleat:* "Pale, ghastly" (*OED,* s.v. *blate*); glossed by the first *bleak.*

7. *Blay:* "A small, white river fish; called also a *bleak*" (*Dictionary*).

8. *Blister* is repeated here as a gloss on *bleb.*

9. *Blabber-lip't:* "Having thick projecting lips" (*OED,* s.v. *babber-lipped*); not in *Dictionary.*

1. *Bloted:* obsolete form of *bloated* (i.e., cured with salt and smoke; *OED*); so *blote-herrings* or *bloaters.*

2. This sentence is a literal translation of *Grammatica* (pp. 112–13) and inconsistent with SJ's usual opinions on the relationship between sound and sense.

Thus words that begin with *str* intimate the force and effect of the thing signified, as if probably derived from *στρόννυμι*,[3] or *strenuus;*[4] as, *strong, strength, strew, strike, streake, stroke, stripe, strive, strife, struggle, strout,*[5] *strut, stretch, strait, strict, streight,* that is, narrow, *distrain, stress, distress, string, strap, stream, streamer, strand, strip, stray, struggle, strange, stride, straddle.*

St in like manner imply[f] strength, but in a less degree, so much only as is sufficient to preserve what has been already communicated, rather than acquire any new degree; as if it were derived from the Latin *sto:* for example, *stand, stay,* that is, to remain, or to prop; *staff, stay,* that is, to oppose; *stop, to stuff, stifle, to stay,* that is, to stop; *a stay*, that is, an obstacle; *stick, stut,*[6] *stutter, stammer, stagger, stickle, stick, stake,* a sharp pale, and any thing deposited at play; *stock, stem, sting, to sting, stink, stitch, stud, stanchion, stub, stubble, to stub* up, *stump,* whence *stumble, stalk, to stalk, step, to stamp* with the feet, whence *to stamp,* that is, to make an impression and a stamp; *stow, to stow, to bestow, steward* or *stoward,*[7] *stead, steady, steadfast,*[g] *stable, a stable, a stall, to stall,*[8] *stool, stall,*[9] *still, stall, stallage,*[1] *stall, stage, still* adj. and *still* adv. *stale, stout, sturdy, steed, stoat, stallion, stiff, stark-dead, to starve* with hunger or cold;[h] *stone, steel, stern, stanch, to stanch* blood, *to stare, steep, steeple, stair, standard,* a stated measure, *stately*. In all these, and perhaps some others,[i] *st* denote[j] something firm and fixed.

f. imply *73*] implies *55a, 55b, 65*
g. steadfast *55a, 55b, 73*] stedfast *65*
h. cold; *55a, 55b, 73*] cold, *65*
i. others, *55a, 55b, 73*] others *65*
j. denote *73*] denotes *55a, 55b, 65*

---

3. *στρόννυμι*: to spread or strew (Liddell, Scott, and Jones, *Greek-English Lexicon,* s.v. *στόρνυμι*).

4. *Strenuus:* active, vigorous, unrelated to *στόρνυμι* (*Oxford Latin Dictionary*).

5. *Strout:* obsolete form of *strut* (*OED*).

6. *Stut:* "to stammer" (*Dictionary*).

7. *Stoward:* a supposed etymology of *steward: stow* (a place) plus *ward* (guard) (*OED*).

8. *To stall: Grammatica* glosses this instance as *saturare* (p. 114), to satiate (see *OED,* s.v. *to stall* [1], sense 12).

9. *Stall: sedile,* or *seat* (*Grammatica,* ibid.).

1. *Stallage:* "Rent paid for a stall" (*Dictionary,* sense 1); related to preceding use of *stall.*

Thr imply[k] a more violent degree of motion, as *throw, thrust, throng, throb, through, threat, threaten, thrall, throws.*

Wr imply[l] some sort of obliquity or distortion, as *wry, to wreathe, wrest, wrestle, wring, wrong, wrinch,*[2] *wrench, wrangle, wrinkle, wrath, wreak, wrack, wretch, wrist, wrap.*

Sw imply[m] a silent agitation, or a softer kind of lateral motion; as *sway, swag, to sway, swagger, swerve, sweat, sweep, swill, swim, swing, swift, sweet, switch, swinge.*

Nor is there much difference of *sm* in *smoothe, smug, smile, smirk, smite,* which signifies the same as to *strike,* but is a softer word; *small, smell, smack, smother, smart,* a *smart* blow properly signifies such a kind of stroke as with an originally silent motion implied in *sm,* proceeds to a quick violence, denoted by *ar* suddenly ended, as is shewn by *t.*

Cl denote[n] a kind of adhesion or tenacity, as in *cleave, clay, cling, climb, clamber, clammy, clasp, to clasp, to clip, to clinch, cloak, clog, close, to close, a clod, a clot,* as a *clot* of blood, *clouted* cream, *a clutter, a cluster.*

Sp imply[o] a kind of dissipation or expansion, especially a quick one, particularly if there be an *r,* as if it were from *spargo* or *separo:*[3] for example, *spread, spring, sprig, sprout, sprinkle, split, splinter, spill, spit, sputter, spatter.*

Sl denote[p] a kind of silent fall, or a less observable motion; as in *slime, slide, slip, slipper, sly, sleight, slit, slow, slack, slight, sling, slap.*

And so likewise *ash,* in *crash, rash, gash, flash, clash, lash, slash, plash, trash,* indicate[q] something acting more nimbly and sharply. But *ush,* in *crush, rush, gush, flush, blush, brush, hush, push,* implies something as acting more obtusely and

k. imply *73*] implies *55a, 55b, 65*
l. imply *55a, 55b, 73*] implies *65*
m. imply *55a, 55b, 73*] implies *65*
n. denote *55a, 55b, 73*] denotes *65*
o. imply *73*] implies *55a, 55b, 65*
p. denote *73*] denotes *55a, 55b, 65*
q. indicate *73*] indicates *55a, 55b, 65*

2. *Wrinch:* obsolete variant of *wrench* (*OED*).

3. *Spargo* or *separo:* Latin, scatter, separate.

dully. Yet in both there is indicated a swift[r] and sudden motion, not instantaneous, but gradual, by the continued sound *sh.*

Thus in *fling, sling, ding, swing, cling, sing, wring, sting,* the tingling of the termination *ng,* and the sharpness of the vowel *i,* imply the continuation of a very slender motion or tremor, at length indeed vanishing, but not suddenly interrupted. But in *tink,*[4] *wink, sink, clink, chink, think,* that end in a mute consonant, there is also indicated a sudden ending.

If there be an *l,* as in *jingle, tingle, tinkle, mingle, sprinkle, twinkle,* there is implied a frequency, or iteration of small acts. And the same frequency of acts, but less subtile by reason of the clearer vowel *a,* is indicated in *jangle, tangle, spangle, mangle, wrangle, brangle,*[5] *dangle;* as also in *mumble, grumble, jumble, tumble, stumble, rumble, crumble, fumble.* But at the same time the close *u* implies something obscure or obtunded; and a congeries of consonants *mbl,* denotes a confused kind of rolling or tumbling, as in *ramble, scamble,*[6] *scramble, wamble, amble;* but in these there is something acute.

In *nimble,* the acuteness of the vowel denotes celerity. In *sparkle,*[s] *sp* denotes dissipation, *ar* an acute crackling, *k* a sudden interruption, *l* a frequent iteration; and in like manner in *sprinkle,* unless *in* may imply the subtility of the dissipated guttules.[7] *Thick* and *thin* differ, in that the former ends with an obtuse consonant, and the latter[t] with an acute.

In like manner, in *squeek,*[8] *squeak, squeal, squall, braul, wraul,*

r. swift *55a, 55b, 73*] swift, *65*

s. *sparkle, 55a, 55b, 73*] *sparkle 65*

t. latter *55b, 65*] later *55a, 73;* later *is not listed in* Dictionary. *In* Dictionary *under* former (*adj., sense* 2), *an illustrative quotation from Pope reads in part:* "a man may be the *former* merely through the misfortune of an ill judgment; but he cannot be the latter without both that and an ill temper." *See also p. 307, n.c.*

---

4. *To tink:* "To make a sharp shrill noise" (*Dictionary*).

5. *Brangle:* "Squabble, wrangle; litigious contest" (*Dictionary*).

6. *Scamble:* "To be turbulent and rapacious; to scramble; to get by struggling with others" (*Dictionary,* sense 1).

7. *Guttules:* an anglicized form of *Grammatica*'s Latin *guttularum* (p. 117), meaning "drops."

8. *Squeek:* an obsolete form of the verb *to squeak* (*OED*), not in *Dictionary.*

yaul, spaul,[9] *screek, shreek, shril, sharp, shrivel, wrinkle, crack, crash, clash, gnash, plash, crush, hush, hisse, sisse,*[u] *whist, soft, jarr, hurl, curl, whirl, buz, bussle,*[v1] *spindle, dwindle, twine, twist,* and in many more, we may observe the agreement of such sort of sounds with the things signified:[w] and this so frequently happens, that scarce any language which I know can be compared with ours. So that one monosyllable word, of which kind are almost all ours, emphatically expresses what in other languages can scarce be explained but by compounds, or decompounds, or sometimes a tedious circumlocution.

We have many words borrowed from the Latin; but the greatest part of them were communicated by the intervention of the French; as *grace, face, elegant, elegance, resemble.*

Some verbs, which seem borrowed from the Latin, are formed from the present tense, and some from the supines.

From the present are formed *spend, expend,* expendo; *conduce,* conduco; *despise,* despicio; *approve,* approbo; *conceive,* concipio.

From the supines, *supplicate,* supplico; *demonstrate,* demonstro; *dispose,* dispono; *expatiate,* expatior; *suppress,* supprimo; *exempt,* eximo.

Nothing is more apparent, than that Wallis goes too far in quest of originals. Many of these which seem selected as immediate descendents from the Latin, are apparently French, as *conceive, approve, expose, exempt.*[2]

Some words purely French, not derived from the Latin, we have transferred into our language; as, *garden, garter, buckler, to advance, to cry, to plead,* from the French *jardin, jartier, bou-*

u. *sisse emend.* (*as in Wallis*)] *fisse 55a, 55b, 65, 73, 84, 85a, 85b*
v. *bussle, 55a, 73*] *busle, 55b, 65*
w. signified: *55a, 55b, 73*] signified; *65*

9. *Braul, wraul, yaul, spaul:* SJ regularly spells such words with *w* instead of *u; wrawl* (not in *Dictionary*) means "to bawl" (*OED*); *to spawl* means "To throw moisture out of the mouth" (*Dictionary*).

1. *Bussle:* earlier form of *bustle* (*OED*), not in *Dictionary.*

2. This isolated paragraph repeats a criticism of Wallis and most earlier etymologists that SJ expresses in *Dictionary,* thereby showing an awareness of contemporary trends in linguistic theory, if not innovation. He returns to his translation of *Grammatica* in the next paragraph.

clier, avancer, cryer, plaider; though indeed, even of these, part is of Latin original.

As to many words which we have in common with the Germans, it is doubtful whether the old Teutons borrowed them from the Latins, or the Latins from the Teutons, or both had them from some common original; as, *wine,* vinum; *wind,* ventus; *went,* veni;[x] *way,* via; *wall,* vallum; *wallow,* volvo; *wool,* vellus; *will,* volo; *worm,* vermis; *worth,* virtus; *wasp,* vespa; *day,* dies; *draw,* traho; *tame,* domo, δαμάω; *yoke,* jugum, ζεῦγος; *over, upper,* super, ὑπερ; *am,* sum, ειμι; *break,* frango; *fly,* volo; *blow,* flo. I make no doubt but the Teutonick is more ancient than the Latin: and it is no less certain, that the Latin, which borrowed a great number of words, not only from the Greek, especially the Æolick, but from other neighbouring languages, as the Oscan[3] and others, which have long become obsolete, received not a few from the Teutonick. It is certain, that the English, German, and other Teutonick languages, retained some derived from[y] the Greek, which the Latin has not; as *ax,*[z] *achs, mit, ford,*[a] *pfurd, daughter, tochter, mickle, mingle, moon, sear, grave, graff, to grave, to scrape, whole,* from[b] ἀξίνη.[c] μετα, πορθμος, θυγατὴρ, μεγάλος,[d] μιγνύω, μῆνη, ξῆρός, γράφω, ὅλος.[e] Since they received these immediately from the Greeks, without the intervention of the Latin language, why may not other words be derived immediately from the same fountain, though they be likewise found among the Latins?[f][4]

Our ancestors were studious to form borrowed words, how-

x. veni; *55a, 55b, 73*] veni: *65*
y. from *55b, 65, 73*] form *55a*
z. as *ax, 73*] as *path, pfad, ax, 55a, 55b, 65*
a. *ford, 55a, 73*] *foad, 55b, 65*
b. *whole,* from *73*] *whole, heal,* from *55a, 55b, 65*
c. from ἀξίνη, *73*] from πάγος, ἀξίνη, *55a, 55b, 65*
d. πορθμός, θυγατὴρ, μεγάλος, *73*] πορθμός, μεγάλος, *55a, 55b, 65*
e. ὅλος. *73*] ὅλος, εἰλέω. *55a, 55b, 65*
f. Latins? *73*] Latins. *55a, 55b, 65*

3. *Oscan:* an Italic language of the Campania, displaced by Latin.

4. This speculation on the history of European languages is Wallis's (*Grammatica,* pp. 121–22), not SJ's. The notion that "Teutonick" was older than Latin was supported by a misinterpretation of the Greek element in the Codex Argenteus (see History, pp. 126–27, nn. 6, 7, above).

ever long, into monosyllables; and not only cut off the formative terminations, but cropped the first syllable, especially in words beginning with a vowel; and rejected not only vowels in the middle, but likewise consonants of a weaker sound, retaining the stronger, which seem the bones of words, or changing them for others of the same organ,[5] in order that the sound might become the softer; but especially transposing their order, that they might the more readily be pronounced without the intermediate vowels. For example, in expendo, *spend;* exemplum, *sample;* excipio, *scape;* extraneus, *strange;* extractum, *stretch'd;* excrucio, *to screw;* exscorio, *to scour;* excorio, *to scourge;* excortico, *to scratch;* and others beginning with *ex:* as also, emendo, *to mend;* episcopus, *bishop;* in Danish *Bisp;* epistola, *pistle;*[6] hospitale, *spittle;*[7] Hispania, *Spain;* historia, *story.*

Many of these etymologies are doubtful, and some evidently mistaken.[8]

The following are somewhat harder, *Alexander, Sander; Elisabetha, Betty;* apis, *bee;* aper,[9] *bar; p* passing into *b,* as in *bishop;* and by cutting off *a* from the beginning, which is restored in the middle; but for the old *bar* or *bare,* we now say *boar;* as for *lang, long;* for *bain, bane;* for *stane, stone;* aprugna,[1] *brawn, p* being changed into *b,* and *a* transposed, as in *aper,* and *g* changed into *w,* as in pignus, *pawn;* lege, *law;* ἀλοπήξ, *fox,* cutting off the beginning, and changing *p* into *f,* as in pellis, *a fell;* pullus, *a foal;* pater, *father;* pavor, *fear;* polio, *file;* pleo, impleo, *fill, full;* piscis, *fish;* and transposing *o* into the middle, which was taken from the beginning; apex, *apice;*[g2]

g. *apice emend.*(*as in Wallis*)] *a piece 55a, 55b, 65, 73, 84, 85a, 85b*

5. *Organ:* one of a group of stops on a full organ, such as *great organ* or *choir organ* (*OED,* 2.c); following Wallis, who used Latin *organum* (p. 122), SJ uses the word metaphorically to mean a related group of sounds.

6. *Pistle:* obsolete; an aphetic form of *epistle* (*OED*).

7. *Spittle:* "[Corrupted from *hospital,* and therefore better written *spital,* or *spittal.*] Hospital. It is still retained in Scotland" (*Dictionary*).

8. SJ interposes this remark, but the next paragraph is again all *Grammatica* (pp. 123–24).

9. *Aper:* Latin, *boar,* for which SJ, following *Grammatica,* gives the old form *bar.*

1. *Aprugna:* Latin, adj., of a boar.

2. *Apice:* a reflex and a translation of

peak, *pike;* zophorus, *freese;*[3] mustum, *stum;*[4] defensio, *fence;* dispensator, *spencer;*[5] asculto, escouter, Fr. *scout;* exscalpo, *scrape,* restoring *l* instead of *r,* and hence *scrap, scrable, scrawl;* exculpo, *scoop;* exterritus, *start;* extonitus, attonitus, *stonn'd;*[6] stomachus, *maw;* offendo, *fined;*[7] obstipo, *stop;* audere, *dare;* cavere, *ware,* whence *a-ware, be-ware, wary, warn, warning;* for the Latin *v* consonant formerly sounded like our *w,* and the modern sound of the *v* consonant was formerly that of the letter *f,* that is, the Æolick digamma, which had the sound of φ,[8] and the modern sound of the letter *f* was that of the Greek φ or *ph;* ulcus, ulcere, *ulcer, sore,* and hence *sorry, sorrow, sorrowful;* ingenium, *engine, gin;* scalenus, *leaning,* unless you would rather derive it from χλίνω, whence inclino; infundibulum, *funnel;* gagates, *jett;*[9] projectum, *to jett*[h] *forth, a jetty;* cucullus, *a cowl.*

There are syncopes somewhat harder; from tempore, *time;* from nomine, *name;* domina, *dame;* as the French *homme, femme, nom,* from homine, fœmina, nomine. Thus pagina, *page;* ποτήριον, *pot;* κυπελλα, *cup;* cantharus, *can;* tentorium, *tent;* precor, *pray;* præda, *prey;* specio, speculor, *spy;* plico, *ply;* implico, *imply;* replico, *reply;* complico, *comply;* sedes episcopalis, *see.*

A vowel is also cut off in the middle, that the number of the syllables may be lessened; as, amita, *aunt;* spiritus, *spright;*

h. *jett 55a, 73*] *jet 55b, 65*

Latin *apex* (top); c.f. *Dictionary:* "*APICES of a flower* . . . Little knobs that grow on the tops of the stamina, in the middle of a flower." SJ's italics in listing the word indicate that he considered it not fully naturalized.

3. *Freese:* a variant of *frieze.*

4. *Stum:* "Wine yet unfermented; must" (*Dictionary*).

5. *Spencer:* "a steward or butler" (*OED*).

6. *Stonn'd:* an earlier form of *stunned.*

7. *Fined:* "come to an end" (*OED,* v1, sense 2); this obsolete word is not in *Dictionary.*

8. Digamma is the sixth letter in the oldest Greek alphabets. Written ϝ, it supplied the shape for the Latin *f,* but it was a *w* consonant, and may sometime in Greek have become a *v* but probably not an f, or φ sound. Richard Bentley made the purpose of the letter widely known in his work on Homer beginning in 1713; see John Edwin Sandys, *A History of Classical Scholarship* (3 vols., 1908), II.407.

9. *Jett:* "*Jet* is a very beautiful fossil, of a fine and very even structure, and of a smooth surface . . ." (*Dictionary*).

debitum, *debt;* dubito, *doubt;* comes, comitis, *count;* clericus, *clerk;* quietus, *quit, quite;* acquieto, *to acquit;* separo, *to spare;* stabilis, *stable;* stabulum, *stable;* pallacium, *palace, place;* rabula, *rail, rawl, wraul,*[1] *brawl, rable, brable;*[2] quæsitio, *quest.*

As also a consonant, or at least one of a softer sound, or even a whole syllable; rotundus, *round;* fragilis, *frail;* securus, *sure;* regula, *rule;* tegula, *tile;* subtilis, *subtle;* nomen, *noun;* decanus, *dean;* computo, *count;* subitaneus, *suddain,*[3] *soon;* superare, *to soar;* periculum, *peril;* mirabile, *marvel;* as[i] magnus, *main;* dignor, *deign;* tingo, *stain;* tinctum, *taint;* pingo, *paint;* prædari, *reach.*

The contractions may seem harder, where many of them meet, as κυριακὸς, *kyrk, church;* presbyter, *priest;* sacristanus, *sexton;* frango, fregi, *break, breach;* fagus, φὴγα, *beech, f* changed into *b,* and *g* into *ch,* which are letters near a-kin;[j] frigesco, *freeze;* frigesco, *fresh, sc* into[k] *sh,* as above in *bishop, fish,* so in scapha,[l] *skiff, ship,*[m] and refrigesco, *refresh;* but viresco, *fresh;* phlebotomus, *fleam;*[4] bovina, *beef;* vitulina, *veal;* scutifer, *squire;* pœnitentia, *penance;* sanctuarium, *sanctuary, sentry;* quæsitio, *chase;* perquisitio, *purchase;* anguilla, *eel;* insula, *isle, ile, island, iland;* insuletta, *islet, ilet; eyght* and more contractedly *ey,*[5] whence *Owsney, Ruley, Ely;*[6] examinare, *to scan,* namely, by rejecting from the beginning and end *e* and *o,* according to the usual manner, the remainder *xamin,* which the Saxons, who did not use *x,* writ *csamen,* or *scamen* is contracted into *scan;* as from dominus, *don;* nomine, *noun;* abo-

i. as *55a, 73*] as, *55b, 65*
j. near a-kin *55b, 65, 73*] near-a-kin *55a*
k. *sc* into *sh 55a, 55b, 65*] *sc* in *sh 73*
l. scapha *84, 85a, 85b*] *scapha 55a, 55b, 65, 73*
m. *ship emend.* (as in Wallis)] *skip 55a, 55b, 65, 73, 84, 85a, 85b*

1. *Rawl* and *wraul* are variants of *wrawl;* see p. 338, n. 9, above.

2. *Rable* and *brable* are variants of *rabble* and *brabble.*

3. *Suddain:* an old form of *sudden.*

4. *Fleam:* "An instrument used to bleed cattle, which is placed on the vein, and then driven by a blow" (*Dictionary*).

5. *Eyght, ey:* "Ait, or Eyght . . . A small island in a river" (*Dictionary*).

6. *Owsney, Ruley, Ely: Grammatica* glosses these place names as "Isidis insula" (the island of Isis), "regalis insula" (the island of the ruler), and "anguillaris insula" (the island of eels), respectively (p. 126).

mino, *ban;* and indeed *apum examen*[7] they turned into *sciame;* for which we say *swarme,* by inserting *r* to denote the murmuring; thesaurus, *store;* sedile, *stool;* νετὸς, *wet;* sudo, *sweat;* gaudium, *gay;* jocus, *joy;* succus, *juice;* catena, *chain;*[n] caliga, calga;[o] chause, chausse, Fr. *hose;* extinguo, *stanch, squench,*[8] *quench, stint;* foras, *forth;* species, *spice;* recito, *read;* adjuvo, *aid;* αἰὼν, ævum, *ay, age, ever;* floccus, *lock;*[9] excerpo, *scrape, scrabble, scrawl;* extravagus, *stray, straggle;* collectum, *clot, clutch;* colligo, *coil;* recolligo, *recoil;* severo, *swear;* stridulus, *shrill;* procurator, *proxy;* pulso, *to push;* calamus, *a quill;* impetere, *to impeach;* augeo, auxi, *wax;* and vanesco, vanui, *wane;* syllabare, *to spell;* puteus, *pit;* granum, *corn;* comprimo, *cramp, crump, crumple, crinkle.*

Some may seem harsher, yet may not be rejected, for it at least appears, that some of them are derived from proper names, and there are others whose etymology is acknowledged by every body; as, Alexander, *Elick, Scander, Sander, Sandy, Sanny;* Elizabetha,[p] *Elizabeth, Elisabeth,*[1] *Betty, Bess;* Margareta, *Margaret, Marget, Meg, Peg;* Maria, *Mary, Mal, Pal, Malkin, Mawkin, Mawkes;* Matthæus, *Mattha, Matthew;* Martha, *Matt, Pat;* Gulielmus, *Wilhelmus, Girolamo, Guillaume, William, Will, Bill, Wilkin, Wicken, Wicks, Weeks.*

Thus cariophyllus, flos; gerofilo, Ital. giriflee, gilofer, Fr. *gilliflower,* which the vulgar call *julyflower,* as if derived from the month *July;* petroselinum, *parsly;* portulaca, *purslain;* cydonium, *quince;* cydoniatum, *quiddeny;*[2] persicum, *peach;* eruca, *eruke,*[3] which they corrupt to *ear-wig,* as if it took its

n. *chain; 55a, 55b, 73*] *chain, 65*
o. calga; *55a, 73*] calga, *55b 65*
p. Elizabetha, *55b, 65, 73*] Elizabeth, *55a*

7. *Apum examen:* a swarm of bees.

8. *Squench:* a dialectical word meaning "to extinguish" (*OED*).

9. *Lock:* "A quantity of hair or wool hanging together" (*Dictionary,* sense 5).

1. *Grammatica* has *Elsibeth* in this place, which, unlike *Elisabeth,* is truly different from *Elizabeth* (p. 127). It is remarkable that SJ did not add *Tetty,* his nickname for his wife Elizabeth.

2. *Quiddeny:* variant of *quiddany,* "Marmalade; confection of quinces made with sugar" (*Dictionary*).

3. *Eruke,* meaning *caterpillar,* is unrelated to *ear-wig* formally and semantically, despite the testimony of Wallis

name from the ear; annulus[q] geminus, *a gimmal* or *gimbal ring;*[r] and thus the word *gimbal* and *jumbal* is transferred to other things thus interwoven;[4] quelques choses, *kickshaws.* Since the origin of these, and many others, however forced, is evident, it ought to appear no wonder to any one if the ancients have thus disfigured many, especially as they so much affected monosyllables; and, to make them sound the softer, took this liberty of maiming, taking away, changing, transposing, and softening them.

But while we derive these from the Latin, I do not mean to say, that many of them did not immediately come to us from the Saxon, Danish, Dutch, and Teutonick languages, and other dialects, and some taken more lately from the French or Italians, or Spaniards.

The same word, according to its different significations, often has a different origin; as, *to bear a burden,* from *fero;* but to *bear,* whence *birth, born, bairn,* comes from *pario;* and a *bear,* at least if it be of Latin original, from *fera.* Thus *perch,* a fish, from *perca;* but *perch,* a measure, from *pertica,*[5] and likewise *to perch. To spell* is from *syllaba;* but *spell,* an inchantment, by which it is believed that the boundaries are so fixed in lands, that none can pass them against the master's will,[6] from *expello;* and *spell,* a message,[s] from *epistola;* whence *gospel, good-spel,* or *god-spell.* Thus *freese,* or *freeze,* from *frigesco;* but *freeze,* an architectonic word, from *zophorus;* but *freese,*[7] for *cloth,* from *Frisia,* or perhaps from *frigesco,* as being more fit than any other for keeping out the cold.

q. annulus *55a, 73*] annullus *55b, 65*

r. *gimbal ring 55a, 73*] *gimbal-ring 55b, 65*

s. message *emend.* (*Wallis's Latin* nuncium)] messenger *55a, 55b, 65, 73, 84, 85a, 85b*

---

and grammarians like Greenwood and SJ who repeat him.

4. *annulus geminus:* a twin finger-ring, which is one of the meanings of *gimmal,* or *gemel,* and *gimmal-ring* (*OED*); *gimbal* is a form of *gimmal; jumbal* is "A kind of fine sweet cake or biscuit, formerly often made up in the form of rings or rolls" (*OED*).

5. *Perch:* "A measure of five yards and a half; a pole" (*Dictionary*); *pertica,* Latin, *pole* or *staff.*

6. Cf. *spell:* "A charm consisting of some words of occult power" (*Dictionary,* sense 1).

7. *Freese:* a form of *frieze,* "A coarse warm cloth, made perhaps first in *Friesland*" (*Dictionary*).

There are many words among us, even monosyllables,[t] compounded of two or more words, at least serving instead of compounds, and comprising the signification of more words than one; as, from *scrip* and *roll* comes *scroll;* from *proud* and *dance, prance;* from *st*[u] of the verb *stay,*[v] or *stand* and *out,*[w] is made *stout;* from *stout* and *hardy, sturdy;* from *sp* of *spit* or *spew,* and *out,*[x] comes *spout;* from the same *sp,* with the termination *in,* is *spin;* and adding *out, spin out;* and from the same *sp,* with *it,* is *spit,* which only differs from *spout* in that it is smaller, and with less noise and force; but *sputter* is, because of the obscure *u,* something between *spit* and *spout;* and by reason of adding *r,* it intimates a frequent iteration and noise, but obscurely confused: whereas *spatter,* on account of the sharper and clearer vowel *a,* intimates a more distinct noise, in which it chiefly differs from *sputter.* From the same *sp,* and the termination *ark,* comes *spark,* signifying a single emission of fire with a noise; namely, *sp* the emission, *ar* the more acute noise, and *k,* the mute consonant, intimates its being suddenly terminated; but adding *l,* is made the frequentative *sparkle.* The same *sp,* by adding *r,* that is *spr,* implies a more lively impetus of diffusing or expanding itself; to which adding the termination *ing,* it becomes *spring;* its vigour *spr* imports, its sharpness the termination *ing,* and lastly *in* acute and tremulous, ends in the mute consonant *g,* denotes the sudden ending of any motion, that it is meant in its primary signification, of a single, not a complicated exilition.[8] Hence we call *spring* whatever has an elastick force; as also a fountain of water, and thence the origin of any thing; and to *spring,* to germinate;[y] and *spring,* one of the four seasons. From the same *spr* and *out,* is formed *sprout,* and with the termination *ig, sprig;*

t. monosyllables, *55a, 73*] monosyllables *55b, 65*
u. *st 55a, 55b, 65*] *st, 73*
v. *stay, 55a*] *stay 55b, 65, 73*
w. *out 55b, 65, 73*] *stout 55a*
x. *out 55a, 73*] out *55b, 65*
y. germinate; *55a, 55b, 73*] germinate: *65*

---

8. *Exilition:* "The act of springing or rushing out suddenly" (*Dictionary*).

of which the following,[z] for the most part, is the difference: *sprout,* of a grosser sound, imports a fatter or grosser[a] bud; *sprig,* of a slenderer sound, denotes a smaller shoot. In like manner, from *str* of the verb *strive,* and *out,* comes *strout*[b9] and *strut.* From the same *str,* and the termination *uggle,* is made *struggle;* and this *gl* imports, but without any great noise, by reason of the obscure sound of the vowel *u.* In like manner, from *throw* and *roll* is made *trull;* and almost in the same sense is *trundle,* from *throw* or *thrust,* and *rundle.* Thus *graff* or *grough*[1] is compounded of *grave* and *rough;* and *trudge* from *tread* or *trot,* and *drudge.*

In these observations it is easy to discover great sagacity and great extravagance, an ability to do much defeated by the desire of doing more than enough. It may be remarked,

1. That Wallis's derivations are often so made, that by the same licence any language may be deduced from any other.

2. That he makes no distinction between words immediately derived by us from the Latin, and those which being copied from other languages, can therefore afford no example of the genius of the English language, or its laws of derivation.

3. That he derives from the Latin, often with great harshness and violence, words apparently Teutonick; and therefore, according to his own declaration, probably older than the tongue to which he refers them.

4. That some of his derivations are apparently erroneous.

z. following, *55a, 55b, 73*] following *65*
a. grosser *55b, 65*] crosser *55a, 73*
b. *strout 55a, 55b, 73*] *strout, 65*

9. *Strout:* obsolete form of *strut* (*OED*).

1. *Grough:* apparently an unrecorded variant of *graff,* "A ditch; a moat" (*Dictionary*).

PART III.[c]

SYNTAX.

The established practice of grammarians requires that I should here treat of the Syntax; but our language has so little inflection, or variety of terminations, that its construction neither requires nor admits many rules. Wallis therefore has totally neglected[d] it; and Johnson, whose desire of following the writers upon the learned languages made him think a syntax indispensably necessary, has published such petty observations as were better omitted.[2]

The verb, as in other languages, agrees with the nominative in number and person; as, *Thou fliest from good; He runs to death.*

Our adjectives and pronouns are invariable.

Of two substantives the noun possessive is the genitive; as, *His father's glory; The sun's heat.*

Verbs transitive require an oblique case; as, *He loves me; You fear him.*

All prepositions require an oblique case: *He gave this* to *me; He took this* from *me; He says this* of *me; He came* with *me.*

PART IV.[e]

PROSODY.

It is common for those that deliver the grammar of modern languages, to omit their Prosody. So that of the Italians is neglected by *Buomattei;*[3] that of the French by *Desmarais;*[4]

c. PART III. *65*] PART III. *absent 55a, 55b, 73*
d. neglected *73*] omitted *55a, 55b, 65*
e. PART IV. *65*] PART IV. *absent 55a, 55b, 73*

2. *English Grammar,* 528–51.

3. Benedetto Buommattei, *Della lingua Toscana* (1623; 3d ed. rev. Florence, 1643). On this monumental work, which was still authoritative in SJ's time, and its debt to Joseph Scaliger's Latin grammar, see G. A. Padley, *Grammatical Theory in Western Europe, 1500–1700: Trends in Vernacular Grammar,* 2 vols. (1985–88), I.254–68.

4. Abbé François Séraphin Regnier-Desmarais, *Traite de la grammaire Françaíse* (Paris, 1705). Like the scholar in *Rambler* 95, Desmarais was called Pertinax.

and that of the English by *Wallis, Cooper,* and even by *Johnson* though a poet.[5] But as the laws of metre are included in the idea of a grammar, I have thought it proper to insert them.

Prosody comprises *orthoepy,*[ee] or the rules of pronunciation; and *orthometry,* or the laws of versification.

§I.[f]

PRONUNCIATION is just, when every letter has its proper sound, and when every syllable has its proper accent, or[g] which in English versification is the same, its proper quantity.

The sounds of the letters have been already explained; and rules for the accent or quantity are not easily to be given, being subject to innumerable exceptions. Such however as I have read or formed, I shall here propose.

1. Of dissyllables formed by affixing a termination, the former syllable is commonly accented, as[h] *chíldish, kíngdom, fástest,*[i] *ácted, tóilsome, lóver, scóffer, faírer,*[j] *fóremost,*[k] *zéalous, fúlness, gódly, méekly, ártist.*

2. Dissyllables formed by prefixing a syllable to the radical word, have commonly the accent on the latter; as, *to begét, to beseém, to bestów.*

3. Of dissyllables, which are at once nouns and verbs, the verb has commonly the accent on the latter, and the noun on the former syllable; as, *to descánt, a déscant; to cemént, a cément; to contráct, a cóntract.*

This rule has many exceptions. Though verbs seldom have

ee. *orthoepy* 84a] *orthoephy 55, 55a, 65, 73*
f. §I. *65*] §I. *absent 55a, 55b, 73*
g. or *55a, 73*] or, *55b, 65*
h. as *55a, 73*] as, *55b, 65*
i. *fástest* emend. (conjecture)] *áctest* 55a, 55b, 65, 73, 84, 85a, 85b
j. *faírer 55a, 55b, 73*] *fáirer 65*
k. *fóremost 55b 65*] *forémost 55a, 73*

5. Citing Julius Caesar Scaliger and Petrus Ramus, Jonson says, "*Prosodie,* and *Orthography,* are not parts of *Grammar,* but diffus'd, like the blood, and spirits through the whole" (*English Grammar,* 466–67). In his *Grammatica Linguae Anglicanae* (1685) and his translation of the first two parts, *The English Teacher* (1687), Christopher Cooper advocated orthographical reform.

their accent on the former, yet nouns often have it on the latter syllable; as, *delíght, perfúme.*

4. All dissyllables ending in *y,* as *cránny;*[l] in *our,* as *lábour, fávour;*[m] in *ow,* as *wíllow, wállow,* except *allów;* in *le,* as *báttle, bíble;* in *ish,* as *bánish;* in *ck,* as *cámbrick, cássock;* in *ter,* as *to bátter;* in *age,* as *coúrage;* in *en,* as *fásten;* in *et,* as *quíet,* accent the former syllable.

5. Dissyllable nouns in *er,* as *cánker, bútter,*[n] have the accent on the former syllable.

6. Dissyllable verbs terminating in a consonant and *e* final, as *compríse, escápe;* or having a diphthong in the last syllable, as *appéase, revéal;* or ending in two consonants, as *atténd;*[o] have the accent on the latter syllable.

7. Dissyllable nouns having a diphthong in the latter syllable, have commonly their accent on the latter syllable, as *applaúse;* except words in *ain,* as[p] *cértain, moúntain.*

8. Trissyllables formed by adding a termination, or prefixing a syllable, retain the accent of the radical word, as *lóveliness, ténderness, contémner, wágonner,*[q] *phýsical, bespátter, cómmenting,*[r] *comménding, assúrance.*

9. Trissyllables ending in *ous,* as *grácious, árduous;* in *al,* as *cápital;* in *ion,* as *méntion,* accent the first.

10. Trissyllables ending in *ce, ent,* and *ate,* accent the first syllable, as *coúntenance, cóntinence, ármament, ímminent, élegant, própagate,* except they be derived from words having the accent on the last, as *connívence,*[6] *acquáintance;* or the middle syllable hath a vowel before two consonants, as *promúlgate.*

11. Trissyllables ending in *y,* as *éntity, spécify, líberty, víctory, súbsidy,* commonly accent the first syllable.

l. *cránny 65*] *cranny 55a, 55b, 73*
m. *lábour, fávour; 65*] *labour, favour; 55a, 55b, 73*
n. *bútter, 55a, 55b, 65*] *bútter; 73*
o. *atténd; 55a, 55b, 65*] *atténd, 73*
p. *ain,* as *65*] *ain, certain 55a, 55b, 73*
q. *wágonner 55a, 55b, 73*] *wágoner 65*
r. *cómmenting 73*] *comménting 55a, 55b, 65*

---

6. *Connívence:* "Connívance" in *Dictionary.*

12. Trissyllables in *re* or *le* accent the first syllable, as *légible, théatre,* except *discíple,* and some words which have a position,[7] as *exámple, epístle.*

13. Trissyllables in *ude* commonly accent the first syllable, as *plénitude.*

14. Trissyllables ending in *ator* or *atour,* as *creátour,* or having in the middle syllable a diphthong, as *endeávour;* or a vowel before two consonants, as *doméstick,* accent the middle syllable.

15. Trissyllables that have their accent on the last syllable are commonly French, as *acquiésce, repartée, magazíne,* or words formed by prefixing one or two syllables to an acute syllable, as *immatúre, overchárge.*

16. Polysyllables, or words of more than three syllables, follow the accent of the words from which they are derived, as *árrogating, cóntinency, incóntinently, comméndable, commúnicableness.* We should therefore say *dispútable, indispútable,* rather than *dísputable, indísputable;* and *advertísement* rather than *advértisement.*[s]

17. Words in *ion* have the accent upon the antepenult, as *salvátion, perturbátion, concóction;* words in *atour* or *ator* on the penult, as *dedicátor.*

18. Words ending in *le* commonly have the accent on the first syllable, as *ámicable,* unless the second syllable have a vowel before two consonants, as *combústible.*

19. Words ending in *ous* have the accent on the antepenult, as *uxórious, volúptuous.*

20. Words ending in *ty*[t] have their accent on the antepenult, as *pusillanímity, actívity.*

These rules are not advanced as complete[u] or infallible, but proposed as useful. Almost every rule of every language

s. We . . . *advértisement.* *73*] *commúnicableness.* *55a, 55b, 65*
t. *ty 65, 73*] *ly 55a, 55b*
u. complete *55b, 65,73*] compleat *55a*

7. *Position:* "The state of a vowel placed before two consonants, as *pómpous;* or a double consonant, as *áxle*" (*Dictionary,* sense 4).

has its exceptions;[v] and in English, as in other tongues, much must be learned by example and authority. Perhaps more and better rules may be given that have escaped my observation.

§II.[w]

VERSIFICATION is the arrangement of a certain number of syllables according to certain laws.

The feet of our verses are either iambick, as *alóft, creáte;* or trochaick, as *hóly, lófty.*

Our iambick measure comprises verses

Of four syllables,

Most good, most fair,
Or things as rare,
To call you's lost;
For all the cost
Words can bestow,
So poorly show
Upon your praise,
That all the ways
Sense hath, come short.

Drayton.[8]

With ravish'd ears[x]
The monarch hears.

Dryden.[9]

Of six,

This while we are abroad,
Shall we not touch our lyre?

v. exceptions; *55a, 73*] exceptions: *55b, 65*
w. §II. *65*] §II. *absent 55a, 55b, 73*
x. ears *55a, 55b, 73*] ears. *65*

8. Michael Drayton, "An Amouret Anacreontick," II.1–9; *Works* (1748), p. 420. SJ marked up his copy of this edition for use in *Dictionary.*

9. "Alexander's Feast," ll. 37–38.

Shall we not sing an ode?
Shall[y] that holy fire,
In us that strongly glow'd,
In this cold air expire?

Though in the utmost Peak[z]
A while we do remain,
Amongst the mountains bleak,
Expos'd to sleet and rain,
No sport our hours shall break,
To exercise our vein.

Who though bright Phœbus' beams[a]
Refresh the southern ground,
And though the princely Thames
With beauteous nymphs abound,
And by old Camber's[b] streams
Be many wonders found.[c]

Yet many rivers clear
Here glide in silver swathes,
And what of all most dear,
Buxton's delicious baths,
Strong ale and noble chear,
T' asswage breem[1] winter's scathes.

In places far or near,
Or famous, or obscure,
Where wholesom[d] is the air,
Or where the most impure,

y. Shall *55a, 55b, 73*] Or shall *65*
z. Peak *55a, 73*] peak *55b, 65*
a. beams *55a, 55b, 73*] beams, *65*
b. Camber's *55a, 55b, 65*] Cambers *73*
c. found. *73*] found; *55a, 55b, 65*
d. wholesom *55a, 55b, 65*] wholsom *73*

1. *Breem: breme* in *Dictionary:* "Cruel: sharp; severe; not used."

All times, and every where,
The muse is still in ure.

Drayton.[2]

Of eight, which is the usual measure for short poems,

And may at last my weary age
Find out the peaceful hermitage,
The hairy gown, and mossy cell,
Where I may sit, and nightly spell
Of ev'ry star the sky doth shew,
And ev'ry herb that sips the dew.

Milton.[3]

Of ten, which is the common measure of heroick and tragick poetry.

Full in the midst of this created space,
Betwixt heav'n, earth, and skies, there stands a place
Confining on all three; with triple bound; }
Whence all things, though remote, are view'd around, }[4]
And thither bring their undulating sound. }
The palace of loud Fame, her seat of pow'r,
Plac'd on the summit of a lofty tow'r;
A thousand winding entries long and wide
Receive of fresh reports a flowing tide.
A thousand crannies in the walls are made;
Nor gate nor bars exclude the busy trade.
'Tis built of brass, the better to diffuse
The spreading sounds, and multiply the news;
Where echo's in repeated echo's play:
A mart for ever full; and open night and day.
Nor silence is within, nor voice express,

---

2. "An Ode Written in the Peake" (stanzas 2 and 6 omitted), *Works,* p. 421; Drayton's fourth stanza begins "What though."

3. "Il Penseroso," ll. 167–72; cited under *hermitage* in *Dictionary.*

4. Elsewhere SJ criticized the use of brackets around the triplet: "Surely there is something unskilful in the necessity of such mechanical direction" ("Life of Dryden," *Lives,* I.468; par. 350).

But a deaf noise of sounds that never cease;
Confus'd, and chiding, like the hollow rore
Of tides, receding from th' insulted shore;
Or like the broken thunder, heard from far,
When Jove to distance drives the rolling war.
The courts are fill'd with a tumultuous din
Of crouds, or issuing forth, or entring in:
A thorough-fare of news; where some devise
Things never heard, some mingle truth with lies:
The troubled air with empty sounds they beat,
Intent to hear, and eager to repeat.

Dryden.[5]

In all these measures the accents are to be placed on even syllables; and every line considered by itself is more harmonious, as this rule is more strictly observed. The variations necessary to pleasure belong to the art of poetry, not the rules of grammar.[e6]

Our trochaick measures are
Of three syllables,

Here we may
Think and pray,
Before death
Stops our breath:
Other joys
Are but toys.

Walton's Angler.[f7]

e. The . . . grammar. *73*] observed. *55a, 55b, 65*
f. *Walton's Angler. 73*] *Walton's Angler. absent 55a, 55b, 65*

5. "The Twelfth Book of Ovid his Metamorphoses," ll. 56–82; cited in part under *death* (sense 4) and in part under *thoroughfare* (sense 1) in *Dictionary.*

6. On the possible significance of this fourth-edition change to a more flexible notion of metrical stress, see Paul Fussell, "A Note on Samuel Johnson and the Rise of Accentual Prosodic Theory," *Philological Quarterly,* XXXIII (1954), 431–33.

7. Izaak Walton, *The Compleat Angler* (1653; ed. Jonquil Bevan, 1983), p. 149; SJ substitutes "Here" for "There."

Of five,

In the days of old,
Stories plainly told,
Lovers felt annoy.

Old Ballad.[g8]

Of seven,

Fairest piece of well-form'd[h] earth,
Urge not thus your haughty birth.

Waller.[i9]

In these measures the accent is to be placed on the odd syllables.

These are the measures which are now in use, and above the rest those of seven, eight, and ten syllables. Our ancient poets wrote verses sometimes of twelve syllables, as Drayton's Polyolbion.

Of all the Cambrian shires their heads that bear so high,
And farth'st survey their soils with an ambitious eye,
Mervinia for her hills, as for their matchless crowds,
The nearest that are said to kiss the wand'ring clouds,
Especial audience craves, offended with the throng,
That she of all the rest neglected was so long;
Alledging for herself, when through the Saxons[j] pride,
The godlike race of Brute to Severn's setting side

g. *Old Ballad. 73] Old Ballad. absent 55a, 55b, 65*

h. well-form'd *65*] welform'd *55a, 55b, 73 . Under* well (*adv., sense 13*) *in* Dictionary, *SJ cites this couplet, with the "well-form'd" spelling.*

i. *Waller. 73] Waller. absent 55a, 55b, 65*

j. Saxons 55a, 55b, 65] Saxon's *73*

8. Thomas Deloney, "The King of France's Daughter," included in Thomas Percy, *Reliques of Ancient English Poetry* (3 vols., 1765), III.161–64, ll. 1, 3–4; the six-syllable second line ("When faire France did flourish") is omitted in SJ's transcription. SJ could have seen the ballad in *A Collection of Old Ballads* (2 vols., 1723), I.181, or in Percy's manuscript; see *Bishop Percy's Folio Manuscript*, ed. John W. Hales and Frederick J. Furnivall (1868), III.441–49.

9. Edmund Waller, "To Zelinda," ll. 1–2; cited under *well* in *Dictionary* (sense 16).

Were cruelly inforc'd, her mountains did relieve
Those whom devouring war else every where did grieve.
And when all Wales beside (by fortune or by might)
Unto her ancient foe resign'd her ancient right,
A constant maiden still she only did remain,
The last her genuine laws which stoutly did retain.
And as each one is prais'd for her peculiar[k] things;
So only she is rich, in mountains, meres, and springs,
And holds herself as great in her superfluous waste,
As others by their towns, and fruitful tillage grac'd.[1]

And of fourteen, as Chapman's Homer.

And as the mind of such a man, that hath a long way gone,
And either knoweth not his way, or else would let alone
His purpos'd journey, is distract.[2]

The measures of twelve and fourteen syllables, were often mingled by our old poets, sometimes in alternate lines, and sometimes in alternate couplets.[l]

The verse of twelve syllables,[m] called an *Alexandrine,* is now only used to diversify heroick lines.

Waller was smooth, but Dryden taught to join
The varying verse, the full-resounding line,
The long majestick march, and energy divine.[n]

Pope.[o3]

k. her peculiar *55a, 65, 73*] for peculiar *55b*
l. The . . . couplets. *73*] distract. *55a, 55b, 65*
m. syllables *65*] lines *55a, 55b, 73*
n. *The . . . divine. 73*] The . . . divine. *55a, 55b, 65*
o. *Pope. 73*] *Pope. inside parenthesis 65*] *Pope. absent 55a, 55b*

1. *Polyolbion,* IX.1–18; *Works* (1748), p. 278.

2. George Chapman, *Iliads of Homer* (1616), XV.79–81.

3. "First Epistle of the Second Book of Horace Imitated," ll. 267–69; quoted in part under *full* (sense 11) and completely under *march* (sense 2) in *Dictionary;* quoted in full in the "Life of Dryden" (*Lives* I.465; par. 342) and the "Life of Pope" (*Lives* III.232; par. 333).

The pause in the Alexandrine must be at the sixth syllable.[4]

The verse of fourteen syllables is now broken into a soft lyrick measure of verses, consisting alternately of eight syllables and six.

She to receive thy radiant name,
Selects a whiter space.

Fenton.[p5]

When all shall praise, and ev'ry lay
Devote a wreath to thee,
That day, for come it will, that day
Shall I lament to see.

Lewis to Pope.[q6]

Beneath this tomb an infant lies
To earth whose body lent,
Hereafter shall more glorious rise,
But not more innocent.
When the Archangel's trump shall blow,
And souls to bodies join,
What crowds shall wish their lives below
Had been as short as thine.

Wesley.[r7]

p. *Fenton.* 73] *Fenton* 65] *Fenton. absent* 55a, 55b
q. *Lewis to Pope.* 73] *Lewis.* 65] *Lewis to Pope. absent* 55a, 55b
r. Beneath . . . *Wesley.* 73] Beneath . . . *Wesley. absent* 55a, 55b, 65

4. Discussing Milton's pentameter verse in *Rambler* 90 (Yale IV.114–15; pars. 14–15), SJ says, "The noblest and most majestic pauses which our versification admits, are upon the fourth and sixth syllables . . . But far above all others, if I can give credit to my own ear, is the rest upon the sixth syllable, which taking in a complete compass of sound, such as is sufficient to constitute one of our lyrick measures, makes a full and solemn close."

5. Elijah Fenton, "An Ode, to the Right Hon. John Lord Gower," ll. 89–90.

6. David Lewis, "To Pope," substituting "all shall praise" for "none shall rail." The verses appear in a note to Pope's *Dunciad* (A) (1728), II.134. See *Life,* IV.307: SJ repeated the verses from memory, with a different misreading, and identified the anonymous author.

7. Samuel Wesley, "Epitaph on an Infant," cited inaccurately and quoted

We have another measure very quick and lively, and therefore much used in songs, which may be called the *anapestick,* in which the accent rests upon every third syllable.

May I góvern my pássions with ábsolute swáy,
And grow wíser and bétter as lífe wears awáy.

Dr. *Pope.*[s8]

In this measure a syllable is often retrenched from the first foot, as

Dióǵenes súrly and proúd.

Dr. *Pope.*[t9]

When présent, we lóve, and when ábsent agrée,[u]
I thínk not of I´ris, nor I´ris of mé.

Dryden.[v1]

These measures are varied by many combinations, and sometimes by double endings, either with or without rhyme, as in the heroick measure.

s. Dr. *Pope.* *73*] Dr. *Pope.* *absent 55a, 55b, 65*
t. Dr. *Pope.* *73*] Dr. *Pope.* *absent 55a, 55b, 65*
u. When . . . agrée, *73*] When . . . agrée, *absent 55a, 55b, 65*
v. *Dryden.* *73*] *Dryden.* *absent 55a, 55b, 65*

---

under *trump* (sense 1) in *Dictionary;* see *Poems on Several Occasions. By Samuel Wesley* (1736), p. 12.

8. Walter Pope, "Doctor Pope's Wish," ("correct and finished copy," 1693), sometimes entitled "The Old Man's Wish," the chorus, ll. 1–2 (mutatis). Bennet Langton reported to Boswell an undated incident in which SJ, "rebuking" a "clergyman's" deliberate failure to quote Pope's "song" accurately, recited the lines correctly, laying special stress on "May I govern my passions with absolute sway" (*Life,* IV.19).

9. "The Tipling Philosophers" (1710), actually by Edward Ward, l. 177.

1. "Mercury's Song to Phaedra," from *Amphitryon,* IV.i.490–91 (*Works of John Dryden,* California edition, XV [1976], 299).

'Tis the divinity that stirs *within us,*[w]
'Tis Heav'n[x] itself that points out an *hereafter,*[y]
And intimates eternity to man.

Addison.[z2]

So in that of eight syllables,

They neither added nor confounded,
They neither wanted nor abounded.

Prior.[a3]

In that of seven,

For resistance I could fear none,
But with twenty ships had done,
What thou, brave and happy Vernon,
Hast atchiev'd with six alone.

Glover.[b4]

In that of six,

'Twas when the seas were roaring,[c]
With hollow blasts of wind,
A damsel lay deploring,
All on a rock reclin'd.

Gay.[d5]

w. 'Tis . . . *us, 73*] 'Tis . . . *us, absent 55a, 55b, 65*
x. Heav'n *73*] heav'n *55a, 55b, 65*
y. *hereafter 73*] hereafter *55a, 55b, 65*
z. *Addison. 73*] *Addison. absent 55a, 55b, 65*
a. *Prior. 73*] *Prior. absent 55a, 55b, 65*
b. *Glover. 73*] *Glover. absent 55a, 55b, 65*
c. roaring, *55a, 55b, 73*] roaring *65*
d. *Gay. 73*] *Gay. absent 55a, 55b, 65*

---

2. Joseph Addison, *Cato,* V.i.7–9; cited under *divinity* and *hereafter* in *Dictionary.*

3. Matthew Prior, "An Epitaph," ll. 45–46.

4. Richard Glover, "Admiral Hosier's Ghost" (1740), ll. 49–52. This political ballad contrasts the sad fate of Admiral Francis Hosier and his men—who in 1726 were forbidden to attack the Spanish port of Portobello (in Panama) and succumbed en masse to disease and, in the case of the admiral, supposedly to "a broken heart"—with Admiral Edward Vernon's successful assault in 1739.

5. The first four lines of a traditional

In the anapestick,

> When terrible tempests assail[e] us,
> And mountainous billows affright,
> Nor power nor wealth can avail us,
> But skilful industry steers right.
>
> *Ballad.*[f6]

To these measures, and their laws, may be reduced every species of English verse.

Our versification admits of few licences, except a *synalœpha,* or elision of *e* in *the* before a vowel, as *th'eternal;* and more rarely of *o* in *to,* as *t'accept;* and a *synæresis,* by which two short vowels coalesce into one syllable, as *question, special;* or a word is contracted by the expulsion of a short vowel before a liquid, as *av'rice, temp'rance.*

Thus have I collected rules and examples, by which the English language may be learned, if the reader be already acquainted with grammatical terms, or taught by a master to those that are more ignorant. To have written a grammar for such as are not yet initiated in the schools, would have been tedious, and perhaps at last ineffectual.[g]

e. assail *55a, 55b, 73*] assails *65*
f. *Ballad. 73*] *Ballad. absent 55a, 55b, 65*
g. *No text after* ineffectual. *55a, 65, 73*] The END of the GRAMMAR. *on separate line below* ineffectual *55b*

song, reprinted, e.g., in *The Aviary: or, Magazine of British Meoldy* (1745?); pp. 535–36; cited as a melodic source by John Gay, *The Beggar's Opera,* II, scene 9, air 28.

6. Lewis Theobald, "The Sailor's Ballad," st. 2, ll. 5–8, in *Perseus and Andromeda* (1730); 5th ed. (1731), pp. 23–24; slight differences in the text suggest that Johnson may have recalled the lines from memory. Theobald's brief entertainment was performed, nearest SJ's composition of the Grammar, on 16–17 October 1752 at Covent Garden, as an afterpiece to *King Lear.*

A DICTIONARY OF THE ENGLISH LANGUAGE, FIRST ABRIDGED EDITION (1756)

THE PREFACE

EDITOR'S INTRODUCTION

Composition and Publication

No details are known concerning Johnson's composition of the short Preface to his two-volume octavo abridgment—"abstract or epitome," as he called it—of his massive, two-volume folio *Dictionary of the English Language.* Indeed, the primary sources of information about the entire enterprise apparently consist only of William Strahan's ledgers, which record the printing of the 5,000 copies in 1755; newspaper advertisements, which provide the cost, ten shillings—the price of the folio was four pounds, ten shillings—and date of publication, 5 January 1756;[1] and the edition itself, specifically, the title page ("Abstracted from the FOLIO EDITION, By the AUTHOR SAMUEL JOHNSON, A. M." and, below, the names of the bookseller proprietors of the folio); and Johnson's Preface.

Guided by these facts, several scholars have validly concluded, in the words of Allen Reddick, the latest and most circumstantial investigator: "With an expensive and potentially valuable property on their hands, the booksellers saw the opening in the market for an abridgement of their dictionary. They may have intended all along to publish an abridgement, delaying its publication in order not to discourage potential buyers from purchasing the two-volume folio edition. They also probably hoped to compete with" the Joseph Nicol Scott–Nathan Bailey *New Universal Etymological Dictionary.* Reddick goes on to emphasize that in his Preface Johnson, the obvious choice as abridger, makes a direct appeal to "the common reader," not those who "aspire to exactness of

1. For Strahan's printing of the 5,000 copies, and the advertisements of the price and date of publication, see Sledd-Kolb, pp. 114, 231 n. 38, 148, 238 n. 49; Reddick, pp. 86, 216 n. 103.

criticism or elegance of style" (p. 367 below).[2] Mindful of his habitual speed in writing, we add our guess that he composed the Preface in a single sitting, after the completion of the main task. It is uncertain whether he was paid for his work.

Johnson's intended readers of the Preface not only resemble those of his *Plan* (see pp. 29–30 above) more closely than those of his folio Preface, they also exhibit marked likenesses to the prospective users singled out in various earlier dictionaries. For example, Robert Cawdrey's *A Table Alphabeticall* (1604), accounted the first English lexicon, specifies on its title page "Ladies, Gentlewomen, or any other unskilfull persons" as the beneficiaries of its contents. Besides "Ladies and Gentlewomen," Henry Cockeram's *The English Dictionarie* (1623) names "young Schollers, Clarkes, Merchants, as also Strangers of any Nation," on its comparable list. *A New English Dictionary* (1702), by "J. K." (probably John Kersey), recognizes similar groups. So does Kersey's *Dictionarium Anglo-Britannicum* (1708), in a list largely echoing J. K.'s. Nathan Bailey's octavo *Universal Etymological English Dictionary* (1721)—the "most popular of all dictionaries antedating Johnson" and more catholic, more wittily discriminating, than its predecessors—is designed, we are told, "as well for the Entertainment of the Curious, as the Information of the Ignorant, and for the Benefit of young Students, Artificers, Tradesmen and Foreigners"—a designation virtually identical to that in Bailey's *Dictionarium Britannicum* (1730). Lastly, John Wesley's "address to the reader" in his *Complete English Dictionary* (1753) must have captivated its perusers by its extraordinary blend of frankness and disinterestedness. "As incredible as it may appear," he says, "I must avow, that this dictionary is not published to get money, but to assist persons of common sense and no learning, to understand the best *English* authors: and that, with as little expense of either time or money, as the nature of the thing would allow."[3]

While stressing in the Preface the superior features of his

2. Reddick, p. 86.

3. For this information about the dictionaries from Cawdrey to Wesley, see Starnes-Noyes, pp. 13, 26, 70, 95, 98–99, 118, 172–73.

"abstract," Johnson displays a predictable familiarity with previous dictionaries (including at least some of those mentioned above) that were directed at much the same audience as his. Before his death in 1784, he was surely aware, too, of the abridgment's much greater popularity than that of the original work; it "appeared, from 1756 to 1786, in eight [proprietorial] editions [alone] of 5,000 copies each."[4] This disparity, it should be noted, continued after his death and far into the nineteenth century.[5]

Text

Seven proprietors' editions of Johnson's abridged (octavo) *Dictionary* were published in his lifetime (1756, 1760, 1766,[6] 1770, 1773, 1778, and 1783). Our collation of the "Preface" in all of them disclosed only one small substantive variant and six equally small accidental differences: nothing to suggest any kind of authorial revision or the need for any emendation. Therefore, we have retained first-edition readings throughout the text.[7]

4. Sledd-Kolb, p. 114.

5. For a detailed description of all the abridgments, see *Bibliography,* pp. 486–556.

6. According to Fleeman, "Of the 70 sheets in this edition, William Strahan printed 45 in 5,000 copies for Andrew Millar in Aug. 1765" (*Bibliography,* p. 492).

7. This paragraph is drawn, with minor changes, from our article "Preliminaries." The list of octavo editions appears on pp. xlvii–xlviii above. We collated Gwin Kolb's copies of all the editions.

THE PREFACE

Having been long employed in the study and cultivation of the English language, I lately published a dictionary like those compiled by the academies of Italy and France, for the use of such as aspire to exactness of criticism[a] or elegance of style.[1]

But it has been since considered that works of that kind are by no means necessary to the greater number of readers, who, seldom intending to write or presuming to judge, turn over books only to amuse their leisure, and to gain degrees of knowledge suitable to lower characters, or necessary to the common business of life: these know not any other use of a dictionary[b] than that of adjusting orthography, or[c] explaining terms of science[2] or words of infrequent occurrence, or remote derivation.

For these purposes many dictionaries have been written by different[d] authors, and with different degrees of skill; but none of them have yet fallen into my hands by which even the lowest expectations could be satisfied. Some of their authors wanted industry, and others literature:[3] some knew not their own defects, and others were too idle to supply them.

For this reason a small dictionary appeared yet to be wanting to common readers:[e4] and, as I may without arrogance

a. criticism *56, 60, 66*] criticism, *70, 73 abr., 78, 83*
b. a dictionary *56, 60, 66, 73 abr., 78, 83*] adictionary *70*
c. or *56, 60*] and *66, 70, 73 abr., 78, 83*
d. different *56, 60, 66, 70, 78, 83*] different, *73 abr.*
e. readers: *56*] readers; *60, 66, 70, 73 abr., 78, 83*

---

1. SJ often compared his work to that of the Continental academies; see e.g., Preface, p. 112 above.

2. *Science:* "Any art or species of knowledge" (*Dictionary*, sense 4).

3. *Literature:* "Learning; skill in letters" (*Dictionary*).

4. Several editions of Bailey's *An Universal Etymological Dictionary* (1st ed., 1721) were small, as were Dyche and

claim to myself a longer acquaintance with the lexicography of our language than any other writer has had,[5] I shall hope to be considered as having more experience at least than most of my predecessors, and as more likely to accommodate the nation with a vocabulary of daily use. I therefore offer to the publick[f] an abstract or epitome of my former work.

In comparing this with other dictionaries of the same kind[g] it will be found to have several advantages.

I. It contains many words not to be found in any other.[6]

II. Many barbarous terms and phrases by which other dictionaries may vitiate the style are rejected from this.

III. The words are more correctly spelled, partly by attention to their etymology, and partly by observation of the practice of the best authors.

IV. The etymologies and derivations, whether from foreign languages or from native roots, are more diligently traced, and more distinctly noted.

V. The senses of each word are more copiously ennumerated, and more clearly explained.

VI. Many words occurring in the elder authors, such as Spenser, Shakespeare, and Milton, which had been hitherto omitted, are here carefully inserted; so that this book may serve as a glossary or expository index to the poetical writers.[7]

VII. To the words, and to the different senses of each word,

f. publick *56, 60, 66*] public *70, 73 abr., 78, 83*
g. kind *56, 60, 66, 70*] kind, *73 abr., 78, 83*

Pardon's *A New General English Dictionary* (1735) and the anonymous *A Pocket Dictionary* (1753); see Starnes and Noyes.

5. SJ glances at Joseph Nicol Scott, who, without any previous lexicographical experience, lightly revised Bailey to produce a direct competitor to *Dictionary, A New Universal Etymological Dictionary* (1755).

6. This may be true but Bailey-Scott (1755) had over half again as many words as *Dictionary* (Starnes and Noyes, p. 185).

7. Cf. SJ's letter to Thomas Warton, 16 July 1754: "The Reason why the authours which are yet read of the sixteenth Century are so little understood is that they are read alone, and no help is borrowed from those who lived with them or before them. Some part of this ignorance I hope to remove by my book [*Dictionary*] which now draws towards its end" (*Letters,* I. 81).

are subjoined from the large dictionary the names of those writers by whom they have been used; so that the reader who knows the different periods of the language, and the time of its authors, may judge of the elegance or prevalence of any word, or meaning of a word; and without recurring to other books, may know what are antiquated, what are unusual, and what are recommended by the best authority.

The words of this dictionary, as opposed to others, are more diligently collected, more accurately spelled, more faithfully explained, and more authentically ascertained. Of an abstract it is not necessary to say more; and I hope, it will not be found that truth requires me to say less.

A DICTIONARY OF THE ENGLISH LANGUAGE, FOURTH FOLIO EDITION (1773)

ADVERTISEMENT TO THIS EDITION

EDITOR'S INTRODUCTION

Composition and Publication

Nothing is known about Johnson's composition of the short "Advertisement" to the fourth, extensively revised, folio edition of his *Dictionary*. The proprietors, who had published the third folio edition in 1765, proposed[1] the revised fourth to Johnson well before 29 August 1771, when he wrote Bennet Langton, "I am engaging in a very great work the revision of my Dictionary. . . ." His chief task, the creation of printer's copy, apparently ended on 8 October 1772, when he wrote William Strahan, "I am now within about two hours or less of the end of my work."[2]

The composition of the "Advertisement" occurred, we guess, markedly later[3]—and in a single sitting. The edition appeared on 25 January 1773, as David Fleeman has shown,[4] not in March, as is commonly supposed. Johnson received £300 for his labor,[5] including, presumably, the writing of the "Advertisement," whose title, we speculate, resulted from the inclusion of Johnson's first-edition Preface in the fourth folio[6]–and seemingly in every other unabridged edition.

1. See Reddick, pp. 89–90.

2. See *Letters* I, 381–82, 397.

3. Fleeman remarks that "probably the last six sheets [of the fourth folio] to be worked off" included the "Advertisement" (*Bibliography,* p. 429).

4. Fleeman cites an advertisement in the *Public Advertiser* and notes that "advts. recur over the following three months" (*Bibliography,* p. 429).

5. *Life,* II.498; *Bibliography,* p. 429.

6. The Preface is followed immediately by the "Advertisement." Confusion about the use of the word "Preface" produced at least one amusing incident in the history of SJ's *Dictionary:* reviewing the first volume (1866) of R. G. Latham's edition, F. J. Furnivall "mistook the Preface of Johnson for one by Latham" (W. P. Courtney and D. Nichol Smith, *A Bibliography of Samuel Johnson* [1915; reissued, together with R. W. Chapman and Allen T. Hazen, *Johnsonian Bibliography: A Supplement to Courtney,* 1984], p. 61).

Text

The fifth (1784),[7] sixth (1785), and seventh (1785)[8] editions of the proprietors' unabridged *Dictionary* all reprint Johnson's "Advertisement" to the fourth edition (1773). Our collation of the three versions turned up no substantive, and only five accidental, variants and no evidence of textual corruption. Consequently, we have retained everywhere the original readings in the fourth edition.[9]

7. The date of "1784" appears on the title pages of the two volumes, but "William Strahan printed 1,000 copies of this edn. in Oct. 1783" (*Bibliography,* 435).

8. This edition contains the same setting of type as the sixth; see p. 71, n. 5, above.

9. This paragraph is drawn, with the change of "six" to "five," from "Preliminaries," p. 132. We collated Gwin Kolb's copies of the fourth, fifth, sixth, and seventh editions.

ADVERTISEMENT to this EDITION

MANY are the works of human industry, which to begin and finish are hardly granted to the same man. He that undertakes to compile a Dictionary, undertakes that, which, if it comprehends the full extent of his design, he knows himself unable to perform. Yet his labours, though deficient, may be useful, and with the hope of this inferior praise, he must incite his activity, and solace his weariness.

Perfection is unattainable, but nearer and nearer approaches may be made;[1] and finding my Dictionary about to be reprinted, I have endeavoured, by a revisal, to make it less reprehensible. I will not deny that I found many parts requiring emendation, and more capable of improvement. Many faults I have corrected, some superfluities I have taken away, and some deficiencies I have supplied. I have methodised some parts that were disordered, and illuminated some that were obscure. Yet the changes or additions bear a very small proportion to the whole.[2] The critic[a] will now have less to object, but the student who has bought any of the former copies,[b] needs not repent; he will not, without nice collation, perceive how they differ,[c] and usefulness seldom depends upon little things.

For negligence or deficience, I have perhaps not need of more apology than the nature of the work will furnish;[d] I have left that inaccurate which never was[e] made exact, and that imperfect which never was completed.

a. critic *73*] critick *85a, 85b*
b. copies, *73*] copies *85a, 85b*
c. differ, *73*] differ; *85a, 85b*
d. furnish; *73*] furnish: *85a, 85b*
e. never was *73*] was never *85a, 85b*

---

1. On perfection, see *Plan,* p. 49, and Preface, p. 101 above.

2. SJ abridged many long citations from technical dictionaries and encyclopedias; added 2,500–3,000 new quotations; changed definitions and etymologies; and extensively reordered the senses of words. Arthur Sherbo counted more than 700 changes in the letter *M* alone, an average of 7 per page ("1773: The Year of Revision," *Eighteenth-Century Studies,* VII [1973–74], 18–39). For an extensive discussion of SJ's revision, see Reddick.

APPENDICES

The holograph manuscript of "A Short Scheme for compiling a new Dictionary of the English Language" and the fair copy of *The Plan of a Dictionary of the English Language* in the hand of a professional amanuensis are reproduced with the kind permission of the late Mary Hyde Eccles and the Houghton Library at Harvard University. The transcription of the "Scheme" is our work, but we benefited from an earlier transcription published in *The R. B. Adam Library Relating to Dr. Samuel Johnson and His Era* (4 vols., 1929–30), II.1–19. We received advice on our transcription from Bruce Redford, but we are solely responsible for any errors that may be found. Johnson's handwriting is difficult, and cross-outs and other marks make this manuscript unusually hard to decipher. One letter in particular gave us trouble: we often had to guess whether Johnson wrote a capital or a lower case *S*. The plates are printed from new photographs, made with the assistance of the Department of Rare Books and Special Collections at Princeton University. For a discussion of the importance of these manuscripts in the composition of the *Plan*, see our introduction to the *Plan* (pp. 3–16 above).

We have used the standard font of this edition (Baskerville) to represent Johnson's writing in the manuscript. Italics represent our editorial comments, as do any marks enclosed in square brackets. The *ITC Officina Serif* font is used to signal the additions of the first and most voluble reader of the manuscript. The infrequent comments of the second reader are represented in bold letters in the standard font (see fol. 10 verso, e.g.). Underlines and cross-through lines represent the handwritten versions of the same. No transcription of the fair copy is provided because, unlike the "Short Scheme," it is quite legible.

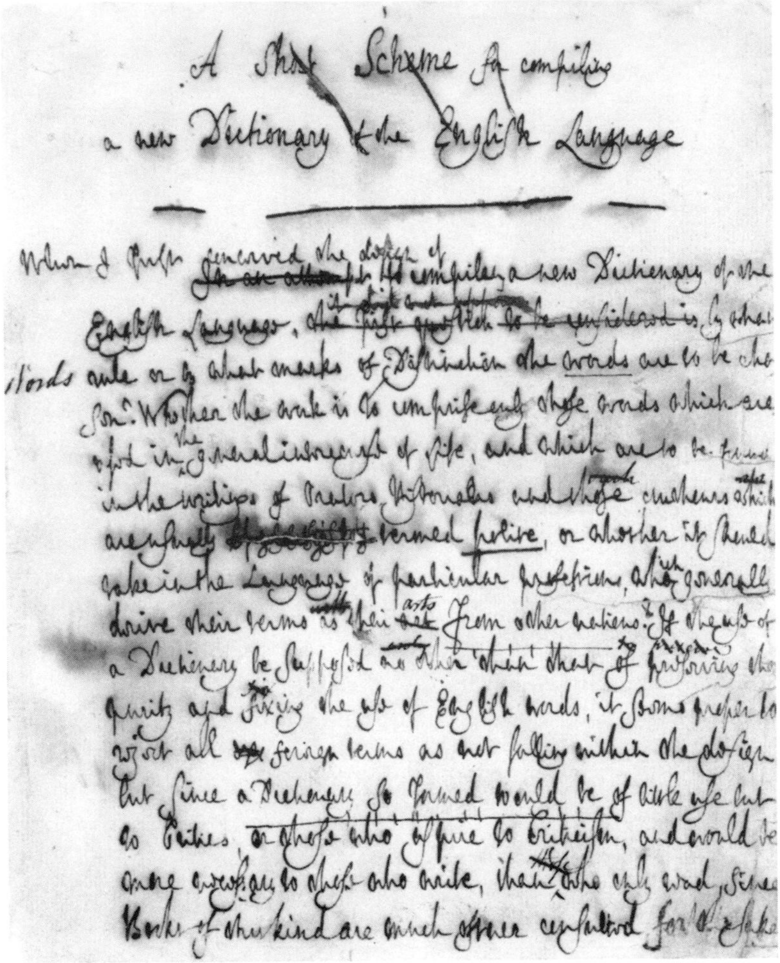

A Short Scheme for compiling
a new Dictionary of the English Language

When I first conceived the design of compiling a new Dictionary of the English Language, the first question to be considered is, by what rule or by what marks of distinction the words are to be chosen. Whether the work is to comprise only those words which are used in the general intercourse of life, and which are to be found in the writings of orators, historians and those authors which are usually termed polite, or whether it should take in the language of particular professions, which generally derive their terms with their arts from other nations. If the use of a Dictionary be supposed any other than that of preserving the purity and fixing the use of English words, it seems proper to reject all foreign terms as not falling within the design, but since a Dictionary so formed would be of little use but to critics, or those who aspire to criticism, and would be more necessary to those who write, than those who only read, since Books of this kind are much oftener consulted for the sake

~~A Short Scheme for compiling a new Dictionary of the English Language~~

~~In an attempt to~~ When I first conceived the design of compiling a new Dictionary of the English Language, ~~the first question~~ Words ~~to be considered is~~ it did not appear by what rule or by what marks of Distinction the words are to be chosen? Whether the work is to comprise only those words which are used in the general intercourse of Life, and which are to be found in the writings of Orators, Historians and those ~~such~~ authours which ~~as~~ are usually ~~*illegible word*~~ termed polite, or whether it should take in the Language of particular professions, wh~~o~~ ich generally derive their terms as ~~with~~ their ~~art~~ arts from other nations? If the use of a Dictionary be supposed no other than that of preserving ~~only to preserve~~ the purity and fixing ~~fix~~ the use of English words, it seems proper to reject all ~~*illegible word*~~ foreign terms as not falling within the design but since a Dictionary so formed would be of little use but to Critics, ~~or those who aspire to Criticism~~, and would be more necessary to those who write, than ~~those~~ who only read, since Books of this kind are much oftner consulted for the sake

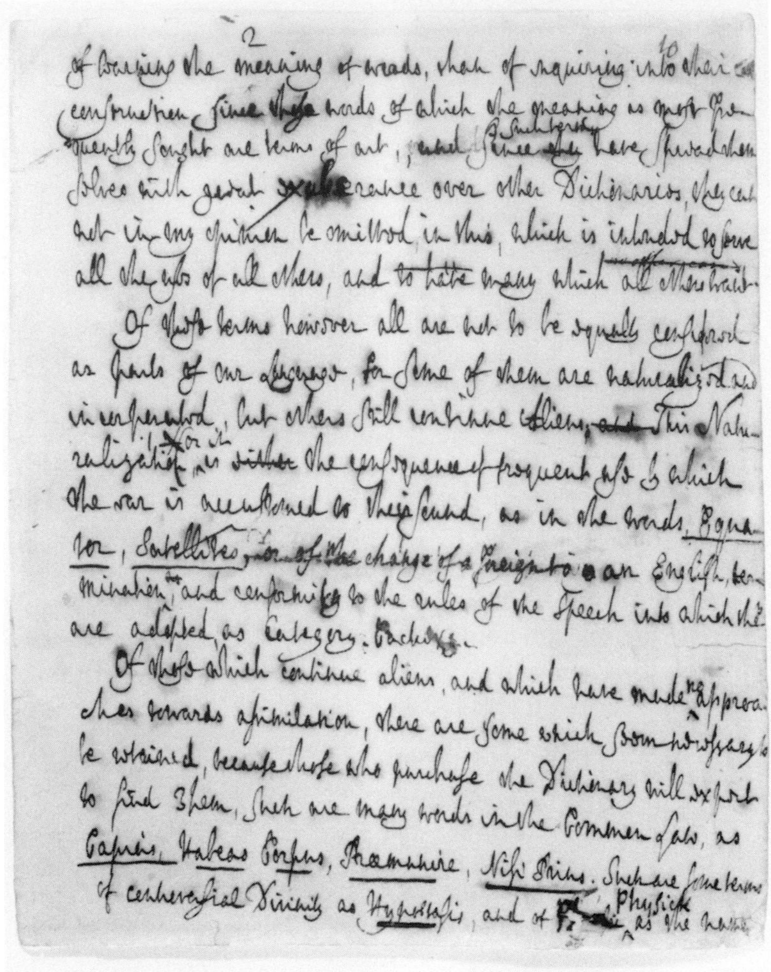

2 10

of knowing the meaning of words, than of enquiring into their construction. Since those words of which the meaning is most frequently sought are terms of art, and since they have spread themselves with great exuberance over other Dictionaries, they cannot in my opinion be omitted in this, which is intended to serve all the uses of all others, and many which all others have wanted.

Of these terms however all are not to be equally considered as parts of our Language, for some of them are naturalized and incorporated, but others still continue Aliens. This Naturalization is either the consequence of frequent use by which the ear is accustomed to their sound, as in the words Equator, Satellites, or of the change of a foreign to an English termination, and conformity to the rules of the Speech into which they are adopted, as Category, Cachexy.

Of those which continue aliens, and which have made no approaches towards assimilation, there are some which seem necessary to be retained, because those who purchase the Dictionary will expect to find them. Such are many words in the Common Law, as Capias, Habeas Corpus, Præmunire, Nisi Prius. Such are some terms of controversial Divinity as Hypostasis, and of Physick as the names

2

of learning the meaning of words, than of enquiring into their construction since those words of which the meaning is most frequently sought are terms of art, and since ~~they~~ such terms have spread themselves with great exuberance over other Dictionaries, they cannot in my opinion be omitted in this, which is intended to serve all the uses of all other, and ~~to have~~ many which ~~no others can~~ all others want

Of these terms however all are not to be equally considered as parts of our Language, for some of them are naturalized and incorporated, but others still continue Aliens. ~~and~~ This Naturalization ~~*illegible characters*~~ or it is [sic] ~~either~~ the consequence of frequent use by which the ear is accustomed to their sound, as in the words, Equator, Satellites, or of the change of a foreign to ~~*illegible character*~~ an English, termination, ~~as~~ and conformity to the rules of the speech into which they are adopted, as Category, Cachexy.[?]

Of those which continue aliens, and which have made no approaches towards assimilation, there are some which seem necessary to be retained, because those who purchase the Dictionary will expect to find Them, such are many words in the Common Law, as Capias, Habeas Corpus, Praemunire, Nisi Prius. Such are some terms of controversial Divinity as Hypostasis, and of ~~Physic~~ [*tear in leaf*] Physick as the names

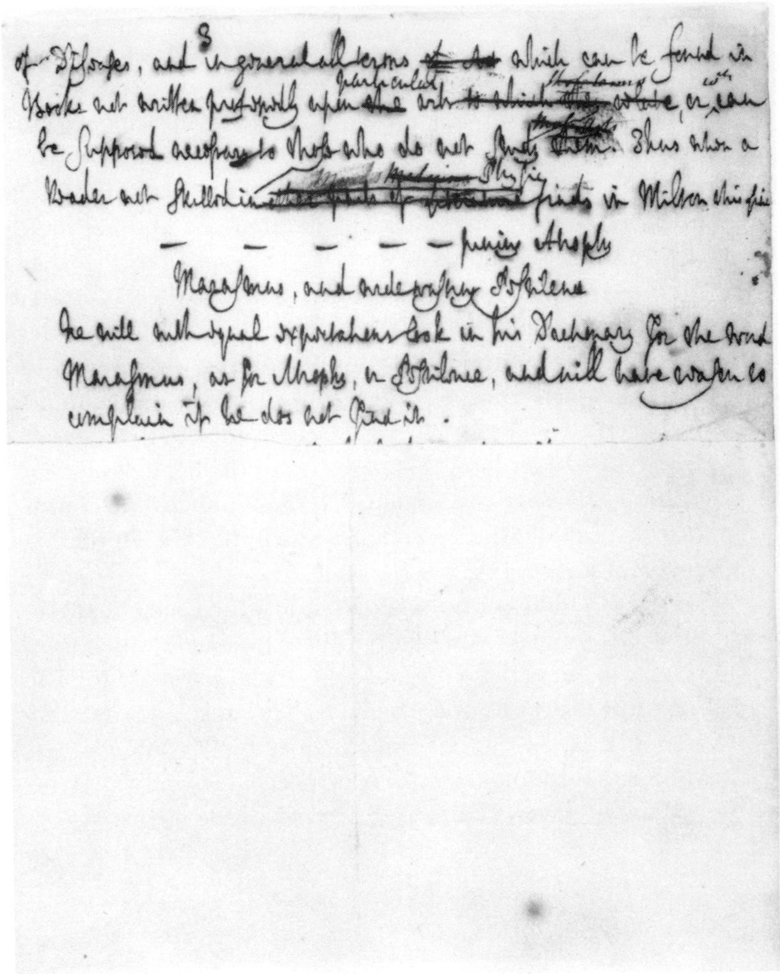
of Diseases, and in general all terms which can be found in
Books not written professedly upon particular arts, or can
be supposed necessary to those who do not study them. Thus when a
Reader not skilled in Physic finds in Milton this line
— — — — — pining Atrophy
Marasmus, and wide-wasting Pestilence
he will with equal expectation look in his Dictionary for the word
Marasmus, as for Atrophy, or Pestilence, and will have reason to
complain if he does not find it.

3

of Diseases, and in general all terms ~~of Art~~ which can be found in Books not written professedly upon ~~the~~ particular arts ~~to which they relate~~, ~~those terms~~ or wch can be supposed necessary to those who do not study ~~those Arts~~ them. Thus when a Reader not skilled in ~~other parts of Literature~~ ~~*illegible word*~~ ~~Medicine~~ Physic finds in Milton this Line

——— pining Atrophy
Marasmus, and widewasting Pestilence

he will with equal expectations look in his Dictionary for the word Marasmus, as for Atrophy, or Pestilence, and will have reason to complain if he dos [sic] not find it.

[*The remainder of leaf 3 is missing*]

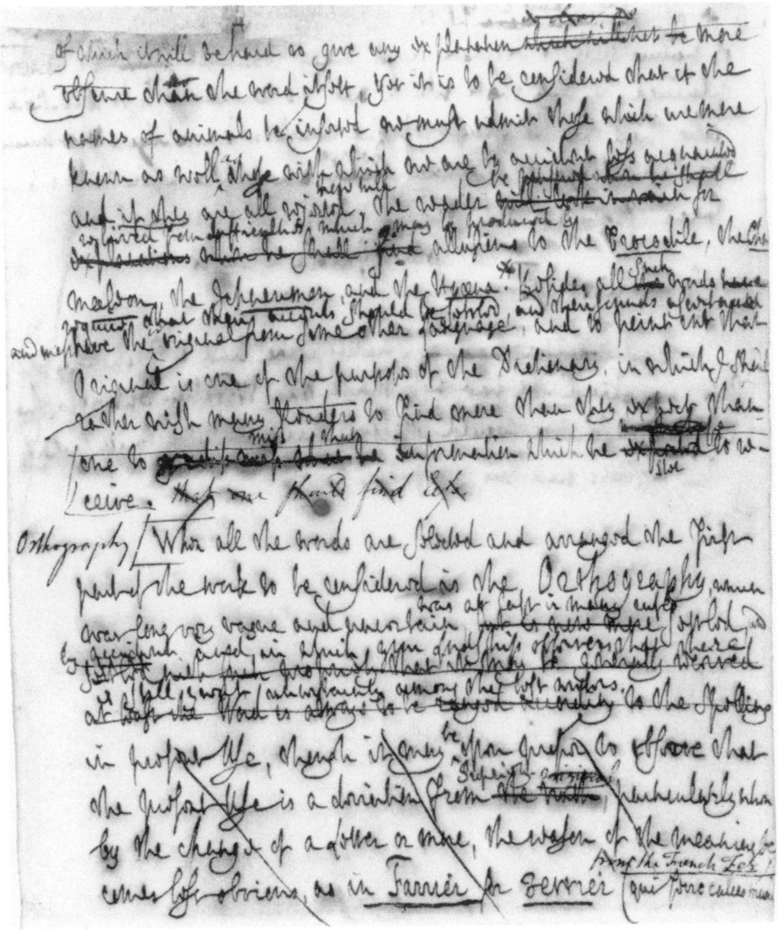

[4]

of which it will be hard to give any explanation ~~which will~~ not ~~be so clear as~~ more obscure than ~~as~~ the word itself, Yet it is to be considered that if the names of animals be inserted we must admit those which are more known as well as those with which we are by accident less acquainted and if they are all rejected, how will the reader ~~will look in vain~~ for ~~explanations which he shall find~~ be ~~satisfied when he shall~~ relieved from difficulties which may be produced by allusions to the Crocodile, the Chamaeleon, the Ichneumon, and the Hyaena.#[1] Besides all ~~the~~ such words ~~have~~ require that their accents should be settled, and their sounds ascertained and must have their original from some other Language, and to point out that Original is one of the purposes of the Dictionary, in which I shoul[d] rather wish many Readers to find more than they expect than one to ~~*illegible words*~~ miss that information which he ~~expected~~ stet ~~*illegible word*~~ to receive. ~~that one should find less.~~

Orthography When all the words are selected and arranged the first part of the work to be considered is the Orthography, which was long very vague and uncertain, ~~but is now more~~ was at last in many cases settled, and settled ~~with such propriety that it may be generally received at least the Word is always to be ranged according to the Spelling in present Use, though it may be often proper to observe that the present Use is a deviation from the truth, Propriety~~ [?] ~~original particularly when by the change of a Letter or more, the reason of the meaning becomes less obvious, as in Farrier for Ferrier from the French Fer (qui ferro calces mun)~~[2] by accident and in which your Lordship observes that there is still great uncertainty among the best writers.

1. See fol. 4, verso, for insertion here.
2. "one who makes shoes from iron."

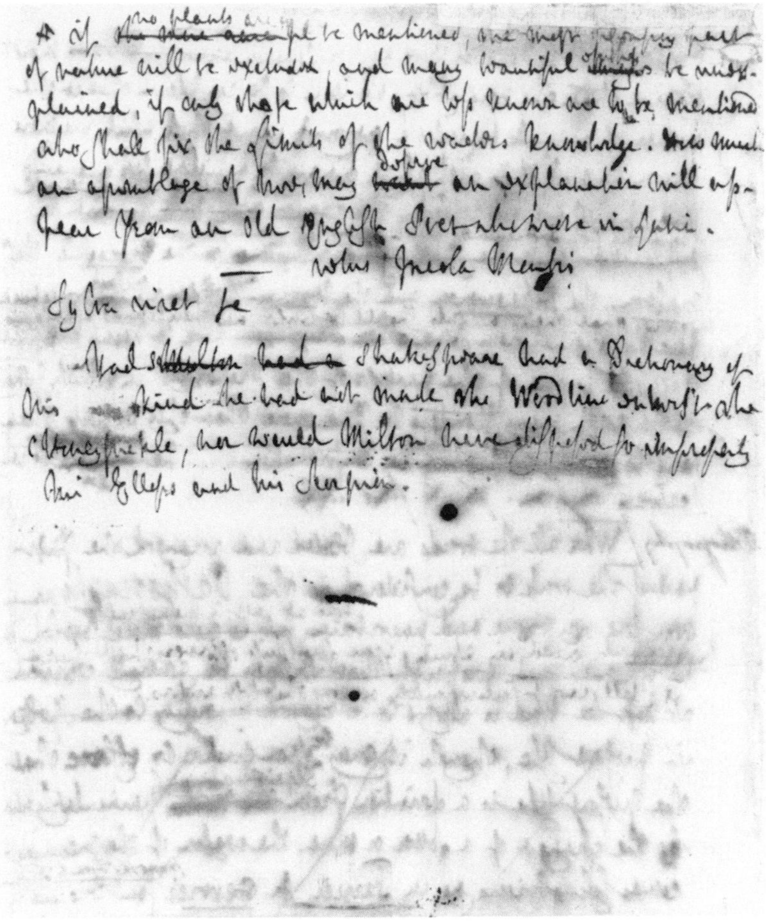
if ~~the same acc~~ no plants are to be mentioned, the most pleasing part
of nature will be excluded, and many beautiful objects be unexplained, if only those which are less known are to be mentioned
who shall fix the limits of the readers knowledge. Thus amidst
an assemblage of trees may ~~want~~ do you an explanation will appear from an Old English Poet who wrote in Latin.
[illegible]
Sylva virent [illegible]
~~Had Milton had a~~ Shakespeare had a Dictionary of
this kind he had not made the Woodbine entwist the
Honeysuckle, nor would Milton have disposed so improperly
his Ellops and his Scorpion.

[4 verso]

#[3] if ~~the more rare~~ pl no plants are to be mentioned, the most pleasing part of nature will be excluded, and many beautiful ~~images~~ epithets be unexplained, if only those which are less known are to be mentioned who shall fix the Limits of the readers knowledge. How much an assemblage of trees may ~~want~~ deserve an explanation will appear from an Old English Poet who wrote in Latin.

———vetus Incola Montis
Sylva viret &c

Had s[?] ~~Milton had a~~ Shakespeare had a Dictionary of this ~~*illegible characters*~~ kind he had not made the Woodbine entwist the Honeysuckle, nor would Milton have disposed so improperly his Ellops and his Scorpion.

3. This is the addition referred to on fol. 4, recto.

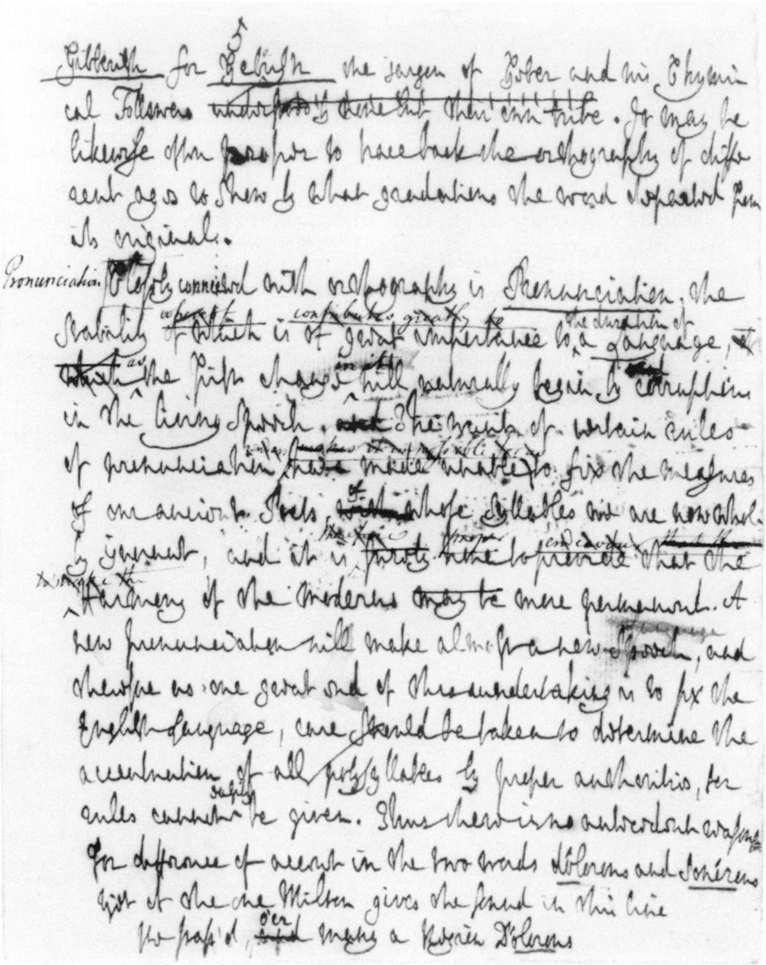

Gibberish for Geberish the jargon of Geber and his Chymical Followers understood by none but their own tribe. It may be likewise often proper to trace back the orthography of different ages to shew by what gradations the word departed from its original.

Pronunciation. Closely connected with orthography is Pronunciation, the Stability of which is of great importance to the duration of a Language, as the first change will naturally begin by corruption in the Living Speech. The want of certain rules of pronunciation has made it impossible to fix the measures of our ancient Poets, of whose Syllables we are now wholly ignorant, and it is therefore time to provide that the harmony of the moderns may be more permanent. A new pronunciation will make almost a new Speech, and therefore as one great end of this undertaking is to fix the English Language, care should be taken to determine the accentuation of all polysyllables by proper authorities, for rules cannot safely be given. Thus there is no antecedent reason for difference of accent in the two words dolorous and sonorous yet of the one Milton gives the sound in this line

He pass'd o'er many a region dolorous

5

Gibberish for Geberish the jargon of Geber and his Chymical Followers ~~understood by none but their own tribe.~~ It may be likewise often proper to trace back the orthography of different ages to shew by what gradations the word departed from its original.

Pronunciation Closely connected with orthography is Pronunciation, the stability of which ~~whereof~~ is of great importance ~~contributes greatly to~~ to the duration of a Language, ~~of which~~ as the first change ~~*illegible word*~~ will naturally begin by corruptions ~~*illegible word*~~ in the living Speech. ~~and~~ The want of certain rules of pronunciation ha~~ve~~ made unable [*sic*] ~~*illegible word*~~ ~~makes it impossible for us~~ to fix the measures of our ancient Poets, ~~with~~ of whose Syllables we are now wholly ignorant, and it is surely time ~~therefore proper~~ to provide that the ~~endeavour~~ ~~that the~~ ~~to make the~~ Harmony of the Moderns may be more permanent. A new pronunciation will make almost a new ~~Speech~~ Language, and therefore as one great end of this undertaking is to fix the English Language, care should be taken to determine the accentuation of all polysyllables by proper authorities, for rules cannot easily be given. Thus there is no antecedent reason for difference of accent in the two words dólorous and sonórous yet of the one Milton gives the sound in this line

He pass'd, ~~*illegible word*~~ o'er many a Region Dólorous

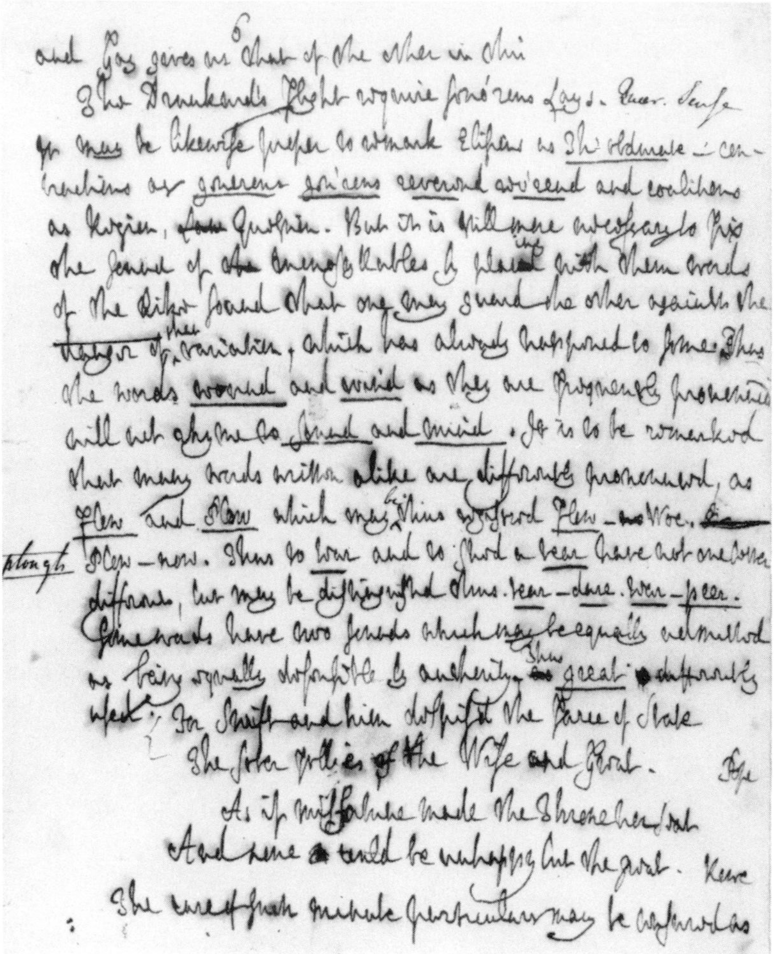
and Gay gives us that of the other in this
Thou Drunkards flight require sonorous Lays. — Gay. Sense
It may be likewise proper to remark Elisions as Th' oldness — contractions as generous gen'rous reverend rev'rend and coalitions as region, question. But it is still more necessary to fix the sound of the monosyllables by placing with them words of the like sound that one may guard the other against the danger of that variation, which has already happened to some. Thus the words wound and wind as they are frequently pronounced will not rhyme to sound and mind. It is to be remarked that many words written alike are differently pronounced, as Flow and Plow which may be thus registered Flow — woe.
plough. Plow — now. Thus to tear and to shed a tear have not one common difference, but may be distinguished thus. tear — dare. tear — peer.
Some words have two sounds which may be equally admitted as being equally defensible by authority. Thus great is differently used.
For Swift and him despis'd the Farce of State
The sober follies of the Wise and Great. Pope
As if misfortune made the Throne her seat
And none could be unhappy but the great. Rowe
The care of such minute particulars may be censured as

6

and Gay gives us that of the other in this

The Drunkard's flight require sonórous Lays. Quær. Sense

It may be likewise proper to remark Elisions as Th' obdurate—contractions as generous gen'rous reverend rev'rend and coalitions as Region, ~~*illegible word*~~ Question. But it is still more necessary to fix the sound of ~~the~~ monosyllables by plac ~~ed~~ ing with them words of the like sound that one may guard the other against the danger of that variation, which has already happened to some. Thus the words wound and wind as they are frequently pronounced will not rhyme to sound and mind. It is to be remarked that many words written alike are differently pronounced, as Flow and Plow which may be thus registered Flow–~~wo~~ Woc. ~~*illegible word*~~ plough Plow–now. Thus to tear and to shed a tear have not one letter different, but may be distinguished thus. tear-dare. tear-peer. Some words have two sounds which may be equally admitted as being equally defensible by authority. ~~as~~ Thus great is differently used.

For Swift and him despis'd the farce of State
The sober follies of the Wise and Great. Pope

As if misfortune made the Throne her seat
And none ~~*illegible character*~~ could be unhappy but the great.
Rowe

The care of such minute particulars may be censured as

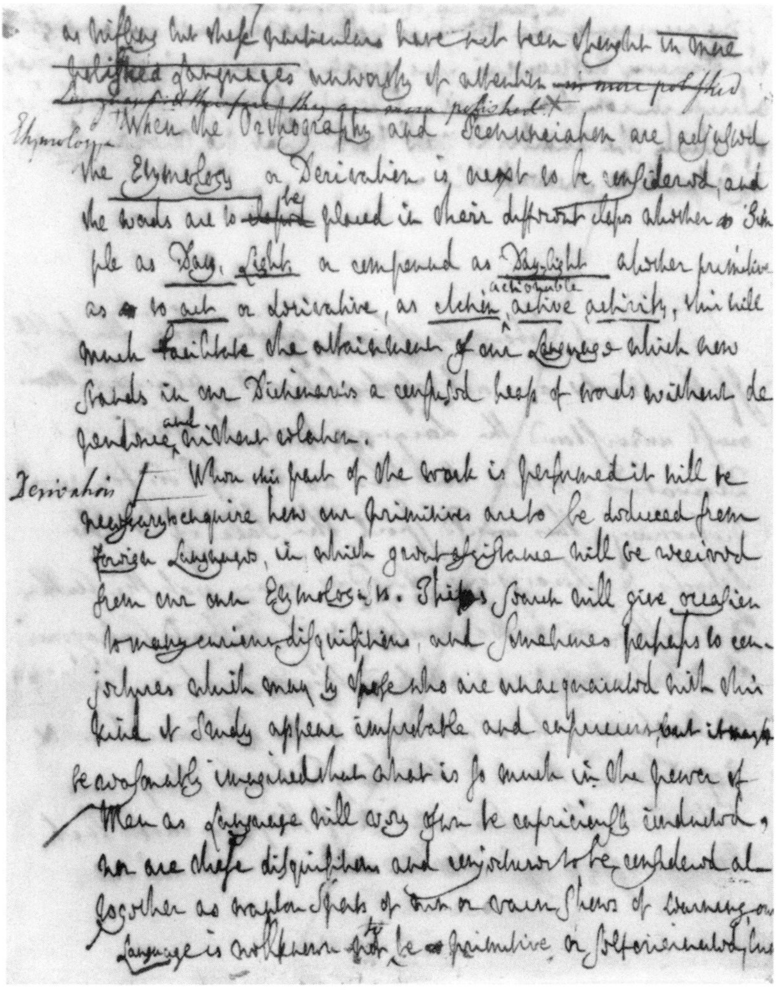

as trifling but these particulars have not been thought in more polished Languages unworthy of attention ~~in more polished~~ ~~Languages~~

Etymology When the Orthography and Pronunciation are adjusted the Etymology or Derivation is next to be considered, and the words are to be placed in their different classes whether simple as Day, Light or compound as Daylight whether primitive as to act or derivative, as Action, actionable, active, activity, this will much facilitate the attainment of our Language which now stands in our Dictionaries a confused heap of words without dependence and without relation.

Derivation When this part of the work is performed it will be necessary to enquire how our primitives are to be deduced from foreign Languages, in which great assistance will be received from our own Etymologists. This search will give occasion to many curious disquisitions, and sometimes perhaps to conjectures which may to those who are unacquainted with this kind of study appear improbable and capricious, but it may be reasonably imagined that what is so much in the power of Men as Language will very often be capriciously conducted, nor are these disquisitions and conjectures to be considered altogether as wanton sports of wit or vain shews of Learning, our Language is well known not to be primitive or selforiginated, but

7

as [sic] trifling but these particulars have not been thought in more polished Languages unworthy of attention in ~~more polished Languages & therefore they are more polished.~~*4

Etymology†5 When the Orthography and Pronunciation are adjusted the Etymology or Derivation is next to be considered, and the words are to ~~classed~~ be placed in their different classes whether ~~*illegible mark*~~ Simple as Day, Light, or compound as Day-light whether primitive as ~~*illegible word*~~ to act or derivative, as Action, actionable active, activity, this will much facilitate the attainment of our Language which now stands in our Dictionaries a confused heap of words without dependence and without relation.

Derivation When this part of the work is performed it will be necessary to enquire how our primitives are to be deduced from Foreign Languages, in which great assistance will be received from our own Etymologists. This search will give occasion to many curious disquisitions, and sometimes perhaps to conjectures which may by those who are unacquainted with this kind of Study appear improbable and capricious, but it may *illegible character* be reasonably imagined that what is so much in the power of Men as Language will very often be capriciously conducted, nor are these disquisitions and conjectures to be considered altogether as wanton Sports of wit or vain shews of Learning, our Language is well known not to be ~~*illegible mark*~~ primitive or self orie [sic] inated, but

4. See fol. 7, verso, for the corresponding addition.
5. See fol. 7, verso, for the corresponding addition.

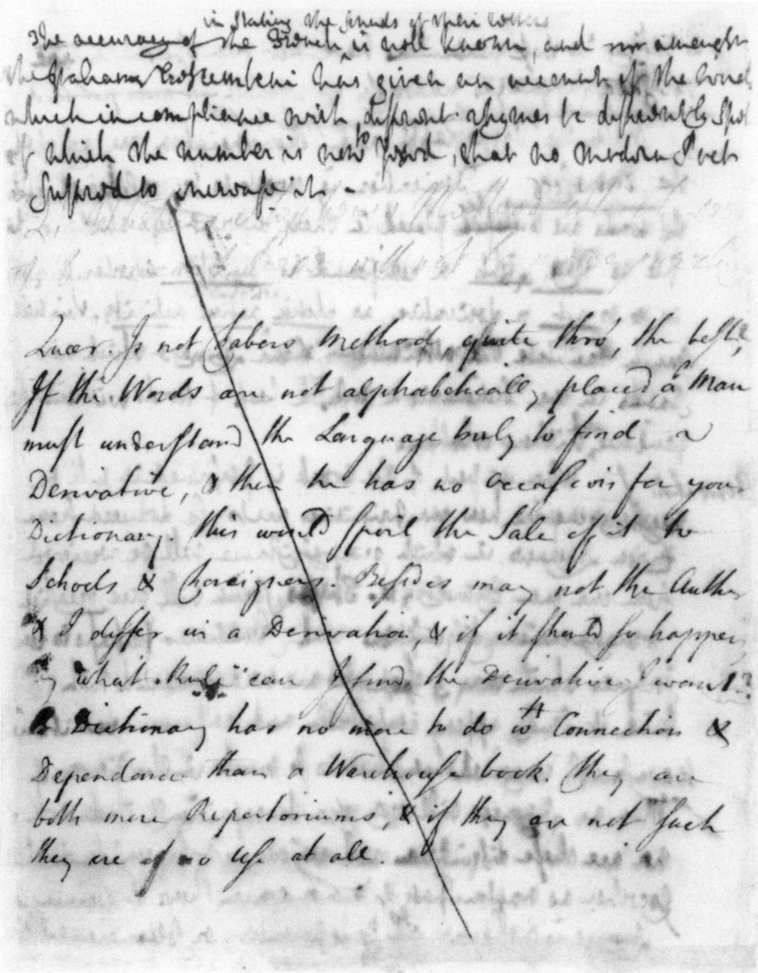

The accuracy of the French in stating the sounds of their letters is well known, and amongst the Italians Buommattei has given an account of the vowel which in compliance with different organs be differently spoken of which the number is now fixed, that no modern Poet is suffered to increase it. –

Quer. Is not Labbes Method quite thro' the best. If the Words are not alphabetically placed a Man must understand the Language truly to find a Derivative, & then he has no Occasion for your Dictionary. This would spoil the Sale of it to Schools & Foreigners. Besides may not the Author & I differ in a Derivation, & if it should so happen by what Rule can I find the Derivative I want? A Dictionary has no more to do wth Connection & Dependance than a Warehouse book. They are both mere Repertoriums, & if they are not such they are of no Use at all.

[7 verso]

The accuracy of the French in stating the sounds of their letters is well known, and now amongst the Italians Crescembeni has given an account of the word[s] which in compliance with different rhymes be differently spel[t] of which the number is now so fixed, that no Modern Poet suffered [sic] to encrease it.

Q^r Whether Stephen's Method which seems to be meant here will not be more puzzling? [*This sentence is too light to be visible in the plate*]

Quær. Is not Fabers method, quite thro', the best? If the Words are not alphabetically placed, a Man must understand the Language only to find a Derivative, & then he has no occasion for your Dictionary. This would spoil the Sale of it to Schools & Foreigners. Besides may not the Author & I differ in a Derivation, & if it should so happen, by what Rule can I find the Derivative I want? A Dictionary has no more to do wth Connections & Dependance than a Warehouse book. They are both mere Repertoriums, & if they are not such they are of no use at all.

[*leaf 8 is missing*]

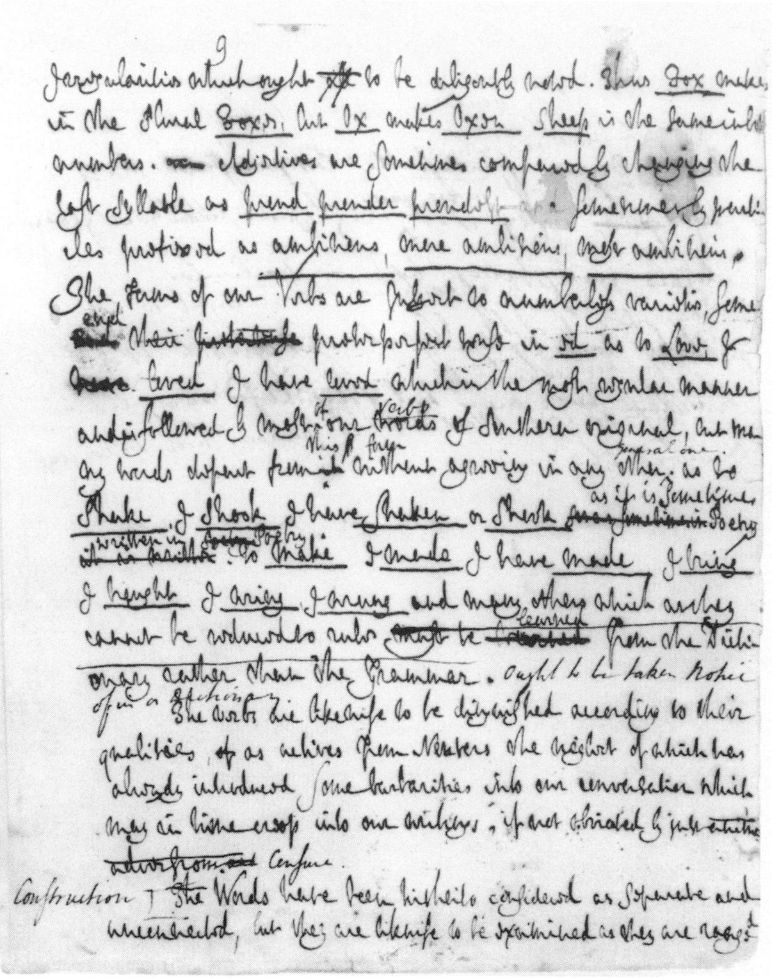

Irregularities which ought to be diligently noted. Thus Box makes in the Plural Boxes, but Ox makes Oxen. Sheep is the same in both numbers. Adjectives are sometimes compared by changing the last Syllable as proud, prouder, proudest, and sometimes by particles prefixed as ambitious, more ambitious, most ambitious. The forms of our Verbs are subject to innumerable varieties, some end their preterperfect tense in ed as to Love, I loved, I have loved which is the most regular manner and is followed by most of our verbs of Southern original, but many words depart from this form without agreeing in any other general one. as to Shake, I Shook, I have Shaken or Shook as it is sometimes written in Poetry, to Make, I made, I have made, I bring, I brought, I wring, I wrung and many others which as they cannot be reduced to rules must be learned from the Dictionary rather than the Grammar. ought to be taken notice of in a Dictionary.

The verbs are likewise to be distinguished according to their qualities, as actives from Neuters, the neglect of which has already introduced some barbarities into our conversation which may in time creep into our writings, if not obviated by just criticism.

Construction ¶ The Words have been hitherto considered as separate and unconnected, but they are likewise to be examined as they are ranged

9

Irregularities which ought ~~all~~ to be diligently noted. Thus Fox makes in the Plural Foxes, but Ox makes Oxen Sheep is the same in both numbers. ~~*illegible character*~~ Adjectives are sometimes compared by changing the last Syllable as proud prouder proudest and sometimes by particles prefixed as ambitious, more ambitious, most ambitious.[6] The forms of our Verbs are subject to numberless varieties, some ~~*illegible word*~~ end their ~~pretertense~~ preterperfect tense in ed as to Love, I ~~have~~ loved I have loved which is the most regular manner and is followed by most of our ~~words~~ verbs of Southern original, but many words depart from ~~it~~ this ~~*illegible character*~~ form without agreeing in any other. general one. as to Shake, I Shook I have Shaken or Shook[7] ~~for as sometimes in~~ Poetry ~~it is written~~. as it is sometimes written in ~~Poetry~~[?] Poetry. to make I made I have made I bring I brought I wring, I wrung and many others which as they cannot be reduced to rules must be ~~derived~~[?] learned from the Dictionary rather than the Grammar. ought to be taken Notice of in a Dictionary.

The verbs are likewise to be distinguished according to their qualities, ~~of~~ as actives from Neuters the neglect of which has already introduced some barbarities into our conversation which may in time creep into our writings, if not obviated by just ~~animadversions. and~~ Censure.

Construction The Words have been hitherto considered as separate and unconnected, but they are likewise to be examined as they are ranged

6. See fol. 9, verso.
7. See fol. 9, verso.

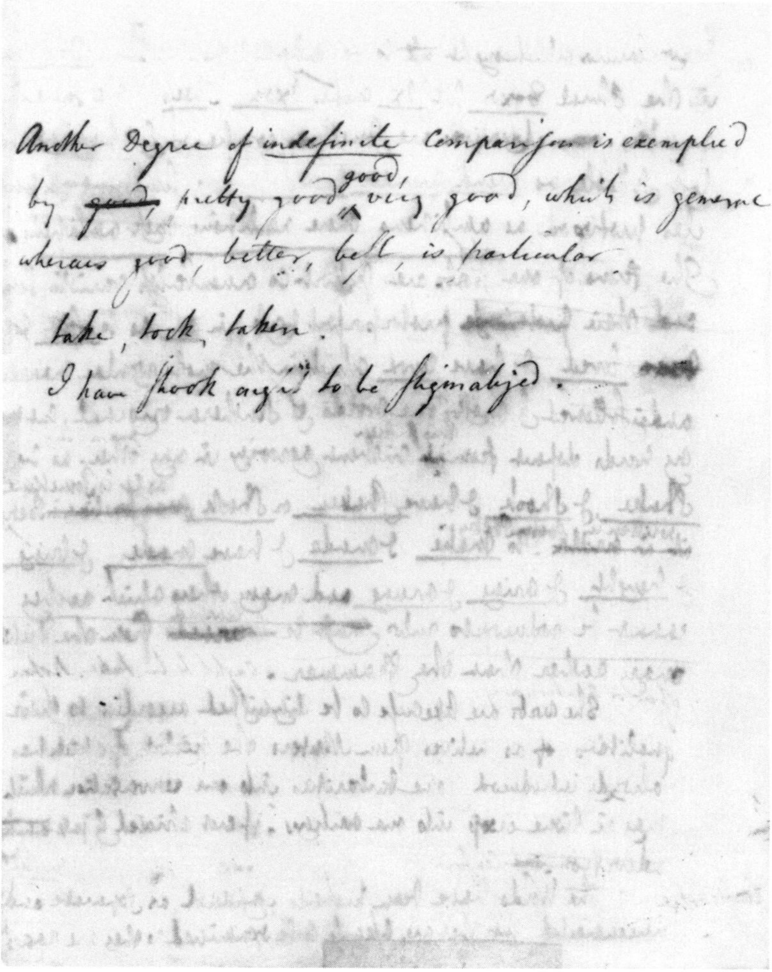
Another Degree of indefinite Comparison is exemplied by ~~good~~ pretty good, good, very good, which is general whereas good, better, best, is particular

take, took, taken.

I have shook argu'd to be stigmatized.

[9 verso]

Another Degree of indefinite comparison is exemplified by ~~good~~, pretty good, good, very good, which is general whereas good, better, best, is particular

take, took, taken.

I have shook ought to be stigmatised.

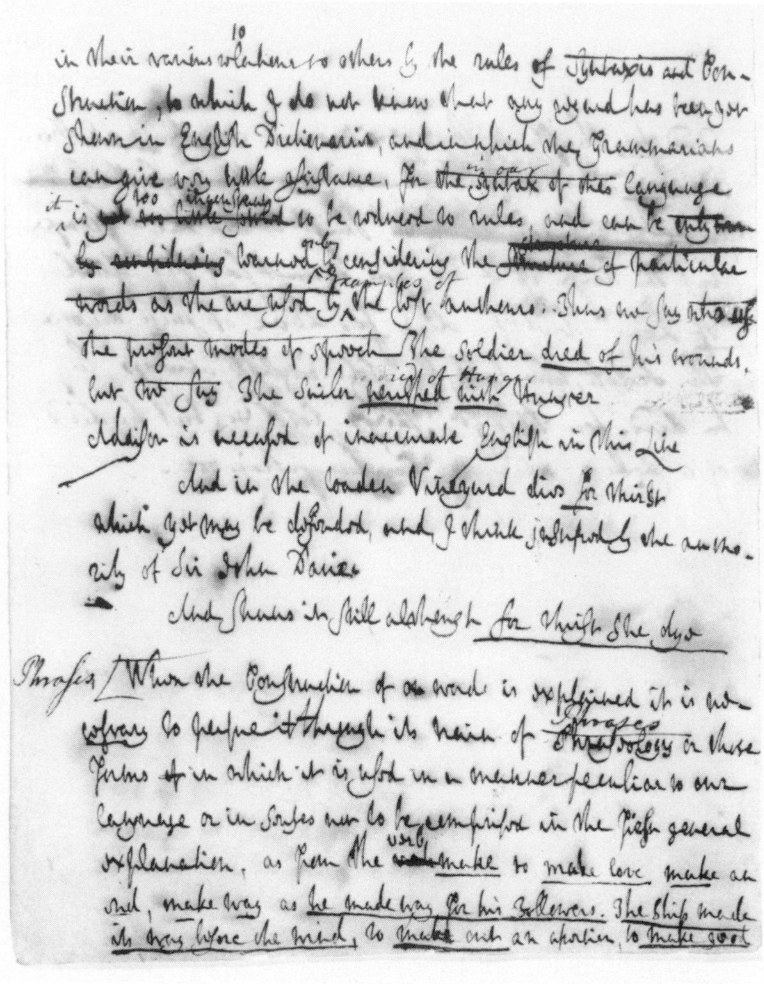

in their various relations to others by the rules of ~~Syntaxis and~~ Construction, to which I do not know that any regard has been yet shewn in English Dictionaries, and in which the Grammarians can give very little assistance. For the ~~Syntax of this~~ Language in our it is ~~yet too little fixed~~ too inconstant to be reduced to rules, and can be ~~only~~ learned ~~by considering~~ only by considering the ~~Structure~~ of particular ~~words as they are used~~ examples of by the best authors. Thus we say according to the present modes of speech The soldier died of his wounds, but we say The sailor perished with Hunger died of Hunger

Addison is accused of inaccurate English in this Line

And in the London Vineyard dies for thirst

which yet may be defended, and I think justified by the authority of Sir John Davies

And shews in still a lethargy for thirst she dyes

Phrases / When the Construction of a word is explained it is necessary to pursue it through its train of ~~Phraseology~~ Phrases or those forms in which it is used in a manner peculiar to our language or in senses not to be comprised in the first general explanation, as from the verb make to make love, make an end, make way as he made way for his followers. The ship made its way before the wind, to make out an assertion, to make good

10

in their various relations to others by the rules of Syntaxis and Construction, to which I do not know that any regard has been yet shewn in English Dictionaries, and in which the Grammarians can give very little assistance, for the syntax of the in our language it is ~~yet too little settled~~ too inconstant to be reduced to rules, and can be only ~~*illegible word* by considering~~ learned only by [?] considering the ~~structure structure~~ of particular words as the[y] are used by examples of the best authours. Thus we say who use the present modes of speech The Soldier died of his wounds, but we say The Sailor perished with Hunger. or died of Hunger Addison is accused of inaccurate English in this Line

And in the loaden Vineyard dies for thirst[8]

which yet may be defended, and, I think justified by the authority of Sir John Davies

And shuns it still although for thirst she dye

Phrasis When the Construction of a word is explained it is necessary to persue it through its train of Phraseology Phrases or those forms ~~of~~ in which it is used in a manner peculiar to our language or in senses not to be comprised in the first general explanation, as from the word[?] verb make to make love make an end, make way as he made way for his Followers. The Ship made its way before the wind, to make out an assertion, to make good

8. See fol. 10, verso.

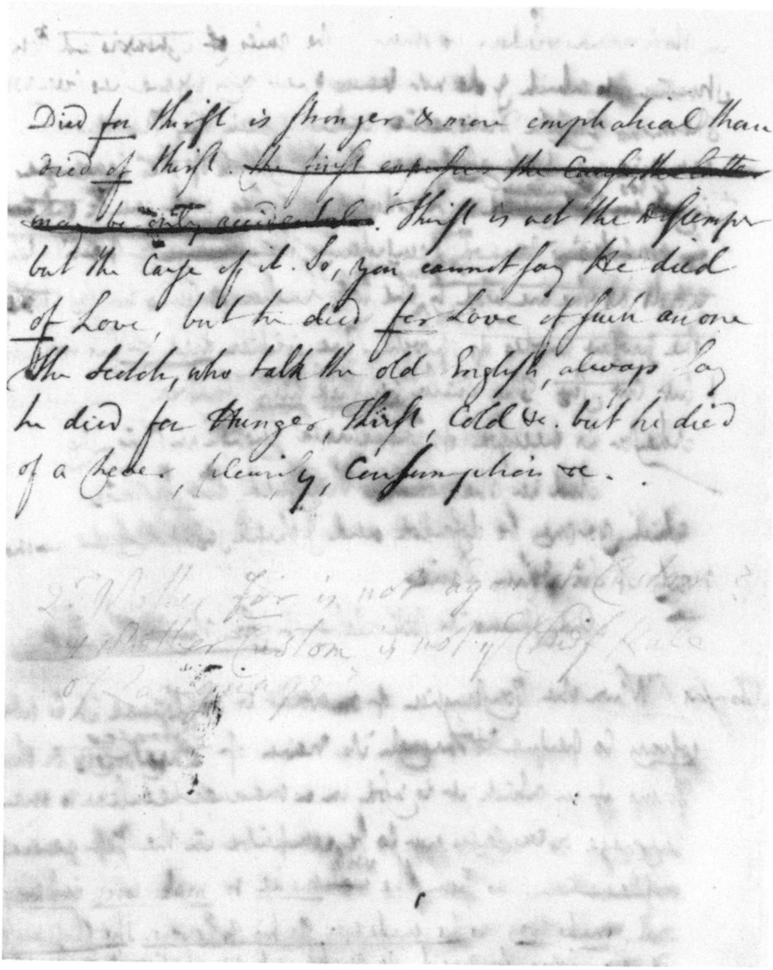

Died *for* thirst is stronger & more emphatical than died *of* thirst. ~~The first expresses the Cause, the latter may be only accidental~~. Thirst is not the Distemper but the Cause of it. So, you cannot say He died of Love, but he died *for* Love of such an one. The Scotch, who talk the old English, always say he died for Hunger, Thirst, Cold &c. but he died of a Fever, Pleurisy, Consumption &c.

[10 verso]

Died for thirst is stronger & more emphatical than died of thirst. ~~The first exposes the Cause, the latter may be only accidental.~~ Thirst is not the Distemper but the Cause of it. So, you cannot say He died of Love, but he died for Love of such an one The Scotch, who talk the old English, always say he died for Hunger, Thirst, Cold &c. but he died of a fever, pleurisy, consumption &c.

Q^{r} Whether for is not against Custom? & whether Custom is not y^{e} Chief Rule of Language? [*These lines are too light to be visible in the plate*]

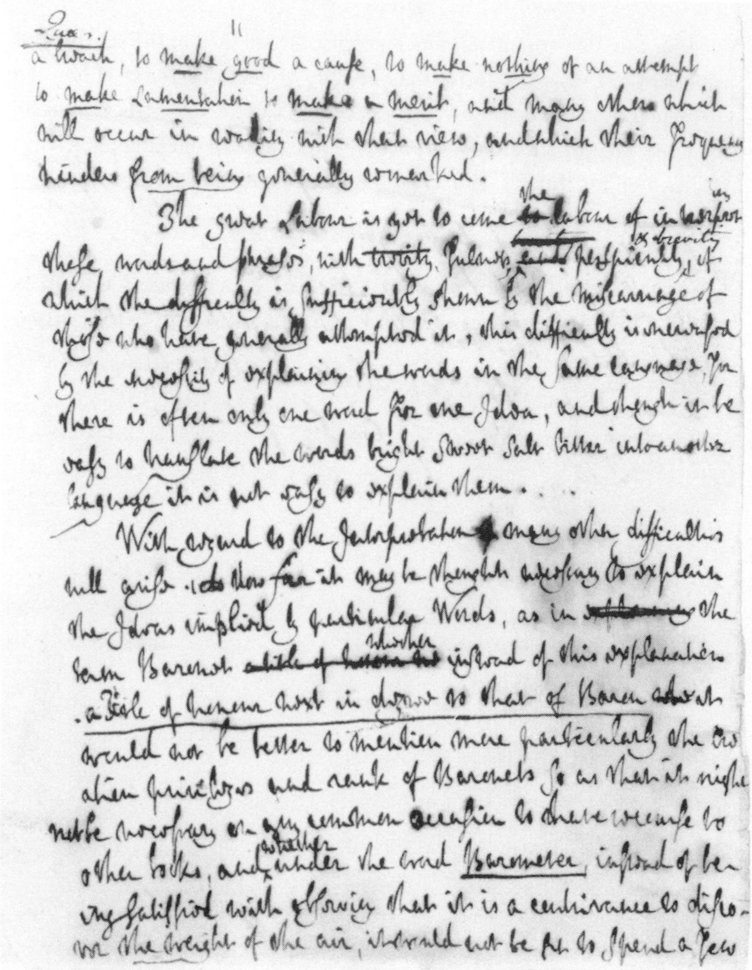

Quæ.

a breach, to make good a cause, to make nothing of an attempt
to make Lamentation to make a merit, and many others which
will occur in reading with that view, and which their frequency
hinders from being generally remarked.

The great labour is yet to come the labour of interpreting
these words and phrases with brevity, fulness, & perspicuity, of
which the difficulty is sufficiently shewn by the miscarriage of
those who have generally attempted it, this difficulty is increased
by the necessity of explaining the words in the same language, for
there is often only one word for one Idea, and though it be
easy to translate the words bright sweet salt bitter into another
language it is not easy to explain them. . .

With regard to the Interpretation many other difficulties
will arise. as how far it may be thought necessary to explain
the Ideas implied by particular Words, as in the
term Baronet whether instead of this explanation
a Title of honour next in degree to that of Baron it
would not be better to mention more particularly the creation privileges and rank of Baronets so as that it might
not be necessary on any common occasion to have recourse to
other books, and whether under the word Barometer, instead of being satisfied with shewing that it is a contrivance to discover the weight of the air, it would not be fit to spend a few

11

Quær.

a breech, to make good a cause, to make nothing of an attempt to make Lamentation to make a merit, and many others which will occur in reading[?] with that view, and which their frequency hinders from being generally remarked.

The great Labour is yet to come ~~to~~ the Labour of interpreting these words and phrases, with ~~brevity~~, fulness, ~~and~~ ~~*illegible word*~~ perspicuity, & brevity of which the difficulty is sufficiently shewn by the miscarriage of those who have generally attempted it, this difficulty is encreased by the necessity of explaining the words in the same language, for there is often only one word for one Idea, and though it be easy to translate the words bright sweet salt bitter into another language it is not easy to explain them.

With regard to the Interpretation ~~*illegible character*~~ many other difficulties will arise. As[?] How far it may be thought necessary to explain the Ideas implied by particular Words, as in ~~explaining~~ the term Baronet ~~a title of honour~~ ~~*illegible word*~~ whether instead of this explanation a Title of honour next in degree to that of Baron ~~*illegible word*~~ it would not be better to mention more particularly the creation privileges and rank of Baronets so as that it night [sic] not be necessary on any common occasion to have recourse to other books, and whether under the word Barometer, instead of being satisfied with observing that it is a contrivance to discover the weight of the air, it would not be fit to spend a few

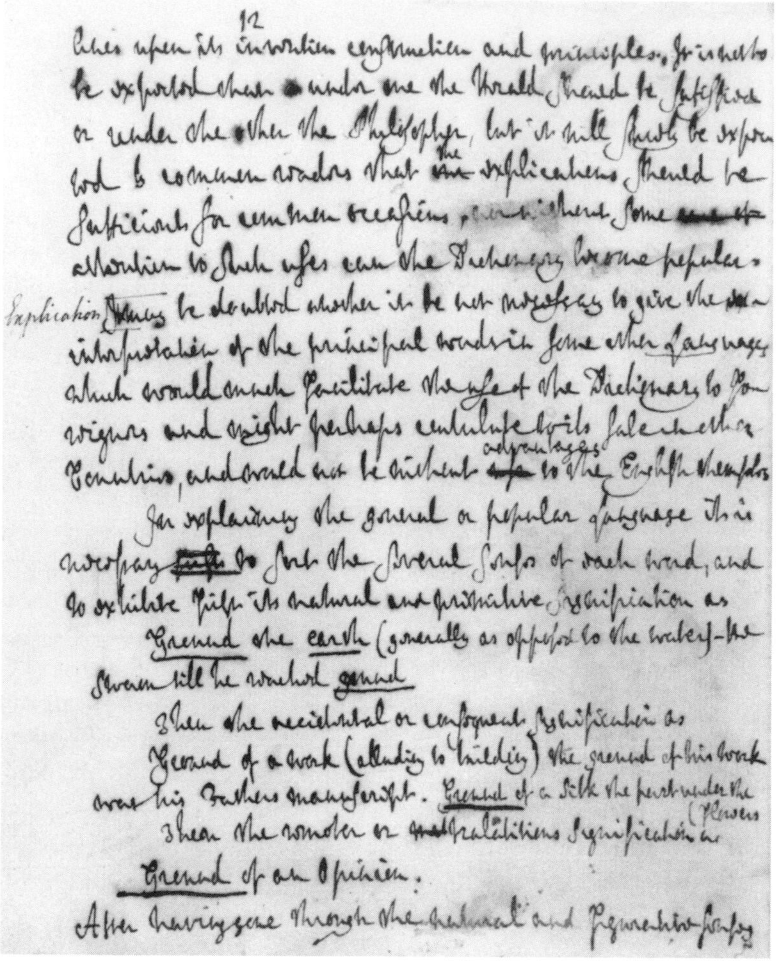

12

lities upon its invention construction and principles. It is not to be expected that under one the World should be satisfied or under the other the Philosopher, but it will surely be expected by common readers that the explications should be sufficient for common occasions, and without some attention to such uses can the Dictionary become popular.

Explication It may be doubted whether it be not necessary to give the interpretation of the principal words in some other Language which would much facilitate the use of the Dictionary to foreigners and might perhaps contribute to its sale in other Countries, and would not be without advantages to the English themselves.

In explaining the general or popular Language it is necessary to sort the several senses of each word, and to exhibit first its natural and primitive signification as

Ground the earth (generally as opposed to the water)–the stream till he reached ground

Then the accidental or consequent signification as

Ground of a work (alluding to building) the ground of his work was his Fathers manuscript. Ground of a silk the part under the flowers

Then the remoter or metaphorical signification as

Ground of an Opinion.

After having gone through the natural and figurative senses

12

lines upon its invention construction and principles. It is not to be expected that ~~*illegible character*~~ under one the Herald should be satisfied or under the other the Philosopher, but it will surely be expected by common readers that ~~one~~ the explications should be sufficient for common occasions, nor[?] without some ~~*illegible word* of~~ attention to such uses can the Dictionary become popular.

Explication It may be doubted whether it be not necessary to give the ~~ex~~ interpretation of the principal words in some other Languages which would much facilitate the use of the Dictionary to foreigners and might perhaps contribute to its sale in other Countries, and would not be without ~~use~~ advantages to the English themselves

In explaining the general or popular Language it is necessary ~~first~~ to sort the several senses of each word, and to exhibite first its natural and primitive signification as

Ground the earth (generally as opposed to the water)—He swam till he reached ground

Then the accidental or consequent signification as

Ground of a work (alluding to building) the ground of his work was his Fathers manuscript. Ground of a Silk the part under the flowers

Then the remoter or ~~*illegible word*~~ tralatitious Signification as Ground of an Opinion.

After having gone through the natural and figurative senses

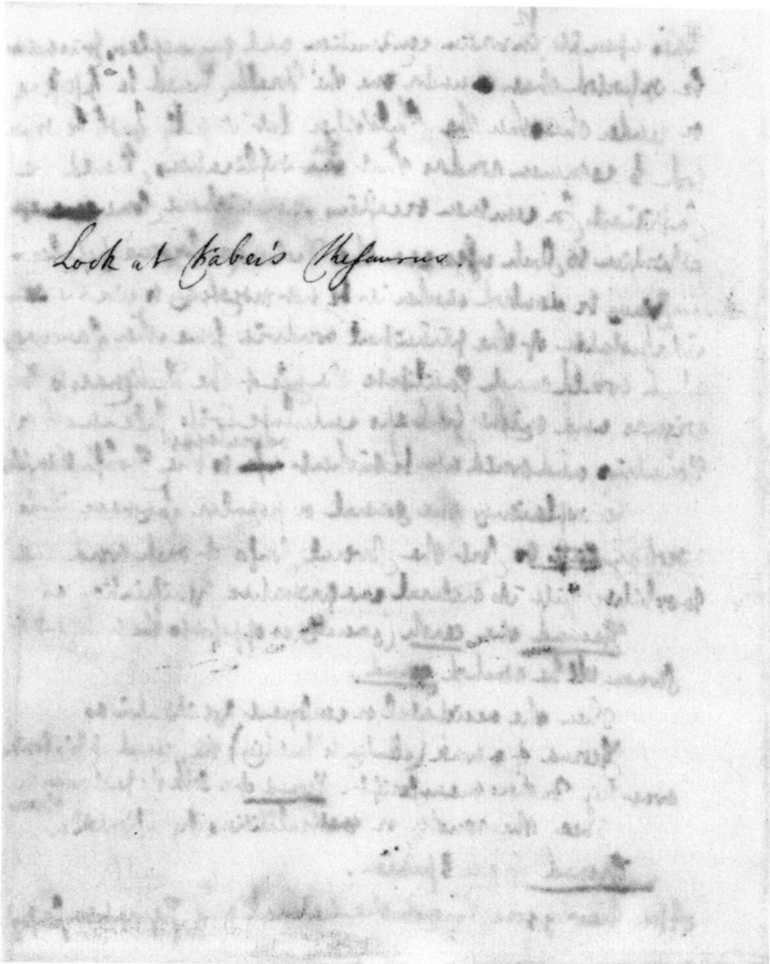
Look at Faber's Thesaurus.

[12 verso]

Look at Faber's Thesaurus

13

It will be proper to subjoin the Poetical sense of each word where it differs from that which is in common use, as wanton applied to any thing of which the motion is irregular, and Philips in In wanton ringlets curl'd her hair,

— curls the wanton Wave.

So the poetical sense may succeed the Familiar as of bite used for a cheat

— more a dupe than wit

Sappho can tell you how this Man was bit. Pope

And the Familiar may be followed by the burlesque as of mellow applied to good-fellowship

In all thy humours whether grave or mellow. Addison

And lastly may be produced the peculiar sense in which it is used by any great author, as file in Shakespeare signifies the proper Rank

Then if you have a Station in the file

And not in the last Rank of manhood, say it.

The signification of adjectives may be often ascertained by uniting them to Substantives as simple Swain simple Sheep and sometimes the sense of a Substantive may be elucidated by the epithets annexed to it by good authors as the boundless ocean the open Lawns, and where such advantages can be gained by a short quotation it is not to be omitted.

~~14~~ 13

it will be proper to subjoin ~~the~~ the Poetical ~~use~~ sense of each word where it differs from ~~that~~ that which ~~as~~[?] is in common use as wanton applied to any thing of which the motion is irregular ~~without terrour,~~ ~~as~~ and pleasing as

In wanton ringlets curl'd her hair,

———curls the wanton Wave.

To the poetical sense may succeed the familiar as of bite used for a cheat

———more a dupe than wit

Sappho can tell You how this Man was bit Pope

And the familiar may be followed by the burlesque as of mellow applied to good fellowship

In all thy humours whether grave or mellow Addison

And lastly may be produced the ~~particular~~ ~~sense in which~~ peculiar Sense ~~in which is found in~~ in which it is used by any great authour, ~~has used them~~ ~~Word~~, as File in Shakespeare signifies the foremost Rank

Then if You have a Station in the file

And not in the last Rank of Manhood shew it.[9]

The signification of Adjectives may be often ~~better~~ ascertained by *illegible character* uniting them to Substantives as simple swain simple Sheep and sometimes the sense of a Substantive may be elucidated by the epithets annexed to it by good authours as the boundless ocean the open Lawns, and where such advantage can be gained by a short quotation it is not to be ~~ad~~omitted.

9. See fol. 13, verso.

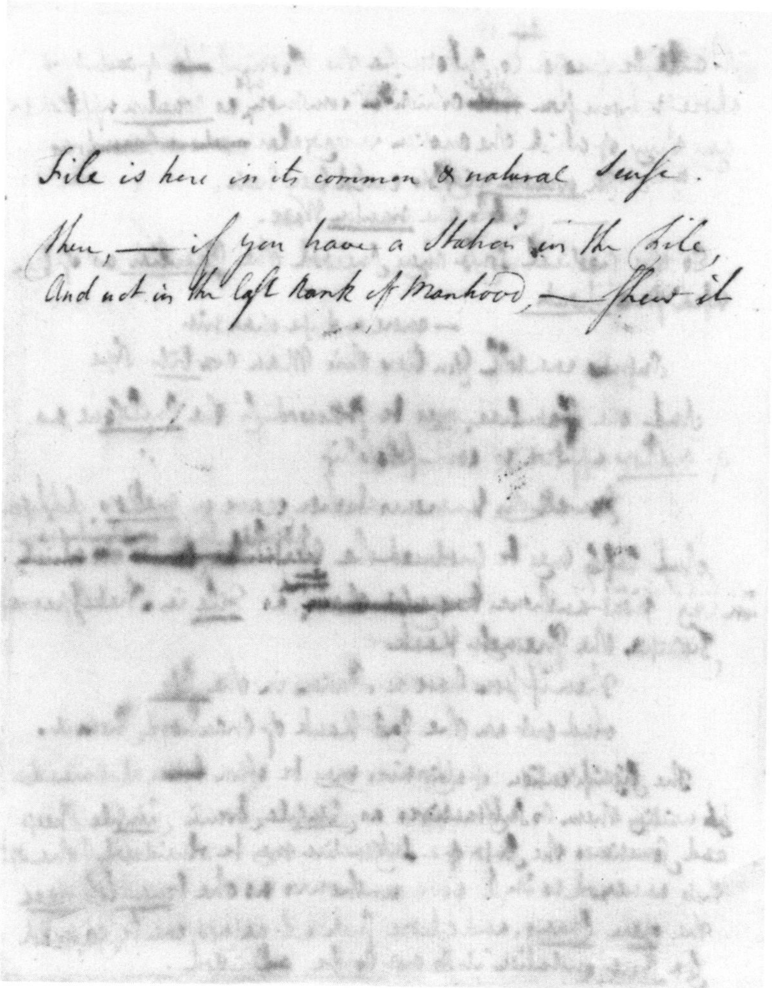
File is here in its common & natural Sense.

Then, — if you have a Station in the File,
And not in the last Rank of Manhood, — Shew it

[13 verso]

File is here in its common & natural Sense.

Then, —if you have a Station in the File,
And not in the last Rank of Manhood, —shew it

Synonimy ~~13~~ 14

The difference of signification in words generally accounted synonimous ought to be carefully observed, as in Pride Haughtiness Arrogance, and the strict and critical sense ought to be distinguished from that which is loose and popular, as in the word perfection, which in its usual application means only an high degree of excellence.

It is necessary likewise to explain many words by their opposition to others, for contraries are best seen when they stand together, thus the verb stand has one sense as opposed to fall and another as opposed to fly, for want of attending to which distinction however obvious Bentley has squandered his Criticism to no purpose on these lines of the Paradise Lost.

— — — — — In heaps
Chariot and Charioteer lay overturn'd
And fiery foaming Steeds, what stood, recoil'd
Orewearied through the faint Satanic host,
Defensive scarce, or with pale fear surpris'd
Fled ignominious —

Here says the Critic, as the words are now read, we find that what stood, fled, ~~swift~~ and therefore he proposes an alteration which he might have spared if he had consulted a dictionary, and found that nothing more was affirmed

~~13~~ 14

Synomimy [sic]

The difference of Signification in words generally accounted synonimous ought to be carefully observed, as in Pride Haughtiness Arrogance, and the strict and critical sense ought to be distinguished from that which is loose and popular, as in the word perfection, which in its usual application means only an high degree of excellence.

It is necessary likewise to explain many words by their opposition to others, for contraries are best seen when they stand together, thus the verb stand has one sense opposed to fall and another ~~as~~[?] opposed to fly for want of attending to which distinction however obvious Bentley has squandred his Criticisms to no purpose on these Lines of the Paradise lost.

——————————In heaps
Chariot and Charioteer lay overturn'd
And fiery foaming Steeds, what stood, recoil'd
Oerwearied through the faint Satanic host,
Defensive scarce, or with pale fear surpris'd
Fled ignominious———

Here, says the Critic, as the words are now read, we find that what stood, Fled, ~~but if~~ and therefore he proposes an alteration which he might have spared if he had consulted a dictionary, and found that nothing more was affirmed than those #15 flod who did not fail.

In explaining such meanings as seem accidental and adventitious it is proper to give an account of the means by which these meanings were introduced, thus to eke out any thing signifies to lengthen it beyond its just dimensions by some low artifice, because the word eke was the usual refuge of our old writers when they wanted a syllable. Thus buxom which means only obedient is now made in familiar phrases to signify wanton because in an ancient form of marriage before the reformation, the Bride promised complaisance and obedience in these terms "I will "be bonair and buxom in bed and at board."

Classing — There remains yet to be considered the Distribution of words into their proper classes, or that part of Lexicography which is strictly critical. The popular Part of the Language which includes all words not appropriated to particular Sciences admits of many distinctions and subdivisions; as, into words of general use, words employed chiefly in poetry, words obsolete, words which are admitted only by particular Writers yet not in themselves improper, words used only in burlesque writing, and words impure and barbarous.

~~14~~ 15

than that those fled who did not fall.

In explaining ~~the~~ such meanings as seem accidental and adventitious it is proper to give an account of the means by which these meanings were introduced, thus to eke out any thing signifies to lengthen it beyond its just dimensions by some low artifice, because the word eke was the usual refuge of our old writers when they wanted a Syllable. Thus buxom ~~is~~ which means only obedient is now made in familiar ~~*illegible word*~~ phrases to signify wanton because in an ancient form of marriage before the reformation, the Bride promised complaisance and obedience in these terms "I will "be bonair and buxom in bed and at board."

Classing There remains yet to be considered the Distribution of words into their proper classes, or that part of Lexicography which is ~~properly~~ strictly critical. The popular ~~or general~~ *illegible character* Part of the Language which includes all words not appropriated to particular Sciences ~~is not~~ admits of many distinctions and subdivisions; as, into words of general use, words ~~employed~~ employed chiefly in poetry, words obsolete, ~~and~~ words which are admitted only by particular Writers yet not in themselves improper, Words used only in burlesque writing and words impure and barbarous.

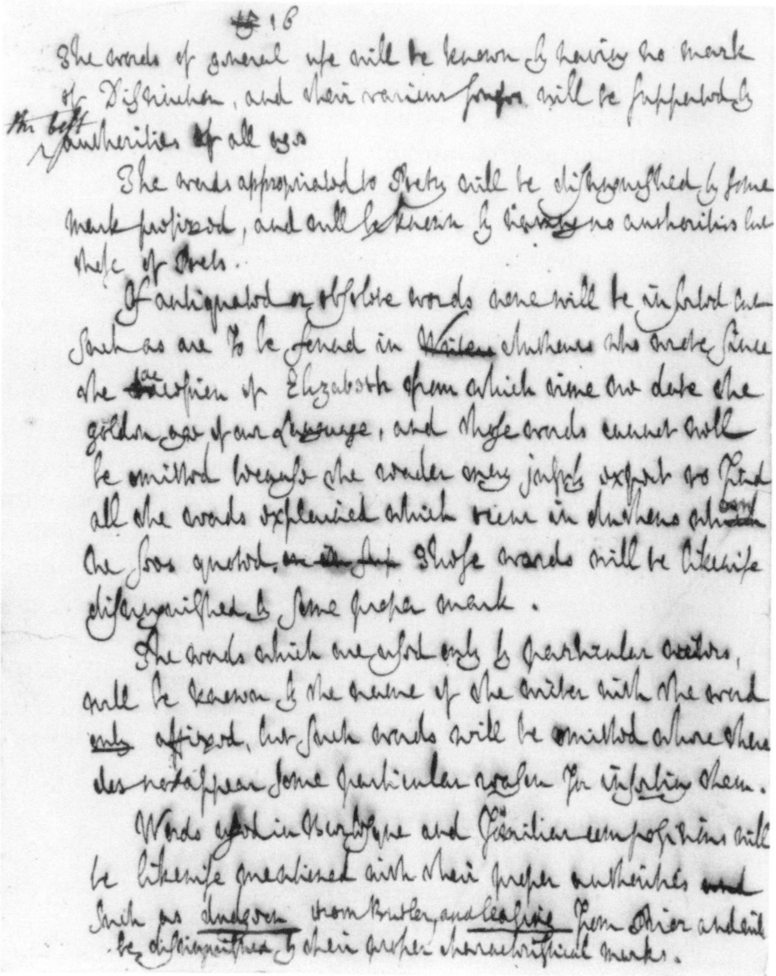

#16

The words of general use will be known by having no mark of Distinction, and their various senses will be supported by [the best] authorities of all ages.

The words appropriated to Poetry will be distinguished by some mark prefixed, and will be known by having no authorities but those of Poets.

Of antiquated or obsolete words none will be inserted but such as are to be found in ~~Writers~~ Authors who wrote since the accession of Elizabeth from which time we date the golden age of our Language, and these words cannot well be omitted because the reader may justly expect to find all the words explained which occur in Authors ~~which~~ are so quoted. ~~or [illegible]~~ Those words will be likewise distinguished by some proper mark.

The words which are used only by particular writers, will be known by the name of the writer with the word only affixed, but such words will be omitted where there does not appear some particular reason for inserting them.

Words of low burlesque and familiar composition will be likewise mentioned with their proper authorities ~~and~~ such as dudgeon from Butler and leasing from Prior and will be distinguished by their proper characteristical marks.

~~15~~ 16

The words of general use will be known by having no mark of Distinction, and their various senses will be supported by the best authorities of all ages

The words appropriated to Poetry will be distinguished by some mark prefixed, and will be known by having no authorities but those of Poets.

Of antiquated or obsolete words none will be inserted but such as are to be found in ~~Writers~~ Authours who wrote since the ~~*illegible characters*~~ accession of Elizabeth from which time we date the golden age of our Language, and those words cannot well be omitted because the reader may justly expect to find all the words explained which occur in Authours wh~~ich~~om he sees quoted. ~~as *illegible words*~~ These words will be likewise distinguished by some proper mark.

The words which are used only by particular writers, will be known by the name of the writer with the word <u>only</u> affixed, but such words will be omitted where there dos [sic] not appear some particular reason for inserting them.

Words used in Burlesque and Familiar compositions will be likewise mentioned with their proper authorities ~~and~~ such as <u>dudgeon</u> from Butler, and <u>leasing</u> from Prior and wil[l] be distinguished by their proper characteristical marks.

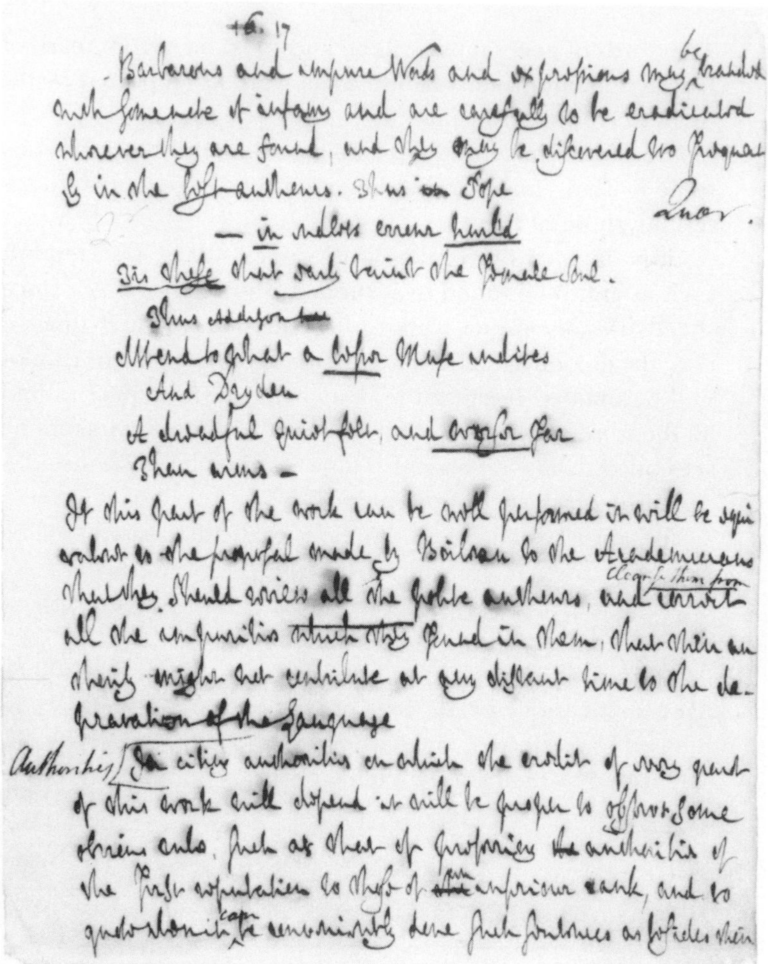

17

Barbarous and impure Words and expressions may be branded with some note of infamy and are carefully to be eradicated wherever they are found, and they may be discovered too frequently in the best authours. Thus in Pope

Luxur.

— in endless errour hurl'd

'Tis these that early taint the Female Soul.

Thus Addison

Attend to what a lesser Muse indites

And Dryden

A dreadful quiet felt, and worser far

Than arms —

If this part of the work can be well performed it will be equivalent to the proposal made by Boileau to the Academicians that they should review all the polite authours, and cleanse them from all the impurities found in them, that their authority might not contribute at any distant time to the depravation of the Language

Authorities) In citing authorities on which the credit of every part of this work will depend it will be proper to observe some obvious rules, such as that of preferring the authorities of the first reputation to those of an inferiour rank, and to quote when it can be conveniently done such sentences as besides their

~~16~~ 17

Barbarous and impure Words and expressions may be branded with some note of infamy and are carefully to be eradicated wherever they are found, and they may be discovered too frequently in the best authours. Thus ~~in~~ Pope

Q[r] ———in endless errour hurl'd Quær.

Tis these that early taint the female Soul.

Thus Addison ~~has~~[?]

Attend to what a lesser Muse indites

And Dryden

A dreadful quiet felt, and worser far

Than arms—

If this part of the work can be well performed it will be equivalent to the proposal made by Boileau to the Academicians that they should review all the polite authours, and correct cleanse them from all the impurities which they found in them, that their authority might not contribute at any distant time to the depravation of the Language

Authorities In citing authorities on which the credit of every part of this work will depend it will be proper to observe some obvious rules, such as that of preferring ~~the~~ authorities of the first reputation to those of ~~the~~ an inferiour rank, and to quote when it can be conveniently done such sentences as besides their

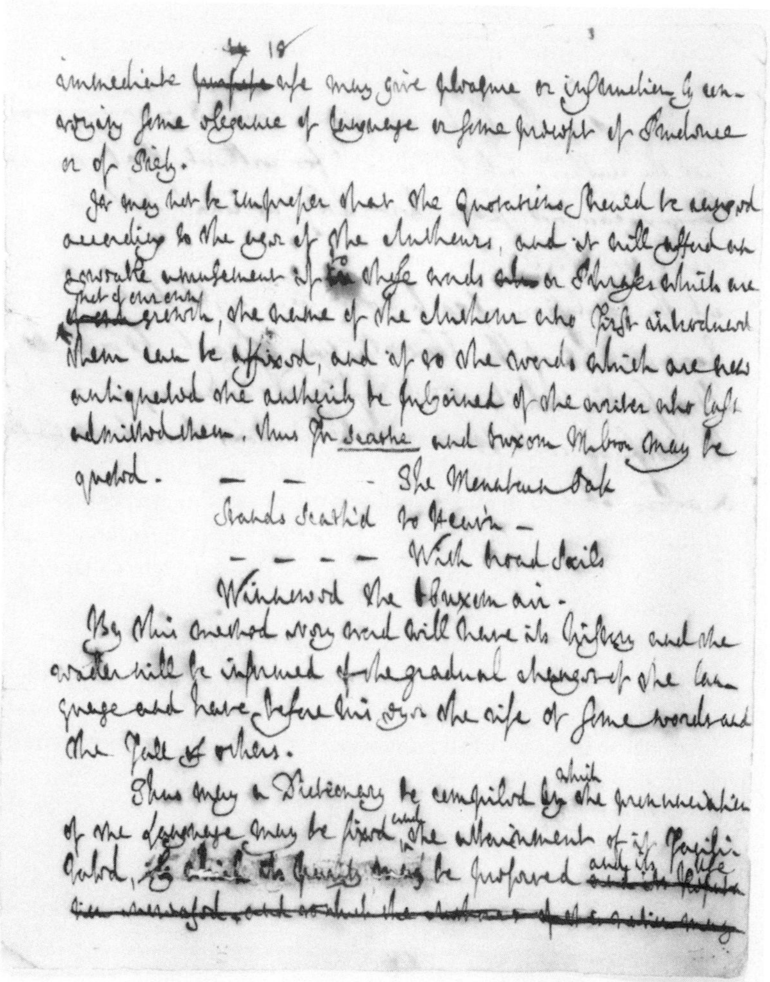

immediate ~~purpose~~ use may give pleasure or information by conveying some elegance of language or some precept of prudence or of piety.

It may not be improper that the Quotations should be ranged according to the ages of the Authors, and it will afford an agreeable amusement if to those words ~~or~~ or Phrases which are not of our own growth, the name of the Author who first introduced them can be affixed, and if to the words which are now antiquated the authority be subjoined of the writer who last admitted them. Thus for scathe and buxom Milton may be quoted. — — — The Mountain Oak

Stands scath'd to Heav'n —

— — — — With broad Sails

Winnow'd the buxom air.

By this method every word will have its history and the reader will be informed of the gradual changes of the language and have before his eyes the rise of some words and the fall of others.

Thus may a Dictionary be compiled by which the pronunciation of the Language may be fixed and the attainment of it facilitated, ~~by which~~ the purity may be preserved and its use ~~[illegible]~~

~~[illegible]~~

~~17~~ 18

immediate ~~purpose~~ use may give pleasure or instruction by conveying some elegance of language or some precept of Prudence or of Piety.

It may not be improper that the Quotations should be ranged according to the ages of the Authours, and it will afford an agreeable amusement if ~~*illegible character*~~ to these words ~~wh~~[?] or Phrases which are ~~of our~~ not of our own growth, the name of the Authour who first introduced them can be affixed, and if to the words which are now antiquated the authority be subjoined of the writer who last admitted them. thus for <u>Scathe</u> and buxom Milton may be quoted.

———The Mountain Oak
Stands Scath'd to Heav'n—
———With broad Sails
Winnowed the buxom air.[1]

By this method every word will have its history and the reader will be informed of the gradual changes of the language and have before his eyes the rise of some words and the fall of others.

Thus may a Dictionary be compiled by which the pronunciation of the Language may be fixed, and the attainment of it facilitated, by which its purity may be preserved ~~and its Reputation encreased and to which the Authours of the nation may~~ and its Use

1. See fol. 18, verso.

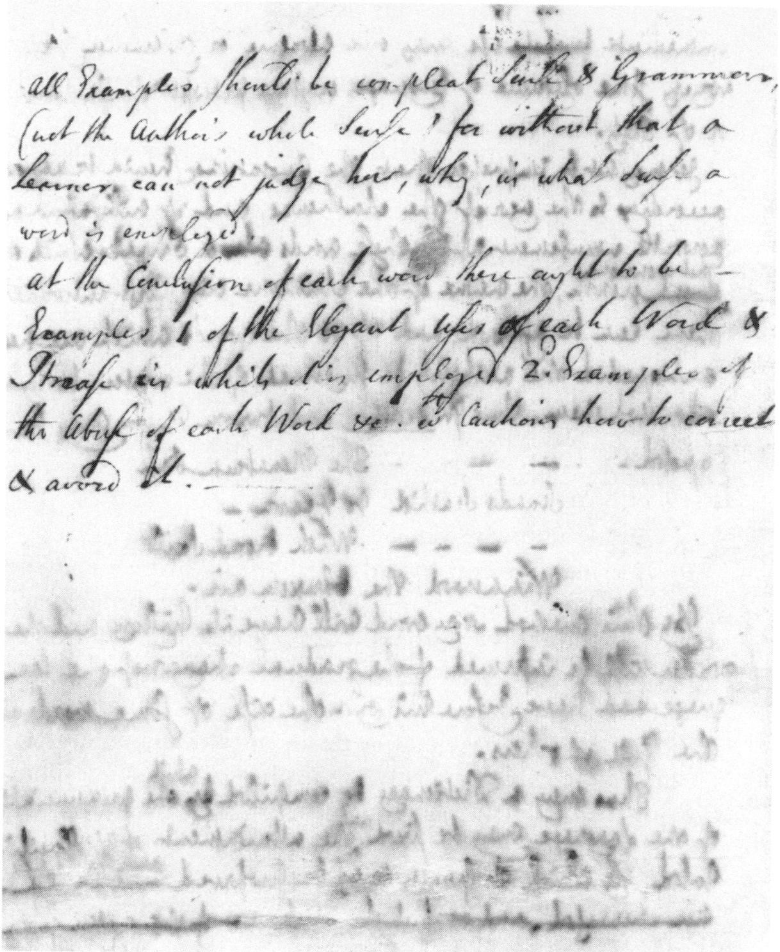
all Examples should be compleat Sense & Grammar,
(not the Author's whole Sense) for without that a
Learner can not judge how, why, or what Sense a
word is employed.
at the Conclusion of each word there ought to be —
Examples 1 of the Elegant uses of each Word &
Phrase in which it is employed 2. Examples of
the Abuse of each Word &c. or Cautions how to correct
& avoid it.

[18 verso]

All Examples should be compleat Sense & Grammar, (not the Author's whole Sense) for without that a Learner can not judge how, why, in what Sense a word is employed.

At the Conclusion of each word there ought to be Examples 1 of the Elegant uses of each Word & Phrase in which it is employed 2. Examples of the Abuse of each Word &c wth Cautions how to correct & avoid it.

ascertained, its Reputation everywhere, and its duration lengthened
and to which therefore the Authors of this Nation may perhaps owe
great part of the Praises ~~which~~ that they shall receive from Posterity.

April 30-1746

19

ascertained, its Reputation encreased, and its duration lengthend and to which therefore the Authours of this Nation may perhaps owe part of the Praises ~~which~~ that they shall receive from Posterity.

April 30. 1746

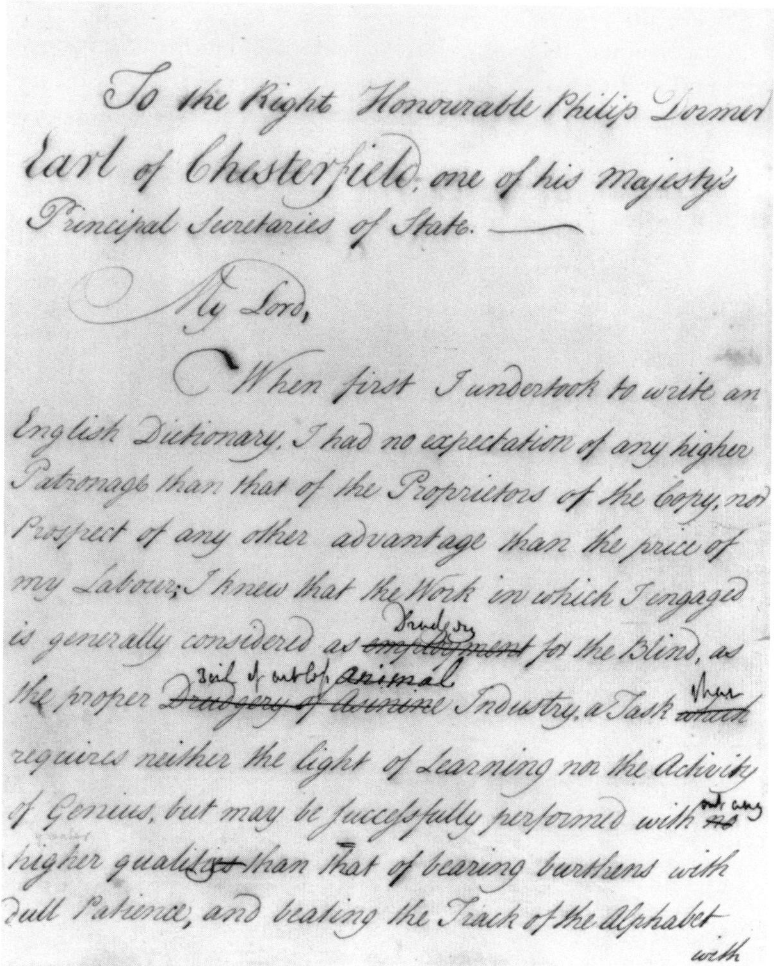

To the Right Honourable Philip Dormer
Earl of Chesterfield; one of his Majesty's
Principal Secretaries of State. —

My Lord,

When first I undertook to write an English Dictionary, I had no expectation of any higher Patronage than that of the Proprietors of the Copy, nor Prospect of any other advantage than the price of my Labour; I knew that the Work in which I engaged is generally considered as ~~employment~~ Drudgery for the Blind, as the proper ~~Drudgery of Animal~~ toil of artless animal Industry, a Task ~~which~~ that requires neither the light of Learning nor the Activity of Genius, but may be successfully performed with~~no~~out any higher qualit~~ies~~y than that of bearing burthens with dull Patience, and beating the Track of the Alphabet with

Folio 1

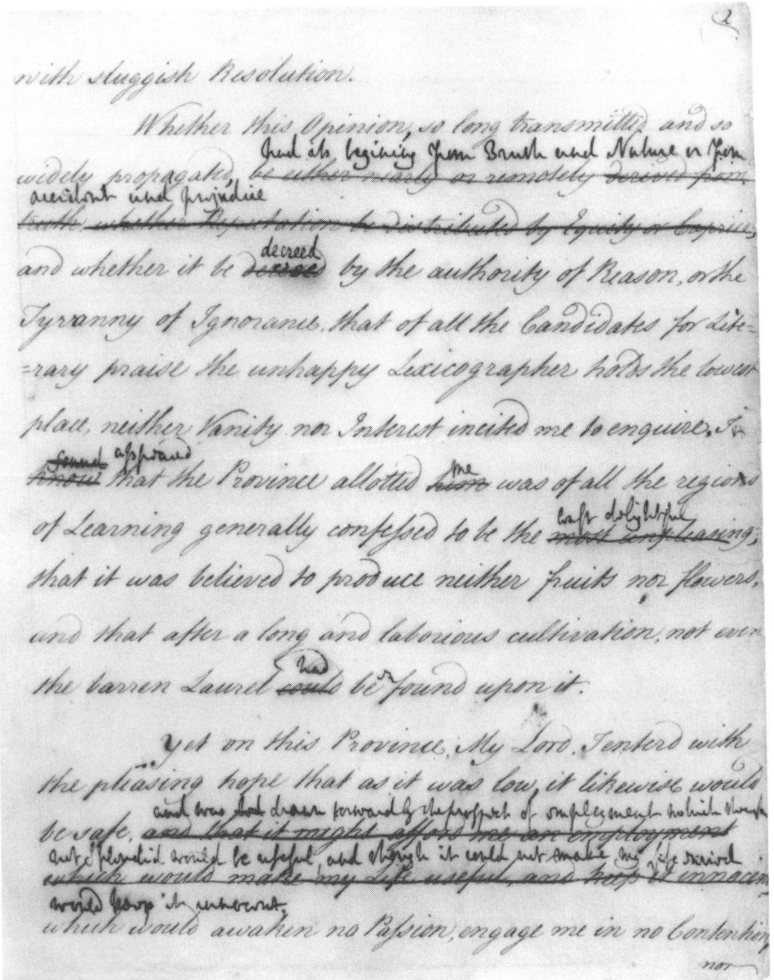
2

with sluggish Resolution.

Whether this Opinion, so long transmitted and so widely propagated, had its beginning from Truth and Nature or from accident and prejudice ~~be either nearly or remotely derived from truth: whether Reputation be distributed by Equity or Caprice,~~ and whether it be decreed ~~decreed~~ by the authority of Reason, or the Tyranny of Ignorance, that of all the Candidates for Lite=rary praise the unhappy Lexicographer holds the lowest place, neither Vanity nor Interest incited me to enquire. I ~~found~~ knew ~~know~~ that the Province allotted me ~~him~~ was of all the regions of Learning generally confessed to be the least delightful ~~most unpleasing~~; that it was believed to produce neither fruits nor flowers, and that after a long and laborious cultivation, not even the barren Laurel had ~~could~~ be found upon it.

Yet on this Province, My Lord, I enterd with the pleasing hope that as it was low, it likewise would be safe, and was not drawn forward by the prospect of employment which though not splendid would be useful, and though it could not make my life envied would keep it innocent ~~and that it might afford me an employment which would make my Life useful, and keep it innocent~~ which would awaken no Passion, engage me in no Contention, nor

Folio 2

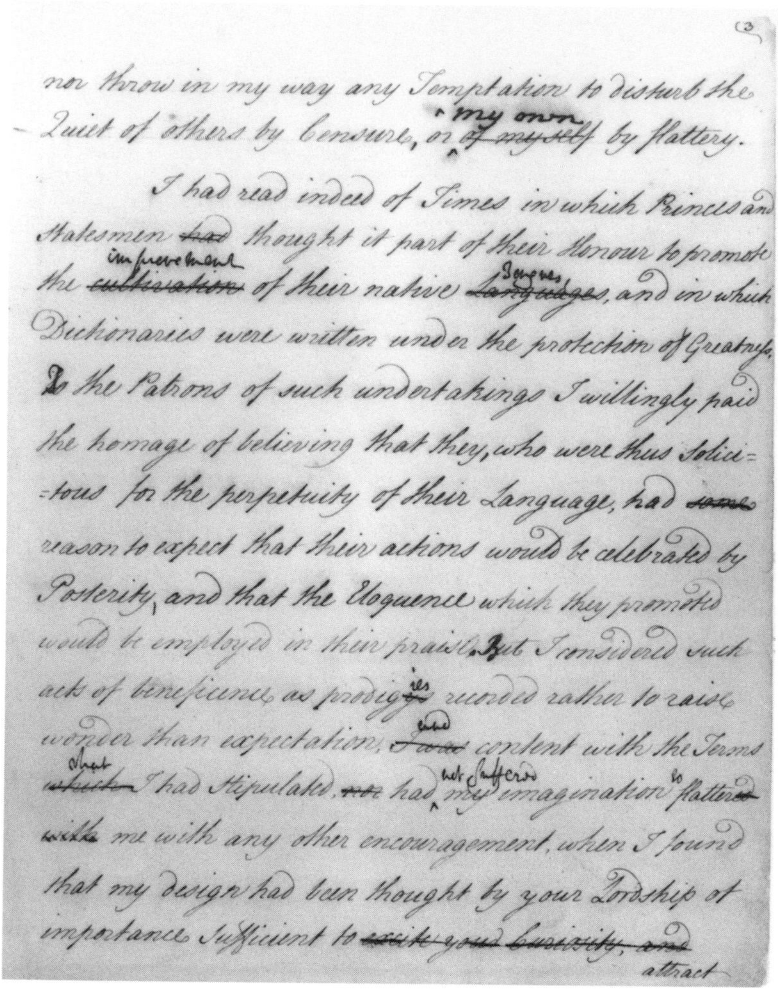

nor throw in my way any Temptation to disturb the
Quiet of others by Censure, or [my own] ~~of myself~~ by flattery.

I had read indeed of Times in which Princes and
Statesmen ~~had~~ thought it part of their Honour to promote
the [improvement] ~~cultivation~~ of their native [Tongues] ~~Languages~~, and in which
Dictionaries were written under the protection of Greatness.
To the Patrons of such undertakings I willingly paid
the homage of believing that they, who were thus Solici=
=tous for the perpetuity of their Language, had ~~some~~
reason to expect that their actions would be celebrated by
Posterity, and that the Eloquence which they promoted
would be employed in their praise. But I considered such
acts of beneficence as prodigies recorded rather to raise
wonder than expectation, ~~I was~~ [and] content with the Terms
[that] ~~which~~ I had stipulated, ~~nor~~ had [not suffered] ~~my~~ imagination [to] flatter~~ed~~
~~with~~ me with any other encouragement, when I found
that my design had been thought by your Lordship of
importance sufficient to ~~excite your Curiosity, and~~
attract

Folio 3

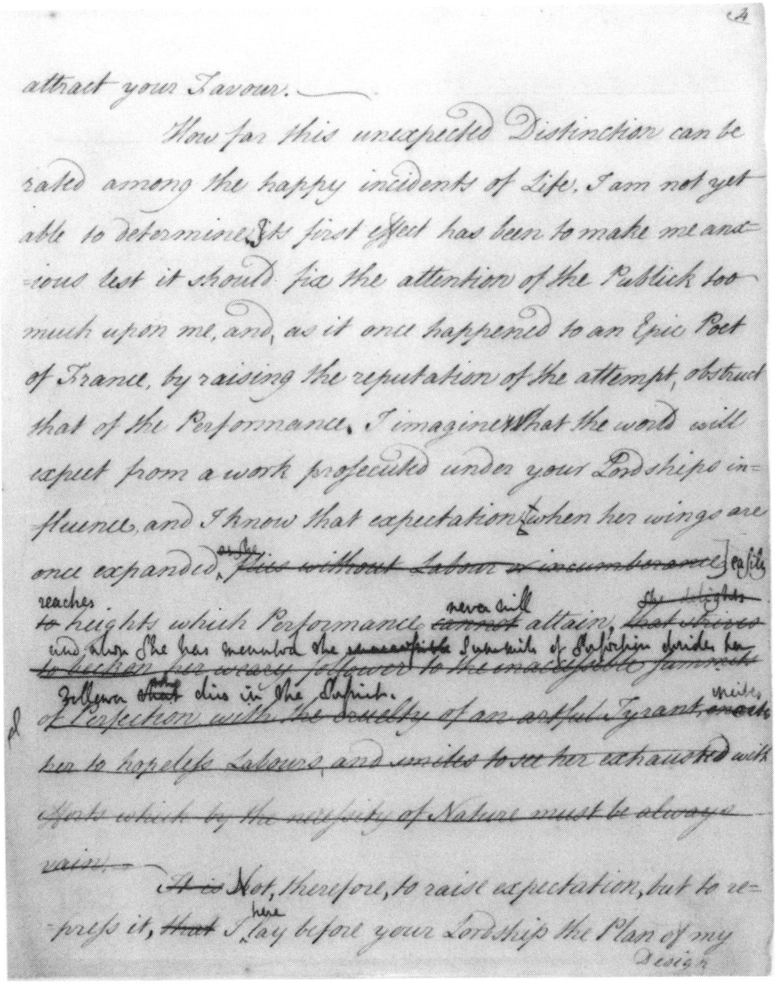

4

attract your Favour. —

How far this unexpected Distinction can be rated among the happy incidents of Life, I am not yet able to determine. Its first effect has been to make me anxious lest it should fix the attention of the Publick too much upon me, and, as it once happened to an Epic Poet of France, by raising the reputation of the attempt, obstruct that of the Performance. I imagine that the world will expect from a work prosecuted under your Lordships influence, and I know that expectation when her wings are once expanded, ~~flies without Labour or incumbrance~~ easily reaches ~~to~~ heights which Performance ~~cannot~~ never will attain, ~~that strives~~ ~~to beckon her weary follower to the inaccessible summits of Perfection with the cruelty of an artful Tyrant, mocks her to hopeless Labours, and smiles to see her exhausted with efforts which by the necessity of Nature must be always vain.~~ —

~~It is~~ Not, therefore, to raise expectation, but to repress it, ~~that~~ I here lay before your Lordship the Plan of my Design

Folio 4

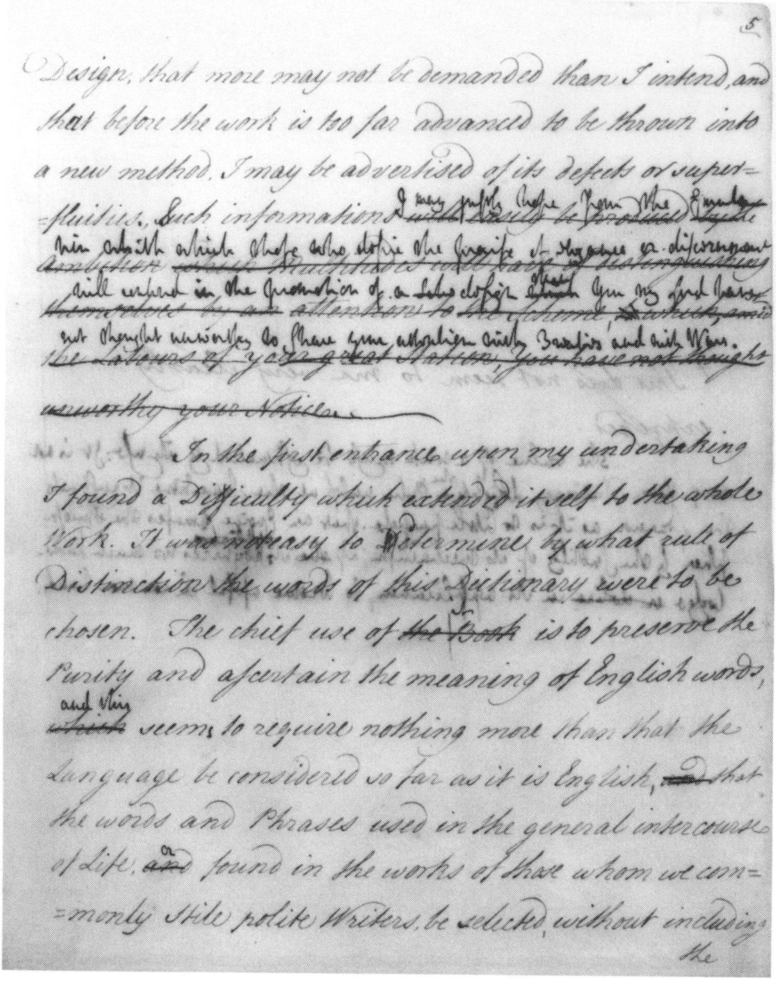

5

Design, that more may not be demanded than I intend, and that before the work is too far advanced to be thrown into a new method, I may be advertised of its defects or super=
=fluities. Such information I may justly hope from the Emulation with which those who desire the praise of elegance or discernment must contend in the promotion of a design that you my Lord have not thought unworthy to share your attention with Treaties and with Wars. ~~will hardly be procured by the ambition which naturally urges of distinguishing themselves by an attention to the scheme, to which, amid the Labours of your great Station, you have not thought unworthy your Notice.~~

In the first entrance upon my undertaking I found a Difficulty which extended it self to the whole Work. It was not easy to determine by what rule of Distinction the words of this Dictionary were to be chosen. The chief use of ~~the Book~~ is to preserve the Purity and ascertain the meaning of English words, and this ~~which~~ seems to require nothing more than that the Language be considered so far as it is English, ~~and~~ that the words and Phrases used in the general intercourse of Life, or ~~and~~ found in the works of those whom we com=
=monly Stile polite Writers, be selected, without including the

Folio 5

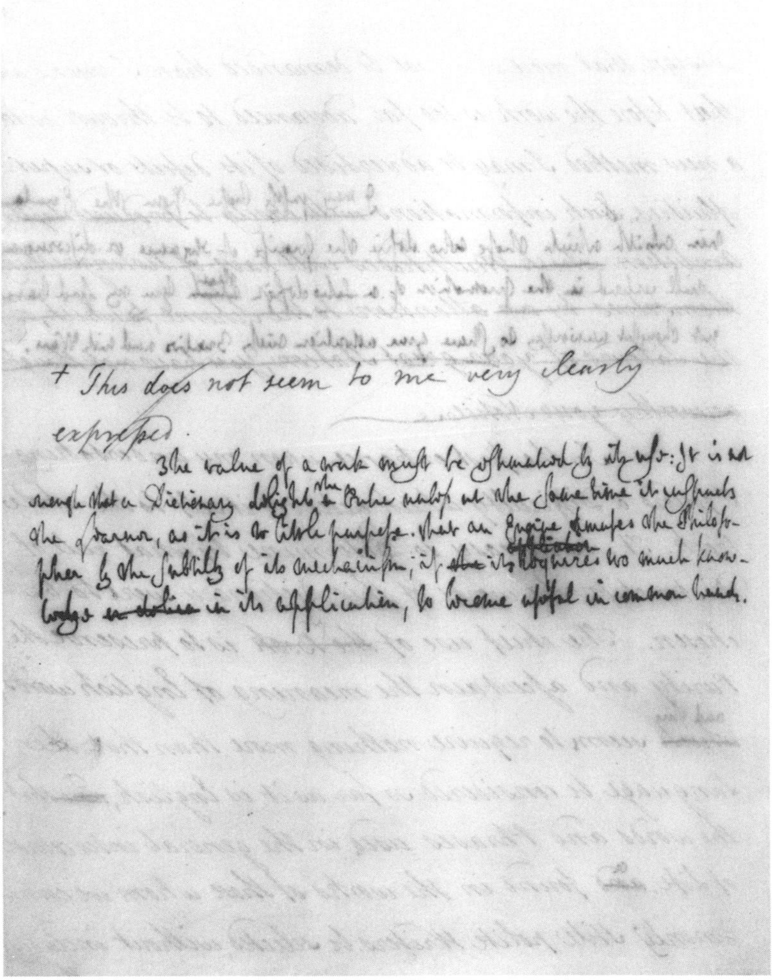
+ This does not seem to me very clearly expressed.

The value of a work must be estimated by its use: It is not enough that a Dictionary delights the Critic unless at the same time it instructs the Learner, as it is to little purpose, that an Engine amuses the Philosopher by the subtilty of its mechanism, if it requires so much knowledge in its application, to become useful in common hands.

Folio 5 verso

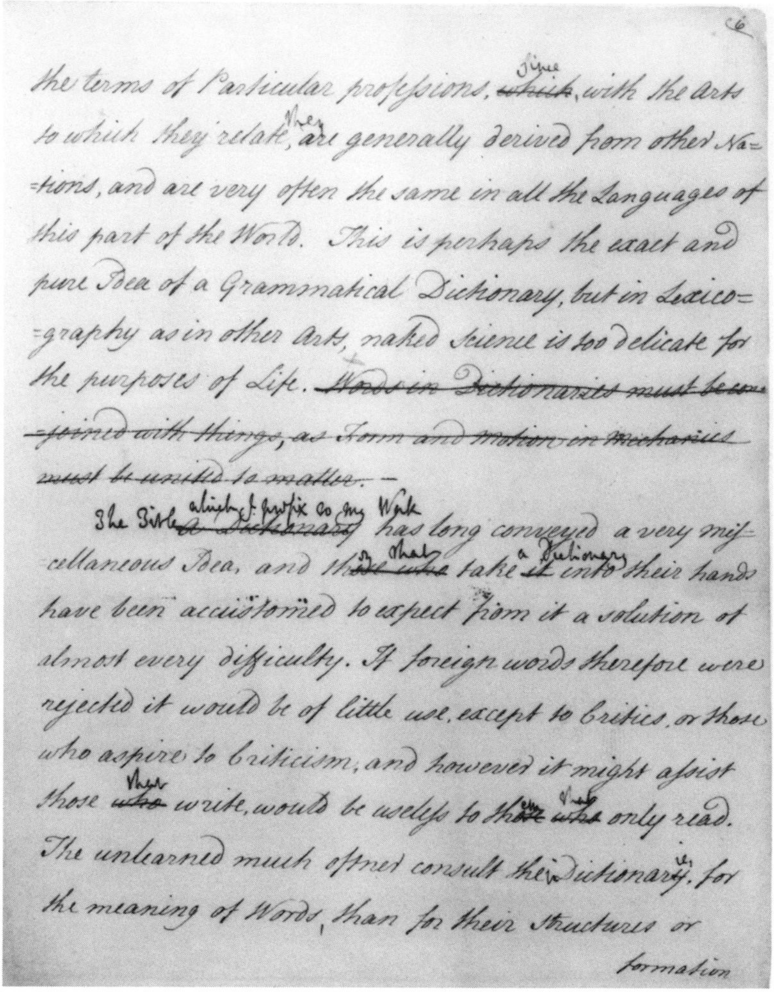
6
the terms of Particular professions, ~~which~~ [since], with the Arts
to which they relate, [they] are generally derived from other Na=
=tions, and are very often the same in all the Languages of
this part of the World. This is perhaps the exact and
pure Idea of a Grammatical Dictionary, but in Lexico=
=graphy as in other Arts, naked Science is too delicate for
the purposes of Life. ~~Words in Dictionaries must be com=~~
~~=joined with things, as Form and Motion in Mechanics~~
~~must be united to matter.~~ —
The Title ~~a Dictionary~~ [which I prefix to my Work] has long conveyed a very mis=
=cellaneous Idea, and ~~those who~~ [they that] take ~~it~~ [a Dictionary] into their hands
have been accustomed to expect from it a solution of
almost every difficulty. If foreign words therefore were
rejected it would be of little use, except to Critics, or those
who aspire to Criticism; and however it might assist
those ~~who~~ [that] write, would be useless to ~~those who~~ [them that] only read.
The unlearned much oftner consult the Dictionar[ies] for
the meaning of Words, than for their structures or
formation

Folio 6

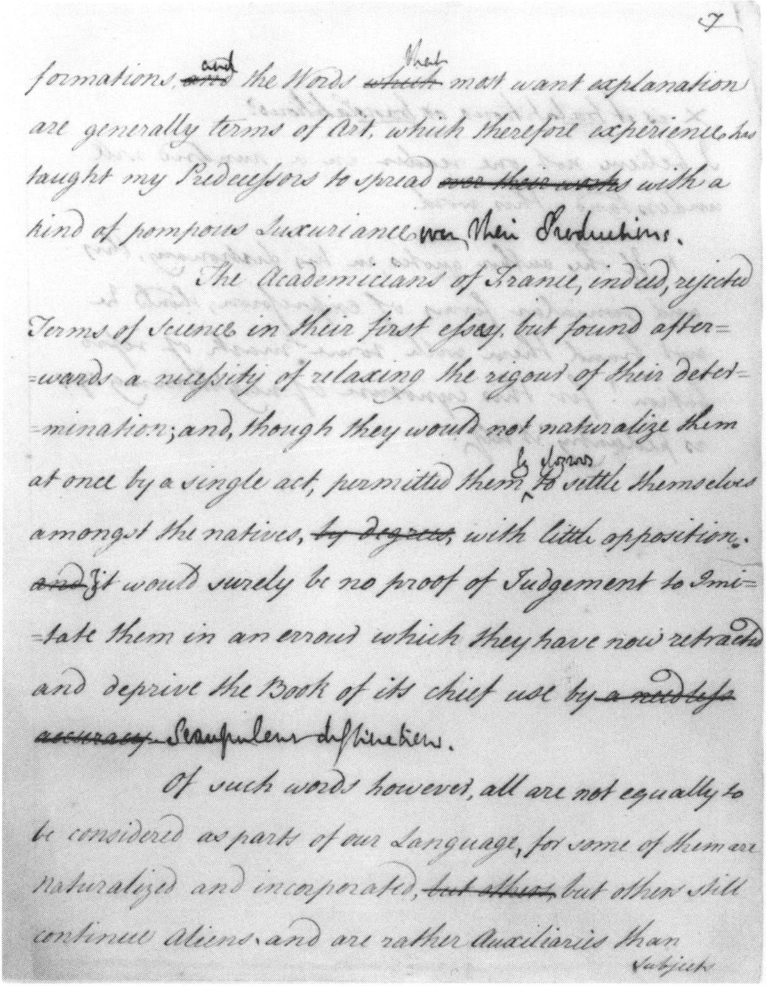

7

formations, ~~and~~ and the Words ~~which~~ that most want explanation
are generally terms of Art, which therefore experience has
taught my Predecessors to spread ~~over their works~~ with a
kind of pompous Luxuriance over their Productions.

The Academicians of France, indeed, rejected
Terms of Science in their first essay, but found after=
=wards a necessity of relaxing the rigour of their deter=
=mination; and, though they would not naturalize them
at once by a single act, permitted them by degrees to settle themselves
amongst the natives, ~~by degrees,~~ with little opposition.
~~and~~ It would surely be no proof of Judgement to Imi=
=tate them in an errour which they have now retracted
and deprive the Book of its chief use by ~~a needless~~
~~accuracy~~ scrupulous distinctions.

Of such words however, all are not equally to
be considered as parts of our Language, for some of them are
Naturalized and incorporated, ~~but others~~ but others still
continue aliens, and are rather Auxiliaries than
Subjects

Folio 7

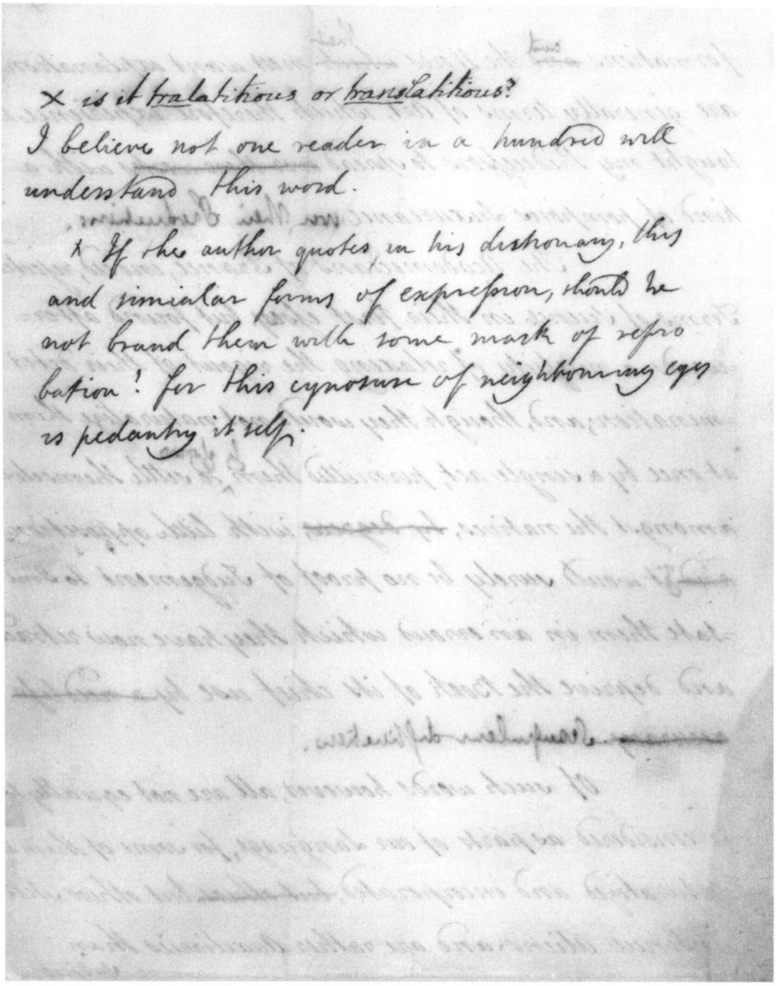

× is it tralatitious or translatitious?
I believe not one reader in a hundred will
understand this word.
× If the author quotes in his dictionary, this
and similar forms of expression, should he
not brand them with some mark of repro
bation! for this cynosure of neighbouring eyes
is pedantry itself.

Folio 7 verso

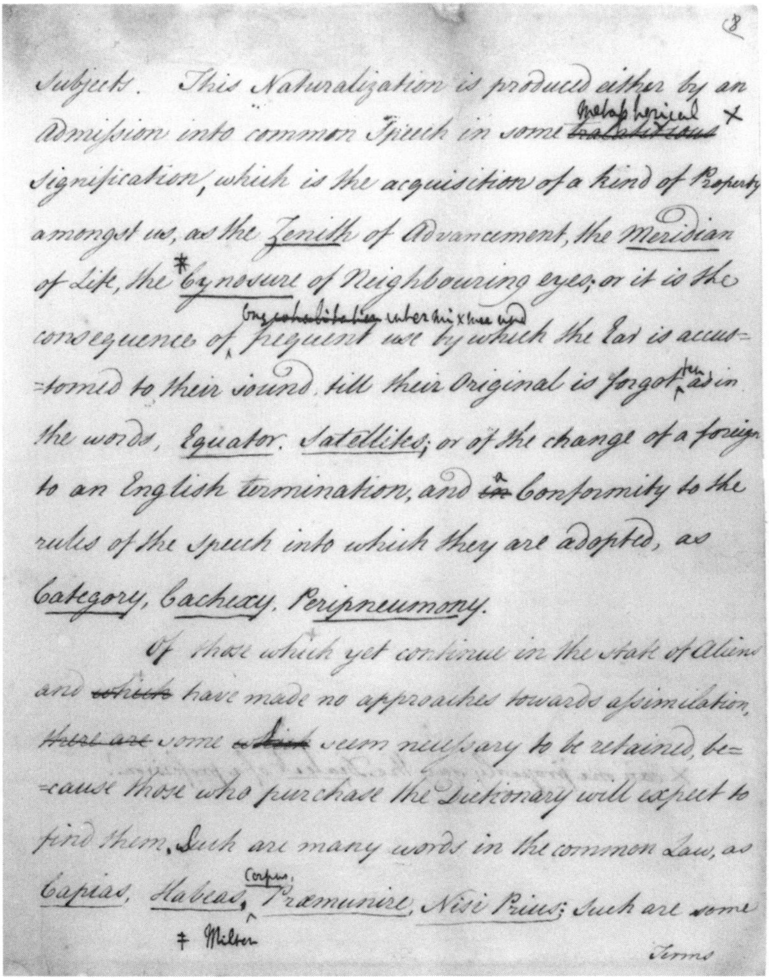

8

Subjects. This Naturalization is produced either by an Admission into common Speech in some ~~translatitious~~ metaphorical × signification, which is the acquisition of a kind of Property amongst us, as the Zenith of Advancement, the Meridian of Life, the *Cynosure of Neighbouring eyes; or it is the consequence of long ~~cohabitation~~ intermixture and frequent use by which the Ear is accus=tomed to their sound, till their Original is forgot, ten as in the words, Equator, Satellites; or of the change of a foreign to an English termination, and ~~in~~ a Conformity to the rules of the speech into which they are adopted, as Category, Cachexy, Peripneumony.

Of those which yet continue in the state of Aliens and ~~which~~ have made no approaches towards assimilation, ~~there are~~ some ~~which~~ seem necessary to be retained, be=cause those who purchase the Dictionary will expect to find them. Such are many words in the common Law, as Capias, Habeas, Corpus, Præmunire, Nisi Prius; Such are some

‡ Milton

Terms

Folio 8

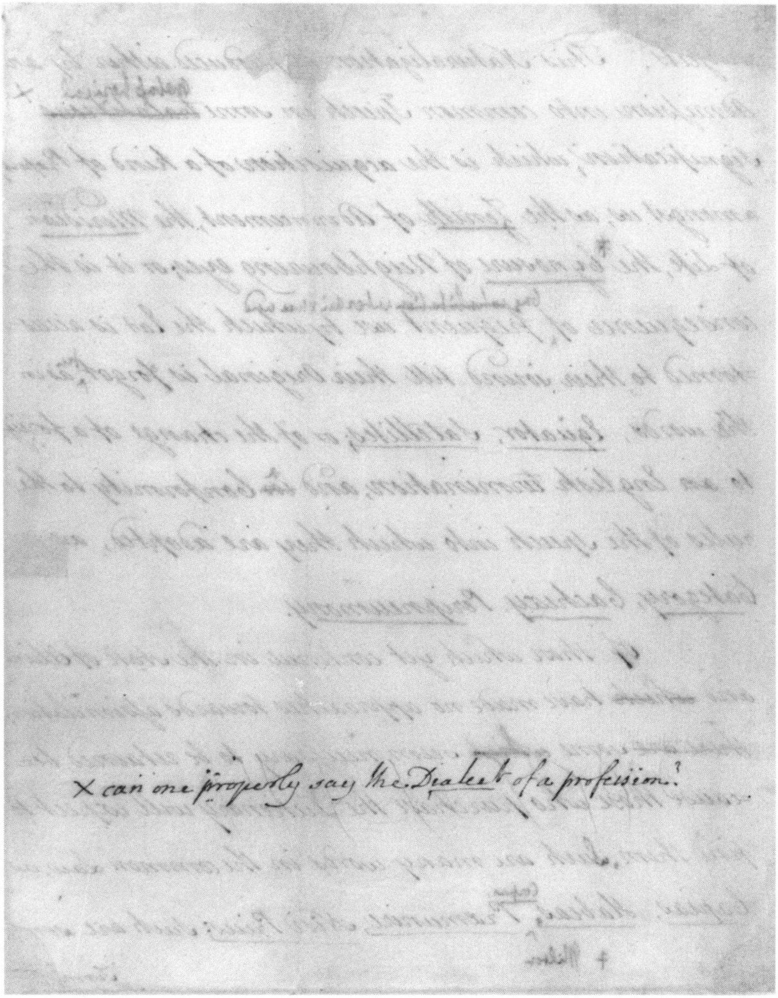
× can one properly say the Dialect of a profession?

Folio 8 verso

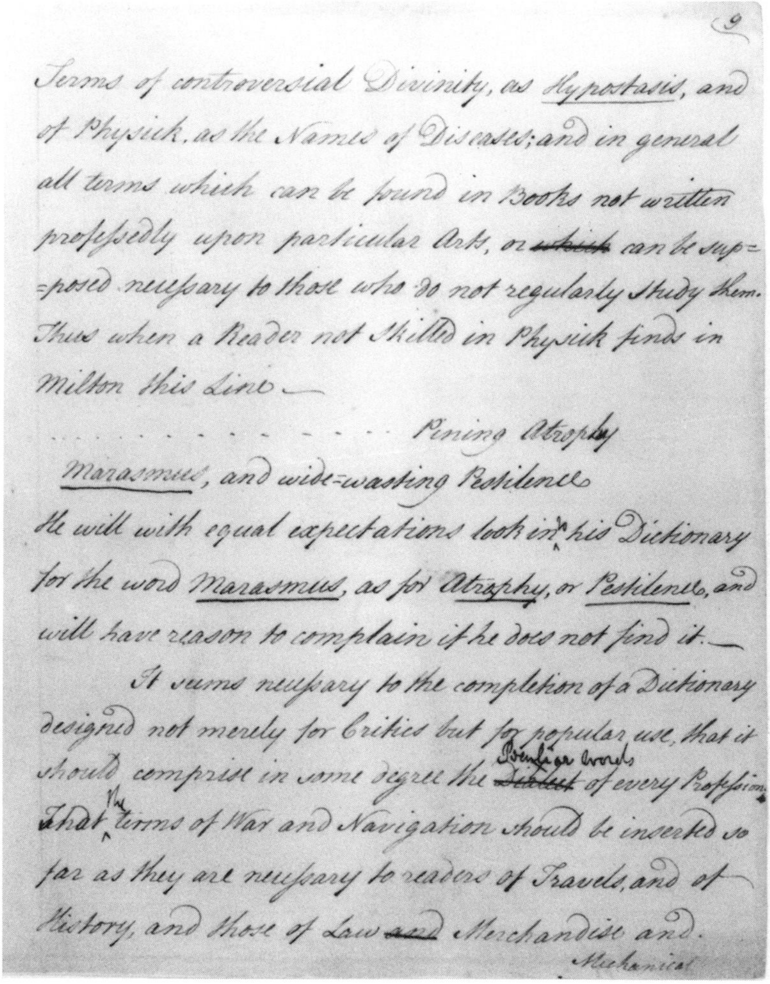

9

Terms of controversial Divinity, as <u>Hypostasis</u>, and
of Physick, as the Names of Diseases; and in general
all terms which can be found in Books not written
professedly upon particular Arts, or ~~which~~ can be sup=
=posed necessary to those who do not regularly study them.
Thus when a Reader not skilled in Physick finds in
Milton this Line —

. . . . Pining Atrophy
<u>Marasmus</u>, and wide-wasting Pestilence

He will with equal expectations look in his Dictionary
for the word <u>Marasmus</u>, as for <u>Atrophy</u>, or <u>Pestilence</u>, and
will have reason to complain if he does not find it.—

It seems necessary to the completion of a Dictionary
designed not merely for Criticks but for popular use, that it
should comprise in some degree the ~~Dialect~~ peculiar words of every Profession.
That the terms of War and Navigation should be inserted so
far as they are necessary to readers of Travels, and of
History, and those of Law ~~and~~ Merchandise and
Mechanical

Folio 9

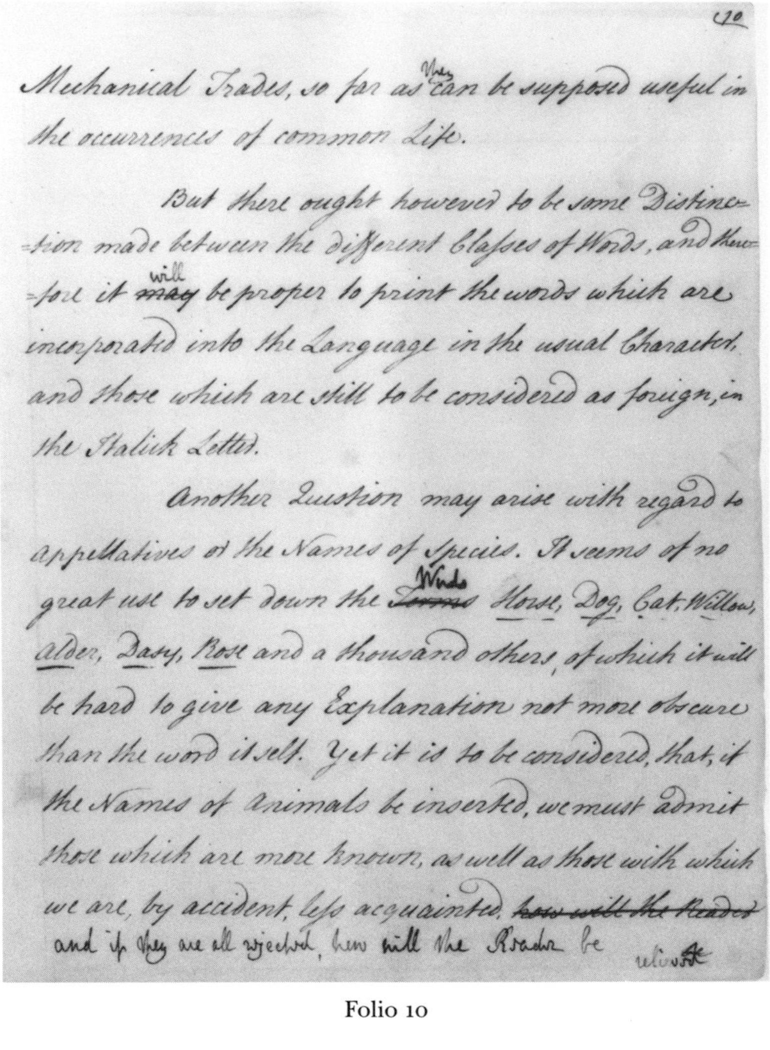

10

Mechanical Trades, so far as they can be supposed useful in the occurrences of common Life.

But there ought however to be some Distinction made between the different Classes of Words, and therefore it ~~may~~ will be proper to print the words which are incorporated into the Language in the usual Character, and those which are still to be considered as foreign, in the Italick Letter.

Another Question may arise with regard to appellatives or the Names of Species. It seems of no great use to set down the ~~Terms~~ Words Horse, Dog, Cat, Willow, alder, Dasy, Rose and a thousand others, of which it will be hard to give any Explanation not more obscure than the word itself. Yet it is to be considered, that, if the Names of Animals be inserted, we must admit those which are more known, as well as those with which we are, by accident, less acquainted. ~~how will the Reader~~ and if they are all rejected, how will the Reader be relieved

Folio 10

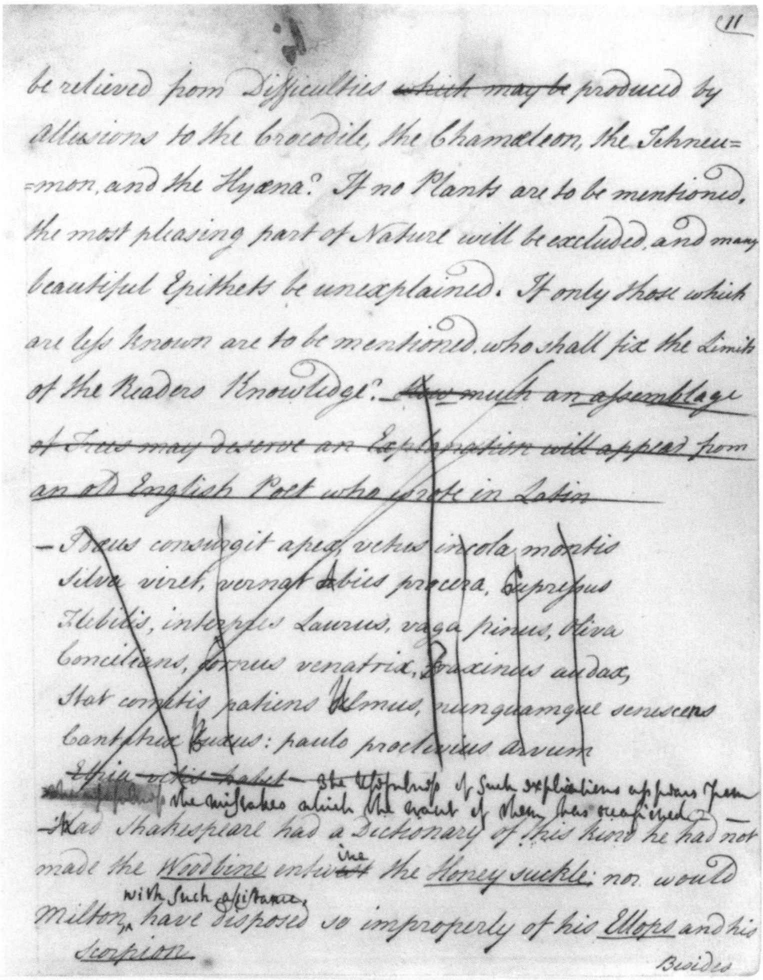

11

be relieved from Difficulties ~~which may be~~ produced by Allusions to the Crocodile, the Chamaeleon, the Ichneu=mon, and the Hyæna. If no Plants are to be mentioned, the most pleasing part of Nature will be excluded, and many beautiful Epithets be unexplained. If only those which are less known are to be mentioned, who shall fix the Limits of the Readers Knowledge? ~~How much an assemblage of Trees may deserve an Explanation will appear from an old English Poet who wrote in Latin~~

~~– Idaeus consurgit apex, vetus incola montis~~
~~Silva viret, vernat abies procera, cupressus~~
~~Flebilis, interpres Laurus, vaga pinus, oliva~~
~~Concilians, cornus venatrix, fraxinus audax,~~
~~Stat comitis patiens ulmus, nunquamque senescens~~
~~Cantatrix buxus: paulo proclivius arvum~~
~~Ethiu … habet~~ – The usefulness of such explications appears from the mistakes which the want of them has occasioned. – Had Shakespeare had a Dictionary of this kind he had not made the <u>Woodbine</u> entwine the <u>Honey suckle</u>; nor would Milton, with such assistance, have disposed so improperly of his <u>Ellops</u> and his <u>Scorpion</u>.

Besides

Folio 11

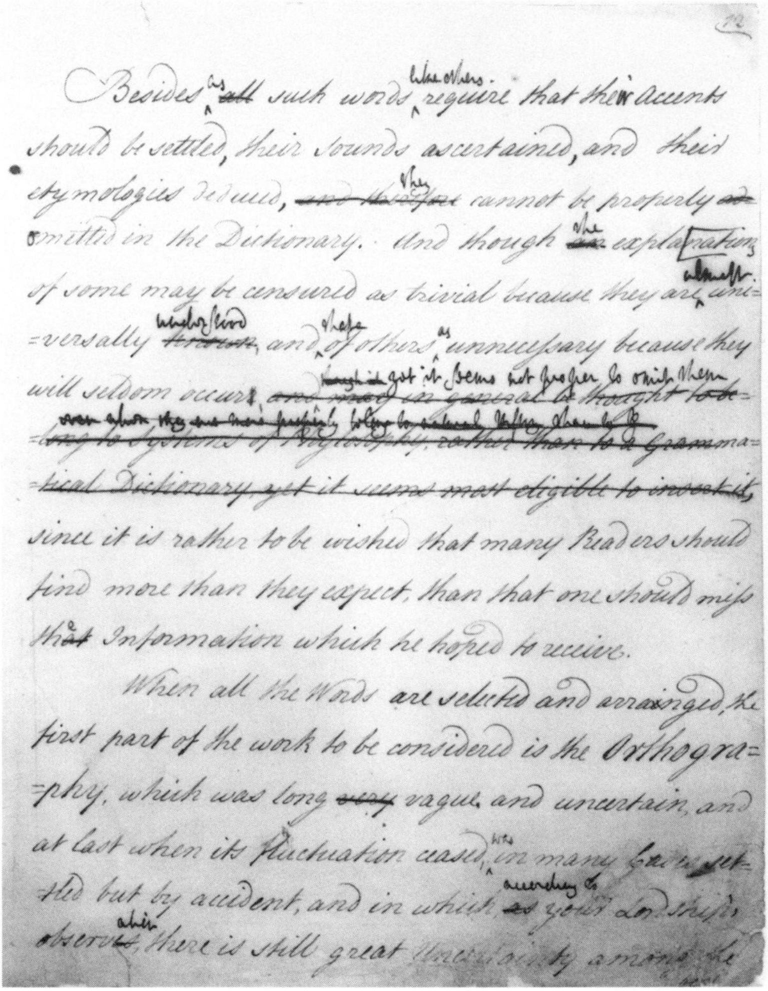

12

Besides, as ~~all~~ such words, like others, require that their accents should be settled, their sounds ascertained, and their etymologies deduced, ~~and therefore~~ they cannot be properly ~~so~~ omitted in the Dictionary. And though the ~~ex~~ explanations of some may be censured as trivial because they are almost universally ~~known~~ understood, and those of others as unnecessary because they will seldom occur, ~~though it~~ yet it seems not proper to omit them ~~and may in general be thought to be~~ ~~even when they are more properly belong to natural history than to~~ ~~long to Systems of Philosophy, rather than to a Grammatical Dictionary, yet it seems most eligible to insert it,~~ since it is rather to be wished that many Readers should find more than they expect, than that one should miss that Information which he hoped to receive.

When all the Words are selected and arranged, the first part of the work to be considered is the Orthography, which was long ~~very~~ vague and uncertain, and at last when its fluctuation ceased, was in many cases settled but by accident, and in which, according to ~~as~~ your Lordship observes, there is still great uncertainty among the

Folio 12

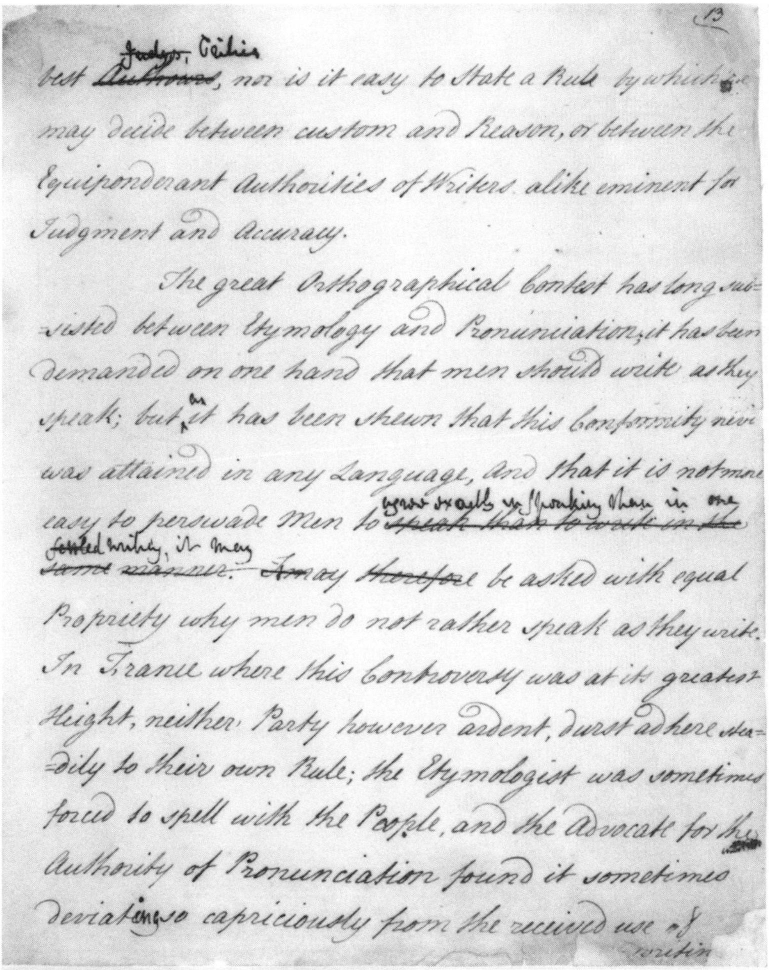
13

best ~~Authors~~ Judges, Critics, nor is it easy to State a Rule by which we may decide between custom and Reason, or between the Equiponderant Authorities of Writers alike eminent for Judgment and Accuracy.

The great Orthographical Contest has long sub=sisted between Etymology and Pronunciation; it has been demanded on one hand that men should write as they speak; but as it has been shewn that this conformity never was attained in any Language, and that it is not more easy to perswade Men to agree exactly in speaking than in one settled writing, it may ~~speak than to write in the same manner. It~~ may ~~therefore~~ be asked with equal Propriety why men do not rather speak as they write. In France where this Controversy was at its greatest Height, neither Party however ardent, durst adhere stea=dily to their own Rule; the Etymologist was sometimes forced to spell with the People, and the Advocate for the Authority of Pronunciation found it sometimes deviating so capriciously from the received use of writin

Folio 13

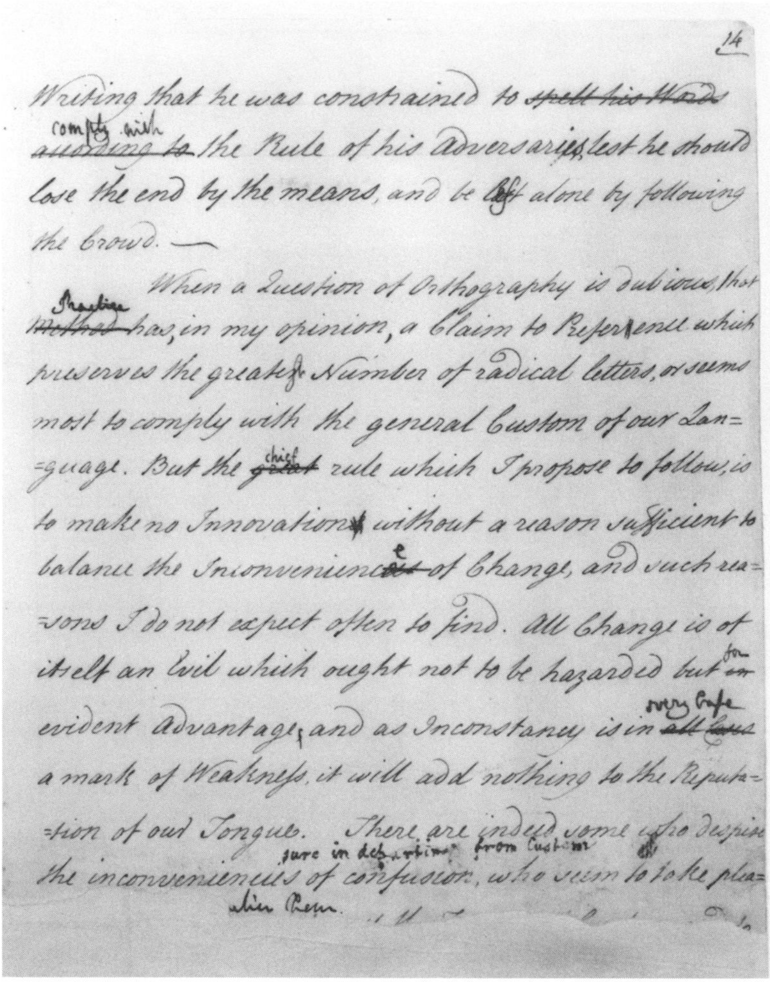
14

Writing that he was constrained to ~~spell his Words~~ ~~according to~~ comply with the Rule of his Adversaries, lest he should lose the end by the means, and be left alone by following the crowd. —

When a Question of Orthography is dubious, that ~~Method~~ Practice has, in my opinion, a Claim to Preference which preserves the greatest Number of radical letters, or seems most to comply with the general Custom of our Lan=guage. But the ~~great~~ chief rule which I propose to follow, is to make no Innovations without a reason sufficient to balance the Inconvenience of Change, and such rea=sons I do not expect often to find. All Change is of itself an Evil which ought not to be hazarded but ~~on~~ for evident Advantage; and as Inconstancy is in ~~all Cases~~ every Case a mark of Weakness, it will add nothing to the Reputa=tion of our Tongue. There are indeed some who despise the inconveniences of confusion, who seem to take plea=sure in departing from Custom

Folio 14

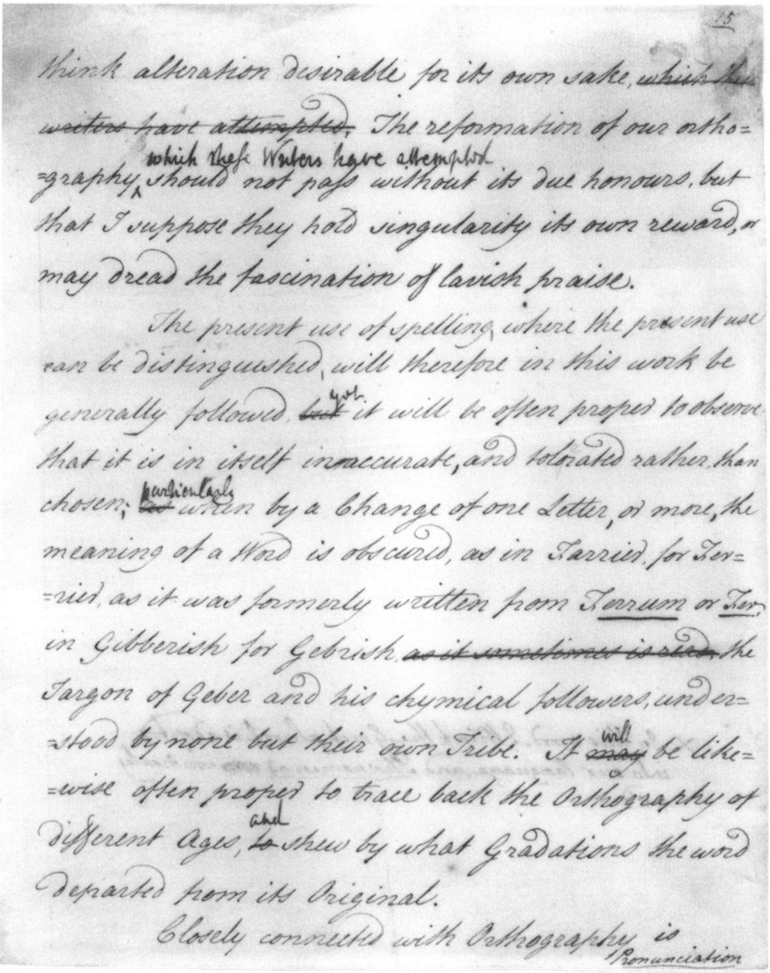

15

think alteration desirable for its own sake, ~~which these writers have attempted.~~ The reformation of our ortho=graphy, which these Writers have attempted should not pass without its due honours, but that I suppose they hold singularity its own reward, or may dread the fascination of lavish praise.

The present use of spelling, where the present use can be distinguished, will therefore in this work be generally followed, ~~but~~ yet it will be often proper to observe that it is in itself inaccurate, and tolerated rather than chosen; ~~as~~ particularly when by a Change of one Letter, or more, the meaning of a Word is obscured, as in Farrier, for Ferrier, as it was formerly written from Ferrum or Fer; in Gibberish for Gebrish, ~~as it sometimes is seen,~~ the Jargon of Geber and his chymical followers, under=stood by none but their own Tribe. It ~~may~~ will be like=wise often proper to trace back the Orthography of different Ages, ~~to~~ and shew by what Gradations the word departed from its Original.

Closely connected with Orthography is Pronunciation

Folio 15

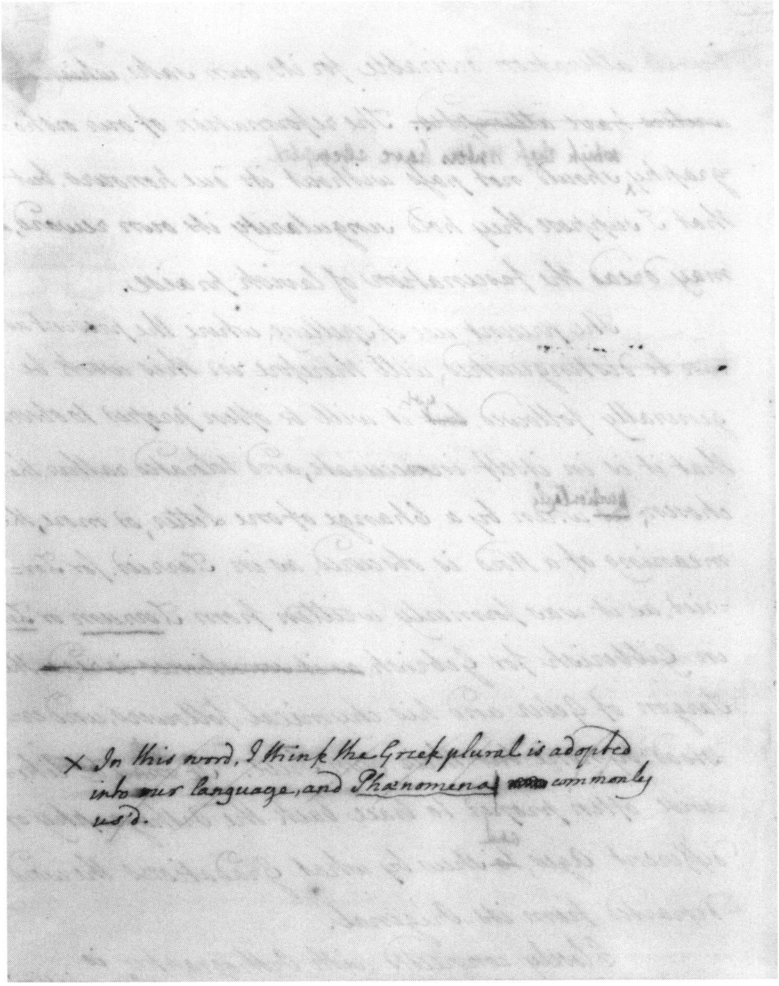
× In this word, I think the Greek plural is adopted into our language, and Phænomena commonly us'd.

Folio 15 verso

16

<u>Pronunciation</u>, the Stability of which is of great Im=
=portance to the duration of a Language, because the
first change will naturally begin by corruptions in
the living Speech. The want of certain rules for the
pronunciation of former ages has made us wholly ~~unable~~
ignorant of the metrical art ~~to discover the measures~~ of our ancient Poets, and since ~~of whose~~
those who study their sentiments ~~must~~ regret the loss of their numbers
~~Versification we are now wholly ignorant, and~~ it is
surely time to provide that the Harmony of the Mo=
=derns may be more permanent. ~~more permanent.~~

A new pronunciation will make almost
a new Speech, and therefore as one great end of this
undertaking is to fix the English Language, care
will ~~should~~ be taken to determine the accentuation of all
Polysyllables by proper Authorities, as it is one of those
capricious Phænomena which cannot be easily redu=
=ced to rules. Thus there is no antecedent reason
for difference of accent in the two words <u>dolorous</u>, and
<u>sonorous</u>, yet of the one Milton gives the sound in
this Line

He pass'd o'er many a Region <u>Dolorous</u>

and

Folio 16

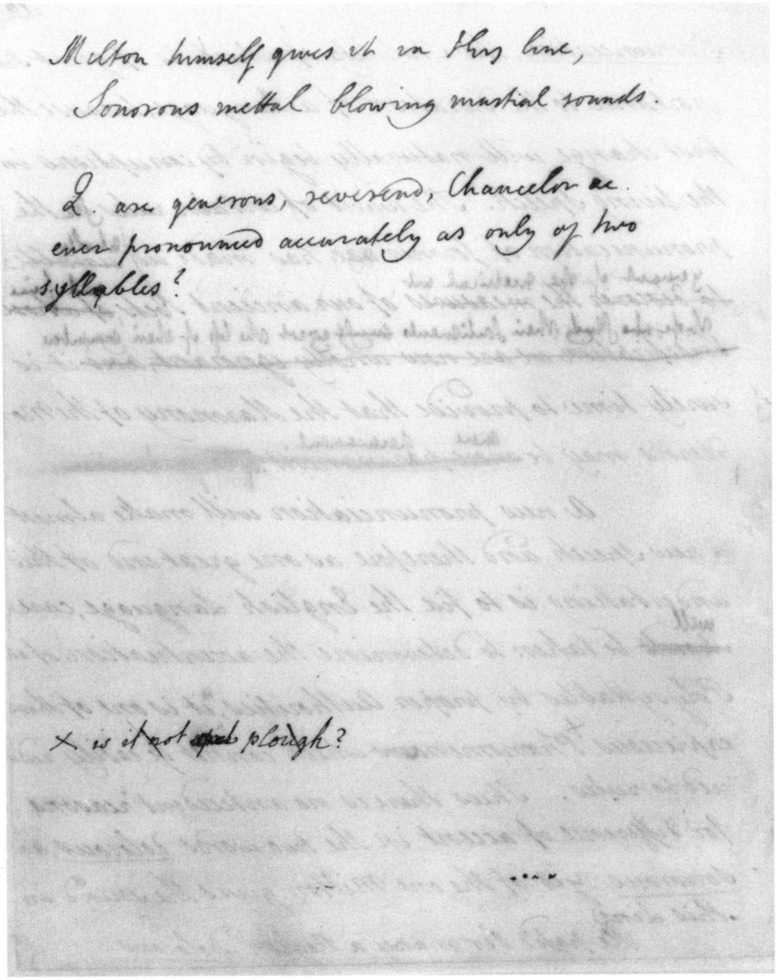

Milton himself gives it in this line,
Sonorous mettal blowing martial sounds.

Q. are generous, reverend, Chancelor &c.
ever pronounced accurately as only of two
syllables?

× is it not ~~[illegible]~~ plough?

Folio 16 verso

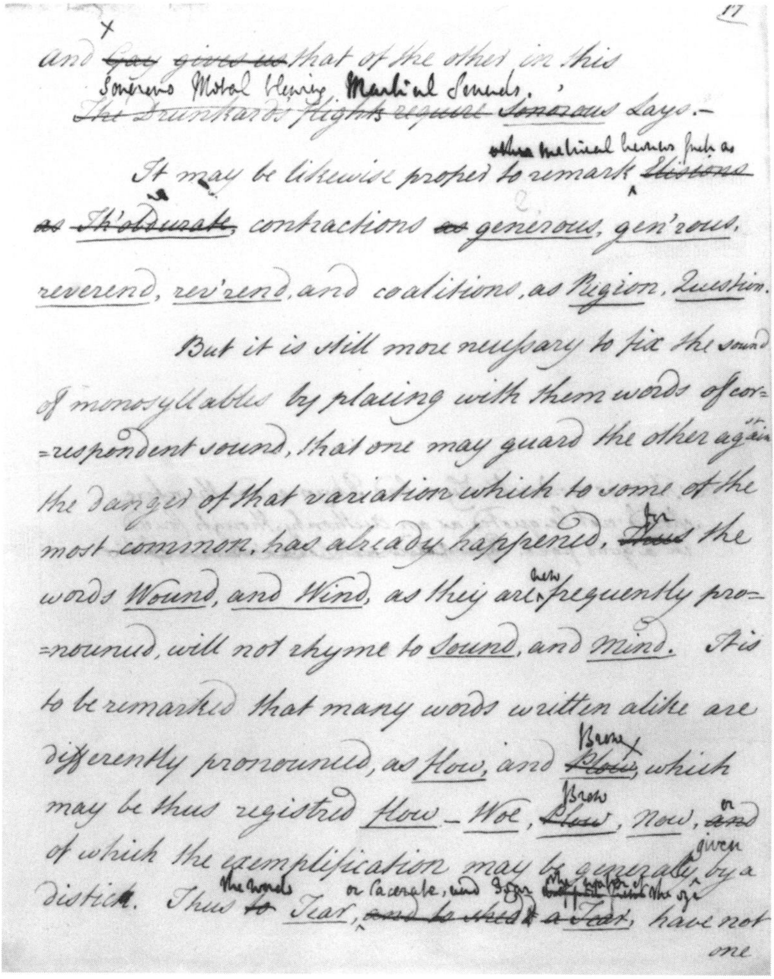
17

and ~~Gay~~ ~~gives us~~ that of the other in this
Sonorous Metal blowing Martial Sounds.
~~The Drunkards flights require~~ ~~Sonorous~~ Lays.–

It may be likewise proper to remark other metrical licenses such as ~~Elisions~~ ~~as~~ ~~Th'obdurate,~~ contractions ~~as~~ generous, gen'rous, reverend, rev'rend, and coalitions, as Region, Question.

But it is still more necessary to fix the sound of monosyllables by placing with them words of cor=respondent sound, that one may guard the other against the danger of that variation which to some of the most ~~common~~, has already happened, ~~Thus~~ for the words Wound, and Wind, as they are now frequently pro=nounced, will not rhyme to Sound, and Mind. It is to be remarked that many words written alike are differently pronounced, as Flow, and ~~Blow~~ Brow, which may be thus registred Flow – Woe, ~~Blow~~ Brow, Now, ~~and~~ or of which the exemplification may be generally given by a distich. Thus ~~to~~ the words Tear, or lacerate, and Tear ~~[illegible]~~ the eye ~~and to shed a Tear~~, have not one

Folio 17

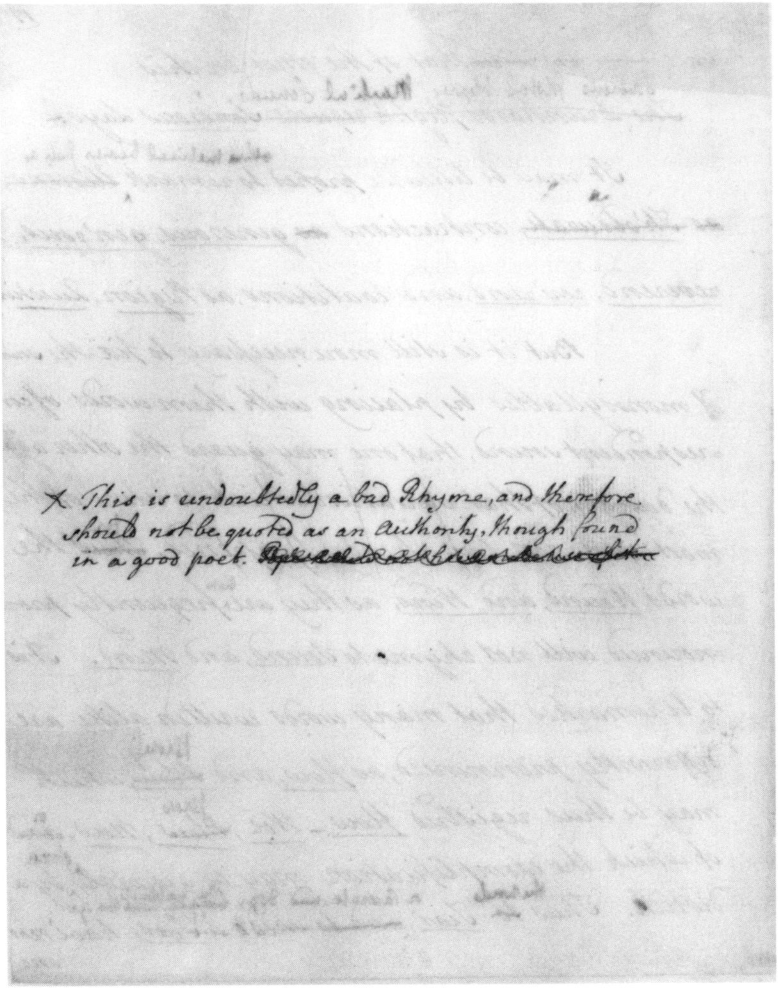

× This is undoubtedly a bad Rhyme, and therefore should not be quoted as an Authority, though found in a good poet.

Folio 17 verso

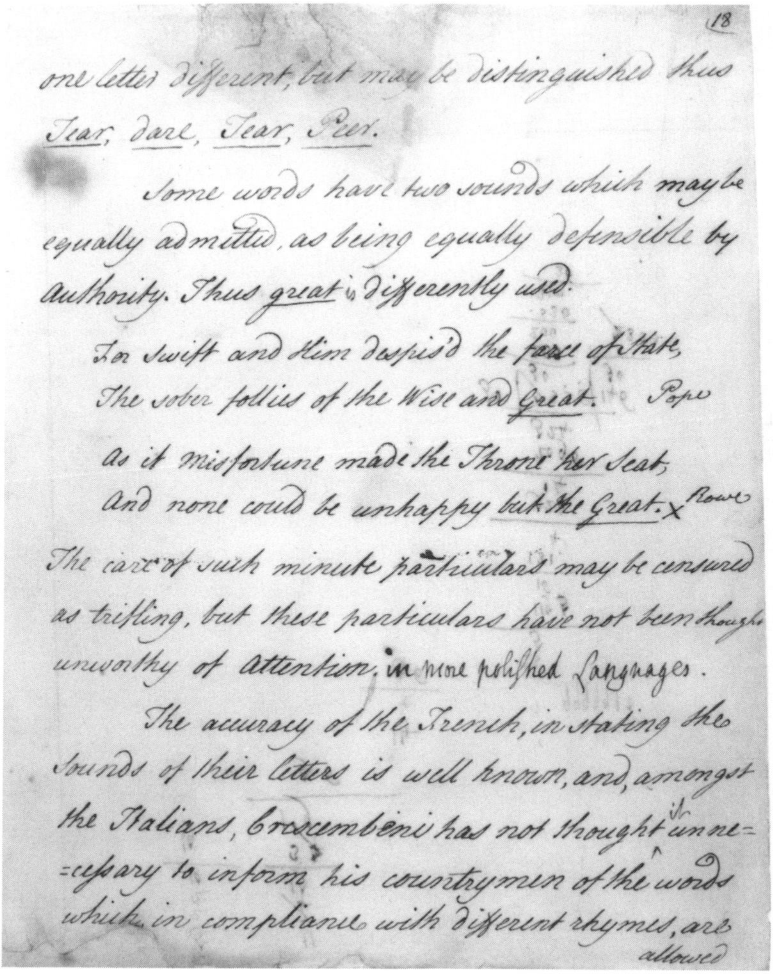
18

one letter different, but may be distinguished thus
Tear, dare, Tear, Peer.

Some words have two sounds which may be equally admitted, as being equally defensible by authority. Thus great is differently used.

For Swift and Him despis'd the farce of State,
The sober follies of the Wise and Great. Pope

As if misfortune made the Throne her Seat,
And none could be unhappy but the Great. × Rowe

The care of such minute particulars may be censured as trifling, but these particulars have not been thought unworthy of attention in more polished Languages.

The accuracy of the French, in stating the sounds of their letters is well known, and, amongst the Italians, Crescembeni has not thought it unne=
=cessary to inform his countrymen of the words which in compliance with different rhymes, are allowed

Folio 18

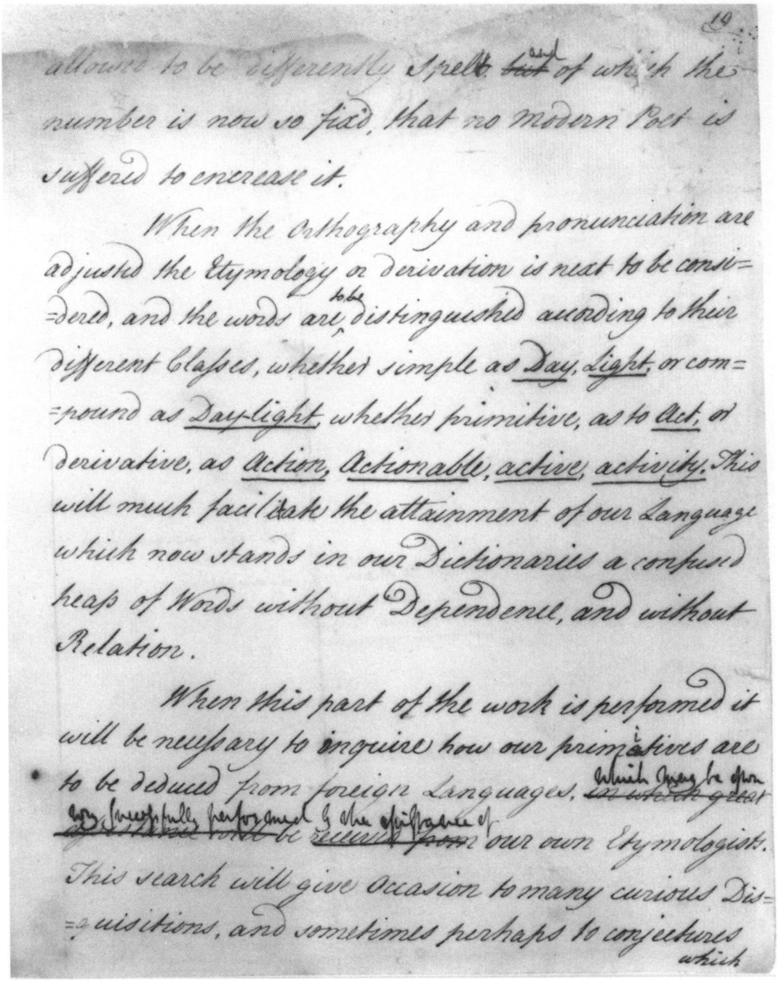

19

allowed to be differently spelt ~~but~~ and of which the number is now so fixed, that no Modern Poet is suffered to encrease it.

When the Orthography and pronunciation are adjusted the Etymology or derivation is next to be consi=dered, and the words are to be distinguished according to their different Classes, whether simple as Day, Light, or com=pound as Day-light, whether primitive, as to Act, or derivative, as Action, Actionable, active, activity. This will much facilitate the attainment of our Language which now stands in our Dictionaries a confused heap of Words without Dependence, and without Relation.

When this part of the work is performed it will be necessary to inquire how our primitives are to be deduced from foreign Languages, which may be often very successfully performed by the assistance of ~~in which great assistance will be received from~~ our own Etymologists. This search will give Occasion to many curious Dis=quisitions, and sometimes perhaps to conjectures which

Folio 19

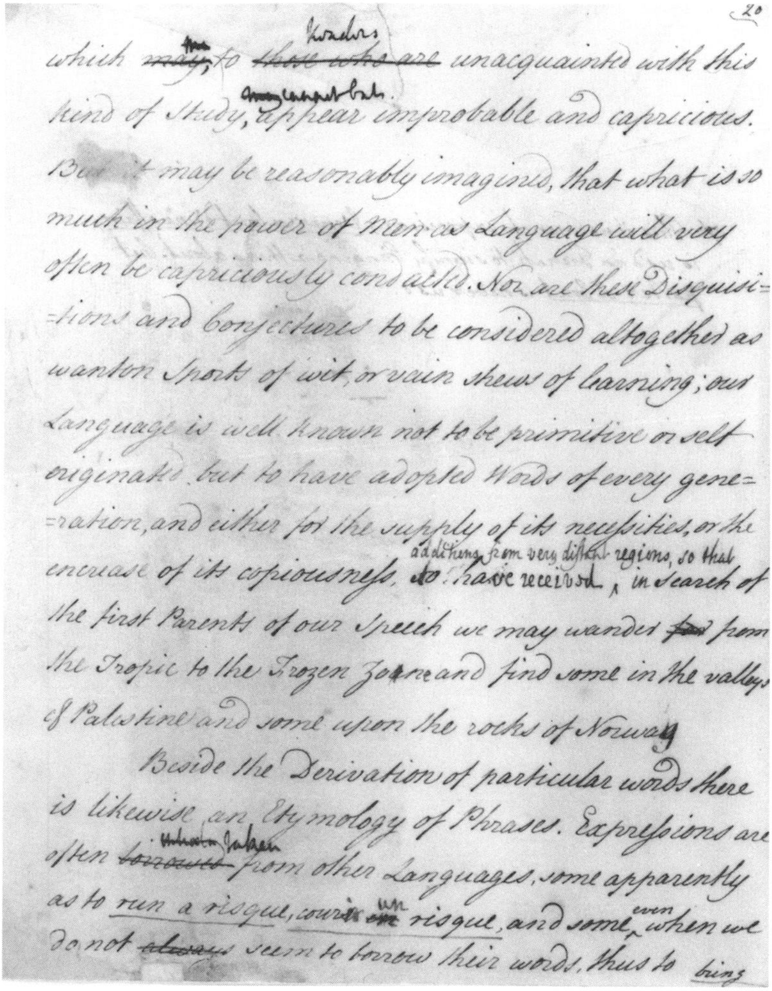

20

which ~~may,~~ to ~~those who are~~ wonders unacquainted with this kind of Study, appear improbable and capricious. But it may be reasonably imagined, that what is so much in the power of Men as Language will very often be capriciously conducted. Nor are these Disquisi=tions and Conjectures to be considered altogether as wanton Sports of wit, or vain shews of learning; our Language is well known not to be primitive or self originated but to have adopted Words of every gene=ration, and either for the supply of its necessities, or the encrease of its copiousness, ~~to~~ have received additions from very distant regions, so that in search of the first Parents of our Speech we may wander ~~far~~ from the Tropic to the Frozen Zone and find some in the valleys of Palestine and some upon the rocks of Norway.

Beside the Derivation of particular words there is likewise an Etymology of Phrases. Expressions are often ~~borrowed~~ taken from other Languages, some apparently as to run a risque, courir un risque, and some even when we do not ~~always~~ seem to borrow their words, thus to bring

Folio 20

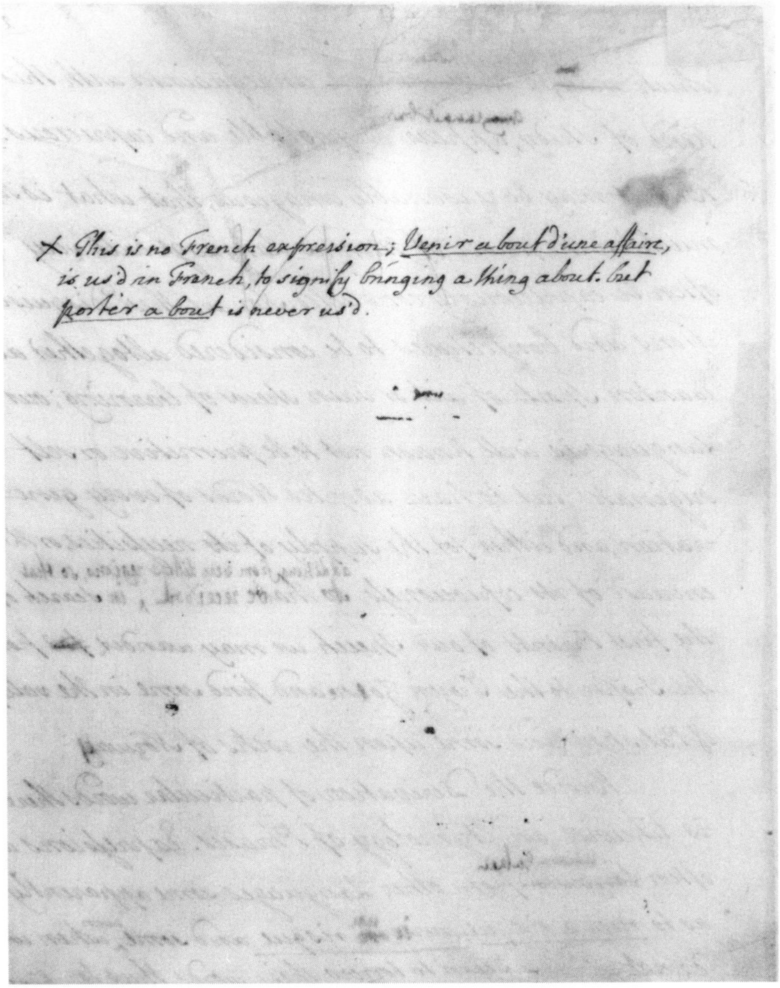
× This is no French expression; Venir a bout d'une affaire, is us'd in French, to signify bringing a thing about. but porter a bout is never us'd.

Folio 20 verso

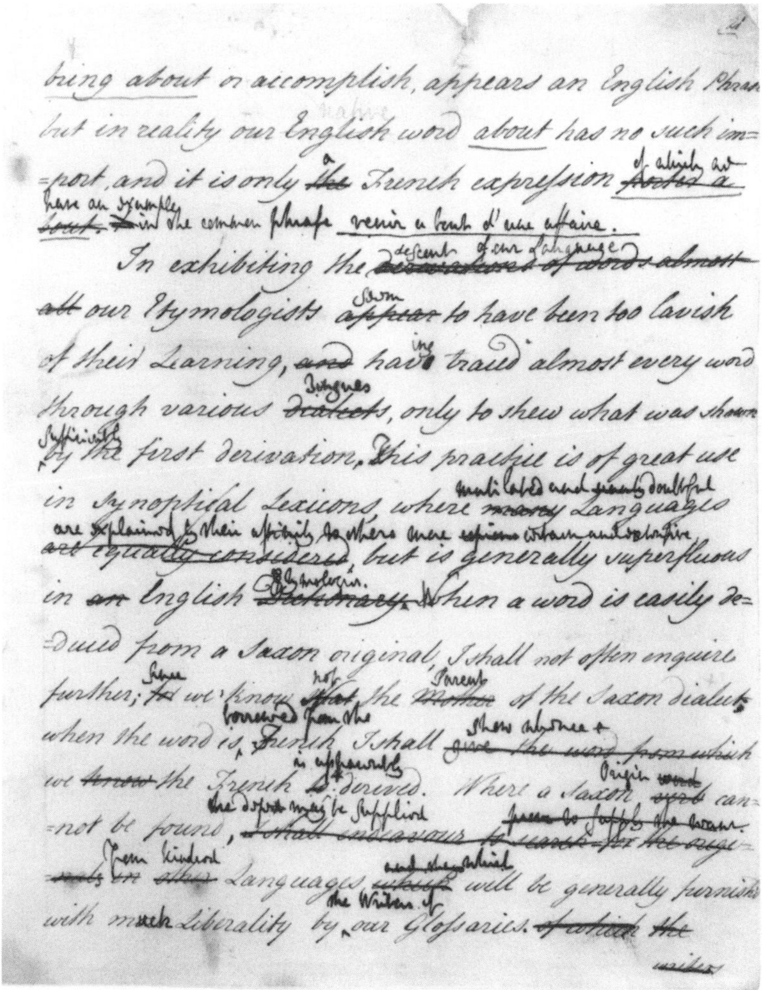

bring about or accomplish, appears an English Phrase but in reality our native English word about has no such im=port, and it is only a ~~the~~ French expression of which we have an example ~~borrowed a bout~~ in the common phrase venir a bout d'une affaire.

In exhibiting the descent of our Language ~~derivations of words almost all~~ our Etymologists seem ~~appear~~ to have been too lavish of their Learning, ~~and~~ having traced almost every word through various Tongues ~~dialects~~, only to shew what was shewn sufficiently by the first derivation. This practice is of great use in synoptical Lexicons, where mutilated and doubtful ~~many~~ Languages are explained by their affinity to others more certain and extensive ~~are equally considered~~, but is generally superfluous in ~~an~~ English Etymologies ~~Dictionary~~. When a word is easily de=duced from a Saxon original, I shall not often enquire further; since ~~for~~ we know not ~~what~~ the Parent ~~Mother~~ of the Saxon dialect; when the word is borrowed from the French I shall shew whence + ~~give the word from which~~ we ~~know~~ the French is apparently derived. Where a Saxon Origin ~~word~~ can=not be found, the defect may be supplied ~~I shall endeavour to search for the origi=nals in other~~ from kindred Languages and which ~~which~~ will be generally furnish'd with much Liberality by the Writers of our Glossaries. ~~of which the writers~~

Folio 21

22

~~Writers~~ Writers who deserve often the highest praise, both of Judgment and Industry, and may expect at least to be mentioned with honour by me ~~from me they claim particular gratitude~~ when ~~since~~ they have freed ~~me~~ from the greatest ~~a~~ part of a very labori=ous work ~~work~~ and on whom they ~~at worst~~ have imposed at worst ~~upon me~~ only the easy task ~~work~~ of rejecting Superfluities. —

By tracing ~~having~~ in this manner every word to its =original, and not admitting, but with great caution, those of which no original can be found, we shall secure our Language from being overrun with cant, from being crouded with low terms the spawn of Folly or affecta=tion, which arise from no just principles of Speech, and of which therefore no legitimate ~~the~~ derivation can ~~not be shown~~ be shewn.

When the Etymology is thus adjusted the Analogy of our Language is next to be considered; when we have discovered whence our words are derived, we are to exa=mine by what rules they are governed, and how they are inflected through ~~by~~ their various terminations. The termi=nations of our Language are few, but those few have hitherto

Folio 22

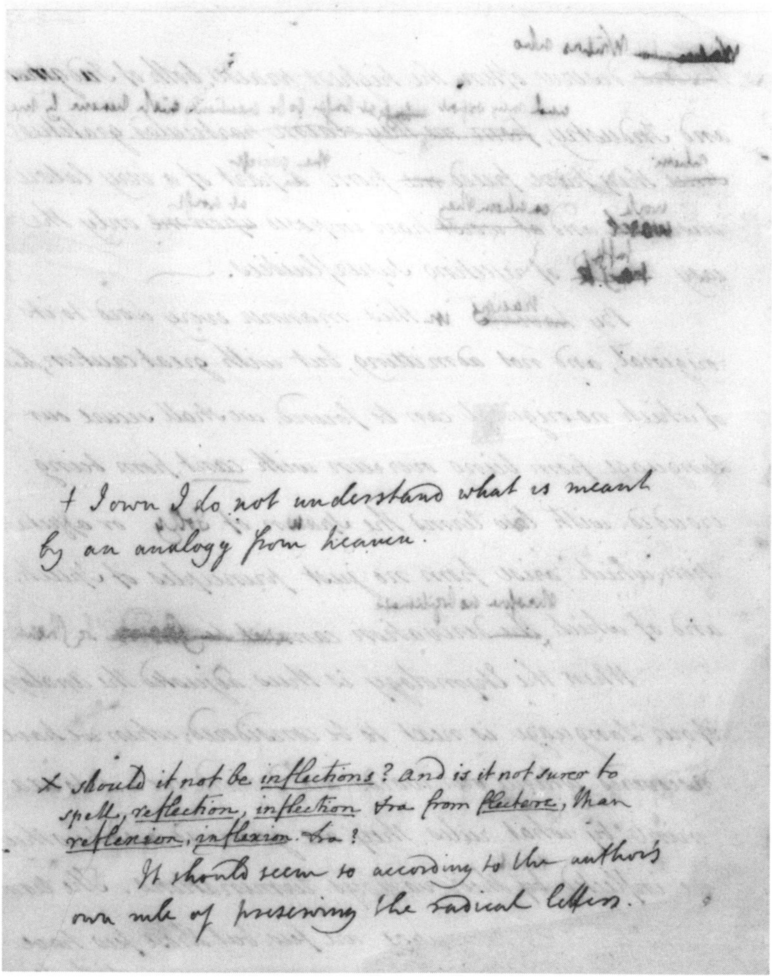

† I own I do not understand what is meant by an analogy from heaven.

× should it not be inflections? and is it not surer to spell, reflection, inflection &c from flectere, than reflexion, inflexion &c?

It should seem so according to the author's own rule of preserving the radical letters.

Folio 22 verso

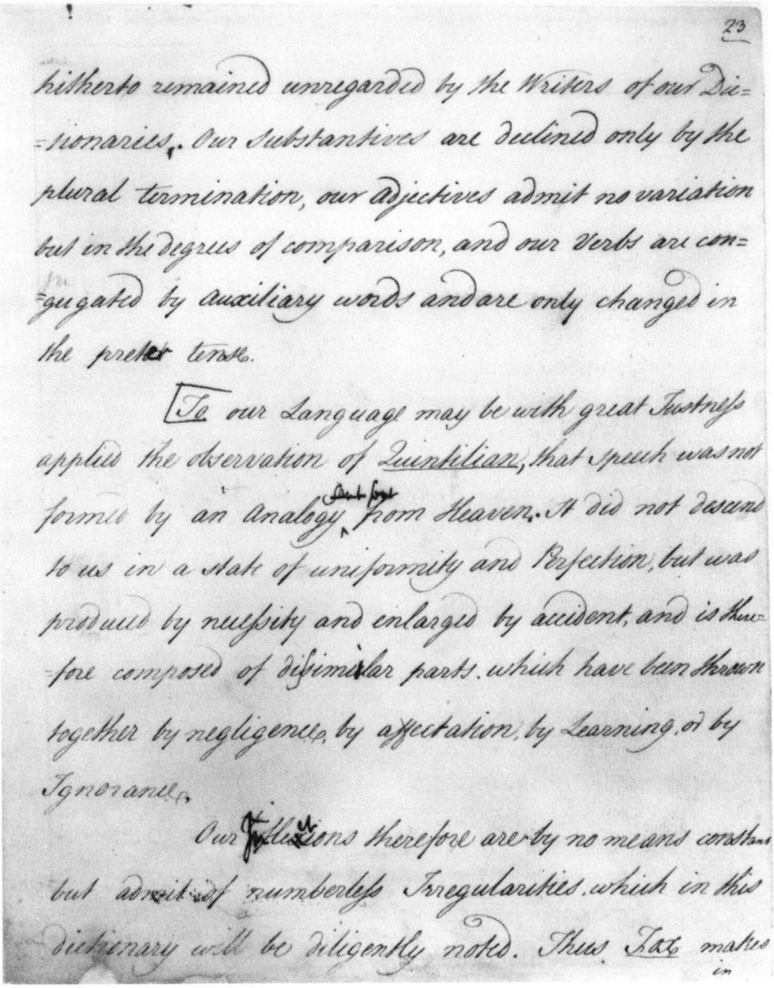

23

hitherto remained unregarded by the Writers of our Dic=
=tionaries. Our Substantives are declined only by the
plural termination, our Adjectives admit no variation
but in the degrees of comparison, and our Verbs are con=
=jugated by auxiliary words and are only changed in
the preter tense.

To our Language may be with great Justness
applied the observation of Quintilian, that speech was not
formed by an Analogy sent from Heaven. It did not descend
to us in a state of uniformity and Perfection, but was
produced by necessity and enlarged by accident, and is there=
=fore composed of dissimilar parts. which have been thrown
together by negligence, by affectation, by Learning, or by
Ignorance.

Our inflections therefore are by no means constant
but admit of numberless Irregularities. which in this
dictionary will be diligently noted. Thus Fox makes
in

Folio 23

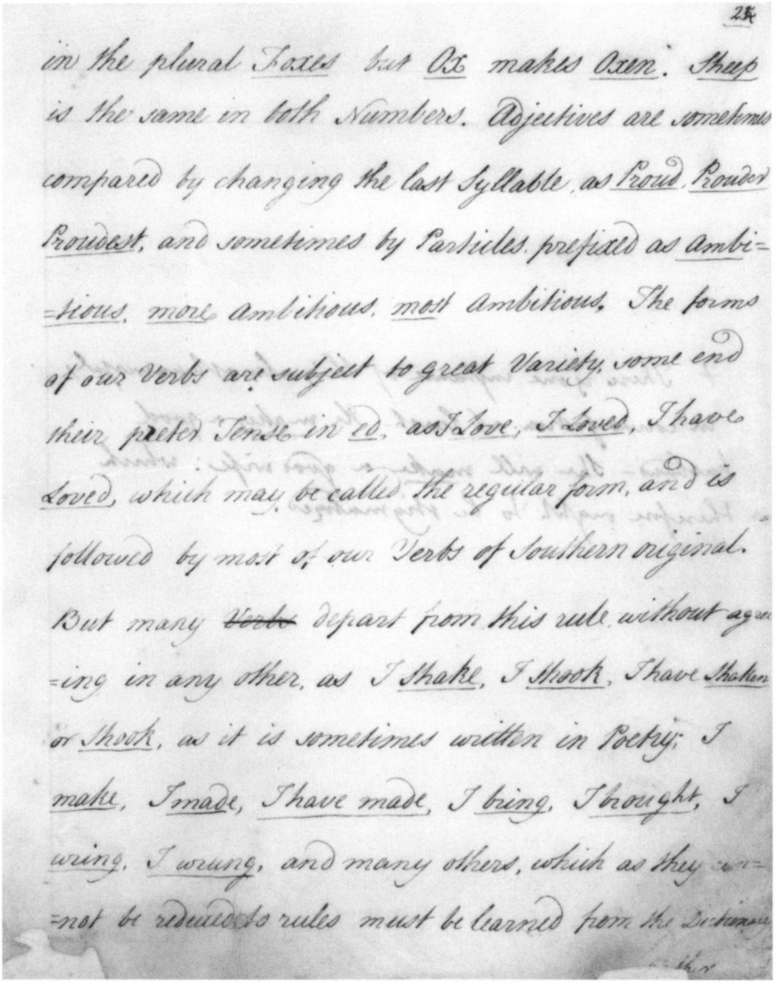
25

in the plural Foxes but Ox makes Oxen. Sheep
is the same in both Numbers. Adjectives are sometimes
compared by changing the last Syllable, as Proud, Prouder
Proudest, and sometimes by Particles prefixed as Ambi-
=tious, more ambitious, most ambitious. The forms
of our Verbs are subject to great Variety, some end
their preter Tense in ed, as I Love, I Loved, I have
Loved, which may be called the regular form, and is
followed by most of our Verbs of Southern original.
But many ~~Verbs~~ depart from this rule without agree-
=ing in any other, as I Shake, I Shook, I have Shaken
or Shook, as it is sometimes written in Poetry; I
make, I made, I have made, I bring, I brought, I
wring, I wrung, and many others, which as they can-
=not be reduced to rules must be learned from the Dictionary

Folio 24

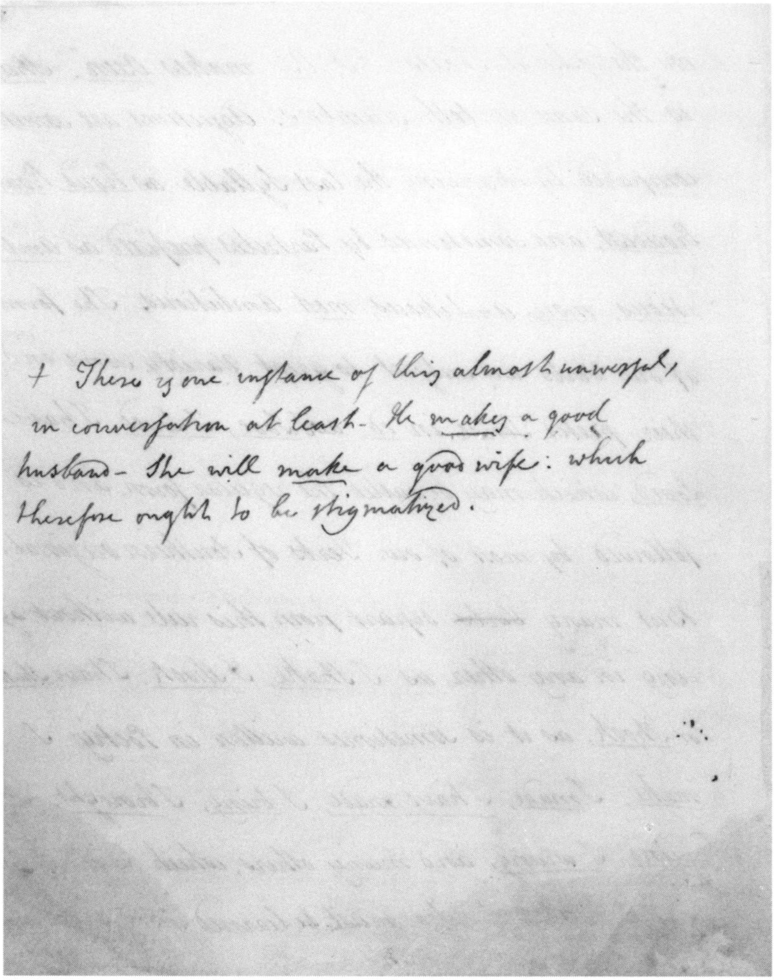
+ There is one instance of this almost universal, in conversation at least – He makes a good husband – She will make a good wife: which therefore ought to be stigmatized.

Folio 24 verso

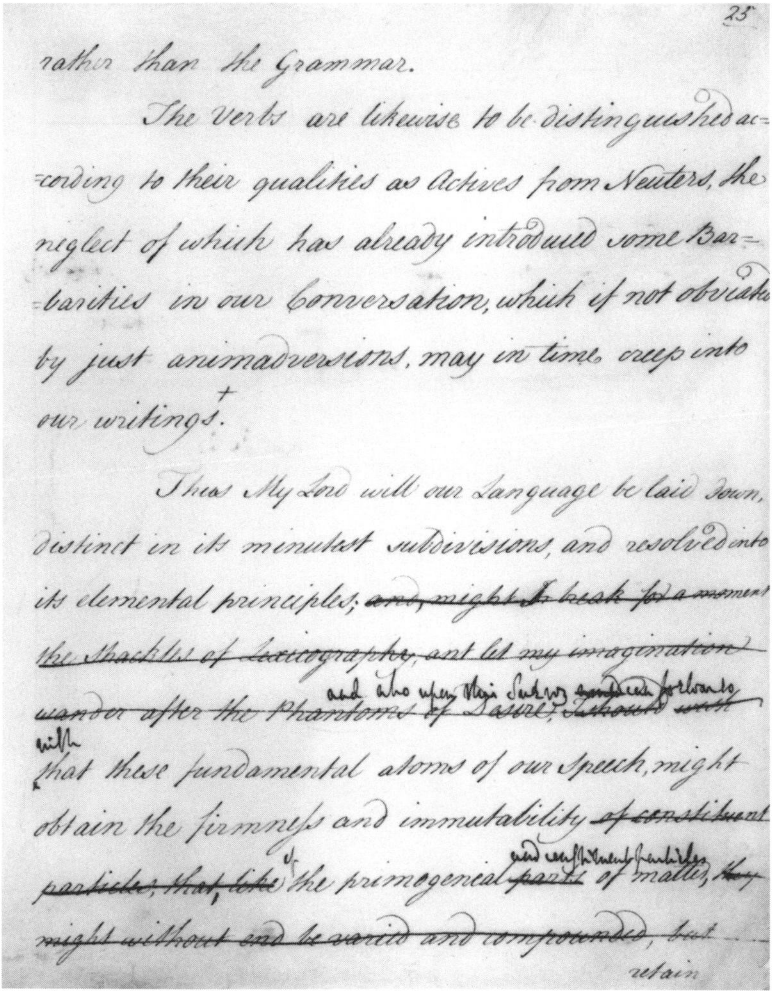

25

rather than the Grammar.

The Verbs are likewise to be distinguished according to their qualities as Actives from Neuters, the neglect of which has already introduced some Barbarities in our Conversation, which if not obviated by just animadversions, may in time creep into our writings.+

Thus My Lord will our Language be laid down, distinct in its minutest subdivisions, and resolved into its elemental principles; ~~and, might I break for a moment the shackles of Lexicography, and let my imagination wander after the Phantoms of Desire, I should wish~~ and who upon this survey can forbear to wish that these fundamental atoms of our Speech, might obtain the firmness and immutability ~~of constituent particles; that, like~~ of the primogenial ~~parts~~ and constituent particles of matter, ~~they might without end be varied and compounded, but~~

retain

Folio 25

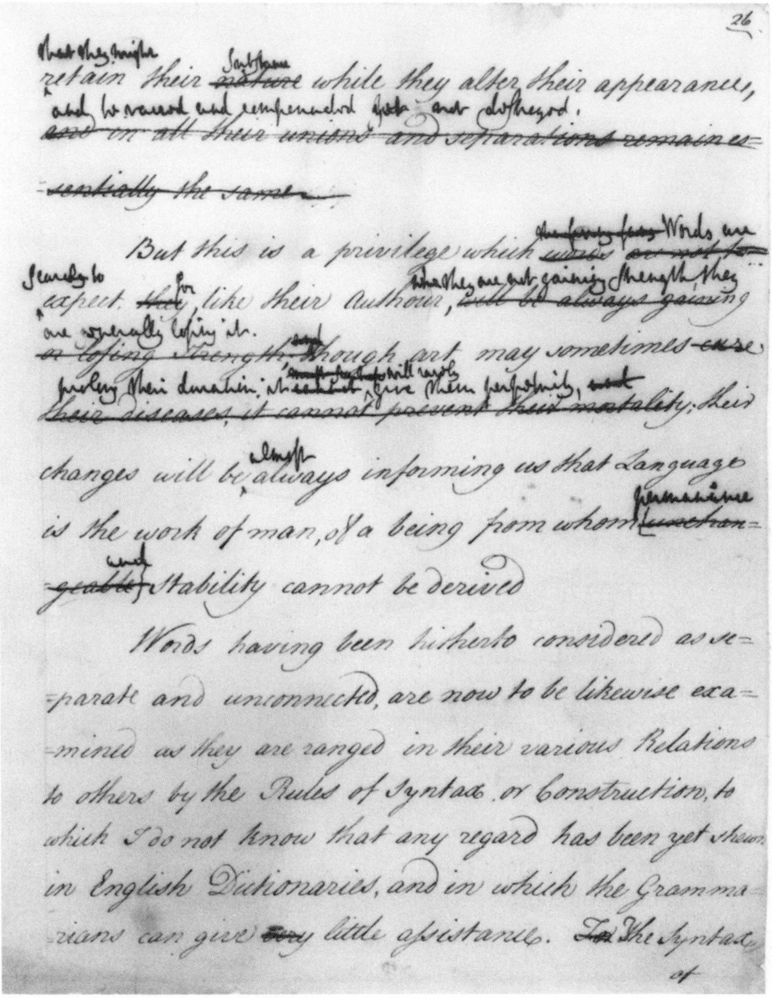

26

that they might retain their ~~nature~~ substance while they alter their appearance, and be varied and compounded yet not destroyed. ~~and in all their unions and separations remain essentially the same.~~

But this is a privilege which ~~the former few~~ Words are ~~words are not to~~ scarcely to expect: ~~they~~ for like their Authour, whether they are not gaining strength, they ~~will be always gaining~~ are generally losing it. ~~or losing strength,~~ and though art may sometimes ~~ease~~ prolong their duration, it ~~cannot~~ will rarely give them perpetuity, ~~and their diseases, it cannot prevent their mortality~~; their changes will be almost ~~always~~ informing us that Language is the work of man, of a being from whom permanence ~~unchangeable~~ and Stability cannot be derived

Words having been hitherto considered as separate and unconnected, are now to be likewise examined as they are ranged in their various Relations to others by the Rules of Syntax or Construction, to which I do not know that any regard has been yet shewn in English Dictionaries, and in which the Grammarians can give ~~very~~ little assistance. ~~To~~ The Syntax of

Folio 26

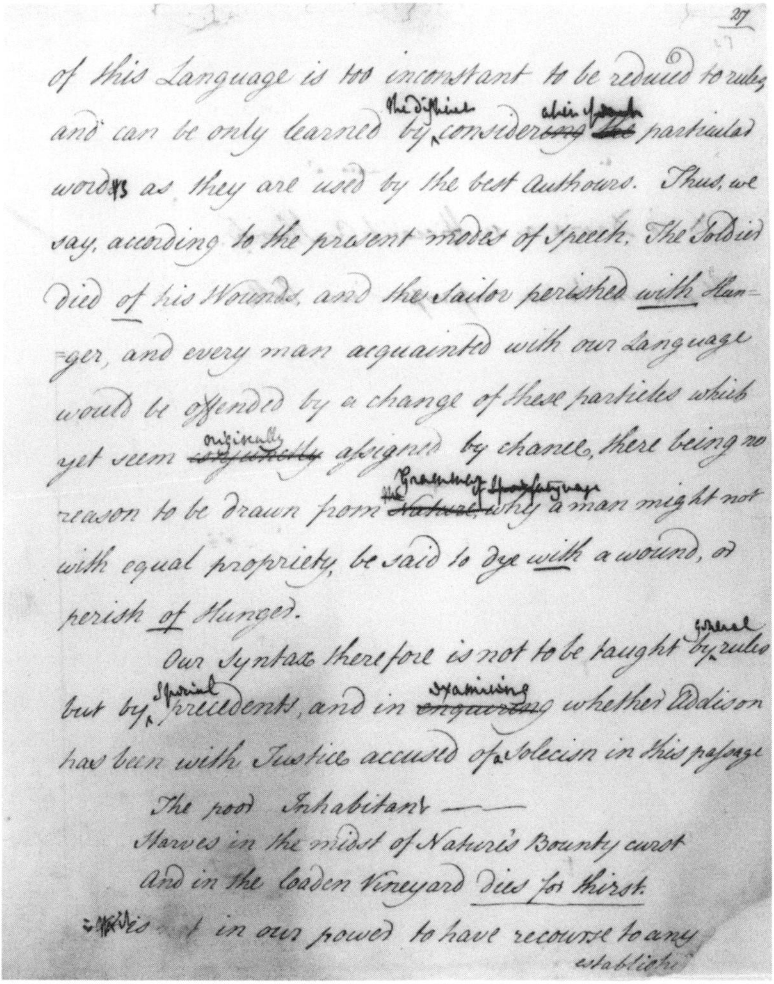
27

of this Language is too inconstant to be reduced to rules,
and can be only learned by the different considerations the particular
words as they are used by the best Authours. Thus, we
say, according to the present modes of Speech, The Soldier
died of his Wounds, and the Sailor perished with Hun-
-ger, and every man acquainted with our Language
would be offended by a change of these particles which
yet seem originally assigned by chance, there being no
reason to be drawn from Grammar of Language why a man might not
with equal propriety, be said to dye with a wound, or
perish of Hunger.

Our Syntax therefore is not to be taught by general rules
but by special precedents, and in examining whether Addison
has been with Justice accused of a Solecism in this passage

The poor Inhabitant ——
Starves in the midst of Nature's Bounty curst
And in the loaden Vineyard dies for thirst.

[illegible] in our power to have recourse to any
establishi

Folio 27

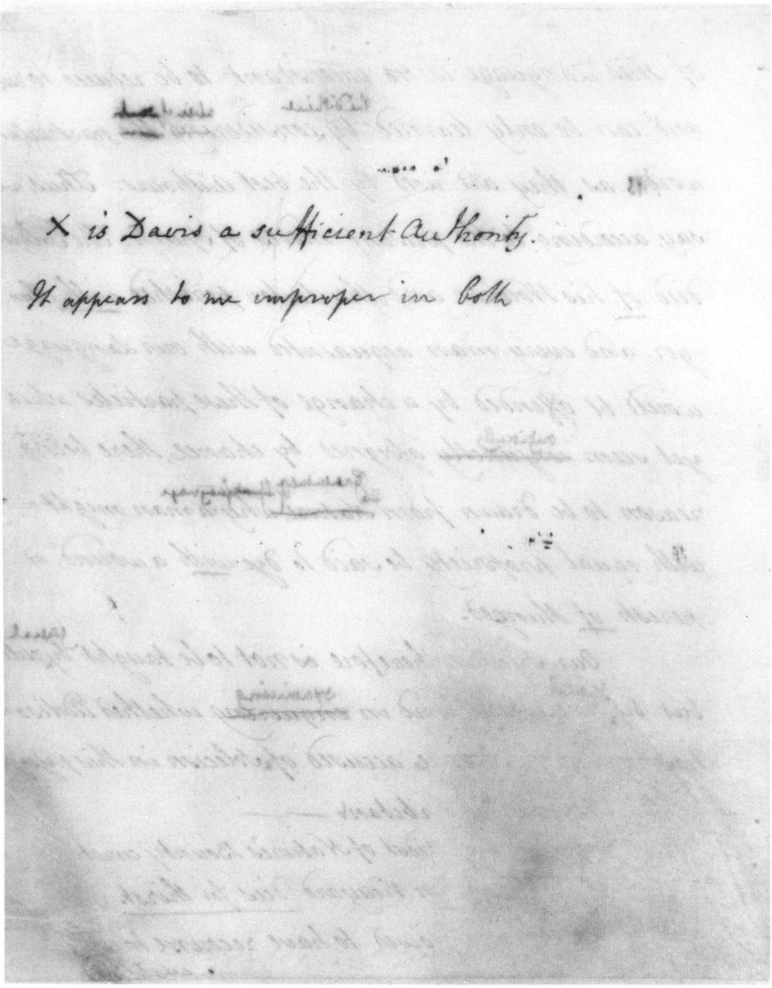
X is Davis a sufficient Authority.

It appears to me improper in both

Folio 27 verso

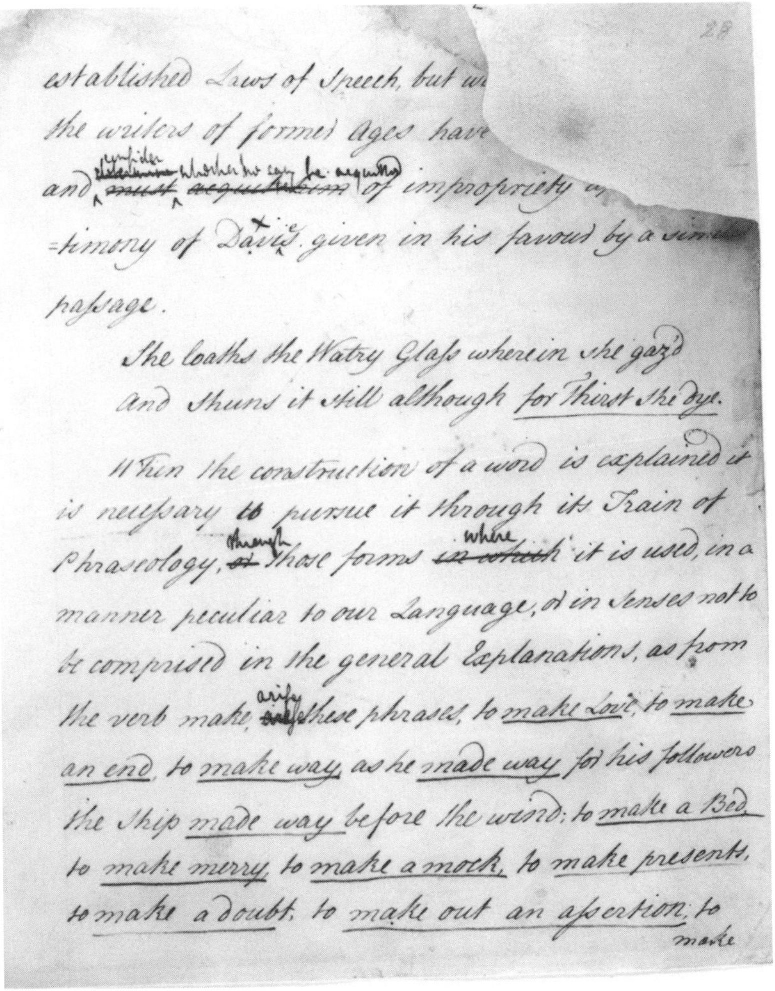

28

established Laws of Speech, but w[...]
the writers of former Ages have [...]
and ~~determine~~ consider ~~must~~ whether he can be acquitted ~~acquit him~~ of impropriety [...]
=timony of Davies given in his favour by a simi[...]
passage.

She loaths the Watry Glass wherein she gaz'd
And shuns it still although for Thirst she dye.

When the construction of a word is explained it
is necessary ~~to~~ pursue it through its Train of
Phraseology, ~~at~~ through those forms ~~in which~~ where it is used, in a
manner peculiar to our Language, or in senses not to
be comprised in the general Explanations, as from
the verb make, ~~arise~~ arise these phrases, to make Love, to make
an end, to make way, as he made way for his followers
the Ship made way before the wind: to make a Bed,
to make merry, to make a mock, to make presents,
to make a doubt, to make out an assertion; to
make

Folio 28

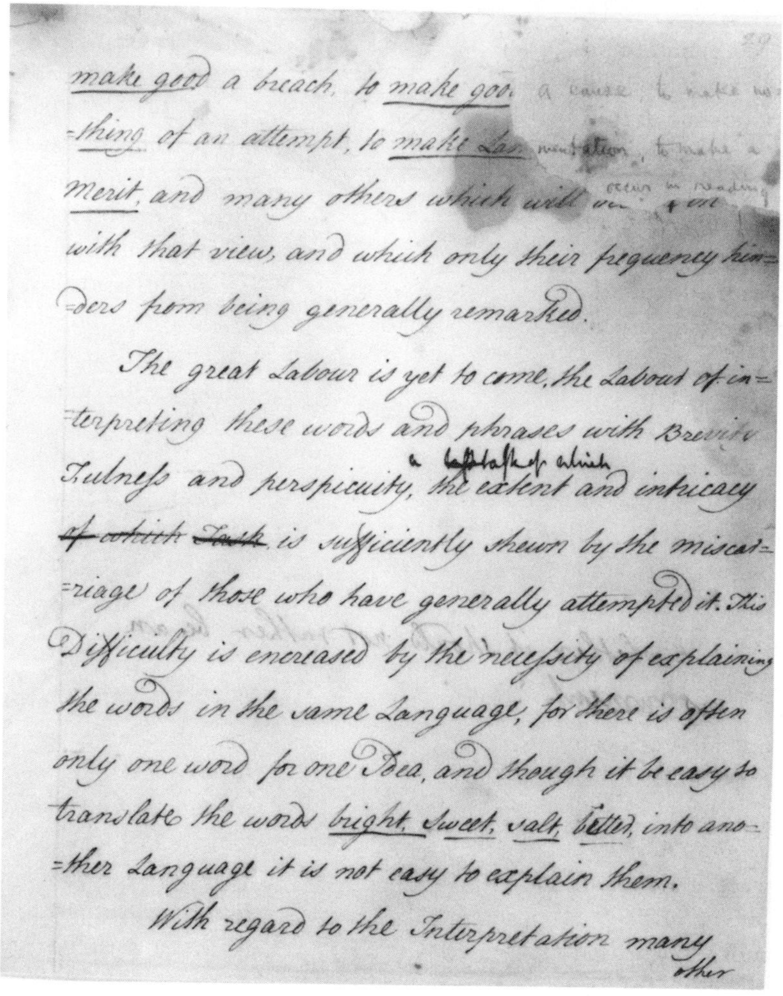
make good a breach, to make good a cause, to make no-
-thing of an attempt, to make Lamentation, to make a
Merit, and many others which will occur in reading
with that view, and which only their frequency hin-
-ders from being generally remarked.

The great Labour is yet to come, the Labour of in-
-terpreting these words and phrases with Brevity
Fulness and perspicuity, a task of which the extent and intricacy
~~of which Task~~ is sufficiently shewn by the miscar-
-riage of those who have generally attempted it. This
Difficulty is encreased by the necessity of explaining
the words in the same Language, for there is often
only one word for one Idea, and though it be easy to
translate the words bright, sweet, salt, bitter, into ano-
-ther Language it is not easy to explain them.

With regard to the Interpretation many
other

Folio 29

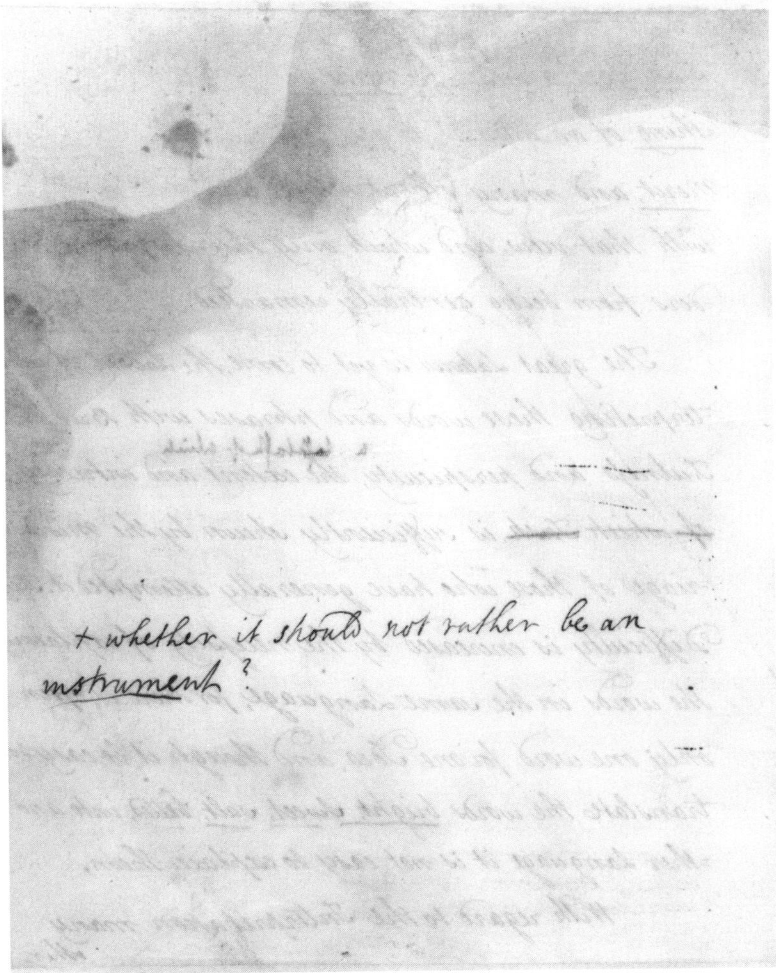

Folio 29 verso

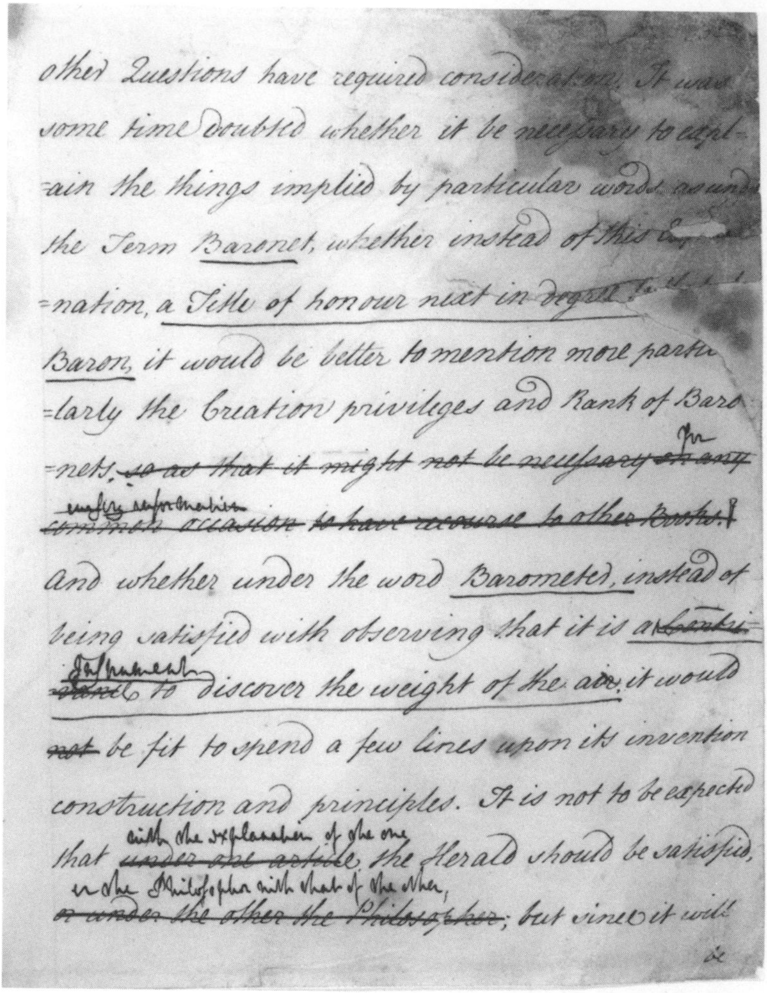

other Questions have required consideration. It was
some time doubted whether it be necessary to expl-
=ain the things implied by particular words as under
the Term Baronet, whether instead of this Expl-
=nation, a Title of honour next in ~~degree~~ to that of
Baron, it would be better to mention more partic-
=larly the Creation privileges and Rank of Baro-
=nets; ~~so as that it might not be necessary on any~~ for
~~common occasion~~ ~~to have recourse to other Books~~: enquiry information
And whether under the word Barometer, instead of
being satisfied with observing that it is a ~~Machi-~~
~~=ne~~ Instrument to discover the weight of the air, it would
~~not~~ be fit to spend a few lines upon its invention
construction and principles. It is not to be expected
that ~~under one article~~ with the explanation of the one the Herald should be satisfied,
~~or under the other the Philosopher~~ or the Philosopher with that of the other; but since it will
&c

Folio 30

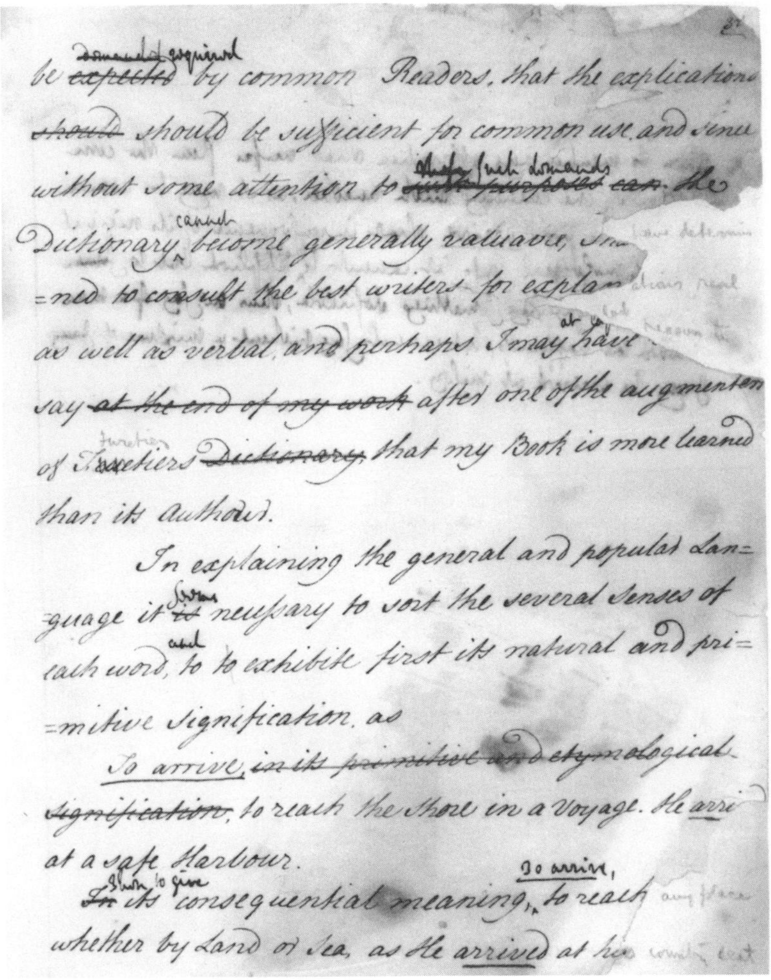

be ~~expected~~ ~~demanded~~ required by common Readers, that the explications
~~should~~ should be sufficient for common use, and since
without some attention to ~~such purposes can~~ ~~these~~ such demands the
Dictionary cannot become generally valuable, I have determi=
=ned to consult the best writers for explanations real
as well as verbal, and perhaps I may at last have reason to
say ~~at the end of my work~~ after one of the augmenters
of Furetiers ~~Dictionary~~, that my Book is more learned
than its Author.

In explaining the general and popular Lan=
=guage it ~~is~~ seems necessary to sort the several Senses of
each word, and to exhibit first its natural and pri=
=mitive signification, as

To arrive, ~~in its primitive and etymological signification~~, to reach the Shore in a Voyage. He arrived at a safe Harbour.

~~In~~ Then to give its consequential meaning, To arrive, to reach any place whether by Land or Sea, as He arrived at his country seat

Folio 31

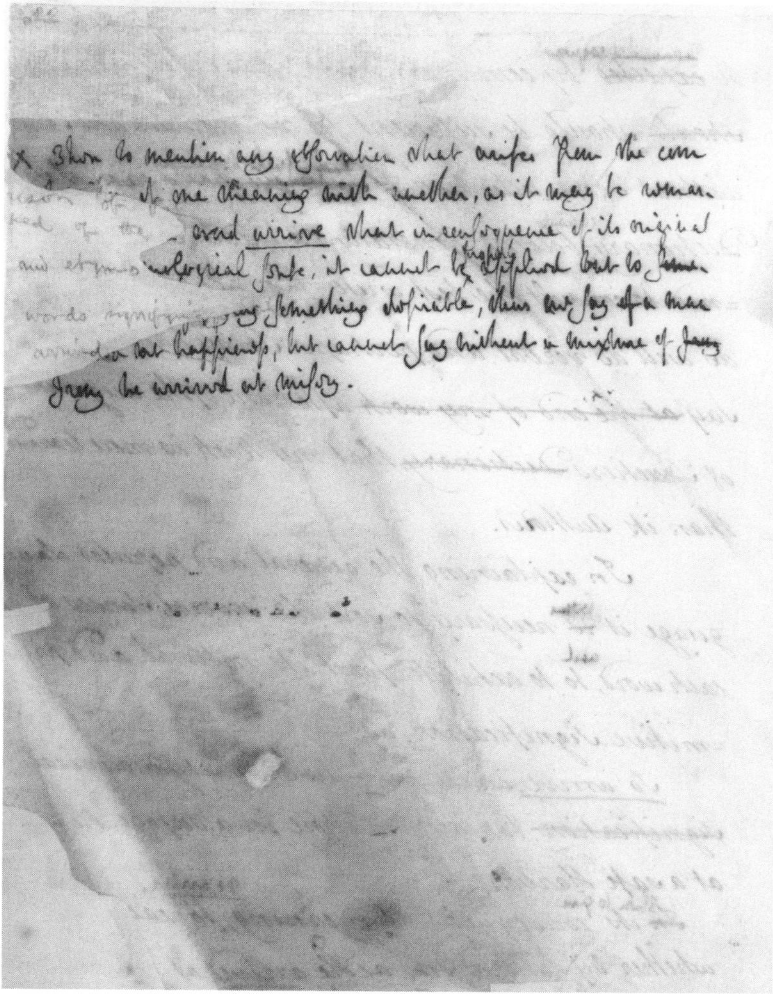
x Then to mention any observation that arises from the connection of one meaning with another, as it may be remarked of the word arrive that in consequence of its original and etymological sense, it cannot be properly applied but to some words signifying something desirable, thus we say of a man arrived at happiness, but cannot say without a mixture of irony he arrived at misery.

Folio 31 verso

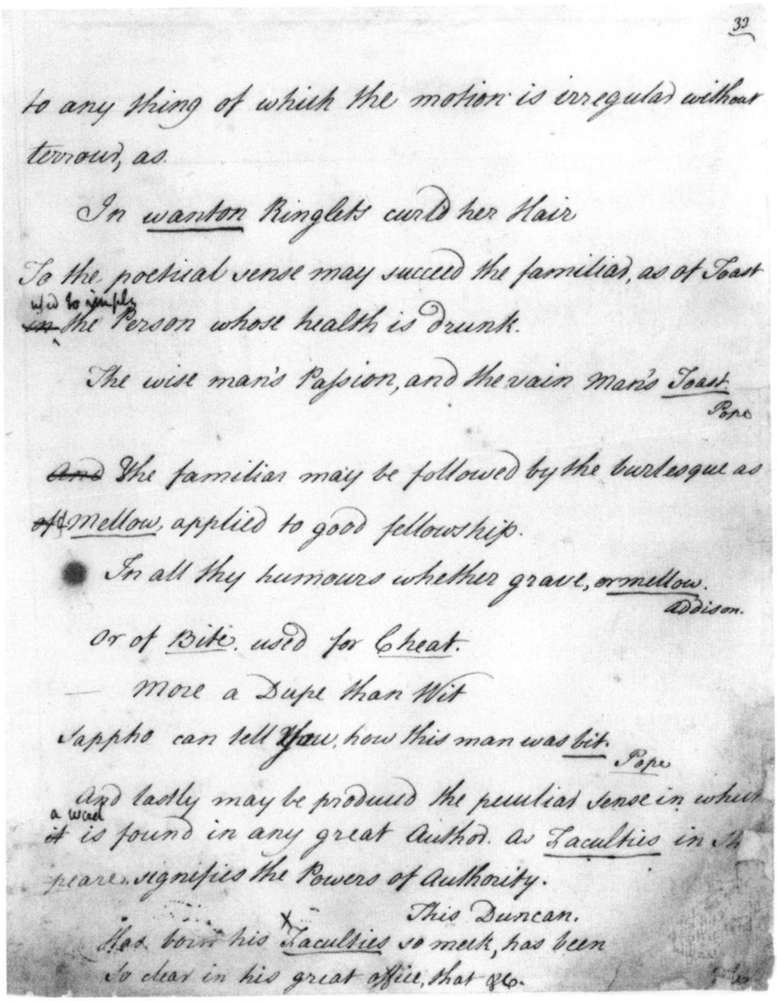

33

to any thing of which the motion is irregular without terrour, as

In wanton Ringlets curl'd her Hair

To the poetical sense may succeed the familiar, as of Toast ~~in~~ used to imply the Person whose health is drunk.

The wise man's Passion, and the vain man's Toast. Pope

~~And~~ The familiar may be followed by the burlesque as ~~of~~ Mellow, applied to good fellowship.

In all thy humours whether grave, or mellow. Addison.

Or of Bite. used for Cheat.

— More a Dupe than Wit

Sappho can tell ~~y~~ you, how this man was bit. Pope

And lastly may be produced the peculiar sense in which ~~it~~ a word is found in any great Author. as Faculties in Shakespeare. signifies the Powers of Authority.

This Duncan.

Has born his Faculties so meek, has been

So clear in his great office, that &c.

Folio 33 [Folio 32 is missing]

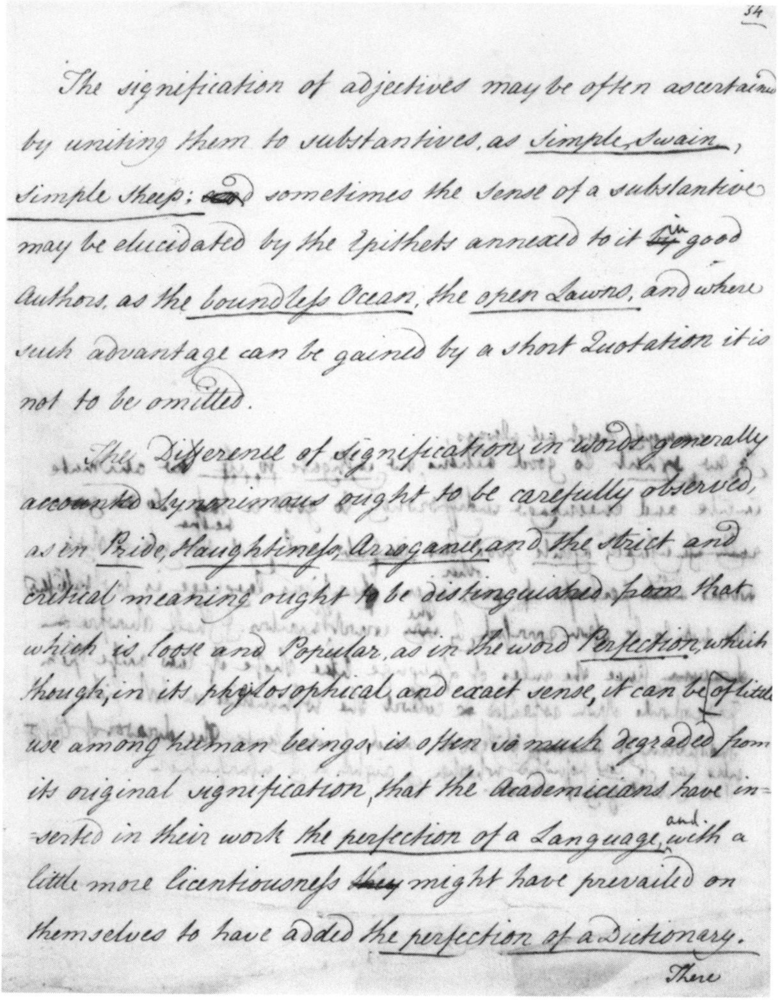

34

The signification of adjectives may be often ascertained by uniting them to substantives, as simple swain, simple sheep; ~~and~~ sometimes the sense of a substantive may be elucidated by the Epithets annexed to it ~~by~~ in good Authors, as the boundless Ocean, the open Lawns, and where such advantage can be gained by a short Quotation it is not to be omitted.

The Difference of signification in words generally accounted Synonimous ought to be carefully observed, as in Pride, Haughtiness, Arrogance, and the strict and critical meaning ought to be distinguished from that which is loose and Popular, as in the word Perfection, which though, in its phylosophical and exact sense, it can be of little use among human beings, is often so much degraded from its original signification, that the Academicians have in=serted in their work the perfection of a Language, and with a little more licentiousness ~~they~~ might have prevailed on themselves to have added the perfection of a Dictionary.

There

Folio 34

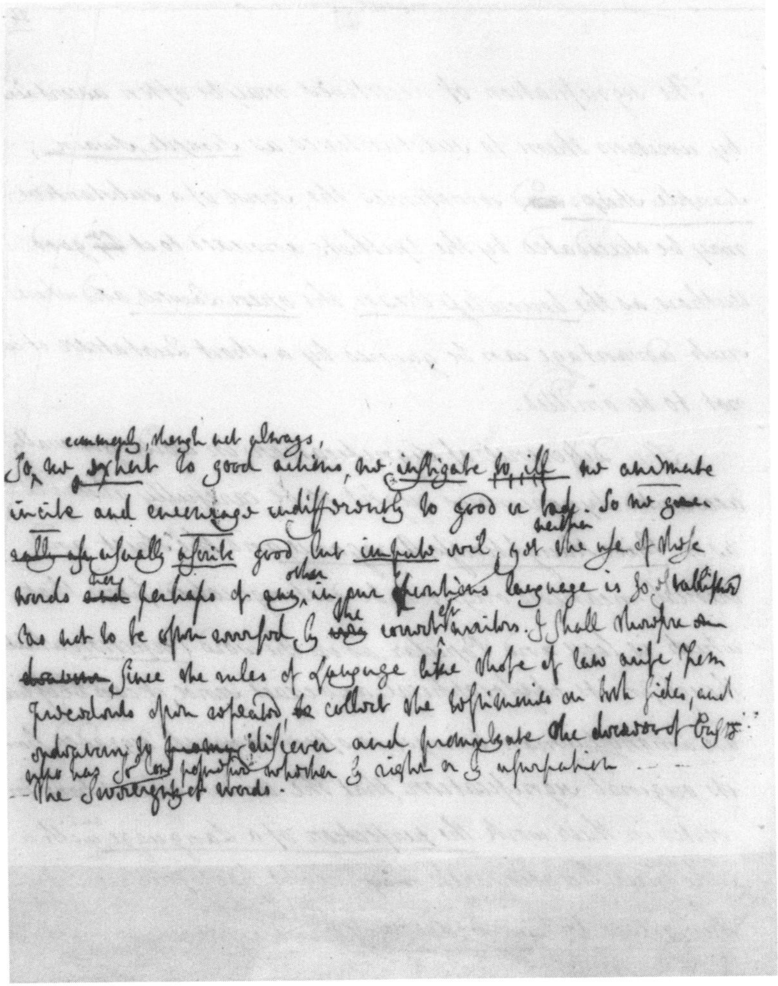
So, we commonly, though not always, exhort to good actions, we instigate to ill; we animate incite and encourage indifferently to good or bad. So we generally ascribe good, but impute evil; yet neither the use of these words nor perhaps of any other in our licentious language is so established as not to be often reversed by the correct writers. I shall therefore since the rules of language like those of law arise from precedents often repeated collect the testimonies on both sides, and endeavour to discover and promulgate the decrees of custom who has so long possessed whether by right or by usurpation — the sovereignty of words.

Folio 34 verso

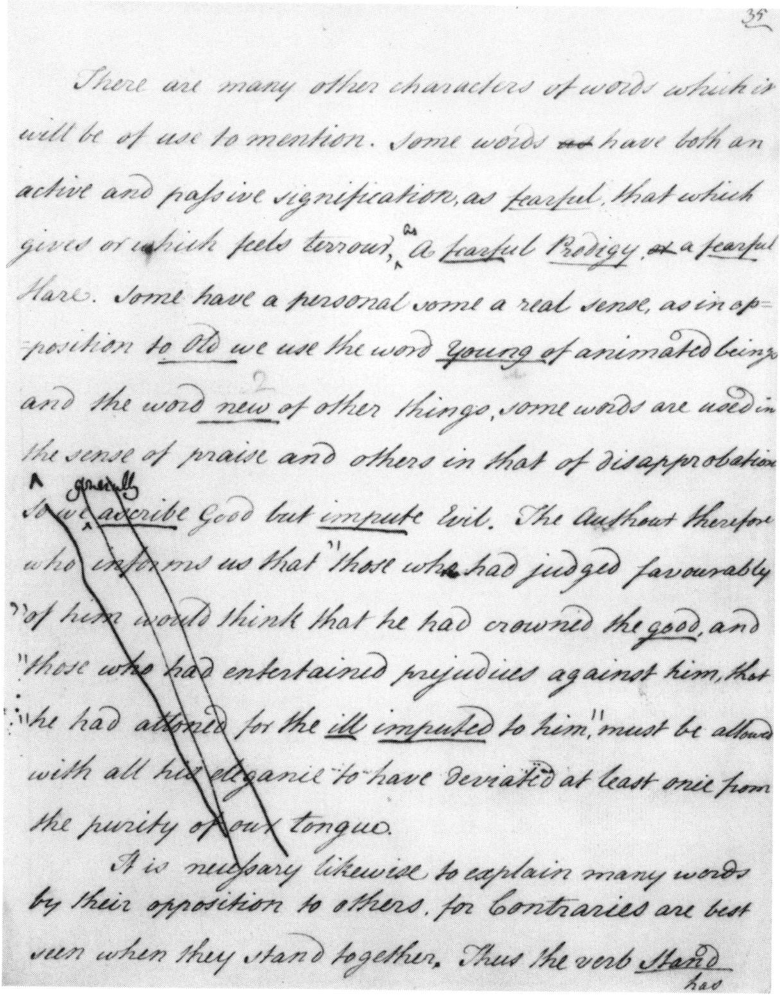

35

There are many other characters of words which it will be of use to mention. Some words ~~as~~ have both an active and passive signification, as fearful, that which gives or which feels terrour, as A fearful Prodigy, ~~or~~ a fearful Hare. Some have a personal some a real sense, as in op=position to Old we use the word Young of animated beings and the word new of other things, some words are used in the sense of praise and others in that of disapprobation. So we generally ascribe Good but impute Evil. The Authour therefore who informs us that "those who had judged favourably "of him would think that he had crowned the good, and "those who had entertained prejudices against him, that "he had attoned for the ill imputed to him," must be allowed with all his elegance to have deviated at least once from the purity of our tongue.

It is necessary likewise to explain many words by their opposition to others, for Contraries are best seen when they stand together. Thus the verb Stand has

Folio 35

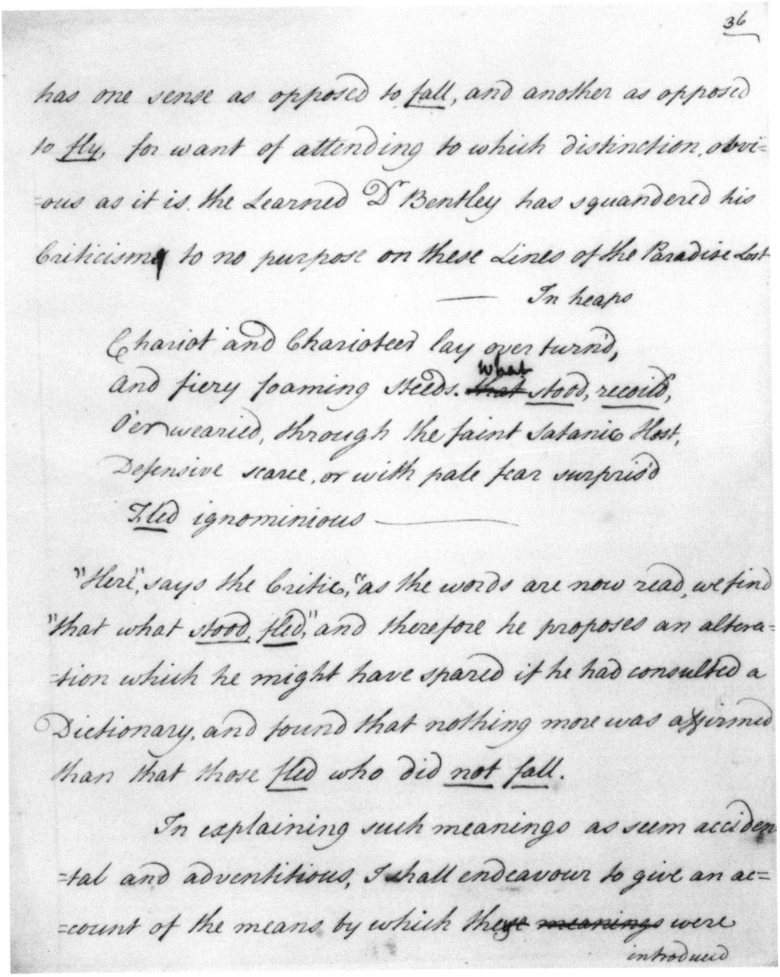

36

has one sense as opposed to fall, and another as opposed to fly, for want of attending to which distinction, obvious as it is, the Learned Dr Bentley has squandered his Criticisms to no purpose on these Lines of the Paradise Lost

— In heaps
Chariot and Charioteer lay over turn'd,
And fiery foaming Steeds. ~~that~~ What stood, recoil'd,
O'er wearied, through the faint Satanic Host,
Defensive scarce, or with pale fear surpris'd
Fled ignominious —

"Here", says the Critic, "as the words are now read, we find "that what stood, fled," and therefore he proposes an alteration which he might have spared if he had consulted a Dictionary, and found that nothing more was affirmed than that those fled who did not fall.

In explaining such meanings as seem accidental and adventitious, I shall endeavour to give an account of the means by which the~~se meanings~~ were introduced

Folio 36

37

introduced. Thus to <u>eke out</u> any thing, signifies to lengthen it beyond its just Dimensions, by some low artifice, be=cause the word <u>eke</u> was the usual refuge of our old writers when they wanted a Syllable. And <u>buxom</u>, which means only <u>obedient</u>, is now made, in familiar phrases, to signify <u>wanton</u>, because in an antient form of marriage, before the Reformation, the Bride promised complaisance and obedience in these Terms "I will be bonair and <u>buxom in</u> "Bed and at board."

I know well, My Lord, how trifling many of these remarks will appear separately considered, and how easi=ly they may give occasion to the ~~contemptuous~~ [slow] merri=ment of [sportive] Idleness, and the ~~gloomy~~ [slow] censures of [arrogant] Stupidity, but dulness it is easy to despise, and laughter it is easy to ~~return~~ [pay]. I shall [not be solicitous what is thought of my work by] ~~not allow those to judge of my work~~ ~~those who are~~ [such as] ~~Strangers~~ know not the difficulty or importance of philological ~~studies~~ ~~who cannot understand it,~~ ~~nor think those who have done~~ Studies, nor shall think ~~~~ [those who that have done] nothing qualified to condemn me for doing little.

Folio 37

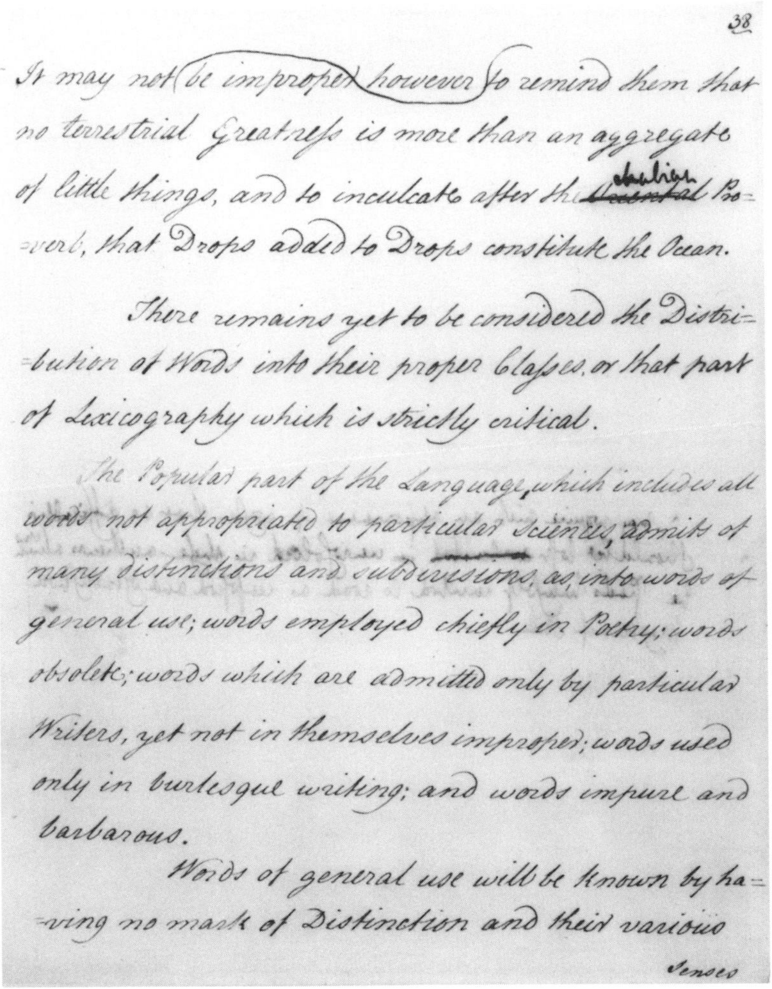

38

It may not (be improper however) to remind them that no terrestrial Greatness is more than an aggregate of little things, and to inculcate after the ~~Oriental~~ Arabian Proverb, that Drops added to Drops constitute the Ocean.

There remains yet to be considered the Distribution of Words into their proper Classes, or that part of Lexicography which is strictly critical.

The Popular part of the Language, which includes all words not appropriated to particular Sciences, admits of many distinctions and subdivisions, as, into words of general use; words employed chiefly in Poetry; words obsolete; words which are admitted only by particular Writers, yet not in themselves improper; words used only in burlesque writing; and words impure and barbarous.

Words of general use will be known by having no mark of Distinction and their various

senses

Folio 38

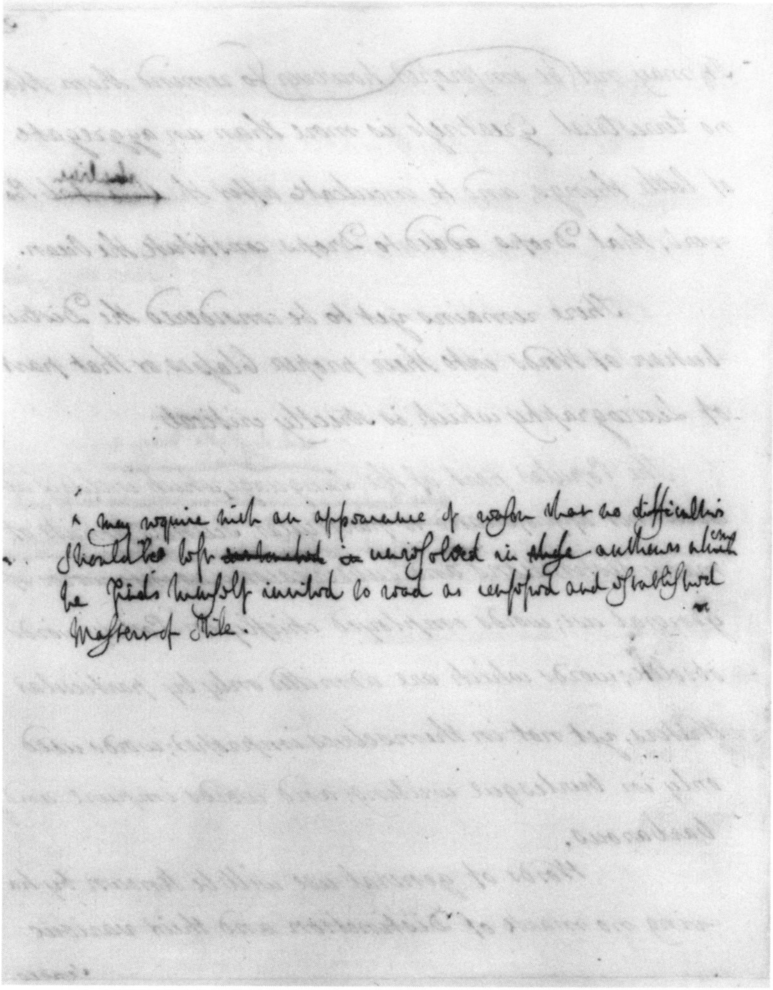
may require such an appearance of reason that no difficulties should be left unresolved in any authors which he finds himself invited to read as confirmed and established Masters of Stile.

Folio 38 verso

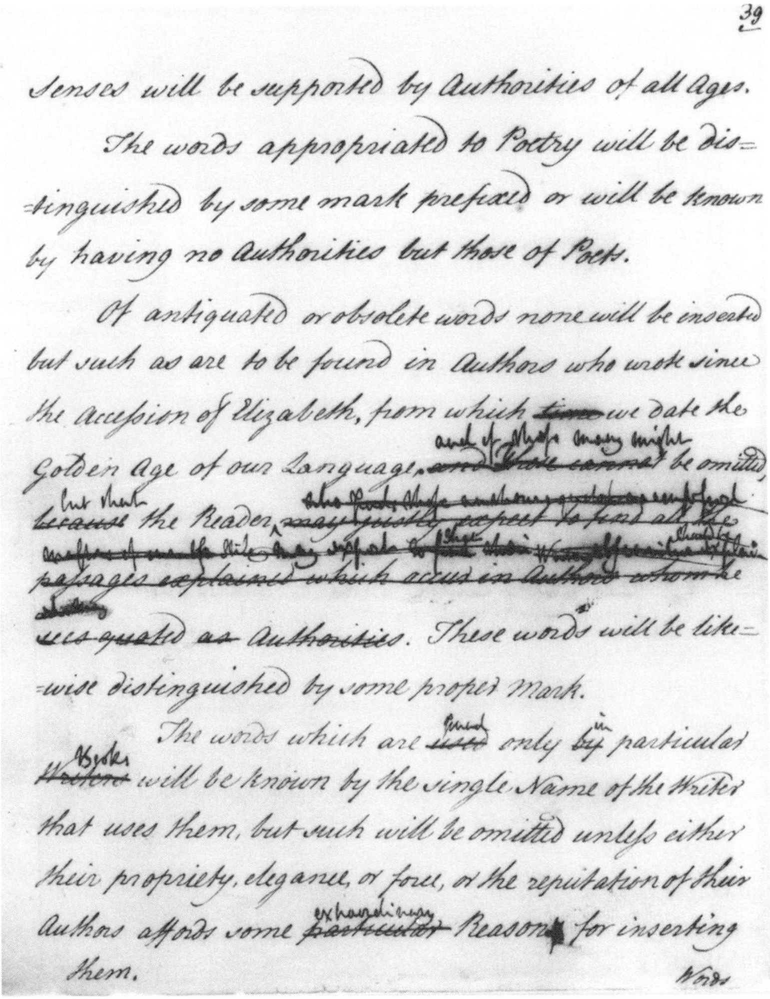
39
Senses will be supported by Authorities of all Ages.
The words appropriated to Poetry will be dis=tinguished by some mark prefixed or will be known by having no Authorities but those of Poets.
Of antiquated or obsolete words none will be inserted but such as are to be found in Authors who wrote since the accession of Elizabeth, from which ~~time~~ we date the Golden Age of our Language, and of these many might ~~and these cannot~~ be omitted, but that ~~because~~ the Reader [illegible] ~~may justly expect to find all the~~ [illegible] ~~passages explained which occur in Authors whom he sees quoted as Authorities~~. These words will be like=wise distinguished by some proper Mark.
The words which are found ~~used~~ only in ~~by~~ particular Books ~~Writers~~ will be known by the single Name of the Writer that uses them, but such will be omitted unless either their propriety, elegance, or force, or the reputation of their Authors affords some extraordinary ~~particular~~ Reason for inserting them.
Words

Folio 39

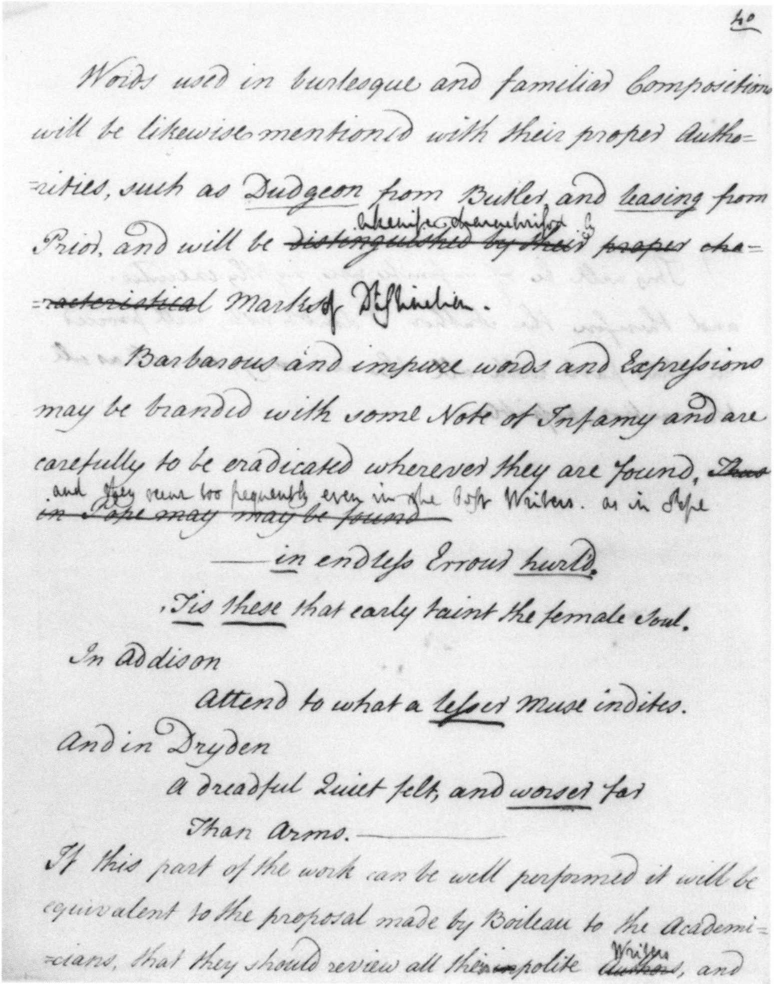

40

Words used in burlesque and familiar Compositions will be likewise mentioned with their proper Autho=rities, such as Dudgeon from Butler, and leasing from Prior, and will be [illegible] ~~distinguished by their~~ ~~proper cha=racteristical~~ Marks of Distinction.

Barbarous and impure words and Expressions may be branded with some Note of Infamy and are carefully to be eradicated wherever they are found, ~~Thus in Pope may may be found~~ and they occur too frequently even in the best Writers. as in Pope

—— in endless Errours hurl'd.

'Tis these that early taint the female Soul.

In Addison

Attend to what a lesser Muse indites.

And in Dryden

A dreadful Quiet felt, and worser far
Than Arms. ——

If this part of the work can be well performed it will be equivalent to the proposal made by Boileau to the Academi=cians, that they should review all their polite ~~Authors~~ Writers, and

Folio 40

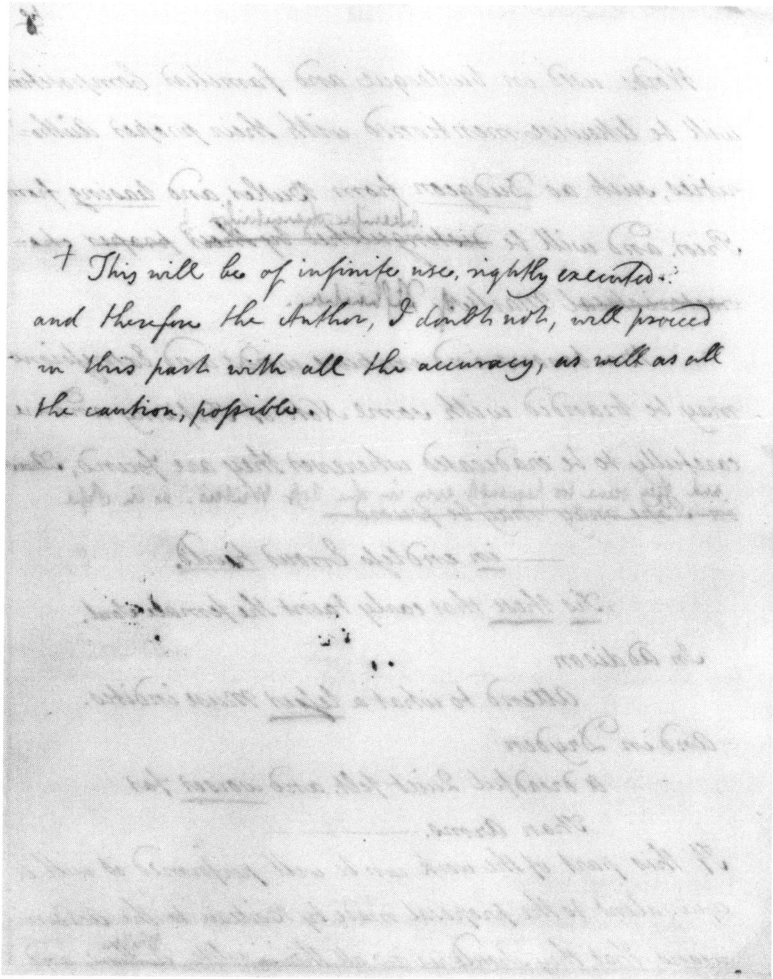

+ This will be of infinite use, rightly executed:
and therefore the Author, I doubt not, will proceed
in this part with all the accuracy, as well as all
the caution, possible.

Folio 40 verso

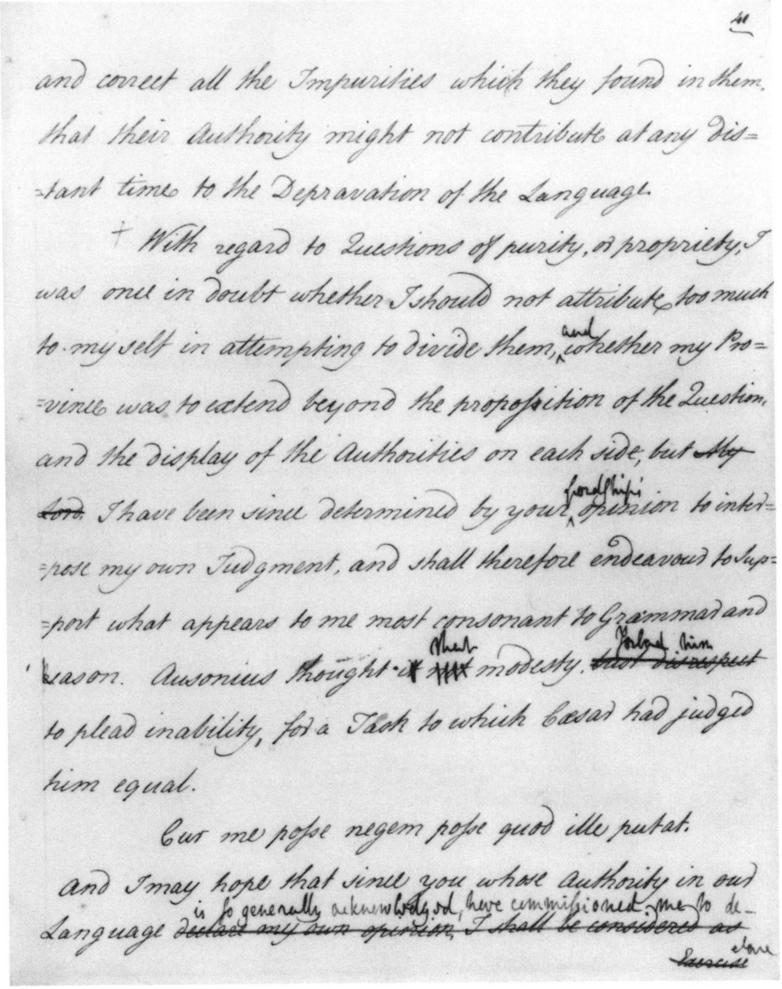

41

and correct all the Impurities which they found in them. that their Authority might not contribute at any dis=
=tant time to the Depravation of the Language.

+ With regard to Questions of purity, or propriety, I was once in doubt whether I should not attribute too much to my self in attempting to divide them, and whether my Pro=
=vince was to extend beyond the proposition of the Question, and the display of the Authorities on each side; but ~~My Lord~~ I have been since determined by your Lordships opinion to inter=
=pose my own Judgment, and shall therefore endeavour to sup=
=port what appears to me most consonant to Grammar and Reason. Ausonius thought ~~it~~ that ~~[illegible]~~ modesty forbid him ~~that he expect~~ to plead inability, for a Task to which Cæsar had judged him equal.

Cur me posse negem posse quod ille putat.

And I may hope that since you whose Authority in our Language is so generally acknowledged, have commissioned me to de- ~~declare my own opinion, I shall be considered as~~ ~~[illegible]~~ clare

Folio 41

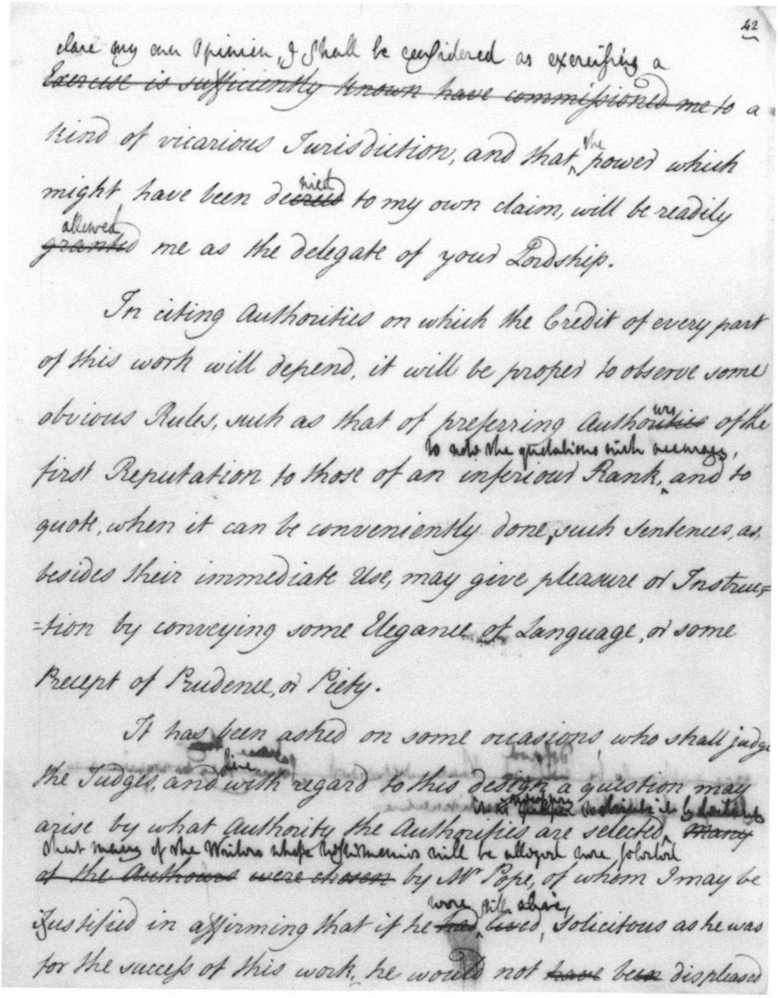
42

clare my own Opinion, I shall be considered as exercising a ~~Exercise is sufficiently known have commissioned me~~ to a kind of vicarious Jurisdiction; and that the power which might have been denied to my own claim, will be readily allowed ~~granted~~ me as the delegate of your Lordship.

In citing authorities on which the Credit of every part of this work will depend, it will be proper to observe some obvious Rules, such as that of preferring Authours of the first Reputation to those of an inferiour Rank, and to note the quotations with accuracy; and to quote, when it can be conveniently done, such Sentences as, besides their immediate Use, may give pleasure or Instruction by conveying some Elegance of Language, or some Precept of Prudence, or Piety.

It has been asked on some occasions who shall judge the Judges, and since with regard to this design a question may arise by what authority the Authorities are selected, [illegible] that many of the Writers whose testimonies will be alleged were selected ~~Many of the Authours were chosen~~ by Mr Pope, of whom I may be justified in affirming that if he were still alive, ~~had lived~~, solicitous as he was for the success of this work, he would not ~~have been~~ be displeased

Folio 42

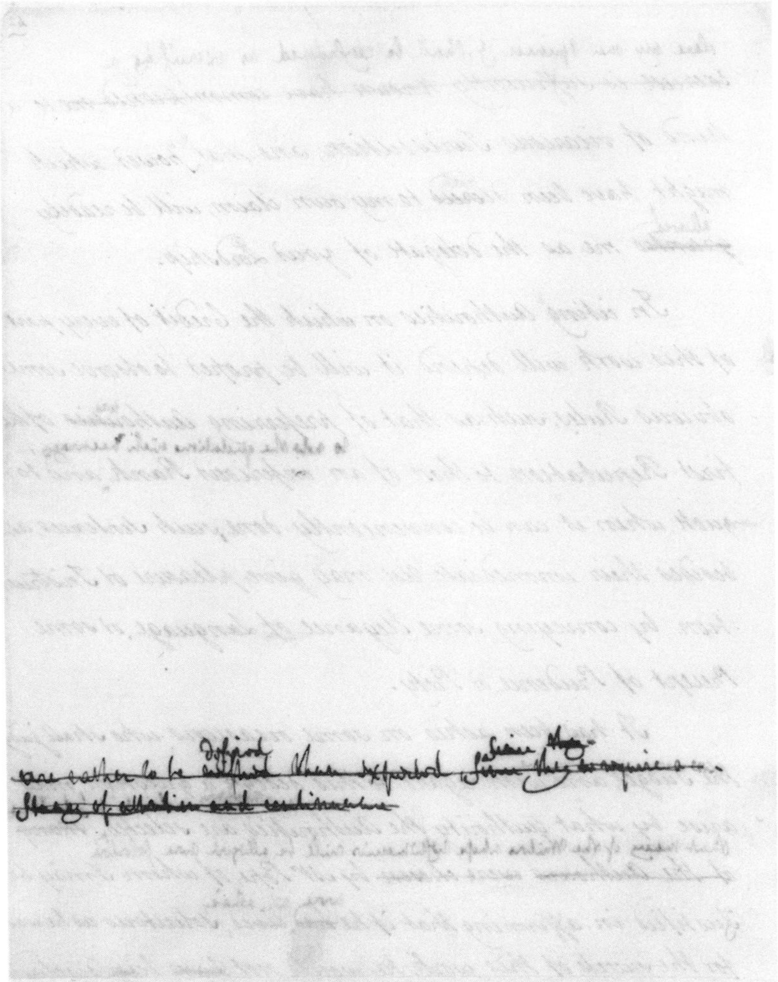

Folio 42 verso

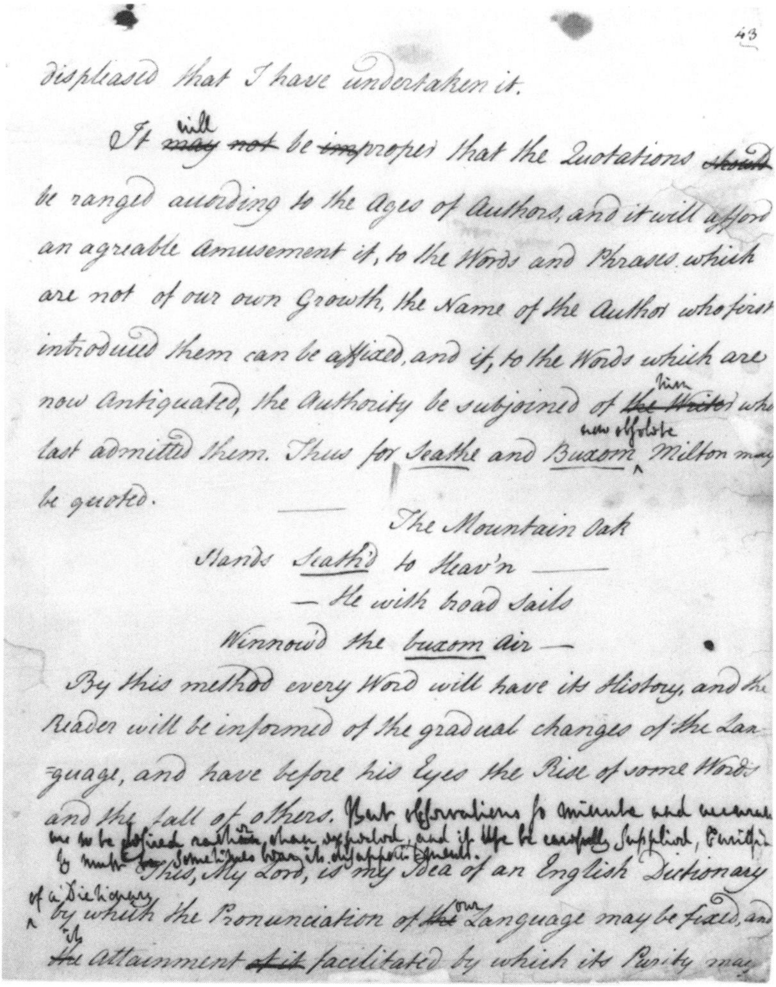

43

displeased that I have undertaken it.

It ~~may not~~ [will] be ~~im~~proper that the Quotations ~~should~~ be ranged according to the Ages of Authors, and it will afford an agreable Amusement if, to the Words and Phrases which are not of our own Growth, the Name of the Author who first introduced them can be affixed, and if, to the Words which are now Antiquated, the Authority be subjoined of ~~the Writer~~ [him] who last admitted them. Thus for Scathe and Buxom, [now obsolete] Milton may be quoted.

— The Mountain Oak
Stands Scath'd to Heav'n —
— He with broad Sails
Winnow'd the buxom Air —

By this method every Word will have its History, and the Reader will be informed of the gradual changes of the Language, and have before his Eyes the Rise of some Words and the Fall of others. But observations so minute and accurate are to be desired rather than expected, and if use be carefully supplied, curiosity must sometimes bear its disappointment. This, My Lord, is my Idea of an English Dictionary [of a Dictionary] by which the Pronunciation of ~~the~~ [our] Language may be fixed, and ~~the~~ [its] Attainment ~~of it~~ facilitated by which its Purity may

Folio 43

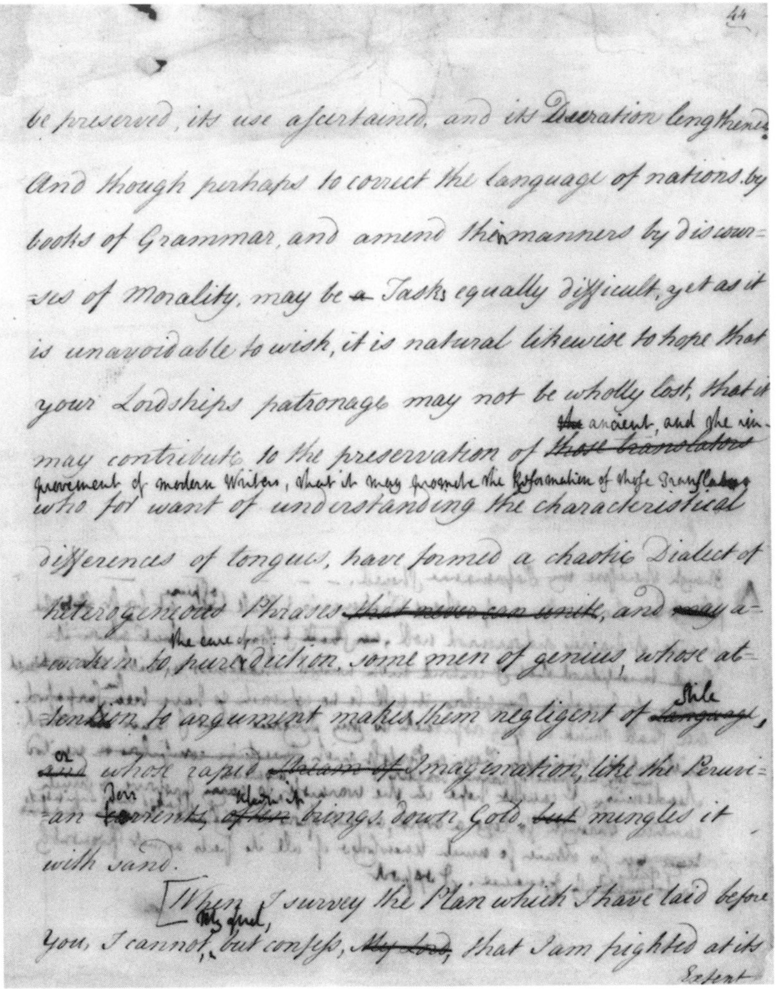
44

be preserved, its use ascertained, and its ~~Duration~~ lengthened.
And though perhaps to correct the language of nations by
books of Grammar, and amend their manners by discour=
=ses of Morality, may be ~~a~~ Tasks equally difficult, yet as it
is unavoidable to wish, it is natural likewise to hope that
your Lordships patronage may not be wholly lost, that it
may contribute to the preservation of ~~the~~ ancient, and the im-
provement of modern Writers, that it may promote the Reformation of those Translators ~~those translators~~
who for want of understanding the characteristical
differences of tongues, have formed a chaotic Dialect of
heterogeneous Phrases ~~that never can unite~~, and ~~may~~ a-
waken to the care purer diction, some men of genius, whose at-
=tention to argument makes them negligent of ~~Language~~ Stile,
~~and~~ or whose rapid ~~stream of~~ Imagination, like the Peruvi=
=an ~~torrents~~ Torr when it ~~often~~ brings down Gold, ~~but~~ mingles it
with sand.
[When I survey the Plan which I have laid before
you, I cannot, My Lord, but confess, ~~My Lord~~, that I am frighted at its
Extent

Folio 44

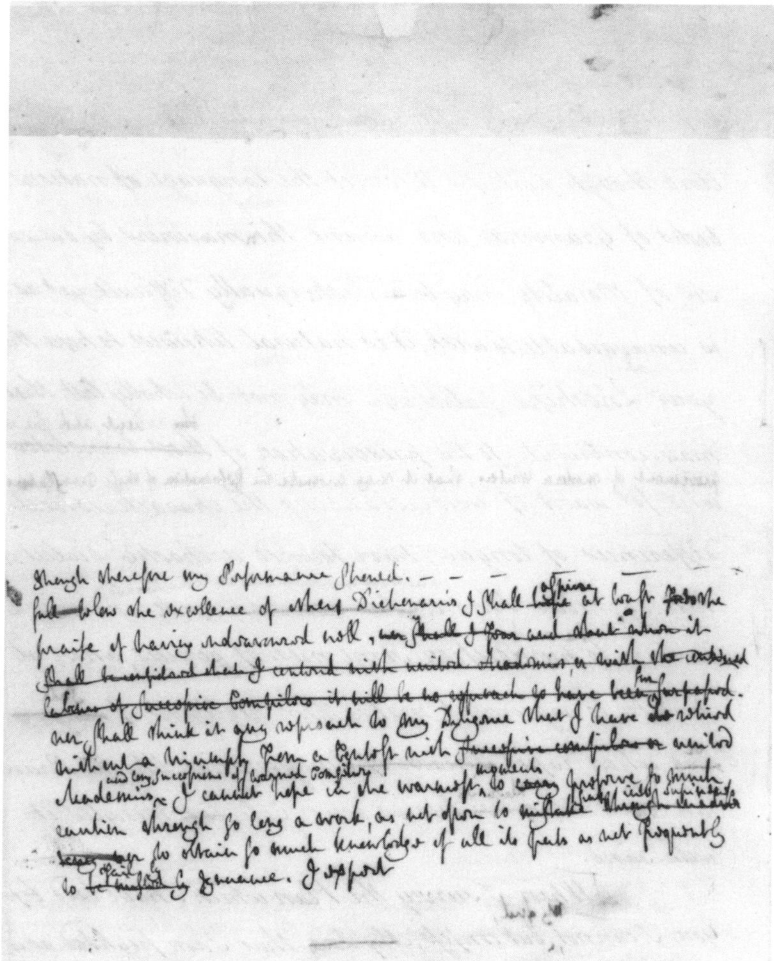

Folio 44 verso

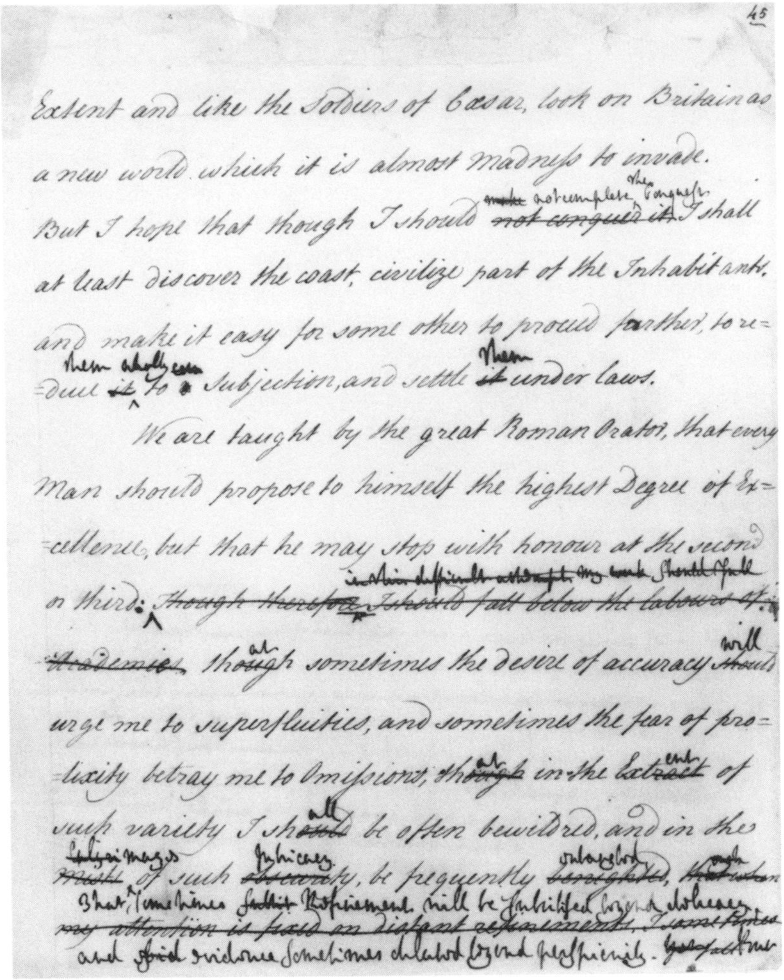

45

Extent and like the Soldiers of Cæsar, look on Britain as a new world which it is almost madness to invade. But I hope that though I should ~~make~~ not complete the conquest ~~not conquer it~~ I shall at least discover the coast, civilize part of the Inhabitants, and make it easy for some other to proceed farther, to re=duce them wholly ~~it~~ to ~~a~~ subjection, and settle them ~~it~~ under laws.

We are taught by the great Roman Orator, that every Man should propose to himself the highest Degree of Ex=cellence, but that he may stop with honour at the second or third: ~~though therefore I should fall below the labours of Academies~~ though sometimes the desire of accuracy will ~~should~~ urge me to superfluities, and sometimes the fear of pro=lixity betray me to Omissions; though in the ~~extract~~ of such variety I shall be often bewildered, and in the ~~mist~~ of such ~~obscurity~~, be frequently ~~benighted~~, ~~that when my attention is fixed on distant refinements, I sometimes~~ That, sometimes refinement will be subtilised beyond exactness and evidence sometimes dilated beyond perspicuity.

Folio 45

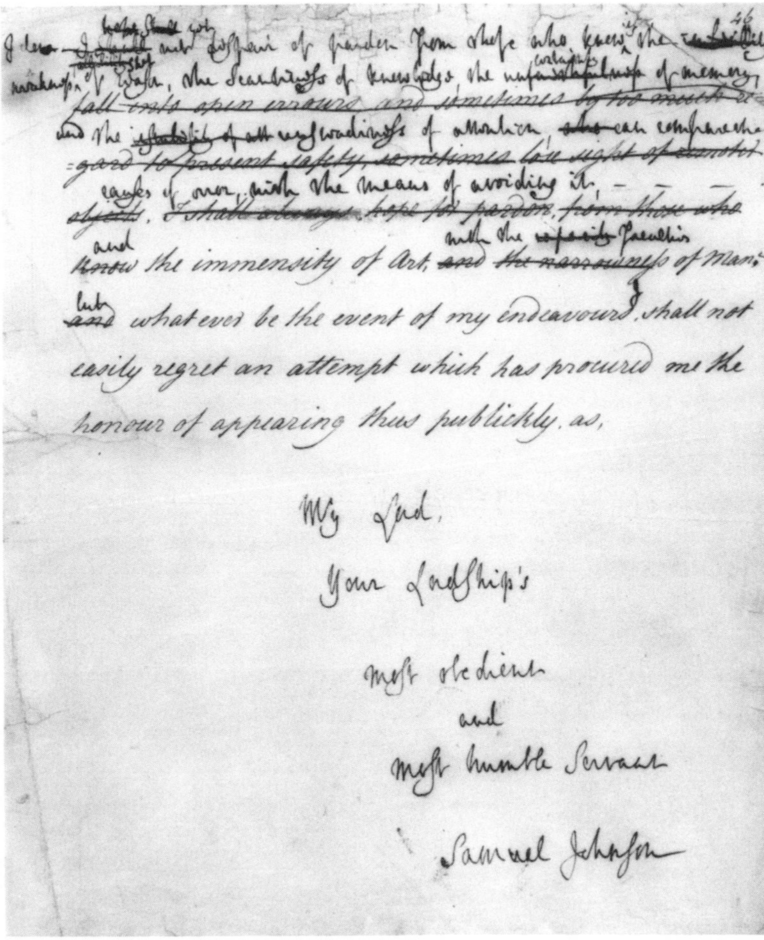

know the immensity of Art, and the narrowness of Man;

and whatever be the event of my endeavours, I shall not easily regret an attempt which has procured me the honour of appearing thus publickly, as,

My Lord,

Your Lordship's

most obedient

and

most humble Servant

Samuel Johnson

Folio 46

INDEX